ANNUAL REVIEW OF SOCIOLOGY

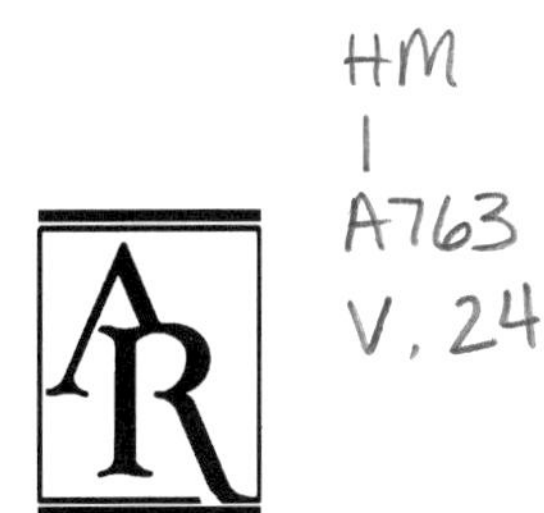

ANNUAL REVIEW OF SOCIOLOGY

VOLUME 24, 1998

JOHN HAGAN, *Co-Editor*
University of Toronto

KAREN S. COOK, *Co-Editor*
Duke University

http://www.AnnualReviews.org science@annurev.org 650-493-4400

ANNUAL REVIEWS 4139 EL CAMINO WAY P.O. BOX 10139 PALO ALTO, CALIFORNIA 94303-0139

ANNUAL REVIEWS
Palo Alto, California, USA

International Standard Serial Number: 0360-0572
International Standard Book Number: 0-8243-2224-X
Library of Congress Catalog Card Number: 75-648500

The paper used in this publication meets the minimum requirements of American National Standards for Information Sciences—Permanence of Paper for Printed Library Materials, ANZI Z39.48-1992

TYPESETTING BY RUTH M. SAAVEDRA AND THE ANNUAL REVIEWS EDITORIAL STAFF
PRINTED AND BOUND IN THE UNITED STATES OF AMERICA

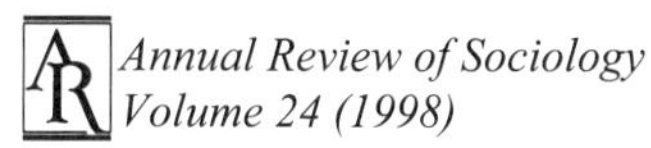
Annual Review of Sociology
Volume 24 (1998)

CONTENTS

PREFATORY CHAPTER

SOCIAL CAPITAL: Its Origins and Applications in Modern Sociology, *Alejandro Portes* 1

THEORY AND METHODS

DIFFUSION IN ORGANIZATIONS AND SOCIAL MOVEMENTS: From Hybrid Corn to Poison Pills, *David Strang and Sarah A. Soule* 265

COMMENSURATION AS A SOCIAL PROCESS, *Wendy Nelson Espeland and Mitchell L. Stevens* 313

MEASURING MEANING STRUCTURES, *John W. Mohr* 345

CONTEMPORARY DEVELOPMENTS IN SOCIOLOGICAL THEORY: Current Projects and Conditions of Possibility, *Charles Camic and Neil Gross* 453

USING COMPUTERS TO ANALYZE ETHNOGRAPHIC FIELD DATA: Theoretical and Practical Considerations, *Daniel Dohan and Martín Sánchez-Jankowski* 477

NARRATIVE ANALYSIS, OR WHY (AND HOW) SOCIOLOGISTS SHOULD BE INTERESTED IN NARRATIVE, *Roberto Franzosi* 517

SOCIAL PROCESSES

BREAKDOWN THEORIES OF COLLECTIVE ACTION, *Bert Useem* 215

WARMER AND MORE SOCIAL: Recent Developments in Cognitive Social Psychology, *Norbert Schwarz* 239

WAS IT WORTH THE EFFORT? THE OUTCOMES AND CONSEQUENCES OF SOCIAL MOVEMENTS, *Marco G. Giugni* 371

INSTITUTIONS AND CULTURE

FUNDAMENTALISM ET AL: Conservative Protestants in America, *Robert D. Woodberry and Christian S. Smith* 25

FORMAL ORGANIZATIONS

NETWORK FORMS OF ORGANIZATIONS, *Joel M. Podolny and Karen L. Page* 57

(continued)

POLITICAL AND ECONOMIC SOCIOLOGY

COMPUTERIZATION OF THE WORKPLACE, *Beverly H. Burris* 141
GLOBALIZATION AND DEMOCRACY, *Kathleen C. Schwartzman* 159

DIFFERENTIATION AND STRATIFICATION

INTERMARRIAGE AND HOMOGAMY: Causes, Patterns, and Trends, *Matthijs Kalmijn* 395

INDIVIDUAL AND SOCIETY

REACTIONS TOWARD THE NEW MINORITIES OF WESTERN EUROPE, *Thomas F. Pettigrew* 77
SOCIAL MEMORY STUDIES: From "Collective Memory" to the Historical Sociology of Mnemonic Practices, *Jeffrey K. Olick and Joyce Robbins* 105
SOCIAL DILEMMAS: The Anatomy of Cooperation, *Peter Kollock* 183
ALCOHOL, DRUGS, AND VIOLENCE, *Robert Nash Parker and Kathleen Auerhahn* 291
ETHNIC AND NATIONALIST VIOLENCE, *Rogers Brubaker and David D. Laitin* 423

SOCIOLOGY OF WORLD REGIONS

SOCIOLOGICAL WORK IN JAPAN, *Keiko Nakao* 499

INDEXES

Subject Index 555
Cumulative Index of Contributing Authors 574
Cumulative Index of Chapter Titles 579

SOME RELATED ARTICLES IN OTHER *ANNUAL REVIEWS*

From the *Annual Review of Anthropology,* Volume 27, 1998

Nationalism and Archaeology: On the Constructions of Nations and the Reconstructions of the Remote Past, P. L. Kohl
The Archaeology of Symbols, J. Robb
Globalization and the Future of "Cultural Areas": Melanesianist Anthropology in Transition, R. Lederman
Multiple Modernities: Christianity, Islam, and Hinduism in a Globalizing Age, R. W. Hefner

From the *Annual Review of Political Science,* Volume 1 (1998)

Social Capital and Politics, R. W. Jackman and R. A. Miller
The Intellectual Legacy of Leo Strauss (1899–1973), N. Behnegar
Communication and Opinion, D. R. Kinder
Social Science and Scientific Change: A Note on Thomas S. Kuhn's Contribution, N. W. Polsby

From the Annual Review of Psychology, Volume 49 (1998)

Sibling Relationship Quality: Its Causes and Consequences, G. H. Brody
Intergroup Contact Theory, T. F. Pettigrew
Adolescent Development: Challenges and Opportunities for Research Programs, and Policies, R. M. Lerner and N. L. Galambos
Human Abilities, R. J. Sternberg and J. C. Kaufman

From the *Annual Review of Public Health,* Volume 19 (1998)

Public Health in Central and Eastern Europe and the Role of Environmental Pollution, R. E. Little
Preventing Youth Violence: What Works, A. L. Kellermann

ANNUAL REVIEWS is a nonprofit scientific publisher established to promote the advancement of the sciences. Beginning in 1932 with the *Annual Review of Biochemistry,* the Company has pursued as its principal function the publication of high-quality, reasonably priced *Annual Review* volumes. The volumes are organized by Editors and Editorial Committees who invite qualified authors to contribute critical articles reviewing significant developments within each major discipline. The Editor-in-Chief invites those interested in serving as future Editorial Committee members to communicate directly with him. Annual Reviews is administered by a Board of Directors, whose members serve without compensation.

ANNUAL REVIEWS OF

Anthropology
Astronomy and Astrophysics
Biochemistry
Biophysics and Biomolecular Structure
Cell and Developmental Biology
Computer Science
Earth and Planetary Sciences
Ecology and Systematics
Energy and the Environment
Entomology
Fluid Mechanics
Genetics
Immunology
Materials Science
Medicine
Microbiology
Neuroscience
Nuclear and Particle Science
Nutrition
Pharmacology and Toxicology
Physical Chemistry
Physiology
Phytopathology
Plant Physiology and Plant Molecular Biology
Political Science
Psychology
Public Health
Sociology

SPECIAL PUBLICATIONS
Excitement and Fascination of Science, Vols. 1, 2, 3, and 4

For the convenience of readers, a detachable order form/envelope is bound into the back of this volume.

Annu. Rev. Sociol. 1998. 24:1–24

SOCIAL CAPITAL: Its Origins and Applications in Modern Sociology

Alejandro Portes
Department of Sociology, Princeton University, Princeton, New Jersey 08540

KEY WORDS: social control, family support, networks, sociability

ABSTRACT

This paper reviews the origins and definitions of social capital in the writings of Bourdieu, Loury, and Coleman, among other authors. It distinguishes four sources of social capital and examines their dynamics. Applications of the concept in the sociological literature emphasize its role in social control, in family support, and in benefits mediated by extrafamilial networks. I provide examples of each of these positive functions. Negative consequences of the same processes also deserve attention for a balanced picture of the forces at play. I review four such consequences and illustrate them with relevant examples. Recent writings on social capital have extended the concept from an individual asset to a feature of communities and even nations. The final sections describe this conceptual stretch and examine its limitations. I argue that, as shorthand for the positive consequences of sociability, social capital has a definite place in sociological theory. However, excessive extensions of the concept may jeopardize its heuristic value.

Alejandro Portes: Biographical Sketch

Alejandro Portes is professor of sociology at Princeton University and faculty associate of the Woodrow Wilson School of Public Affairs. He formerly taught at Johns Hopkins where he held the John Dewey Chair in Arts and Sciences, Duke University, and the University of Texas-Austin. In 1997 he held the Emilio Bacardi distinguished professorship at the University of Miami. In the same year he was elected president of the American Sociological Association. Born in Havana, Cuba, he came to the United States in 1960. He was educated at the University of Havana, Catholic University of Argentina, and Creighton University. He received his MA and PhD from the University of Wisconsin-Madison.

0360-0572/98/0815-0001$08.00

Portes is the author of some 200 articles and chapters on national development, international migration, Latin American and Caribbean urbanization, and economic sociology. His most recent books include *City on the Edge, the Transformation of Miami* (winner of the Robert Park award for best book in urban sociology and of the Anthony Leeds award for best book in urban anthropology in 1995); *The New Second Generation* (Russell Sage Foundation 1996); *Caribbean Cities* (Johns Hopkins University Press); and *Immigrant America, a Portrait.* The latter book was designated as a centennial publication by the University of California Press. It was originally published in 1990; the second edition, updated and containing new chapters on American immigration policy and the new second generation, was published in 1996.

Introduction

During recent years, the concept of social capital has become one of the most popular exports from sociological theory into everyday language. Disseminated by a number of policy-oriented journals and general circulation magazines, social capital has evolved into something of a cure-all for the maladies affecting society at home and abroad. Like other sociological concepts that have traveled a similar path, the original meaning of the term and its heuristic value are being put to severe tests by these increasingly diverse applications. As in the case of those earlier concepts, the point is approaching at which social capital comes to be applied to so many events and in so many different contexts as to lose any distinct meaning.

Despite its current popularity, the term does not embody any idea really new to sociologists. That involvement and participation in groups can have positive consequences for the individual and the community is a staple notion, dating back to Durkheim's emphasis on group life as an antidote to anomie and self-destruction and to Marx's distinction between an atomized class-in-itself and a mobilized and effective class-for-itself. In this sense, the term social capital simply recaptures an insight present since the very beginnings of the discipline. Tracing the intellectual background of the concept into classical times would be tantamount to revisiting sociology's major nineteenth century sources. That exercise would not reveal, however, why this idea has caught on in recent years or why an unusual baggage of policy implications has been heaped on it.

The novelty and heuristic power of social capital come from two sources. First, the concept focuses attention on the positive consequences of sociability while putting aside its less attractive features. Second, it places those positive consequences in the framework of a broader discussion of capital and calls attention to how such nonmonetary forms can be important sources of power and influence, like the size of one's stock holdings or bank account. The potential fungibility of diverse sources of capital reduces the distance between the sociological and economic perspectives and simultaneously engages the attention of policy-makers seeking less costly, non-economic solutions to social problems.

In the course of this review, I limit discussion to the contemporary reemergence of the idea to avoid a lengthy excursus into its classical predecessors. To an audience of sociologists, these sources and the parallels between present social capital discussions and passages in the classical literature will be obvious. I examine, first, the principal authors associated with the contemporary usage of the term and their different approaches to it. Then I review the various mechanisms leading to the emergence of social capital and its principal applications in the research literature. Next, I examine those not-so-desirable consequences of sociability that are commonly obscured in the contemporary literature on the topic. This discussion aims at providing some balance to the frequently celebratory tone with which the concept is surrounded. That tone is especially noticeable in those studies that have stretched the concept from a property of individuals and families to a feature of communities, cities, and even nations. The attention garnered by applications of social capital at this broader level also requires some discussion, particularly in light of the potential pitfalls of that conceptual stretch.

Definitions

The first systematic contemporary analysis of social capital was produced by Pierre Bourdieu, who defined the concept as "the aggregate of the actual or potential resources which are linked to possession of a durable network of more or less institutionalized relationships of mutual acquaintance or recognition" (Bourdieu 1985, p. 248; 1980). This initial treatment of the concept appeared in some brief "Provisional Notes" published in the *Actes de la Recherche en Sciences Sociales* in 1980. Because they were in French, the article did not garner widespread attention in the English-speaking world; nor, for that matter, did the first English translation, concealed in the pages of a text on the sociology of education (Bourdieu 1985).

This lack of visibility is lamentable because Bourdieu's analysis is arguably the most theoretically refined among those that introduced the term in contemporary sociological discourse. His treatment of the concept is instrumental, focusing on the benefits accruing to individuals by virtue of participation in groups and on the deliberate construction of sociability for the purpose of creating this resource. In the original version, he went as far as asserting that "the profits which accrue from membership in a group are the basis of the solidarity which makes them possible" (Bourdieu 1985, p. 249). Social networks are not a natural given and must be constructed through investment strategies oriented to the institutionalization of group relations, usable as a reliable source of other benefits. Bourdieu's definition makes clear that social capital is decomposable into two elements: first, the social relationship itself that allows individuals to claim access to resources possessed by their associates, and second, the amount and quality of those resources.

Throughout, Bourdieu's emphasis is on the fungibility of different forms of capital and on the ultimate reduction of all forms to economic capital, defined as accumulated human labor. Hence, through social capital, actors can gain direct access to economic resources (subsidized loans, investment tips, protected markets); they can increase their cultural capital through contacts with experts or individuals of refinement (i.e. embodied cultural capital); or, alternatively, they can affiliate with institutions that confer valued credentials (i.e. institutionalized cultural capital).

On the other hand, the acquisition of social capital requires deliberate investment of both economic and cultural resources. Though Bourdieu insists that the outcomes of possession of social or cultural capital are reducible to economic capital, the processes that bring about these alternative forms are not. They each possess their own dynamics, and, relative to economic exchange, they are characterized by less transparency and more uncertainty. For example, transactions involving social capital tend to be characterized by unspecified obligations, uncertain time horizons, and the possible violation of reciprocity expectations. But, by their very lack of clarity, these transactions can help disguise what otherwise would be plain market exchanges (Bourdieu 1979, 1980).

A second contemporary source is the work of economist Glen Loury (1977, 1981). He came upon the term in the context of his critique of neoclassical theories of racial income inequality and their policy implications. Loury argued that orthodox economic theories were too individualistic, focusing exclusively on individual human capital and on the creation of a level field for competition based on such skills. By themselves, legal prohibitions against employers' racial tastes and implementation of equal opportunity programs would not reduce racial inequalities. The latter could go on forever, according to Loury, for two reasons—first, the inherited poverty of black parents, which would be transmitted to their children in the form of lower material resources and educational opportunities; second, the poorer connections of young black workers to the labor market and their lack of information about opportunities:

> The merit notion that, in a free society, each individual will rise to the level justified by his or her competence conflicts with the observation that no one travels that road entirely alone. The social context within which individual maturation occurs strongly conditions what otherwise equally competent individuals can achieve. This implies that absolute equality of opportunity,…is an ideal that cannot be achieved. (Loury 1977, p. 176)

Loury cited with approval the sociological literature on intergenerational mobility and inheritance of race as illustrating his anti-individualist argument. However, he did not go on to develop the concept of social capital in any detail.

He seems to have run across the idea in the context of his polemic against orthodox labor economics, but he mentions it only once in his original article and then in rather tentative terms (Loury 1977). The concept captured the differential access to opportunities through social connections for minority and nonminority youth, but we do not find here any systematic treatment of its relations to other forms of capital.

Loury's work paved the way, however, for Coleman's more refined analysis of the same process, namely the role of social capital in the creation of human capital. In his initial analysis of the concept, Coleman acknowledges Loury's contribution as well as those of economist Ben-Porath and sociologists Nan Lin and Mark Granovetter. Curiously, Coleman does not mention Bourdieu, although his analysis of the possible uses of social capital for the acquisition of educational credentials closely parallels that pioneered by the French sociologist.[1] Coleman defined social capital by its function as "a variety of entities with two elements in common: They all consist of some aspect of social structures, and they facilitate certain action of actors—whether persons or corporate actors—within the structure" (Coleman 1988a: p. S98, 1990, p. 302).

This rather vague definition opened the way for relabeling a number of different and even contradictory processes as social capital. Coleman himself started that proliferation by including under the term some of the mechanisms that generated social capital (such as reciprocity expectations and group enforcement of norms); the consequences of its possession (such as privileged access to information); and the "appropriable" social organization that provided the context for both sources and effects to materialize. Resources obtained through social capital have, from the point of view of the recipient, the character of a gift. Thus, it is important to distinguish the resources themselves from the ability to obtain them by virtue of membership in different social structures, a distinction explicit in Bourdieu but obscured in Coleman. Equating social capital with the resources acquired through it can easily lead to tautological statements.[2]

Equally important is the distinction between the motivations of recipients and of donors in exchanges mediated by social capital. Recipients' desire to

[1]The closest equivalent to human capital in Bourdieu's analysis is embodied cultural capital, which is defined as the habitus of cultural practices, knowledge, and demeanors learned through exposure to role models in the family and other environments (Bourdieu 1979).

[2]Saying, for example, that student A has social capital because he obtained access to a large tuition loan from his kin and that student B does not because she failed to do so neglects the possibility that B's kin network is equally or more motivated to come to her aid but simply lacks the means to do. Defining social capital as equivalent with the resources thus obtained is tantamount to saying that the successful succeed. This circularity is more evident in applications of social capital that define it as a property of collectivities. These are reviewed below.

gain access to valuable assets is readily understandable. More complex are the motivations of the donors, who are requested to make these assets available without any immediate return. Such motivations are plural and deserve analysis because they are the core processes that the concept of social capital seeks to capture. Thus, a systematic treatment of the concept must distinguish among: (*a*) the possessors of social capital (those making claims); (*b*) the sources of social capital (those agreeing to these demands); (*c*) the resources themselves. These three elements are often mixed in discussions of the concept following Coleman, thus setting the stage for confusion in the uses and scope of the term.

Despite these limitations, Coleman's essays have the undeniable merit of introducing and giving visibility to the concept in American sociology, highlighting its importance for the acquisition of human capital, and identifying some of the mechanisms through which it is generated. In this last respect, his discussion of closure is particularly enlightening. Closure means the existence of sufficient ties between a certain number of people to guarantee the observance of norms. For example, the possibility of malfeasance within the tightly knit community of Jewish diamond traders in New York City is minimized by the dense ties among its members and the ready threat of ostracism against violators. The existence of such a strong norm is then appropriable by all members of the community, facilitating transactions without recourse to cumbersome legal contracts (Coleman 1988a:S99).

After Bourdieu, Loury, and Coleman, a number of theoretical analyses of social capital have been published. In 1990, WE Baker defined the concept as "a resource that actors derive from specific social structures and then use to pursue their interests; it is created by changes in the relationship among actors" (Baker 1990, p. 619). More broadly, M Schiff defines the term as "the set of elements of the social structure that affects relations among people and are inputs or arguments of the production and/or utility function" (Schiff 1992, p. 161). Burt sees it as "friends, colleagues, and more general contacts through whom you receive opportunities to use your financial and human capital" (Burt 1992, p. 9). Whereas Coleman and Loury had emphasized dense networks as a necessary condition for the emergence of social capital, Burt highlights the opposite situation. In his view, it is the relative absence of ties, labeled "structural holes," that facilitates individual mobility. This is so because dense networks tend to convey redundant information, while weaker ties can be sources of new knowledge and resources.

Despite these differences, the consensus is growing in the literature that social capital stands for the ability of actors to secure benefits by virtue of membership in social networks or other social structures. This is the sense in which it has been more commonly applied in the empirical literature although, as we will see, the potential uses to which it is put vary greatly.

Sources of Social Capital

Both Bourdieu and Coleman emphasize the intangible character of social capital relative to other forms. Whereas economic capital is in people's bank accounts and human capital is inside their heads, social capital inheres in the structure of their relationships. To possess social capital, a person must be related to others, and it is those others, not himself, who are the actual source of his or her advantage. As mentioned before, the motivation of others to make resources available on concessionary terms is not uniform. At the broadest level, one may distinguish between consummatory versus instrumental motivations to do so.

As examples of the first, people may pay their debts in time, give alms to charity, and obey traffic rules because they feel an obligation to behave in this manner. The internalized norms that make such behaviors possible are then appropriable by others as a resource. In this instance, the holders of social capital are other members of the community who can extend loans without fear of nonpayment, benefit from private charity, or send their kids to play in the street without concern. Coleman (1988a: S104) refers to this source in his analysis of norms and sanctions: "Effective norms that inhibit crime make it possible to walk freely outside at night in a city and enable old persons to leave their houses without fear for their safety." As is well known, an excessive emphasis on this process of norm internalization led to the oversocialized conception of human action in sociology so trenchantly criticized by Wrong (1961).

An approach closer to the undersocialized view of human nature in modern economics sees social capital as primarily the accumulation of obligations from others according to the norm of reciprocity. In this version, donors provide privileged access to resources in the expectation that they will be fully repaid in the future. This accumulation of social chits differs from purely economic exchange in two aspects. First, the currency with which obligations are repaid may be different from that with which they were incurred in the first place and may be as intangible as the granting of approval or allegiance. Second, the timing of the repayment is unspecified. Indeed, if a schedule of repayments exists, the transaction is more appropriately defined as market exchange than as one mediated by social capital. This instrumental treatment of the term is quite familiar in sociology, dating back to the classical analysis of social exchange by Simmel ([1902a] 1964), the more recent ones by Homans (1961) and Blau (1964), and extensive work on the sources and dynamics of reciprocity by authors of the rational action school (Schiff 1992, Coleman 1994).

Two other sources of social capital exist that fit the consummatory versus instrumental dichotomy, but in a different way. The first finds its theoretical underpinnings in Marx's analysis of emergent class consciousness in the industrial proletariat. By being thrown together in a common situation, workers learn to identify with each other and support each other's initiatives. This solidarity is not the result of norm introjection during childhood, but is an emergent product of a common fate (Marx [1894] 1967, Marx & Engels [1848] 1947). For this reason, the altruistic dispositions of actors in these situations are not universal but are bounded by the limits of their community. Other members of the same community can then appropriate such dispositions and the actions that follow as their source of social capital.

Bounded solidarity is the term used in the recent literature to refer to this mechanism. It is the source of social capital that leads wealthy members of a church to anonymously endow church schools and hospitals; members of a suppressed nationality to voluntarily join life-threatening military activities in its defense; and industrial proletarians to take part in protest marches or sympathy strikes in support of their fellows. Identification with one's own group, sect, or community can be a powerful motivational force. Coleman refers to extreme forms of this mechanism as "zeal" and defines them as an effective antidote to free-riding by others in collective movements (Coleman 1990, pp. 273–82; Portes & Sensenbrenner 1993).

The final source of social capital finds its classical roots in Durkheim's ([1893] 1984) theory of social integration and the sanctioning capacity of group rituals. As in the case of reciprocity exchanges, the motivation of donors of socially mediated gifts is instrumental, but in this case, the expectation of repayment is not based on knowledge of the recipient, but on the insertion of both actors in a common social structure. The embedding of a transaction into such structure has two consequences. First, the donor's returns may come not

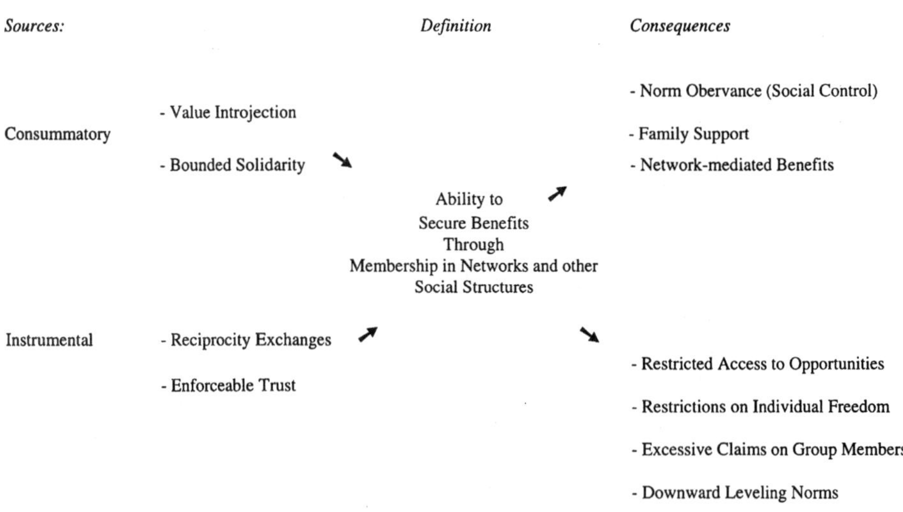

Figure 1 Actual and potential gains and losses in transactions mediated by social capital

directly from the recipient but from the collectivity as a whole in the form of status, honor, or approval. Second, the collectivity itself acts as guarantor that whatever debts are incurred will be repaid.

As an example of the first consequence, a member of an ethnic group may endow a scholarship for young co-ethnic students, thereby expecting not repayment from recipients but rather approval and status in the collectivity. The students' social capital is not contingent on direct knowledge of their benefactor, but on membership in the same group. As an example of the second effect, a banker may extend a loan without collateral to a member of the same religious community in full expectation of repayment because of the threat of community sanctions and ostracism. In other words, trust exists in this situation precisely because obligations are enforceable, not through recourse to law or violence but through the power of the community.

In practice, these two effects of enforceable trust are commonly mixed, as when someone extends a favor to a fellow member in expectation of both guaranteed repayment and group approval. As a source of social capital, enforceable trust is hence appropriable by both donors and recipients: For recipients, it obviously facilitates access to resources; for donors, it yields approval and expedites transactions because it ensures against malfeasance. No lawyer need apply for business transactions underwritten by this source of social capital. The left side of Figure 1 summarizes the discussion in this section. Keeping these distinctions in mind is important to avoid confusing consummatory and instrumental motivations or mixing simple dyadic exchanges with those embedded in larger social structures that guarantee their predictability and course.

Effects of Social Capital: Recent Research

Just as the sources of social capital are plural so are its consequences. The empirical literature includes applications of the concept as a predictor of, among others, school attrition and academic performance, children's intellectual development, sources of employment and occupational attainment, juvenile delinquency and its prevention, and immigrant and ethnic enterprise.[3] Diversity of effects goes beyond the broad set of specific dependent variables to which social capital has been applied to encompass, in addition, the character and meaning of the expected consequences. A review of the literature makes it possible to distinguish three basic functions of social capital, applicable in a variety of contexts: (*a*) as a source of social control; (*b*) as a source of family support; (*c*) as a source of benefits through extrafamilial networks.

[3]The following review does not aim at an exhaustive coverage of the empirical literature. That task has been rendered obsolete by the advent of computerized topical searches. My purpose instead is to document the principal types of application of the concept in the literature and to highlight their interrelationships.

As examples of the first function, we find a series of studies that focus on rule enforcement. The social capital created by tight community networks is useful to parents, teachers, and police authorities as they seek to maintain discipline and promote compliance among those under their charge. Sources of this type of social capital are commonly found in bounded solidarity and enforceable trust, and its main result is to render formal or overt controls unnecessary. The process is exemplified by Zhou & Bankston's study of the tightly knit Vietnamese community of New Orleans:

> Both parents and children are constantly observed as under a "Vietnamese microscope." If a child flunks out or drops out of a school, or if a boy falls into a gang or a girl becomes pregnant without getting married, he or she brings shame not only to himself or herself but also to the family. (Zhou & Bankston 1996, p. 207)

The same function is apparent in Hagan et al's (1995) analysis of right-wing extremism among East German youth. Labeling right-wing extremism a subterranean tradition in German society, these authors seek to explain the rise of that ideology, commonly accompanied by anomic wealth aspirations among German adolescents. These tendencies are particularly strong among those from the formerly communist eastern states. That trend is explained as the joint outcome of the removal of social controls (low social capital), coupled with the long deprivations endured by East Germans. Incorporation into the West has brought about new uncertainties and the loosening of social integration, thus allowing German subterranean cultural traditions to re-emerge.

Social control is also the focus of several earlier essays by Coleman, who laments the disappearance of those informal family and community structures that produced this type of social capital; Coleman calls for the creation of formal institutions to take their place. This was the thrust of Coleman's 1992 presidential address to the American Sociological Association, in which he traced the decline of "primordial" institutions based on the family and their replacement by purposively constructed organizations. In his view, modern sociology's task is to guide this process of social engineering that will substitute obsolete forms of control based on primordial ties with rationally devised material and status incentives (Coleman 1988b, 1993). The function of social capital for social control is also evident whenever the concept is discussed in conjunction with the law (Smart 1993, Weede 1992). It is as well the central focus when it is defined as a property of collectivities such as cities or nations. This latter approach, associated mainly with the writings of political scientists, is discussed in a following section.

The influence of Coleman's writings is also clear in the second function of social capital, namely as a source of parental and kin support. Intact families and those where one parent has the primary task of rearing children possess more of this form of social capital than do single-parent families or those where both parents work. The primary beneficiaries of this resource are, of course, the children whose education and personality development are enriched accordingly. Coleman (1988a:S110) thus cites approvingly the practice of Asian immigrant mothers who not only stay at home but often purchase second copies of school textbooks to help their offspring with their homework.

A second example of this function is in McLanahan & Sandefur's monograph *Growing Up with a Single Parent* (1994), which examines the consequences of single parenthood for school achievement and attrition, teenage pregnancy, and other adolescent outcomes. Social capital tends to be lower for children in single-parent families because they lack the benefit of a second at-home parent and because they tend to change residences more often, leading to fewer ties to other adults in the community. This deficit is not the only causal factor but certainly plays an important role in bringing about less desirable educational and personality outcomes among single-parent children. Along the same lines, Parcel & Menaghan (1994a,b) have conducted extensive quantitative analyses of national surveys to examine the effect of parental work on children's cognitive and social development. They conclude that parental intellectual and other resources contribute to the forms of family capital useful in facilitating positive children outcomes, but that common beliefs about a negative effect of maternal work during early infancy are overgeneralized.

A third example is Hao's (1994) analysis of kin support and out-of-wedlock motherhood. Like financial capital, social capital influences transfers made by parents to daughters and behavioral outcomes such as teen pregnancy, educational attainment, and labor force participation. Social capital is greater in two-parent families, those with fewer children, and those where parents have high aspirations for their young. These conditions foster greater parental attention, more hours spent with children, and the emergence of an achievement orientation among adolescents.

Two interesting final examples highlight the role of family support as a counterweight to the loss of community bounds. In their longitudinal study of adolescents in Toronto, Hagan et al (1996) confirm Coleman's finding about the deleterious effect of multiple family moves on children's emotional adjustment and educational achievement. Leaving a community tends to destroy established bonds, thus depriving family and children of a major source of social capital. These authors find, however, an interaction effect leading to an exacerbation of the loss among children whose parents provide them with weak support and to a partial neutralization among those in the opposite situation. Parental support leads to higher educational achievement, both directly and indirectly through compensating for the loss of community among migrants.

Along the same lines, Gold (1995) highlights the change in parental roles among Israeli immigrant families in the United States. In Israel, close community bonds facilitate supervision and rearing of children because other adults know the young and assume responsibility for their well-being. In the more anomic American environment, mothers are assigned the role of compensating for the lack of community ties with exclusive dedication to their children. Thus, female labor force participation is much greater in Israel than among Israelis in the United States as mothers endeavor to preserve an appropriate cultural environment for their young. Note that in both of these examples, reduction of social capital in its first form—community social bonds and control—is partially compensated by an increase of social capital in its second form, familial support.

By far, however, the most common function attributed to social capital is as a source of network-mediated benefits beyond the immediate family. This definition comes closest to that of Bourdieu (1979, 1980), for whom parental support of children's development is a source of cultural capital, while social capital refers to assets gained through membership in networks. This third function is illustrated by Anheier et al's (1995) use of blockmodeling techniques to map social ties among artists and intellectuals in the German city of Cologne. Results of their analysis show very strong networks among core members of the city's intellectual elite along with more restricted access to them for those in peripheral and commercial pursuits. From a methodological standpoint, this article is one of the most sophisticated applications of Bourdieu's ideas to the sociology of culture.

Yet, the most common use of this third form of social capital is in the field of stratification. It is frequently invoked here as an explanation of access to employment, mobility through occupational ladders, and entrepreneurial success. The idea that connections are instrumental in furthering individual mobility is central to Loury's analysis, as seen previously, and is also found among a number of authors who do not conceptualize it explicitly as social capital. Granovetter (1974), for example, coined the term "strength of weak ties" to refer to the power of indirect influences outside the immediate circle of family and close friends to serve as an informal employment referral system. The idea was original because it ran contrary to the commonsense notion that dense networks such as those available through family circles would be most effective in finding jobs. Almost two decades later, Burt (1992) built on Granovetter's insight by developing the concept of "structural holes." As we have seen, Burt did employ the term social capital and, like Bourdieu's, his definition is instrumental. In Burt's case, however, social capital is based on the relative paucity of network ties rather than on their density.

Another noteworthy early effort was by Nan Lin, Walter Ensel, and John C Vaughn (1981), *Social Resources and Strength of Ties*, which points precisely in the opposite direction. Although Lin and his colleagues did not use the term social capital, Coleman (1988a) cites their work approvingly because of a common emphasis on dense networks as a resource. This alternative stance which, in contrast to Granovetter and Burt, may be labeled "the strength of strong ties" is also evident in other areas of the social-networks-and-mobility literature. One of the most noteworthy is the study of immigrant and ethnic entrepreneurship, in which networks and the social capital that flows through them are consistently identified as a key resource for the creation of small businesses. Light, for example, has emphasized the importance of rotating credit associations (RCAs) for the capitalization of Asian immigrant firms in the United States. RCAs are informal groups that meet periodically, with every member contributing a set amount to a common pool that is received by each in turn. Social capital in this case comes from the trust that each participant has in the continuing contribution of others even after they receive the pooled funds. Without such trust, no one will contribute and each will be deprived of this effective means to gain access to finance (Light 1984, Light & Bonacich 1988).

The role of social networks is equally important in studies of ethnic business enclaves and ethnic niches. Enclaves are dense concentrations of immigrant or ethnic firms that employ a significant proportion of their co-ethnic labor force and develop a distinctive physical presence in urban space. Studies of New York's Chinatown (Zhou 1992); of Miami's Little Havana (Portes 1987, Portes & Stepick 1993, Perez 1992); and of Los Angeles' Koreatown (Light & Bonacich 1988, Nee et al 1994) consistently highlight the role of community networks as a source of vital resources for these ethnic firms. Such resources include but are not limited to start-up capital; others are tips about business opportunities, access to markets, and a pliant and disciplined labor force.

Ethnic niches emerge when a group is able to colonize a particular sector of employment in such a way that members have privileged access to new job openings, while restricting that of outsiders. Examples documented in the literature range from restaurant work and garment factories all the way to police and fire departments and certain branches of the New York and Miami civil services (Waters 1994, Doeringer & Moss 1986, Bailey & Waldinger 1991, Waldinger 1996, Stepick 1989). As in the case of enclaves, mobility opportunities through niches are entirely network-driven. Members find jobs for others, teach them the necessary skills, and supervise their performance. The power of network chains is such that entry level openings are frequently filled by contacting kin and friends in remote foreign locations rather than by tapping other available local workers (Sassen 1995).

The opposite of this situation is the dearth of social connections in certain impoverished communities or their truncated character. Since publication of Carol Stack's *All Our Kin* (1974), sociologists know that everyday survival in poor urban communities frequently depends on close interaction with kin and friends in similar situations. The problem is that such ties seldom reach beyond the inner city, thus depriving their inhabitants of sources of information about employment opportunities elsewhere and ways to attain them. Wacquant & Wilson (1989) and Wilson (1987, 1996) also emphasize how the departure of both industrial employment and middle-class families from black inner city areas have left the remaining population bereft of social capital, a situation leading to its extremely high levels of unemployment and welfare dependency.

The same point is central to Mercer Sullivan's (1989) comparative ethnographies of Puerto Rican, black, and working-class white youth in three New York communities. Sullivan challenges blanket assertions about youth subcultures as determinants of deviant behavior by showing that access to regular jobs and participation in deviant activities are both network mediated. As Granovetter (1974) had noted earlier, teenagers seldom find jobs; instead jobs come to them through the mediation of parents and other adults in their immediate community. Sullivan shows how such networks are much feebler in the case of black youth because of the scarcity of occupants of influential positions in the adult generation. Thrown back on their own resources, black adolescents are seldom able to compete successfully for good regular jobs; thus they become available for alternative forms of income earning.

In her analysis of teenage pregnancy in Baltimore's ghetto, Fernandez-Kelly (1995) notes how the dense but truncated networks of inner-city black families not only cut off members from information about the outside world, but simultaneously support alternative cultural styles that make access to mainstream employment even more difficult. In this isolated context, teenage pregnancy is not the outgrowth of carelessness or excess sexuality but, more commonly, a deliberate means to gain adult status and a measure of independence.

Similarly, Stanton-Salazar & Dornbush (1995) have investigated the relationship between outside social networks and academic achievement and aspirations among Mexican high school students in the San Francisco area. They find positive correlations among these variables, although the strongest associations are with bilingualism, suggesting the role of cultural capital in status attainment. In a related article, Valenzuela & Dornbush (1994) highlight the role of family networks and a familistic orientation in the academic achievement of Mexican-origin students. Paralleling the studies of Hagan et al (1996) and Gold (1995), these articles suggest that immigrant families compensate for the absence of the third form of social capital—outside networks—with an emphasis on social capital in the form of familial support, including preservation of the cultural orientations of their home country.

As in the case of the various sources of social capital outlined in the last section, it is also important to keep in mind the differing functions of the concept both to avoid confusion and to facilitate study of their interrelationships. It is possible, for example, that social capital in the form of social control may clash with social capital in the form of network-mediated benefits, if the latter consists precisely on the ability to bypass existing norms. The capacity of authorities to enforce rules (social control) can thus be jeopardized by the existence of tight networks whose function is precisely to facilitate violation of those rules for private benefit. These paradoxical outcomes point to the need of a closer look at the actual and potential gainers and losers in transactions mediated by social capital. The right side of Figure 1 summarizes the previous discussion and that of the next section.

Negative Social Capital[4]

The research literature on social capital strongly emphasizes its positive consequences. Indeed it is our sociological bias to see good things emerging out of sociability; bad things are more commonly associated with the behavior of homo economicus. However, the same mechanisms appropriable by individuals and groups as social capital can have other, less desirable consequences. It is important to emphasize them for two reasons: first, to avoid the trap of presenting community networks, social control, and collective sanctions as unmixed blessings; second, to keep the analysis within the bounds of serious sociological analysis rather than moralizing statements. Recent studies have identified at least four negative consequences of social capital: exclusion of outsiders, excess claims on group members, restrictions on individual freedoms, and downward leveling norms. I summarize them next.

First, the same strong ties that bring benefits to members of a group commonly enable it to bar others from access. Waldinger (1995) describes the tight control exercised by white ethnics—descendants of Italian, Irish, and Polish immigrants—over the construction trades and the fire and police unions of New York. Other cases include the growing control of the produce business by Korean immigrants in several East Coast cities, the traditional monopoly of Jewish merchants over the New York diamond trade, and the dominance of Cubans over numerous sectors of the Miami economy. In each instance, social capital generated by bounded solidarity and trust are at the core of the group's economic advance. But, as Waldinger (1995, p. 557) points out, "the same social relations that...enhance the ease and efficiency of economic exchanges among community members implicitly restrict outsiders."

Ethnic groups are not the only ones that use social capital for economic advantage. Two centuries ago, Adam Smith ([1776] 1979, p. 232) complained that meetings of merchants inevitably ended up as a conspiracy against the public. The public, of course, are all those excluded from the networks and mu-

[4]This section is partially based on Portes & Sensenbrenner (1993) and Portes & Landolt (1996).

tual knowledge linking the colluding groups. Substitute for "merchants" white building contractors, ethnic union bosses, or immigrant entrepreneurs, and the contemporary relevance of Smith's point becomes evident.

The second negative effect of social capital is the obverse of the first because group or community closure may, under certain circumstances, prevent the success of business initiatives by their members. In his study of the rise of commercial enterprises in Bali, Geertz observed how successful entrepreneurs were constantly assaulted by job and loan-seeking kinsmen. These claims were buttressed by strong norms enjoining mutual assistance within the extended family and among community members in general (Geertz 1963). The result was to turn promising enterprises into welfare hotels, checking their economic expansion.

Granovetter (1995), who calls attention to this example, notes that it is an instance of the problem that classic economic development theory identified among traditional enterprises. Weber ([1922] 1965) made the same point when he stressed the importance of impersonal economic transactions guided by the principle of universalism as one of the major reasons for Puritan entrepreneurial success. Thus, cozy intergroup relations of the kind found in highly solidary communities can give rise to a gigantic free-riding problem, as less diligent members enforce on the more successful all kinds of demands backed by a shared normative structure. For claimants, their social capital consists precisely of privileged access to the resources of fellow members. In the process, opportunities for entrepreneurial accumulation and success are dissipated.[5]

Third, community or group participation necessarily creates demands for conformity. In a small town or village, all neighbors know each other, one can get supplies on credit at the corner store, and children play freely in the streets under the watchful eyes of other adults. The level of social control in such settings is strong and also quite restrictive of personal freedoms, which is the reason why the young and the more independent-minded have always left. Boissevain (1974) reports such a situation in his study of village life in the island of Malta. Dense, "multiplex"[6] networks tying inhabitants together created the

[5]A related problem has been observed in inner city neighborhoods where kin networks form a key survival resource through mutual assistance and ready access to favors and small loans. By the same token, the norm that dictates that incoming resources (such as a money prize) be shared with relatives and friends effectively prevents any sustained accumulation or entrepreneurial investment by individuals. Those wishing to pursue that route must distance themselves from their former partners (see Uehara 1990, Fernandez-Kelly 1995, Stack 1974).

[6]Multiplexity refers to overlapping social networks where the same people are linked together across different roles. In small towns, for example, the same individuals may be simultaneously kin, neighbors, and co-workers thus intensifying the intensity and capacity for mutual monitoring of their ties (Boissevain 1974, p. 31–33).

ground for an intense community life and strong enforcement of local norms. The privacy and autonomy of individuals were reduced accordingly.

This is an expression of the age-old dilemma between community solidarity and individual freedom analyzed by Simmel ([1902] 1964) in his classic essay on "The Metropolis and Mental Life." In that essay, Simmel came out in favor of personal autonomy and responsibility. At present, the pendulum has swung back, and a number of authors are calling for stronger community networks and norm observance in order to re-establish social control. This may be desirable in many instances, but the downside of this function of social capital must also be kept in mind.

Constraints on individual freedom may be responsible for Rumbaut's findings that high levels of familistic solidarity among recent immigrant students are negatively related to four different educational outcomes, including grades and standardized test scores. According to this author, "family ties bind, but sometimes these bonds constrain rather than facilitate particular outcomes" (Rumbaut 1977, p. 39).

Fourth, there are situations in which group solidarity is cemented by a common experience of adversity and opposition to mainstream society. In these instances, individual success stories undermine group cohesion because the latter is precisely grounded on the alleged impossibility of such occurrences. The result is downward leveling norms that operate to keep members of a downtrodden group in place and force the more ambitious to escape from it. In his ethnographic research among Puerto Rican crack dealers in the Bronx, Bourgois (1991, 1995) calls attention to the local version of this process, which singles out for attack individuals seeking to join the middle-class mainstream. He reports the views of one of his informants:

> When you see someone go downtown and get a good job, if they be Puerto Rican, you see them fix up their hair and put some contact lenses in their eyes. Then they fit in and they do it! I have seen it!...Look at all the people in that building, they all "turn-overs." They people who want to be white. Man, if you call them in Spanish it wind up a problem. I mean like take the name Pedro—I'm just telling you this as an example—Pedro be saying (imitating a whitened accent) "My name is Peter." Where do you get Peter from Pedro? (Bourgois 1991, p. 32)

Similar examples are reported by Stepick (1992) in his study of Haitian-American youth in Miami and by Suarez-Orozco (1987) and Matute-Bianchi (1986, 1991) among Mexican-American teenagers in Southern California. In each instance, the emergence of downward leveling norms has been preceded by lengthy periods, often lasting generations, in which the mobility of a particular group has been blocked by outside discrimination. That historical experience underlines the emergence of an oppositional stance toward the mainstream and a solidarity grounded in a common experience of subordination.

Once in place, however, this normative outlook has the effect of helping perpetuate the very situation that it decries.

Notice that social capital, in the form of social control, is still present in these situations, but its effects are exactly the opposite of those commonly celebrated in the literature. Whereas bounded solidarity and trust provide the sources for socioeconomic ascent and entrepreneurial development among some groups, among others they have exactly the opposite effect. Sociability cuts both ways. While it can be the source of public goods, such as those celebrated by Coleman, Loury, and others, it can also lead to public "bads." Mafia families, prostitution and gambling rings, and youth gangs offer so many examples of how embeddedness in social structures can be turned to less than socially desirable ends. The point is particularly important as we turn to the more recent and more celebratory versions of social capital.

Social Capital as a Feature of Communities and Nations[7]

As seen in previous sections, sociological analyses of social capital have been grounded on relationships between actors or between an individual actor and a group. Throughout, the focus has been on the potential benefit accruing to actors because of their insertion into networks or broader social structures. An interesting conceptual twist was introduced by political scientists who equate social capital with the level of "civicness" in communities such as towns, cities, or even entire countries. For Robert Putnam, the most prominent advocate of this approach, social capital means "features of social organizations, such as networks, norms, and trust, that facilitate action and cooperation for mutual benefit." The collective character of this version of the concept is evident in the next sentence: "Working together is easier in a community blessed with a substantial stock of social capital" (Putnam 1993, pp. 35–36).

In practice, this stock is equated with the level of associational involvement and participatory behavior in a community and is measured by such indicators as newspaper reading, membership in voluntary associations, and expressions of trust in political authorities. Putnam is not shy about the expected reach and significance of this version of social capital:

> This insight turns out to have powerful practical implications for many issues on the American national agenda—for how we might overcome the poverty and violence of South Central Los Angeles…or nurture the fledgling democracies of the former Soviet empire. (Putnam 1993: 36, 1996)

The prospect of a simple diagnosis of the country's problems and a ready solution to them has attracted widespread public attention. Putnam's article, "Bowling Alone: America's Declining Social Capital," published in the *Jour-*

[7]This section is partially based on Portes & Landolt (1996).

nal of Democracy in 1995, created something of a sensation, earning for its author a tête-à-tête with President Clinton and a profile in *People* magazine. The nostalgic image evoked by the lonely bowler resonated with many powerful members of the American establishment and even inspired passages in Clinton's State of the Union address in 1995 (Pollitt 1996, Lemann 1996). Putnam buttressed his case with figures about rapidly declining levels of voting and membership in such organizations as the PTA, the Elks Club, the League of Women Voters, and the Red Cross. He then identified the immediate determinant of the decreasing national stock of social capital, namely the passage from the scene of the civic generation active during the 1920s and 1930s and the succession of an uncivic generation—the baby boomers—born and raised after World War II:

> ...the very decades that have seen a national deterioration in social capital are the same decades during which the numerical dominance of a trusting and civic generation has been replaced by this domination of post-civic cohorts....Thus a generational analysis leads almost inevitably to the conclusion that the national slump in trust and engagement is likely to continue. (Putnam 1996, pp. 45–46)

Critics have focused on the question of whether voluntarism and civic spirit have actually declined in America and on the unacknowledged class bias in Putnam's thesis. Lay reviewers such as Lemann in *The Atlantic Monthly* and Pollitt in *The Nation* questioned whether American civic virtue is on the wane or has simply taken new forms different from the old-style organizations cited in Putnam's article. They also note the elitist stance of the argument, where responsibility for the alleged decline of social capital is put squarely on the leisure behavior of the masses, rather than on the economic and political changes wrought by the corporate and governmental establishment. In her trenchant review of Putnam's thesis, Skocpol (1996, p. 25) also stresses this point:

> How ironic it would be if, after pulling out of locally rooted associations, the very business and professional elites who blazed the path toward local civic disengagement were now to turn around and successfully argue that the less privileged Americans they left behind are the ones who must repair the nation's social connectedness....

These critiques are valid but do not address a more fundamental problem with Putnam's argument, namely its logical circularity. As a property of communities and nations rather than individuals, social capital is simultaneously a cause and an effect. It leads to positive outcomes, such as economic development and less crime, and its existence is inferred from the same outcomes. Cities that are well governed and moving ahead economically do so because they have high social capital; poorer cities lack in this civic virtue. This circularity is well illustrated in passages like the following:

> Some regions of Italy...have many active community organizations....These "civic communities" value solidarity, civic participation, and integrity. And here democracy works. At the other end are "uncivic" regions, like Calabria and Sicily, aptly characterized by the French term *incivisme*. The very concept of citizenship is stunted here. (Putnam 1993, p. 36)

In other words, if your town is "civic," it does civic things; if it is "uncivic," it does not.

Tautology in this definition of social capital results from two analytic decisions; first, starting with the effect (i.e. successful versus unsuccessful cities) and working retroactively to find out what distinguishes them: second, trying to explain all of the observed differences. In principle, the exercise of seeking to identify post-factum causes of events is legitimate, provided that alternative explanations are considered. In fairness to Putnam, he does this in his analysis of differences between the well-governed towns of the Italian north and the poorly governed ones of the south (Putnam 1993, Lemann 1996). Such retroactive explanations can only be tentative, however, because the analyst can never rule out other potential causes and because these explanations remain untested in cases other than those considered.

More insidious, however, is the search for full explanation of all observed differences because the quest for this prime determinant often ends up by relabeling the original problem to be explained. This happens as the elimination of exceptions reduces the logical space between alleged cause and effect so that the final predictive statement is either a truism or circular.[8] In Putnam's analysis of Italian cities, such factors as differences in levels of economic development, education, or political preferences proved to be imperfect predictors. Thus, the search for a prime determinant gradually narrowed to something labeled (following Machiavelli) *vertu civile* (civic virtue). It is present in those cities whose inhabitants vote, obey the law, and cooperate with each other and whose leaders are honest and committed to the public good (Putnam 1993, 1995).

The theory then goes on to assert that civic virtue is the key factor differentiating well-governed communities from poorly governed ones. It could hardly be otherwise given the definition of the causal variable. Thus, cities where everyone cooperates in maintaining good government are well governed. To avoid saying the same thing twice, the analyst of social capital must observe certain logical cautions: first, separating the definition of the concept, theoreti-

[8]The method of analytic induction, popular in American sociology in the 1940s and 1950s, consisted precisely in this process of seeking to explain all cases and gradually eliminate all exceptions. It went rapidly out of favor when it was discovered that it basically gave rise to tautologies by redefining the essential characteristics of the phenomenon to be explained. The only way of guaranteeing closure or zero exceptions turns out to be an explanation that is a logical corollary of the effect to be explained. On analytic induction, see Turner (1953) and Robinson (1951).

cally and empirically, from its alleged effects; second, establishing some controls for directionality so that the presence of social capital is demonstrably prior to the outcomes that it is expected to produce; third, controlling for the presence of other factors than can account for both social capital and its alleged effects; fourth, identifying the historical origins of community social capital in a systematic manner.

This task is doable, but time-consuming. Instead, the intellectual journey that transformed social capital from an individual property into a feature of cities and countries tended to disregard these logical criteria. The journey was fast, explaining major social outcomes by relabeling them with a novel term and then employing the same term to formulate sweeping policy prescriptions. While I believe that the greatest theoretical promise of social capital lies at the individual level—exemplified by the analyses of Bourdieu and Coleman—there is nothing intrinsically wrong with redefining it as a structural property of large aggregates. This conceptual departure requires, however, more care and theoretical refinement than that displayed so far.[9]

Conclusion

Current enthusiasm for the concept reviewed in this article and its proliferating applications to different social problems and processes is not likely to abate soon. This popularity is partially warranted because the concept calls attention to real and important phenomena. However, it is also partially exaggerated for two reasons. First, the set of processes encompassed by the concept are not new and have been studied under other labels in the past. Calling them social capital is, to a large extent, just a means of presenting them in a more appealing conceptual garb. Second, there is little ground to believe that social capital will provide a ready remedy for major social problems, as promised by its bolder proponents. Recent proclamations to that effect merely restate the original problems and have not been accompanied so far by any persuasive account of how to bring about the desired stocks of public civicness.

At the individual level, the processes alluded to by the concept cut both ways. Social ties can bring about greater control over wayward behavior and provide privileged access to resources; they can also restrict individual freedoms and bar outsiders from gaining access to the same resources through particularistic preferences. For this reason, it seems preferable to approach these

[9]A promising effort in this direction has been made by Woolcock (1997), who seeks to apply the concept of social capital to the analysis of national and community development in Third World countries. After an extensive review of the literature, he notes that "definitions of social capital should focus primarily on its sources rather than its consequences since long-term benefits, if and when they occur, are the result of a combination of different...types of social relations, combinations whose relative importance will, in all likelihood, shift over time" (Woolcock 1997, p. 35).

manifold processes as social facts to be studied in all their complexity, rather than as examples of a value. A more dispassionate stance will allow analysts to consider all facets of the event in question and prevent turning the ensuing literature into an unmitigated celebration of community. Communitarian advocacy is a legitimate political stance; it is not good social science. As a label for the positive effects of sociability, social capital has, in my view, a place in theory and research provided that its different sources and effects are recognized and that their downsides are examined with equal attention.

ACKNOWLEDGMENTS

I acknowledge the assistance of Patricia Landolt and Clemencia Cosentino in the preparation of the article and the comments on an earlier version from John Logan and Robert K Merton. Responsibility for the contents is exclusively mine.

Literature Cited

Anheier HK, Gerhards J, Romo FP. 1995. Forms of social capital and social structure in cultural fields: examining Bourdieu's social topography. *Am. J. Sociol.* 100: 859–903

Bailey T, Waldinger R. 1991. Primary, secondary, and enclave labor markets: a training system approach. *Am. Sociol. Rev.* 56: 432–45

Baker WE. 1990. Market networks and corporate behavior. *Am. J. Sociol.* 96:589–625

Blau PM. 1964. *Exchange and Power in Social Life.* New York: Wiley

Boissevain J. 1974. *Friends of Friends: Networks, Manipulators, and Coalitions.* New York: St. Martin's Press

Bourdieu P. 1979. Les trois états du capital culturel. *Actes Rech. Sci. Soc.* 30:3–6

Bourdieu P. 1980. Le capital social: notes provisoires. *Actes Rech. Sci. Soc.* 31:2–3

Bourdieu P. 1985. The forms of capital. In *Handbook of Theory and Research for the Sociology of Education,* ed. JG Richardson, pp. 241–58. New York: Greenwood

Bourgois P. 1991. *Search of respect: the new service economy and the crack alternative in Spanish Harlem.* Presented at Conf. Poverty, Immigr. Urban Marginality Adv. Soc., Maison Suger, Paris, May 10–11

Bourgois P. 1995. *In Search of Respect: Selling Crack in El Barrio.* New York: Cambridge Univ. Press

Burt RS. 1992. *Structural Holes, The Social Structure of Competition.* Cambridge, MA: Harvard Univ. Press

Coleman JS. 1988a. Social capital in the creation of human capital. *Am. J. Sociol.* 94: S95–121

Coleman JS. 1988b. The creation and destruction of social capital: implications for the law. *Notre Dame J. Law, Ethics, Public Policy* 3:375–404

Coleman JS. 1990. *Foundations of Social Theory.* Cambridge: Belknap Press of Harvard Univ. Press

Coleman JS. 1993. The rational reconstruction of society (1992 Presidential Address). *Am. Sociol. Rev.* 58:1–15

Coleman JS. 1994a. A rational choice perspective on economic sociology. In *Handbook of Economic Sociology,* ed. NJ Smelser, R Swedberg, pp. 166–80. Princeton, NJ: Princeton Univ. Press

Coleman JS. 1994b. The realization of effective norms. In *Four Sociological Traditions: Selected Readings*, ed. R Collins. pp. 171–89. New York: Oxford Univ. Press

Doeringer P, Moss P. 1986. Capitalism and kinship: do institutions matter in the labor market? *Indust. Labor Relat. Rev.* 40: 48–59

Durkheim E. 1984. (1893). *The Division of Labor in Society.* New York: Free Press

Fernández-Kelly MP. 1995. Social and cultural capital in the urban ghetto: implications for the economic sociology of immigration. See Portes 1995, pp. 213–47

Geertz C. 1963. *Peddlers and Princes.* Chicago: Univ. Chicago Press

Gold SJ. 1995. Gender and social capital among Israeli immigrants in Los Angeles. *Diaspora* 4:267–301

Granovetter MS. 1974. *Getting a Job: A Study of Contacts and Careers.* Cambridge, MA: Harvard Univ. Press

Granovetter MS. 1995. The economic sociology of firms and entrepreneurs. See Portes 1995, pp. 128–65

Hagan J, Merkens H, Boenhke K. 1995. Delinquency and disdain: social capital and the control of right-wing extremism among East and West Berlin youth. *Am. J. Sociol.* 100:1028–52

Hagan J, MacMillan R, Wheaton B. 1996. New kid in town: social capital and the life course effects of family migration in children. *Am. Sociol. Rev.* 61:368–85

Hao L. 1994. *Kin Support, Welfare, and Out-of-Wedlock Mothers.* New York: Garland

Homans GC. 1961. *Social Behavior: Its Elementary Forms.* New York: Harcourt, Brace & World

Lemann N. 1996. Kicking in groups. *Atlantic Mon.* 277(April):22–26

Light I. 1984. Immigrant and ethnic enterprise in North America. *Ethn. Racial Stud.* 7: 195–216

Light I, Bonacich E. 1988. *Immigrant Entrepreneurs: Koreans in Los Angeles 1965–1982.* Berkeley: Univ. Calif. Press

Lin N, Ensel WM, Vaughn JC. 1981. Social resources and strength of ties: structural factors in occupational attainment. *Am. Sociol. Rev.* 46: 393–405

Loury GC. 1977. A dynamic theory of racial income differences. In *Women, Minorities, and Employment Discrimination,* ed. PA Wallace, AM La Mond, pp. 153–86. Lexington, MA: Heath

Loury GC. 1981. Intergenerational transfers and the distribution of earnings. *Econometrica* 49:843–67

Marx K. 1967. (1894). *Capital,* Vol. 3. New York: International

Marx K, Engels F. 1947. (1848). *The German Ideology.* New York: International

Matute-Bianchi ME. 1986. Ethnic identities and patterns of school success and failure among Mexican-descent and Japanese-American students in a California high school. *Am. J. Educ.* 95:233–55

Matute-Bianchi ME. 1991. Situational ethnicity and patterns of school performance among immigrant and non-immigrant Mexican-descent students. In *Minority Status and Schooling: A Comparative Study of Immigrant and Involuntary Minorities,* ed. MA Gibson, JU Ogbu, pp. 205–47. New York: Garland

McLanahan S, Sandefur G. 1994. *Growing Up with a Single Parent: What Hurts, What Helps.* Cambridge, MA: Harvard Univ. Press

Nee V, Sanders JM, Sernau S. 1994. Job transitions in an immigrant metropolis: ethnic boundaries and the mixed economy. *Am. Sociol. Rev.* 59:849–72

Parcel TL, Menaghan EG. 1994. *Parents' Jobs and Children's Lives.* New York: Aldine de Gruyter

Parcel TL, Menaghan EG. 1994a. Early parental work, family social capital, and early childhood outcomes. *Am. J. Sociol.* 99:972–1009

Perez L. 1992. Cuban Miami. In *Miami Now,* ed. GJ Grenier, A Stepick, pp. 83–108. Gainesville: Univ. Press Fla.

Pollitt K. 1996. For whom the ball rolls. *The Nation* 262(April 15):9

Portes A. 1987. The social origins of the Cuban enclave economy of Miami. *Sociol. Perspect.* 30:340–72

Portes A. 1995, ed. *The Economic Sociology of Immigration.* New York: Russell Sage

Portes A, Landolt P. 1996. The downside of social capital. *Am. Prospect* 26:18–22

Portes A, Sensenbrenner J. 1993. Embeddedness and immigration: notes on the social determinants of economic action. *Am. J. Sociol.* 98:1320–50

Portes A, Stepick A. 1993. *City on the Edge: The Transformation of Miami.* Berkeley: Univ. Calif. Press

Portes A, Zhou M. 1993. The new second generation: segmented assimilation and its variants among post-1965 immigrant youth. *Ann. Am. Acad. Polit. Soc. Sci.* 530: 74–96

Putnam RD. 1993. The prosperous community: social capital and public life. *Am. Prospect* 13:35–42

Putnam RD. 1995. Bowling alone: America's declining social capital. *J. Democr.* 6:65–78

Putnam RD. 1996. The strange disappearance of civic America. *Am. Prospect* 24: 34–48

Robinson WS. 1951. The logical structure of analytic induction. *Am. Sociol. Rev.* 16: 812–18

Rumbaut RG. 1977. Ties that bind: immigration and immigrant families in the United States. In *Immigration and the Family: Research and Policy on US Immigrants,* ed. A Booth, AC Crouter, N Landale, pp. 3–45. Mahwah, NJ: Erlbaum

Sassen S. 1995. Immigration and local labor markets. See Portes 1995, pp. 87–127

Schiff M. 1992. Social capital, labor mobility, and welfare. *Ration. Soc.* 4:157–75

Simmel G. 1964. [1902]. The metropolis and mental life. In *The Sociology of Georg Simmel,* ed./transl. KH Wolff, pp. 409–24. New York: Free Press

Skocpol T. 1996. Unraveling from above. *Am. Prospect* 25:20–25

Smart A. 1993. Gifts, bribes, and guanxi: a reconsideration of Bourdieu's social capital. *Cult. Anthropol.* 8:388–408

Smith A. 1979. (1776). *The Wealth of Nations.* Baltimore, MD: Penguin

Stack C. 1974. *All Our Kin.* New York: Harper & Row

Stanton-Salazar RD, Dornbusch SM. 1995. Social capital and the reproduction of inequality: information networks among Mexican-origin high school students. *Sociol. Educ.* 68:116–35

Stepick A. 1989. Miami's two informal sectors. In *The Informal Economy: Studies in Advanced and Less Developed Countries,* ed. A Portes, M Castells, LA Benton, pp. 111–34. Baltimore, MD: Johns Hopkins Univ. Press

Stepick A. 1992. The refugees nobody wants: Haitians in Miami. In *Miami Now,* ed. GJ Grenier, A Stepick, pp. 57–82. Gainesville: Univ. Fla. Press

Suarez-Orozco MM. 1987. Towards a psychosocial understanding of hispanic adaptation to American schooling. In *Success or Failure? Learning and the Languages of Minority Students,* ed. HT Trueba, pp. 156–68. New York: Newbury House

Sullivan ML. 1989. *Getting Paid: Youth Crime and Work in the Inner City.* Ithaca, NY: Cornell Univ. Press

Turner R. 1953. The quest for universals in sociological research. *Am. Sociol. Rev.* 18: 604–11

Valenzuela A, Dornbusch SM. 1994. Familism and social capital in the academic achievement of Mexican origin and anglo adolescents. *Soc. Sci. Q.* 75:18–36

Wacquant LJD, Wilson WJ. 1989. The cost of racial and class exclusion in the inner city. *Ann. Am. Acad. Polit. Soc. Sci.* 501:8–26

Waldinger R. 1986. *Through the Eye of the Needle: Immigrants and Enterprise in the New York's Garment Trade.* New York: New York Univ. Press

Waldinger R. 1995. The "Other Side" of embeddedness: a case study of the interplay between economy and ethnicity. *Ethn. Racial Stud.* 18:555–80

Waldinger R. 1996. *Still the Promised City? African-Americans and New Immigrants in Post-Industrial New York.* Cambridge, MA: Harvard Univ. Press

Waters M. 1994. West Indian immigrants, African Americans, and whites in the workplace: different perspectives on American race relations. Presented at Meet. Am. Sociol. Assoc., Los Angeles

Weber M. 1965. (1922, 1947.) *The Theory of Social and Economic Organization.* New York: Free Press. Originally published as *Wirtsch. Ges.,* Part I

Weede E. 1992. Freedom, knowledge, and law as social capital. *Int. J. Unity Sci.* 5: 391–409

Wilson WJ. 1996. *When Work Disappears: The World of the New Urban Poor.* New York: Knopf

Wilson WJ. 1987. *The Truly Disadvantaged: The Inner-City, the Underclass, and Public Policy.* Chicago: Univ. Chicago Press

Woolcock M. 1997. Social capital and economic development: towards a theoretical synthesis and policy framework. *Theory Soc.* In press

Wrong D. 1961. The oversocialized conception of man in modern sociology. *Am. Sociol. Rev.* 26:183–93

Zhou M. 1992. *New York's Chinatown: The Socioeconomic Potential of an Urban Enclave.* Philadelphia: Temple Univ. Press

Zhou M, Bankston CL. 1996. Social capital and the adaptation of the second generation: the case of Vietnamese youth in New Orleans. In *The New Second Generation,* ed. A Portes, pp. 197–220. New York: Russell Sage Found.

Annu. Rev. Sociol. 1998. 24:25–56

FUNDAMENTALISM ET AL: Conservative Protestants in America

Robert D. Woodberry and Christian S. Smith

Sociology Department, University of North Carolina, Chapel Hill, North Carolina 27599-3210; e-mail: cssmith@email.unc.edu

KEY WORDS: religious right, "culture wars," family, tolerance, survey measurement

ABSTRACT

Since the rise of the religious right, scholars have become increasingly interested in studying conservative Protestantism. Not only do conservative Protestants (CPs) make up at least a quarter of the US population; they differ from many Americans in gender-role attitudes, childrearing styles, political orientation, and other ways as well. In fact, religious factors often predict people's political views better than do either class or gender, even though the latter two have received far more attention in the scholarly literature (Manza & Brooks 1997, Kellstedt et al 1996b). Unfortunately research in this area has been hampered by imprecise measurement and poor understanding of the various movements grouped together as CPs. This has muddied statistical results, stifled theoretical development, and blinded researchers to promising areas of analysis. Thus, in this chapter we first discuss the history and distinctive qualities of the various CP movements, then we use these insights to propose better survey measures, and finally we apply this knowledge to several substantive areas (i.e., gender-role attitudes, childrearing styles, tolerance, the "culture wars," the religious right, and the reasons for the religious vitality of CP groups).

PARAMETERS OF THIS CHAPTER

Defining conservative Protestantism is difficult because conservative Protestants (CPs) belong to such a jumble of different denominations and movements, and they do not agree on any one label or set of beliefs (Dayton & Johnston 1991, Marsden 1987a, Kellstedt et al 1996a,c). To add to the confusion, many social scientists and journalists use the terms "fundamentalist," "evangelical," "born again," "conservative Protestant," and "religious right" indiscriminately without considering the differing meanings of these terms (Kellstedt & Smidt 1996). Survey researchers also employ widely varying measurement strategies,

0360-0572/98/0815-0025$08.00

which can create seemingly contradictory results. Even the label "conservative" Protestant is problematic. Although CPs are generally conservative on some theological issues, they are often innovative on others, breaking patterns of classical Protestant thought, creating new worship styles, etc. Their resistance to modernity is highly selective (Oldfield 1996, p. 49, Dayton 1991).

Moreover, not all CPs are conservative politically. A sizable portion are Democrats and economically liberal (Hart 1992, Jelen 1987). If anything, the average white CP is more economically liberal than mainline Protestants. This is especially true for biblical literalists and members of holiness or Pentecostal denominations (though "Baptist-fundamentalists" tend to be more economically conservative) (Iannaccone 1993, Pyle 1993).[1] On social issues CPs are generally more conservative (as measured by their statistical mean) but often also have greater diversity in their views than the general public (i.e., a significantly larger standard deviation) (Gay et al 1996, Gay & Ellison 1993, DiMaggio et al 1996).

To avoid the problem of confusing religious and political "conservatism," many scholars use the term "evangelical" to describe all CPs. These scholars also argue that "evangelical" and "mainline" Protestantism are identifiably historic traditions, whereas other categorizations have more arbitrary dividing lines. However, using the general "evangelical" category has two problems. First, not all CPs accept the label, and some actively deny it (Dayton 1991). Although there may be a loose affinity between the groups categorized as "evangelical," it is not clearly the only or best label. Second, the term evangelical is confusing, because scholars simultaneously use it to describe the moderate wing of contemporary CPs, CPs as a whole, and nineteenth century revivalism (often in the same text). Thus, those not familiar with the movements have difficulty determining when the term refers to moderate CPs and when to all of them. To avoid this problem we use "CP" as the general term, and "evangelical" for the moderate wing of CPs which emerged after World War II. In doing this, we are adjusting the terminology of scholars like Kellstedt et al (1996a); we are not challenging their definition of the broad "evangelical" category or their division of Protestant denominations into "mainline," "evangelical," and "black Protestant" categories. In the history section we also refer to nineteenth century Protestant revivalistic movements as "evangelical." This matches the historical literature and is distinct enough in time to avoid undue confusion. Our terminology creates problems as well, but we have not discovered any unproblematic terms.[2]

[1]Conservative Protestants may be becoming more economically conservative (see Kellstedt et al 1996d).

[2]Alternative solutions would be to call all CPs "traditional Protestants" or "theologically conservative Protestants" or to call all CPs "evangelicals" and moderate CPs "neo-evangelicals." We do not recommend dividing Protestants into "conservatives," "moderates," and "liberals." Unfortunately, however, our terminology may create some confusion with this alternative categorization.

This chapter focuses on white CPs. Although black CPs are conservative theologically, they are very different politically and are separated institutionally from white CPs. Thus, most researchers analyze them as a distinct group. For good summaries of research on black CPs, see Lincoln & Mamiya (1990), Payne (1995), and Sernett (1991). Scholars have generally ignored Asian-American and Latino/a-American CPs. Fortunately, an edited volume that includes chapters on these is forthcoming (Warner & Wittner 1998).

A substantial literature also compares "fundamentalisms" around the world [e.g., the five-volume series edited by Marty & Appleby (1991–1995)].[3] A number of scholars have criticized these works for conflating conservative religious movements with postcolonial nationalist religious movements and for brushing over the substantial differences between, for example, American Protestant fundamentalism and Lebanese Muslim fundamentalism [see Munson 1995a,b, Billings & Scott 1994, and review symposiums in the *Review of Religious Research* 35(1), (4), 37(4)]. Others contend that as long as proper qualifications are made, comparison facilitates new insights (Appleby 1995). This chapter focuses exclusively on CPs in the United States.

HISTORICAL CONTEXT

Fundamentalists and Evangelicals

Modern American fundamentalism grew out of the nineteenth century evangelical movement. In the first half of the century, the revivalistic evangelical tradition grew rapidly, outstripping the Congregationalists, old-light Presbyterians, and Anglicans who had dominated the colonial religious map but did not adjust well to the challenges of the expanding frontier (Finke & Stark 1992). Northern evangelicals were active social reformers and provided the major impetus behind abolitionism, temperance, and a number of similar social movements (Carwardine 1993, Marsden 1987a, Smith 1957); they were also early advocates of the separation of church and state (McLoughlin 1971).

Following the Civil War, tensions developed between Northern evangelical leaders over Darwinism and higher biblical criticism; Southerners remained unified in opposition to both (Marsden 1980, 1991). Modernists attempted to update Christianity to match their view of science. They denied biblical miracles and argued that God manifests himself through the social evolution of society. Conservatives resisted these changes. These latent tensions erupted to the surface after World War I in what came to be called the fundamentalist/modernist split.

[3]Other literature examines the social and political implications of the spread of American CP movements overseas (Hallum 1996, Walls 1996, Brusco 1995, Cox 1995, Martin 1990). For good or ill, these movements are profoundly influencing Asia, Africa, and Latin America; yet social scientists have paid little attention to them (Cox 1995).

Shortly before the war, conservative scholars published a series of monographs called *The Fundamentals of the Christian Religion*, which argued for the authority of Scripture, the veracity of biblical miracles, and salvation through Christ alone. They claimed that these doctrines are so fundamental to the Christian faith that those who deny them are outside the Christian tradition. As a result they were labeled "fundamentalists." Many fundamentalists viewed the rise of Bolshevism as the natural outcome of modernism, and the barbarity of "civilized" Europe during World War I as a resounding disproof of modernist beliefs in the perfectibility of society and the goodness of human nature. Society was not becoming better, it was becoming worse; social reform and education could not overcome human sinfulness.

Modernists had their greatest strength among Northern denominational leaders and seminary professors; fundamentalists, among pastors and laity. Thus, Northern fundamentalists struggled to wrest control of denominational hierarchies and seminaries from modernists. But when inclusive moderates sided with the modernists for the sake of tolerance, the fundamentalists were defeated. Fundamentalists also experienced a humiliating public-opinion defeat in the Scopes trial of 1925 and increasingly withdrew from the public spotlight to build their own separate institutions.[4] Some formed separate denominations; others stayed in existing denominations but developed networks of parachurch organizations outside denominational control (Marsden 1980, Carpenter 1997).

However, significant tension still existed within fundamentalism about how much to "separate from the world." Many fundamentalist leaders were embarrassed by the fractious, anti-intellectual image of fundamentalism and sought to differentiate themselves from the more extreme elements of the movement. They wanted a more open, intellectually engaged version of classical Protestantism, and therefore they called themselves "neo-evangelicals," in reference to the nineteenth century evangelical movement.[5] Initially most neoevangelical institutions were in the North and West, although the movement spread to the South as well. Eventually the "neo" dropped away, and these CPs became "evangelicals" (Marsden 1987a, 1987b).[6]

Currently, "fundamentalism" properly refers to a small subset of CPs (although it is often misused to refer to all CPs). Fundamentalists emphasize a strict literal interpretation of the Bible, dispensational theology, premillennial eschatology, and institutional separation from "apostasy" (i.e., liberal Protestants and Catholics) (see Weber 1991, Marsden 1987a, 1991, Ammerman

[4]See Numbers (1993) for a history of creationism from the mid-1800s to the mid-1980s.

[5]The seminal work on fundamentalism between the 1920s and the rise of neoevangelism is Carpenter (1997).

[6]For a list of resources and annotated bibliographies about CPs, see Blumhofer & Carpenter (1990) and Magnuson & Travis (1990, 1997).

1987). Although fundamentalists have some loose national associations, such as Jerry Falwell's Baptist Bible Fellowship, power remains predominantly with individual pastors.[7]

Pentecostals and Charismatics

Conservative Protestantism also contains two other major movements: Pentecostalism and the charismatic renewal. Pentecostals emerged around the turn of the century from the "Holiness" wing of nineteenth century evangelicalism. They emphasized the gifts of the Holy Spirit (especially divine healing, prophecy, and speaking in tongues) and spread primarily among socially marginalized groups (i.e., poor whites, blacks, and immigrants) (Anderson 1987, Oldfield 1996). In some early revivals (e.g., Azusa Street), blacks and whites worshipped together, but each soon formed separate institutions (Sernett 1991). Like fundamentalists, Pentecostals have traditionally been separatistic (Anderson 1987),[8] but fundamentalists and Pentecostals have not gotten along well with each other either. One area of contention is the basis of religious authority. For fundamentalists, miraculous signs (especially prophecy and speaking in tongues) ended when the writing and compilation of the Bible was completed; religious authority is based on a "literal" interpretation of these sacred texts.[9] Pentecostals, on the other hand, believe that God still continues to reveal his will through prophets. To fundamentalists this seems to challenge the final authority of Scripture. Fundamentalists emphasized doctrine; Pentecostals, experience (also see Wilcox 1996, pp. 28–30).

These antipathies have had important implications for recent political mobilizations. For example, even though Jerry Falwell (a fundamentalist) and Pat Robertson (a charismatic/Pentecostal) are both Southern, Republican, theologically conservative, and politically conservative, both have had difficulty gaining support among the others' constituencies (Oldfield 1996, Wilcox 1996, Green 1996). Traditionally neoevangelicals have distanced themselves from both fundamentalists and Pentecostals because of disagreements about how much Christians must separate themselves from the world (although class and regional differences probably also play a role). Most evangelicals also tend to feel uncomfortable with the more exuberant aspects of Pentecostal worship and with claims of prophesy, healing, etc. Politically, Pentecostals are

[7]Fundamentalists are further divided over the strictness of separation; strict separatists are a very small group, less separatist groups are larger (see Marsden 1991).

[8]Some Pentecostals have become more ecumenical and joined the National Association of Evangelicals (e.g., the Assemblies of God).

[9]Fundamentalists tend to be "dispensationalists." According to this theory, God interacts with his people in different ways during different phases of history (i.e. different dispensations). Miracles were necessary in biblical times to establish the authority of the apostles and prophets who wrote the Bible, but in the current dispensation ("the age of the church"), they are not.

the most conservative on abortion and other social issues, the most liberal on welfare spending, and statistically the least likely to vote, even when socioeconomic status is controlled (Kellstedt et al 1996c, Smidt et al 1996, Pyle 1993).

In the 1960s a fourth movement developed within conservative Protestantism—the charismatic renewal. Like Pentecostalism, the charismatic movement emphasized speaking in tongues and miraculous healing. But unlike Pentecostalism, it spread among Catholics and members of mainline and evangelical denominations. Charismatics were also more middle-class and Northern (Wilson 1984) and probably as a result were less separatistic (Anderson 1987). Thus, unlike Pentecostals, charismatics generally stayed within existing denominations and became a bridge among evangelicals, Pentecostals, mainline Protestants, and Catholics. Pentecostals have increased in socioeconomic status to levels similar to those of charismatics and share many beliefs with them, but still most charismatics do not identify as Pentecostals and vice versa (Smidt et al 1996).[10]

Charismatics and Pentecostals comprise approximately 12% of the US population[11] and have had a profound impact on African, Latin American, and Asian Christianity. They are the fastest growing segment of Christianity worldwide, and yet social scientists have paid little attention to them (Smidt et al 1996, Anderson 1987). Most research surveys don't ask even a single question that would identify them (e.g., questions about speaking in tongues, or religious movement identity, or detailed denominational categories). Thus, most scholars and journalists did not realize that in the 1988 presidential campaign Pat Robertson's political support was limited almost exclusively to the "Spirit filled" (Green 1996, Oldfield 1996, Smidt & Penning 1990).[12]

Although these distinctions within conservative Protestantism may not seem important to many contemporary social scientists, they are important to adherents, and they have important social and political implications (Smith et al 1998, Green et al 1996b, Kirkpatrick 1993). Moreover, in the United States, each of these four groups is probably as large as all non-Christian religious groups combined and none shows any sign of declining. Thus, presumably they deserve a similar amount of scholarly attention.

Regional Variation

There are also important regional variations among CPs. Southern CPs have their own unique religious style and distinct networks of institutions. They also

[10]The major theological distinction between the two is that Pentecostals believe that those who do not speak in tongues have not been baptized by the Holy Spirit; charismatics disagree.

[11]Many of the estimates in this paper are based on phone polls. Phone polls oversample regular church attenders and thus may oversample some religious groups as well (Woodberry 1998).

[12]For annotated bibliographies and resource lists on charismatics and Pentecostals see Mills 1985, Dayton 1985, Burgess & McGee 1988, and Jones 1983,1995.

tend to be more separatistic and socially conservative than Northern CPs (Shibley 1996, Ammerman 1990, Carpenter 1984). This is the result of the South's distinct historical experience.

During the colonial period, evangelicalism was weak in the South. Most white Southerners were Anglican or nonpracticing, and they viewed evangelicals with suspicion. Initially, Northern evangelical missionaries to the South openly condemned slavery, had mixed-race meetings, and emphasized more egalitarian gender roles. The Methodists even attempted to bar all slave holders from membership. However, these practices caused such opposition that evangelicals moderated them to avoid alienating potential followers (Heyrman 1997). As the movement became indigenous, Southern evangelicals increasingly defended slavery based on a literal interpretation of scripture. Southern evangelicals also resisted Northern evangelical social reform movements and perfectionist theology because they were associated with abolitionism (Carwardine 1993, Smith 1957). As the Civil War approached, most evangelical denominations and mission boards split over slavery (Northerners dominated national-level organizations because of their larger population), and a number of separatist religious movements swept through the South that rejected church organization beyond the local level as unbiblical. These movements had a lasting impact on Southern religion (Ammerman 1990, pp. 33–34, 343).

The toll of the Civil War on the South was enormous and left deep resentments against Northern cultural impositions. In the cultural crisis that followed defeat, Southerners struggled to regain the honor and identity they had lost. Many believed that their unfaithfulness to God's law had caused their defeat; for God to bless them again, they needed to uphold his law more diligently than ever before. The result was a series of revivals that swept through the South. Southerners emphasized that they were not morally inferior; on the contrary, it was the Northerners who had become increasingly involved in secular social reform, while the South upheld the true faith (Hill 1980, p. 106, Ammerman 1990, pp. 38–39).[13] Southern denominations perpetuated distinctions from their Northern counterparts and successfully lobbied Southern states to block authorization of Northern home missionaries in the South (Ammerman 1990, pp. 37–38). Thus, many denominations remained organizationally disconnected from the fundamentalist/modernist split and the later neoevangelical movement. Meanwhile, the North was becoming increasingly diverse, while the South stayed more religiously homogeneous and CPs maintained a denominate position in society (Hill 1980). Because of this homogeneity, few Southerners objected to prayer or Bible reading in public schools (Shibley

[13]Not only did these experiences influence Southern symbols and schema, they influenced Northern ones as well. Even today Northerners often associate Southern religion with racism and backwardness.

1996, Ammerman 1990, p. 55); laws against such practices easily appeared as further examples of Northern cultural domination.

As Southerners migrated to the North and West in search of opportunity, they often felt uncomfortable with Northern churches and set up churches similar to those back home (Shibley 1996, Ammerman 1990).[14] These migrations occurred in several waves (i.e., after the Civil War, during the Great Depression, and after World War II). In the 1930s, impoverished Dust Bowl farmers migrated from Arkansas, Oklahoma, and Texas to the agricultural regions of California and the Pacific Northwest (Shibley 1996, p. 34). Today nearly one eighth of Californians, and nearly half of those who reside in the San Joaquin Valley, can trace their ancestry to Oklahoma (Haslam 1989). Other Southerners migrated to the factories of Ohio, Indiana, and southern Michigan. Many Pentecostal, fundamentalist, and Southern Baptist churches in the North and West were planted as a result of these migrations. By 1990 there were over 7300 Southern Baptist churches outside the South with over 2.8 million members (Shibley 1996, Ammerman 1990, pp. 50–51).[15] Although many of the members of these churches do not have Southern ancestry, these churches remain in contact with their roots through the seminary training of pastors, networks of relationships, denominational bulletin inserts, Sunday school material, etc. These networks facilitate the flow of new theological, social, and political ideas between the North and the South.

In spite of the differences described by historians and ethnographers, few social scientists have analyzed differences between Northern and Southern CPs. Strangely, even students of politics in the South have largely neglected religious factors (Green et al 1988a). Yet many of the political leaders of the religious right (RR) are Southerners, and some of the issues associated with the movement seem strongly influenced by regional identity (Woodberry et al 1996).[16] Moreover, the massive movement of Southerners from the Democratic to Republican party may be central to the rise of the New Right.

There is important variation among Southern CPs as well (e.g., Jimmy Carter, Billy Graham, and Al Gore are all Southern CPs), and the RR has gained

[14]The reverse has also happened more recently with Northerners moving to the South.

[15]Dozens of Southern CPs have also become famous as televangelists—e.g., Oral Roberts, Jimmy Swaggart, Jim Bakker, Pat Robertson, and Jerry Falwell (Shibley 1996, Oldfield 1996, p. 135).

[16]Jerry Falwell, Pat Robertson, Oliver North, Donald Wildmon, Ralph Reed, James Kennedy, and Jesse Helms are all Southerners; many RR organizations are/were headquartered in the South (e.g., the Moral Majority, the Christian Coalition, the American Family Association, *World Magazine*, the Christian Action Council, Operation Rescue); and many of the most conservative leaders of the Republican revolution in Congress are also from the South (e.g., Newt Gingrich, Trent Lott, Dick Armey, Strom Thurmond, Tom DeLay, Jesse Helms), although many are not part of the RR (Nixon 1996). The areas of California, Oregon, Washington, Michigan, and Ohio with the strongest RR activism seem to coincide with areas of high Southern migration, although establishing this connection would require further research.

support among non-Southerners. However, it seems plausible that the historical Southern experience of defeat and ridicule could have shaped the political beliefs of Southern CPs differently than Northern CPs, just as the African-American experience of oppression has shaped the political beliefs of black CPs differently than white CPs. Some (although not all) of the issues associated with the RR seem to be influenced by this experience. The concerns of the RR cannot be reduced to class and regional conflicts, but they may be accentuated by them.[17]

MEASUREMENT

Contemporary sociological research about CPs is generally not as developed as historical research. Few social scientists or journalists are religiously active—especially in CP denominations (Wuthnow 1985, Lichter & Rothman 1981, Thalheimer 1973)—and perhaps because of this lack of familiarity, religious factors are frequently ignored or measured poorly (Kellstedt et al 1996a, Woodberry 1997, Hart 1996, C Smith 1996, Larson et al 1994, Thomas & Cornwall 1990, Wuthnow & Hodgkinson 1990, Gorsuch 1988, Hood 1983).

Further, distinguishing fundamentalists, evangelicals, charismatics, and Pentecostals is complex. Researchers can divide denominations into mainline, CP, and black Protestant denominational families. They can also distinguish Pentecostal denominations. However, they cannot easily identify fundamentalists, evangelicals, and charismatics in this way. Some denominations are clearly part of each of these movements, but these movements cross-cut denominations and even denominational families. They are better understood as loosely connected networks of ministerial associations, parachurch organizations, schools, seminaries, magazines, etc. Only recently have scholars begun developing measures to differentiate these groups (see Green et al 1996b, chapters 10–13); most research focuses only on identifying CPs as a whole.

The three major approaches to identifying CPs are denomination, beliefs, and self-identification. Although these approaches overlap, they have important distinctions as well. These differences cause many of the apparent contradictions in the literature. Indeed, whether "fundamentalists" are less educated than the general population depends on whether they are identified by denomination or doctrine or are self-identified (Kellstedt & Smidt 1996). Without multiple measures these distinctions are impossible to identify. However, this

[17]Unfortunately Southern identity is usually measured poorly on surveys. Given the mobility between the North and South, the differences between black and white Southerners, and the great variation in the strength of people's regional identity, merely controlling for state of residence does not seem sufficient.

type of detail is extremely rare. On most surveys, it is fortunate if there is even one good measure.

Another weakness is that scholars do not generally connect qualitative interviews with quantitative survey data. Thus, scholars have difficulty determining how representative case studies, "insider documents," or interviews are, and they have difficulty deciphering the rich contextual meanings of isolated survey responses. This increases the danger that scholars will either overgeneralize the views of small, unrepresentative groups and leaders or project alien meanings on respondents' statements and practices. For example, some of CPs' positions on government intervention seem contradictory but make more sense once scholars understand the moral metaphors that motivate them (Lakoff 1996).

Denominational Affiliation

The most commonly available measure of CPs is denominational affiliation. Unfortunately it is seldom measured with sufficient care or precision.[18] For example, Northern Baptists (i.e., American Baptists in the USA and General Conference Baptists) are more moderate than Southern Baptists, Missionary Baptists, and Independent Baptists. Missouri Synod and Wisconsin Synod Lutherans are more conservative than the Evangelical Lutheran Church in America.[19] The generic categories Baptist, Lutheran, Presbyterian, etc, mask these distinctions and muddy statistical results. Without detailed denominational categories and specific follow-up questions, valuable information is lost and scholars have difficulty recoding respondents into CP, mainline, and black Protestants (let alone into Pentecostal or Northern- and Southern-based denominations). When respondents say they are "Lutheran" or "Presbyterian," researchers need to ask, "Which kind?"

The next problem is separating this jumble of denominations into useful categories. Perhaps the most commonly used categorization is that of Roof & McKinney (1987). However, their denominational categories are broad and incomplete and can cause significant measurement error. Major denominations like the Nazarenes are not even listed. One advantage of their approach, however, is that black Protestant denominations are separated from white ones.

The General Social Survey (GSS) coding is more complete but also has problems (especially before 1983). It recodes all denominations into the categories "fundamentalist," "moderate," and "liberal" (see T Smith 1990). This applies the category "fundamentalist" to over 30% of the US population, a label most would actively deny. This also assumes that all respondents can be

[18]Indeed, most surveys record only whether a respondent is "Protestant," "Catholic," "Jewish," or "Other." These categories are too broad to be of much use (Demerath & Roof 1976, Kellstedt et al 1996a).

[19]In this case "Evangelical" refers to the Protestant Reformation in Germany.

categorized along a single continuum based on the fundamentalist/modernist split of the 1920s, which is questionable even among Protestants, let alone Buddhists and Hindus (Kellstedt et al 1996a). The GSS codes all Catholics as "moderates" and all nonaffiliated as "liberal." Political views also seem to influence how some denominations and religious groups are coded. For example, many black CP denominations are coded as "moderates," although theologically they probably belong in the "fundamentalist" category, and all Jews are coded as "liberal," even those who are theologically conservative (Regnerus et al 1997).[20] The GSS also lumps "nondenominational" Protestants in the same category as those with no denomination. This is unfortunate because the growth of nondenominational Protestants is one of the most important and least documented religious changes taking place in the United States. The overwhelming majority are CPs and do not belong in the "moderate" or "liberal" category. Those who claim "no denomination" do not resemble them either socially or politically (Smidt et al 1996, Shibley 1996).

Fortunately, political scientists have developed some excellent tools to distinguish CP denominations. Kellstedt et al (1996a) is probably the most thorough published version, but similar categorizations are available on the American National Election Studies 1996 cumulative file, the fall 1996 Southern Focus Poll, and several Pew data sets.[21] Interviews with those who conducted these surveys suggest that detailed denomination questions take little survey time and create little respondent or interviewer burden. Developing CATI skip patterns and recoding denominations into useful categories are complicated, but these can be copied from existing surveys. These detailed categorizations also allow scholars to distinguish Pentecostals, black Protestants, and Northern- and Southern-based denominations.

Beliefs

Although many surveys have questions about religious belief, few of these are useful for distinguishing CPs. "Biblical literalism" or "biblical inerrancy" are the most common beliefs used, but these are usually measured poorly. First, the conservative response categories are generally too broad. About 35% of the US population claim the Bible should be interpreted "literally," and many more say it is true but should not always be interpreted literally (both of these are theologically appropriate responses for CPs). However, there are major differences in what people mean by "literal" or "without error" (Bartkowski 1996, Shibley 1996). The limited response options mask these differences.

[20]Controlling for race does not solve the problems caused by the lack of a black Protestant category.

[21]Melton (1989) describes the origins and beliefs of almost every religious group in the United States. It is helpful for more detailed categorizations of denominations. Many small denominations are not coded on most surveys, including the GSS.

Second, many better-educated evangelicals are not literalists or inerrantists. They prefer to say the Bible is "trustworthy for all matters of faith and practice." As a result, biblical literalism is more strongly correlated with education than either CP movement identification or denominational affiliation (Kellstedt & Smidt 1996). Thus, when scholars use these measures to identify CPs, they influence CPs' demographics and attitudes.

Moreover, using a single belief to categorize a complex group like CPs causes substantial measurement error; thus coefficients are no longer BLUE (i.e., unbiased and consistent) (Bollen 1989). When possible, it is better to measure conservative Protestantism as a latent variable using several beliefs. Generally CPs emphasize a personal relationship with Jesus Christ, believe in the importance of converting others to their faith, have a strong view of biblical authority, and believe that salvation is through Christ alone.[22] Unfortunately, few surveys have such detailed belief questions. Almost none ask respondents whether they think it is important to convert others, whether they speak in tongues, or about their views on Jesus Christ, biblical prophecy, or separation from the world. Yet historians use many of these exact measures to distinguish different types of CPs (see e.g., Marsden 1987a). This makes connecting historical and social science literature difficult. Moreover, many of these beliefs predict people's behavior better than the more typical questions about whether they believe in God or the afterlife (about 70–90+% say they do—too many to be very useful), and certainly more than the many detailed questions the GSS asks every year on how people view God or heaven (e.g., "Do you see God as more a savior or redeemer?" "More as a creator or healer?"). Even when surveys have multiple indicators, most researchers use them separately or additively (e.g., CPs are biblical literalists, who are "born again" and have shared their faith with others). This also causes measurement problems because, for example, CPs may be biblical literalists and "born again," but too shy to share their faith. Measuring conservative Protestantism as a latent variable avoids these problems. Still these problems are minor in comparison to the typical single measure approach.

Movement Identification

Until recently, few surveys asked respondents whether they identify with particular religious movements (e.g., fundamentalism, evangelicalism).[23] Yet

[22]For a more detailed discussion of identifying CPs with belief measures, see Green et al 1996b, chapters 10–13. They also discuss ways to identify subgroups within conservative Protestantism.

[23]Some surveys ask if respondents are "born again," but this has several disadvantages. First, it provides less detailed information than a movement ID question; second, the number of people who are "born again" varies significantly based on context and definition; and third, many avoid the label because they cannot pinpoint the time of their conversion or because of negative connotations (see Schumm & Silliman 1990).

movement ID generally predicts people's attitudes and political behavior better than denomination or generic religious beliefs (Smith et al 1998, appendix B, Kellstedt et al 1996c). Among Protestants, we think the most useful categories are "theologically liberal," "mainline," "Pentecostal," "charismatic," "evangelical," and "fundamentalist."[24] Surprisingly, given the widespread use of the term "mainline-liberal," almost no one chooses both of those self-IDs. Few people also choose both the charismatic and Pentecostal IDs (also see Smidt et al 1996).

Despite the predictive power of movement IDs, there are some potential problems with using them. First, people can be part of a religious movement without knowing it. Second, some people have multiple IDs. Third, the terms may mean different things to different people. For example, some may choose the label "fundamentalist" because they believe the fundamentals (e.g., the virgin birth of Christ, the authority of the Bible) and not because they are separatistic, premillenial dispensationalists, or connected to ministers like Jerry Falwell, Bob Jones, or Jack Hyles. Some politically liberal CPs may also avoid using the term "evangelical" because of its association with fundamentalism and the RR (see Kellstedt et al 1996c, p. 259, Johnston 1991). Even those who identify themselves as evangelicals do not always feel close to them, presumably for these same reasons. Fourth, the meaning of the terms is gradually changing as people try to associate themselves with particular groups (or distance themselves from them). Since the late 1970s, journalists and scholars have applied the term "fundamentalist" to Muslim religious movements, some of which use terrorist tactics. In the 1990s, Ralph Reed and the Christian Coalition began to use the term "evangelical" (Jerry Falwell was a fundamentalist and Pat Robertson a Southern charismatic/Pentecostal). Jouranlists covering the RR use a variety of terms, often indiscriminately. In time, these public uses of the terms may change who is willing to use them.

However, despite these possible problems, our analysis suggests that IDs work relatively well. As part of the Religious Identity and Influence Survey, we selected a sample of Protestant respondents from the phone survey and conducted qualitative face-to-face interviews with them. Their explanations of what they meant by "evangelical," etc., generally matched our expectations (although many "fundamentalists" are not as separatistic as expected). For all measures, this type of checking is important because respondents often do not mean what researchers assume.

[24]"Mainline" is probably not a religious movement per se, but it allows respondents to avoid choosing one of the other movement labels.

Religiosity

Although some surveys have multiple measures of religiosity, few researchers use more than one. They generally do not analyze the multiple dimensions of religiosity or combine identifiers to measure latent religiosity variables. Many also analyze religiosity without analyzing religious affiliation or any other aspects of religion (Thomas & Cornwall 1990). This assumes that religiosity is generic, that it does not matter what people believe or what the social context of their worship is. However, sometimes denomination strongly influences the impact of church attendance. Why people attend is also important. For example, those who attend for personal or religious reasons tend to be less prejudiced against ethnic minorities; those who attend for social reasons are more prejudiced (Gorsuch 1988). However, when researchers put multiple measures of religious involvement in the same regression, they must carefully decipher what the individual religion variables represent. For example, it is not clear what conservative Protestantism net of the impact of religiosity is.

Using Multiple Measures

Green et al (1996b, 1997) have found even stronger results by combining all the above measures. For example, those who attend a CP denomination, identify with a CP movement, have conservative religious beliefs, and have higher religiosity have more conservative abortion attitudes and are more Republican than those who are missing some of these CP identifiers. However, this type of analysis works better with crosstabs and multiple classification analysis than with regression. In structural equation modeling, these multiple measures could be used to identify an underlying latent variable or variables.

SUBSTANTIVE AREAS

Gender and Family

Evangelical and Pentecostal groups were the first to ordain women, and some Pentecostal denominations still ordain higher proportions of women than any other denominations (Dayton 1991, Chaves 1996, Lindley 1996). Still, most CP groups have resisted this and limit the participation of women in church leadership. Lobbying by certain CP groups also effectively prevented the bestselling New International Version of the Bible from changing its translation to use gender-inclusive terms. Moreover, CPs are generally more supportive of traditional roles for women (Gay et al 1996), and a higher proportion of them are full-time homemakers. A vast literature has developed about this. Yet little of it contemplates why, in spite of this, women are more active in CP churches than men (Pevey et al 1996) and also more active in missions and evangelism for these groups (Hutchison 1987, Neill 1986, Ryan 1978; also see Brusco 1995).

Recently, several scholars have begun to examine the complexity in prescribed women's roles among CPs (Bartkowski 1996, 1997, Ingersoll 1995) and to interview CP women about their experience and acceptance of these roles. These studies show that CP attitudes and practices in the area of gender and family life (e.g., household division of labor, female employment, marital decision making) are more nuanced and negotiated than previously recognized (Brasher 1997, Ellison & Bartkowski 1997, Gallagher 1996, Pevey et al 1996, Ozorak 1996, Demmitt 1992, Rose 1987, McNamara 1984) and that there is significantly more disagreement about gender-role attitudes among CPs than in the general population (i.e., their standard deviation is significantly larger) (Gay et al 1996). This complexity is often missed in survey analysis because of distinct subcultural usages of terms like "headship" (Gallagher 1996, Pevey et al 1996).

Many scholars also theorize that CPs are more patriarchal and therefore more likely to physically or verbally abuse their wives (e.g., Straus et al 1988, pp. 7–8, 21). However, both self-report and spousal-report suggest that CP men are not more likely than other religious groups to physically abuse their wives and are significantly less likely than the religiously nonaffiliated (Ellison et al 1996, Brinkerhoff et al 1992; also see Straus et al 1988, pp. 128, 138).[25] Neither are they more likely to use verbal or symbolic aggression (Brinkerhoff et al 1992). Moreover, most available evidence suggests that regular church attenders are significantly less likely to abuse their spouse (Ellison et al 1996, Ferguson et al 1986), although in one Canadian study the relationship is curvilinear, with irregular attenders being the most abusive (Brinkerhoff et al 1992).

Although few scholars have analyzed CP family involvement (Wilcox 1997), research does show that "biblical literalists" are more likely to value obedience in children and to use corporal punishment (Ellison & Sherkat 1993a,b, Ellison 1996).[26] Some researchers suggest that as a result, CPs may legitimate and encourage child abuse (Maurer 1982, Capps 1992). However, Ellison (1996) argues that the available evidence does not demonstrate this. According to Ellison, most studies on the negative impact of corporal punishment are seriously flawed, especially as it applies to conservative Protestants. These studies combine spanking, beating, threats, and assault with weapons, and they do not control for attenuating factors like parental involvement, affection, and communication. Definitive conclusions are difficult because almost no research analyzes the impact of mild-to-moderate corporal punishment. Generally, CP authors carefully delimit how and when corporal punishment

[25]The exceptions to this rule are the relatively few cases in which the husband attends church far more or is far more theologically conservative than his wife. In these cases husbands are more likely to use violence (Ellison et al 1996). Studies disagree about whether CP women are more or less likely to use violence against their husbands (Brinkerhoff et al 1992, Ellison et al 1996).

[26]They are not less likely to value intellectual autonomy (Ellison & Sherkat 1993b).

can be used (i.e., only for willful disobedience by pre-teens, not when parents are angry or feel loss of control, and only when the reason for the punishment is carefully explained and followed by "a period of loving intimacy") (Ellison & Sherkat 1993a, Ellison 1996, Bartkowski 1996). However, ordinary people may not necessarily follow these injunctions. Still, recent research on fatherhood by W Bradford Wilcox (1997) suggests that CP fathers are more likely to hug and praise their children, less likely to yell at them, and are among the most involved in their children's daily lives. [27] This may or may not attenuate the possible negative consequences of corporal punishment.

Thus, CP women may be willing to accept more traditional roles in order to get men to be more committed to their marriage and child-raising. Qualitative research suggests that CP women use biblical injunctions to hold their husbands to higher standards of emotional intimacy and support (Gallagher 1996, Pevey et al 1996). In any case, both regular church attenders and CPs report greater life satisfaction and greater commitment to and dependence on their marriages (Larson & Goltz 1989, Wilson & Musick 1996, Ellison 1991, Ellison et al 1989). The more religiously active also have greater marital stability and report higher levels of marital satisfaction (Call & Heaton 1997, Thomas & Cornwall 1990, Lehrer & Chiswick 1993, Filsinger & Wilson 1984, Hunt & King 1978). Studies disagree over whether CPs have higher or lower marital satisfaction and stability than other religious respondents (Call & Heaton 1997, Schumm et al 1989, Wilson & Filsinger 1986, Chi & Houseknecht 1985, Hunt & King 1978). Much of the difference seems to depend on how conservative Protestantism is measured, what is controlled for, and to whom CPs are compared.

Tolerance

Much research suggests that CPs have selective tendencies toward greater intolerance than do other Americans (e.g., Gay & Ellison 1993, Wilcox & Jelen 1990). CPs are not more anti-Semitic than other Americans. Two studies commissioned by the American Jewish Committee show CPs are stronger supporters of Israel, feel closer to Jews, are more likely to view Jews as God's chosen people, and have high social and political acceptance of Jews (e.g., 96% would vote for a Jewish president). Their major "intolerant" attitude is that they generally believe Jews must accept Jesus to be saved (although they believe this for all non-Christians, not just Jews) (T Smith 1994, 1996, Whalen 1996, Guth et al 1996a,c, Abrams 1997). CPs are also not more racist than other Americans.[28]

[27]However, religiosity is not controlled in this analysis; thus greater religiousity rather than CPism may be the important factor.

[28]Some extremist-right groups use Christian rhetoric. However, these have little support or recognition among CPs. For example, of politically/socially conservative white CPs who know David Duke, only 5% "admire" or "somewhat admire" him, compared to 6% of the rest of the white population (T Smith 1994, 1996).

They differ little from other Americans on attitudes toward blacks, Asians, Catholics, Hispanics, or immigrants (T Smith 1996, Davis & Robinson 1996, also see Guth et al 1996c, pp. 308–9).[29]

Conservative Protestants do hold less tolerant views of militarists, racists, atheists, homosexuals, feminists, and Moslems (Wilcox & Jelen 1990, Tamney & Johnson 1997, T Smith 1996). They are also more likely to think "dangerous" books should not be in the public libraries. These kind of findings are reflected in most tolerance scales.

However, some scholars argue that much of this tolerance research is flawed (e.g., Sullivan et al 1982, Smidt & Penning 1982, Davis & Robinson 1996, Jelen & Wilcox 1990, Hood 1983). First, some studies do not have adequate controls. Second, they have no measures of behavior. Some "tolerance" items may measure attitudinal "moral relativism" rather than actual behavioral graciousness toward those with whom one disagrees. Third, most studies treat tolerance as a single unidimensional attitude that people either possess or do not, despite the fact that different groups may be tolerant to some target groups but not others. Fourth, Smidt & Penning (1982) argue that most tolerance scales (e.g., the GSS tolerance scale) are biased against CPs (also see Sullivan et al 1982, pp. 137, 249–50).[30] A better method of measuring tolerance is to let respondents choose the group they dislike most. This methodology eliminates the difference in tolerance between Protestants, Catholics, and Jews and greatly reduces the difference between liberals and conservatives (Sullivan et al 1982, pp. 135–39). Unfortunately it is difficult to determine what happens to CPs' tolerance level because the measures of religion in Sullivan et al are so crude.

However, even if scales were less biased, on average CPs would probably be less tolerant. The fact that CP intolerance does not appear to be ideologically selective—they are as intolerant of militarists and racists (Wilcox & Jelen 1990, Tamney & Johnson 1997) as of atheists and homosexuals—suggests that the distinction between CPs and others may ultimately derive from competing moral visions. Standing in the old tradition of political conservatism (á la Burke), CPs appear to prioritize the conservation of what is in their view the moral basis of the "common good," over the liberal ethic of tolerance.

[29]The relationship between religiosity and prejudice is curvilinear. Those who are peripherally involved in religion are the most prejudiced, and those who are heavily involved the least. People's motivations for attending are also important (Gorsuch 1988, Kirkpatrick 1993). Although some scholars question their motives and methods, CP groups like Promise Keepers have made significant attempts to promote racial reconciliation (e.g., see Olsen 1997).

[30]These scales ask about attitudes toward homosexuals, atheists, communists, and feminists (left-wing target groups), but not about people's attitudes toward fundamentalists, gender-role traditionalists, etc (right-wing target groups). They ask whether it is okay to have books that advocate atheism in the public library but not about books that advocate conversion to Christianity.

Finally, however, even using the traditional tolerance scales, there is a significantly higher variance in tolerance attitudes among CPs than in the general population (Gay & Ellison 1993). This suggests that some subgroups within conservative Protestantism are highly tolerant and others are highly intolerant. Much of this intolerance seems to result from fundamentalism rather than religious orthodoxy per se (Green et al 1994, Kirkpatrick 1993). Tolerance is also influenced by how much a group feels marginalized and threatened (Green et al 1994, Sullivan et al 1982, p. 251).

Culture Wars?

With the rise of the religious right (RR), many scholars and journalists have become convinced that America is involved in a culture war in which CPs play a leading role (e.g., Hunter 1991). However, at the grass roots this does not appear to be the case (C Smith et al 1998, Williams 1997, Manza & Brooks 1997, DiMaggio et al 1996, Davis & Robinson 1996, Iannaccone 1993). After analyzing multiple attitudinal measures on the GSS and NES, DiMaggio et al (1996) conclude that the attitudes of liberals and conservative religionists have actually converged since the 1970s. The only area of increased polarization they found is in abortion attitudes. Since the 1970s, liberals have become more pro-choice and more unified in their views; conservative religionists have become more internally polarized (pp. 733–34). The gender-role and racial attitudes of both groups have also become more liberal and less polarized over time. The authors analyze a number of other possible cleavage lines in society, but only party ID showed increased cleavage (i.e., the attitudes of self-identified Democrats and Republicans have become more polarized). This may have resulted because conservative Southern Democrats have increasingly joined the Republican party, which makes Democrats appear more liberal and Republicans more conservative.

There is also little evidence of a massive increase in the number of CPs (Guth 1996a, T Smith 1992, Wuthnow 1992). Some people convert to CP denominations, but higher birth rates and greater retention of CP children cause much of the relative growth. However this has been a slow, gradual process (Guth 1996a, Finke & Stark 1992).

Moreover, according to Manza & Brooks (1997) white CPs have not become more Republican or increased their presidential voting behavior between 1960 and 1992, although liberal Protestants have become increasingly Democratic. This seems to contradict the research of most other scholars (e.g., Kellstedt et al 1996d, Layman 1997). However, different starting years and methodologies seem to have caused these apparent contradictions.[31] Manza & Brooks started

[31]Manza & Brooks divided Protestant into conservatives, moderates, and liberals. Kellstedt et al divided them into evangelicals and mainliners. However, this does not seem to explain the different results. Manza & Brooks' analysis shows no trend for either conservative or moderate Protestants (which include the denominations in Kellstedt et al's evangelical category).

their analysis in 1960; most others start around 1980 (e.g., Layman 1997). However, Manza & Brooks' analysis shows that CPs moved strongly into the Democratic party to support fellow evangelical Jimmy Carter in both the 1976 and 1980 elections. Thus, this temporary Democratic shift is the anomaly, not their gradual drift back into the Republican party.

The second difference is the type of controls used. Manza & Brooks controlled for the overall trend in presidential voting; the others did not. On average, the general population voted more Republican in presidential elections between 1960 and 1988; thus, in cross-tabulated analysis without controls, CPs seem to have become more Republican and mainline Protestants to have remained unchanged in their political loyalties (see Kellstedt et al 1996d). However, this does not necessarily contradict a proper reading of Manza & Brooks' tables. According to their tables CPs have become no more Republican than the general population has, while liberal Protestants have resisted the general trend. Thus, if the CP trend does not differ significantly from the general population, it seems unlikely that the RR had a major impact on CP presidential voting or party ID, at least up to the 1992 elections. This interpretation is reinforced by the fact that CP voter participation peaked in the 1976 and 1980 Carter elections and has declined since (Manza & Brooks 1997).[32]

Why then do CPs have so much greater public visibility? First, CPs' increased wealth and education have led to increased community involvement and greater organizational skills. Now CPs as a whole are almost even with mainline Protestants in education, income, and middle-class identity (Guth 1996a). Some groups of CPs always were middle-class and college educated, but others, like Pentecostals, have made significant recent gains. Second, some CPs have set up political pressure groups that attempt to speak for the CP community and have mobilized activists to participate in the Republican party organization (which previously was dominated by mainline Protestants). These organizations allowed previously marginalized groups to inject their concerns into the public arena (see Regnerus & Smith 1998). They also facilitate rapid dissemination of political information to CP constituents. As with the rise of Catholic involvement in politics earlier in this century, the new political visibility of CPs has raised concern among older elites. Third, CPs are more visible because of a restructuring of the political spectrum. Traditionally, Catholics, Jews, minorities, and Southerners voted Democratic, and white non-Southern Protestants voted Republican. However, according to Manza & Brooks (1997), liberal Protestants have moved strongly toward the Democratic party and conservative Southerners into the Republican party. This has radically shifted party coalitions and rhetoric. Thus, whites, Jews, secularists,

[32]This analysis focuses on presidential elections: CPs may have increased their voting in non-presidential elections, or since 1992. Research by Green et al (1996a,b) suggests that this is the case.

and social liberals have become the new core of the Democratic party. This has left more conservative Protestants as the core of the Republican party (Manza & Brooks 1997, Green et al 1996b, p. 4).[33]

According to Manza & Brooks, decomposition of the regression coefficients suggests that this shift in the party alignment of liberal Protestants was caused by their increasingly liberal views on social issues, especially abortion (no doubt the rise of the RR helped speed them on their way). The shift of liberal Protestants and Southerners has increased the internal consistency of both parties on social issues and made it in the interest of party elites to manipulate religious and regional issues to mobilize political support and demobilize opposition. Social issues may mobilize some CPs, but fear of the RR is also an effective counter-mobilization tool (Wald 1995, Rozell & Wilcox 1995c).

The Religious Right[34]

In the 1960s and 1970s, a number of CPs became increasingly concerned about the direction in which the United States was moving. Stricter enforcement of the separation of church and state, the legalization of abortion, the sexual revolution, the gay rights movement, the removal of religion from public education, the increasing sexual explicitness of TV and movies, the spread of pornography, and challenges to traditional gender roles all raised concern (Guth 1996a). These issues were strongly linked to the family and the socialization of the next generation of believers (Davis & Robinson 1996, Oldfield 1996).[35] Also, CPs' growing socioeconomic status allowed them to develop stronger institutional structures.

However, the 1976 campaign of Jimmy Carter provided the initial spark. Carter was openly evangelical, and CPs moved strongly into the Democratic party to support him in the 1976 election. Despite common beliefs to the contrary, CPs disproportionately supported Carter against Ronald Reagan in the 1980 election (Woodberry et al 1996; also see Manza & Brooks 1997, Lipset & Raab 1981, p. 29).[36] However, the 1976 election drew the attention of New Right strategists (most of whom were not CPs) (Oldfield 1996, p. 100, Guth

[33]This religious cleavage is even more evident among party elites than at the grass roots (Kellstedt et al 1996d).

[34]For more extended summaries of research on the RR, see the introductory chapter of Rozell & Wilcox 1996, Wilcox 1996, pp. 25–57, Oldfield 1996, and Guth 1996a.

[35]RR activists often use the rhetoric of a persecuted minority (Oldfield 1996, pp. 31, 55; Reed 1994).

[36]Woodberry et al (1996) selected white CPs by denomination and then further separated respondents by region and age into Northern and Southern CPs from three different age cohorts. In 1980, all groups except Northern baby-boomer CPs supported Carter at rates similar to those in 1976 (young Northerners seem the least likely to have been influenced by the RR). Mainline Protestants were far more likely to abandon Carter. In fact, all mainline groups did, except Northern baby-boomers (who increased in their support).

1996a). They realized that they could win the presidency and a substantial portion of Congress with the CP vote and began to court its politically conservative wing. At the same time, repeated intervention of the government in Southern fundamentalist schools (many of which had grown significantly during desegregation), and frequent inquiries by the Securities and Exchange Commission and the IRS into the fund-raising of TV ministers, helped convince formally apolitical leaders like Jerry Falwell and Pat Robertson of the importance of political involvement (Guth 1996a). New Right activists eagerly showed them the political ropes. This helps explain why the economic rhetoric of the RR is more conservative than that of its CP constituency. From its inception the RR has been just one part of a new right-wing political coalition (Iannaccone 1993; also see Oldfield 1996, pp. 100, 218–19).

Despite the attention the RR received in the press, it was initially very weak. The Moral Majority, the Religious Round Table, and The Christian Voice predominantly mobilized fundamentalist ministers from the Sunbelt (Guth 1996b).[37] The Moral Majority was composed mostly of Independent Baptists and some conservative Southern Baptists and Presbyterians. The leadership was almost exclusively pastors in Jerry Falwell's Baptist Bible Fellowship. Although mobilizing the ministers in his denomination allowed Falwell to list organizations in 47 states (which looked good on paper), most of the organizations did very little. Many pastors were either not interested or too busy running their churches to do much politically. The Moral Majority gave a total of only $25,000 to political candidates and had little grass-roots mobilization, even among CPs (Guth 1996a, Guth & Green 1996a, Georgiana 1989).[38] A survey of contributors to 60 political action committees (PACs) shows that conservative political attitudes, not demographic or religious factors, best predicted support for the Moral Majority (Guth & Green 1996a).

Nevertheless, these organizations collapsed within a few years. Initially many observers claimed the RR had died, but to their surprise it rose again with the presidential campaign of Pat Robertson in 1988. Robertson received few votes but surprised journalists and opponents with the size of his activist following (Oldfield 1996, Green 1996). Other candidates raised more money, but he received contributions from more individuals than the rest of the Republican candidates combined. These supporters were primarily middle-class urban Pentecostals and charismatics from the Sunbelt, areas where secular and traditional religious values are increasingly in tension (Green 1996). Those who voted for him were also primarily Pentecostals and charismatics (Smidt et al 1996, Rozell & Wilcox 1995b, Oldfield 1996). However, Robertson failed to

[37]Pentecostals were also an important element of the Christian Voice (Smidt et al 1996).

[38]Even Jerry Falwell's television audience was small, ranging from about 1,440,000 in 1981 to 300,000 in 1988 (W Martin 1981, Winzenburg 1988).

gain wide support even among CP clergy. A survey of ministers indicates that only about one tenth of Southern Baptist ministers and one fourth of Assemblies of God ministers supported him (Green 1996).[39] Still, his campaign was important because it tapped a largely unmobilized segment of CPs (Pentecostals and charismatics), established the first truly grass-roots RR organization, and created the foundation for the Christian Coalition (Green 1996, Smidt et al 1996, Oldfield 1996).

After his failed presidential campaign, Pat Robertson asked Ralph Reed to form the Christian Coalition with the remnants of his political organization. Reed attempted to broaden the coalition to include evangelicals, Catholics, Mormons, black CPs, and conservative Jews. He framed the movement in more moderate terms, laced his speeches and books with seemingly liberal language about the rights of women, condemnation of racism, and repentance for past wrongs perpetuated by CPs (e.g., Reed 1994, 1996). The Christian Coalition actually established a grass-roots organization and has expanded the coalition to include a significant number of evangelicals and Mormons. Support by Catholics, blacks, and Jews is still minor (Green 1995, Rozell & Wilcox 1995b). As religious activists have integrated into the political system and gained more experience, they have lost some of their original militancy and become increasingly willing to compromise (Wilcox 1996, pp. 105–11, Moen 1995, Soper 1995, Billings & Scott 1994). The RR now has strong influence in the Republican parties of Utah, Kansas, Nebraska, and ten Southern states. It has contested influence in Virginia, Arizona, Iowa, Minnesota, Idaho, and the five Pacific-rim states, and modest-to-weak influence elsewhere (Green et al 1998b).

Despite impressive mobilization of activists, the RR's political impact has been minimal. Many of its victories have been symbolic, such as influencing the wording of the Republican party platform (Green & Guth 1996, Rozell & Wilcox 1995a). Most scholars now believe the RR will not disappear but will not become a dominant influence in politics either (Oldfield 1996, Wilcox 1996, Guth 1996a, Rozell & Wilcox 1995a, Green 1995).

There are several reasons for this. First, the RR has a limited constituency. Through the 1980s and 1990s, approximately 10% to 15% of survey respondents reported support for RR organizations.[40] A somewhat larger group supports specific issues on the RR's agenda; a much smaller number are active

[39]The Assemblies of God is the largest Pentecostal denomination in the United States (Green 1996).

[40]These percentages may be too high. According to T Smith (1996), when surveys ask about support for the "Religious Right," most respondents do not understand that this applies to a political movement. Support for the "Religious Right political movement" is much lower than for the "Religious Right." Even among supporters of the political movement, 47% had read little or nothing about it, and about 40% lacked awareness or admiration of even one of the major leaders (Pat Robertson, Jerry Falwell, or Ralph Reed).

participants (Rozell & Wilcox 1995b; also see T Smith 1996, p. 27). Even in Virginia, only 15% of voters said endorsement by Falwell, Robertson, or the Christian Coalition would increase their support for a candidate; most said it would reduce it (Rozell & Wilcox 1995c, p. 125). Yet Virginia is the home of Falwell, Robertson, the Christian Coalition, and numerous other RR organizations. The RR has limited support even within the Christian religious community (Jelen 1987, Guth & Green 1996a). Many (if not most) CP ministers remain solidly apolitical; only fundamentalist ministers seem to have responded with enthusiasm to the RR's call (Guth 1996a, p. 12). Even among Southern Baptist ministers, about half think political activism usually hurts the church (another third are not sure), and half think some Southern Baptist leaders have gone too far in mixing religion and politics (Guth 1996b). Many people who welcome religious people into the public square still fear the intolerance of RR leaders. Although a number of RR issues have broad support in the general public, openly identifying with the RR usually hurts candidates politically (Gilbert & Peterson 1995, Wald 1995). RR organizations and leaders are considerably less popular than the messages they intend to convey (Jelen 1987).

Second, there is a residual antipolitical bias among many CPs. Even with demographics controlled, CPs as a whole are still less likely to vote in presidential elections than are all other religious groups (Manza & Brooks 1997). Many CPs fear politics will dilute the church's spirituality, destroy internal harmony, debase its moral authority, and divert attention from evangelism (Guth et al 1996b, Oldfield 1996). Large groups like the National Association of Evangelicals and influential evangelical magazines like *Christianity Today* have supported selected RR initiatives but have resisted endorsing candidates or involvement in elections, and they have consistently counseled moderation (Guth 1996a). Third, both CPs and the RR are internally divided, with many competing organizations, leaders, and agendas (Green 1995).[41] CP organizations can be found on multiple sides of most political issues.

Fourth, the RR is isolated from many of the mainstream culture-shaping institutions.[42] Few Baptist, Pentecostal-Holiness, or other CPs are among the "power elite," few are CEOs, and few are listed in *Who's Who* (Pyle 1996, Davidson et al 1995, Manza & Brooks 1997). Few CPs are in the movie or TV industries (Rothman & Lichter 1984, Lichter et al 1983); few work at prominent newspapers, magazines, or TV newsrooms (Jelen & Wilcox 1995, Lichter & Rothman 1981), and few work in academia—especially in the humanities and social sciences (Jelen & Wilcox 1995, Wuthnow 1985, Gorsuch

[41]See McAdam (1982) for how a similar complexity of organizations hampered the effectiveness of the Civil Rights Movement after the mid-1960s.

[42]They do have access to "subcultural shaping" institutions of their own.

1988).[43] Many of these sources also suggest that these elites are more socially liberal than the general public and especially than CPs. Thus, the RR has one type of power (i.e., votes, donations, activism), but RR activists have little power to determine how their movements will be framed in the national media or to influence which people and statements will be highlighted to represent their causes.[44] Their attempts to censor or influence textbook and media content must be done in public through boycotts and letter campaigns; they cannot do these things behind the scenes, or make others censor themselves through their control of promotions and resources.

Still the RR enjoys something like a veto power in the Republican party. On their own, the constituents of the RR cannot determine the Republican presidential candidate, and any candidate too closely tied to the movement would probably lose. But the Republicans would have difficulty nominating a candidate they directly oppose. Thus, Republican candidates must at least give lip service to their cause.[45]

The RR has primarily been successful where its activists have been part of a broad coalition of allies, when their role is not highlighted, where state and party organizations have less control over committee memberships, candidates, and interest group activities, and where they have a mass constituency of CPs and other conservatives (Green et al 1998b, Guth & Green 1996a, Green et al 1996a, Wald 1995). Thus, they have gained substantial influence on the Republican party in the South and in Utah. However, in most other places RR activism arouses intense opposition (e.g., California, Oregon, and Minnesota). Because of the high commitment of CP activists, they are also influential in low-turnout elections and caucuses (where political participation has greater cost) (Oldfield 1996).

Why Conservative Churches Grow

Dean Kelley's 1972 book, *Why Conservative Churches Are Growing*, demonstrated that CP churches tend to thrive numerically, while more liberal churches languish. Since then, scholars have advanced several theories seeking to explain why. For example, status discontent approaches focus on threats

[43]In Jelen & Wilcox's academic sample (professors of political science, sociology, history, and English), 90% thought "Evangelicals/Religious Right" have too much power, 86% had the strongest view of the separation of church and state, and 75% thought "Evangelicals/Religious Right" are a threat to democracy (only 36% mentioned "Nazis/KKK/Racist Right").

[44]Conflict may be accentuated because RR organizations use boycotts and letter campaigns to challenge the economic interests of the media conglomerates that produce many television shows, movies, and news programs.

[45]Ronald Reagan did this skillfully by, for example, promoting a constitutional amendment allowing school prayer, but only after he knew there were not enough Congressional votes for it to pass (Sider 1997).

to the social or economic status of religious groups. They suggest that religious identities become more salient, commitments more firm, and resources more easily mobilized, the more a religious group feels their social status is threatened. Originally developed to explain right-wing political extremism, and largely unfashionable among contemporary sociologists, versions of status discontent theory still find occasional proponents among scholars of religion (e.g., Wald et al 1989, Lorentzen 1980, Page & Clelland 1978; see Thurow 1996, p. 232).

Another theoretical approach, "strictness" theory, focuses on the differential impact of the microlevel normative demands religious groups impose on their members. In short, "strict" religious groups thrive, while "lenient" religious groups decline. Kelley (1972, 1978) argued that religions that deliver substantial meaning to their adherents thrive. Religions produce meaning by demanding that their followers respond to their beliefs by committing their time, money, energy, reputations, and selves in a way that validates and invests in those ideas. "Meaning = concept + demand" (1972, p. 52). More recently, Iannaccone (1992, 1994) suggests that strict religions thrive because they screen out free-riders (i.e., people who enjoy many of the benefits of the religious group while contributing little to the group). Strict churches demand that their members contribute their fair share of time, money, and emotional energy to generate the collective religious goods all enjoy. Strict CP churches that screen out free-riders enjoy higher degrees of commitment, solidarity, and mutual rewards, all of which make them thrive and grow.

A third theory of religious vitality, based on the economic model of rational choice, is called the "religious economies" or "supply side" theory (Finke & Stark 1988, 1989, 1992, Finke & Iannaccone 1993, Finke et al 1996). This theory claims that religious regulation and monopolies create lethargic religions, but pluralistic, competitive environments allow entrepreneurial religious groups to thrive. In these environments, religious "firms" (denominations and traditions) that possess superior organizational structures (denominational polities), sales representatives (evangelists and clergy), products (religious messages), and marketing (evangelistic techniques) flourish (Finke & Stark 1989). Those that cannot successfully compete, decline. CP vitality, then, is a result of unregulated religious environments that stimulate aggressive CP religious entrepreneurs to promote more diverse religious products that satisfy ever-expanding markets of religious consumers.

Finally, seeking to elaborate sociology of religion's "new paradigm" (Warner 1993) in cultural and structural rather than economistic terms, Smith et al (1998) advance a "subcultural identity" theory of evangelical church vitality. It suggests that in a pluralistic society, those religious groups will be relatively stronger that better possess and employ the cultural tools needed to create both clear distinction from, and significant engagement and tension with, other relevant outgroups (short of becoming genuinely countercultural). Smith et al (1998) argue that evangelicalism possesses precisely these cultural tools. Formulated in contrast to older modernization-secularization interpretations of evangelicalism (e.g., Hunter 1983, 1987), the subcultural identity theory attempts to demonstrate how and why American evangelicalism thrives within its modern, pluralistic environment. The elaborated theory suggests that the human drives for meaning and belonging are satisfied primarily by locating human selves within social groups that sustain distinctive, morally orienting identities; that social groups construct and maintain collective identities by drawing symbolic boundaries between themselves and relevant outgroups; that modern believers establish stronger religious identities and commitments through individual choice than through ascription; that people define their values and evaluate themselves in relation to specific reference groups; that modern pluralism promotes the formation of strong subcultures and potentially deviant identities; and that inter-group conflict in a pluralistic context typically strengthens in-group identity, solidarity, resources mobilization, and membership retention.

Theories of CP organizational vitality remain contested (see Marwell 1996, Bibby 1978, Chaves 1989, Hunter 1987, pp. 203–6, Perrin & Mauss 1993), and more empirical research is needed to evaluate their usefulness.

CONCLUSION

Conservative Protestantism represents at least a quarter of the US population and significantly influences its adherents' attitudes and behaviors. Conceptual problems and measurement difficulties have obscured the importance of CP faith in many previous sociological studies. We suggest that greater clarity in definitions, understanding of history, use of sophisticated measurement tools, and attention to complex and nuanced qualitative data should significantly enhance our understanding of conservative Protestantism and its social significance in the years ahead. This type of research is already beginning to alter our understanding of CPs' gender-role attitudes, childrearing strategies, tolerance, and political behavior.

Literature Cited

Abrams E. 1997. *Faith or Fear: How Jews Can Survive in a Christian America*. New York: Free

Ammerman NT. 1987. *Bible Believers: Fundamentalists in the Modern World*. New Brunswick, NJ: Rutgers Univ. Press

Ammerman NT. 1990. *Baptist Battles: Social Change and Religious Conflict in the Southern Baptist Convention*. New Brunswick, NJ: Rutgers Univ. Press

Anderson RM. 1987. Pentecostal and charismatic Christianity. In *The Encyclopedia of Religion,* ed. M Eliade, 11:229–35. New York: Macmillan

Appleby SR. 1995. But all crabs are crabby: valid and less valid criticisms of the Fundamentalism project. *Contention* 4(3): 195–202

Bartkowski J. 1996. Beyond biblical literalism and inerrancy: conservative Protestants and the hermeneutic interpretation of scripture. *Soc. Relig.* 57(3):259–72

Bartkowski J. 1997. Debating patriarchy: discursive disputes over spousal authority among evangelical family commentators. *J. Sci. Stud. Relig.* 36(3):393–410

Bibby RW. 1978. Why conservative churches really are growing: Kelley revisited. *J. Sci. Stud. Relig.* 17(2):129–38

Billings DB, Scott SL. 1994. Religion and political legitimation. *Annu. Rev. Sociol.* 20: 173–201

Blumhofer EW, Carpenter JA. 1990. *Twentieth-Century Evangelicalism: A Guide to the Sources*. New York: Garland

Bollen KA. 1989. *Structural Equations with Latent Variables*. New York: Wiley

Brasher BE. 1997. My beloved is all radiant: two case studies of congregational-based Christian Fundamentalist female enclaves and the religious experiences they cultivate among women. *Rev. Relig. Res.* 38(3): 231–46

Brinkerhoff MB, Grandin E, Lupri E. 1992. Religious involvement and spousal violence: the Canadian case. *J. Sci. Stud. Relig.* 31(1):15–31

Brusco EE. 1995. *The Reformation of Machismo: Evangelical Conversion and Gender in Colombia*. Austin: Univ. Texas Press

Burgess SM, McGee GB, ed. 1988. *Dictionary of Pentecostal and Charismatic Movements*. Grand Rapids, MI: Regency Ref. Library

Call VRA, Heaton TB. 1997. Religious influence on marital stability. *J. Sci. Stud. Relig.* 36(3):382–92

Capps D. 1992. Religion and child abuse: perfect together. *J. Sci. Stud. Rel.* 31(1):1–14

Carpenter JA. 1984. Fundamentalism. In *Encyclopedia of Religion in the South,* ed. S Hill, pp. 275–78. Macon, GA: Mercer Univ. Press

Carpenter JA. 1997. *Revive Us Again: The Reawakening of American Protestantism*. New York: Oxford Univ. Press

Carwardine RJ. 1993. *Evangelicals and Politics in Antebellum America*. New Haven, CT: Yale Univ. Press

Chaves M. 1989. Secularization and religious revival: evidence from U.S. church attendance rates, 1972–1986. *J. Sci. Stud. Relig.* 28(4):464–77

Chaves M. 1996. Ordaining women: the diffusion of an organizational innovation. *Am. J. Sociol.* 101(4):840–73

Chi SK, Houseknecht SK. 1985. Protestant Fundamentalism and marital success: a comparative approach. *Sociol. Soc. Res.* 69(3):351–75

Cox HG. 1995. *Fire From Heaven: The Rise of Pentecostal Spirituality and the Reshaping of Religion in the Twenty-First Century*. Reading, MA: Addison-Wesley

Davidson JD, Pyle RE, Reyes DV. 1995. Persistence and change in the Protestant establishment, 1930–1992. *Soc. Forc.* 74(1): 157–75

Davis NJ, Robinson RV. 1996. Are the rumors of wars exaggerated? Religious orthodoxy and moral progressivism in America. *Am. J. Sociol.* 102(3):756–87

Dayton DW, ed. 1985. *The Higher Christian Life: A Bibliographic Overview*. New York: Garland

Dayton DW. 1991. Some doubts about the usefulness of the category 'Evangelical.' In *The Variety of American Evangelicalism,* ed. D Dayton, R Johnston, pp. 245–51. Downers Grove, IL: InterVarsity

Dayton DW, Johnston RK. 1991. *The Variety of American Evangelicalism*. Downers Grove, IL: InterVarsity

Demerath NJ, Roof WC. 1976. Religion—recent strands of research. *Annu. Rev. Sociol.* 2:19–33

Demmitt K. 1992. Loosening the ties that bind: the accommodation of dual-earner families in a conservative Protestant church. *Rev. Relig. Res.* 34(1):3–19

DiMaggio P, Evans J, Bryson B. 1996. Have Americans' social attitudes become more polarized? *Am. J. Sociol.* 102(3): 690–755

Ellison CG. 1991. Religious involvement and

subjective well-being. *J. Health Soc. Behav.* 32(1)80–99

Ellison CG. 1996. Conservative Protestantism and the corporal punishment of children: clarifying the issue. *J. Sci. Stud. Rel.* 35(1)1–16

Ellison CG, Bartkowski JP. 1997. *Conservative Protestantism and the household division of labor.* Presented at Assoc. Sociol. Relig., Toronto, Canada

Ellison CG, Bartkowski JP, Anderson KL. 1996. *Are there religious variations in domestic violence?* Presented at Assoc. Sociol. Relig., New York

Ellison CG, Gay DA, Glass TA. 1989. Does religious commitment contribute to individual life satisfaction? *Soc. Forc.* 68(1): 100–23

Ellison CG, Sherkat DE. 1993a. Conservative Protestantism and support for corporal punishment. *Am. Sociol. Rev.* 58(1): 131–44

Ellison CG, Sherkat DE. 1993b. Obedience and autonomy: religion and parental values reconsidered. *J. Sci. Stud. Rel.* 32(4): 313–29

Ferguson DM, Horwood LJ, Kershaw KL, Shannon FT. 1986. Factors associated with reports of wife assault in New Zealand. *J. Marriage Fam.* 48(2):407–12

Filsinger E, Wilson M. 1984. Religiosity, socioeconomic rewards and family development: predictors of marital adjustment. *J. Marriage Fam.* 46(3):663–70

Finke R, Guest A, Stark R. 1996. Religious pluralism in New York state, 1855 to 1865. *Am. Sociol. Rev.* 61(2):203–18

Finke R, Iannaccone L. 1993. Supply-side explanations for religious change. *Ann. Am. Acad. Polit. Soc. Sci.* 527:27–39

Finke R, Stark R. 1988. Religious economies and sacred canopies: religious mobilization in American cities, 1906. *Am. Sociol. Rev.* 53(1):41–49

Finke R, Stark R. 1989. How the upstart sects won America: 1776-1850. *J. Sci. Stud. Relig.* 28(1):27–44

Finke R, Stark R. 1992. *The Churching of America 1776–1990: Winners and Losers in Our Religious Economy.* New Brunswick, NJ: Rutgers Univ. Press

Gallagher SK. 1996. *Symbolic traditionalism and pragmatic egalitarianism: contemporary evangelicals, family, and gender.* Presented at Assoc. Sociol. Relig., New York

Gay DA, Ellison CG. 1993. Religious subcultures and political tolerance: Do denominations still matter? *Rev. Relig. Res.* 34(4): 311–32

Gay DA, Ellison CG, Powers DA. 1996. In search of denominational subcultures: religious affiliation and "pro-family" issues revisited. *Rev. Relig. Res.* 38(1):3–17

Georgiana SL. 1989. *The Moral Majority and Fundamentalism.* Lewiston, NY: Mellon

Gilbert CP, Peterson DA. 1995. Minnesota: Christians and Quistians in the GOP. In *God at the Grass Roots,* ed. M Rozell, C Wilcox, pp. 169–89. Lanham, MD: Rowman & Littlefield

Gorsuch RL. 1988. Psychology of religion. *Annu. Rev. Psychol.* 39:201–21

Green JC. 1995. The Christian right and the 1994 elections: an overview. In *God at the Grass Roots,* ed. M Rozell, C Wilcox, pp. 1–18. Lanham, MD: Rowman & Littlefield

Green JC. 1996. A look at the "invisible army": Pat Robertson's 1988 activist corps. See Green et al 1996b, pp. 44–61

Green JC, Guth JL. 1996. The Christian Right in the Republican party: The case of Pat Robertson's supporters. See Green et al 1996b, pp. 86–102

Green JC, Guth JL, Hill K. 1996a. Faith and election: the Christian Right in congressional campaigns 1978–1988. See Green et al 1996b, pp. 103–16

Green JC, Guth JL, Kellstedt LA, Smidt CE. 1994. Uncivil challenges?: Support for civil liberties among religious activists. *J. Polit. Sci.* 22:25–49

Green JC, Guth JL, Kellstedt LA, Smidt CE. 1998a. The soul of the South. In *The New Politics of the Old South,* ed. C Bullock, M Rozell, pp. 261–76. Lanham, MD: Rowman & Littlefield

Green JC, Guth JL, Smidt CE, Kellstedt LA. 1996b. *Religion and the Culture Wars: Dispatches from the Front.* Lanham, MD: Rowman & Littlefield

Green JC, Guth JL, Wilcox C. 1998b. Less than conquerors: the Christian Right in the state Republican Parties. In *Social Movements and American Political Institutions,* ed. A Costain, A McFarland, pp. 117–35. Lanham, MD: Rowman & Littlefield. In press

Green JC, Kellstedt LA, Guth JL, Smidt CE. 1997. Who elected Clinton: a collision of values. *First Things* 75:35–40

Guth JL. 1996a. The politics of the Christian Right. See Green et al 1996b, pp. 7–29

Guth JL. 1996b. The bully pulpit: Southern Baptist clergy and political activism 1980–1992. See Green et al 1996b, pp. 146–73

Guth JL, Fraser CR, Green JC, Kellstedt LA, Smidt CE. 1996a. Religion and foreign policy attitudes: the case of Christian Zionism. See Green et al 1996b, pp. 330–60

Guth JL, Green JC. 1996a. The moralizing minority: Christian Right support among po-

litical contributors. See Green et al 1996b, pp. 30–43
Guth JL, Green JC. 1996b. Politics in a new key: religiosity and participation among political activists. See Green et al 1996b, pp. 117–45
Guth JL, Green JC, Kellstedt LA, Smidt CE. 1996b. Onward Christian soldiers: religious activist groups in American politics. See Green et al 1996b, pp. 62–85
Guth JL, Green JC, Kellstedt LA, Smidt CE. 1996c. The political relevance of religion: the correlates of mobilization. See Green et al 1996b, pp. 300–29
Hallum AM. 1996. *Beyond Missionaries: Toward an Understanding of the Protestant Movement in Central America.* Lanham, MD: Rowman & Littlefield
Hart S. 1992. *What Does the Lord Require? How American Christians Think About Economic Justice.* New York: Oxford Univ. Press
Hart S. 1996. The cultural dimension of social movements: a theoretical reassessment and literature review. *Soc. Relig.* 57(1):87–100
Haslam G. 1989. Dust bowl legacy. *Los Angeles Times Mag.* March 26, p. 8 ff
Heyrman CL. 1997. *Southern Cross: The Beginnings of the Bible Belt.* New York: Knopf
Hill SS Jr. 1980. *The South and the North in American Religion.* Athens: Univ. Georgia Press
Hodgkinson VA, Weitzman MS, Kirsch AD. 1990. From commitment to action: how religious involvement affects giving and volunteering. In *Faith and Philanthropy in America,* ed. R Wuthnow, V Hodgkinson, pp. 93–114. San Francisco: Jossey-Bass
Hood RW Jr. 1983. Social psychology and religious fundamentalism. In *Rural Psychology,* ed. AW Childes, GB Melton, pp. 169–98. New York: Plenum
Hunt RA, King MB. 1978. Religiosity and marriage. *J. Sci. Stud. Relig.* 17(4): 399–406
Hunter JD. 1983. *American Evangelicalism: Conservative Religion and the Quandary of Modernity.* New Brunswick, NJ: Rutgers Univ. Press
Hunter JD. 1987. *Evangelicalism: the Coming Generation.* Chicago: Univ. Chicago Press
Hunter JD. 1991. *Culture Wars: The Struggle to Define America.* New York: Basic Books
Hutchison WR. 1987. *Errand to the World: American Protestant Thought and Foreign Missions.* Chicago: Univ. Chicago Press
Iannaccone LR. 1992. Sacrifice and stigma: reducing free-riding in cults, communes, and other collectives. *J. Polit. Econ.* 100(2):271–92
Iannaccone LR. 1993. Heirs to the Protestant ethic? The economics of American Fundamentalists. In *Fundamentalisms and the State,* ed. M Marty, R Appleby, pp. 342–366. Chicago: Univ. Chicago Press
Iannaccone LR. 1994. Why strict churches are strong. *Am. J. Sociol.* 99(5):1180–1211
Ingersoll JJ. 1995. Which tradition, which values? "Traditional family values" in American Protestant fundamentalism. *Contention* 4(2):91–103
Jelen TG. 1987. The effects of religious separatism on white Protestants in the 1984 presidential election. *Sociol. Anal.* 48(1): 30–45
Jelen TG, Wilcox C. 1990. Denominational preferences and the dimensions of political tolerance. *Sociol. Anal.* 51(1):69–81
Jelen TG, Wilcox C. 1995. *Public Attitudes Toward Church and State.* Armonk, NY: Sharpe
Johnston RK. 1991. American Evangelism: an extended family. In *The Variety of American Evangelism,* ed. D Dayton, R Johnston. pp. 252–72. Downers Grove, IL: InterVarsity
Jones CE. 1983. *A Guide to the Study of the Pentecostal Movement.* Metuchen, NJ: Scarecrow
Jones CE. 1995. *The Charismatic Movement: A Guide to the Study of Neo-Pentecostalism.* Metuchen, NJ: Scarecrow
Kelley D. 1972. *Why Conservative Churches are Growing.* New York: Harper & Row
Kelley D. 1978. Why conservative churches are still growing. *J. Sci. Stud. Relig.* 17(2): 165–72
Kellstedt LA, Green JC, Guth JL, Smidt CE. 1996a. Grasping the essentials: the social embodiment of religion and political behavior. See Green et al 1996b, pp. 174–92
Kellstedt LA, Green JC, Guth JL, Smidt CE. 1996b. Has Godot finally arrived? Religion and realignment. See Green et al 1996b, pp. 291–99
Kellstedt LA, Green JC, Smidt CE, Guth JL. 1996c. The puzzle of Evangelical Protestantism: core, periphery, and political behavior. See Green et al 1996b, pp. 240–66
Kellstedt LA, Green JC, Smidt CE, Guth JL. 1996d. Religious voting blocs in the 1992 election: the year of the Evangelical? See Green et al 1996b, pp. 267–90
Kellstedt LA, Smidt CE. 1996. Measuring Fundamentalism: an analysis of different operational strategies. See Green et al 1996b, pp. 193–218
Kirkpatrick LA. 1993. Fundamentalism, Christian orthodoxy, and intrinsic religious orientation as predictors of discrimi-

natory attitudes. *J. Sci. Stud. Relig.* 32(3): 256–68

Lakoff G. 1996. *Moral Politics: What Conservatives Know that Liberals Don't.* Chicago: Univ. Chicago Press

Larson L, Goltz J. 1989. Religious, participation and marital commitment. *Rev. Relig. Res.* 30(4):387–400

Larson DB, Sherrill KA, Lyons JS. 1994. Neglect and misuse of the R word: systematic reviews of religious measures in health, mental health, and aging. In *Religion in Aging and Health*, ed. J Levin, pp. 178–95. Thousand Oaks, CA: Sage

Layman GC. 1997. Religion and political behavior in the United States: the impact of beliefs, affiliations, and commitment from 1980 to 1994. *Pub. Opin. Q.* 61(2):288–316

Lehrer E, Chiswick C. 1993. Religion as a determinant of marital stability. *Demography* 30(3):385–404

Lichter LS, Lichter SR, Rothman S. 1983. Hollywood and America: the odd couple. *Pub. Opin.* 5(6):54–58

Lichter SR, Rothman S. 1981. Media and business elites. *Pub. Opin.* 4(5):42–46, 59–60

Lincoln EC, Mamiya LH. 1990. *The Black Church in the African American Experience.* Durham, NC: Duke Univ. Press

Lindley SH. 1996. *"You Have Stept Out of Your Place": A History of Women and Religion in America.* Louisville, KY: Westminster John Knox

Lipset SM, Raab E. 1981. The election and the evangelicals. *Commentary* 71(3):25–31

Lorentzen LJ. 1980. Evangelical life style concerns expressed in political action. *Sociol. Anal.* 41(2):144–54

Magnuson NA, Travis WG. 1990. *American Evangelicalism: An Annotated Bibliography.* West Cornwall, CT: Locust Hill

Magnuson NA, Travis WG. 1997. *American Evangelicalism II: First Bibliographical Supplement 1990–1996.* West Cornwall, CT: Locust Hill

Manza J, Brooks C. 1997. The religious factor in U.S. presidential elections, 1960–1992. *Am. J. Sociol.* 103(1):38–81

Marsden GM. 1980. *Fundamentalism and American Culture: The Shaping of Twentieth-Century Evangelicalism 1870–1925.* New York: Oxford Univ. Press

Marsden GM. 1987a. Evangelical and fundamental Christianity. In *The Encyclopedia of Religion,* ed. M Eliade, 15:190–97. New York: Macmillan

Marsden GM. 1987b. *Reforming Fundamentalism: Fuller Seminary and the New Evangelicalism.* Grand Rapids, MI: Eerdmans

Marsden GM. 1991. Fundamentalism and American evangelicalism. In *The Variety of American Evangelicalism,* ed. D Dayton, R Johnston, pp. 22–35. Downers Grove, IL: InterVarsity

Martin D. 1990. *Tongues of Fire: The Explosion of Protestantism in Latin America.* Cambridge, MA: Blackwell's

Martin W. 1981. The birth of a media myth. *Atlantic* 247(6):7–11

Marty ME, Appleby R ed. 1991–1995. *The Fundamentalism Project.* Chicago: Univ. Chicago Press

Marwell G. 1996. We still don't know if strict churches are strong, much less why: comment on Iannaccone. *Am. J. Sociol.* 101(4): 1097–1103

Maurer A. 1982. Religious values and child abuse. In *Institutional Abuse of Children and Youth,* ed. R Hanson, pp. 57–63. New York: Haworth

McAdam D. 1982. *Political Process and the Development of Black Insurgency, 1930–1970.* Chicago: Univ. Chicago Press

McLoughlin WG. 1971. *New England Dissent, 1630–1833: The Baptists and the Separation of Church and State.* Cambridge, MA: Harvard Univ. Press

McNamara PH. 1985. Conservative Christian families and their moral world: some reflections for sociologists. *Sociol. Anal.* 46(2): 93–99

Melton JG, ed. 1989. *The Encyclopedia of American Religions.* (Vol 1–3). Tarrytown, NY: Triumph

Mills WE. 1985. *Charismatic Religion in Modern Research: A Bibliography.* Macon, GA: Mercer Univ. Press

Moen MC. 1995. Political and theological adjustment in the U.S. Christian right. *Contention* 4(2):75–90

Munson H Jr. 1995a. Not all crustaceans are crabs: reflections on the comparative study of fundamentalism and politics. *Contention* 4(3):151–66

Munson H Jr. 1995b. Response to Appleby. *Contention* 4(3):207–9

Neill S. 1986. *A History of Christian Missions.* New York: Penguin

Nixon R. 1996. The dixification of America. *Southern Exposure* 24(3):19–22

Numbers RL. 1993. *The Creationists.* Berkeley: Univ. Calif. Press

Oldfield DM. 1996. *The Right and the Righteous: The Christian Right Confronts the Republican Party.* Lanham, MD: Rowman & Littlefield

Olsen T. 1997. Racial reconciliation emphasis intensified. *Christianity Today* 41(1):67

Ozorak EW. 1996. The power, but not the glory: how women empower themselves through religion. *J. Sci. Stud. Relig.* 35(1): 17–29

Page A, Clelland D. 1978. The Kanawha County textbook controversy: a study of the politics of life style concern. *Soc. Forc.* 57(1):265–81

Payne WJ, ed. 1995. *Directory of African American Religious Bodies: A Compendium by the Howard University School of Divinity*. Washington, DC: Howard Univ. Press

Perrin R, Mauss A. 1993. Strictly speaking...: Kelley's quandary and the Vineyard Christian Fellowship. *J. Sci. Stud. Relig.* 32(2): 125–35

Pevey C, Williams CL, Ellison CG. 1996. Male God imagery and female submission: lessons from a Southern Baptist ladies' Bible class. *Qual. Sociol.* 19(2):173–93

Pyle RE. 1993. Faith and commitment to the poor: theological orientation and support for government assistance measures. *Soc. Relig.* 54(4):385–401

Pyle RE. 1996. *Persistence and Change in the Protestant Establishment*. Westport, CT: Praeger

Reed R. 1994. *Politically Incorrect: The Emerging Faith Factor in American Politics*. Dallas, TX: Word

Reed R. 1996. *Active Faith: How Christians are Changing the Soul of American Politics.* New York: Free

Regnerus MD, Smith CS. 1998. Selective deprivatization among American religious traditions: the great reversal of the great reversal. *Soc. Forc.* 76(4):In press

Regnerus MD, Woodberry RD, Robinson L, Wilcox WB, Park J, Steensland B. 1997. *Re-classifying Protestant denominations: improving the General Social Survey's measurement of religious affiliation.* Presented at Southern Assoc. Pub. Opin. Res., Raleigh, NC

Roof WC, McKinney W. 1987. *American Mainline Religion: Its Changing Shape and Future*. New Brunswick, NJ: Rutgers Univ. Press

Rose SD. 1987. Women warriors: the negotiation of gender in a charismatic community. *Sociol. Anal.* 48(3)245–58

Rothman S, Lichter SR. 1984. What are moviemakers made of? *Pub. Opin.* 6(6): 14–18

Rozell MJ, Wilcox C. 1995a. *God at the Grass Roots: The Christian Right in the 1994 Election*. Lanham, MD: Rowman & Littlefield

Rozell MJ, Wilcox C. 1995b. The past as prologue: the Christian Right in the 1996 election. See Rozell & Wilcox 1995a, pp. 253–63

Rozell MJ, Wilcox C. 1995c. Virginia: God, guns, and Oliver North. See Rozell & Wilcox 1995a, pp. 109–131

Rozell MJ, Wilcox C. 1996. *The Second Coming: The New Christian Right in Virginia Politics*. Baltimore, MD: Johns Hopkins Univ. Press

Ryan MP. 1978. A woman's awakening: Evangelical religion and the families of Utica, New York, 1800–1840. *Am. Q.* 30(4):602–23

Schumm WR, Obiorah FC, Silliman B. 1989. Marital quality as a function of conservative religious identification in a sample of Protestant and Catholic wives from the Midwest. *Psychol. Rep.* 64(1):124–26

Schumm WR, Silliman B. 1990. A research note and commentary on Dixon, Levy and Lowery's asking the 'born-again' question. *Rev. Relig. Res.* 31(4):413–15

Sernett MG. 1991. Black religion and the question of evangelical identity. In *The Variety of American Evangelism,* ed. D Dayton, R Johnston, pp. 135–47. Downers Grove, IL: InterVarsity

Shibley MA. 1996. *Resurgent Evangelicalism in the United States: Mapping Cultural Change Since 1970*. Columbia: Univ. South Carolina Press

Sider RJ. 1997. Can we agree to agree? *Books Culture* 3(1):27

Smidt CE, Green JC, Kellstedt LA, Guth JL. 1996. The Spirit-filled movement and American politics. See Green et al 1996b, pp. 219–39

Smidt C, Penning JM. 1982. Religious commitment, political conservatism and political and social tolerance in the United States: a longitudinal analysis. *Sociol. Anal.* 43(3):231–46

Smidt C, Penning JM. 1990. A party divided? *Polity* 23(1):127–38

Smith C. 1996. Correcting a curious neglect, or bringing religion back in. In *Disruptive Religion: The Force of Faith in Social-Movement Activism,* ed. C Smith, pp. 1–25. New York: Routledge

Smith C, with Emerson M, Gallagher S, Kennedy P, Sikkink D. 1998. *American Evangelicals: Embattled and Thriving*. Chicago: Univ. Chicago Press

Smith TL. 1957. *Revivalism and Social Reform in Mid-Nineteenth-Century America*. New York: Abingdon

Smith TW. 1990. Classifying Protestant denominations. *Rev. Relig. Res.* 31(3): 224–45

Smith TW. 1992. Are conservative churches growing? *Rev. Relig. Res.* 33(4):305–29

Smith TW. 1994. *Anti-Semitism in Contemporary America. Work. Pap. on Contemp. Anti-Semitism.* New York: Am. Jewish Com.

Smith TW. 1996. *A Survey of the Religious*

Right: Views on Politics, Society, Jews and Other Minorities. Work. Pap. on Contemp. Anti-Semitism. New York: Am. Jewish Com.

Soper CJ. 1995. California: Christian conservative influence in a liberal state. See Rozell & Wilcox 1995a, pp. 211–26

Straus MA, Gelles RJ, Steinmetz SK. 1988. *Behind Closed Doors: Violence in the American Family.* Newbury Park, CA: Sage

Sullivan JL, Piereson J, Marcus G. 1982. *Political Tolerance and American Democracy.* Chicago: Univ. Chicago Press

Tamney JB, Johnson SD. 1997. Christianity and public book banning. *Rev. Relig. Res.* 38(3):263–71

Thalheimer F. 1973. Religiosity and secularization in the academic profession. *Sociol. Educ.* 46(2):183–202

Thomas DL, Cornwall M. 1990. Religion and family in the 1980's: discovery and development. *J. Marriage Fam.* 52(4):983–92

Thurow LC. 1996. *The Future of Capitalism.* New York: William Morrow

Wald KD. 1995. Florida: running globally and winning locally. See Rozell & Wilcox 1995a, pp. 19–46

Wald K, Owen D, Hill S. 1989. Evangelical politics and status issues. *J. Sci. Stud. Relig.* 28(1):1–16

Walls AF. 1996. *The Missionary Movement in Christian History: Studies in the Transmission on Faith.* Maryknoll, NY: Orbis

Warner RS. 1993. Work in progress toward a new paradigm for the sociological study of religion in the United States. *Am. J. Sociol.* 98(5):1044–93

Warner RS, Wittner JG, ed. 1998. *Gatherings in Diaspora: Religious Communities and the New Immigration.* Philadelphia: Temple Univ. Press. In press

Weber TP. 1991. Premillennialism and the branches of evangelicalism. In *The Variety of American Evangelicalism,* ed. D Dayton, R Johnston, pp. 5–21. Downers Grove, IL: InterVarsity

Whalen RK. 1996. Christians love the Jews!: the development of American Philo-Semitism, 1790–1860. *Relig. Am. Cult.* 6(2):225–60

Wilcox C. 1996. *Onward Christian Soldiers? The Religious Right in American Politics.* Boulder, CO: Westview

Wilcox C, Jelen T. 1990. Evangelicals and political tolerance. *Am. Polit. Q.* 18(1):25–46

Wilcox WB. 1997. *Religion and fatherhood: exploring the links between religious affiliation, gender roles attitudes, and paternal practices. Dep. Sociol. Work. Pap. No. 13-97.* Princeton Univ., NJ

Williams RH, ed. 1997. *Cultural Wars in American Politics: Critical Reviews of a Popular Myth.* Hawthorne, NY: Aldine de Gruyter

Wilson J. 1984. The Charismatic movement. In *The Encyclopedia of Religion in the South,* ed. S Hill, pp. 144–46. Macon, GA: Mercer Univ. Press

Wilson J, Musick M. 1996. Religion and marital dependency. *J. Sci. Stud. Relig.* 35(1): 30–40

Wilson MR, Filsinger EE. 1986. Religiosity and marital adjustment: multidimensional interrelationships. *J. Marriage Fam.* 48(1):147–51

Winzenburg S. 1988. On understanding TV evangelists. *Broadcasting* 115(3):25

Woodberry RD. 1997. *The Place of Religion in American Sociology.* Presented at Assoc. Sociol. Relig., Toronto, Canada

Woodberry RD. 1998. When surveys lie and people tell the truth: how surveys oversample church attenders. *Am. Sociol. Rev.* 63(1):9–12

Woodberry RD, Brick P, Babic L. 1996. *Evangelicals and politics: surveying a contemporary Mason-Dixon line.* Presented at Am. Sociol. Assoc., New York

Wuthnow R. 1985. Science and the sacred. In *The Sacred in a Secular Age,* ed. P Hammond, pp. 187–203. Berkeley: Univ. Calif. Press

Wuthnow R. 1992. *Rediscovering the Sacred.* Grand Rapids, MI: Eerdmans

Wuthnow R, Hodgkinson VA, ed. 1990. *Faith and Philanthropy in America.* San Francisco: Jossey-Bass

Annu. Rev. Sociol. 1998. 24:57–76

NETWORK FORMS OF ORGANIZATION

Joel M. Podolny and Karen L. Page
Graduate School of Business, Stanford University, Stanford, California 94305-5015; e-mail: podolny_joel@gsb.stanford.edu

KEY WORDS: networks, organization, alliances, governance, trust

ABSTRACT

Initial sociological interest in network forms of organization was motivated in part by a critique of economic views of organization. Sociologists sought to highlight the prevalence and functionality of organizational forms that could not be classified as markets or hierarchies. As a result of this work, we now know that network forms of organization foster learning, represent a mechanism for the attainment of status or legitimacy, provide a variety of economic benefits, facilitate the management of resource dependencies, and provide considerable autonomy for employees. However, as sociologists move away from critiquing what are now somewhat outdated economic views, they need to balance the exclusive focus on prevalence and functionality with attention to constraint and dysfunctionality. The authors review work that has laid a foundation for this broader focus and suggest analytical concerns that should guide this literature as it moves forward.

INTRODUCTION

Over the past decade or so, sociological interest in network forms of organization has blossomed. Sociologists have become increasingly intrigued by the plethora of organizational configurations that fail to conform to traditional definitions of markets or hierarchies. Part of the interest in these alternative organizational arrangements is no doubt due to what some regard as their increased empirical prevalence (Kanter 1991).

0360-0572/98/0815-0057$08.00

While a number of scholars have convincingly challenged the view that these forms are more prevalent now than at other times in history (e.g., Clawson 1980, Granovetter 1995, Laumann 1991), it nonetheless remains true that changes in the US regulatory environment greatly facilitated the ability of US firms to engage in cooperative activities with their market competitors. For example, the National Cooperative Research Act enabled coordinated research and development activity across firm boundaries to an extent that had not been allowed in the past. Such regulatory changes were themselves a consequence of another empirical phenomenon in the 1980s that also increased scholarly interest in these network forms of organization: the worldwide competitive success of Japanese and, to a lesser extent, other Asian firms. Because Japanese firms seemed to rely extensively on network forms of organization, there emerged great interest on the part of both scholars and practitioners in understanding the extent to which that reliance was itself a determinant of competitive success (Lincoln et al 1996, Gerlach 1992, Orr et al 1991).

Yet, if part of the motivation was empirical, another part was that the existence, prevalence, and functionality of these organizational arrangements represented a challenge to economic views of organization that were becoming popular during this time period (Granovetter 1985). Prior to the middle 1970s, economists had largely regarded the organization as a black box that is to be understood as a production function converting inputs to outputs. In the middle 1970s and early 1980s, economists started to look inside the black box, and two perspectives in particular became quite prominent: principal-agent theory and transaction cost economics. At least when they first emerged, each perspective was grounded in a dichotomous view of economic organization: markets, on the one hand, and hierarchies, on the other.

While this dichotomous view was perhaps more implicit than explicit in the principal-agent tradition, it was quite explicit in transaction cost economics. For example, whereas Oliver Williamson, one of the leading figures of the transaction cost perspective, acknowledged that other forms of organization existed, he nonetheless asserted two points. First, the alternatives to pure markets and pure hierarchies can be interpreted as intermediate or hybrid forms, combining elements of markets and hierarchies (Williamson 1991). Second, the distribution of organizations along the markets-hierarchies continuum is "thick in the tails" (Williamson 1985). That is, pure types tend to prevail over the mixed forms.

Sociological research on network forms of organization sought to challenge both of these points. First, sociologists argued that network forms of organization could not be considered hybrids of markets or hierarchies; rather, network forms of organization represented a unique alternative possessing its own logic (Powell 1990). Second, sociologists argued that the network form of organization has a number of distinct efficiency advantages not possessed by pure markets or pure hierarchies, and because of these efficiency advantages, network forms are quite prevalent (Bradach & Eccles 1989).

In the following pages, we review and highlight a number of important insights into the nature and functionality of the network form of organization. At the same time, we question whether the emphasis on the functionality of the network form has perhaps gone too far. In elucidating functions, sociologists are prone to neglect constraints that underlie the formation of network forms of organization, problems that arise in their governance, and boundary conditions on their functionality. We may have a good understanding of why economic actors want to utilize network forms of organization, but we have less understanding of why they do not. That is, we have little understanding of the reasons why variance exists in the utilization of network forms of organization or why a given focal actor would pursue one network partner and not another.

WHAT IS A NETWORK FORM OF ORGANIZATION?

From a purely structural perspective, the trichotomy among market, hierarchy, and network forms of organization is a false one. Markets and hierarchies are simply two pure types of organization that can be represented with the basic network analytic constructs of nodes and ties (Laumann 1991). For example, one might operationalize a spot market as a population of isolates. Each market actor is a node that lacks any ties to the other actors/nodes. One could operationalize a hierarchy as a centralized network in which the vast majority of ties flow to or from one particular node. In effect, from a structural perspective, every form of organization is a network, and market and hierarchy are simply two manifestations of the broader type.

However, when considered as a form of governance, the network form can be distinctly characterized. *We define a network form of organization as any collection of actors ($N \geq 2$) that pursue repeated, enduring exchange relations with one another and, at the same time, lack a legitimate organizational authority to arbitrate and resolve disputes that may arise during the exchange.* In a pure market, relations are not enduring, but episodic, formed only for the purpose of a well-specified transfer of goods and resources and ending after the transfer. In hierarchies, relations may endure for longer than a brief episode, but a clearly recognized, legitimate authority exists to resolve disputes that arise among actors.

This definition of a network form of organization includes a wide array of joint ventures, strategic alliances, business groups, franchises, research consortia, relational contracts, and outsourcing agreements. This definition excludes most pure market arrangements such as short-term contracts or spot market transactions, and it excludes employment relations. Yet, while it is tempting to provide a list of formal organizational arrangements that can or cannot be categorized as network forms of organization, any such list would obscure important variance within formal organizational types. For example, consider syndicates—collections of (typically financial) actors that pool assets to support a high-risk endeavor in exchange for profits from that endeavor. Syndicates can differ in the extent to which authority for managing the syndicate is vested in one actor, and they can differ in terms of their time horizon. In fact, an important trend among investment banks in the twentieth century was the increasingly transitory character of syndicates for the underwriting of securities (Carosso 1970, Eccles & Crane 1987). Such decentralization affected the extent to which this particular interorganizational arrangement conformed to the definition of the network form.

More generally, a significant sociological finding is that many of the economic arrangements that are formally labeled markets and hierarchies may conform empirically to the definition of network organization laid out above. For example, in his work on transfer pricing within organizations, Eccles (1985) discusses a number of cases in which organizational divisions lack a legitimate authority to set the price for the internal transfer of goods and arrive at prices based on negotiation. Therefore, while we provide a list of formal organizations typically regarded as manifestations of network forms of organization for the sake of illustration, we emphasize that there is no clear mapping of formal organizational arrangements onto the network form.

Even though network forms of organization cannot be identified according to some limited set of labels for formal organizational arrangements, a number of scholars have argued that network forms of organization can be characterized by a distinct ethic or value-orientation on the part of exchange partners. In his analysis of long-term buyer-supplier relations among Japanese firms, Ronald Dore (1983) points to what he calls the "spirit of goodwill" underlying these relationships. The central elements of this spirit of goodwill are a commitment to use "voice" rather than "exit" (cf. Hirschman 1970) to resolve disputes and a high level of trust between the parties. The buyer tries to work with the seller to address any deficiencies in the seller's performance rather than simply moving to another seller. Buyer and seller are both willing to make relationship-specific investments without contractual guarantees protecting those investments because each party expects that the other will not use the relationship-specific investments to its own advantage. Similarly, Powell (1990) argues that a norm of reciprocity is a guiding principle underlying network forms of organization. Each member of the network feels a sense of obligation to the other party or parties rather than a desire to take advantage of any trust that may have been established. In his analysis of business groups, Granovetter (1995) also points to a high level of trust and obligation among members of the group. He argues that a distinctive feature of such groups is that they constitute a moral community insofar as "trustworthy behavior can be expected, normative standards understood, and opportunism foregone." Finally, in a treatise on what he calls "small firm networks," Perrow (1993) identifies trust as a critical element of small firm production networks.

Probably the most vivid illustration of trustworthiness and obligation in a network form of organization comes from Uzzi's (1997) examination of subcontracting relationships in the New York garment industry. Uzzi is particularly interested in what he refers to as "embedded ties," strong enduring relations between manufacturers and subcontractors. He describes the case of a manufacturer that had decided to move all of its production facilities overseas to Asia. Because of this upcoming move, the manufacturer would no longer be relying on its subcontractors in New York. He writes:

> As a result [of this move], this manufacturer had strong incentives not to tell its contractor that it intended to leave. Doing so put it at risk of receiving low-quality goods from contractors who now saw the account as temporary and had to redirect their efforts to new manufacturers who could replace the lost business. Yet the CEO of this manufacturer personally notified his embedded ties, because his relationships with them obliged him to help them adapt to the closing of his business, and his trust in them led him to believe that they would not shirk on quality. Consistent with his account, one of his contractors said that the jobber's personal visit to his shop reaffirmed their relationship, which he repaid with quality goods. This same manufacturer, however, did not inform those contractors with which it had arms-length ties. (Uzzi 1997, p. 55)

This example is noteworthy because there exists no shadow of the future to ensure cooperation in the present. Moreover, because the manufacturer is moving overseas, it has no need to preserve its local reputation. Cooperation does not arise as a route to future gains.

While there may be subtle differences in each author's understanding of the trusting ethic guiding economic exchange in network forms of organization, these subtle differences need not concern us here. What is important is that this more trusting ethic is one of the defining elements of a network form of governance, and the network form of governance is therefore not reducible to a hybridization of market and hierarchical forms, which, in contrast, are premised on a more adversarial posture.

To be sure, it is probably true that a moral community or spirit of goodwill is not a functional necessity for a network form of organization to exist. If two economic actors wish to enter into an enduring relation and lack a legitimate authority to resolve disputes, they may enter into a long-term contract in order to place restrictions on the opportunistic behavior of one another. In the contract, they can include provisions that allow for anticipated changes or allow for recontracting at a later date based on unanticipated changes. However, in the face of unexpected changes to the opportunities and constraints confronting parties to the exchange, an exchange relation governed by a contract with provisions only for anticipated changes will generally be less flexible than an exchange governed by a norm of reciprocity. Moreover, a contract allowing for recontracting at a later date based on unanticipated changes to circumstance requires some level of trust that the other party will act in good faith at the time of recontracting. In short, while a long-term contract may represent a substitute for what some have identified as a moral community, spirit of goodwill, or norm of reciprocity, such a contract is not likely to allow for the same flexibility and adaptability as these ethics of exchange.

FUNCTIONS OF NETWORK FORMS OF ORGANIZATION

An increasingly large volume of research has sought to highlight the functionality of network forms of organization. Sociologists and organizational scholars have claimed that network forms allow participating firms to learn new skills or acquire knowledge, gain legitimacy, improve economic performance, and manage resource dependencies. In addition, the widespread use of network forms of organization may have unintended social welfare benefits. We consider each of these proposed advantages separately.

Learning

A number of scholars have emphasized the learning benefits of network forms of organization (Dore 1983, Powell 1990, Uzzi 1997, Hamel 1991). Network forms of organization foster learning because they preserve greater diversity of search routines than hierarchies and they convey richer, more complex information than the market. As Powell (1990) writes, "the most useful information is rarely that which flows down the formal chain of command in an organization, or that which can be inferred from price signals. Rather, it is that which is obtained from someone you have dealt with in the past and found to be reliable" (p. 304).

There are two ways in which network forms of organization can foster learning. First, they can encourage learning by promoting the rapid transfer of self-contained pieces of information. In this view, network ties are conduits or channels (e.g., Contractor & Lorange 1988b, Root 1988, Hamel 1991, Kogut 1988b). Hamel (1991) is perhaps the most explicit in examining how interfirm collaborations provide participating firms with opportunities to internalize one another's skills. Conceiving firms as portfolios of skills, Hamel argues that network forms of organization are less a compromise between market and hierarchy (Grant 1996), to use Williamson's (1975) terminology, and more an alternative to other modes of skill acquisition. This understanding of learning through networks is quite consistent with some of the early network research on information transfer. For example, in Granovetter's (1974) seminal research on job search, information on jobs resides at nodes and is transferred through the ties linking nodes.

Alternatively, as Powell & Brantley (1992) contend, network forms of organization may foster learning by encouraging novel syntheses of information that are qualitatively distinct from the information that previously resided within the distinct nodes. That is, rather than simply facilitating the transfer of information between two nodes, the existence of an enduring exchange relation may actually yield new knowledge. In effect, the network becomes the locus of innovation rather than the nodes that comprise the network.

In a study of the biotechnology industry, Powell et al (1996) attempt to test empirically the claim that when the knowledge of an industry is broadly distributed and rapidly changing, the locus of innovation will be found in interorganizational networks of learning, rather than in individual firms. In their study, the authors find some evidence of a liability of unconnectedness; strong-performing biotechnology firms have larger, more diverse alliance networks than do weak-performing firms. While this result is consistent with the authors' hypothesis, it is also consistent with a number of others. First, the link between connectedness and performance does not necessarily mean that learning and innovation constitute the intervening process between structure and performance. As we discuss further below, network ties may serve a number of other functions such as managing resource dependencies or enhancing legitimacy, both of which have positive effects on performance. Second, even if the tie count reflects learning, it is not clear whether ties are conduits for information flow or are actually loci of innovation that would not arise in the absence of the ties.

Using a firm's position in a network of patent citations as a measure of technological position, Stuart & Podolny (1996, 1997) attempt to establish a closer connection between alliances and learning. The authors illustrate how patent citations can be used to establish (*a*) the technological distance of a firm from its alliance partners and (*b*) the extent to which a firm's current inventions differ considerably in content from its past inventions. Stuart & Podolny (1997) find that the greater a firm's technological distance from its alliance partners, the higher the likelihood that the focal firm produces inventions that are considerably different in content from its previous inventions. Such a finding provides more direct support for the learning hypothesis, but it does not distinguish between the two means of learning identified above.

To know whether alliances yield novel syntheses, we would need to know not only whether a firm's inventions were significant departures from past inventions but also whether the firm's inventions were qualitatively distinct from its alliance partners' past inventions. If alliances yield inventions that are qualitatively distinct from the inventions of either partner, then we can more confidently assert that the locus of innovation is in the network itself rather than the nodes of that network. While such research has not yet been conducted, it seems a straightforward extension of the current work using patent citations as proxies for technological distance.

Legitimation and Status

A number of scholars have argued that if an actor's partner in a network form of organization possesses considerable legitimacy or status, then the actor may derive legitimacy or status through the affiliation. This legitimacy or status may in turn have a number of positive economic benefits for the actor, ranging from survival to organizational growth to profitability. For example, in a study of daycare centers, Baum & Oliver (1992) find that a tie to a legitimate institutional actor, such as a church or governmental entity, has a positive effect on the life chances of an organization. In a study of the investment banking industry, Podolny & Phillips (1996) find that the higher the status of a bank's management partners in underwriting syndicates at time t, the greater its status growth between time t and $t + 1$. This enhanced status, in turn, has positive economic advantages for the organization (Podolny 1993).

In one of the more compelling demonstrations of the economic value of ties to legitimate or high-status actors, Stuart et al (1997) examine the economic effects of the interorganizational networks of privately held biotechnology firms. These authors find that an affiliation with a prominent alliance partner increases the market value of the biotechnology firm. What is particularly notable about this study is that the authors seek to empirically disentangle the legitimating or status-enhancing effects of these ties from the resources that would flow from such ties. The authors argue that the legitimating or status-enhancing effects of an affiliation with a prominent actor should vary with the age of the start-up. When a start-up is young, there is considerable investor uncertainty about its quality. As the start-up ages, this uncertainty inevitably declines since investors have more history on which to base their inferences. If ties to prominent actors are primarily symbolic in their significance, then the effect of such ties should be greatest for the young start-ups, whose quality is most uncertain. Conversely, if the ties to prominent actors are simply proxies for superior resource flows, then the effect should not vary with age; older and younger firms should benefit equally from superior resource flows. Consistent with an interpretation of these ties as carriers of legitimacy, Stuart and his associates find that the effect of affiliations varies inversely with the age of the start-up.

Finally, Stark (1996) offers one of the most intriguing accounts of the legitimating effects of network ties. Stark examines the development of organizational forms in postsocialist Hungary. In this transitional period, multiple socioeconomic and sociopolitical orders exist simultaneously, with different and sometimes contradictory bases on which organizations can lay legitimate claims to resources. Decentralized networks of organizations emerge, and assets and liabilities are reallocated within the network in such a way that the network represents a hedge against uncertainty in the political and economic environment. In Stark's account, status and legitimacy are acquired not by virtue of a tie to an actor that is generally regarded as high status or legitimate. Rather, legitimacy is attained through a distribution of liabilities and assets within the organizational network that is robust with respect to the multiple, contending sociopolitical and socioeconomic orders.

Whereas all of the above accounts of legitimacy emphasize benefits that flow from one network partner to another, Baum & Oliver (1991, 1992) make the additional claim that a focal organization's tie to a legitimate actor has positive externalities for others in the focal organization's population. A tie to a legitimate actor outside of the organizational population helps to institutionalize the population as a whole. Sharfman et al (1991) make a similar argument.

Economic Benefits

In elaborating functions fulfilled by the network form of organization, it is important not to overlook the direct economic benefits of this form in terms of costs and quality. Williamson (1991) lays out conditions under which network forms of organization lower transaction costs, though it bears repeating that the transaction cost perspective does not see trusting or altruistic behavior as particularly germane to the network form of organization. A number of economists and strategy scholars attempt to assess empirically the relevance of the transaction cost perspective to the network form of organization (Hennert 1988, 1991, Zajac & Olsen 1993, Parkhe 1993, Buckley & Casson 1988, Stuckley 1983). Perhaps because they seek to elaborate a view of network forms of organization that is distinct from economic views, sociologists downplay or reject the role of transaction costs in the adoption of the network form (e.g., Powell et al 1996, Lazerson 1993, Bradach & Eccles 1989). Moreover, when sociologists see transaction costs reduced through the network form, they emphasize the reliance on trust rather than contractual provisions as the primary basis on which transaction costs are reduced (e.g., Dore 1983).

Perhaps more importantly, sociologists stress quality advantages rather than costs as the primary economic benefit. For example, comparing long-term or embedded subcontracting relations to arms-length subcontracting relations, Uzzi (1997) argues that the former are more conducive to high-quality production because they enable richer communication between buyer and supplier on issues pertaining to quality.

Some sociologists also claim that one of the economic benefits of the network form of organization is the adaptability of this form to unanticipated environmental changes (Powell 1990, Kanter 1991). By fostering greater communication than the market does, network forms of organization facilitate greater coordination in the face of changes whose significance cannot be completely conveyed or understood through price signals. At the same time, because the boundaries of network forms of organization are generally easier to adjust than the boundaries of hierarchies, it is easier to modify the composition of network organizations to respond to those changes (Sorenson 1997).

Other Benefits of the Network Form of Organization

In addition to the benefits just listed, at least two other advantages are emphasized by sociologists and organizational scholars. First, following Selznick's (1949) initial insights regarding organizational cooptation, resource dependence scholars posit that organizations can alleviate sources of external constraint or uncertainty by strengthening their relationship with the particular sources of dependence. Pfeffer & Nowak (1976) apply this general insight to the formation of joint ventures. They find that that oligopolistic industries (i.e., industries of intermediate concentration) have the highest proportion of firms engaged in within-industry joint ventures. Since oligopolistic industries are those in which firms face the highest uncertainty about the actions of their competitors, Pfeffer & Nowak take this finding as evidence that joint ventures are a means for reducing that uncertainty. Second, Perrow (1993) identifies a number of social welfare benefits with what he refers to as small firm networks, or networks of small producers. He argues that in comparison to larger, bureaucratic forms of organization, small firm networks provide individuals with greater autonomy, lead to less inequality in the distribution of wealth, and foster a greater sense of community.

WHY ARE THERE MARKETS AND HIERARCHIES?

While this list of functions or benefits of the network form of organization is perhaps not exhaustive, it captures the vast majority of those that sociologists and organization scholars have identified. This research has yielded some important insights. Yet, a review of the work does raise an important question: Why do not all actors within an organizational population rely exclusively on the network form? That is, if a network form of governance can result in superior learning, enhanced legitimacy and prestige, greater control over the external environment, and economic benefits, why are there any markets and hierarchies remaining? In effect, this attention to the functionality of network forms of organization explains why economic actors rely on network forms of organization, but it does not explain why they do not.

To be sure, this work potentially provides some understanding of cross-industry or cross-population variance in the utilization of network forms of organization. For example, to the extent that network form fosters learning, the form should be more prevalent in industries where knowledge is broadly dispersed and knowledge is rapidly updated (Powell & Brantley 1992). Based on this argument, one would expect the form to be more prevalent in the biotechnology industry than in the steel industry, for example.

But what explains the variance in the utilization of this form within the biotechnology industry? More generally, what are the determinants of intrapopulation or intraindustry variance in the utilization of network forms of organization? This concern with intrapopulation variation in the utilization of network forms of organization can be framed as two research questions. First, what determines the extent to which an economic actor chooses to rely on a network form of governance? Second, to the extent that an economic actor wishes to employ a network form of governance, what are the constraints on the pattern of network relationships that the actor may form?

In an examination of relationships between corporations and investment bankers, Baker (1990) attempts to answer this first question. Baker distinguishes three market interfaces that can link an investment bank to its corporate issuers: a relationship interface involving long-term ties with at most a few banks; a transaction interface involving short-term ties with numerous banks; and a hybrid interface representing an intermediate category between the other two. The relationship interface obviously corresponds to the network form of governance, whereas a transactional interface corresponds to market governance. Using a number of measures of a corporation's power, such as its size or its availability of resource alternatives, Baker finds that a more transactional orientation is associated with greater corporate power. Only those corporations that are weaker and more dependent on investment banks adopt the relationship interface.

These findings are important insofar as they provide some initial insight into why actors would adopt a network form of organization. However, further work must be done to integrate these findings with the literature emphasizing the functionality of the network form of governance. In Baker's work, corporations only adopt the network form when they are too weak to adopt an alternative, more transactional interface. If network forms of organization are functional for the reasons elaborated above, then it is difficult to understand why only weak corporations would prefer this form. One possibility is that powerful firms are in less need of the benefits yielded by alliances. However, given the broad set of advantages claimed for the network form of governance, this proposition seems difficult to sustain. Another possibility is that unique features of the investment banking industry limit the benefits of the network form of organization. This conclusion, too, is difficult to sustain in light of research highlighting functional benefits of the relationship interface in this industry (Eccles & Crane 1987).

While not necessarily directed toward the specific topic of network forms of organization, ecological arguments on inertia (Hannan & Freeman 1989) may nonetheless provide some analytical leverage in understanding intrapopulation variance in the adoption of this form. Drawing on Stinchcombe's (1965) arguments about organizational imprinting, ecologists argue that important features of an organization's structure are established early in an organization's history, and these features can be difficult to alter. For example, older firms in the computer industry such as IBM or DEC are vertically integrated. At the time of their entry into the computer industry, such firms had strong functional reasons for a high level of vertical integration. An absence of efficient markets for various components of computers drove firms to integrate vertically. In contrast, younger computer firms such as Sun Computers, Compaq, and Silicon Graphics are vertically disintegrated, relying extensively on outsourcing relationships. These younger firms emerged during a time when efficient markets existed for many of the various components within computers. Because of the difficulties involved in significant organizational restructuring, older firms have been either unable or unwilling to modify their vertically integrated structures to take advantage of the more efficient markets for computer components.

A third basis for variance in the propensity to adopt the network form of organization is nationality. Cultural and legal differences across countries can be the basis for differences in the propensity of organizations to adopt network forms of organization. Dore (1983), for example, argues that the ethic underlying a network form of organization is more consistent with a collectivist orientation and thus more prevalent in countries where individuals subscribe to the collectivist orientation. In Italy, tax laws favor small employers. Such laws greatly encourage the formation of small-firm networks over the formation of large hierarchies.

Power, conditions at time of founding, and nationality have thus been identified as three factors that potentially affect intrapopulation or intraindustry variance in the adoption of the network form. Yet, of these three factors, only two can explain within-country variance, and of these two, one is difficult to reconcile with the view that network organizations are—at least at times—functional and desirable rather than a response to a weakened power position. Moreover, the organizational imprinting argument does not by itself explain why network forms were more prominent in some periods than in others. Further research obviously needs to be undertaken to explain differences in the propensity of economic actors to adopt the network form of organization.

We now shift from work focusing on the propensity of an actor to adopt a network form to work that seeks to explain the pattern of network ties that arise among a population of actors. Some research suggests that the pattern of relations follows a functional logic. That is, a network tie arises when it is most likely to foster one of the functions listed above. For example, Lincoln et al (1992) examine transaction cost and resource dependence motivations underlying the pattern of ties among leading Japanese firms. In addition, implicit in Hamel's (1991) assertion that firms form alliances to obtain skills is a hypothesis that a firm will form alliances with those that are most able to provide the skill set needed by the firm.

Though there is value in linking the functions of the network form of organization to the pattern of ties that arise among a population of actors, a central feature of the sociological perspective is its attention to constraints on action that lie outside of the purposive behavior of individual actors. Even if a particular network tie would convey one of the functional advantages listed above, there may still be reasons why a dyad would be unable to form an enduring exchange relation in the absence of a legitimate authority. Nevertheless, despite the centrality of the constraint emphasis to the sociological perspective, there is surprisingly little work that highlights these constraints.

Mowery et al (1996) draw on Cohen & Levinthal's (1989, 1990) concept of absorptive capacity to explain the pattern of technology-sharing alliances. They contend that a firm's ability to absorb knowledge from a potential partner is contingent on the stock of related knowledge. Therefore, a firm is unlikely to enter into an alliance with another firm whose technology is highly different from its own. At the same time, the authors assert that a firm is unlikely to enter into an alliance with a partner that possesses redundant technology. Accordingly, the authors hypothesize and find evidence that a firm is most likely to form technology-sharing alliances with a firm whose technology is at an intermediate technological distance.

Podolny (1994) examines the pattern of syndicate relations among investment banks. He argues that in markets where there is high uncertainty about the quality of a good or service that an actor brings to market, an actor's status may limit the potential exchange partners to which the actor has access. High status actors must avoid affiliating with low status actors in order to avoid risking a loss of their own status, and low status actors are thereby constrained in their ability to enter into exchange relations with high status actors.

Gulati (1995) offers probably the most general account of the constraints underlying the pattern of network tie formation. In a multi-industry examination of alliance formation, he argues that one of the most important determinants of the pattern of alliances at time t is the preexisting pattern of alliances at $t-1$. More specifically, Gulati hypothesizes that the probability that points in a dyad will enter into an alliance with one another is a function of past direct contact between the pair and the presence of indirect network connections through others in the industry. Gulati asserts and finds evidence that these indirect ties serve both a referral and a control function. They provide information on each potential partner's reliability, and they represent a source of peer sanctioning when one party does not act in good faith in the context of the alliance. Powell et al (1996) also develop some similar hypotheses as to how the previous pattern of ties predicts the existing patterns of ties. Framing these results in terms of constraint, a firm will generally be unwilling or unable to form a tie with another if it lacks some indirect connection to that other.

Of course, any endogenous explanation of tie formation, in which ties at one time period lay a foundation for ties at a subsequent time period, begs the question: What are the determinants of the initial ties in which a firm is involved? Especially in rapidly growing industries like biotechnology, where so many new organizations enter each year without ties, the presence of previous direct or indirect ties cannot be a critical explanatory variable in understanding the distribution of ties within a population. Gulati & Gargiulo (1997) have started to respond to this concern by situating the endogenous dynamic in a broader evolutionary framework.

As work on constraints underlying the pattern of network relations moves forward, it will be important to attend to two observations. First, the pattern is a function not only of the formation of new ties but of the persistence of established ties, and, second, constraints operate not only on tie formation but also on tie persistence. For example, consider Gulati's finding that a firm's ability to form an alliance with another is contingent on the presence of previously existing indirect ties to that firm. To the extent that this claim is true, a firm has an incentive to preserve an alliance simply to help lay the foundation for future alliances with others even if that focal alliance provides no tangible benefit itself. Moreover, given the importance of trust and obligation to the successful operation of network ties, there are inevitably limits on how much an actor can alter its network in response to changes in self-interest (Portes & Sensenbrenner 1993).

The existence of constraints on the breaking of ties has clear, specific implications for the previously mentioned claims regarding the adaptability of network forms of organization. If there are reputational costs from breaking ties, then there are at least some circumstances in which market and hierarchical forms of governance, which are not premised on trust and obligation, will be more adaptable than a network form, which is. More generally, if there are constraints on the dissolution of ties, then it seems quite reasonable to conclude that network ties can often outlive the duration of their functionality. A network tie that may have originated for strongly functional reasons persists only for the purpose of preserving reputation.

WHY ARE THERE NO NETWORK FAILURES?

This discussion of constraints on the dissolution of network ties naturally leads to another topic that has received scant attention in sociological research on network forms of organization: the dysfunctionalities that arise through the operation of the network. One possible reason for the inattention to dysfunctionalities is that network forms of organization may indeed constitute a superior organizational form. A number of scholars (e.g., Kanter 1991, Powell 1990, Perrow 1993) seem at least implicitly to make the claim that alliance capitalism is simply more efficient and effective than a capitalism premised on arms-length transactions among large hierarchies, especially when efficiency and efficacy hinge on the coordination of a complex array of elements.

However, this enthusiasm for network forms of organization seems difficult to reconcile with an important fact: An extremely large fraction of network forms of organization do not perform the function for which they were designed (Kogut 1988a, Killing 1982, Inkpen 1996). While there are essentially no scientific studies of the failure rate of network forms of organization, journalistic and managerial sources are essentially unanimous in the conclusion that an extremely large proportion of at least one common type of network organization—strategic alliances—result in failure. For example, the Boston Consulting Group, which undertook a study of the performance of alliances in the airline industry—an industry with 401 alliances in 1995—estimated that fewer than 40% of regional alliances and fewer than 30% of international alliances should be considered successes (*The Economist* 1995). Similarly, Savona (1992) refers to a study finding that the average joint venture lasts less than 3.5 years and that fewer than one third of joint ventures are considered successes.

Obviously, such findings must be supplemented with more scientific analyses. Enthusiasts for the network form of organization could perhaps respond to such a finding by observing that the dysfunctionality of a particular form is relative, and one would need to compare the failure rate of alliances to the failure rate of other organizational structures. Fair enough. Such an analysis would clearly be of value to establishing the relative performance of the network form of governance.

However, even in the absence of such a study, it seems important to pay more attention to conditions under which network forms of organization meet their objective and those under which they do not. While there is some acknowledgment that networks do fail (e.g., Powell & Smith-Doerr 1994), such acknowledgments have not yet had a significant impact on the focus of empirical research. We suspect that one of the reasons that there has been little work on this topic is that it is quite difficult to obtain longitudinal data on the performance of a population of network organizations. Moreover, for network forms such as strategic alliances, data on dates of founding are generally much better than on the dates of failure. Failure rarely occurs on a specific date, and even if an alliance is formally terminated on a particular date, the participating actors often do not publicly announce the termination. As a consequence, researchers cannot rely on archival data to establish failures.

One initial attempt to reconcile the concern with functionality and dsyfunctionality is Uzzi (1996, 1997). He argues that embedded transactions are more functional than arms-length transactions, though he posits an inverted U-relationship between embeddedness and performance. That is, while embedded transactions are superior to unembedded ones, it nonetheless remains possible for an organization to depend too much on embedded ties. If a disproportionate number of an organization's ties are embedded, then the organization becomes trapped by these relationships. However, even here, dysfunctionality is at the level of an actor's entire network rather than at the level of individual ties, and the above data on failure are at the tie level, not at the level of the entire network.

Some research suggests that the ability to operate in a network form of organization is a skill or capability that must be learned, and as a consequence the likelihood of failure is related to the experience of the actors with the form. Acknowledging the difficulties inherent in working with unrelated entities, Powell & Brantley note that "successful firms are those who learn most rapidly how to gain from external linkages without creating enemies or behaving opportunistically" (1992, p. 371). That is, the ability to exploit the substantive knowledge gained through network relationships without killing the proverbial goose can be viewed as an important capability in its own right (Levitt & March 1988), to be learned through experience in network forms of organizations (Powell et al 1996, Mody 1993, Gulati et al 1994, Gulati 1995, Westney 1988, Balakrishnana & Koza 1993). The implication of this research is that the likelihood that a network organization will fail decreases with the partners' experience with the form.

In addition to this general insight on the importance of experience, some qualitative field research provides clues and insights into the behavioral determinants of success and failure at the dyad level (e.g., Doz 1996, Liebeskind et al 1996, Parkhe 1991, Larson 1992). For example, Doz (1996) argues that a number of factors such as the level of task integration, similarity of organizational cultures, and commonality of organizational goals affect the ability of alliance partners to learn from one another. Parkhe (1991) also looks at learning and adaptation as critical processes underlying the longevity and effectiveness of alliances, focusing in particular on how the firms' diversity affects learning and adaptation.

Unfortunately, with the exception of Larson's (1992) study, these field studies tend to fall outside of the sociological literature. As a result, they do not link up with the theoretical constructs that have been of greatest interest to sociologists. Further work needs to be done to establish a more substantial linkage. Especially given the importance of trust in sociological accounts, it would be valuable to have some more direct insight into the social and psychological processes by which trust in network forms of organization is built up and breaks down. Though their analysis is more at the level of interpersonal networks than network organizations, the work of Burt & Knez (1995) provides a model for such an examination.

One could perhaps draw on some of the research on constraints to develop hypotheses about dysfunctionalities. For example, as noted above, Gulati (1995) demonstrates that the probability that an alliance will form between two actors is a function of the indirect connections that these actors have to one another. These indirect connections are conduits for information about reputation and peer control. We suspect that these should be relevant not only to the likelihood of formation but also to the likelihood of failure. That is, less information about reputation and less peer control increase the likelihood that a strategic alliance will end in failure.

Yet, regardless of the direction pursued in future research, it is clear that more attention must be given to the factors that determine the success and failure of network forms of organization. Once the possibilities for failure are acknowledged, one can no longer simply add up the number of network ties and assume that more ties imply greater learning or greater legitimacy. It seems quite plausible to assume that a failed tie with a high status or legitimate actor may have more adverse consequences than no tie at all.

CONCLUSION: A BALANCED APPROACH TO THE NETWORK FORM

A large volume of research has documented the functionality of the network form of organization. As noted in the introduction, we suspect that the initial impetus for this concern with the functionality of the network form was to critique and challenge economic views of organization, as is made quite explicit in the writings of Granovetter (1985) and Powell (1990). When explicitly linked to a critique, the primary objective was to show that at least under some conditions, nonmarket, nonhierarchical forms or organization are functional. However, as the literature has evolved, it has become decoupled from such an explicit critique. Such a decoupling seems a necessary and important stage in the evolution of this literature; however, in moving away from the explicit critique, researchers must counterbalance the focus on prevalence and functionality with an equally strong focus on constraint and dysfunctionality. Otherwise, the literature runs the risk of succumbing to a naive functionalism.

In moving toward this more balanced consideration of the network form, it is important to recognize that the network form represents one of three alternative forms of governance, not one of two. In the past, sociologists have typically made pairwise comparisons when evaluating network organizations. For example, when discussing the richness of information conveyed through network ties, the comparison is to arms-length contracts. When discussing the autonomy of the network form, the comparison is to hierarchy. However, does the network form provide richer information than hierarchies and more autonomy than the market? Only by considering all three forms simultaneously can objective assessments of the strengths and weaknesses of the form be made.

ACKNOWLEDGMENTS

The authors wish to thank Woody Powell for helpful comments on this review.

Literature Cited

Baker WE. 1990. Market networks and corporate behavior. *Am. J. Sociol.* 96:589–625

Balakrishnana S, Koza MP. 1993. Information asymmetry, market failure and joint ventures: theory and evidence. *J. Econ. Behav. Org.* 20:99–117

Baum JAC, Oliver C. 1991. Institutional linkages and organizational mortality. *Admin. Sci. Q.* 36:187–218

Baum JAC, Oliver C. 1992. Institutional embeddedness and the dynamics of organizational populations. *Am. Sociol. Rev.* 57: 540–59

Bourdieu P, Coleman JS, eds. 1991. *Social Theory for a Changing Society.* Boulder, CO: Westview

Bradach JL, Eccles RG. 1989. Price, authority, and trust: from ideal types to plural forms. *Annu. Rev. Sociol.* 15:97–118

Buckley PJ, Casson M. 1988. A theory of cooperation in international business. See Contractor & Lorange 1988a, pp. 31–53

Burt RS, Knez M. 1995. Kinds of third-party effects on trust. *Ration. Soc.* 7:255–92

Carosso VP. 1970. *Investment Banking in America: A History.* Cambridge, MA: Harvard Univ. Press

Clawson D. 1980. *Bureaucracy and the Labor Process: The Transformation of U.S. Industry, 1860–1920.* New York: Monthly Rev.

Cohen WM, Levinthal DA. 1989. Innovation and learning: the two faces of R&D. *Econ. J.* 99:569–96

Cohen WM, Levinthal DA. 1990. Absorptive capacity: a new perspective on learning and innovation. *Admin. Sci. Q.* 35:128–52

Contractor FJ, Lorange P, eds. 1988a. *Cooperative Strategies in International Business.* Lexington, MA: Lexington Books

Contractor FJ, Lorange P. 1988b. Why should firms cooperate: the strategy and economic basis for cooperative ventures. See Contractor & Lorange 1988a, pp. 3–30

Dore R. 1983. Goodwill and the spirit of market capitalism. *Br. J. Sociol.* 34:459–82

Doz YL. 1996. The evolution of cooperation in strategic alliances: initial conditions or learning processes? *Strat. Manage. J.* 17: 55–83 (Sum. Suppl.)

Eccles RG. 1985. *The Transfer Pricing Problem.* Lexington, MA: Lexington Books

Eccles RG, Crane DB. 1987. Managing through networks in investment banking. *Calif. Manage. Rev.* 30:176–95

Editors. 1995. Flying in formation. *The Economist* 336(7924):59–60

Gerlach ML. 1992. *Alliance Capitalism: The Social Organization of Japanese Business.* Berkeley: Univ. Calif. Press

Granovetter MS. 1974. *Getting a Job; a Study of Contacts and Careers.* Cambridge, MA: Harvard Univ.

Granovetter MS. 1985. Economic action and social structure: the problem of embeddedness. *Am. J. Sociol.* 91:481–510

Granovetter MS. 1995. Coase revisited: business groups in the modern economy. *Ind. Corp. Change* 4:93–131

Grant RM. 1996. Prospering in dynamically-competitive environments: organizational capability as knowledge integration. *Org. Sci.* 7:375–87

Gulati R. 1995. Social structure and alliance formation patterns: a longitudinal analysis. *Admin. Sci. Q.* 40:619–52

Gulati R, Gargiulo M. 1997. *Where do networks come from?* Work. Pap. Northwestern Univ. Grad. Sch. Mgmt.

Gulati R, Khanna T, Nohria N. 1994. Unilateral commitments and the importance of process in alliances. *Sloan Manage. Rev.* 35(3):61–69

Hamel G. 1991. Competition for competence and inter-partner learning within international strategic alliances. *Strat. Manage. J.* 12:83–103 (Summ. Suppl.)

Hannan MT, Freeman J. 1989. *Organizational Ecology*. Cambridge, MA: Harvard Univ. Press

Hennart J. 1988. A transaction costs theory of equity joint ventures. *Strat. Manage. J.* 9: 361–74

Hennart J. 1991. The transaction costs theory of joint ventures: an empirical study of Japanese subsidiaries in the United States. *Manage. Sci.* 37:483–97

Hirschman AO. 1970. *Exit, Voice, and Loyalty: Responses to Decline in Firms, Organizations, and States*. Cambridge, MA: Harvard Univ. Press

Inkpen AC. 1996. Creating knowledge through collaboration. *Calif. Manage. Rev.* 39:123–40

Kanter RM. 1991. The future of bureaucracy and hierarchy in organizational theory: a report from the field. See Bourdieu & Coleman 1991, pp. 63–90

Killing JP. 1982. How to make a global joint venture work. *Harvard Bus. Rev.* 60:3

Kogut B. 1988a. A study of the life cycle of joint ventures. *Manage. Int. Rev.* 28:39–52

Kogut B. 1988b. Joint ventures: theoretical and empirical perspectives. *Strat. Manage. J.* 9:319–32

Larson A. 1992. Network dyads in entrepreneurial settings: study of the governance of exchange relationships. *Admin. Sci. Q.* 37: 76–104

Laumann EO. 1991. Comment on "The Future of Bureaucracy and Hierarchy in Organizational Theory: A Report from the Field." See Bourdieu & Coleman 1991, pp. 90–93

Lazerson M. 1993. Future alternatives of work reflected in the past: the putting-out production in Modena. In *Explorations in Economic Sociology,* ed. R Swedberg, pp. 403–28. New York: Russell Sage Found.

Levitt B, March JG. 1988. Organizational learning. *Annu. Rev. Sociol.* 14:319–40

Liebeskind JP, Oliver AL, Zucker LG, Brewer M. 1996. Social networks, learning, and flexibility: sourcing scientific knowledge in new biotechnology firms. *Org. Sci.* 7: 428–43

Lincoln JR, Gerlach ML, Ahmadjian C. 1992. Keiretsu networks in the Japanese economy: a dyad analysis of intercorporate ties. *Am. Sociol. Rev.* 1992:57:561–85

Lincoln JR, Gerlach ML, Ahmadjian C. 1996. Keiretsu networks and corporate performance in Japan. *Am. Sociol. Rev.* 61:67–88

Mody A. 1993. Learning through alliances. *J. Econ. Behav. Org.* 20:151–70

Mowery DC, Oxley JE, Silverman BS. 1996. Strategic alliances and interfirm knowledge transfer. *Strat. Manage. J.* 17:77–91 (Summ. Suppl.)

Orru M, Biggart NW, Hamilton GG. 1991. Organizational isomophism in East Asia. In *The New Institutionalism in Organizational Analysis,* ed. WW Powell, PJ DiMaggio, pp. 361–89. Chicago: Univ. Chicago

Parkhe A. 1991. Interfirm diversity, organizational learning, and longevity in global strategic alliances. *J. Int. Bus. Stud.* 22: 579–601

Parkhe A. 1993. Strategic alliance structuring: a game theoretic and transaction cost examination of interfirm cooperation. *Acad. Manage. J.* 36:794–829

Perrow C. 1993. Small firm networks. In *Explorations in Economic Sociology,* ed. R Swedberg, pp. 277–402. New York: Russell Sage Found.

Pfeffer J, Nowak P. 1976. Joint-ventures and interorganizational interdependence. *Admin. Sci. Q.* 21:398–418

Podolny JM. 1993. A status-based model of market competition. *Am. J. Sociol.* 98: 829–72

Podolny JM. 1994. Market uncertainty and the social character of economic exchange. *Admin. Sci. Q.* 39:458–83

Podolny JM, Phillips DJ. 1996. The dynamics of organizational status. *Ind. Corp. Change* 5:453–72

Portes A, Sensenbrenner J. 1993. Embeddedness and immigration: notes on the social determinants of economic action. *Am. J. Sociol.* 98:1320–50

Powell WW. 1990. Neither market nor hierarchy: network forms of organization. In *Research in Organizational Behavior*, ed. B Staw, LL Cummings, 12:295–336. Greenwich, CT: JAI

Powell WW, Brantley P. 1992. Competitive cooperation in biotechnology: learning through networks? In *Networks and Organizations: Structure, Form and Action,* ed. N Nohria, R Eccles, pp. 366–94. Boston: Harvard Bus. Sch.

Powell WW, Koput KW, Smith-Doerr L. 1996. Interorganizational collaboration and the locus of innovation: networks of learning in biotechnology. *Admin. Sci. Q.* 41:116–45

Powell WW, Smith-Doerr L. 1994. Networks and economic life. In *The Handbook of Economic Sociology,* ed. NJ Smelser, R Swedberg, pp. 368–402. Princeton, NJ: Princeton Univ. Press

Root RR. 1988. Some taxonomies of international cooperative arrangements. See Contractor & Lorange 1988a, pp. 69–80

Savona D. 1992. When companies divorce. *Int. Bus.* 5(11):48–51

Selznick P. 1949. *TVA and the Grass Roots.* Berkeley, CA: Univ. Calif. Press

Sharfman MP, Gray B, Yan A. 1991. The context of interorganizational collaboration in the garment industry: an institutional perspective. *J. Appl. Behav. Sci.* 27:181–208

Sørenson O. 1997. *Complexity catastrophe: interdependence and adaptability in organizational evolution.* Work. Pap. Univ. Chicago Grad. Sch. Bus.

Stark D. 1996. Recombinant property in East European capitalism. *Am. J. Sociol.* 101: 993–1027

Stinchcombe A. 1965. Social structures and organizations. In *Handbook of Organizations,* ed. JG March, pp. 142–93. Chicago: Rand McNally

Stuart TE, Hoang H, Hybels R. 1997. *Interorganizational endorsements and the performance of entrepreneurial ventures.* Work. Pap. Univ. Chicago Grad. Sch. Bus.

Stuart TE, Podolny JM. 1996. Local search and the evolution of capabilities. *Strat. Manage. J.* 17:21–38

Stuart TE, Podolny JM. 1997. *Positional causes and consequences of strategic alliances in the semiconductor industry.* Work. Pap. Univ. Chicago Grad. Sch. Bus.

Stuckley JA. 1983. *Vertical Integration and Joint Ventures in the Aluminum Industry.* Cambridge, MA: Harvard Univ.

Uzzi B. 1996. The sources and consequences of embeddedness for the economic performance of organizations: the network effect. *Am. Sociol. Rev.* 61:674–98

Uzzi B. 1997. Networks and the paradox of embeddedness. *Admin. Sci. Q.* 42:35–67

Westney DE. 1988. Domestic and foreign learning curves in managing international cooperative strategies. See Contractor & Lorange 1988a, pp. 339–46

Williamson OE. 1975. *Markets and Hierarchies.* New York: Free

Williamson OE. 1985. *The Economic Institutions of Capitalism.* New York: Free

Williamson OE. 1991. Comparative economic organization: the analysis of discrete structural alternatives. *Admin. Sci. Q.* 36: 269–96

Zajac EJ, Olsen CP. 1993. From transaction cost to transactional value analysis: implications for the study of interorganizational strategies. *J. Manage. Stud.* 30:131–45

Annu. Rev. Sociol. 1998. 24:77–103

REACTIONS TOWARD THE NEW MINORITIES OF WESTERN EUROPE

Thomas F. Pettigrew
University of California, Santa Cruz, California 95064;
e-mail: PETTIGR@CATS.UCSC.EDU

KEY WORDS: new minorities, blatant prejudice, subtle prejudice

ABSTRACT

Millions of ex-colonials, "guest workers," refugees, and other immigrants have settled in western Europe during recent decades. Extensive research on this phenomenon broadens sociology's understanding of intergroup relations in industrial societies. Unlike African Americans, these new Europeans are often viewed as not "belonging," and gaining citizenship can be difficult. The chapter discusses four major reactions to the new minorities: prejudice, discrimination, political opposition, and violence. Both blatant and subtle forms of prejudice predict anti-immigrant attitudes. And between 1988 and 1991, a hardening took place in these attitudes. Similarly, direct and indirect discrimination against the new minorities is pervasive. Moreover, anti-discrimination efforts have been largely ineffective. Far-right, anti-immigration political parties have formed to exploit this situation. These openly racist parties have succeeded in shifting the political spectrum on the issue to the right. In addition, violence against third-world immigrants has increased in recent years, especially in nations such as Britain and Germany where far-right parties are weakest. The chapter concludes that these phenomena are remarkably consistent across western Europe. Furthermore, the European research on these topics supports and extends North American research in intergroup relations.

INTRODUCTION

The world is experiencing two major intergroup trends—massive migration and increased group conflict. An estimated 80 million migrants, almost 2% of

0360-0572/98/0815-0077$08.00

the world's population, live permanently or for long periods of time outside their countries of origin (Castles 1993, p. 18). And headlines of intergroup strife fill our newspapers.

These trends are especially evident in western Europe (Solomos & Wrench 1993, Thraenhardt 1992a). Somalis in London's East End (Griffiths 1997) and Cypriot entrepreneurs in the city's garment industry (Panayiotopoulos 1996), Russian Jews in Berlin (Doomernik 1997), Peruvian house servants in Barcelona (Escriva 1997), Senegalese street vendors in Italian cities (Campani 1993)—every western European city reveals the arrival of immigrants over recent decades. And every western European nation has seen harsh, often violent, reactions to these new minorities.

An extensive research literature has developed on these groups. This chapter outlines this work with an eye toward enlarging the sociological understanding of intergroup processes. Such a comparison is important for American sociology. The discipline has focused on black-white relations in the United States. This situation is atypical of the world's intergroup situations on many dimensions. African Americans endured two centuries of slavery and another of legal segregation. They still face intense racial barriers. They remain the most residentially segregated and have the lowest intermarriage rates with whites of any American minority (Pettigrew 1988). Nonetheless, African Americans "belong" in the United States (Landes 1955). Not even racists question their citizenship. Moreover, they share a language, religion, and a national culture with other Americans. Indeed, they are major contributors to the most distinctive elements of American culture.

In short, the position of African Americans is vastly different from that of Europe's new minorities. Yet it is the American black-white situation upon which much of sociology's study of intergroup dynamics rests. Hence, current scholarship on the unfolding scene of majority-minority relations in western Europe offers a welcome opportunity to broaden our perspective. Though only a ninth of the chapter's citations are from non-English literatures, works in English by leading European scholars help to compensate.

THE NEW MINORITIES

A Rich Variety of Groups and Contexts

The variety of new minorities within contrasting national contexts enhances the comparative value of intergroup phenomena in western Europe. The new Europeans come from Africa, Asia, the Caribbean, the Middle East, and South America. And they typically have cultural backgrounds sharply different from those of their host nations. Seven million, for instance, are Muslims (Peach & Glebe 1995).

This is not an entirely novel experience for the continent. There were mass movements of people after World War I and following the Russian Revolution (Kulischer 1948). And western Europe has long had indigenous minorities—such as the Frisians of the Netherlands and Germany, the Bretons and Corsicans of France, the Scots and Welsh of Great Britain, and the Basques and Catalans of Spain (Foster 1980). But the new minorities offer a more culturally diverse intergroup situation than the traditionally emigrating continent has experienced.

FOUR DECADES OF IMMIGRATION Driven by both economic opportunities and the decline of European empires, colonial minorities began arriving during the 1950s. Before independence of their native lands, French colonials were French citizens and began coming in growing numbers to France for greater opportunities. In Great Britain, London transport and other employers recruited West Indians for low-wage jobs. While only 2,000 immigrated from the islands in 1952, 26,441 came in 1956. By late 1959, Britain's West Indian population numbered 126,000 (Rich 1990, pp. 181, 188).

An especially troubled group were the South Moluccans. Prized soldiers of the Dutch East Indian Army, they had fought to maintain Dutch colonization. When Indonesia won independence in 1948, many of these soldiers and their families migrated to the Netherlands. But, upon arrival, the Dutch decommissioned them. Stripped of their specialty, many Moluccans became unemployed and remain today dependent on welfare. Their dream of returning to a sovereign South Molucca heightens their plight. Their island is now firmly in Indonesia's grip, and their dream has retarded their adjustment to Dutch society.

The 1960s saw the arrival of contract workers who were not colonials. Many of these misnamed "guest workers" were Europeans. Spanish and Portuguese came to France; Italians to France, Germany, and Belgium; Yugoslavs and Greeks to Germany; and Turks to the Netherlands and Germany. North Africans came soon after to France and the low countries. There were economic and other push factors as well as economic pull factors. Portuguese men, for example, avoided induction into their nation's colonial armies fighting to maintain African colonies.

Rapid industrial expansion in western Europe in the 1960s fueled the worker recruitment. West Germany, undergoing its "economic miracle," desperately needed more workers. It made recruitment treaties with Italy (1955), Spain (1960), Turkey (1961–1964), Morocco (1963), Portugal (1964), Greece (1965), Tunisia (1965), Yugoslavia (1968), and even South Korea (1968) (Thraenhardt 1992b, p. 25). Almost 35,000 North Africans entered France each year during this decade (Creamean 1996, p. 51). Indeed, most western European countries took part in such recruitment efforts in this period.

The boom years ended with rising oil prices in the 1970s and consequent unemployment. Labor recruitment abruptly stopped, and governments developed schemes to encourage the "guest workers" to leave. Yet their numbers fell only slightly. By the 1980s, the new minorities were again growing in size from three sources: family reunion, the high birth and low death rates of their young populations, and increasing numbers of refugees. By 1995, resident foreign populations ranged from 3.6% in the United Kingdom to 18.9% in Switzerland. More than half of these foreigners are from non–European Union countries (Waldrauch & Hofinger 1997, p. 274).

DIFFERENT STATUSES Today the new minorities hold an array of statuses. We distinguish seven types. (For a detailed scheme, see Husbands 1991a.)

1. The most favored are the national migrants—those considered citizens who are seen as returning "home." The special case of the "Saxons" from Romania illustrates the extremes this social construction can assume. Though separated by eight centuries from Germany, these Aussiedler "return" with full citizenship automatically granted them (McArthur 1976, Verdery 1985, Wilpert 1993).
2. Citizens of European Union (EU) countries living in other EU countries also are a favored class. Though "foreigners," they have full rights under EU agreements. Of 13 million foreign residents in western Europe in 1993, six million were western Europeans (Muenz 1996, p. 211). Hence, they often constitute a large segment of a nation's foreign residents—such as the Portuguese in France and Italians in Belgium (Martiniello 1992a, 1993; Vranken & Martiniello 1992). Today, however, only rural Portuguese are still migrating in large numbers. Many EU migrants return to their native lands. Among those who remain, many are second- and third-generation residents.
3. Ex-colonial peoples form a large contingent. These groups usually arrived familiar with the host country's culture and language. They include Indians, Pakistanis, and West Indians in the United Kingdom, North Africans and Southeast Asians in France, Eritreans and Somalis in Italy, and Surinamers in the Netherlands. Distinctions are often made among these groups. In Britain, "new commonwealth peoples" is the euphemism for ex-colonials of color (Miles & Phizacklea 1984, Miles & Cleary 1992, p. 131).
4. Recruited workers from such noncolonial countries as Turkey form a fourth group. Germany patterned the "guest worker" (Gastarbeiter) system after the Swiss treatment of Italian workers. The intention was for the recruits to rotate before planting family roots. But the Swiss plan involved mostly service workers. Skilled work required training, and companies were unwilling to rotate their "guests" and lose their human capital investment.

Soon families joined the workers, and migratory chains formed. The guests had come to stay (Thraenhardt 1992b).

5. Refugees and asylum seekers are an increasingly large cluster among the new minorities. About 15 million people throughout the world claim this status, though most go from one third-world country to another. While only 5% are in western Europe (Santel 1992, p. 107), their arrivals in EU countries rose rapidly during the 1980s—from 65,000 in 1983 to 289,000 in 1989 (Castles 1993, p. 18). It reached a peak in 1992 with 700,000 applications but, with tightened regulations, declined to 300,000 in 1994 (Koser 1996, p. 153).
6. Accepted illegal immigrants are those who, while not legal, are known to authorities and tolerated as long as they are economically useful. Polish construction workers in Germany and African harvest workers in Italy are two examples. These groups are vulnerable to the whims of officials and the economy, and they receive no social welfare benefits. In contrast, such prosperous illegals as the English in Portugal do not register so as to avoid taxes (Miles 1993).
7. Rejected illegal immigrants are the true illegals. Since there is no perceived economic need for them, authorities often deport them. Organized criminal groups from eastern Europe and Russia are often in this group. Many generalize justifiable opposition to such groups into opposition to all immigrants.

The fuzzy boundaries of these types overlap. Asylum seekers are a highly diverse group and constitute an especially slippery social construction (Castles 1993, p. 19, Joly 1996, Koser 1996, Santel 1992). The 1951 Geneva Convention of the United Nations defined a "political refugee" narrowly: persons with a "well-founded fear" of persecution in their native lands because of their race, religion, nationality, or political opinions. This definition excludes victims of generalized oppression, civil wars, or natural disasters as well as economic refugees. With rapid population and slow economic growth in much of the world, more asylum seekers try to escape poverty—not persecution as the United Nations defines it.

In the 1990s, the European Parliament enunciated its "safe country of origin principle." Designed to harmonize EU policies toward asylum seekers, the Parliament returned to the narrow UN definition to exclude many "unfounded applications" (European Parliament 1997). The policy has had a chilling effect. In the Netherlands, for instance, the number of asylum seekers declined from 53,000 in 1994 to about 21,000 in 1996 (Muus 1996/7).

Belongingness and Citizenship

The new minorities often find citizenship to be a major barrier. Without the New World's immigration traditions, Europeans lack a "melting pot" metaphor and a sense that immigration is "normal." Nationality often carries biological connotations—"British stock," as Margaret Thatcher phrased it (Thraenhardt 1992b, p. 16). Thus, many view the new minorities as not belonging—even the growing numbers of the second- and third-generation who have lived only in the host nation.

This sense of not belonging interacts with citizenship. Here the nations vary widely (Thraenhardt 1992b). Sweden and the Netherlands are "the most welcoming for immigrants" (Waldrauch & Hofinger 1997, p. 278). They boast the highest rates of naturalization relative to their populations, and they allow voting in local elections for immigrants before citizenship (Hammar 1993). Although becoming more selective (Alund & Schierup 1993), Sweden provides courses in its language and culture, and naturalization for immigrants after five years.

Britain and France, though increasingly restrictive, have allowed extensive naturalization for ex-colonial peoples. And most of the second generation born in the United Kingdom or France receive citizenship. Three nations without former colonial subjects—Germany, Austria, and Switzerland—are by far the most restrictive (Waldrauch & Hofinger 1997). Turks provide a revealing example. By the mid-1990s, less than 5% of resident Turks had gained citizenship in Germany compared to more than a fifth in the Netherlands. In 1995, the Netherlands granted the largest number of naturalizations in its history—71,000, twice that of 1992 (Muus 1996/7).

A Time of Threat and Change

Western Europe has experienced dramatic economic changes during the final decades of this century. The oil shocks of the 1970s reminded Europeans of the vulnerability of their economies. As in the United States, European governments began to give deficit reduction and global competitiveness priority over social and distributive justice (Stasiulis 1997). "Downsizing" the work force took hold, and unemployment mounted. Guest-worker programs ended, but the foreigners did not leave. Indeed, more immigrants arrived as families reunited, and the entry of refugees increased. Thus, the urban concentrations of the new minorities expanded. As unemployment intensified from the economic restructuring in the 1980s, it became easy to blame the foreigners.

These economic phenomena took place in a context of equally sweeping political alterations. The power of nation-states began to erode as European unity advanced, while regional claims for autonomy grew. The Communist regimes in the East imploded, the Berlin Wall fell, Yugoslavia broke up into contending ethnic enclaves, and German unification came suddenly. Societal disequilibria swept central and eastern Europe.

Many worried that a "flood" of eastern Europeans would "pour" in. Germany introduced a new Gastarbeiter policy in 1990 involving eastern European governments (Rudolph 1996). Germany now has about a million East European nationals within its borders, most of whom are Polish or from the former Yugoslavia (Carter et al 1993, p. 492). Overlooked in the public debate is that every western European nation's natural increase (births over deaths) has declined since 1960 while its economy has expanded—making immigration essential for continued prosperity (Munz 1996, Thraenhardt 1996).

Nevertheless, such events create threat. They set the scene for scapegoating the culturally different "others" in their midst. Quillian (1995) shows that group threat is important. Defined as the interaction of high non-EU minority percentage and low gross national product, it accounts for 70% of the variance in anti-immigrant attitude means across the 12 EU nations (also see Fuchs et al 1993).

MAJORITY PREJUDICE AGAINST THE NEW MINORITIES

We can assess attitudes toward the new minorities with a rich data source. In 1988, the Eurobarometer Survey 30 asked seven probability samples a range of prejudice measures about a variety of minorities (Reif & Melich 1991). In West Germany, the survey asked 985 majority respondents about Turks. In France, it asked 455 about North Africans and 475 about southeastern Asians. In the Netherlands, it asked 462 about Surinamers and 476 about Turks. And in Great Britain, it asked 471 about West Indians and 482 about Pakistanis and Indians (Pettigrew et al 1998, Zick 1997).

Blatant and Subtle Prejudice

Two key measures distinguish between blatant and subtle types of prejudice (Pettigrew & Meertens 1995). Blatant prejudice is the traditional form; it is hot, close, and direct. The ten items that tap it involve open rejection of minorities based on presumed biological differences. Subtle prejudice is the modern form; it is cool, distant, and indirect. The ten items that measure it are not readily recognized as indicators of prejudice. They tap the perceived threat of the minority to traditional values, the exaggeration of cultural differences with the minority, and the absence of positive feelings toward them. American researchers have studied similar distinctions (Pettigrew 1989, Sears 1988). And, as various writers had proposed (Barker 1982, Bergmann & Erb 1986, Essed 1990), it proved equally useful in Europe.

Figure 1 shows the *blatant* and *subtle* scale means for the seven samples. Four major findings emerge. 1. The *subtle* means are consistently higher than those of the *blatant* scale, because the *subtle* items are covert and more socially acceptable (Pettigrew & Meertens 1995, 1996). 2. The means for *blatant*

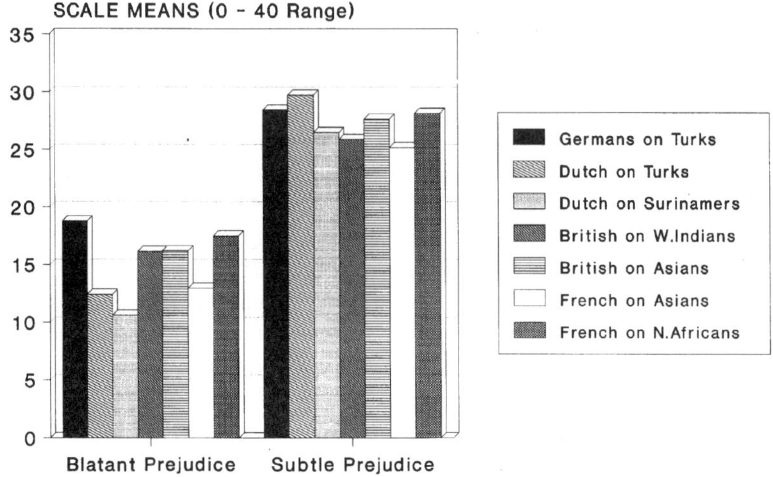

Source: Pettigrew et al. 1997.

Figure 1 Blatant and subtle prejudice across seven samples

prejudice are conspicuously higher for German attitudes toward Turks and French attitudes toward North Africans. This result suggests that norms against the open expression of prejudice are weakest in these two instances. The means for *subtle* prejudice, however, reveal less variability. 3. Target differences exist in two nations—less French prejudice against Asians than North Africans, and less Dutch prejudice against Surinamers than Turks. Note these preferences place greater weight on cultural than racial similarities. 4. Observe, too, the distinctive data of the Dutch. They are significantly lower on *blatant* prejudice, but not on *subtle* prejudice. The contrast is striking when we compare similar target groups. The Dutch *blatant* mean for Turks is significantly lower than that of the Germans for Turks. And the Dutch *blatant* mean for Surinamers is significantly lower than that of the British for West Indians. Yet the Dutch *subtle* means are higher than these comparisons. In normative terms, this unique pattern outlines the famed "tolerance" of the Netherlands. There exists a stern Dutch norm against *blatant* prejudice. But *subtle* prejudice slips in under the norm, unrecognized as prejudice (Pettigrew & Meertens 1996).

Across the seven samples, the *blatant* and *subtle* prejudice scales correlate between +.48 and +.70. The two measures share the same correlates in all samples (Meertens & Pettigrew 1997). Both the blatantly and subtly prejudiced are less educated and older. They report less interest in politics but more pride in their nationality. They less often think of themselves as "Europeans" (Petti-

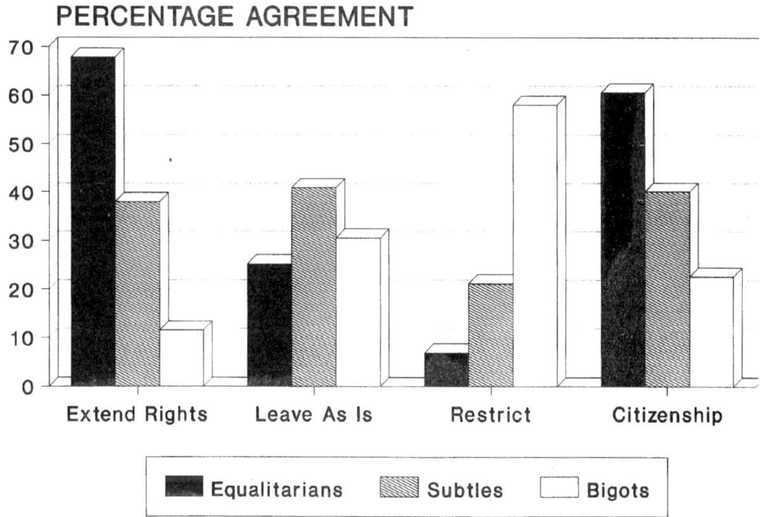

Source: Meertens & Pettigrew 1997.

Figure 2 Three prejudice types and attitudes on immigrant rights

grew 1998). They are more politically conservative; but subtle prejudice is not, as some claim, simply a reflection of conservatism (Meertens & Pettigrew 1997). The prejudiced also are more likely to have only ingroup friends (Pettigrew 1997). Finally, they reveal a strong sense of group, but not individual, relative deprivation. Thus, the prejudiced sense a group threat to "people like themselves" from minorities, but not a sense of personal threat. These correlates replicate findings of American research. Since these extensive data involve seven independent samples, four nations, and six target minorities, this replication is of theoretical significance.

Attitudes Toward Immigration

Do the blatant and subtle prejudice measures predict attitudes toward the salient issue of immigration? Consider the differences among three types of respondents. Equalitarians are those who score below the central point (not the mean) of both the blatant and subtle scales. Bigots score above the central points of both scales. The subtles are the most interesting; they score low on blatant but high on subtle prejudice. They reject crude expressions of prejudice. Still, they view the new minorities as "a people apart" who violate traditional values and for whom they feel little sympathy or admiration. (A fourth logical type, those high on blatant but low on subtle prejudice, occurs in less than 3% of the sample.)

Figures 2 and 3 show the results for all 3800 majority respondents, and these results replicate in all seven samples. In Figure 2, most Bigots wish to restrict immigrants' rights further. Most Equalitarians favor extending immigrants' rights. By contrast, many Subtles simply wish to leave the issue as it is. When asked if government should make citizenship easier for immigrants, the three types line up as expected. While most Equalitarians think naturalization procedures should be easier, most Subtles and Bigots disagree.

The surveys also included a scale of immigration positions that allowed multiple responses. "... The government should... (1) send all Asians, even those born in France, back to their own country. (2) Send only those Asians who were not born in France back.... (3) Send only those Asians back who are not contributing to the economic livelihood of France. (4) Send only those Asians who have committed severe criminal offenses back... (5) Send only those Asians who have no immigration documents back... (6) The government should not send back to their own country any of the Asians now living in France."

In Figure 3, differences between the types also appear on this measure. Many Bigots want to send all immigrants home. Equalitarians often favor not sending back any immigrants. Subtles typically support sending immigrants home only when there is an ostensibly nonprejudicial reason for doing so—if they have committed crimes or do not have their documents. These differences among the types are statistically significant in all samples.

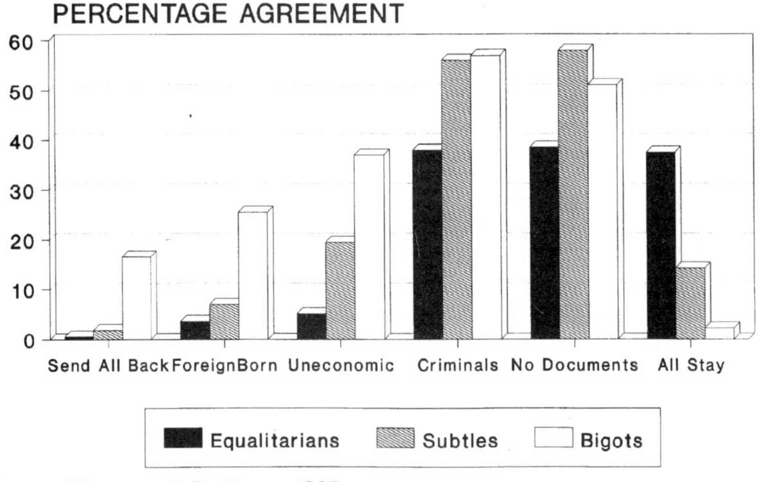

Figure 3 Three prejudice types and preferred immigration policies. Total sample: N = 3783

Are Attitudes Toward Foreigners Becoming More Negative?

Unfortunately, the Eurobarometer surveys have not repeated the extensive 1988 measures of prejudice. They have, however, repeatedly asked several relevant questions (Melich 1995). Figure 4 shows the rising percentage of Europeans who believe there are "too many" non-EU foreigners in their country. For each national sample shown and the 12 EU nations (EU12) combined, the sharpest increase occurs between 1988 and 1991. (Preunification 1988 data for East Germany were not attainable.) Clear majorities in Belgium, West Germany, France, and Italy agreed during the early 1990s that the number of foreigners is excessive. There was, however, less of this feeling by 1994, especially in Germany and Italy. The decline in Germany may well reflect changes in the constitution that made it difficult for asylum seekers to gain entry.

Figure 5 tells a similar story. Abrupt increases in the numbers of those who wish to restrict the rights of non-EU nationals again occur between 1988 and 1991. Yet not all indicators show this effect. The percentage of respondents who find the presence of non-EU nationals "disturbing" does not rise much over these years. Hence, western European opinion toward foreigners did harden during the years when the issue took center stage and political leaders defined immigration as a serious problem. Yet the increases in negative attitudes are not so large as to explain the rise in political and violent actions against immigrants.

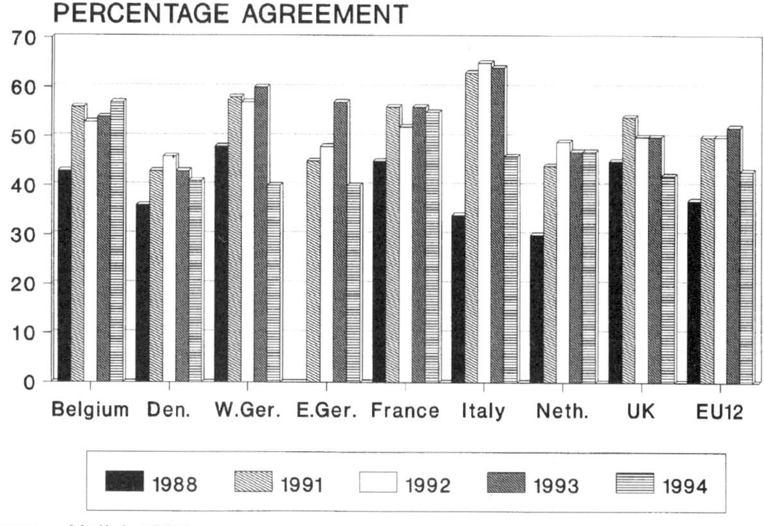

Figure 4 Too many non–European Union nationals in the country, 1988–1994

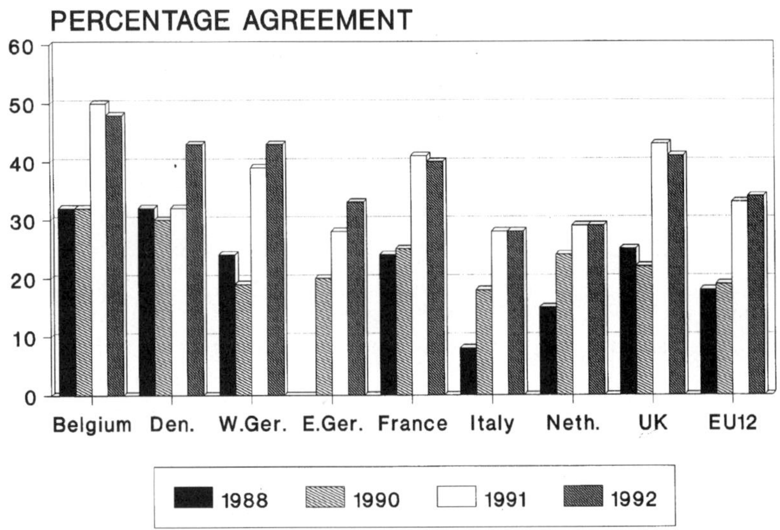

Figure 5 The rights of non-EU nationals should be restricted, 1988–1992

DISCRIMINATION AGAINST THE NEW MINORITIES

Direct and Indirect Discrimination

Discrimination against the new minorities is pervasive throughout western Europe (Castles 1984, MacEwen 1995, World Council of Churches Migration Secretariat 1980). But, save for the United Kingdom and the Netherlands, the problem has received far less attention than that of violence.

Both direct and indirect discrimination are involved (Pettigrew & Taylor 1991). Direct discrimination, like blatant prejudice, is straightforward. It occurs at points where inequality is generated, often intentionally. Indirect discrimination, like subtle prejudice, is less obvious. It involves the perpetuation or magnification of the original injury. It occurs when the inequitable results of direct discrimination are used as a basis for later decisions ("past-in-present discrimination") or decisions in related institutions ("side-effect discrimination"; Feagin & Feagin 1986). Indirect discrimination, a result of systemic patterns, is largely unrecognized in Europe.

Investigators have repeatedly uncovered direct discrimination in England (Amin et al 1988, Daniel 1968, Gordon & Klug 1984, Smith 1976). Controlled tests reveal the full litany of discriminatory forms involving employment, public accommodations, housing, the courts, insurance, banks, even car rentals.

One study sent identical letters for 103 advertised, nonmanual jobs from native white, West Indian, and Asian applicants. The letters contained multiple cues of ethnicity. Firms refused the white an interview only six times when they granted one to a minority candidate. But on 49 occasions, they called the white for an interview and refused to interview the minority candidates (Hubbuck & Carter 1980).

In Germany, a reporter dyed his moustache black, dressed in guest-worker style, and tried to get a drink in bars and cafes throughout Frankfurt. Repeatedly, he was refused service and thrown out (Castles 1984, p. 191). Better-controlled field studies by social scientists reveal differential, face-to-face treatment of the new minorities in Britain, Germany, and the Netherlands (Den Uyl et al 1986, Klink & Wagner 1998, Sissons 1981). Their results closely resemble those of similar field studies of discriminatory acts in the United States (Crosby et al 1980).

Employment discrimination poses the most serious problem. In every western European nation, foreigners have far higher unemployment rates than do natives. In 1990 in the Netherlands, Moroccans and Turks had unemployment rates above 40%, and the Surinamese 27% compared with the native Dutch rate of 13% (Pettigrew & Meertens 1996). During the 1974–1977 recession, West German manufacturing reduced its labor force by 765,000—42% of whom were foreign workers (Castles 1984, p. 148).

There are many reasons in addition to discrimination for this situation. The "last-in, first-out" principle selectively affects the younger foreign workers. Being typically less skilled, they are more affected by job upgrading. Foreigners also are more likely to be in older, declining industries in such areas as the Ruhr Valley. Indeed, planners put Gastarbeiter into these industries for cheaper labor precisely because of their decline. Some emphasize these factors to deny any role for discrimination. Yet these factors offer insufficient explanations for the greater unemployment of foreigners. Veenman & Roelandt (1990) tested how much education, age, sex, region, and employment level account for the large group discrepancies in Dutch unemployment rates. They found that these factors explained only a small portion of the differential rates.

Indirect discrimination operates when the inability to obtain citizenship restricts the opportunities of non-EU minorities in most institutions. It restricts their ability to get suitable housing, employment, and schooling for children. A visa is required for travel to other EU countries. In short, the lives of noncitizens are severely circumscribed (Wilpert 1993).

Castles (1984) contends that the guest-worker system was itself a state-controlled system of institutional discrimination. It established the newcomers as a problematic and stigmatized outgroup, suitable for low-status jobs but not for citizenship. For initial victims of such direct discrimination, indirect discrimination in all areas of life was inevitable.

Wilpert goes further. She asserts that Germany's institutions are based on "a dominant ideology which distributes rights according to ethnic origins..." (Wilpert 1993, p. 70). The revealing comparison is between the almost two million Aussiedler and the Gastarbeiter. Officials regard the former as kin often on the thinnest of evidence, though since 1996 a language test must be taken. Aussiedler readily become citizens and receive favorable government treatment. Yet even third-generation Turks, who are at least as culturally "German" as the Aussiedler, are largely denied citizenship and given unfavorable treatment.

Anti-Discrimination Remediation

Basic rights in Germany are guaranteed only to citizens. So, the disadvantages of noncitizenship include limited means to combat discrimination (Layton-Henry & Wilpert 1994). Extensive German legislation combats anti-Semitism and Nazi ideology, but these laws have proved difficult to apply to noncitizens.

The German constitution explicitly forbids discrimination on the basis of origin, race, language, beliefs, or religion—but not citizenship. Indeed, the Federal Constitutional Court (Bundesverfassungsgericht) has ruled that differential treatment based on citizenship is constitutional if there is a reasonable basis for it, and if it is not wholly arbitrary. In practice, this has meant a court has upheld charging foreign bar owners higher taxes than German bar owners. And restaurants can refuse service to Turks and others on the grounds that their entry might lead to intergroup disturbances. According to the German legal specialist Dan Leskien, Germany needs anti-discrimination legislation with broad enforcement powers and an effective monitoring system (Layton-Henry & Wilpert 1994, pp. 19–22).

Few means of combating discrimination are available in France either. Commentators often view discrimination as "natural," as something universally triggered when a "threshold of tolerance" (*seuil de tolerance*) is surpassed (MacMaster 1991). Without supporting evidence, this rationalization supports quotas and dispersal policies that limit minority access to suitable housing.

The Netherlands, United Kingdom, and Sweden have enacted anti-discrimination legislature that specifically applies to the new minorities. Not coincidentally, these countries make citizenship much easier to obtain than Germany. Yet this legislation has been largely ineffective for two interrelated reasons. First, European legal systems do not allow class action suits—a forceful North American weapon to combat discrimination. Second, European efforts rely heavily on individual complaints rather than systemic remediation. Britain's 1976 Act gave the Commission for Racial Equality power to cast a broad net, but individual complaints remain the chief tool (MacEwen 1993, 1995).

It is a sociological truism that individual efforts are unlikely to alter such systemic phenomena as discrimination. Mayhew (1968) showed how individual suits and complaints are largely nonstrategic. Minorities bring few charges against the worst discriminators, because they avoid applying to them. Complaints about job promotion are common, but they are made against employers who hire minorities. Thus, effective anti-discrimination laws must provide broad powers to an enforcement agency to initiate strategic, institutionwide actions that uproot the structural foundations of discrimination.

POLITICAL RESPONSES

The Rise of Far-Right Anti-Immigration Parties

By the 1980s, the new Europeans elicited an increasingly hostile reaction from sectors of the native populations that felt especially threatened. Throughout western Europe, extreme right-wing groups seized on the threat as their central issue. In each election for the European Parliament, the average vote for these anti-immigration parties has risen—3.4% in 1979, 4.9% in 1984 to 5.1% in 1989. By 1994, with an average of 11.1% unemployment in the European Union, the far-right parties garnered 6.9% of the vote and 25 seats (3 from Belgium, 11 each from France and Italy). Indeed, a close relationship is found across countries between the extreme right's share of the European Parliament votes and unemployment (Baimbridge et al 1994, 1995).

It is a mistake to view the new European right as simply Nazi revivals. To be sure, they share the classic authoritarian personality orientation—calls for a strong leader and law and order, beliefs in conspiracy theories, and an exclusionary view of citizenship. But, as Kitschelt (1995) makes clear, times have changed and so has the radical right. He distinguishes four types of far right. Two have only tiny constituencies—traditional fascists and "welfare chauvinists." Two other types, however, have attracted strong followings—the new radical right and "populist anti-statists." Unlike the first two varieties, these right-wing movements heartily endorse free market capitalism. They are political, not economic, populists. And the anti-statists gain ground in Italy and Austria, where patronage is based on the traditional party system. Yet one central theme runs through all four types—nativism and stern opposition to immigration.

AUSTRIA Begun after World War II under a former member of the Nazi SS, Austria's Freedom Party (FPO) met with only modest success until Joerg Haider became its leader in 1986. A multimillionaire with a populist flair,

Haider fashioned the FPO into the strongest far-right party in western Europe and a major party of Austria. He gained international notoriety when, as governor of Carinthia province, he praised Nazi labor practices as a good way to reduce the welfare rolls (Feen 1996, Wise 1995). Not surprisingly, Haider and his party vigorously oppose immigration, bilingual education, and immigrants' rights.

In 1994, Haider's Freedom Party won 42 of 183 parliamentary seats with more than 22% of the vote. In 1996, the party won 29 seats in Vienna's city council with the anti-immigration slogan, "Vienna must not become like Chicago" (Shanker 1996). Despite Haider's ambiguous remarks about Nazis, he claims the party is leaving its Nazi roots. Indeed, the FPO has strong free market and anti-statist positions (Betz 1994, Kitschelt 1995, Parkinson 1989). It offers a classic case of Kitschelt's (1995) anti-statist type. Nonetheless, violent groups in Austria, such as the one that desecrated a new Jewish cemetery in November 1992, use Nazi symbols and proclaim support for Haider and his party (Husbands 1993, p. 113).

BELGIUM Until 1979, the Volksunie was the only nationalist party of Flanders. Then dissidents formed the Vlaams Blok (VB)—a prime example of Kitschelt's "new radical right" type. This party stands for a separate Flanders that would someday join the Netherlands, and it opposes non-European residents. It would set up a fund for their repatriation, expel them after three months of unemployment, prohibit family reunion, and levy a tax on their employers. With this program, the VB has increased its vote in every general election since 1981. Centered in Antwerp, it now attracts about one eighth of Belgium's Flemish voters (Govaert 1995).

FRANCE The best known of Europe's far-right parties is Jean-Marie Le Pen's Front National (FN)—another example of "the new radical right." Formed in 1972, the FN suffered repeated electoral reverses until the 1980s. It gained respectability in 1983 when conservatives joined them in a second ballot in the small city of Dreux. From 1984 to the present, the party has consistently attracted between 9% and 16% of the vote in a variety of national elections (Singer 1991; Husbands 1991b, Table 3). In 1995, for example, Le Pen received more than four million votes for president—more than 15% of the total.

The FN is a nationalist and populist party that has carved out a stable slot in French politics (Birenbaum 1992, Fysh & Wolfreys 1992, Husbands 1991a, Marcus 1995, Mayer & Perrineau 1992, Shields 1989, Tezenas du Montcel 1995). It is especially strong in cities of the Southeast and Northeast—areas hit hardest by industrial decline and "the exhaustion of the working-class movement" (Wieviorka 1993, p. 64). Yet it also has secured a modest hold throughout the country.

It has a broad policy program, but its key position is anti-immigration. Its leader, Le Pen, expresses blatant bigotry against a range of immigrants and minorities—from Jews to the Harkis who fought with the French against Algerian independence. "Two million unemployed" he asserts, "that's two million immigrants too many" (Gunn 1989, p. 23). Increasingly, the French understand Le Pen's position. National surveys show 53% in 1996, compared with 43% in 1990, "understand the Le Pen vote" considering "the behavior of certain immigrants" (Commission Nationale Consultative des Droits de l'Homme 1997, p. 371).

Given its broad base, the FN's voters do not differ from the general French electorate as much as some writers suggest (Husbands 1991b). There are, however, consistent findings in the many studies of the phenomenon. Like supporters of other radical right parties, FN voters are typically males (women are more attracted to European Green parties; Betz 1994, p. 143). And they are particularly numerous among small businessmen and craftsmen as well as white ex-colonials. Since 1984, the FN has attracted an increasing percentage of manual workers. Yet most of their gains are at the expense of other right-wing parties, not the declining French Communists, as some claim. And those French who live in communities with more than 10% foreign populations are less prejudiced and more accepting of immigrants than are other French (Commission Nationale Consultative des Droits de l'Homme 1997, p. 388). There also is a vigorous anti-FN countermovement (Mayer 1995), fueled by students (Husbands 1991b).

GERMANY Le Pen's success inspired the German right. In the 1986 Bavarian state elections, the Christian Social Union (CSU) began a furious campaign against third-world refugees. Their electoral success put the issue on center stage.

This event also saw a new far-right party split from the CSU. With anti-immigration its chief issue, the Republikaners under their leader, Franz Schoenhuber—a former SS member—offered a populist-nationalist alternative similar to that of the Front National. While centered in Bavaria, the Republikaners enjoyed success in elections elsewhere from 1989 to 1993. In 1989, they won 90,000 votes and 11 parliament seats in West Berlin. And they garnered more than two million votes and six seats in a European Parliament election. They also did well in state elections in Baden Wuerttemberg in 1992 and Hessen in 1993. However, the Kohl government's partial adoption of their program blunted their appeal (Atkinson 1993, Thraenhardt 1992b, Wilpert 1993). By the 1994 European Parliament election, their strength had dissipated.

GREAT BRITAIN From the 1950s till the late 1960s, a policy consensus on immigration existed between the Labor and Conservative parties. It depoliticized race, allowed limited nonwhite immigration, but did little to improve the status of immigrants (Messina 1989, Rich 1990). The crowning achievement of this era—the 1968 Race Relations Act—lacked the necessary enforcement powers to be effective. North American specialists (including the writer) had warned the act's drafters of the need for structural teeth, but their advice was ignored.

Ending this cozy arrangement, Enoch Powell began an anti-minority campaign in 1968 (Schoen 1977). A maverick Conservative member of Parliament, Powell predicted "rivers of blood" if nonwhites continued to come to Britain. He opposed anti-discrimination legislation and called for immigration restrictions and nonwhite repatriation. His message struck a popular chord in British opinion. So popular, in fact, it broke the consensus and molded the Conservatives into an anti-immigration party. "Almost single-handedly," writes Messina (1989, p. 105), "Powell prepared the intellectual groundwork for the emergence of Margaret Thatcher as Conservative party leader in 1975."

In 1967, England's National Front mobilized far-right opposition to the new minorities. It had minor success, especially in the 1977 elections of the Greater London Council. Yet, as in Germany, the government assumed much of the Front's position. Thatcher won election in 1979, aided by her anti-immigration stand. She slashed the budget of the Commission for Racial Equality and pushed through revisions of the immigration rules designed to end primary nonwhite entry.

THE NETHERLANDS Unlike Britain, the major Dutch parties have maintained an enlightened consensus throughout this period. The focus of this consensus, however, has shifted. In the 1980s, it emphasized the collective integration of minorities. Now it stresses the integration of minority individuals into the labor market (Fermin 1997). Still, a misnamed Centrum Party formed in 1980 to exploit the immigration issue. Two years later, it secured one seat in the lower house of parliament (Tweede Kamer). In 1986, the party split into two—the Centrum Party 86 and the Centrum Democrats. Only the latter has secured seats in the Tweede Kamer—one in 1989, three in 1994. Some members sit on municipal councils (van Donselaar 1993). Yet, with only modest strength in a few urban pockets, the Dutch far-right has failed to crack the dominant consensus on the new minorities.

SWITZERLAND Economic insecurity is a facilitating factor in far-right opposition to immigration. Yet prosperous Switzerland shows that it is not a necessary factor. An extremist alliance, National Action Against the Swamping of the People and Homeland, came forward with a radical initiative in 1970. It proposed to cut the foreign population almost in half, and the initiative won the support of 46% of Swiss voters. The alliance later split into two small parties, both with parliamentary representation. They have kept immigration controversial, and gained power in Geneva as vigilants (Thraenhardt 1992b, pp. 42–44).

SOUTHERN EUROPE For Greece, Italy, Portugal, and Spain, large-scale immigration is a new phenomenon. Long accustomed to emigration, these nations have been slow to adjust to their new situation. Italy has attracted the most immigrants, many of them illegals. Under EU pressure, Italy belatedly began to formulate immigration policies in 1986 (Campani 1993, Martiniello 1992b). Its mishandling of Albanian refugees in 1991, however, revealed how Italy remains unprepared to be an immigrant receiving country (Vasta 1993).

Figures 4 and 5 record the pointed rise in Italian concern over immigration after 1988. This suggests that a sudden increase in foreigners, rather than the actual proportion of foreigners, is key to predicting change in European attitudes toward immigration. In Italy, both national and regional political parties have exploited the public's changing attitudes. At the national level, a neofascist party (Movimento Sociale Italiano) and the Partito Repubblicano Italiano have taken anti-immigration positions. And so have regional secessionist parties, especially the Leagues of Tuscany and Lombardy (Martiniello 1992b, Vasta 1993). Indeed, a blatantly racist platform helped the Lega Lombarda gain success in the local elections of May 1990. More recently, the Lega Nord and the Alleanza Nazionale have added to anti-immigration agitation.

The Thraenhardt Thesis

Thraenhardt (1995) contends that these political phenomena are similar across France, Germany, and the United Kingdom. While far-right efforts have gained only minimal power directly, they have shifted the entire political spectrum to the right on immigration. Left-wing and center politicians have equivocated, sometimes even collaborated. Conservative politicians have exploited the situation for two reasons. First and foremost, they see an opportunity to obscure economic issues and seize a share of the left's labor vote. And, second, they fear the loss of supporters to the far right. Thraenhardt (1992b, p. 49) credits racist appeals as vital to conservative victories in all three nations.

Conservative governments have made repeated concessions to antiminority sentiments. They have "played an important role in promoting xenophobia and putting it on the public agenda" (Thraenhardt 1995, p. 337). Former Prime Ministers Thatcher and Major in the United Kingdom, Chancellor Kohl in Germany, and President Chirac in France have all espoused restrictions on immigration and citizenship that partly meet the far right's demands. Note these similarities across the three nations emerged despite sharp differences in their immigrant populations. Note also the policy inconsistency: Conservative parties actively pursued immigration to provide cheap labor for industry; now they stigmatize and scapegoat the foreigners who they earlier had invited.

The Thraenhardt thesis applies beyond Europe. Recall 1968 in the United States when Alabama Governor George Wallace helped to create a climate that moved President Nixon to the right on civil rights. The Republican Party has played "the race card" ever since, and converted the white South into its major base of support (Carmines & Stimson 1989, Kinder & Sanders 1996). Similarly in Australia, the rise of a far-right, populist politician, Pauline Hanson, has pushed Prime Minister John Howard's Liberal Government further to the right on racial and immigration issues.

VIOLENCE AGAINST THE NEW MINORITIES

Increasing Anti-Immigrant Violence

Playing "the race card" heightens intergroup tensions and risks violence. Indeed, Europe's political shift to the right accompanied a rise in anti-minority violence (Bjorgo & Witte 1993, Koopmans 1995, Witte 1995). In 1990, violent attacks against African street vendors in Florence, Italy, and the desecration of Jewish graves in Carpentras, France, made headlines.

The most publicized attacks occurred in Germany (Atkinson 1993, Heitmeyer 1993). In September 1991, a mob attacked and besieged a residence of asylum seekers in Hoyerswerda. Soon imitative acts of brutality erupted, the worst being riots and murders in Rostock, Moelln, Solingen, and Magdeburg. Passive onlookers and ineffective police characterized these horrendous events. Initially, Asian and African refugees were the primary targets. Later, Turks also became victims (Wagner & Zick 1997). Moreover, the intensity of the political debates on the constitutional rights of asylum seekers closely paralleled these acts of extreme-right violence (Gerhard 1992, Koopmans 1995, p. 27, Zick & Wagner 1993).

Germany was not alone. Britain (Gordon 1993), France (Lloyd 1993), the Netherlands (van Donselaar 1993), Scandinavia (Bjorgo 1993, Loow 1993), and the rest of Europe have all experienced patterned, anti-minority violence. Differences in record keeping and definitions of violence preclude precise cross-national comparisons (Koopmans 1995, Witte 1995). Nonetheless, sharp differences in racist violence exist. Per million inhabitants over the 1988–1993 period, England and Wales have had as many or even more racist acts as Germany. France, Norway, and Denmark have far lower rates. Switzerland has a high rate of deaths due to racist and extreme-right violence (Koopmans 1995, pp. 9–14). Save for Switzerland, however, the lethality of this European violence has not rivaled that of sectarian violence in Northern Ireland or of the Ku Klux Klan in the late nineteenth century in the southern United States.

The far-right does not commit all the racist violence. Some youthful perpetrators evince little or no right-wing ideology (Willems 1995). Their violence often involves the affect-arousing context of sports (Holland 1995). And not all right-wing targets are minorities. Still, in Germany and the Netherlands in the early 1990s, low-status minorities were the targets of roughly three fourths of far-right violence (Buijs & van Donselaar 1994, pp. 69–70). Significantly, other immigrants—from the EU, Japan, or North America—were rarely victims (Witte 1995, p. 494).

The Koopmans Thesis

Using social movement theory, Koopmans (1995) offers a two-part explanation for the sharp differences in racist violence among European nations. Following from Thraenhardt's thesis, he first emphasizes the significance of political elites who legitimize the far-right's view of foreigners as unbearable burdens. Thus, respected leaders convert the new minorities into problems. Such legitimization, Koopmans (1995, p. 34) argues, furthers far-right mobilization "...with high mass media resonance and favorable chances of substantive success."

This mobilization, however, need not invoke violence. It also can activate far-right political parties, as shown by the Vlaams Blok and Front National. Hence, Koopmans' second point highlights the importance of such parties. He shows that countries with influential racist parties, such as France, Denmark, and Norway, have experienced relatively low levels of racist violence. By contrast, countries with weak racist parties, such as Germany and the United Kingdom, have had high levels. Even the Netherlands and Sweden, with low levels of general violence and without strong racist parties, have endured mid-levels of such racist attacks.

This second part of Koopmans' thesis is problematic. Aggregate data from only a few nations provide the quantitative support. And Europe's experience between the world wars contradicts the argument. Fascist parties and political violence developed together during those turbulent years. Two divergent theories of human aggression are at issue. Koopmans is following Freud's (1930) steam-boiler model of a finite amount of aggression. If it can be channeled into political action, then right-wing aggression against minorities should decline. Allport's (1954) feedback model of aggression predicts precisely the opposite. Have the far-right mobilize anti-immigrant feelings, and aggression will increase and spill over into more violence against the new minorities.

Americans can readily apply the first part of Koopmans' thesis. The regressive 1980s and 1990s have seen the erosion in the United States of the sense of inevitability of continued racial progress. Repeated attacks by leading public officials on civil rights, affirmative action, and immigration have produced an intergroup climate comparable to that shaped by Thatcher, Kohl, and Chirac in Europe (Kinder & Sanders 1996). And violence against minorities, especially on college campuses, appears to have risen over these years (US Commission on Civil Rights 1990). Koopman's emphasis on the role of political leaders in violence is also consistent with recent time-series analyses by Green and his colleagues (Green et al 1997) of ethnic hate crimes in New York City. They find little relationship between these crimes and such macroeconomic conditions as unemployment rates.

CONCLUSIONS

This chapter emphasizes the negative reactions to western Europe's new minorities. There also is a positive side to the picture. Native populations are slowly adjusting to the new cultures. Parisians have developed a taste for hummus, Berliners for kabab; the Indonesian rijsttafel is a basic of Dutch cuisine.

More importantly, western Europe now boasts anti-racist movements. When the wave of atrocities against foreigners swept Germany in 1992, hundreds of thousands of Germans protested. With torchlight vigils and candlelight demonstrations, they countered "hatred and violence" in Berlin, Hamburg, Munich, and other cities and towns. When the French government tried to discontinue the naturalization of French-born children of foreign parents, students protested with the slogan, "Don't touch my buddy."

Still, increased prejudice, direct and indirect discrimination, political opposition, and extensive violence are major European reactions to the new minorities. These responses represent serious social problems worthy of study for practical, policy reasons. In addition, attention to these problems broadens our understanding of intergroup conflict in industrial societies.

The research to date reveals remarkable agreement across societies. Despite sharp differences in national histories, political systems, and minorities, this new work reveals considerable consistency across the nations of western Europe. It also largely replicates and extends, rather than rebuts, the North American literature.

This chapter has noted many such convergencies. Blatant and subtle prejudice measures scale in nearly identical ways across four nations and diverse minority targets. The scales also share the same correlates across the seven samples, and these correlates replicate North American research. Both types of prejudice also predict attitudes toward immigration in all samples. And throughout the EU, attitudes toward immigrants hardened during the tense 1989–1992 period.

Moreover, a host of established social psychological processes, such as intergroup contact and group relative deprivation, operate in comparable ways in Europe. They typically act as proximal causes of prejudice, serving as mediators for the distal effects of cultural and structural factors (Pettigrew et al 1998).

The comparabilities extend to discrimination. Examples of both direct and indirect forms abound throughout western Europe. And efforts to combat discrimination have been weak across the continent. In those countries that resist granting citizenship to their new minorities, efficacious remediation of discrimination is extremely difficult. In those countries that have legislated against discrimination, the reliance upon individual complaints limits their effectiveness—again comparable to the North American experience.

Western European nations have seen the rise of far-right political opposition to immigration and the new minorities. While none of these parties has risen to power, this right-wing surge has succeeded in moving the entire political spectrum to the right on the issue. The process closely resembles that of the Wallace movement in the United States and the current Hanson movement in Australia.

Finally, similar patterns of racist violence have swept western Europe. While there is variability across nations in the number of reported incidents, the timing of this violence is similar. In particular, the elite framing of the immigration discourse, especially defining the new minorities as unbearable burdens, relates closely to the violence patterns.

The new European research supports and broadens earlier North American research in intergroup relations. It also extends our understanding in important ways. The chapter has described two of these extensions: the Thraenhardt thesis on the political exploitation of xenophobia and the Koopmans thesis on the mobilization of racist violence.

ACKNOWLEDGMENTS

I wish to thank James Jackson and Myriam Torres of the University of Michigan, Roel W. Meertens of the University of Amsterdam, Ulrich Wagner of the Philipps University of Marburg, and Andreas Zick of the University of Wuppertal for their invaluable help with data and bibliography. I also greatly appreciate the helpful comments on earlier drafts of this chapter by William Domhoff, Roel Meertens, Amelie Mummendey, Ann Pettigrew, Bernd Simon, Dietrich Thraenhardt, and Ulrich Wagner.

Literature Cited

Allport GW. 1954. *The Nature of Prejudice*. Reading, MA: Addison-Wesley. 537 pp.

Alund A, Schierup CU. 1993. The thorny road to Europe: Swedish immigrant policy in transition. See Solomos & Wrench 1993, pp. 99–114

Amin K, Fernandes M, Gordon P. 1988. *Racism and Discrimination in Britain: A Select Bibliography, 1984–87*. London: Runnymede Trust. 98 pp.

Atkinson G. 1993. Germany: nationalism, Nazism and violence. See Bjorgo & Witte 1993, pp. 154–66

Baimbridge M, Burkitt B, Macey M. 1994. The Maastricht Treaty: exacerbating racism in Europe? *Ethn. Racial Stud.* 17: 420–41

Baimbridge M, Burkitt B, Macey M. 1995. The European Parliamentary election of 1994 and racism in Europe. *Ethn. Racial Stud.* 18:128–30

Barker M. 1982. *The New Racism: Conservatives and the Ideology of the Tribe*. Frederick, MD: Aletheia. 183 pp.

Bergmann W, Erb R. 1986. Kommunikationslatenz, moral und offentliche meinung. *Koln. Zeitschr. Soziol. Sozialpsychol.* 38:223–46

Betz HG. 1994. *Radical Right-Wing Populism in Western Europe*. New York: St. Martin's Press. 226 pp.

Birenbaum G. 1992. *Le Front National en Politique*. Paris: Balland. 358 pp.

Bjorgo T. 1993. Terrorist violence against immigrants and refugees in Scandinavia: patterns and motives. See Bjorgo & Witte 1993, pp. 29–45

Bjorgo T, Witte R, eds. 1993. *Racist Violence in Europe*. New York: St. Martin's Press. 261 pp.

Buijs FJ, van Donselaar J. 1994. *Extreem-Rechts: Aanhang, Gewald en Onderzoek*. Leiden: LISWO. 67 pp.

Campani G. 1993. Immigration and racism in southern Europe: the Italian case. *Ethn. Racial Stud.* 16:507–35

Carmines EG, Stimson JA. 1989. *Issue Evolution: Race and the Transformation of American Politics*. Princeton, NJ: Princeton Univ. Press. 217 pp.

Carter FW, French RA, Salt J. 1993. International migration between East and West Europe. *Ethn. Racial Stud.* 16:467–91

Castles S. 1984. *Here for Good: Western Europe's New Ethnic Minorities*. London: Pluto. 259 pp.

Castles S. 1993. Migrations and minorities in Europe. Perspectives for the 1990s: eleven hypotheses. See Solomos & Wrench 1993, pp. 17–34

Commission Nationale Consultative des Droits de l'Homme. 1997. *Rapport de la Commission Nationale Consultative des Droits de l'Homme*. Paris: La Documentation francaise. 442 pp.

Creamean L. 1996. Membership of foreigners: Algerians in France. *Arab Stud. Q.* 18: 49–67

Crosby F, Bromley S, Saxe L. 1980. Recent unobtrusive studies of black and white discrimination and prejudice: a literature review. *Psychol. Bull.* 87:546–63

Daniel WW. 1968. *Racial Discrimination in England*. Harmondsworth, UK: Penguin. 272 pp.

Den Uyl R, Choenni CE, Bovenkerk F. 1986. *Mag het ook een Buitenlander Wezen? Discriminatie bij Uitzendburo's*. Utrecht, The Netherlands: Natl. Bur. Against Racism. 45 pp.

Doomernik J. 1997. Adaptation strategies among Soviet Jewish immigrants in Berlin. *New Community* 23:59–73

Escriva A. 1997. Control, composition and character of new migration to south-west Europe: the case of Peruvian women in Barcelona. *New Community* 23:43–57

Essed P. 1990. *Everyday Racism: Reports from Women of Two Cultures*. Claremont, CA: Hunter House. 288 pp.

European Parliament. 1997. *Asylum in the European Union: The "Safe Country of Origin Principle.". Strasbourg, France: Eur. Parliament. 41 pp.*

Feagin JR, Feagin CB. 1986. *Discrimination American Style: Institutional Racism and Sexism*. Malabar, FL: Krieger. 246 pp. 2nd ed.

Feen RH. 1996. Thunder on the right: Austria's Jorg Haider and Freedom Party. *Migration World Mag.* 24(1–2):49–50

Fermin A. 1997. Dutch political parties on minority policy, 1977–1995. *Merger* 4(2):14–15

Foster CR, ed. 1980. *Nations Without a State: Ethnic Minorities in Western Europe*. New York: Praeger. 215 pp.

Freud S. 1930. *Civilization and Its Discontents*. Transl. J Riviere. New York: Cape & Smith. 144 pp.

Fuchs D, Gerhards J, Roller E. 1993. Wir und die Anderen. Ethnozentrismus in der zwoelf Landeren der europaeischen Gemeinshaft. *Koln. Zeitschr. Soziol. Sozialpsychol.* 45:238–53

Fysh P, Wolfreys J. 1992. Le Pen, the National

Front and the extreme-right in France. *Parliam. Aff.* 45:309–26

Gerhard U. 1992. Wenn Fluchtlinge und Einwanderer zu 'Asylantenfluten' werden—zum Anteil des Mediendiskurses an rassistischen Pogromen. *Osnabrucker Beitr. Sprachtheor.* 46:163–78

Gordon P. 1993. The police and racist violence in Britain. See Bjorgo & Witte 1993, pp. 167–78

Gordon P, Klug F. 1984. *Racism and Discrimination in Britain: A Select Bibliography, 1970–83.* London: Runnymede Trust. 143 pp.

Govaert S. 1995. Flander's radical nationalism: how and why the Vlaams Blok ascended. *New Community* 4:537–49

Green DP, Strolovitch DZ, Wong JS. 1997. Defended neighborhoods, integration, and hate crime. Unpublished ms. Yale Univ. Inst. for Social and Policy Stud., New Haven, CT

Griffiths D. 1997. Somali refugees in Tower Hamlets: clanship and new identities. *New Community* 23:5–24

Gunn S. 1989. *Revolution of the Right: Europe's New Conservatives.* London: Pluto. 135 pp.

Hammer T. 1993. Political participation and civil rights in Scandinavia. See Solomos & Wrench 1993, pp. 115–28

Heitmeyer W. 1993. Hostility and violence towards foreigners in Germany. See Bjorgo & Witte 1993, pp. 17–28

Holland B. 1995. Kicking racism out of football: an assessment of racial harassment in and around football grounds. *New Community* 21:567–86

Hubbuck J, Carter S. 1980. *Half a Chance? A Report on Job Discrimination Against Young Blacks in Nottingham.* London: Comm. Racial Equal. 63 pp.

Husbands CT. 1991a. The mainstream right and the politics of immigration in France: developments in the 1980s. *Ethn. Racial Stud.* 14:170–98

Husbands CT. 1991b. The support for the Front National: analyses and findings. *Ethn. Racial Stud.* 14:382–416

Husbands CT. 1993. Racism and racist violence: some theories and policy perspectives. See Bjorgo & Witte 1993, pp. 113–27

Joly D. 1996. *Haven or Hell? Asylum Policies and Refugees in Europe.* New York: St. Martin's Press. 215 pp.

Kinder DR, Sanders LM. 1996. *Divided by Color: Racial Politics and Democratic Ideals.* Chicago: Univ. Chicago Press. 391 pp.

Kitschelt H. 1995. *The Radical Right in Western Europe: A Comparative Analysis.* Ann Arbor, MI: Univ. Mich. Press. 332 pp.

Klink A, Wagner U. 1998. Discrimination against ethnic minorities in Germany: going back to the field. *J. Appl. Soc. Psychol.* In press

Koopmans R. 1995. *A Burning Question: Explaining the Rise of Racist and Extreme Right Violence in Western Europe.* Berlin: Wiss.zent. Berlin Soz.forsch. 38 pp.

Koser K. 1996. European migration report: recent asylum migration in Europe. *New Community* 22:151–58

Kulischer E. 1948. *Europe on the Move: War and Population Changes, 1917–47.* New York: Columbia Univ. Press. 377 pp.

Landes R. 1955. Biracialism in American society: a comparative view. *Am. Anthropol.* 57:1253–63

Layton-Henry Z, Wilpert C. 1994. *Discrimination, Racism and Citizenship: Inclusion and Exclusion in Britain and Germany.* London: Anglo-German Found. Study Indust. Soc. 30 pp.

Lloyd C. 1993. Racist violence and anti-racist reactions: a view of France. See Bjorgo & Witte 1993, pp. 207–20

Loow H. 1993. The cult of violence: the Swedish racist counterculture. See Bjorgo & Witte 1993, pp. 62–79

MacEwen M. 1993. *Enforcing anti-discrimination law in Britain: Here they be monsters.* Presented at Discrim., Racism and Citizenship Conf., Anglo-German Found. Study Indust. Soc., Berlin, Ger.

MacEwen M. 1995. *Tackling Racism in Europe: An Examination of Anti-Discrimination Law in Practice.* Washington, DC: Berg. 223 pp.

MacMaster N. 1991. The "seuil de tolerance": the uses of a "scientific" racist concept. In *Race, Discourse and Power in France,* ed. M Silverman, pp. 14–28. Aldershot, UK: Avebury. 129 pp.

Marcus J. 1995. *The National Front and French Politics: The Resistible Rise of Jean-Marie Le Pen.* London: Macmillan. 212 pp.

Martiniello M. 1992a. *Leadership et Pouvoir dans les Communautes d'Origine Immigree.* Paris: CIEMI/L'Harmattan. 317 pp.

Martiniello M. 1992b. Italy—the late discovery of immigration. See Thraenhardt 1992a, pp. 195–218

Martiniello M. 1993. Ethnic leadership, ethnic communities' political powerlessness and the state in Belgium. *Ethn. Racial Stud.* 16:237–55

Mayer N. 1995. The dynamics of Anti-Front National countermovement. *French Polit. Soc.* 13(4):12–32

Mayer N, Perrineau P. 1992. Why do they vote for Le Pen? *Eur. J. Polit. Res.* 22:123–41

Mayhew LH. 1968. *Law and Equal Opportunity: A Study of the Massachusetts Commission Against Discrimination.* Cambridge, MA: Harvard Univ. Press. 313 pp.

McArthur M. 1976. The "Saxon" Germans: political fate of an ethnic identity. *Dialect. Anthropol.* 1:349–64

Meertens RW, Pettigrew TF. 1997. Is subtle prejudice really prejudice? *Public Opin. Q.* 61:54–71

Melich A. 1995. *Comparative European trend survey data on racism and xenophobia.* Presented at Workshop Racist Parties Eur., Inst. d'Etudes Polit. de Bordeaux, France

Messina AM. 1989. *Race and Party Competition in Britain.* New York: Oxford Univ. Press. 200 pp.

Miles R. 1993. Introduction—Europe 1993: the significance of changing patterns of migration. *Ethn. Racial Stud.* 16:459–66

Miles R, Cleary P. 1992. Britain: post-colonial migration in context. See Thraenhardt 1992a, pp. 121–44

Miles R, Phizacklea A. 1984. *White Man's Country: Racism in British Politics.* London: Pluto. 184 pp.

Munz R. 1996. A continent of migration: European mass migration in the 20th century. *New Community* 22:201–26

Muus P. 1996/1997. International migration to the Netherlands. *Merger* 4(1):4

Panayiotopoulos PI. 1996. Challenging orthodoxies: Cypriot entrepreneurs in the London garment industry. *New Community* 22: 437–60

Parkinson F, ed. 1989. *Conquering the Past: Austrian Nazism Yesterday and Today.* Detroit, MI: Wayne State Univ. Press. 345 pp.

Peach C, Glebe G. 1995. Muslim minorities in western Europe. *Ethn. Racial Stud.* 18: 26–45

Pettigrew TF. 1988. Integration and pluralism. In *Eliminating Racism: Profiles in Controversy,* ed. PA Katz, D Taylor, pp. 19–30. New York: Plenum. 380 pp.

Pettigrew TF. 1989. The nature of modern racism in the United States. *Rev. Int. Psychol. Soc.* 2:291–303

Pettigrew TF. 1997. Generalized intergroup contact effects on prejudice. *Pers. Soc. Psychol. Bull.* 23:173–85

Pettigrew TF. 1998. *Systematizing the predictors of prejudice: an empirical approach.* Univ. Calif., Santa Cruz. Unpubl. ms

Pettigrew TF, Jackson J, Ben Brika J, Lemain G, Meertens RW, et al. 1998. Outgroup prejudice in western Europe. *Eur. Rev. Soc. Psychol.* In press

Pettigrew TF, Meertens RW. 1995. Subtle and blatant prejudice in western Europe. *Eur. J. Soc. Psychol.* 25:57–75

Pettigrew TF, Meertens RW. 1996. The verzuiling puzzle: understanding Dutch intergroup relations. *Curr. Psychol.* 15:3–13

Pettigrew TF, Taylor MC. 1991. Discrimination. In *The Encyclopedia of Sociology,* ed. EF Borgatta, ML Borgatta, 1:498–503. New York: Macmillan. 519 pp.

Quillian L. 1995. Prejudice as a response to perceived group threat: population composition and anti-immigrant and racial prejudice in Europe. *Am. Sociol. Rev.* 60: 586–611

Reif K, Melich A. 1991. *Euro-Barometer 30: Immigrants and Out-Groups in Western Europe, October-November 1988.* Ann Arbor, MI: Inter-Univ. Consort. Polit. Soc. Res. 780 pp.

Rich PB. 1990. *Race and Empire in British Politics.* New York: Cambridge Univ. Press. 274 pp. 2nd ed.

Rudolph H. 1996. The new gastarbeiter system in Germany. *New Community* 22: 287–300

Santel B. 1992. European community and asylum seekers: the harmonization of asylum policies. See Thraenhardt 1992a, pp. 103–16

Schoen DE. 1977. *Enoch Powell and the Powellites.* New York: St. Martin's Press. 317 pp.

Sears DD. 1988. Symbolic racism. In *Eliminating Racism: Profiles in Controversy,* ed. PA Katz, DA Taylor, pp. 53–84. New York: Plenum. 380 pp.

Shanker T. 1996. City hell. *New Republic* 215(22):14–15

Shields JG. 1989. Campaigning on the fringe: Jean-Marie Le Pen. In *The French Presidential Elections of 1988: Ideology and Leadership in Contemporary France,* ed. J Gaffney, pp. 140–57. Aldershot, UK: Dartmouth. 241 pp.

Singer D. 1991. The resistible rise of Jean-Marie Le Pen. *Ethn. Racial Stud.* 14: 368–81

Sissons M. 1981. Race, sex and helping behavior. *Br. J. Soc. Psychol.* 20:285–92

Smith DJ. 1976. *The Facts of Racial Disadvantage: A National Survey.* London: PEP. 257 pp.

Solomos J, Wrench J, eds. 1993. *Racism and Migration in Western Europe.* Oxford, UK: Berg. 293 pp.

Stasiulis DK. 1997. International migration, rights, and the decline of "actually existing liberal democracy." *New Community* 23: 197–214

Tezenas du Montcel A. 1995. Le Pen: la strategie de la fourmi. *Le Nouvel Econ.* 24: 56–60

Thraenhardt D, ed. 1992a. *Europe: A New Immigration Continent.* Muenster, Ger: Lit. 252 pp.

Thraenhardt D. 1992b. Europe—a new immigration continent: policies and politics since 1945 in comparative perspective. See Thraenhardt 1992a, pp. 15–74

Thraenhardt D. 1995. The political uses of xenophobia in England, France and Germany. *Party Polit.* 1:323–45

Thraenhardt D. 1996. European migration from East to West: present patterns and future directions. *New Community* 22: 227–42

US Commission on Civil Rights. 1990. *Bigotry and Violence on American College Campuses.* Washington, DC: US Comm. Civil Rights. 80 pp.

van Donselaar J. 1993. The extreme right and racist violence in the Netherlands. See Bjorgo & Witte 1993, pp. 46–61

Vasta E. 1993. Rights and racism in a new country of immigration: the Italian case. See Solomos & Wrench 1993, pp. 83–98

Veenman J, Roelandt T. 1990. Allochtonen: achterstand en achterstelling. In *Arbeidsmarkt en Maatschappelijke Ongelijkheid,* ed. JJ Schippers, pp. 88–114. Groningen, The Netherlands: Wolters-Noordhoff. 281 pp.

Verdery K. 1985. The unmaking of an ethnic collectivity: Transylvania's Germans. *Am. Ethnol.* 12:62–83

Vranken J, Martiniello M. 1992. Migrants, guest workers and ethnic minorities. Historical patterns, recent trends and social implications of migration in Belgium. See Thraenhardt 1992a, pp. 219–51

Wagner U, Zick A. 1997. Auslanderfeindlichkeit, Vorurteile und diskriminierendes Verhalten. In *Aggression und Gewalt,* ed. HW Bierhoff, U Wagner, pp. 145–64. Stuttgart: Kohlhammer. 268 pp.

Waldrauch H, Hofinger C. 1997. An index to measure the legal obstacles to the integration of immigrants. *New Community* 23: 271–85

Wieviorka M. 1993. Tendencies to racism in Europe: Does France represent a unique case, or is it representative of a trend? See Solomos & Wrench 1993, pp. 55–65

Willems H. 1995. Right-wing extremism, racism or youth violence? Explaining violence against foreigners in Germany. *New Community* 21:501–23

Wilpert C. 1993. Ideological and institutional foundations of racism in the Federal Republic of Germany. See Solomos & Wrench 1993, pp. 67–81

Wise MZ. 1995. Spandau spandex: Meet Austria's latest fascist. *New Republic* 213(26): 16–17

Witte R. 1995. Racist violence in western Europe. *New Community* 21:489–500

World Council of Churches Migration Secretariat, ed. 1980. *Migrant Workers and Racism in Europe.* Geneva: World Counc. Churches. 158 pp.

Zick A. 1997. *Vorurteile und Rassismus: Eine Sozialpsychologische Analyse.* Muenster, Germ: Waxmann. 494 pp.

Zick A, Wagner U. 1993. Den Turken geht es besser als uns. Wie Fremde zu Feinden werden. *Psychol. Heute* 20:48–53

Annu. Rev. Sociol. 1998. 24:105–40

SOCIAL MEMORY STUDIES: From "Collective Memory" to the Historical Sociology of Mnemonic Practices

Jeffrey K. Olick and Joyce Robbins[1]
Department of Sociology, Columbia University, New York, New York 10027;
e-mail: jko5@Columbia.edu

KEYWORDS: sociology of knowledge, identity and memory,

ABSTRACT

Despite substantial work in a variety of disciplines, substantive areas, and geographical contexts, social memory studies is a nonparadigmatic, transdisciplinary, centerless enterprise. To remedy this relative disorganization, we (re-)construct out of the diversity of work addressing social memory a useful tradition, range of working definitions, and basis for future work. We trace lineages of the enterprise, review basic definitional disputes, outline a historical approach, and review sociological theories concerning the statics and dynamics of social memory.

Introduction

> ...the time is past in which time did not matter. Modern man no longer works at what cannot be abbreviated...
>
> Paul Valéry

Scholars have viewed social memory narrowly as a subfield of the sociology of knowledge (Swidler & Arditi 1994) and broadly as "the connective structure of societies" (Assmann 1992, p. 293). They have seen it as involving particular

[1]Direct all correspondence to Jeffrey K. Olick, Department of Sociology, 324M Fairweather Hall, Columbia University, New York, New York 10027; e-mail: jko5@Columbia.edu

0360-0572/98/0815-0105$08.00

sets of practices like commemoration and monument building and general forms like tradition, myth, or identity. They have approached it from sociology, history, literary criticism, anthropology, psychology, art history, and political science, among other disciplines. They have studied it in simple and complex societies, from above and below, across the geographical spectrum. Social memory studies is nevertheless, or perhaps as a result, a nonparadigmatic, transdisciplinary, centerless enterprise. While this relative disorganization has been productive, it now seems possible to draw together some of these dispersed insights. Our goal in this essay is therefore to (re-)construct out of the diversity of work addressing social memory a useful tradition, range of working definitions, and basis for future work in a field that ironically has little organized memory of its own.

Lineages

Memory, of course, has been a major preoccupation for social thinkers since the Greeks. Yet it was not until the late nineteenth and earlier twentieth centuries that a distinctively social perspective on memory became prominent. The first explicit use of the term collective memory we could find was by Hugo von Hofmannsthal in 1902, who referred to "the dammed up force of our mysterious ancestors within us" and "piled up layers of accumulated collective memory" (Schieder 1978, p. 2). Contemporary usages are usually traced to Maurice Halbwachs, who published his landmark *Social Frameworks of Memory* in 1925. Halbwachs' Strasbourg colleague, historian Marc Bloch (1925), also used the term collective memory in 1925 as well as later in his book on feudal society (Bloch 1974 [1939]). The art historian Aby Warburg used the term social memory to analyze artworks as repositories of history. Walter Benjamin as well, though he never used the terms social or collective memory, analyzed the material world as accumulated history, brilliantly emphasizing not only the manifold traces of the past in the artifacts of commodity culture, but the relations between commodity culture and particular forms of historicity as well (Buck-Morss 1989).

Bartlett (1932) is usually credited as the first modern psychologist to attend to the social dimensions of memory, attributing decisive importance to group dynamics in individual remembering. Anthropologist Evans-Pritchard (1940) developed a notion of "structural amnesia" in his famous study of the Nuer. Interesting but largely forgotten works in other fields include Janet's (1927) study of the evolution of memory and the concept of time, Vygotsky's 1929 claim that memory takes narrative form and is wholly shaped by cultural influences (Bakhurst 1990), and Czarnowski's 1919 Durkheimian analysis of festivals and rituals celebrating Saint Patrick (Schwartz 1996, pp. 275–76).

In about the same period, American sociologists Cooley (1918) and Mead (1959 [1932]) also theorized about the social context of remembering, but their important ideas—especially Mead's—have usually been ascribed to extrasociological interests (Maines et al 1983). Among the emerging European classical theorists, Durkheim (1951 [1915]) is insightful about temporality but addresses memory directly only in his brief discussion of commemorative rituals, and there only as a feature of primitive societies. Social reproduction is perhaps *the* central category of Marx's thought, but the Marxist tradition emphasizes the automatic and unconscious quality of the process; conscious attention to the past is characterized as an irrational residue of earlier social forms: "The tradition of the dead generations," Marx (1852) writes in *The Eighteenth Brumaire*, "weighs like a nightmare on the minds of the living." Simmel (1959) wrote that "All the uncertainties of change in time and the tragedy of loss associated with the past find in the ruin a coherent and unified expression." This remark is prescient of later theories that see memory traces as evidence of loss, but Simmel did not develop it more than aphoristically. Weber, too, had little to say about memory, despite his interest in traditional legitimation: "by its very 'progressiveness' [civilized society]... gives death the imprint of meaninglessness" (1946). Meaningful death is elusive because memory is inadequate to hold together the diversity of our life experiences. But this is an intriguing aside rather than the beginning of a theory of memory.

Shils (1981, p. 9) explains this shared neglect of tradition and memory by demonstrating how Weber and his contemporaries were the victims of their own overdrawn dichotomies. The classical theorists, Shils writes, "oversubscribed to the naive view that modern society was on the road to traditionlessness...." From such a perspective, an interest in how the past works on the present was antiquarian, or at least useful only as a contrast to the ways modern societies work. In his discussion of Tönnies, Terdiman (1993) notes how unusual this lack of interest in memory and tradition was in a fin de siècle culture he describes as otherwise obsessed with memory.

Between this early period of scattered work on the social foundations of memory and the present, relatively little attention was paid to the issue. Even major works like Lloyd Warner's *The Living and the Dead* (1959) were considered exotic. Since about 1980, however, both the public and academia have become saturated with references to social or collective memory. Why has public interest in memory grown so in the last two decades? Kammen (1995) explains it in terms of the rise of multiculturalism, the fall of Communism, and a politics of victimization and regret, among other factors. Schwartz (1997) explains a decline in presidential reputations under the rubric of postmodernity. Nora, Hutton, Le Goff, Matsuda, and Huyssen pursue similar lines of explanation through an enterprise they label "the history of memory," which we review in greater detail below.

It is a slightly different matter to trace the rise of scholarly interest in the memory problematic and the associated rediscovery of Halbwachs; analytical paradigms appear to have at least a semiautonomous dynamic. Schwartz (1996) identifies three related aspects of 1960s–1970s intellectual culture that gave rise to interest in the social construction of the past. First, multiculturalists identify historiography as a source of cultural domination and challenge dominant historical narratives in the name of repressed groups. Second, postmodernists attack the conceptual underpinnings of linear historicity, truth, and identity, thereby raising interest in the relations linking history, memory, and power. Finally, hegemony theorists provide a class-based account of the politics of memory, highlighting memory contestation, popular memory, and the instrumentalization of the past.

Hutton (1993) traces the memory problematic to the history of mentalities that has dominated French historiography since the 1960s. Foucault's "archaeological" stance provided general philosophical support for a desacralization of traditions. Historians like Ariès (1974) and Agulhon (1981), Hutton writes, began to study the history of commemorative practices, which they saw as mechanisms of political power, thus shifting historiographical interest from ideology to imagery and from meaning to manipulation. Writers like Hobsbawm—whose much-cited *Invention of Tradition* was a hallmark work in this vein—extended this desacralization, seeing traditions as disingenuous efforts to secure political power. According to Hutton, it was on this foundation that interest in Halbwachs revived; his apparently presentist position was seen as anticipating postmodernism. The recent effort by Nora to document all the "realms of memory" in French society (discussed below), Hutton argues, is the crowning moment in this tradition.

Analogously, sociology has moved from the study of social structures and normative systems to that of "practice" (Bourdieu 1984, Ortner 1984), expanding the functionalist definition of culture as norms, values, and attitudes to culture as the constitutive symbolic dimension of all social processes (Crane 1994). The view that all meaning frameworks have histories and that explicitly past-oriented meaning frameworks are prominent modes of legitimation and explanation leads to increased interest in social memory because it raises questions about the transmission, preservation, and alteration of these frameworks over time. Social memory studies also draw on the Mannheimian tradition in the sociology of knowledge and the Mertonian tradition in the sociology of science as well as on Berger & Luckmann's (1966) social constructionism, for which many sociologists of memory seem to have a special affinity. Social memory studies thus fit squarely within the reorientation of cultural sociology, much like that of recent historiography, from interest in "ideas developed by knowledge specialists… [to] structures of knowledge or consciousness that shape the thinking of laypersons" (Swidler & Arditi 1994) as well as drawing on older sociological interests.

Delimiting the Field

Through this reconstruction of intellectual lineages for social memory studies, it is possible to limn a conceptual core for our contemporary efforts. The place to begin is Durkheim's response to philosophical positions, in contradistinction to which he demanded a social account of temporality. For Halbwachs, Durkheim's student, this meant that studying memory was not a matter of reflecting philosophically on inherent properties of the subjective mind; memory is a matter of how minds work together in society, how their operations are not simply mediated but are structured by social arrangements: "[I]t is in society that people normally acquire their memories. It is also in society that they recall, recognize, and localize their memories..." (Halbwachs 1992, p. 38). Nonetheless, because questions of social memory involve issues of temporality, mind, and, as we see shortly, narrative and historicity, social studies of memory have remained close to philosophy.

Halbwachs developed his concept of collective memory not only beyond philosophy but against psychology, though the very idea of a social memory appropriates psychological terminology. Freud had argued that the individual's unconscious acts as a repository for all past experiences. Forgetting, rather than remembering, is what takes work in the form of repression and the substitution of "screen" memories that block access to more disturbing ones. Halbwachs rejects this Freudian and other purely psychological accounts. He argues that it is impossible for individuals to remember in any coherent and persistent fashion outside of their group contexts: "There is [thus] no point," he argues, "in seeking where... [memories] are preserved in my brain or in some nook of my mind to which I alone have access: for they are recalled by me externally, and the groups of which I am a part at any time give me the means to reconstruct them..." (Halbwachs 1992, p. 38).

Writers in other traditions have rejected an individual-psychological approach to memory as well: Gadamer (1979), for instance, has written, "It is time to rescue the phenomenon of memory from being regarded as a psychological faculty and to see it as an essential element of the finite historical being of man" (Hutton 1993). Contemporary psychologists Middleton & Edwards (1990) as well encourage their discipline to recover Bartlett's and Halbwachs' more social insights. Neisser (1982) implicitly calls for a more social perspective on memory when he argues that the standard experimental methods of cognitive psychology have been inadequate due to the artificiality of the experimental setting. Pennebaker, Paez, and Rimé (1997) take an explicitly *social* psychological perspective in their studies of collective memory of political events. Preserving more of the individualist perspective, some authors have suggested possible benefits of linking social, neuropsychological, and paleoanthropological inquiries into memory (Schachter 1995, Leroi-Gourhan 1993).

The third, and perhaps most contested, boundary for social memory studies is its relation to historiography. Halbwachs was very decisive about his solution: History is dead memory, a way of preserving pasts to which we no longer have an "organic" experiential relation. On the surface, this understanding of the distinction negates the self-image of historiography as the more important or appropriate attitude toward the past: History's epistemological claim is devalued in favor of memory's meaningfulness. At a deeper level, however, the distinction is the same that traditional historians would draw between history and memory: Only the former is engaged in a search for truth. In this vein, Yerushalmi (1982, p. 95) draws a sharp contrast between Jewish memory and Jewish historiography, arguing that until the eighteenth century, the former excluded the latter. On the one hand, he laments this condition because, as he writes, "...collective memory... is drastically selective. Certain memories live on; the rest are winnowed out, repressed, or simply discarded by a process of natural selection which the historian, uninvited, disturbs and reverses." On the other hand, he critiques history for its sterile posture of distance from meaning and relevance: "...Jewish historiography can never substitute for Jewish memory.... A historiography that does not aspire to be memorable is in peril of becoming a rampant growth" (Yerushalmi 1982, p. 101).

Recent approaches within historiography, however, have critiqued this understanding of the relations between history and memory. First, as historiography has broadened its focus from the official to the social and cultural, memory has become central "evidence." Theorists now recognize, moreover, that memory frequently employs history in its service: Professional historians have often provided political legitimation for nationalism and other more reconstructive identity struggles. This involvement calls into question not only the success of historians in being objective, but the very notion of objectivity itself (Novick 1988). Furthermore, postmodernists have challenged the "truth-claim" of professional historiography by questioning the distinction between knowledge and interpretation, and derivatively between history and memory (White 1973, Veyne 1984). Philosophers have argued forcefully that historiography constructs as much as uncovers the "truths" it pursues (Novick 1988, Iggers 1997). History is written by people in the present for particular purposes, and the selection and interpretation of "sources" are always arbitrary. If "experience," moreover, is always embedded in and occurs through narrative frames, then there is no primal, unmediated experience that can be recovered. The distinction between history and memory in such accounts is a matter of disciplinary power rather than of epistemological privilege. Burke (1989) therefore refers to history as social memory, using the term as "a convenient piece of shorthand which sums up the rather complex process of selection and interpretation." Hutton (1993) titles his book *History as an Art of Memory*. Schwartz argues that "Sharp opposition between history and collective memory has been our Achilles Heel, causing us to assert unwillingly, and often despite ourselves, that what is not historical must be 'invented' or 'constructed'—which transforms collective memory study into a kind of cynical muckraking" (B Schwartz, personal communication).

Before turning to the history of memory and to the substantive results of social memory studies, it is possible, on the basis of the preceding reconstruction, to define some of the basic concepts for such an inquiry. Halbwachs distinguished among autobiographical memory, historical memory, history, and collective memory. Autobiographical memory is memory of those events that we ourselves experience, while historical memory is memory that reaches us only through historical records. History is the remembered past to which we no longer have an "organic" relation—the past that is no longer an important part of our lives—while collective memory is the active past that forms our identities. Memory inevitably gives way to history as we lose touch with our pasts. Historical memory, however, can be either organic or dead: We can celebrate even what we did not directly experience, keeping the given past alive for us, or it can be alive only in historical records, so-called graveyards of knowledge.

Though collective memory does seem to take on a life of its own, Halbwachs reminds that it is only individuals who remember, even if they do much of this remembering together. And Coser (1992) points out that, while Durkheim writes "Society" with a capital S, Halbwachs employs the more cautious "groups." Halbwachs characterized collective memory as plural; he shows that shared memories can be effective markers of social differentiation (Wood 1994, p. 126). Some authors, nonetheless, detect the collectivist overtones of the Durkheimian tradition in Halbwachs' work. Fentress & Wickham (1992) worry about "a concept of collective consciousness curiously disconnected from the actual thought processes of any particular person," which risks rendering "the individual a sort of automaton, passively obeying the interiorized collective will."

As a result of these problems, some authors prefer other terms to "collective memory." Sturkin (1997) defines "cultural memory" as "memory that is shared outside the avenues of formal historical discourse yet is entangled with cultural products and imbued with cultural meaning." Fentress & Wickham (1992) refer to "social memory" rather than to collective memory. Olick & Levy (1997) refer to "images of the past" as parts of "political cultural profiles." Assmann (1992) distinguishes among four modes of memory in an effort to capture the range of memory problematics: 1. mimetic memory—the transmission of practical knowledge from the past; 2. material memory—the history contained in objects; 3. communicative memory—the residues of the past in language and communication, including the very ability to communicate in language; and 4. cultural memory—the transmission of meanings from the past, that is, explicit historical reference and consciousness.

Critics who charge that "collective memory" over-totalizes prefer a proliferation of more specific terms to capture the ongoing contest over images of the past: official memory, vernacular memory, public memory, popular memory, local memory, family memory, historical memory, cultural memory, etc. Still others argue that a collective memory concept has nothing to add to older formulations like myth, tradition, custom, and historical consciousness. Gedi & Elam (1996) hold that overuse of the term collective memory is "an act of intrusion… forcing itself like a molten rock into an earlier formation… unavoidably obliterating fine distinctions…." If defined too broadly, as the pattern-maintenance function of society or as social reproduction per se, what is not social memory? On the other hand, Burke (1989) argues that "if we refuse to use such terms, we are in danger of failing to notice the different ways in which the ideas of individuals are influenced by the groups to which they belong." Schwartz uses Herbert Blumer's classical distinction between operational and sensitizing concepts, and classifies collective memory as of the latter sort. He argues that collective memory "is not an alternative to history (or historical memory) but is rather shaped by it as well as by commemorative symbolism and ritual. To conceive collective memory in this way sensitizes us to reality while encouraging us to recognize the many things we can do to reality interpretively" (personal communication).

In this review, we refer to "social memory studies" as a general rubric for inquiry into the varieties of forms through which we are shaped by the past, conscious and unconscious, public and private, material and communicative, consensual and challenged. We refer to distinct sets of mnemonic practices in various social sites, rather than to collective memory as a thing. This approach, we argue, enables us to identify ways in which past and present are intertwined without reifying a mystical group mind and without including absolutely everything in the enterprise. Methodologically, Olick (n.d.) and Schudson (1992) suggest specifying the different institutional fields that produce memory such as politics and the arts; Olick (n.d.) and Reichel (1995) theorize the varying links between media and memory; Wagner-Pacifici (1996) places special emphasis on memory's cultural forms.

The History of Memory

Instead of trying to fix conceptual distinctions theoretically, many scholars have called for a historical approach to social memory, one that sees such distinctions as emerging in particular times and locations and for particular purposes. As Matsuda (1996, p. 16) puts it, "…memory has too often become another analytical category to impose on the past; the point should be to rehistoricize memory and see how it is so inextricably part of the past." Yates' (1966) *The Art of Memory* is the seminal work in this vein, charting the links between memory systems and particular historical orders. Yates traces transformations in *ars memoria*—the rhetorical art of memorizing through spatial images—from Roman times through the Renaissance, where the art of memory persisted in the humanist tradition despite its decline due to the spread of the printing press. Coleman (1992) as well offers a comprehensive history of theories of memory from antiquity through later medieval times, noting the particular sophistication of medieval theories, which address the reconstruction of narratives. Following Yates' lead, Carruthers (1990) demonstrates the persistence of memory training even with the spread of texts, which resulted in the highly mixed oral-literate nature of medieval cultures. Indeed, the dissemination of written materials, she argues, occurred through memorization and oral transmission.

Yet for Yates, Coleman, and Carruthers, memorization remains central: In earlier centuries, this form of remembering was of greater significance than it is today. But even for those periods, an analysis of *ars memoria* reveals little about popular memory due to its elite focus. In response, Geary (1994, p. 8) focuses on ordinary medieval people who, he argues, were actively engaged in creating their past: "Individuals and communities copied, abridged, and revised archival records, liturgical texts, literary documents, doing so with reference to physical reminders from previous generations and a fluid oral tradition...." Geary (1994) also breaks with Yates et al by expanding the definition of memory to include textual transmission as well as oral memorization.

But while ancient arts of memory do persist in the interstices of later mnemonic forms (Matsuda 1996, Casey 1987, Zonabend 1984), it is virtually impossible to discuss collective memory without highlighting historical developments in the material means of memory transmission. While new technological means of recording the past are often seen as "artificial," with time they are incorporated into the accepted cultural construct of memory. By extension, contemporary interest in the social bases of memory may be traced at least partly to a historical shift of memory from the mind to external loci; without externalization of memory in "artificial" sites, the social location of memory is not as clear. Even in earlier cultures, however, direct attention to material forms of memory can yield important insights.

Assmann (1992), for instance, argues that while Babylonian, Egyptian, Greek, and Jewish cultures all developed the technical means for preserving the past (word, text, writing, and book), only the Greek and Jewish persisted as living traditions, due to the peculiarities of their historical experiences. In the Jewish case, where the entire weight of cultural continuity rested on fundamental texts, everything depended on keeping them alive. This led to the development of a new form of reading—commentary—and a new kind of historical consciousness. This study thus contradicts technologically determinist claims about the importance of the alphabet for cultural continuity: While the development of an alphabet was important, it was not sufficient, nor were its effects uniform.

Epochal generalizations about the developing relations between memory and technologies of communication have nonetheless described a broad shift from orality to literacy over millennia. Founding this tradition, McLuhan theorized the effects of electronic communications on typographic culture within a history that includes the move from manuscript to print culture two centuries earlier and from orality to literacy a millennium before that (Hutton 1993). Subsequently, Ong traced a long-range pattern from orality to manuscript literacy, to print culture, to media culture, drawing out implications for memory. The invention of writing in antiquity was the seed for the rise of more abstract thinking. Because that capability resided in the hands of a small elite, however, it was not until the vast expansion of literacy in the seventeenth and eighteenth centuries that the profound possibilities of written culture became a dominant cultural form. In the process, memory became a public affair, and a problematic one at that.

On the basis of this kind of macro-historical theory, many contemporary scholars of memory work with an image of oral culture as richly expressive and of literate culture as detached and introspective (Goody 1986). "Memory," as Hutton (1993, p. 16) puts it, " first conceived as a repetition, is eventually reconceived as a recollection." Where Proust revelled in the "involuntary" memory evoked by the taste of a tea cookie, macro-historical theorists of memory describe modern memory as predominantly "voluntary" or active. Hobsbawm & Ranger (1983), for instance, distinguish sharply between custom and tradition. The former is the unproblematic sense of continuity that undergirds the gradual, living changes of "traditional" societies. Tradition, in contrast, aims at invariance and is the product of explicit ideologies.

In an important synthesis, Le Goff (1992) follows Leroi-Gourhan (1993 [1964–1965]) in identifying five distinct periods in the history of memory.

- First, peoples without writing possessed what Le Goff calls "ethnic memory," in which memory practices are not highly developed arts; Le Goff therefore see societies without writing as free, creative, and vital.
- Second, the move from prehistory to Antiquity involved the development from orality to writing, though writing never fully supplanted oral transmission. This new condition enabled two important new mnemonic practices—commemoration and documentary recording—associated with emerging city structures.
- Third, memory in the Middle Ages involved "the Christianization of memory and of mnemotechnology, the division of collective memory be-

tween a circular liturgical memory and a lay memory little influenced by chronology, the development of the memory of the dead and especially of dead saints…" (p. 68).

- Fourth, memory as it developed from the Renaissance to the present involved the gradual revolution in memory brought about by the printing press, which required the long development of a middle class readership to complete its effect. With a "progressive exteriorization of individual memory," the collective memory grew to such a degree that the individual could no longer assimilate it in toto. In the nineteenth century, Romanticism added to a growing fervor for commemorating, and proliferated multifarious forms for doing so, including coins, medals, postage stamps, statuary, inscriptions, and souvenirs. In the same period, we witness the birth of archives, libraries, and museums, reflecting the interests of different nations seeking to build shared identities within their citizenries.
- Finally, changes in the twentieth century constituted another genuine revolution in memory, the most important element of which was the invention of electronic means of recording and transmitting information, which not only change the way we remember, but provide new ways of conceptualizing memory. Not only computers but image processing and the immune system (Sturkin 1997) now serve as basic models and metaphors for thinking about memory.

A key point in many histories of memory is that a significant transformation in the experience of time occurred at some debatable point between the Middle Ages and the nineteenth century. Many authors describe an existential crisis arising out of the increased possibility for abstract thought discussed above, out of accelerating change resulting from increased industrialization and urbanization, as well as out of the resultant decline of religious worldviews and of traditional forms of political authority. Koselleck (1985), for instance, describes a shift from a "space of experience" to a "horizon of expectation." Through the seventeenth and eighteenth centuries, a wide variety of new experiences and events produced an awareness of the "noncontemporaneity of the contemporaneous," which led, in turn, to a sense of a human future and of the distinctness of history. Ariès's (1974) work on attitudes toward death and dying in Western culture, as well, attributes the rising importance and frequency of commemorative practices in the nineteenth century to an increased sense of change: The past was no longer felt to be immediately present but was something that required preservation and recovery.

Hobsbawm (1972) describes the rise of linear historical consciousness as a necessary solution to the existential problems of rapid transformation: "Paradoxically, the past remains the most useful analytical tool for coping with constant change." Thompson (1995) attributes a similar dynamic largely to transformations in media technology, which extended individuals' experiences beyond the sphere of day-to-day encounters: "The process of self-formation [thus] became more reflexive and open-ended." Jacoby (1975) and Berman (1982), among others, attribute to late modernity a condition—at least partly related to rampant commodification—that makes it harder and harder to relate to the past, producing what Jacoby calls "social amnesia." When the past is no longer obviously connected to the present, memory becomes of diagnostic importance, as Terdiman (1993) puts it. Yerushalmi (1982) specifies much of this in his discussion of Jewish memory: "The modern effort to reconstruct the Jewish past begins at a time that witnesses a sharp break in the continuity of Jewish living and hence also an ever-growing decay of Jewish group memory." In sum, according to Schieder (1978, p. 8), "...historical thought served a compensating function making up for the actual loss of history by exaggerating a consciousness of it."

The connection between nationalism and social memory appears to have been especially important. Cressy (1989) traces a new kind of memory in England to the seventeenth century, a memory that gave expression to a mythic and patriotic sense of national identity: "The calendar became an important instrument for declaring and disseminating a distinctively Protestant national culture... binding the nation to the ruling dynasty and securing it through an inspiring providential interpretation of English history" (Cressy 1989, p. xi). Calendars map the basic temporal structures of societies, enabling and constraining their abilities to remember different pasts (Zerubavel 1981); many have noted how a new calendar served French Republican leaders as effective symbolic markers for their break from the old regime (Hunt 1984, Ferguson 1994). More generally, Gillis (1994) links the construction of national memories to what he calls a cult of new beginnings.

Anderson (1991) combines insights into the spread of print literacy, capitalist commerce, and the decline of religious worldviews to explain the rise of historicizing national identities as a pervasive modern principle. In his account, the transformation of temporality and the associated rise of interest in the past made it possible "to think the nation." Print capitalism, according to Anderson, was the principal agent of this transformation toward what Benjamin (1968) called the "empty, homogeneous time" of the nation-state. Felt communities of fate were secured across wide territories by newspapers and novels, which produced shared culture among people who would never meet. As a result, in Smith's (1986) words, "ethnic nationalism has become a 'surrogate' religion which aims to overcome the sense of futility engendered by the removal of any vision of an existence after death, by linking individuals to persisting communities whose generations form indissoluble links in a chain of memories and identities."

Others have given similar insights a more critical turn. Boyarin (1994), for instance, points out that statist ideologies "involve a particularly potent manipulation of dimensionalities of space and time, invoking rhetorically fixed national identities to legitimate their monopoly on administrative control." Renan is remembered from the nineteenth century for having pointed out the ways in which national identities combine remembering and forgetting, with greater emphasis on the latter: They forget that they are not inevitable and that their internal fissures may be as significant as their external boundaries (Anderson 1991). Duara (1995) writes that the relationship between linear historicity and the nation-state is repressive: "National history secures for the contested and contingent nation the false unity of a self-same, national subject evolving through time..." enabling "conquests of Historical awareness over other, 'nonprogressive' modes of time."

Many writers have pointed to the ways in which national states consciously manipulate and exploit professional history. Smith (1986) writes that "One sign of the formation of the nation out of the protonation is the shifting of the center of collective memory from the temple and its priesthood to the university and its scholarly community." Breisbach (1994) shows that "Historians were called on to mediate between the demands for change and the equally strong desire to see the continuity of past, present, and future preserved.... Presented by careful scholars with great eloquence, these histories became popular possessions rather than scholarly curiosa." Novick (1988) shows how, despite protestations of disinterest and objectivity, American historical scholarship has always been inextricably tied to contemporary political problematics. More generally, Lévi-Strauss (1979) argues that "In our own societies, history has replaced mythology and fulfills the same function...." Nevertheless, Noiriel (1996) has argued that "the degree to which commemoration of historical origins is essential for building political consensus may be treated as a variable." Smith (1986) as well warns against either overgeneralizing or overspecifying the urge toward historical commemoration: Nostalgia exists in every society; in the era of the nation-state nostalgia for the "ethnic past" has merely become more acute.

In a major contribution, Hobsbawm (1983) notes the proliferation in the mid to late nineteenth century of state-led efforts to "invent" useful traditions to shore up their fading legitimacy. Particularly after 1870, in conjunction with the emergence of mass politics, political leaders "rediscovered the importance of 'irrational' elements in the maintenance of the social fabric and the social order." Many thinkers thus advocated the construction of a new "civil religion;" successful leaders sought to imbue educational institutions with nationalist content, to expand public ceremony, and to mass produce public monuments. This impulse spread to nonstate groups as well, producing an interest in genealogies of all sorts, including social registers for the upper classes. With more emphasis on local cultures in the nation-building process, Confino (1997) shows how German nation-building in the nineteenth century (and by extension other nation-building projects elsewhere) required assimilating diverse regional memories into one coherent national identity, which was successful only when the national was mediated through local categories.

Not all thinkers of the nineteenth century, however, championed this proliferation of history. Nietzsche (1983) was highly critical of his age's pervasive production of the past in both its scientific and monumental guises. While recognizing that it is the power to bring the past to life that constitutes the humanity of human beings, Nietzsche also claims that an excess of history can destroy our humanity: "The past," he writes, "has to be forgotten if it is not to become the gravedigger of the present." Many contemporary writers on social memory quote Borges's short story about "Funes the Memorious," depicting the agony of a young man who has lost the ability to forget. Nietzsche sees historicism's scientific attitude as producing "dead" knowledge, while monumental history "inspires the courageous to foolhardiness and the inspired to fanaticism." In another well-known essay, Butterfield (1965 [1931]) warns against an overly interested approach to history writing, what he calls "Whig history," which produces "a story which is the ratification if not the glorification of the present."

Moving to a slightly later period, historians of memory emphasize the importance of the First World War for perceptions of temporality and the status of national memory. Benjamin in particular portrayed the War experience as a decisive moment in a longer-term trend, typified by a decline of storytelling, a process which he sees, however, as "only a concomitant symptom of the secular productive forces of history." The conditions for storytelling, "woven thousands of years ago in the ambience of the oldest forms of craftsmanship" have lost their most basic support "because there is no more weaving and spinning to go on while... [stories] are being listened to." "Boredom," Benjamin (1968) writes, "is the dream bird that hatches the egg of experience. A rustling in the leaves drives him away.... With this, the gift for listening is lost and the community of listeners disappears." For Benjamin, the First World War brought this process into a new phase: "...never has experience been contradicted more thoroughly than strategic experience by tactical warfare, economic experience by inflation, bodily experience by mechanical warfare, moral experience by those in power." This cataclysm left people not only without the conditions for telling stories but without communicable experiences to tell.

With less apocalyptic vision, other writers as well have noted a change in the form of memory after the War. Mosse (1990), in a study of "The Myth of the War Experience," notes that the burial of the dead and commemoration became the tasks of specially formed national commissions during the War. Paradoxically, just as the effect of war was felt more brutally than ever among civilian populations, the tasks of consolation were made more public than ever before. As a result, "The memory of the war was refashioned into a sacred experience which provided the nation with a new depth of religious feeling, putting at its disposal ever-present saints and martyrs, places of worship, and a heritage to emulate." Additionally, Winter (1995) explores the new forms of war memorial that emerged to appropriate the devastation of total war for national purposes, though he emphasizes the proliferation of more introspective forms too. Gillis (1994) notes that World War I marked a massive democratization of the cult of the dead. In a detailed study of war literature that emerged in Great Britain, Fussell (1975) characterizes this corpus as comprising a peculiarly "modern" form of memory.

While the First World War thus created new attitudes toward both the present and the past, the Holocaust is said to have produced an even more decisive crisis of representation. "We are dealing," writes Friedlander (1992, p. 3), "with an event which tests our traditional conceptual and representational categories, an 'event at the limits.'" There is the oft-quoted remark of Adorno that to write lyric poetry after Auschwitz is barbaric. By extension, many have portrayed the Holocaust as challenging the validity of any totalizing view of history (Friedlander 1992, p. 5). In German intellectual circles, this issue has spawned an ongoing debate between those who maintain that the Holocaust was unique and those who call for "historicizing" it. The literature on German debates about the Nazi past is too voluminous to even begin to report. Good starting places are Maier (1988), Evans (1989), and Olick (1993).

Gillis (1994), Mosse (1990), Young (1993), and Koonz (1994) document changes in war memorials after the Second World War, noting that the memory of war is now understood in a new way. Where nationalist leaders exploited a cult of the war dead after the First World War to foment further nationalist sentiment, memory after Auschwitz and Hiroshima has often been more problematic (Bosworth 1993). Where earlier monuments aimed to exacerbate resentment for future campaigns, many later monuments worked to erase a clear burden. Indeed, Young (1992) goes so far as to implicate the very form of monumentalization in the forgetting: "...once we assign monumental form to memory, we have to some degree divested ourselves of the obligation to remember." Adorno (1967) had many years earlier pointed out the association between the words "museum" and "mausoleum."

While some authors make the Holocaust the decisive turning point, others see in it merely one last and most horrible stage in a development already under way—one which included recognition of horrors of colonialism, two world wars, racism, environmental damage, etc—on the road to postmodernity. In either case, from early intimations of postmodernism in Heidegger, through the critical theory of Benjamin and Adorno, to the postmodernist theory of the 1980s, the connected problems of time and memory have been central issues for cultural criticism. Postmodern writers have addressed the ruptured sense of continuity and the multiple temporalities that they see as characterizing our highly mediated society. While many of these theorists have made important insights, we focus very briefly on only two here, Huyssen and Nora. For a critique of the postmodernist account of memory as overly unilinear in its critique of unilinearity, see Schwartz (1997).

In *Twilight Memories,* Andreas Huyssen (1995) characterizes the situation of memory in postmodernity as paradoxical. He notes the simultaneous popularity of museums and the resurgence of the monument and the memorial at the same time there is an "undisputed waning of history and historical consciousness." Novelty, he says, is now associated with new versions of the past rather than with visions of the future. This memory boom, however, is not to be confused with the historical fever to legitimatize nation-states that Nietzsche derided. "In comparison, the mnemonic convulsions of our culture seem chaotic, fragmentary, and free-floating."

His pessimism, however, is not complete, and his analysis is perceptive: "The current obsession with memory," Huyssen writes, "is not simply a function of the fin de siècle syndrome, another symptom of postmodern pastiche. Instead, it is a sign of the crisis of that structure of temporality that marked the age of modernity with its celebration of the new as utopian, as radically and irreducibly other." Where Benjamin and Adorno ascribed the contemporary crisis of memory to the forgetting at the center of the commodity, Huyssen relates the further development of media technologies since their time to "the evident crisis of the ideology of progress and modernization and to the fading of a whole tradition of teleological philosophies of history." As a result, the postmodern condition of memory is not wholly one of loss: "Thus the shift from history to memory represents a welcome critique of compromised teleological notions of history rather than being simply anti-historical, relativistic, or subjective." The contemporary crisis of memory, Huyssen argues, "represents the attempt to slow down information processing, to resist the dissolution of time in the synchronicity of the archive, to recover a mode of contemplation outside the universe of simulation and fast-speed information and cable networks, to claim some anchoring space in a world of puzzling and often threatening heterogeneity, non-synchronicity, and information overload." Where postmodern antiepistemology derides any easy correspondence between experience and memory, Huyssen characterizes that fissure as "a powerful stimulant for cultural and artistic creativity."

French historian Pierre Nora (1992), leading theoretician and editor of a massive seven-volume project on "places" or "lieux" of French memory, also begins by observing the paradoxes of memory in postmodernity. "We speak so much of memory," he writes, "because there is so little of it left." Nora can in this way be seen as the true heir to Halbwachs, who noted the passing of memory into history as we lose a living relation to the past, though Nora sees this process as even more dramatic and irreversible, and as more clearly political, than Halbwachs did. Where premodern societies live within the continuous past, contemporary societies have separated memory from the continuity of social reproduction; memory is now a matter of explicit signs, not of implicit meanings. We now compartmentalize memory as a mode of experience; our only recourse is to represent and invent what we can no longer spontaneously experience (Wood 1994). Nora thus contrasts contemporary "lieux" or places of memory to earlier lived "milieux." The former are impoverished versions of the latter: "If we were able to live within memory, we would not have needed to consecrate lieux de mémoire in its name."

Nora's project is to catalogue all of these places of memory in French society. He organizes the analyses around three principles which he sees as layered on top of one another in telling ways: the Republic, the Nation, and "Les Frances." For Nora, this ordering represents a historical progression from unity, through uncertainty, to multiplicity. The peculiar status of the second, the memory-nation, is the linchpin. In its ascendancy, the memory-nation relied on national historical narratives to provide continuity through identity. In the nineteenth century, change was still slow enough that states could control it through historiography. But, Nora argues, the nation as a foundation of identity has eroded as the state has ceded power to society. The nation itself, earlier shored up by memory, now appears as a mere memory trace. In contrast to theories of the nation discussed above, Nora thus sees the nation-state as declining in salience, the last incarnation of the unification of memory and history, a form in which history could provide the social cohesion memory no longer could. History too has now lost its temporary ability to transmit values with pedagogical authority (Wood 1994). All that is left, as Hutton (1993) characterizes Nora's project, is to autopsy the past, at best to celebrate its celebrations.

Many writers, however, note that older styles of memory persist in the interstices of modern historical consciousness, and they see in this coexistence an indictment of clear dichotomy between memory and history (Zonabend 1984), while others worry that such accounts are inappropriately teleological. Rappaport (1990), moreover, charges that the dichotomy between oral and written modes of memory serves a colonialist mentality that devalues non-Western forms of remembering. These critiques notwithstanding, it is clear that the situation of memory has changed rather dramatically both over the centuries and especially in the last few decades. Nora's approach raises as many questions as it answers: Given the scope of the cataloguing project, what is not a lieu de mémoire? Isn't the attempt to catalogue even what one recognizes as impoverished memory traces itself a political act of recuperation (Englund 1992)? Nonetheless, Nora's theory remains the most comprehensive empirical effort to confront the contemporary situation of memory. Where Yates suggests a history of memory, Nora takes it to a programmatic level.

Processes of Social Memory: Statics and Dynamics

The history of memory outlined above makes clear that memory is not an unchanging vessel for carrying the past into the present; memory is a process, not a thing, and it works differently at different points in time (Zelizer 1995). Sociologists of memory have thus sought to specify at a more middle level how memory processes operate within specific social institutions. Here the quintessential sociological issues of power, stratification, and contestation are central. One merit of Nora's project is that it reminds us of all the different places historical imagery and practices occur. Sociologists have long studied many of these sites and practices in an attempt to understand the statics and dynamics of social reproduction. Key terms here include identity, contestation, malleability, and persistence.

Identity

Erikson (1959) is usually credited with introducing the identity concept to describe psychological development over the life course: personal identity, despite periodic crises, is self-sameness over time. A recent narrative turn in identity theory, however, has warned against essentializing identities; instead, they are seen as ongoing processes of construction in narrative form (Bruner 1990, Calhoun 1994). As MacIntyre (1984, p. 218) puts it, "...all attempts to elucidate the notion of personal identity [and, by extension, group identity] independently of and in isolation from the notions of narrative... are bound to fail." As Hall writes, "Identities [personal or collective] are the names we give to the different ways we are positioned by, and position ourselves in, the narratives of the past" (Huyssen 1995, p. 1). Identities are projects and practices, not properties.

Many recent social theorists have extended the concept to the social level, noting, as MacIntyre does, that "The possession of an historical identity and the possession of a social identity coincide." As Hobsbawm (1972) writes, "To be a member of any human community is to situate oneself with regard to one's (its) past, if only by rejecting it." In a much-quoted formulation, Bellah and coauthors (1985, p. 153) write that "Communities... have a history—in an important sense are constituted by their past—and for this reason we can speak of a real community as a 'community of memory,' one that does not forget its past. In order not to forget that past, a community is involved in retelling its story, its constitutive narrative." "The temporal dimension of pastness," Wallerstein (1991, p. 78) adds, "is central and inherent in the concept of peoplehood."

A crucial link between the literatures on identity and memory concerns how we acquire our personal and social identities. Halbwachs paid particular attention to the role of the family in shaping how we construct the past; Zerubavel (1996) generalizes this insight by discussing what he calls "mnemonic socialization" into "mnemonic communities." "All subsequent interpretations of our early 'recollections,'" he writes, "are only reinterpretations of the way they were originally experienced and remembered within the context of our family." Much of what we "remember," moreover, we did not experience as individuals. "Indeed," Zerubavel writes, "being social presupposes the ability to experience events that happened to groups and communities to which we belong long before we joined them as if they were part of our own past...." This "sociobiographical memory" is the mechanism through which we feel pride, pain, or shame with regard to events that happened to our groups before we joined them.

Another central conceptual tool for analyzing this intersection between individual and collective identities as constituted through shared memories is that of generations. Mannheim's (1952 [1928]) seminal work here argues that social and political events shape generations through major shared experience during their formative years. It is not an accident that the notion of generations flowered in Europe after World War I. The war created a felt community of experience especially among the soldiers. Wohl (1979) refers to "the generation of 1914," whose members, following Mannheim's theory, were in the right place (total war) at the right time (when they were young men) to form a particularly clearly demarked generation. Schuman & Scott (1989) develop and test Mannheim's theories about the connections between generations and social memory by asking different age cohorts to rank various historical events in terms of their perceived importance. Striking response differences, they argue, demonstrate that generational differences in memory are strong, that adolescence and early adulthood are indeed the primary periods for "generational imprinting in the sense of political memories," and that later memories can best be understood in terms of earlier experiences. Shils (1981) points out that new generations define themselves against their elders and thus bear a different relation to the past than previous generations. Theorists of nationalism have pointed out (Smith 1986, Anderson 1991) that nationalist movements almost always centrally involve youth movements.

In the previous section, we saw that the nation-state, despite internal divisions along generational, regional, religious, and other lines, has often claimed to be the primary form of organizing social identity. But in the history of memory, this remains a broad epochal generalization. Sociologists have studied at a closer level how this aim to dominate identity manifests itself through collective mnemonic processes. Collective memory does not merely reflect past experiences (accurately or not); it has an orientational function (Schwartz 1996a). As Schwartz puts it, "collective memory is both a mirror and a lamp—a model of and a model for society" (personal communication).

National and other identities are established and maintained through a variety of mnemonic sites, practices, and forms. Spillman (1997), for instance, compares the role of centennial and bicentennial celebrations in Australia and the United States, demonstrating the different ways each of these countries used commemorations to address diverse issues. Hunt (1984) explores clothing, medals, language, and other symbolic forms as well, as markers of memory and identity. Cerulo (1995) examines national anthems, though she does not make the connection to social memory explicit. Schwartz (1990, 1991) and Goode (1978), not to mention the classical work of Thomas Carlyle (1901), examine the role of heroes in national identity. Coontz (1992) documents nostalgia for earlier "golden ages," as does Smith (1986), who notes the importance of origin myths in creating and maintaining identities. Zerubavel (1995) discusses national mythologies, and associated physical places, as ordering principles for articulations of national memory. Ferguson (1994), Boyer (1994), and Haydon (1995) examine the ways urban form embodies a vision of identity by inscribing the past. Muensterberger (1994) explores collecting as a mnemonic practice, while Bennett (1995) undertakes a history of the museum and of the world's fair as sites for articulating national identities. Rochberg-Halton (1986) studies the role of household objects in establishing the relations between memory and identity. Olick (1993, 1997) examines political speech as mnemonic practice. Dayan & Katz (1992) see the mass media as producing electronic monuments that compete with history writing to frame social memory; Lang & Lang (1989) examine the role of the news in forging collective memory. The literature on film and national memory is enormous.

There are many important case studies of the connections between memory and particular national identities, emphasizing both positive and negative aspects of those historical formations. Rousso (1991) and Maier (1988) study how France and Germany respectively confront their difficult legacies of World War II. Roniger (1997) and Nino (1996) look at how various countries in the Southern Cone, including Chile, Uruguay, and Argentina, confront the memory of human rights violations. Aguilar (1997) discusses the problematic legacy of the Spanish Civil War for subsequent regimes. Trouillot (1995) analyzes the complex memories of colonialism and contemporary struggles over historical identity in Haiti. Sturkin (1997) examines memories of Vietnam and of the AIDS epidemic in the United States as sites for working out national identity. Buruma (1994) compares Japanese and German memories of the Second World War. Gluck (1993) examines different epochs in Japanese memory. A special issue of the journal *Representations* edited by Greenblatt, Rev, and

Starn (1995) studies struggles in Eastern Europe with memory of pre-1989 events; a volume edited by Watson (1994) examines memory under state socialism; Tumarkin (1994) has written on the cult of World War II in Russia. Borneman (1997) analyzes how various central and eastern European countries have settled accounts after 1989 with their Communist pasts, as does Rosenberg (1995).

Herzfeld (1991) uses ethnography to analyze the complex negotiations between local and national memories in a Greek town, as does Confino (1997) for Wilhelmine Germany. Kammen (1991, 1978) is the preeminent analyst of American memory, documenting the changing forms of historical consciousness in American history; Thelen (1989) has edited an important volume on American memory. Mudimbe & Jewsiewicki (1993) explore history making in Africa, while Fabre & O'Meally (1994) explore the role of memory in African-American identity. Segev (1993) and Zerubavel (1995) present rich studies of memory in Israeli collective identity. Darian-Smith & Hamilton (1994) have edited a volume on Australian memory. A massive tome sponsored by the Holocaust Memorial Center (Wyman 1996) contains monographs on how 24 different nations reacted to the Holocaust, exploring how that event shaped national identities and vice versa. Rapaport (1997) and Irwin-Zarecka (1989) research how Jews in contemporary Germany and Poland, respectively, live in the lands of their former oppressors.

One particularly vibrant area of debate concerning the connection between memory and identity has been scholarship concerning heritage. The classic work in this field is Lowenthal's (1985) monumental *The Past Is a Foreign Country*, which documents the ways in which national pasts, particularly their built and geographical remains, are reshaped according to present interests. Heritage sites appear to be especially useful for dramatizing the historicity of the nation, particularly in Great Britain. Indeed, the heritage debate has been most heated in Britain, which possesses an elaborate physical legacy and which has a substantial history of propagating it. Barthel (1996) compares such debates in Great Britain and the United States, finding more democratic and inclusive versions in the United States and more elitist programs in the United Kingdom; Koshar (1994) studies such processes in West Germany. Wright (1985) has provided a detailed account of British debates and, along with Hewison (1987), criticizes the nostalgia "industry" for producing mindless, pacifying, and politically conservative commodifications of the national past. Samuel (1994), on the other hand, sees a redemptive potential in the heritage industry; to argue otherwise is to denigrate popular consciousness in the name of the people. Many others have documented the commercialization of nostalgia, particularly in the form of reconstructed villages, Disneyland versions of the American past, and souvenirs (Davis 1979). For an informative review of the literature on nostalgia, see Vromen (1993).

National identities, of course, are not the only ones available, but hegemonic forces within the nation-state have worked hard to appropriate and silence other identity discourses. As Alonso (1988) explains, "Historical chronologies solder a multiplicity of personal, local, and regional historicities and transform them into a unitary, national time." Almost all of the studies just mentioned, however, highlight not the simplicity or unity of national narratives, but the fact that they are essentially contested: Memory sites and memory practices are central loci for ongoing struggles over identity. As Sturkin (1997) puts it, "Cultural memory is a field of cultural negotiation through which different stories vie for a place in history." This sounds almost too benign and passive; people and groups fight hard for their stories. Contestation is clearly at the center of both memory and identity.

Contestation

Memory contestation takes place from above and below, from both center and periphery. The critical theorists of nationalism discussed above noticed that nation-states not only use history for their purposes, but make historiography into a nationalist enterprise. Indeed, Wilson et al (1996) document how national governments seek to control the very "sources" of professional historiography by limiting access to state archives. "The hegemony of modern nation-states," Alonso writes (1988), "and the legitimacy which accrues to the groups and classes that control their apparatuses, are critically constituted by representations of a national past." This is accomplished through the related strategies of naturalization, departicularization, and idealization. This means that history as a tool has until recently not been easily available to competing identities; as a result, other claimants often have not been very good competitors. As Foucault (1977) put it, "Since memory is actually a very important factor in struggle... if one controls people's memory, one controls their dynamism."

In order to resist the disciplinary power of nationalist historiography, Foucault articulated a notion of "counter-memory," referring to memories that differ from, and often challenge, dominant discourses. In a similar vein, many scholars in the past several decades have sought to redirect historical inquiry away from the nation-state as a unit of analysis in favor of groups and perspectives excluded from traditional accounts. Feminist historians, for instance, have sought to recover the repressed history of women that has been left out of "official" histories. Oral historians (Thompson 1988) see their enterprise as a way of giving "history back to the people in their own words:" It claims to be more democratic than other historiographical methodologies because it provides an alternative viewpoint from below, a viewpoint that conventional methodology disenfranchises. Feminists and oral historians, in fact, have often combined their efforts to recover the lost voices of ordinary women's experience (Leydesdorff et al 1996).

The dominance of national memory over other memories thus not only excludes other contestants for control over the national identity but maintains the primacy of national over other kinds of identity for primary allegiance. On the other hand, counter-memory approaches often employ a rather essentialist notion of authenticity: Counter-memory is sometimes seen as protected and separate from hegemonic forms. To resist this, the *Popular Memory Group* (Johnson et al 1982) and others employing the concept of popular memory (Lipsitz 1990, Wallace 1996) have sought to understand popular memory in terms of ongoing processes of contestation and resistance, a relatively free space of reading and reaction in which official and unofficial, public and private, interpenetrate. Dominant memory is not monolithic, nor is popular memory purely authentic. Some historians of gender argue that "focusing exclusively on the dominated makes a full understanding even of the origins and maintenance of their subordination impossible" (Leydesdorff et al 1996). "The intertwining of power and memory," these authors write, "is very subtle… when we as oral historians try to rescue and interpret these memories… we also inevitably transform their standing and character as memories."

Achieving mnemonic consensus is thus rarely easy, charged as it is with transcending the infinity of differences that constitute and are constituted by it. As Thelen (1989) puts it, "The struggle for possession and interpretation of memory is rooted in the conflict and interplay among social, political, and cultural interests…" "It is a product," Irwin-Zarecka (1994) writes, "of a great deal of work by large numbers of people." Many empirical studies have focused on these struggles, especially over the most public representations of the past to be found in monuments and museums. Wagner-Pacifici & Schwartz (1991), for instance, introduce a notion of cultural entrepreneurship in their study of the struggle for the Vietnam Veterans Memorial. The essays in Linenthal & Engelhardt (1996) document so-called history wars over a proposed Smithsonian exhibit on the bombing of Hiroshima. Savage (1994) characterizes American Civil War memorials as involving "systematic cultural repression, carried out in the guise of reconciliation and harmony." But as much as monumental form strives for permanence, Savage argues, "the cultural contest that monuments seem to settle need not end once they are built and dedicated": Even the most concrete presentations of the past are polysemic. Along these lines, Sandage (1993) showed how African-American civil rights groups appropriated the Lincoln Memorial as a site for articulating their claims.

Groups can also use images of the past and struggles over history as vehicles for establishing their power or, perversely, lack of power. Baker (1985) demonstrates how revolutionaries in eighteenth-century France used memory to achieve their movement aims. Bodnar (1992) shows how various ethnic groups in the 1920s used national holidays to articulate their versions of American identity and to claim a unique place in the cultural landscape. Takezawa (1995) documents the Japanese-American movement for redressing internment during World War II. De Oliver (1996) analyzes the struggle over containing alternative voices at the Alamo historic site. There are numerous other such studies of contestation and social movements demanding an inversion of some past or a new monumental interpretation.

Malleability and Persistence

Noticing the ways in which images of the past are the products of contestation has led varieties of both constructionists and deconstructionists to emphasize that the past is produced in the present and is thus malleable. A powerful line of so-called "presentism" runs through much of the sociological work on memory, work which documents the ways in which images of the past change over time, how groups use the past for present purposes, and that the past is a particularly useful resource for expressing interests. Within presentism, however, it is possible to emphasize either instrumental or meaning dimensions of memory: The former see memory entrepreneurship as a manipulation of the past for particular purposes where the latter see selective memory as an inevitable consequence of the fact that we interpret the world—including the past—on the basis of our own experience and within cultural frameworks. Hobsbawm & Ranger (1983) are paradigmatic examples of instrumental presentism, while Mead (1959 [1932]) and Mannheim (1956) manifest the latter variety; Halbwachs (1992) combines elements of both.

In response to the perceived ascendancy of presentism in social memory studies, a number of authors highlight limits on the malleability of the past. Schudson (1989, 1992), for instance, argues that "The past is in some respects, and under some conditions, highly resistant to efforts to make it over." Three factors, according to Schudson, limit our abilities to change the past: The structure of available pasts presents only some pasts and poses limits to the degree to which they can be changed, while placing other pasts beyond our perceptual reach; the structure of individual choice makes some pasts unavoidable and others impossible to face; and the structure of social conflict over the past means that we are not always the ones deciding which pasts to remember and which to forget. In his important study of Watergate in American memory as well, Schudson (1992) responds to the instrumentalist claim of infinite malleability by taking the limits on such manipulability into account.

In contrast, Schwartz (1991, 1996) responds to the cultural claim of malleability: Certain pasts, while somewhat malleable, are remarkably persistent over time. Schuman & Scott (1989) and Middleton & Edwards (1990) emphasize individual-level processes like generational experience and personal identities, while Schwartz and others look at institutional factors. Schwartz documents how certain meanings remain relevant over long periods of time despite superficial changes in the reading of those meanings as well as in their institutional contexts; certain pasts are constitutive elements of political cultures, and these endure as long as the political culture is not completely superseded. Even when radically new pasts emerge, they often superimpose themselves over older versions without eliminating them. As Shils (1981) sums up a more extreme version of this argument, "traditional patterns of belief and conduct... are very insistent; they will not wholly release their grip on those who would suspend or abolish them." Shils also emphasizes that the persistence of the past can be an explicit goal, as in self-conscious orthodoxies, thus mixing instrumentalist and culturalist positions.

A third aspect of memory persistence and malleability could be termed "inertial." Halbwachs discusses how memories become generalized over time into an "imago," a generalized memory trace. Conservatives see this kind of change in memory as decay and seek ways to recuperate the lost past. Shils (1981) and Assmann (1992), among others, discuss pasts that remain the same simply out of the force of habit. Connerton's (1989) focus on memory "incorporated" in bodily practices (as opposed to that "inscribed" in print, encyclopedias, indexes, etc) suggests this sort of inertia. Drawing on Elias's civilizing process and Bourdieu's work on consumption, he argues for a "mnemonics of the body."

Table 1 summarizes this discussion by identifying six ideal types of mnemonic malleability or persistence: 1. instrumental persistence—actors intentionally seek to maintain a particular version of the past, as in orthodoxy or movements to maintain or recover a past; 2. cultural persistence—a particular past perseveres because it remains relevant for later cultural formations (more general images are more likely to adapt to new contexts than more specific ones); 3. inertial persistence—a particular past occurs when we reproduce a version of the past by sheer force of habit; 4. instrumental change—we intentionally change an image of the past for particular reasons in the present (though we cannot always predict the results of our efforts); 5. cultural

Table 1

	Instrumental	Cultural	Inertial
Persistence	Self-conscious orthodoxy, conservatism, heritage movements	Continued relevance, canon	Habit, routine, repetition, custom
Change	Revisionism, memory entrepreneurship, redress movements, legitimation, invented tradition	Irrelevance, paradigm change, discovery of new facts	Decay, atrophy, saturation, accidental loss, death

change—a particular past no longer fits with present understandings or otherwise loses relevance for the present; and 6. inertial change—the carriers of particular images die, our mnemonic capabilities decay, or we simply forget.

One problem with instrumentalist and inertial accounts of change or persistence is that they locate the statics and dynamics of memory outside of the memories themselves. Even cultural approaches, while emphasizing meanings, seem to locate the source of change in political cultures, not in the textual dynamics of memory itself. To remedy this exogenous bias, Olick & Levy (1997) argue that whether a particular past persists or not depends partly on how it is constituted: Mythic logics produce taboos and duties while rational logics produce prohibitions and requirements; the former require bold acts of transgression to change them while the latter can be changed through argument and refutation. Olick (1997) also refines culturalist theories of mnemonic dynamics by pointing out that cultural persistence or change is not merely a matter of fit or lack of fit with context, nor of whether a particular memory is defensible as accurate or authentic: Memories form genres that unfold over time by referring not only to their contexts and to the "original" event, but to their own histories and memories as texts.

Reputations and Knowledge

Two empirical areas that have seen a great deal of work on the statics and dynamics of memory are reputation studies and the sociology of knowledge. While the sociology of reputation is not an entirely new field—biographies have always dealt with image—it concentrates in an unprecedented way on how individuals are remembered rather than how they lived. Often these studies begin by recognizing that reputations are only loosely correlated with lifetime achievements; not only talent, but social factors play a role in securing and maintaining the outstanding reputations of individuals.

Various authors, including especially Lang & Lang (1988) and Taylor (1996), appear to have converged on explanations in terms of four basic factors in reputational dynamics. First, personal strategizing and political maneuvering by the figure or his or her representatives can control the figure's image. Strategies include seclusion, autobiography, flamboyance, forging relations with patrons, etc. Lang & Lang (1988) note that in order to catch the eyes of dealers, collectors, curators, and art historians, artists have to produce a critical mass of work, keep adequate records to guarantee proper attribution, and make arrangements for custodianship. Institutional practices like record-keeping also favor some kinds of reputation for preservation over others.

Second, image is influenced by those with a stake in a particular reputation. Latour (1988), for instance, argues that Pasteur's reputation spread as doctors and hygienists aligned themselves with the scientist's cause to promote their own professional interests. De Nora (1995) shows how Beethoven benefited from admiration by an aristocratic musical public that was pivotal in shaping the narrative of his genius. Schudson (1990) reveals how Ronald Reagan's popularity was constructed by an oral political culture in Washington, DC. Donoghue (1996) argues that in the eighteenth-century literary market, it was reviewers, and not the authors themselves, who were chiefly responsible for creating narratives of literary careers.

Third, the impact of cultural factors on reputation is theorized in two distinct ways. For those who view cultural patterns as distinct from talent, culture works to boost some reputations at the expense of others as a matter of happenstance. Lang & Lang (1990), for instance, discuss the influence of ideology on reputation, noting that artists' achievements are refracted "through their availability as a symbolic form for a variety of sentiments that may have nothing to do directly with art." In a different approach, cultural theorists (Bourdieu 1984) who focus on the constructed nature of taste show how reputations depend on struggles for prestige and position that employ culture as a tool and as markers. De Nora (1995, p. 180), for instance, details how Beethoven's promotion of a sturdier piano helped create new aesthetic categories within which his music "could make sense and be positively evaluated." Reviews of Beethoven's work became more favorable as personal idiosyncrasies and creativity came to be valued in the music-critical discourse as a "higher" form of music. Similarly, Tuchman & Fortin (1984) show how women were "edged out" of the literary field: As men entered the field, the novel rose to high-culture status while the themes and styles of women's writing were demoted to popular culture. Zelizer (1992) shows how professional journalists used the Kennedy assassination and their eulogies of him to advance their own authoritative status.

A fourth line of work on reputation shows how reputations respond to broader narrative and cultural forms. We have a tendency, theorists of reputation argue, to exaggerate both greatness and evil. One of the earliest reputation studies (Connelly 1977), for instance, demonstrates how the figure of Robert E. Lee was invested with extraordinary import because, across many years, his image acted as a palimpsest on which contemporary concerns could be written and rewritten. Schwartz (1990) documents how Lincoln's image changed from one of simple accessibility to that of a "remote and dignified personage." Schwartz (1991) also shows how Washington's reputational malleability is tied up with the changing needs of different periods in American history, while maintaining a common core of continuity. In his now classic study, Pelikan (1985) shows how the varying representation of Jesus reflected particular preoccupations of different societies in different periods.

From the other side, Ducharme & Fine (1995) show how villains—in their case, Benedict Arnold—are remembered in much worse light than their deeds might warrant; Johnson (1995) discusses the rehabilitation of Richard Nixon. Additionally, Taylor (1996, p. 261) notes that "we are particularly prone to remember stimuli associated with major changes in a niche." It helps one's reputation, Latour (1988) argues, to be associated with the dawn of a new era in a particular field. Others have carried this line of argument even further, arguing that the very possibility of distinctive reputations is tied up with the career of the genius notion in the culture at large. Heinich (1996), for instance, inquires into the history of the category of talent in her study of *The Glory of Van Gogh*, as does Gamson (1994) in his study of the category of celebrity in American culture.

Another empirical field where sociologists have studied the dynamics of memory is the sociology of science and knowledge. Research on scientific knowledge is concerned largely with the problem of forgetting, while investigations of canon formation ask why particular kinds of knowledge are remembered. Kuhn (1962) argues that knowledge depends on paradigmatic conventions: Normal science within paradigms cumulates, but knowledge in different (later) paradigms is incommensurable. Gans (1992) argues, however, that even within paradigms knowledge does not cumulate: Younger researchers repeat findings already reported by earlier practitioners. Gans labels this process "sociological amnesia" and attributes it to institutional factors including academia's reward structure, myths of scientific progress, and the lack of mechanisms for punishing unintentional borrowers. Gans is aware that Sorokin (1956) had already made the same point. Merton (1973) also documented how scientists tend to forget the origins of their ideas: Scientists are committed to an ideology of original discovery, "which is embedded in all the forms of institutional life, along with prizes and naming of plants, animals, measurements, and even diseases after scientists." Good ideas, moreover, are the products of climates of opinion; it is thus often pointless to ask who said something first, as Merton demonstrates in his study of the expression, "on the shoulders of giants" (1985 [1965]).

Some works, figures, and ideas, however, tend to be singled out and preserved as particularly important. Just as for reputation, one important factor is how closely associated with a major rupture a work or idea is, in Kuhn's terms, how close to a paradigm shift. As Levine (1995) notes, moreover, disciplines have collective memories that establish and maintain their identities. Douglas (1986) argues that a theory is more likely to be remembered if it shares basic formulae, equations, and rules of thumb with theories in other fields: "On the principle of cognitive coherence, a theory that is going to gain a permanent place in the public repertoire of what is known will need to interlock with other kinds of theories." Tuchman & Fortin (1984), as already noted, show that these processes can be political: Ideas propagated by powerful groups and for powerful purposes are more likely to be remembered than others. Taylor (1996), among many others, documents the underlying political function of canons as well.

Efforts to revise established knowledge orthodoxies can be tied up with overt political constellations and purposes as well. In the past decade, there has been a proliferation of "historians' disputes," public debates about both the content and meaning of history in several nations, including Germany (Maier 1988), France (Kaplan 1995), and Israel (Ram 1995). The rise of interest in memory, the challenges to the distinction between history and memory, and the status of memory in postmodern society reviewed in this essay are part of the explanation for these debates. It is interesting to note that the term "revisionism" is of relatively recent vintage (Novick 1988); revisionism now is taken to refer to those who deny taken-for-granted truths—like the occurrence of a German genocide of Jews in the 1940s—though it originally meant any attempt to challenge commonly held beliefs about the past, including the "normal" growth of scientific knowledge. Studies of more extreme revisionisms (Lipstadt 1993, Vidal-Naquet 1992) document both that history can serve as a surrogate in more general political struggles as well as that particular images of the past have symbolic import that extends beyond questions of their truth.

Future Directions

The field of social memory studies is clearly vast, the forms of memory work diverse. It should be clear, however, that similar themes occur in different disciplinary, substantive, and geographic areas. Given the epochal character of memory demonstrated by the history of memory, this should not be surprising. As Valéry put it in our epigraph, the time is past in which time did not matter; we experience this condition as a problem of memory. In recent times, the solution has been to designate sites to stand in for lost authenticity, to proliferate new narratives when the old ones no longer satisfy, and to abbreviate—as here—in face of insurmountable accumulation. Social memory studies are therefore part of the phenomenon they seek to explain. But the explanation, we have tried to show, need not be relentlessly particular: The enterprise does have clear lineages just as the phenomenon has general contours, and explanations of the various processes are transposable across cases (e.g. Germany and the United States) and across issues (e.g. reputation, monuments, and knowledge).

We conclude by pointing to four areas that emerge in social memory studies as possible future directions. First, social memory studies clearly fit with the widespread interest in identity in recent social and sociological discourse. Memory is a central, if not the central, medium through which identities are constituted. Inquiries into identity and memory are being related; these research programs, we hope, will illuminate further how, when, and why individuals and groups turn toward their pasts.

Interestingly, both fields have attacked the tendency to reify their foundational concepts; both identity and memory, we now recognize, are ongoing processes, not possessions or properties. This leads directly to our second point: Many sociologists (McDonald 1996) have recently argued that the basic categories of sociological analysis reify temporality. These critiques call for a "processual" or "narrative" approach to social processes, arguing that sociological strategies for approaching the past have heretofore been ahistorical. Appreciating the changing history of mnemonic practices as well as the ways in which these changing practices are the media of temporal experience can and should play a role in this search for a more genuinely historical sociology.

A third point is more practical. As the belief that history and memory are epistemologically and ontologically distinct has eroded and as competing pasts and historical legitimacy claims have proliferated, the ability to settle conflicts over how to represent the past has also diminished. We have certainly gotten better at deconstructing identitarian mythology, but this has left us with a not-always-productive cacophony of claims vying for dominance. While the recent period of inquiry into the history and dynamics of social memory seems to have fed this deconstructive mood (and vice versa), we hope that further research will help us resolve some of the conflicts or at least manage them better.

Our fourth point is connected to this: Until now, it seems that macrosociological theories of modernity and postmodernity have done well at explaining memory as a dependent variable. But social memory is largely absent from our grandest theories. The diverse memory practices reviewed here are not merely symptoms of modernity and postmodernity—they are modernity and postmodernity. Sociological theorists, we argue, thus have a great deal to learn from theorists like Nora, Huyssen, and Koselleck. Recent work by Giddens (1990, 1994) has moved in this direction. More studies of the way memory practices are central features of modern and postmodern life and more theories of these epochal forms with memory at their heart should follow. In sum, all four of these points demonstrate that social memory studies is not a narrow subfield; it provides powerful lessons for sociology as a whole, is consonant with the reformation of historical sociology now occurring, and provides important insights for theory at the broadest level. Sociology, we argue, cannot afford to forget memory.

Acknowledgments

Work on this paper was partially supported by a Council Grant for Research in the Humanities and Social Sciences, Columbia University. The authors thank Priscilla Ferguson, Herbert Gans, Daniel Levy, Michael Schudson, and particularly Barry Schwartz for comments on an earlier draft of this essay.

Literature Cited

Adorno T. 1967. Valéry Proust Museum. In *Prisms*. Transl. S Weber, pp. 173–86. Cambridge, MA: MIT Press

Aguilar P. 1997. Collective Memory of the Spanish Civil War: The Case of the Political Amnesty in the Spanish Transition to Democracy. *Democratization* 4(4) (Winter):88–109.

Agulhon M. 1981. *Marianne into Battle: Republican Imagery and Symbolism in France, 1789–1880*. Transl. J Lloyd. Cambridge, UK: Cambridge Univ. Press

Alonso AM. 1988. The effects of truth: representation of the past and the imagining of community. *J. Hist. Soc.* 1:33–57

Anderson B. 1991. *Imagined Communities: Reflections on the Origin and Spread of Nationalism*. New York: Verso. 2nd ed.

Ariès P. 1974. *Western Attitudes Toward Death from the Middle Ages to the Present*. Baltimore, MD: Johns Hopkins Univ. Press

Assmann J. 1992. *Das kulterelle Gedaechtnis: Schrift, Erinnerung und politische Identitaet in fruehen Hochkulturen*. Munich: CH Beck

Baker KM. 1985. Memory and practice: politics and the representation of the past in eighteenth-century France. *Representations* 11:134–64

Bakhurst D. 1990. Social memory in Soviet thought. See Middleton & Edwards 1990, pp. 203–26

Balibar E, Wallerstein I. 1991. *Race, Nation, Class: Ambiguous Identities*. Transl. C Turner. London: Verso

Barthel DL. 1996. *Historic Preservation: Collective Memory and Historical Identity*. New Brunswick, NJ: Rutgers Univ. Press

Bartlett FC. 1932. *Remembering: A Study in Experimental and Social Psychology*. Cambridge, UK: Cambridge Univ. Press

Bellah RN, Madsen R, Sullivan W, Swidler A, Tipton SM. 1985. *Habits of the Heart: Individualism and Commitment in American Life*. Berkeley: Univ. Calif. Press

Benjamin W. 1968. The storyteller. In *Illuminations*. Transl. H Zohn, pp. 83–109. New York: Schocken

Bennett T. 1995. *The Birth of the Museum: History, Theory, Politics*. New York: Routledge

Berger PL, Luckmann T. 1966. *The Social Construction of Reality: A Treatise in the Sociology of Knowledge*. New York: Doubleday

Berman M. 1982. *All That Is Solid Melts Into Air: The Experience of Modernity*. New York: Penguin

Bhabha HK, ed. 1990. *Nation and Narration*. London: Routledge

Bloch M. 1925. Mémoire collective, tradition, et coutume: a propos dans livre. *Rev. Synth.* 40:

Bloch M. 1974. (1939). *Feudal Society*. Transl. LA Manyon. Chicago: Univ. Chicago Press

Bodnar J. 1992. *Remaking America: Public Memory, Commemoration, and Patriotism in the Twentieth Century*. Princeton, NJ: Princeton Univ. Press

Borneman J. 1997. *Settling Accounts: Violence, Justice, and Accountability in Postsocialist Europe*. Princeton: Princeton Univ. Press

Bosworth RJB. 1993. *Explaining Auschwitz and Hiroshima: History Writing and the Second World War, 1945–1990*. New York: Routledge

Bourdieu P. 1984. *Distinction*. Transl. R Nice, 1979. Cambridge, MA: Harvard Univ. Press

Boyarin J, ed. 1994. *Remapping Memory: The Politics of TimeSpace*. Minneapolis, MN: Univ. Minn. Press

Boyer MC. 1994. *The City of Collective Memory: Its Historical Imagery and Architectural Entertainments*. Cambridge, MA: MIT Press

Breisbach E. 1994. *Historiography: Ancient, Medieval, and Modern*. Chicago: Univ. Chicago Press. 2nd ed.

Bruner JS. 1990. *Acts of Meaning*. Cambridge, MA: Harvard Univ. Press

Buck-Morss S. 1989. *The Dialectics of Seeing: Walter Benjamin and the Arcades Project*. Cambridge, MA: MIT Press

Burke P. 1989. History as social memory. In *Memory: History, Culture and the Mind*, ed. T Butler, pp. 97–113. New York: Blackwell

Buruma I. 1994. *The Wages of Guilt: Memories of War in Germany and Japan*. New York: Farrar, Straus, Giroux

Butterfield H. 1965. (1931). *The Whig Interpretation of History*. New York: Norton

Calhoun C. 1994. Social theory and the politics of identity. In *Social Theory and the Politics of Identity*, ed. C Calhoun, pp. 9–36. Cambridge, MA: Blackwell

Carlyle T. 1901. *On Heroes, Hero-Worship, and the Heroic in History*. New York: Scribner's

Carruthers M. 1990. *The Book of Memory: A Study of Memory in Medieval Culture*. Cambridge, UK: Cambridge Univ. Press

Casey E. 1987. *Remembering: A Phenomenol-*

ogical Study. Bloomington: Indiana Univ. Press

Cerulo KA. 1995. *Identity Designs: The Sights and Sounds of a Nation*. New Brunswick: Rutgers Univ. Press

Coleman J. 1992. *Ancient and Medieval Memories: Studies in the Reconstruction of the Past*. Cambridge, UK: Cambridge Univ. Press

Confino A. 1997. *The Nation as a Local Metaphor: W'fcrtemberg, Imperial Germany, and National Memory, 1871-1918*. Chapel Hill, NC: Univ. N. Carolina Press

Connelly T. 1977. *The Marble Man: Robert E. Lee and His Image in American Society*. New York: Knopf

Connerton P. 1989. *How Societies Remember*. New York: Cambridge Univ. Press

Cooley CH. 1918. *Social Process*. New York: Scribner's

Coontz S. 1992. *The Way We Never Were: American Families and the Nostalgia Trap*. New York: Basic Books

Coser L. 1992. Introduction: Maurice Halbwachs 1877–1945. See Halbwachs 1992, pp. 1–34

Crane D, ed. 1994. *The Sociology of Culture: Emerging Theoretical Perspectives*. Oxford: Blackwell

Cressy D. 1989. *Bonfires and Bells: National Memory and the Protestant Calendar in Elizabethan and Stuart England*. Berkeley: Univ. Calif. Press

Darian-Smith K, Hamilton P, eds. 1994. *Memory and History in Twentieth-Century Australia*. Melbourne: Oxford Univ. Press

Davis F. 1979. *Yearning for Yesterday: A Sociology of Nostalgia*. New York: Free Press

Dayan D, Katz E. 1992. *Media Events: The Live Broadcasting of History*. Cambridge, MA: Harvard Univ. Press

De Nora T. 1995. *Beethoven and the Construction of Genius: Musical Politics in Vienna, 1792–1803*. Berkeley: Univ. Calif. Press

de Oliver M. 1996. Historical preservation and identity: the Alamo and the production of a consumer landscape. *Antipode* 28(1): 1–23

Donoghue F. 1996. *The Fame Machine: Book Reviewing and Eighteenth-Century Literary Careers*. Stanford, CA: Stanford Univ. Press

Douglas M. 1986. *How Institutions Think*. Syracuse, NY: Syracuse Univ. Press

Duara P. 1995. *Rescuing History from the Nation: Questioning Narratives of Modern China*. Chicago: Univ. Chicago Press

Ducharme LJ, Fine GA. 1995. The construction of nonpersonhood and demonization: commemorating the traitorous reputation of Benedict Arnold. *Soc. Forces* 73(4): 1309–31

Durkheim E. 1961. (1915). *The Elementary Forms of the Religious Life*. Transl. JW Swain. New York: Collier Books

Englund S. 1992. The ghost of nation past. *J. Mod. Hist.* 64(June):299–320

Erikson E. 1959. *Identity and the Life Cycle*. New York: Norton

Evans RJ. 1989. *In Hitler's Shadow: West German Historians and the Attempt to Escape from the Nazi Past*. New York: Pantheon

Evans-Pritchard EE. 1940. *The Nuer: A Description of the Modes of Livelihood and Political Institutions of a Nilotic People*. Oxford: Clarendon

Fabre G, O'Meally R, eds. 1994. *History and Memory in African-American Culture*. New York: Oxford Univ. Press

Fentress J, Wickham C. 1992. *Social Memory*. Oxford, UK: Blackwell

Ferguson PP. 1994. *Paris as Revolution: Writing the 19th-Century City*. Berkeley: Univ. Calif. Press

Foucault M. 1977. *Language, Counter-Memory, Practice: Selected Essays and Interviews*. Transl. DF Bouchard, S Simon. Ithaca, NY: Cornell Univ. Press

Friedlander S, ed. 1992. *Probing the Limits of Representation: Nazism and the "Final Solution."* Cambridge, MA: Harvard Univ. Press

Fussell P. 1975. *The Great War and Modern Memory*. New York: Oxford Univ. Press

Gamson J. 1994. *Claims to Fame: Celebrity in Contemporary America*. Berkeley: Univ. Calif. Press

Gans HJ. 1992. Sociological amnesia: the noncumulation of normal social science. *Sociol. Forum* 7(4):701–10

Geary PJ. 1994. *Phantoms of Remembrance: Memory and Oblivion at the End of the First Millennium*. Princeton, NJ: Princeton Univ. Press

Gedi N, Elam Y. 1996. Collective memory—What is it? *Hist. Mem.* 8(2):30–50

Giddens A. 1990. *The Consequences of Modernity*. Stanford, CA: Stanford Univ. Press

Giddens A. 1994. Living in a post-traditional society. In *Reflexive Modernization: Politics, Tradition and Aesthetics in the Modern Social Order,* ed. U Beck, A Giddens, S Lash, pp. 56–109. Stanford, CA: Stanford Univ. Press

Gillis JR, ed. 1994. *Commemorations: The Politics of National Identity*. Princeton, NJ: Princeton Univ. Press

Gluck G. 1993. The past in the present. In *Postwar Japan as History,* ed. A Gordon, pp. 64–95. Berkeley: Univ. Calif. Press

Goode W. 1978. *The Celebration of Heroes:*

Prestige as a Social Control System. Berkeley: Univ. Calif. Press

Goody J. 1986. *The Logic of Writing and the Organization of Society*. New York: Cambridge Univ. Press

Greenblatt S, Rev I, Starn R. 1995. Introduction. *Representations* 49(Winter):1–14

Halbwachs M. 1992. *On Collective Memory*. Transl./ed. LA Coser. Chicago: Univ. Chicago Press

Haydon D. 1995. *The Power of Place: Urban Landscape as Public History*. Cambridge, MA: MIT Press

Heinich N. 1996. *The Glory of Van Gogh: An Anthropology of Admiration*. Transl. PL Browne. Princeton, NJ: Princeton Univ. Press

Herzfeld M. 1991. *A Place in History: Social and Monumental Time in a Cretan Town*. Princeton, NJ: Princeton Univ. Press

Hewison R. 1987. *The Heritage Industry: Britain in a Climate of Decline*. London: Methuen

Hobsbawm E. 1983. Mass-producing traditions: Europe 1870–1914. See Hobsbawm & Ranger 1983, pp. 203–307

Hobsbawm E, Ranger T, eds. 1983. *The Invention of Tradition*. New York: Cambridge Univ. Press

Hobsbawm EJ. 1972. The social function of the past: some questions. *Past Present* 55: 3–17

Hunt L. 1984. *Politics, Culture, and Class in the French Revolution*. Berkeley: Univ. Calif. Press

Hutton P. 1993. *History as an Art of Memory*. Hanover, NH: Univ. Press New Engl.

Huyssen A. 1995. *Twilight Memories: Marking Time in a Culture of Amnesia*. New York: Routledge

Iggers GC. 1997. *Historiography in the Twentieth Century: From Scientific Objectivity to the Postmodern Challenge*. Hanover, NH: Univ. Press N. Engl.

Irwin-Zarecka I. 1989. *Neutralizing Memory: The Jew in Contemporary Poland*. New Brunswick, NJ: Transaction Books

Irwin-Zarecka I. 1994. *Frames of Remembrance: The Dynamics of Collective Memory*. New Brunswick, NJ: Transaction Books

Jacoby R. 1975. *Social Amnesia: A Critique of Conformist Psychology From Adler to Laing*. Boston: Beacon

Johnson R, McLennan G, Schwarz B, Sutton D, eds. 1982. *Making Histories: Studies in History-Writing and Politics*. London: Cent. Contemp. Cult. Stud.

Kammen M. 1978. *A Season of Youth: The American Revolution and the Historical Imagination*. New York: Knopf

Kammen M. 1991. *Mystic Chords of Memory: The Transformations of Tradition in American Culture*. New York: Knopf

Kammen M. 1995. Review of *Frames of Remembrance: The Dynamics of Collective Memory,* by I Irwin-Zarecka. *Hist. Theory* 34(3)(Oct.):245–61

Kaplan SL. 1995. *Farewell, Revolution: Disputed Legacies, France, 1789/1989*. Ithaca, NY: Cornell Univ. Press

Koonz C. 1994. Between memory and oblivion: concentration camps in German memory. See Gillis 1994, pp. 258–80

Koselleck R. 1985. *Futures Past: On the Semantics of Historical Time*. Transl. K Tribe. Cambridge, MA: MIT Press

Koshar R. 1994. Building pasts: historic preservation and identity in twentieth-century Germany. See Gillis 1994, pp. 215–38

Kuhn TS. 1962. *The Structure of Scientific Revolutions*. Chicago: Univ. Chicago Press

Lang GE, Lang KL. 1989. Collective memory and the news. *Communication* 11:123–40

Lang GE, Lang KL. 1990. *Etched in Memory: The Building and Survival of Artistic Reputation*. Chapel Hill: Univ. NC Press

Lang GE, Lang KL. 1988. Recognition and renown: the survival of artistic reputation. *Am. J. Sociol.* 94(1):78–109

Latour B. 1988. *The Pasteurization of France*. Transl. A Sheridan, J Law. Cambridge, MA: Harvard Univ. Press

Le Goff J. 1992. *History and Memory*. New York: Columbia Univ. Press

Leroi-Gourhan A. 1993. (1964–1965). *Gesture and Speech*. Transl. AB Berger. Cambridge, MA: MIT Press

Levine D. 1995. *Visions of the Sociological Tradition*. Chicago: Univ. Chicago Press

Lévi-Strauss C. 1979. *Myth and Meaning*. New York: Schocken

Leydesdorff S, Passerini L, Thompson P. 1996. *Gender and Memory*. Oxford, UK: Oxford Univ. Press

Linenthal ET, Engelhardt T, eds. 1996. *History Wars: The Enola Gay and Other Battles for the American Past*. New York: Holt

Lipsitz G. 1990. *Time Passages: Collective Memory and American Popular Culture*. Minneapolis: Univ. Minn. Press

Lipstadt DE. 1993. *Denying the Holocaust: The Growing Assault on Truth and Memory*. New York: Free Press

Lowenthal D. 1985. *The Past Is a Foreign Country*. New York: Cambridge Univ. Press

MacIntyre AC. 1984. *After Virtue: A Study in Moral Theory*. Notre Dame, IN: Univ. Notre Dame Press

Maier CS. 1988. *The Unmasterable Past: History, Holocaust, and German National Identity*. Cambridge, MA: Harvard Univ. Press

Maines DR, Sugrue NM, Katovich M. 1983. The sociological import of G. H. Mead's theory of the past. *Am. Sociol. Rev.* 48(Apr):161–73

Mannheim K. 1952. (1928). The problem of generations. In *Essays in the Sociology of Culture*, pp. 276–322. London: Routledge & Kegan Paul

Marx K. 1992. (1852). The Eighteenth Brumaire of Louis Bonaparte. In *Surveys From Exile: Political Writings,* 2:143–249. London: Penguin

Matsuda MK. 1996. *The Memory of the Modern*. New York: Oxford Univ. Press

McDonald J, ed. 1996. *The Historic Turn in the Human Sciences*. Ann Arbor: Univ. Mich. Press

Mead GH. 1959. (1932). *The Philosophy of the Present.* La Salle, IL: Open Court

Merton RK. 1973. *The Sociology of Science: Theoretical and Empirical Investigations.* Chicago: Univ. Chicago Press

Merton RK. 1985. (1965). *On the Shoulders of Giants: A Shandean Postscript.* New York: Harcourt Brace Jovanovich

Middleton D, Edwards D, eds. 1990. *Collective Remembering.* Newbury Park, CA: Sage

Miller J. 1990. *One, by One, by One: Facing the Holocaust.* New York: Simon & Schuster

Mosse GL. 1990. *Fallen Soldiers: Reshaping the Memory of the World Wars.* New York: Oxford Univ. Press

Mudimbe VY, Jewsiewicki B, eds. 1993. *History Making in Africa. Hist. Theory* 32. (Entire issue)

Muensterberger W. 1994. *Collecting: An Unruly Passion*. Princeton, NJ: Princeton Univ. Press

Neisser U. 1982. *Memory Observed: Remembering in Natural Contexts*. New York: Freeman

Nietzsche FW. 1983. *Untimely Meditations*. Transl. RJ Hollingdale. Cambridge, MA: Cambridge Univ. Press

Nino CS. 1996. *Radical Evil on Trial*. New Haven: Yale Univ. Press

Noiriel G. 1996. *The French Melting Pot: Immigration, Citizenship, and National Identity*. Transl. G de Laforcade. Minneapolis: Univ. Minn. Press

Nora P, ed. 1992. *Les Lieux de mémoire*, Vol. 7. Paris: Les Frances, La Republique, Le Nation. 7 Vols.

Novick P. 1988. *That Noble Dream: The "Objectivity Question" and the American Historical Profession*. Cambridge, UK: Cambridge Univ. Press

Olick JK. 1993. *The sins of the fathers: the Third Reich and West German legitimation*. PhD thesis. New Haven: Yale Univ. Press

Olick JK. 1997. *The textual dynamics of memory: continuities and departures in German commemoration of May 8, 1945*. Presented at the Annu. Meet. Am. Sociol. Assoc., Toronto

Olick JK, Levy D. 1997. Collective memory and cultural constraint: Holocaust myth and rationality in German politics. *Am. Sociol. Rev.* 62(6):921–36

Ortner S. 1984. Theory in anthropology since the sixties. *Comp. Stud. Soc. Hist.* 26: 126–66

Pelikan J. 1985. *Jesus Through the Centuries: His Place in the History of Culture*. New Haven: Yale Univ. Press

Pennebaker JW, Paez D, Rimé B. 1997. *Collective Memory of Political Events: Social Psychological Perspectives*. Mahwah, NJ: Erlbaum

Ram U. 1995. Zionist historiography and the invention of modern Jewish nationhood: the case of Ben Zion Dinur. *Hist. Mem.* 7(1)(Spring-Summer):91–124

Rapaport J. 1990. *The Politics of Memory: Native Historical Interpretation in the Colombian Andes*. Cambridge, UK: Cambridge Univ. Press

Rapaport L. 1997. *Jews in Germany after the Holocaust: Memory, Identity, and Jewish-German Relations*. New York: Cambridge Univ. Press

Reichel P. 1995. *Politik mit der Erinnerung*. Munich: Carl Hanser Verlag

Rochberg-Halton E. 1986. *Meaning and Modernity: Social Theory in the Pragmatic Attitude*. Chicago: Univ. Chicago Press

Roniger L. 1997. Human rights violations and the reshaping of collective identities in Argentina, Chile, and Uruguay. *Soc. Identities.* Forthcoming

Rosenberg T. 1995. *The Haunted Landscape: Facing Europe '92s Ghosts after Communism*. New York: Random House

Rousso H. 1991. *The Vichy Syndrome: History and Memory in France Since 1944*. Transl. A Goldhammer. Cambridge, MA: Harvard Univ. Press

Samuel R. 1994. *Theatres of Memory.* Vol. 1. *Past and Present in Contemporary Culture.* London: Verso

Sandage S. 1993. A marble house divided: the Lincoln Memorial, the Civil Rights Movement, and the politics of memory, 1939–1963. *J. Am. Hist.* 80(1):135–67

Savage K. 1994. The politics of memory:

Black emancipation and the Civil War monument. See Gillis 1994, pp. 127–49

Schachter D, ed. 1995. *Memory Distortion: How Minds, Brains, and Societies Reconstruct the Past*. Cambridge, MA: Harvard Univ. Press

Schieder T. 1978. The role of historical consciousness in political action. *Hist. Theory* 17:1–18

Schudson M. 1989. The present in the past versus the past in the present. *Communication* 11:105–13

Schudson M. 1990. Ronald Reagan misremembered. See Middleton & Edwards 1990, pp. 108–19

Schudson M. 1992. *Watergate in American Memory: How We Remember, Forget, and Reconstruct the Past*. New York: Basic Books

Schuman H, Scott J. 1989. Generations and collective memory. *Am. Sociol. Rev.* 54: 359–81

Schwartz B. 1996a. Memory as a Cultural System: Abraham Lincoln in World War II. *Am. Sociol. R.* 61(5) (Oct):908–27

Schwartz B. 1990. The reconstruction of Abraham Lincoln. See Middleton & Edwards 1990, pp. 81–107

Schwartz B. 1991. Social change and collective memory: the democratization of George Washington. *Am. Sociol. Rev.* 56(April):221–36

Schwartz B. 1996. Introduction: the expanding past. *Qual. Sociol.* 9(3)(Fall):275–82

Schwartz B. 1997. *Post-modernity and the erosion of historical reputation: Abraham Lincoln in the late twentieth century*. Presented at Annu. Meet. Am. Sociol. Assoc., Toronto

Segev T. 1993. *The Seventh Million: The Israelis and the Holocaust*. Transl. H Watzman. New York: Hill & Wang

Shils E. 1981. *Tradition*. Chicago: Univ. Chicago Press

Simmel G. 1959. The ruin. In *Georg Simmel 1858–1918,* ed. K Wolff, pp. 259–66. Columbus: Ohio State Univ. Press

Smith AD. 1986. *The Ethnic Origins of Nations*. Oxford: Blackwell

Sorokin PA. 1956. *Fads and Foibles in Modern Sociology and Related Sciences*. Chicago: Henry Regnery

Spillman LP. 1997. *Nation and Commemoration: Creating National Identities in the United States and Australia*. New York: Cambridge Univ. Press

Sturkin M. 1997. *Tangled Memories: The Vietnam War, The Aids Epidemic, and the Politics of Remembering*. Berkeley: Univ. Calif. Press

Swidler A, Arditi J. 1994. The new sociology of knowledge. *Annu. Rev. Sociol.* 20: 305–29

Takezawa YI. 1995. *Breaking the Silence: Redress and Japanese-American Ethnicity*. Ithaca, NY: Cornell Univ. Press

Taylor G. 1996. *Cultural Selection*. New York: Basic Books

Terdiman R. 1993. *Present Past: Modernity and the Memory Crisis*. Ithaca: Cornell Univ. Press

Thelen D, ed. 1989. *Memory and American History*. Bloomington: Indiana Univ. Press

Thompson JB. 1995. *The Media and Modernity: A Social Theory of the Media*. Cambridge, UK: Polity

Thompson P. 1988. *The Voice of the Past: Oral History*. Oxford, UK: Oxford Univ. Press. 2nd ed.

Trouillot MR. 1995. *Silencing the Past: Power and the Production of History*. Boston: Beacon

Tuchman G, Fortin NE. 1984. Fame and misfortune: edging women out of the great literary tradition. *Am. J. Sociol.* 90(1):72–96

Tumarkin N. 1994. *The Living and the Dead: The Rise and Fall of the Cult of World War II in Russia*. New York: Basic Books

Veyne P. 1984. *Writing History: Essay on Epistemology*. Transl. M Moore-Rinvolucri. Middletown, CT: Wesleyan Univ. Press

Vidal-Naquet P. 1992. *Assassins of Memory: Essays on the Denial of the Holocaust*. Transl. J Mehlman. New York: Columbia Univ. Press

Vromen S. 1993. The ambiguity of nostalgia. *YIVO Annu.* 21:69–86

Wagner-Pacifici R. 1996. Memories in the making: the shapes of things that went. *Qual. Sociol.* 19(3):301–22

Wagner-Pacifici R, Schwartz B. 1991. The Vietnam Veterans Memorial: commemorating a difficult past. *Am. J. Sociol.* 97(2): 376–420

Wallace M. 1996. *Mickey Mouse History and Other Essays on American Memory*. Philadelphia, PA: Temple Univ. Press

Wallerstein I. 1991. The construction of peoplehood: racism, nationalism, ethnicity. See Balibar & Wallerstein 1991

Warner WL. 1959. *The Living and the Dead: A Study of the Symbolic Life of Americans*. New Haven, CT: Yale Univ. Press

Watson RS, ed. 1994. *Memory, History, and Opposition Under State Socialism*. Santa Fe, NM: Sch. Am. Res. Press

Weber M. 1946. Science as a vocation. In *From Max Weber: Essays in Sociology*. Transl. HH Gerth, CW Mills. New York: Oxford Univ. Press

White H. 1973. *Metahistory: The Historical*

Imagination in Nineteenth-Century Europe. Baltimore, MD: Johns Hopkins Univ. Press

Wilson K, ed. 1996. *Forging the Collective Memory: Government and International Historians Through Two World Wars*. Providence, RI: Berghahn

Winter J. 1995. *Sites of Memory, Sites of Mourning: The Great War in European Cultural History*. New York: Cambridge Univ. Press

Wohl R. 1979. *The Generation of 1914*. Cambridge, MA: Harvard Univ. Press

Wright P. 1985. *On Living in an Old Country: The National Past in Contemporary Britain*. London: Verso

Wyman DS, ed. 1996. *The World Reacts to the Holocaust*. Baltimore, MD: Johns Hopkins Univ. Press

Yates FA. 1966. The *Art of Memory*. Chicago: Univ. Chicago Press

Yerushalmi YH. 1982. *Zakhor: Jewish History and Jewish Memory*. Seattle: Univ. Wash. Press

Young JE. 1992. The counter-monument: memory against itself in Germany today. *Crit. Inq.* 18(2):267–96

Young JE. 1993. *The Texture of Memory: Holocaust Memorials and Meaning*. New Haven, CT: Yale Univ. Press

Zelizer B. 1992. *Covering the Body: The Kennedy Assassination, the Media, and the Shaping of Collective Memory*. Chicago: Univ. Chicago Press

Zelizer B. 1995. Reading the past against the grain: the shape of memory studies. *Crit. Stud. Mass. Commun.* 12(June):214–39

Zerubavel E. 1981. *Hidden Rhythms: Schedules and Calendars in Social Life*. Berkeley: Univ. Calif. Press

Zerubavel E. 1996. Social memories: steps to a sociology of the past. *Qual. Sociol.* 19(3) (Fall):283–300

Zerubavel Y. 1995. *Recovered Roots: Collective Memory and the Making of Israeli National Tradition*. Chicago: Univ. Chicago Press

Zonabend F. 1984. *The Enduring Memory: Time and History in a French Village*. Manchester, UK: Manchester Univ. Press

Annu. Rev. Sociol. 1998. 24:141–57

COMPUTERIZATION OF THE WORKPLACE

Beverly H. Burris

Department of Sociology, University of New Mexico, Albuquerque, New Mexico 87131; e-mail: bburris@unm.edu

KEY WORDS: computers, work, organizations, skill, technology

ABSTRACT

Divergent conceptualizations of the recent changes in work organization that have accompanied computerization include neo-Bravermanian analyses, postindustrial analyses, and contingency analyses. To make sense of these differing views, the paper surveys sociological research on computerization and its impact on three analytically separate dimensions of the workplace: organizational restructuring, changes in worker skill, and power and authority relationships. The review reveals that computerized work organizations typically have fewer hierarchical levels, a bifurcated workforce, frequently with race and sex segregation, a less formal structure, and diminished use of internal labor markets and reliance instead on external credentialing. Variable patterns of centralization and decentralization occur, and workplace power relationships interact with technological change to produce variable political outcomes. With regard to worker skills, recent evidence suggests aggregate upskilling with some deskilling and skill bifurcation. Future research should more closely analyze the process of technological design and implementation.

INTRODUCTION

During the latter part of the twentieth century, the implementation of computerized technology and advanced information systems, in conjunction with related socioeconomic changes, has led to a fundamental restructuring of work organizations. Contemporary sociologists, trying to understand this "second industrial divide" (Piore & Sabel 1984), as nineteenth century sociologists

0360-0572/98/0815-0141$08.00

tried to understand the first industrial revolution, have generated widely divergent conceptualizations. On the one hand, some social scientists have found that recent social and technological changes have created a centralized, neo-Taylorist work organization, deskilling of the labor process, and reduced worker autonomy (Braverman 1974, Feldberg & Glenn 1987, Kraft 1977, 1979, Noble 1977, 1984, Shaiken 1984, Zimbalist 1979). Conversely, other social scientists have concluded that the transformation of production has promoted a postindustrial or postbureaucratic work organization characterized by decentralization and reduction in hierarchy, upskilling of work and a centrality of knowledge workers, and democratization and increased worker autonomy (Attewell 1992, Bell 1973, Block 1990, Clegg 1990, Hirschhorn 1984, Piore & Sabel 1984). Still others have abandoned the search for general theory concerning the impact of technological change on the organization of production in favor of "contextualist" or "contingent" approaches that explore the micro-dynamics of workplace changes (Adler 1992b, Barley 1986, Cornfield 1987, Gallie 1978, Kelley 1990, Thomas 1994). These "contingency theorists" have argued that "the quest for general trends about the development of skill levels, or general conclusions about the impact of technologies, is likely to be in vain and misleading" (Wood 1989, p. 4; see also Vallas & Beck 1996, p. 341 ff for a good review).

We now have a considerable body of empirical research to help make sense of these divergent views. Can we substantiate any empirical or theoretical generalization concerning the impact of advanced technology on the workplace? If recent changes in the organization of production are contingent, can we begin to specify the contingencies? To answer these questions, this paper reviews recent sociological work on computerization and its impact on each of three analytically separate (although practically intertwined) dimensions of the workplace: organizational restructuring, changes in worker skill, and power and authority relationships. Although computerization is a global phenomenon, space constraints necessitate an emphasis here on US workplaces. I conclude with an analysis and interpretation.

ORGANIZATIONAL RESTRUCTURING

If it is true, as Salzman & Rosenthal (1994, p. 4) contend, that "workplaces are shaped by the design of the technology used," then we would expect work organizations centered around computerized systems of production and information to differ structurally from those utilizing other technologies. However, computerized systems are more flexible and variable than previous types of workplace technology; it is therefore not surprising to find variable patterns of implementation. Nonetheless, some trends are observable in the empirical literature.

Reduction in the Hierarchical Division of Labor

In contrast to the specialized division of labor with fine vertical gradations, characteristic of classical bureaucracy and many production workplaces, some researchers have found that computerization has correlated with fewer hierarchical levels and a "two-tier" occupational structure (Baran 1987, Colclough & Tolbert 1992, Kanter 1983, 1984, 1991, Hodson 1985, 1988, Noyelle 1987, Smith 1993, 1996, Wellman et al 1996, Zuboff 1988). Middle-level positions are reduced or eliminated, with a credential barrier typically separating the two sectors of the polarized corporation, with emphasis on external credentialing and recruitment from without (Kanter 1984, 1991, Burris 1983a,b, 1993). This trend appears particularly pronounced in high-tech firms (Kanter 1983, Hodson 1988). However, some observers disagree about whether this reduction in vertical hierarchy is causally related to computerization; Kling (1996a, p. 282) finds that what he terms "delayering" is also found in low-tech organizations and is more related to broader cultural and political changes than to computerization per se.

It appears that the extent and shape of the restructuring of the division of labor are dependent on several factors: the specific type of technology, managerial policies and choices, and the nature of the service or product (Salzman & Rosenthal 1994). When production of goods or services can be standardized and performed largely by the computer system, the workforce is likely to be more bifurcated into skilled technical workers and a smaller number of less skilled production or clerical workers, whereas when computerization is less extensive, the polarization may be less pronounced (Baran 1987, Barley & Orr 1997). With even more extensive computerization, "superautomation," comes a dramatic reduction in the size of the production workforce (Indergaard & Cushion 1987, Office of Technology Assessment 1984, Shaiken 1984).

One corollary associated with this polarization is that the organizational structure becomes less formal. In contrast to conventional bureaucracies, with their clearly defined chains of responsibility and communication channels, restructured bureaucracies rely more on ad hoc teams and task forces (Hodson 1988, Kanter 1983). What has been called an "adhocracy" (Mintzberg 1979) or "matrix organization" (Kanter 1983) emerges in some contexts: organic, integrative, flexible, adaptive, and innovative workplaces with a constantly changing internal structure. For expert-sector workers (managers and professionals), at least, bureaucratic constraints are relaxed to allow for creativity and flexibility (see Burris 1993). Indeed, occupational segregation appears sometimes to be accompanied by a pronounced bifurcation of working conditions. Hodson (1988) found that worker autonomy, input into decision-making, and salaries were dramatically different for high-tech engineers and workers.

A second corollary is that conventional internal labor markets tend to erode, along with mobility prospects for non-expert sector workers (Baran 1987, Hodson 1988, Kanter 1991, Noyelle 1987). External credentialing and promotion from without frequently substitute for in-house training and promotion. In some firms, diminished mobility prospects have translated into impaired worker motivation (Burris 1983a,b, Hodson 1988, Noyelle 1987); some firms have experimented with quality control circles and other worker participation experiments to compensate for the lack of training and mobility opportunities (see Noyelle 1987).

A final corollary of polarization has been the reinforcement of race and sex segregation in some firms (Burris 1989, Cockburn 1985, Colclough & Tolbert 1992, Hodson 1988, Noyelle 1987, Smith 1993). The erosion of internal labor markets has had special implications for women and racial minorities, as the organizational restructuring occurred during the 1970s and 1980s, a period of equal employment legislation and expanding social opportunities. The effect was to thwart legal and social reforms at the organizational level:

> ...at the same time that EEO policies were gaining speed, other forces came into play that began weakening the role of internal labor markets across a broad range of industries. Hence a basic dimension of EEO strategy—aggressive internal promotion of women and minority workers—was undermined. Some women and minority workers continued to advance to higher echelons, but their progress became increasingly dependent upon a different set of factors, involving educational credentials. (Noyelle 1987, p. 15–16)

Quantitative analyses have confirmed this race and sex segregation (Colclough & Tolbert 1992, Glem & Tolbert 1987, Kraft 1987, Mahung 1984, Strober & Arnold 1987). More qualitative analyses have also documented the persistence of gender stereotypes that define femininity as antithetical to technical expertise (Cockburn 1985, 1991, Hacker 1989). However, this pattern of gender segregation may be changing; Wright & Jacobs (1994) found that computer support occupations (i.e. jobs that support other people's use of computer systems—computer programmers, systems analysts, computer and systems engineers) became less gender segregated during the 1980s, with all computer support jobs being 36% female by 1991.

Patterns of Centralization and Decentralization

Traditionally, workplaces have been kept highly centralized, but with computerization come opportunities for new patterns of centralization and decentralization. Computerized numerical control (CNC), for example, can be used to facilitate end-user programming and editing (Noble 1984, Shaiken 1984), and personal computers can serve to link relatively autonomous satellite stations or work teams (Kanter 1991, Murphree 1984). However, the same technology can be used to maintain centralized managerial control and even surveillance (see Office of Technology Assessment 1984, National Research Council 1986). In some contexts, the computer system may assume the form of visible, functional decentralization (e.g. a computer terminal in every office or throughout the shop floor) but with an underlying centralization of control (see Burris 1993, Prechel 1994).

Variable patterns of centralization and decentralization have been documented, as social and political choices interact with technical considerations and system design (Burris 1993, Kling 1996a, Noyelle 1987). Kling (1996a, p. 295–96) discusses two divergent approaches to system design and implementation: "business process reengineering [which] is usually applied by managers and consultants to streamline operations" and increase efficiency, and "sociotechnical systems design," which emphasizes people and their relationships with each other and the technology. The former typically implies more centralizd control, what Clement (1996) calls a "command and control culture," and the latter a more decentralized pattern, and one where end-users sometimes play a substantial role in redesigning their work practices (Kling 1996a, p. 299, Clement 1996). Despite the variable patterns of centralization, however, there is also evidence that traditional centralized patterns are the norm. The National Research Council (1986, p. 150) concludes from its survey of computer automation in diverse white-collar settings that "because innovations can be implemented in broadly different ways, the major determinant of the effects of innovation appears to be management's preexisting employee policies."

Some workplaces have experimented with geographical decentralization in the form of "telecommuting" or "telework." Although currently limited in scope, these experiments are significant and may become more prevalent in the future (Kling 1996a, Wellman et al 1996). A recent report by the Clinton administration (IITF 1994) cites numerous potential benefits from an expansion of telework: reduced automobile pollution and traffic congestion, improved quality of work life, smoother integration of work and family life.

Although research on telework has been limited, some evidence suggests that current telework experiments may also result in teleworkers being less visible to peers, less likely to be promoted, and more difficult to supervise (Forester 1989). Kling (1996a, p. 288) also points out that some employees may lack the self-discipline required to work at home amidst home-based distractions. Olson (1989) in a study of computer professionals working at home full-time found reduced job satisfaction and organizational commitment and higher levels of role conflict. Olson & Primps (1984) found that female teleworkers were particularly likely to assume greater housework and childcare responsibilities and to experience stress deriving from work/family conflicts. Wellman et al (1996) argue that telework may exacerbate workplace bifurcation, for some studies have found that professional teleworkers tend to benefit from computerized social networks and expanded autonomy, whereas clerical teleworkers tend to become more isolated and often more stringently monitored (Olson & Primps 1984).

Telework highlights issues of centralization and control that are also pertinent to computerized workplaces more generally. Computerized systems of production are flexible, although not neutral, and the design of the software is critical. Salzman & Rosenthal (1994, p. 6) in their analysis of software production show in some detail how "technology both shapes and reflects the social matrix of organizations and socioeconomic systems, of which it is a part" and how a new technology can be either "assimilated" into existing organizational structures or "accommodated" by restructuring the organization (1994, p. 23; see also MacKenzie & Wajcman 1985, Thomas 1994). Although there has been a tendency to design and implement computerized technology in a manner consistent with centralized control, this is not inevitable and in fact may lead to organizational contradictions, worker dissatisfaction, and further change (Hirschhorn 1984, Kling 1996b, Noble 1984, Vallas 1990).

CHANGES IN WORKER SKILL

Braverman and the Labor Process Tradition

Braverman's (1974) analysis of Taylorism and the capitalist labor process has been influential for over 20 years, despite some trenchant criticism (Attewell 1987, Friedman 1977, Stark 1980). Braverman analyzed the ways in which scientific management, under the guise of scientific neutrality and objectivity, promoted the interests of capitalist managers (1974, p. 86). Taylor (1913, p. 25) contended that "there is always one method ... which is quicker and better than any of the rest. And this one best method ... can only be discovered or developed through a scientific study and analysis." Braverman showed how Taylorism was implemented so as to deskill the labor process, separating conception from execution and transferring conceptual skills to technical experts and managers (see Burris in press for fuller discussion).

Braverman discusses computerization, a trend far from widespread in 1974, only in passing and in fact appears to see the logic of computerization as antithetic to the logic of Taylorism and capitalism, due to its potential to "re-unify" the labor process (see Braverman 1974, p. 328). However, neo-Marxist sociologists have often found that capitalist social relations tend to shape technological design so as to make computerization consistent with capitalist and managerial imperatives. Noble (1977, 1979, 1984), for instance, showed how numerical control of machining was chosen and implemented in accordance with capitalist and militarist imperatives toward centralized control (see also Shaiken 1984).

Other empirical studies in the labor-process tradition have also found that deskilling of workers results from computerization of production workplaces. Cockburn (1985), for instance, found deskilling, increased managerial control, and race and sex polarization in her study of the garment industry in England. The case studies in Zimbalist (1979) reveal evidence of deskilling in industries ranging from carpentry to coal mining.

Upskilling and Sociotechnical Design Perspectives

As Attewell (1987, 1992; see also Vallas 1990, 1993) points out, however, a contradiction exists between these qualitative case studies, with their evidence of deskilling, and more aggregate, quantitative analyses of the labor force, which have tended to find substantial upgrading due to an expansion of more skilled occupations (Adler 1988, Baran 1987, Spenner 1983). As Barley & Orr (1997, p. 3) demonstrate, since 1950 the fastest growing occupational group has been professional/technical workers, who comprised 17% of all workers in 1991. Wright & Singlemann (1982) and Barley & Orr (1997) discuss how overall occupational upgrading can coexist with deskilling of specific occupations, as the production workforce becomes bifurcated into skilled technicians and less skilled operatives.

In contrast to the neo-Bravermanian labor process literature, then, other empirical studies have found skill upgrading, "upskilling," to be correlated with computerization. The classic study in this tradition is Blauner's (1964) comparison of automation with earlier types of technology, in which he found that continuous-process operators were upskilled, had more opportunities to learn and grow on the job, were less isolated and often worked in teams, and in general were less alienated than workers in industries with less advanced technology.

The sociotechnical conception of work design (Trist et al 1963) emphasizes that the social and technological dimensions of work organizations must be designed to complement one another and that computerized production systems are capable of being designed so as to expand worker skill and autonomy. Sociotechnical analysts assume that advanced technology, expensive and vulnerable to technical problems, leads to a heightened dependence on operators to ensure productivity, cost-effectiveness, and quality control; therefore, to realize the potential of the technology, decentralization and teams of multiskilled workers who understand the total operation of the plant are needed. Hirschhorn (1984) analyzed the interaction between technology and the social organization of production in firms such as Olivetti, Fiat, and General Foods, and his findings are consistent with sociotechnical analysis: When work was organized around self-governing worker teams and worker learning, the result was better quality products and superior market position, whereas when worker deskilling and alienation were the norm, workers were unable to effectively monitor and diagnose the complex technological system, making the operation vulnerable to technical breakdown and lost productivity. Hirschhorn & Mokray (1992, p. 16), in their study of a computer manufacturing plant, show how worker "[c]ompetence is shaped through the interaction of a worker's skills with the role he or she performs," making skill upgrading and worker autonomy necessary for optimal production.

Zuboff's (1988) case studies of the computerization of diverse workplaces is also consistent with the sociotechnical perspective. For Zuboff computerization fundamentally transforms skill by making work more "abstract" (see also Barley & Orr 1997, p. 5 ff, Hirschhorn & Mokray 1992, p. 23). Whereas earlier types of production involved manual skills and the interpretation of visual cues, working with computers involves "the electronic manipulation of symbols. Instead of a sensual activity, it is an abstract one" (Zuboff 1982, p. 145).

For Zuboff (1988, p. 9 ff), computerized technology can be implemented so as to either "automate" or "informate" jobs. When the informating strategy is chosen, information about the overall operation of the system is more available to workers, who are therefore able to learn and develop new skills and comprehensive understanding. In practice, however, Zuboff (1988, p. 252) found that such technological potential is often thwarted by managerial reluctance to share information and power: "Managers perceive workers who have information as a threat. They are afraid of not being the 'expert'" (see also Kanter 1983, Noble 1984).

Zuboff's work indicates general upskilling of production work, with the redefinition of jobs around more abstract skill, but limited expansion of worker autonomy. Similarly, Vallas & Beck (1996), in their study of pulp and paper mills, found significant upskilling of the jobs of manual workers as they learned the computerized system, but no evidence of any expansion of worker autonomy or discretion. Instead, they found a persistence of centralized managerial control in conjunction with increased reliance on degreed engineers as supervisors. Barley & Orr (1997, p. 19) found that the "emergent skills" of technical workers are often neither recognized nor rewarded; Creighton & Hodson (1997) found that technical workers in diverse settings were skilled but lacked power and autonomy. Vallas (1993, p. 184) in his study of AT&T found that "while the use of automated systems has at times increased skill requirements, its overall effects on levels of worker autonomy or responsibility have been far less beneficial..."; Iacono & Kling (1996) found that although "dramatic improvements in office technologies ... have sometimes made many clerical jobs much more interesting, flexible, and skill rich ... these changes, especially those involving increased skill requirements, have not brought commensurate improvements in career opportunities, influence, or clerical salaries" (Kling 1996a, p. 283).

The empirical literature on computerization and skill, then, is somewhat inconsistent and contradictory. Some have preferred to speak of "skill disruption" (Hodson 1988) or "skill restructuring" (Cockburn 1983), thus remaining agnostic on the deskilling vs. upskilling controversy. The more recent empirical work reveals aggregate upskilling, sometimes combined with the deskilling of a small number of jobs (Adler 1992a, Attewell 1992). At least three trends seem pertinent in explaining the increased salience of upskilling: 1. Computerized systems have become more sophisticated, with the development of advanced manufacturing technology and increased reliance on more skilled workers (Attewell 1992, p. 70; see also Hirschhorn & Mokray 1992). 2. The least skilled jobs have been disproportionately eliminated by the technology (Aronowitz & DiFazio 1994, Rifkin 1995). 3. More managers may be choosing to supplement their computer system with skilled workers to maximize productivity (reduce downtime) and quality control (Adler 1992b).

Professional Work

In recent decades professional work has also been transformed as the ideal type of the autonomous, self-employed professional has become the exception rather than the rule. As with other types of work, both empirical findings and conceptualizations of these changes have varied.

Some social scientists have concluded that "deprofessionalization" or "proletarization of the professions" is occurring (Derber 1982, Haug 1973, 1975, 1977, Larson 1977, Rothman 1984). Haug (1973, 1975, 1977), for instance, argues that such developments as rising educational levels among the general population, computerization and greater availability of knowledge, and a growing societal consciousness of the need for professional accountability have contributed to an undermining of professional power and increasing reliance on paraprofessionals. Larson (1977) focuses more on the trend toward professional employment in large bureaucratic organizations and on corporate pressures to maximize profits as leading to a more rigid division of labor, larger professional caseloads, and the routinization and standardization of professional work. She concludes that "technobureaucratic professionalism" results, as "professional status ... no longer insures the incumbent against the predominant relations of production in our society" (Larson 1977, p. 233). Derber (1982, p. 21) highlights another dimension of proletarization: professionals' increased difficulty in owning and controlling their own means of production, making them more dependent on large institutions for their survival.

Others have interpreted recent changes in professional work as more consistent with Weberian bureaucratization, rationalization, and formalization. Freidson (1984, 1986), for instance, argues that conceptualizations such as deprofessionalization and proletarization are exaggerated in that professionals continue to enjoy high status, prestige, and occupational power (see also Derber et al 1990). Computerization may not adversely affect professionals, since "it is the members of each profession who determine what is to be stored and how it is to be done, and who are equipped to interpret and employ what is retrieved effectively" (Freidson 1984, p. 8). Freidson sees the professions as becoming "formalized," as a certain internal stratification into an administrative elite, a knowledge elite, and rank-and-file professionals occurs (Freidson 1986).

Abbott (1988) also focuses upon the increasing systemization and rationalization of the professions and the ongoing redefinition of professional categories and jurisdictional boundaries within the system of professions in recent years owing to technological and organizational changes. Like the deprofessionalization school, Abbott also highlights the "commodification of knowledge," the competition from computerized diagnostic systems, and the ensuing routinization and degradation of some professions (Abbott 1988, p. 126 ff).

Certainly we have seen the creation of many paraprofessional occupations in the last few decades, for instance, in the health care field (McKinlay 1982). Medical diagnostic systems have also been developed, although not widely implemented (Dreyfus & Dreyfus 1986). However, physicians have retained considerable occupational power and workplace autonomy. In fact, some evidence suggests that computerized technology may be enhancing, rather than undermining, the work of the physician (Burris 1993, National Research Council 1986, p. 159).

Similarly, the legal profession and the judiciary have undergone internal stratification and systemization (Heydebrand & Seron 1990, Spangler & Lehman 1982). Heydebrand (1979) speaks of a "technocratic restructuring" of the judiciary in response to a crisis of the judicial system, with increased reliance on computerized data banks, role integration of professional and administrative functions, and more circumscribed and specialized judicial discretion. Others have found that judicial discretion has been enhanced and expanded, even as the judiciary has been reorganized and systematized (Aaronson 1977, Freidson 1984).

Some researchers have found polarization of certain professions. Shaiken (1984), Kraft (1987), and Kunda (1992) all found polarization within the ranks of computer professionals and engineers. Kunda (1992) documents a division between "central" and "marginal" engineers, with cultural normative control characteristic of the central, exempt engineers and more coercive and utilitarian control characteristic of the nonexempt sector.

In sum, it appears that technological changes and other rationalization measures appear to have differential effects on professional work, depending on the relative status of the profession and of the professional within a given profession. Professionals within elite professions may lose a certain degree of autonomy as they become more integrated into complex administrative systems, but discretion over professional work is generally retained (or even expanded). Ideologically and economically, they may be more subject to capitalist and bureaucratic imperatives, but not deprofessionalized. Less elite professionals and paraprofessionals (health care technicians, nurses, teachers, computer programmers) may be more vulnerable to professional rationalization. In some instances they may be deprofessionalized: their work deskilled, their caseloads increased, their contact with clients routinized. For such workers, professionalism may be little more than a legitimating ideology (see Burris 1993, p. 142 ff).

POWER AND AUTHORITY RELATIONSHIPS

Increased Salience of Technical Expertise

With the increased salience of professional and technical workers, it appears that traditional rank authority is deemphasized in favor of technical expertise (Burris 1993, Ilchman 1969). Kanter (1983, p. 55 ft), for instance, found that in the high-tech firms she studied "traditional authority virtually disappears; managers must instead persuade, influence, or convince" (see also Hodson 1988, Kunda 1992). Burris (1983a, 1993, see also Zuboff 1988) found that "conspicuous expertise" and new forms of politicking, centered around expertise, emerge.

Knowledge and information become important sources of power. Zuboff (1988) found that computer conferencing, along with computerized information generally, was restricted to expert-sector workers through the use of passwords, account numbers, and "closed status" designations. Kraft (1977) found that conflicts over the locus of authority occurred between experts and managers, and that these were exacerbated when managers had limited technical knowledge; similarly, Hirschhorn (1984) found that managers of utility companies were sometimes threatened by engineers' expertise and perceived threats to managerial authority. In other contexts, experts and managers have formed unified coalitions, and conflicts between workers and technical experts have been more common (Burris 1993, Zuboff 1988).

Worker Autonomy or More Stringent Managerial Control?

As we have seen, postindustrial analysts have argued that the fundamental logic of advanced technology is most consistent with increased worker autonomy and democratization (Hirschhorn 1984, Piore & Sable 1984, Zuboff 1988). Conversely, some have found that managerial control has been intensified and extended by computerized systems (Applebaum & Albin 1989, Prechel 1994).

Worker participation experiments have been implemented in many workplaces (Applebaum & Batt 1994, Smith 1996, US Department of Labor 1994);

more ambiguous is the significance of these experiments and whether they are causally related to technological change. Some have found the level of worker autonomy and input into decision-making to be minimal, and the significance of the experiments to be largely ideological, a form of "hegemonic" or "consensual" control (Burawoy 1979, 1985, Hodson et al 1993, Vallas 1993). Smith (1996), however, argues that this interpretation, although not without validity, misses the fact that the low-level white-collar workers that she studied perceived the new system of worker participation to be personally beneficial, promoting the acquisition of social/relational skills and "a new step on a constrained mobility ladder" (Smith 1996, p. 177; see also Hodson et al 1993). Kling (1996a, p. 299) also highlights examples of more significant types of worker participation, where workers reorganized the way in which computerization was implemented so as to create more flexible and less regimented jobs for themselves.

Computerization promotes not only production but also social networking (see Wellman et al 1996 for a good review). Office computers can be used for recreation, private "conversation" with other workers, nonwork friends, or family members, and work-related interaction. In some workplaces, computer-mediated communication, with its diminished social presence and greater anonymity, can be used to cross status and power boundaries, promoting a more democratic type of workplace interaction and culture (Wellman et al 1996, Zuboff 1988). For relatively autonomous computer conferencing and collaborative work, now potentially global in scope, computerization can greatly enhance the work process; as Wellman et al (1996) point out, this computerized augmentation of collaboration is more salient among professionals and academics.

Computerization is also consistent with more sophisticated and intensified systems of managerial control. Zuboff (1988), for instance, found that computerization can be implemented so as to promote centralized managerial control by making workers more visible and vulnerable to supervision, a technologically advanced version of the "Panopticon." Others have addressed the issue of computerized monitoring of workers, although there is little consensus about the extent of this practice (Attewell 1987, Kling 1996a, p. 286 ff, Garson 1988, Marx 1996). Management sometimes monitors not only level of productivity and errors, but also the type of on-line activities to ensure "appropriate" use of the technology (Orlikowski et al 1995, Zuboff 1988).

Prechel (1994) found that the large steel corporation he studied, in response to global competition and economic crisis, has implemented a "neo-Fordist" strategy of "hypercentralization," "hyperquantification," and "formalized control'" (Prechel 1994, p. 737 ff), a system that reduced or eliminated the former autonomy of managers and instituted a sophisticated neo-Taylorist system of production control where the "one best way" of doing something is consistently utilized. Prechel's case study demonstrates how a firm can flatten its hierarchy, utilize the computerized system to achieve functional decentralization and flexibility, yet also strengthen centralized managerial authority over production and decision-making.

Another recent conceptualization of changes in managerial control systems is that of "algorithmic" control (Applebaum & Albin 1989, Vallas 1993), which Applebaum & Albin (1989, p. 252) define as the reduction of "decision-making as much as possible to a set of self-contained rules (algorithms) implementable by a computer." Vallas (1993), in his study of AT&T, shows how management, through algorithmic control, can simultaneously upgrade worker skills and extend managerial control over production by "placing information systems at the directive nodes of the productive circuitry and progressively removing workers to more peripheral locations in the labor process… [so that (in the words of one manager)] 'there are no decisions to be made [by workers]'" (Vallas 1993, p. 187).

Finally, Burris (1993) highlights a neo-Taylorist "technocratic" ideology that rests on the increasing centrality of technical expertise and the assumption that technical and system imperatives have displaced traditional workplace politics: that there is one best technical solution to any problem, which can be found only by technical experts. This ideology, in conjunction with the mystique of computers and a sense of technological determinism and progress, serves to legitimate the power and privilege of technical experts, to obscure existing workplace politics, and to promote consensual control of workers (see also Collins 1979).

DISCUSSION AND CONCLUSIONS

Although the trends discussed above appear to correlate with computerization, causal inference is made problematic by the fact that computerization is embedded in a constellation of factors: the internalization of the division of labor, intensified worldwide competition and a corresponding emphasis on innovation, expanded need (and capacity) to manage complex organizations and systems and to perfect long-range planning. Technology interacts with social preferences and political choices in complex ways, making generalization difficult (Thomas 1994). The challenge is to assess the impact of computerization, avoiding both the Scylla of technological determinism and the Charybdis of technological indeterminism.

While there are many contingencies concerning computerization, there are also observable trends in the empirical literature. This review has revealed the need to separate analytically the three dimensions of the workplace examined here: organizational restructuring, worker skill, and power and authority relationships. One pitfall of existing theories has been the tendency to assume correspondence among these dimensions. Thus, postindustrial analyses have tended to assume flatter hierarchies, a more skilled workforce, and worker empowerment to be coterminous. Neo-Bravermanian analyses, on the other hand, have tended to assume that more stringent centralization, worker deskilling, and reduced worker autonomy coexist and reinforce one another.

Recent empirical work indicates, however, that these dimensions do not always line up. We have seen, for instance, that technically skilled workers often do not enjoy autonomy or responsibility on the job (Baran 1987, Barley & Orr 1997, Creighton & Hodson 1997, Iacono & Kling 1996, Vallas & Beck 1996, Zuboff 1988). A reduction in levels of hierarchy does not necessarily imply a more egalitarian workplace; delayering appears more often to result in a polarized, "two-tier" workplace and dramatically unequal working conditions between the two sectors (Baran 1987, Colclough & Tolbert 1992, Kanter 1983, 1984, 1991, Hodson 1985, 1988, Noyelle 1987, Smith 1993, 1996, Zuboff 1988). In some workplaces, centralized decision-making, embedded in the computer system, can be combined with a considerable degree of functional decentralization and flexibility (Burris 1993, Prechel 1994). With regard to the deskilling/upskilling controversy, it has become apparent that both trends can coexist, depending on the unit of analysis: aggregate upskilling with some skill bifurcation, some deskilling, and considerable skill disruption (Adler 1992, Attewell 1992, Barley & Orr 1997).

Rather than abandoning the search for general theories about workplace change, we need to search for more complex and nuanced theory, multidimensional and multilevel theory, to understand both the generality and the contingency of contemporary workplaces. The new types of work and organization emerging along with computerization do not readily conform to existing theories, but this does not imply that they cannot be theorized.

In addition to more relevant theory, we also need more objective research. As a subdiscipline, the field of the sociology of work has tended to be highly politicized, with some researchers influenced by managerial perspectives and others by solidarity with workers (see Abbott 1993). In researching computerization, some have taken the situation of expert-sector, professional workers to be generally representative of working with computers and have therefore emphasized the positive side of computerization; conversely, others have focused upon the situation of non-expert sector workers and have therefore emphasized the negative side of computerization (see Burris 1993). Each perspective is partially valid. One salient contingency in assessing the impact of computerization on contemporary workplaces is one's position within an increasingly bifurcated workforce.

Future research in this area needs to analyze more closely the process of technological design and implementation within work organizations so as to better specify the interaction between existing power relationships and computerized systems (Salzman & Rosenthal 1994, Thomas 1994). We need to understand better not only the impact of computerization on work organizations, but also the impact of work organization on computerization. Only with this more comprehensive understanding can we promote intelligent choices about the workplaces of the future.

ACKNOWLEDGMENTS

The author would like to thank Richard Coughlin, Jesse Dillard, Randy Hodson, Gary LaFree, Steven Vallas, and an anonymous Annual Reviews reviewer for helpful comments on earlier drafts.

Literature Cited

Aaronson D. 1977. *The New Justice*. Washington, DC: Natl. Inst. Law Enforc. Crim. Justice

Abbott A. 1988. *The System of Professions*. Chicago, IL: Univ. Chicago Press

Abbott A. 1993. The sociology of work and occupations. *Annu. Rev. Sociol.* 19: 187–209

Adler PS. 1988. Automation, skill, and the future of capitalism. *Berkeley J. Sociol.* 33(l):1–36

Adler PS. 1992a. *Technology and the Future of Work*. New York: Oxford Univ. Press

Adler PS. 1992b. Introduction. See Adler 1992a, pp. 3–14

Applebaum E, Albin P. 1989. Computer rationalization and the transformation of work. See Wood 1989, pp. 247–65

Applebaum E, Batt R. 1994. *The New American Workplace*. Ithaca, NY: ILR

Aronowitz S, DiFazio W. 1994. *The Jobless Future*. Minneapolis: Univ. Minn. Press

Attewell P. 1987. The deskilling controversy. *Work Occup.* 14(3):323–34

Attewell P. 1992. Skill and occupational changes in U.S. manufacturing. See Adler 1992a, pp. 46–88

Baran B. 1987. The technological transformation of white-collar work. See Hartmann 1987, pp. 25–62

Barley S. 1986. Technology as an occasion for structuring. *Admin. Sci. Q.* 31:78–108

Barley SR, Orr JE. 1997. *Between Craft and Science*. Ithaca, NY: Cornell Univ. Press

Bell D. 1973. *The Coming of Post-Industrial Society*. New York: Basic Books

Blauner R. 1964. *Alienation and Freedom*. Chicago, IL: Univ. Chicago Press

Block F. 1990. *Postindustrial Possibilities*. Berkeley: Univ. Calif. Press

Braverman H. 1974. *Labor and Monopoly Capital*. New York: Monthly Rev.

Burawoy M. 1979. *Manufacturing Consent*. Chicago, IL: Univ. Chicago Press

Burawoy M. 1985. *The Politics of Production*. London: Verso

Burris BH. 1983a. *No Room at the Top*. New York: Praeger

Burris BH. 1983b. The human effects of underemployment. *Soc. Probl.* 31(l):96–109

Burris BH. 1989. Technocracy and gender in the workplace. *Soc. Probl.* 36(2):165–80

Burris BH. 1993. *Technocracy at Work*. Albany: State Univ. NY Press

Burris BH. 1998. Braverman, Taylorism, and Technocracy. In *Rethinking the Labor Process,* ed. M Wardell, T Steiger, P Meiksins. Albany, NY: State Univ. NY Press. In press

Clegg SR. 1990. *Modern Organizations*. Newbury Park, CA: Sage

Clement A. 1996. Computing at work: empowering action by low-level users. See Kling 1996b, pp. 383–406

Cockburn C. 1983. *Brothers*. London: Pluto

Cockburn C. 1985. *Machinery of Dominance*. London: Pluto

Cockburn C. 1991. *In the Way of Women*. Ithaca, NY: ILR

Colclouogh G, Tolbert CM III. 1992. *Work in the Fast Lane*. Albany: State Univ. NY Press

Collins R. 1979. *The Credential Society*. New York: Academic

Cornfield D. 1987. *Workers, Managers, and Technological Change*. New York: Plenum

Creighton S, Hodson R. 1997. Whose side are they on? See Barley & Orr 1997, pp. 82–100

Derber C, ed. 1982. *Professionals as Workers*. Boston: Hall

Derber C, Schwartz WA, Magrass Y. 1990. *Power in the Highest Degree*. New York: Oxford Univ. Press

Dreyfus HL, Dreyfus S. 1986. *Mind Over Machine*. New York: Free Press

Feldberg R, Glenn E. 1987. Technology and the transformation of clerical work. See Kraut 1987, pp. 77–98

Forester T. 1989. The myth of the electronic cottage. In *Computers in the Human Context,* ed. T Forester, pp. 125–54. Cambridge, MA: MIT Press

Freidson E. 1984. The changing nature of professional control. *Annu. Rev. Sociol.* 10: 1–20

Freidson E. 1986. *Professional Powers*. Chicago, IL: Univ. Chicago Press

Friedman AL. 1977. *Industry and Labor*. London: Macmillan

Gallie D. 1978. *In Search of the New Working Class*. New York: Cambridge Univ. Press

Garson B. 1988. *The Electronic Sweatshop*. New York: Penguin

Glenn EN, Tolbert CM. 1987. Technology and emerging patterns of stratification for women of color: race and gender segregation in computer occupations. In *Women, Work, and Technology*, ed. B Wright, M Ferree, G Mellow, L Lewis, M Samper, et al, pp. 318–31. Ann Arbor: Univ. Mich. Press

Hacker S. 1989. *Pleasure, Power, and Technology*. Boston: Unwin & Hyman

Hartmann H, ed. 1987. *Computer Chips and Paper Clips,* Vol. 2. Washington, DC: Natl. Acad. Sci.

Haug M. 1973. Deprofessionalization. *Sociol. Rev. Monogr.* 20:195–211

Haug M. 1975. The deprofessionalization of everyone? *Sociol. Focus* 8:197–213

Haug M. 1977. Computer technology and the obsolescence of the concept of profession. In *Work and Technology,* ed. M Haug, J Dofny, pp. 215–28. Beverly Hills, CA: Sage

Heydebrand W. 1979. The technocratic administration of justice. *Res. Law Soc.* 2: 29–64

Heydebrand W, Seron C. 1990. *Rationalizing Justice*. Albany: State Univ. NY Press

Hirschhorn L. 1984. *Beyond Mechanization*. Cambridge, MA: MIT Press

Hirschhorn L, Mokray J. 1992. Automation and competency requirements in manufacturing: a case study. See Adler 1992a, pp. 15–45

Hodson R. 1985. Working in high-tech: research issues and opportunities for the industrial sociologist. *Sociol. Q.* 26(3): 351–64

Hodson R. 1988. Good jobs and bad management: How new problems evoke old solutions in high-tech settings. In *Sociological and Economic Approaches to Labor Markets,* ed. P England, G Farkas, pp. 247–79. New York: Plenum

Hodson R, Creighton S, Jamison C, Rieble S, Welsh S. 1993. Is worker solidarity undermined by autonomy and participation? *Am. Sociol. Rev.* 58(3):398–416

Iacono S, Kling R. 1996. Computerization, office routines, and changes in clerical work. See Kling 1996b, pp. 309–15

Ilchman WF. 1969. Productivity, administrative reform, and antipolitics. In *Political and Administrative Development*, ed. R Braibanti, pp. 472–526. Durham, NC: Duke Univ. Press

Indergaard M, Cushion M. 1987. Conflict and cooperation in the global auto factory. In *Workers, Managers, and Technological Change,* ed. D Cornfield, pp. 203–28. New York: Plenum

Information Infrastructure Task Force (IITF). 1994. *Promoting Telecommuting.* Washington, DC. URL: gopher://iitfcat.nist.gov:95/0-catitem2/telecom.txt

Kanter RM. 1983. *The Change Masters*. New York: Simon & Schuster

Kanter RM. 1984. Variations in managerial career structures in high-technology firms: the impact of organizational characteristics on internal labor market patterns. In *Internal Labor Markets,* ed. P Osterman, pp. 109–32. Cambridge, MA: MIT Press

Kanter RM. 1991. The future of bureaucracy and hierarchy in organizational theory. In *Social Theory for a Changing Society,* ed. P Bourdieu, J Coleman, pp. 63–86. Boulder, CO: Westview

Kelley M. 1990. New process technology, job design and work organization. *Am. Sociol. Rev.* 55(2):191–208

Kling R. 1996a. Computerization at work. See Kling 1996b, pp. 278–308

Kling R, ed. 1996b. *Computerization and Controversy*. New York: Academic. 2nd ed.

Kraft P. 1977. *Programmers and Managers*. New York: Springer-Verlag

Kraft P. 1979. The industrialization of computer programming. See Zimbalist 1979, pp. 1–17

Kraft P. 1987. Computers and the automation of work. See Kraut 1987, pp. 99–112

Kraut R, ed. 1987. *Technology and the Transformation of White-Collar Work.* Hillsdale, NJ: Erlbaum

Kunda G. 1992. *Engineering Culture*. Philadelphia, PA: Temple Univ. Press

Larson MS. 1977. *The Rise of Professionalism*. Berkeley: Univ. Calif. Press

Machung A. 1984. Word processing: forward for business, backward for women. In *My Troubles Are Going to Have Trouble with Me,* ed. K Sacks, D Remy, pp. 47–62. New Brunswick, NJ: Rutgers Univ. Press

MacKenzie D, Wajcman J, eds. 1985. *The Social Shaping of Technology*. Philadelphia: Open Univ. Press

Marx GT. 1996. The case of the omniscient organization. See Kling 1996b, pp. 316–21

McKinlay JB. 1982. Toward the proletarianization of physicians. See Derber 1982, pp. 156–80

Mintzberg H. 1979. *The Structuring of Organizations*. Englewood Cliffs, NJ: Prentice-Hall

Murphree MC. 1984. Brave new office: the changing world of the legal secretary. In *My Troubles Are Going to Have Trouble with Me*, ed. K Sack, D Remy, pp. 63–90. New Brunswick, NJ: Rutgers Univ. Press

National Research Council. 1986. *Computer Chips and Paper Clips,* Vol. 1. Washington, DC: Natl. Acad. Press

Noble D. 1977. *America by Design*. New York: Knopf

Noble D. 1979. Social choice in machine design. See Zimbalist 1979, pp. 18–50

Noble D. 1984. *Forces of Production*. New York: Knopf

Noyelle T. 1987. *Beyond Industrial Dualism*. Boulder, CO: Westview

Office of Technology Assessment. 1984. *Computerized Manufacturing Automation; Employment, Education, and the Workplace*. Washington, DC: US Gov. Print. Off.

Olson MH. 1989. Work at home for computer professionals. *ACM Trans. Inf. Syst.* 7(4): 317–38

Olson MH, Primps SB. 1984. Working at home with computers. *J. Soc. Issues* 40(3): 97–112

Orlikowski W, Yates J, Okamura K, Fujimoto M. 1995. Shaping electronic communication. *Organ. Sci.* 6(4):423–44

Piore M, Sabel C. 1984. *The Second Industrial Divide*. New York: Basic Books

Prechel H. 1994. Economic crisis and the centralization of control over the managerial process. *Am. Sociol. Rev.* 59:723–45

Rifkin J. 1995. *The End of Work*. New York: Putnam

Rothman R. 1984. Deprofessionalization. *Work Occup.* 11(2):183–206

Salzman H, Rosenthal SR. 1994. *Software by Design*. New York: Oxford Univ. Press

Shaiken H. 1984. *Work Transformed*. New York: Holt, Rinehart & Winston

Smith V. 1993. Flexibility in work and employment: the impact on women. *Res. Sociol. Organ.* 11:195–216

Smith V. 1996. Employee involvement, involved employees. *Soc. Probl.* 43(2): 166–79

Spangler E, Lehman P. 1982. Lawyering as work. See Derber 1982, pp. 190–211

Spenner KI. 1983. Deciphering Prometheus: temporal change in the skill level of work. *Am. Sociol. Rev.* 48:824–37

Stark D. 1980. Class struggle and the labor process: a relational perspective. *Theory Soc.* 9(l):89–130

Strober M, Arnold C. 1987. Integrated circuits/segregated labor: women in computer-related occupations and high-tech industries. See Hartmann 1987, pp. 136–82

Taylor FW. 1913. *The Principles of Scientific Management*. New York: Harper

Thomas RJ. 1994. *What Machines Can't Do*. Berkeley: Univ. Calif. Press

Trist E, Higgin GW, Murray H, Pollock AB. 1963. *Organizational Choice*. London: Tavistock

US Department of Labor. 1994. *Fact Finding Report*. Washington, DC: US Gov. Print. Off.

Vallas SP. 1990. The concept of skill. *Work Occup.* 17(4):379–88

Vallas SP. 1993. *Power in the Workplace*. Albany: State Univ. NY Press

Vallas SP, Beck JP. 1996. The transformation of work revisited: the limits of flexibility in American manufacturing. *Soc. Probl.* 43(3):339–61

Wellman B, Salaff J, Dimitrova D, Garton L, Gulia M, Haythornthwaite C. 1996. Computer networks as social networks: collaborative work, telework, and virtual community. *Annu. Rev. Sociol.* 22:213–38

Wood S. 1989. *The Transformation of Work?* London: Allen & Unwin

Wright EO, Singlemann J. 1982. Proletarianization in the changing American class structure. *Am. J. Sociol.* 88:S176–209

Wright R, Jacobs JA. 1994. Male flight from computer work: a new look at occupational resegregation and ghettoization. *Am. Sociol. Rev.* 59(4):511–36

Zimbalist A, ed. 1979. *Case Studies on the Labor Process*. New York: Monthly Rev.

Zuboff S. 1982. New worlds of computer-mediated work. *Harv. Bus. Rev.* 60(2): 142–52

Zuboff S. 1988. *In the Age of the Smart Machine*. New York: Basic Books

Annu. Rev. Sociol. 1998. 24:159–81

GLOBALIZATION AND DEMOCRACY

Kathleen C. Schwartzman
Department of Sociology, University of Arizona, Tucson, Arizona 85721;
e-mail: KCS@U.Arizona.edu

KEY WORDS: democratization, redemocratization, semiperiphery, global convergence, B-phase, hegemonic shifts, foreign capital investment, foreign intervention, social movements

ABSTRACT

By 1996, 66% of the countries of the world were using elections to choose their top leaders. This wave of democratization was accompanied by a paradigm shift that took the large number of historically clustered democratizations and called it a "wave." The scholarship has moved beyond overly episodic, event-oriented accounts of democratization to comparative work that investigates the impact of global processes on the political regimes of nations. This review examines numerous renderings of the linkage between globalization and democratization, including: favorable climate for democracy, global economic growth, global crises, foreign intervention, hegemonic shifts, and world-system contraction. Those authors who have advanced a stronger theoretical integration of the global and domestic processes offer exceptional insight into the momentous shifts that recently have occurred.

INTRODUCTION

In the last several decades, the world has experienced a democratic revival. In 1974, only 39 countries (25% of the world's independent nations) were democratic. By 1996, 66% were using elections to choose their top leaders (*Wall Street Journal,* June 25, 1996, p. 1). Dismantling totalitarian regimes and replacing them with democratic ones are momentous societal transformations. The new democracies were celebrated in a rich and diverse literature that ad-

0360-0572/98/0815-0159$08.00

dressed the antecedents and causes of the democratic transitions. Democratization in Greece, Spain, and Portugal begot a scholarship that focused on the historical and cultural distinctiveness of the respective cases. A few authors, observing the "historical clustering," offered an analysis of Europe's southern rim. Then, in the 1980s, several Latin American countries embarked on the transition to democracy. A new "transitions" literature connected these 1980 events to those of the 1970s. When that set of democratizations was joined (in the late 1980s and 1990s) by South Korean, Taiwan, Eastern Europe, and even South Africa, the "Third Wave" literature was born.

> A wave of democratization is a group of transitions from nondemocratic to democratic regimes that occur within a specified period of time and that significantly outnumber transitions in the opposite direction during that period of time. A wave also usually involves liberalization or partial democratization in political systems that do not become fully democratic. (Huntington 1991, p. 15)

What has come to be known as the Third Wave heralded a paradigm shift in the contemporary scholarship. The innovation consisted in conceptually assembling these geographically and temporally dispersed events into a "wave." It signaled a radical departure from the country-specific idiographic work which offered explanations that were overly episodic and event-oriented and insufficiently structural or cyclical (Wallerstein 1991, p. 1). The notion of a "wave" compels us to consider theoretical and methodological approaches that are comparative or even global. If observers of the 1970s transitions could comfortably reject internationally oriented theories, later scholars were deprived of this luxury as the number of transitions grew, and as they moved from one continent to another. Once established, the wave concept enveloped all transitions.

Some writers were critical of this warning that the wave is more like a hurricane that sweeps away anything in its path. Bunce argues that "a mere three years after the collapse of state socialism...eastern Europe was in virtually all accounts in 'transition to democracy.' Few paused to ask whether this was the best way to understand what is happening in this region..." (1993, p. 37). And with the exception of Czechoslovakia, Bunce insists, the Eastern European transitions are not like Southern Europe and Latin America (1993, p. 43). Likewise, the cases of the Dominican Republic and Ecuador are very distinct from those mentioned above, yet their transitions (1978 and 1979, respectively) have been grouped into the transition perspective (Conaghan & Espinal 1990).

As the voices of dissent suggest, the Third Wave does indeed have a staggering amplitude: It includes countries with a 50-year history of nondemocratic rule as well as countries that had substantial democratic interludes; it includes those terminating traditional authoritarian regimes, populist dictatorships as well as bureaucratic authoritarian ones; and it includes countries that dismantled their nondemocratic regimes with dramatic feats such as the destruction of a wall, the assassination of former leaders, or the uprising of the military against the authoritarian regime, as well as those in which the military itself negotiated the transition.

This celebratory literature also permits a wide amplitude in the definition of democracy. The debate over the essence of democracy has in no way been resolved in the wave literature. Advocates of popular democracies argue that not only must there be widespread participation of majorities in decision-making, but the democratic process must be used for achieving social and economic justice. Advocates of polyarchy, in contrast, accept a minimalist version in which a small group rules and mass participation in decision-making is confined to restricted choices in periodic elections (Robinson 1996, p. 49). While the former stresses outcomes, the latter stresses processes. Likewise, the debate regarding the measurement of democracy has not been resolved in the wave literature. Should we use a binary measure (presence or absence of some institution associated with democracy) as early scholars did, or should we use a scale that includes numerous measures of liberty (Bollen & Jackman 1989, p. 612). Despite legitimate concerns regarding the classification of nations, I have passed over the definitional debate in order to highlight what authors have written about the causes of those transitions.

Przeworski traces two major strategies in the research on redemocratization: 1. macro-oriented comparative works that focus on objective conditions and speak the language of causal determination; and 2. "micro-oriented studies which tend to emphasize the strategic behavior of political actors embedded in concrete historical situations" (1986, p. 47). The first implies that regime transformations are determined by economic, social, or political conditions. But he asks, "Were all the intentional, self-reflective, strategic actors merely unwitting agents of historical necessity?" (1986, p. 48). Przeworski's resolution is to label the first as constraints that do not determine the outcome and then to ask within those constraints, "How do alternatives become organized?" (1986, p. 53). Many may take this second question as a charge for studying individual choice or social movements in isolation from the macroconstraints. The emergence of a global wave, however, necessitates that we analytically embed the second question within the first.

The principal intellectual challenge is to link global processes with domestic ones and then to show how those domestic processes influence the daily experiences of both those who rule and those who are ruled. The question "How can global change constitute a catalyst for the transition-to-democracy?" can be rewritten as several questions: 1. In what way do global shifts affect domestic economic and/or political processes? 2. How do these domestic changes lead elites to withdraw legitimacy from the nondemocratic regime? 3. How do these domestic changes encourage those who are dominated to mobilize against the regime? and 4. When the walls come tumbling down, must democracy rise from the rubble? These questions are depicted as alternative causal paths to democratization (Figure 1), and each path is given a letter that will be used in summarizing the approaches of individual authors.

Who addresses these questions? The judgment of Kincaid and Portes regarding development studies is pertinent:

> To cover the vast territory [of]...the sociology of development counts with only a relative handful of specialists. The traditional parochialism of American sociology is faithfully reflected in the fact that events affecting the majority of the world's population are usually either ignored or reduced to a few variables in quantitative cross-national studies. (Kincaid & Portes 1994, p. 3)

In the period following the exhaustion of the modernization perspective, area studies remained the domain of a few sociological outliers. Those who had been working on totalitarian states (Goldfarb 1992), authoritarian regimes (Linz & Stepan 1978), underdevelopment, or dependent development (Evans

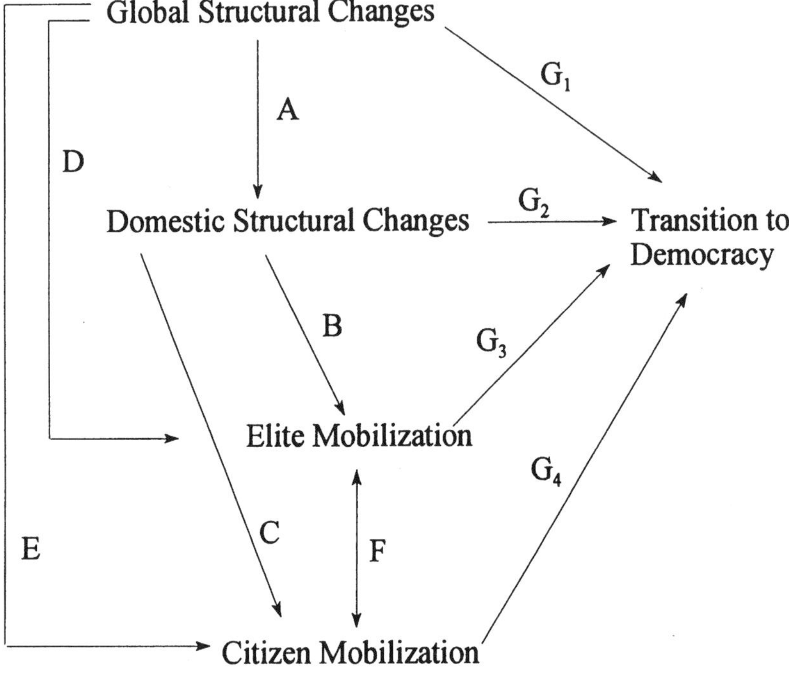

Figure 1 Overview of causal paths

1979) were best positioned and equipped to analyze the new phenomenon of (re)democratization. Those early transition scholars were followed by others who introduced a comparative perspective that was often cross-decade and cross-continental (for example, Seidman 1994 and Zubeck & Gentleman 1994). In contrast to the bibliographies of standard research monographs, which tend to implode in the matter of citations, the literature cited in this review essay draws from a wide range of scholarship.

THYMOS AND MORAL ROT

Why did the authoritarian and totalitarian states wither away? Fukuyama's answer is poetic—the human need for expression (thymos) leads to the perfect political form (democracy). Having achieved global democratic acceptance, he tells us, we have reached the "end of history." Chirot asserts that the economic failures of state socialism and moral rot of the whole system rendered the system morally unbearable for the citizenry. While undeniably cogent, many such ex post facto accounts are silent on the issue of threshold. Why did the thymos quotient reach its tipping point so many centuries after the first Greek model? How did societies live so long with moral rot? In the final analysis, ex post facto models such as these often invoke "loss of legitimacy" as their main explanatory factor. The loss of legitimacy is certainly the quintessential process (Linz & Stepan 1978). It is so quintessential, however, that it borders on the tautological: The regime fell, thus it must have lost its legitimacy. Rather than upgrade lost legitimacy to the principal causal mechanism, we should incorporate it as the critical intervening process and look to models that specify: 1. who specifically withdraws legitimacy, and 2. what accounts for their withdrawal. The transition scholarship includes excellent idiographic and ethnographic studies that cannot all be mentioned here. For this essay, I have drawn from those monographs that grapple with the notion of a global catalyst. By piecing together numerous works that touch on some aspect of the connection between globalization and redemocratization, we can assemble a more comprehensive answer.

THE GLOBAL CONNECTIONS

Authors who utilize a global linkage in their analysis offer prima facie evidence that the Third Wave transitions are not isolated, coincidental, or randomly distributed in time or space. Despite their shared conviction regarding the global or world-system nature of the democratic transitions, they diverge significantly in their designation of a global mechanism. I have sorted the global factors into six categories.

Favorable International Climate

Democratization in one country becomes the favorable climate, and thereby a partial cause, of democratization in others. Huntington argues that a favorable global atmosphere operates through diffusion, a demonstration effect, or snowballing. When knowledge of political events is transmitted around the world, it may trigger comparable events elsewhere (1991, p. 33). Success in some parts of the world may encourage other countries to see democratization as a solution for their problems. Huntington thinks that greater snowballing in the later phase of the Third Wave is due to the expansion of global communications and transportation, particularly satellites, computers, and faxes (1991, p. 101) (Figure 1, path C).

Numerous authors invoke the effect of a favorable international climate. In his analysis of the Greek transition, Diamandouros describes how the climate was favorable to democracy: "In Europe...the disrepute into which authoritarian rule had fallen since the days of Fascist experiments; the widespread acceptance of the legitimacy of democratic rule and of populist politics; the multiplicity of international organizations committed...to the preservation and defense of democratic politics..." (1986, p. 146). The snowballing concept also has been employed in explaining the fate of the Eastern bloc. Holmes argues that Gorbachev's criticisms of socialism and his own proposed reforms, "helped to undermine the legitimacy of communists everywhere" (1997, p. 26). Because of a favorable environment—the conviction that the USSR would not intervene—Eastern Europeans pursued their own goals (Figure 1, path C).

At a very general level, the favorable-climate perspective helps us understand why, at the moment of regime collapse, democracy possesses more legitimacy than monarchy, reformed totalitarianism, or some other alternative. It leaves unspecified, nevertheless, a number of crucial dynamics. What accounts for the shift of the early trendsetters? Why didn't the model diffuse sooner after the Greeks developed it? Why do some nations cast off their democratic form? The favorable-climate answer presumes a model of action—the persuasiveness of an idea—in which some of the main puzzles are simply assumed away. By failing to take seriously the social, economic, and political processes at both the global and domestic levels, the model does not contribute much to our understanding of these tremendous transformations.

Global Industrialization and Development

A second perspective in the literature contends that global economic development promotes global democratization. Global growth has eliminated precapitalist niches and resulted in a shift from capital intensive to technology intensive production. This metamorphosis is sometimes referred to as a "convergence" because it appears as though the preexisting distinction between industrialized and nonindustrialized countries is disappearing. The globalization of production unleashes mechanisms that lay the groundwork for democracy in at least four ways. Some scholars stress the technological innovations in communication and transportation that accompany global capitalism. For other scholars, industrialization brings with it the growth of professional and a middle class, the main carriers of democracy. Still others see industrialization as bringing with it the growth of the working classes, the main agents of democratization. A fourth approach claims that global growth undermines interventionist (nondemocratic) states. Global industrialization lessens the previous gap between industrialized and nonindustrialized countries: Their economic profiles begin to converge.

A first version of the global industrialization argument privileges the role of technology and communications. Technological innovations in communication, it is argued, make it more difficult to withhold information from the masses and under these circumstances, democracy flourishes.

"Just as the growing technology of control helped to shape authoritarian regimes in Latin America, new information technology is shaping Latin American democracies, especially with regard to elections and public debate in the media" (Chalmers 1990, p. 2) (Figure 1, path E,G4).

Markoff offers a plethora of factors, including communication and transportation. He attributes the world-wide subscription to democracy to the rise of communication and transportation, which increases the capacity of ordinary people to develop and sustain social movements (1996, p. 44). He suggests that the rise in communication means that both the governing elites and social movements pay attention to what other social movements and governing elites are doing elsewhere (1996, p. 20). Once the wave begins, Markoff argues, models (of sit-ins, underground cells, symbols, etc) and ideas (of social injustice) can spread throughout the networks of communication and transportation (Figure 1, path D,G3 and E,G4). Verdery, in a similar way, claims that technology and communications undermined socialism and contributed to democratization. Solidarity's strikes in 1980 were "rebroadcast instantly into Poland via Radio Free Europe and the BBC mobilizing millions of Poles against their Party" (1993, p. 19) (Figure 1, path E,G4).

Drawing on a large body of historical literature, Crenshaw ventures an empirical evaluation of the preindustrial legacy and its impact on democracy. He argues that advanced systems of transportation and communication endowed some early agrarian states with higher levels of spatial articulation, which encouraged the adoption of political democracy (1995, p. 715). A rise in his agricultural density index was associated with a rise in the democracy index. While there is a wide intellectual moat between his theoretical exposition and the twelve regression models based on data from 1960 to 1990, the endeavor reflects an enormously creative leap beyond the routinely cited but regularly untested effects of communication and transportation.

Overall, the technology models are appealing, but they ignore the quandary that social and communication networks are content-neutral; fascist and antidemocratic ideas can spread equally well. Such models do not tell us why waves begin or why they are democratic rather than authoritarian. These models have to assume the first perspective, namely that the international climate values democracy rather than some alternative. Such models, Therborn asserts, do not show much interest in the social dynamics (1977, p. 7).

A second rendition of global growth can be found among Huntington's explanatory factors. "[E]conomic development appears to have promoted changes in social structure and values that, in turn, encouraged democratization" (1991, p. 65). He suggests that global economic integration and industrial development provide greater resources for distribution and compromise, create nongovernmental sources of wealth and influence, and open societies "to the impact of the democratic ideas prevailing in the industrialized world" (1991, p. 66). It is akin to the classic Lipset notion (1960): Increased industrialization brings with it the development of the middle class, which serves as a buffer between the wealthy and the impoverished. And, like Lipset, Huntington posits that development increases the literate and educated population who "develop characteristics of trust, satisfaction, and competence that go with democracy" (1991, p. 66). These social strata (as individuals, not as a collectivity) are the carriers of democratic values and the agents in the democratization process. Rueschemeyer et al in their review of the redemocratization literature on Latin America also judge that "the middle classes played a more prominent role in the process of democratization than they had in advanced capitalist societies" (1992, p. 222) (Figure 1, path A,G2).

A third inescapable social transformation that accompanies global capitalism is the growth of the working class. The legal emancipation of labor, the creation of free labor markets, and the concentration of industrial workers create conditions that foster worker strength and invite popular struggles. In cases where the working class needs and/or has allies, the process unfolds as democratization rather than revolution or socialist transformation (Therborn 1977, p. 34). An excellent synthesis of these arguments can be found in the work of Rueschemeyer et al (1992). The works highlighted below are a sample of those that explicitly link the prodemocratic militancy of working classes to a global phenomenon.

Maravall and Santamaria describe how global convergence generated new working classes in Spain and contributed to the breakdown of the Franco regime. Despite the fact that they begin with the obligatory "exhaustion of the economic model and the fragility of the grounds on which the regime was based" (1986, p. 74), their analysis hinges upon a global factor. Spain embarked on a development project that invited foreign capital and linked Spain to international markets. The economic project was accompanied by social transformations such as a rural-to-urban migration and an increase in the industrial population. These social changes reinforced the organization of the democratic opposition and made it difficult to maintain the conservative patterns that had characterized the Franco regime (1986, p. 75). Their analysis points to the working class as the agent of a regime transformation. Whereas the second approach offered individual attitudes of trust and civility as the democratic building blocks, this third approach requires the collective action of workers. And, rather than relying on a favorable climate for democracy, it provides an endogenous understanding of why democracy is the preferred regime replacement. Revolution and democracy offer the best opportunities for workers to satisfy their material needs, and excluding the possibility of a socialist revolution, democracy is the preferred successor to Franco's regime (Figure 1, path A,C,G4). But as Therborn argues, "[T]he working-class movement was nowhere capable of achieving democracy by its own unaided resources..." (1977, p. 34). This suggests then that our analytical framework need go beyond simply pinpointing the strength of one class or another as the carrier of democracy.

A fourth variant of the global growth model is the most nuanced in terms of the interplay between globalized capitalism and class-state relations. As production becomes more electronically based and capital moves quickly around the world without stopping for long periods in production processes, it limits the role of national governments. As globalizing capital hollows out the state, new conflicts emerge between the (nondemocratic) state and fractions of the capitalist class. Huntington's minimalist version is that "broad-based economic development involving significant industrialization may contribute to democratization..." (1991, p. 65) because industrialization leads to a complex, diverse, and interrelated economy that is more difficult for authoritarian regimes to control.

What is named "industrial convergence" at the global level is tantamount to "late industrialization" for individual nations. With the globalization of production, some countries that were previously categorized as peripheral or semiperipheral (because of their integration into the world-system as raw material exporters) have graduated from that rank. Many countries like Brazil, Mexico, and South Africa grew fastest during the golden years of global expansion. The fourth interpretation pinpoints how global convergence alters the relationship that the state has with fractions of capital on one hand and with the working classes on the other.

Seidman's work on South Africa and Brazil exemplifies this analytical perspective. She asks how the elite, who had cooperated with the previous authoritarian state and depended upon it for protection and support, came to challenge that state and to acknowledge the legitimacy of workers' demands; and how "militant strikes and organization...spread from factories to communities...to encompass broad demands for social inclusion and citizenship" (1994, p. 97). The authoritarian state had ushered in structural changes typically associated with late industrialization; specifically, it attracted foreign and domestic capital into heavy industry (1994, p. 11). Such rapid state-sponsored industrialization shifted the composition of the business elite, putting industry in a dominant position over mining. This process was interrupted by the post-1973 international recession, which precipitated conflict between elites and the state over how to sustain the new industrial growth. Entrepreneurs had the perception that they were being closed out of policy-making agendas. Parastatals in both South Africa and Brazil were criticized for unfairly competing with private companies and for spending revenue on relatively unprofitable state-owned energy and arms industries (1994, p. 98). Seidman's state-capitalist class analysis provides the grounds for her observation that fractions of the capitalist class were withdrawing their support from the nondemocratic state.

Turning to the working class, Seidman asks if there is something about late industrializing countries that spurs workers to apply their militant discourse on class to that of citizenship. Rapid industrialization reshaped the industrial working class while denying workers and their families access to political and labor organizations. Seidman suggests that demanding greater access to state decision-making bodies, the industrialists created a political space in which labor movements could begin to demand the right to organize factory-based unions. For her, the timing of the new unionism boosted its chances of survival because dominant groups were already engaged in debates about democratization (1994, p. 10) (Figure 1, path A,B,G3 and C,G3, and F).

These four approaches all posit an affinity between global convergence and democratization, yet history cautions against easy generalizations. The early insight of Lipset (1960) regarding the affinity between development and democracy was turned on its head by a subsequent reverse wave of bureaucratic authoritarianism. What Moon writes about South Korea has been written by many: "[d]emocracy and globalization have not been necessarily complementary. They have often produced ambivalent and conflicting implications" (1996, p. 10). While globalization opens up economic spaces for the private sector, democratization opens up civil society to public interest and progressive social groups. In short, societies still confront the hostility inherent in democratic capitalism—those who own the means of production do not have a monopoly of power, and those who have political power are without ownership of the means of production (Marx 1964).

These authors formally insert class conflict into their interpretations. We learn from the second and third approaches that 1. global convergence has altered the social structure in a way that upsets the previous regime, and 2. these newly created groups, middle classes and workers, prefer democracy. The fourth interpretation traces how convergence reduces the functions of the state and alters the relationship between the state and numerous social classes. This global convergence literature adds social processes that were taken for granted in the "favorable environment" perspective.

Global Shocks

Rather than identifying a secular trend such as global industrialization, another literature identifies global shocks that have had world-wide political reverberations. In a minimalist version, any shock may create a legitimacy crisis that alters the political regime. This is essentially Hobsbawm's argument regarding the 1929 world market collapse and the subsequent fall of ten oligarchic regimes in Latin America (1967, p. 46). Most prominent in the redemocratization literature is, of course, the oil crisis. After the 1973 oil crisis, countries "such as the Philippines, Spain, Portugal, Greece, Brazil, and Uruguay were particularly hard hit" (Huntington 1991, p. 51), and it is in this population of countries that we see the movements toward redemocratization. The second oil crisis in 1979 not only fueled the Third Wave, but in "West Germany, France, Canada, and the United States, incumbent parties were turned out of office" (Huntington 1991, p. 51).

Martins (1986) traces the following path from the global oil shocks to democratization. The first oil shock produced a global recession. The Brazilian government, he argues, inattentive to this, continued with its original development program. Instead of delivering growth, that strategy created a domestic economic crisis exhibited in skyrocketing domestic interest and inflation rates, a drop in industrial production, a rise in the national debt, and an inability to service the debt (1986, p. 90). Such precarious conditions widened the gap between state promises and state accomplishments. This, and the need to renegotiate the debt with the IMF, "deprived the regime of one of its most efficient means of acquiring support from strategic groups" (1986, p. 91) and eventually cost the regime its legitimacy. Capitalists joined with the already existing mass-based opposition groups, undermining the nondemocratic regime.

The literature that enters the account with the third world debt crises of the 1980s also falls into this global shock camp. The debt crisis is the sequel to the oil crisis because windfall petro dollars were reloaned to third world nations, which had acquired substantial trade deficits owing to the increased cost of imported oil (Frieden 1991, p. 63). Castells and Laserna link democratic liberalization in Mexico back to the 1981–1982 debt crisis and the economic restructuring that it necessitated. They trace a process that began with a core nation: 1. "dominant economic aspects of the world economy (the United States) were willing to incorporate Mexico in the dynamic core of that economy"; and 2.

Mexico had the political capacity to pull it off, namely, "the efficient clientelistic system embracing the entire set of relationships between state and society" (1994, p. 68). That economic restructuring increased Mexico's role as an export processing platform, increased Mexico's ability to compete globally via technological modernization, and increased international inter-governmental and inter-firm cooperation. The restructuring and integration led business interests to realize they did not need the state as an intermediary with the United States. Mexico "no longer needed a central state" (1994, p. 73). These newly autonomous business interests generated historic electoral victories for the conservative party (PAN). Reduced state control and state ownership harmed a bureaucratic middle class whose control of the state had been its source of power and prestige. These newly disaffected middle classes provided the basis of electoral success for the Cardenas party (PRD). And finally, restructuring, debt negotiations, and the austerity programs secured Mexico's credibility in the international finance community but led to "popular discontent over the deterioration of living conditions" (1994, p. 73). This too contributed to the electoral success of the leftist party of Cardenas (PRD). Castells and Laserna have constructed an account that goes beyond the global convergence models and offers us insight into the timing and processes of democratization (Figure 1, path A,D,B,G3 and C,G4).

Foreign Intervention

The contemporary foreign intervention scholarship has highlighted the positive role of the United States in promoting democracy. In 1991, the US Congress tied guidelines regarding democracy and human rights to foreign aid (Joseph Gichuhi Njoroge, 1996. "Linkage politics: foreign aid and political changes in Sub-saharan Africa," MS: p. 3). And in 1991 and 1992 the United States and the Paris Club declared a moratorium on aid to Kenya and to Malawi pending the implementation of political reforms such as multiparty democracy, cessation of politically motivated torture and imprisonment, and the like. The analytical framework that attributes the global ascent of the democratic form to foreign intervention faces a colossal challenge. Foreign intervention does not uniformly bring democracy, sometimes it brings dictatorship.

The foreign intervention factor includes both long-term residence and short-term intervention. Regarding the former, many have hypothesized that former British colonies, on the average, had a higher probability of being democratic (Bollen & Jackman 1985, Crenshaw 1995). Rueschemeyer et al point out that limited suffrage even preceded independence in the British settler colonies—the United States, Canada, Australia, and New Zealand. British indirect rule had this beneficial outcome because it transferred representative institutions. In contrast, where the British exercised direct rule, it precluded the emergence of a civil society that might have nurtured democracy at a later time (1992, p. 121). In Arab lands, the British armies "played a major role in organizing the new...profoundly undemocratic monarchies" (Markoff 1996, p. 75). While the legacy of British indirect rule might explain the surge of democratization in the post–World War II decolonization period, it gives us little purchase on the recent Third Wave.

The balance of the literature assesses how the foreign policy objectives of some countries determine the political regimes of others. "How important are the international factors influencing attempts at redemocratization? What motivates governments to proclaim the 'promotion of democracy' as an important goal of foreign policy...?" (Whitehead 1986, p. 3). Roquie argues that the hemispheric policy of successive US administrations—the alternation after 1945 between anti-Communist vigilance and democratizing preoccupations—imparts a rhythm to the phases of autocracy and the waves of demilitarization..." (1986, p. 126). This foreign factor is imposed on nations through the use of imitation and intimidation. The overthrow of Argentine President Frondizi in 1962, for example, was a response to national conflicts that borrowed heavily from the "defensive perspective outlined by the Pentagon in the framework of post-Cuban-Revolution strategic objectives" (1986, p. 126) (Figure 1, path G1). During the post-war period, the Common Market (allegedly) excluded Spain, Greece, and Portugal because of their political regime.[1] While Europe created a "long-term pressure for democratization" (Whitehead 1986, p. 23), the United States relegated the "promotion of democracy" to a lower priority (Whitehead 1986, p. 40). "The greater America's security concern, the stronger was its benevolence toward the authoritarian Right" (1986, p. 42). From the time of Kennedy (who said he would not be averse to the overthrow of the elected Brazilian government) through Reagan, the US government did not behave in ways consistent with its principled advocacy of democracy (Whitehead 1986, p. 7) (Figure 1, path G1).

What then accounts for this shift? The end of the Cold War, a new historical conjuncture, offering the ruling hegemon(s) the luxury to tolerate and even support democracies. Huntington says as early as 1977, the International League for Human Rights indicated that human rights had become a national policy item (1991, p. 94). Carter started the conversation on human rights that Reagan institutionalized in the National Endowment for Democracy (founded in 1984). Yet the support for democracy seemed tenuous in the early years. Steinmetz (1994) asserts that the United States was only a weak champion of democracy to the Shah (Iran), Somozas (Nicaragua), and Marcos (Philippines). By the 1990s, however, the historical conjuncture of supporting dictators appeared to be coming to an end.

[1]Poulantzas argues instead that it was fear of redundancy in agricultural production.

Such explanations for the rise of democracy are deduced from an analysis of the foreign policy needs of hegemonic powers. This literature clearly establishes that decisions to construct particular political regimes are not always endogenous, rather they receive a heavy contribution from exogenous forces. What is still puzzling is why core nations found the promotion of democracy in the developing world better suited to global capitalism. From where comes this good will?

Shifting Global Hegemon

The scholarship on hegemons does not stand totally apart from the above mentioned works, to the contrary it builds upon it. In this section, I refer to authors who explicitly conceptualize the global impact in terms of a shifting global hegemon. Wallerstein (1991), in his analysis of the collapse of the Eastern bloc, offers such a model. The collapse of Eastern Europe is not the triumph of Western liberalism; it is the aftermath of US hegemonic decline. Yalta (and the cold war) allowed the Soviet Union and the United States to keep order in their respective houses. For the USSR, it meant a monopoly over the Communist discourse, permitting it to direct or repress revolutionary socialist tendencies in Eastern Europe and the Third World. When faced with German and Japanese economic competition, US hegemony came undone. As the US hegemony collapsed, so too did the Yalta-approved hold that the Soviets had on its own citizens and those of the Eastern Bloc (Figure 1, path G1).

In his study of the 1970s' transitions, Poulantzas argues that the shift in global hegemon totally undermined the authoritarian regimes. "The fundamental question regarding the overthrow of the dictatorships in Portugal and Greece, and …Spain, is…in what way have the so-called 'external' factors, the changes involved in the present phase of imperialism, been reproduced and internalized actually within the socio-economic and political structures of these countries?" (1976, p. 41). Let me summarize his analytical scheme for the Portuguese case.

Portugal, even in the post–World War II period, still derived its wealth from exploiting its colonies. Its international partners also benefitted from the colonial wealth. The changing world-system, however, shattered this pattern. As labor costs rose in the developed world, capitalists began to export capital to the less developed world (1976, p. 12) where a more intensive exploitation of labor was possible. In the early phase, industrial investments in developing countries were characterized by low levels of technology, expatriated profits, and concentration in manufactured products. Foreign capital entered Portugal in 1960 and boosted the growth in the industrial sector. While the GNP grew 1.5% and 5.9% in the agriculture and service sectors respectively, it grew 9.1% in the industrial sector. The second dimension of his analysis involves the shift from American to European dominance. By 1972, West German capital investments in Portugal had overtaken American capital. British capital was right behind (1976,p. 25). In Greece, Spain, and Portugal, the percentage of trade with the European Union was growing faster than trade with the United States.

The Portuguese project of colonial exploitation had a parallel political formation comprised of a numerically and politically weak working class; a petty bourgeoisie tied to the large state apparatus; and an oligarchy that included land owners who functioned chiefly as commercial and financial intermediaries for foreign capital associated with colonial exploitation. The new wave of foreign investment opened a space for domestic industries and gave birth to a new bourgeoisie (1976, p. 42). This new economic project differed substantially from the earlier one: It needed protected markets and state support to be competitive internationally. Nonetheless, the Estado Novo (the Portuguese authoritarian state) continued to allocate resources to the former project, dedicating, for example, 50% of the state budget to the colonial wars.

The new fractions unsuccessfully sought to renegotiate the compromise that the state had made with the older comprador bourgeoisie and to acquire a political weight equal to their new economic weight (to break the disproportionate grip of agrarian interests). This struggle led to deep conflicts within the power bloc which could not be resolved. Herein lies, for Poulantzas, the answer to the question: Why democracy? To resolve these conflicts without bloodshed, the state needed to be organized in a fashion that would permit ongoing negotiation and resolution, and it needed to allow the various classes to be represented by their own political organizations (Poulantzas 1976, p. 48).

> [T]hese military dictatorships did not enable such contradictions to be regulated by the organic representation of these various fractions within the state apparatus, nor did it allow for the establishment of a compromise equilibrium without serious upsets....We can add here that the fall or decline of these regimes corresponded to a redistribution of the balance of forces within the power bloc in favour of the fraction of capital polarized towards the Common Market and at the expense of the fraction polarized towards the United States, whose interests these regimes preponderantly represented, though not exclusively. (1976, p. 30)

But what are we to make of the role of popular struggles in democratization? The authoritarian regimes never were hegemonic among masses. Opposition existed in Portugal since the 1926 overthrow of its democracy (Schwartzman 1989), yet "(t)here was no frontal mass movement against the dictatorships, and in this sense, the popular struggles were not the direct or principal factor in their overthrow" (1976, p. 78). Nevertheless these struggles were obviously a determining factor. At this point, we can invoke those processes summarized above: The global hegemonic shift that gave rise to the new capitalist class also fostered urban migration and proletarianization of a section of the peasantry. As we have seen, this often increases the volume of class conflict. Since economic protest, such as striking, was illegal under the dictatorship, class struggles became political struggles. Rather than reinforcing authoritarian relations, such transformations gave birth to a new pro-democracy coalition—new domestic fractions of capital and workers. In this aspect, Poulantzas' analysis moves beyond observing the emergence of a new working class. He argues that workers and mass organizations will be tolerated by the new capitalists for two reasons. First, because of the nature of their economic activity (they produce wage goods rather than exported goods), they can tolerate a more open and conciliatory position toward trade unions (1976, p. 56). Second, they need the mobilized masses for their own struggle against the agrarian bloc. After failing to end the dictatorship without the associated risks of mass mobilization, the new fractions of capital reluctantly accepted mass participation (1976, p. 56). Thus, the transition to democracy resulted from

> ...a conjunctural and tactical convergence of interests between the domestic bourgeoisie on the one hand and the working classes and popular masses on the other, its objective being the replacement of these regimes by "democratic" ones. (1976, p. 58) (Figure 1, path A,B,G3 and C,G4 and F)

In a grammatically less obstructed version of Poulantzas' argument, Logan locates the principal conflict in Spain and Portugal between the competing factions of capital tied to irreconcilable strategies of integrating into the world-system (1985, p. 149). Such a line of investigation might have application for the Eastern European cases. Noting the shifting hegemon, "Gorbachev frequently spoke of the USSR's European home" (Bergesen 1992, p. 140).

In Arrighi's interpretation of the new hegemonic environment, the shift from global hegemonic anarchy to a clear bipolar order had an impact on semiperipheral nations. In the postdepression and World War II period, direct investment came to supersede trade and territorial expansion as the leading vehicle of transnational competition: The UK flag of free trade was replaced by the US flag of free enterprise. Arrighi argues that the sustained process of capital investment, particularly under conditions of global competition (the post–World War II split between capitalism and communism), led to the eventual proletarianization of workers, even in rural areas (1985, p. 272). This resulted in a "resurgence of labor movements in forms that fascism could not contain.... [which] pushed political elites towards democratic socialist forms of political-economic regulation" (1985, p. 264). For Arrighi, the hegemonic shift unleashes its influence mainly through labor (1985, p. 273) (Figure 1, path A,C,G4 and F,G3).

In these works, we are supplied a stronger, more explicit relationship between the economic development of core nations and the political transformations in semiperipheral ones. And, at least for Poulantzas, there is an attempt to identify the symbiotic tie between elites and masses as they jointly mobilize for democracy.

World-System Cycles

World-system cycle models, rather than concluding with something episodic or accidental at the global level, invoke the systemic and cyclical nature of the world-system. The world-system develops through cycles of accumulation, which are composed of phases of capital formation, consolidation, and disintegration (Arrighi 1994, p. 10). The periods of stagnation, referred to as the B-phase, are accompanied by numerous phenomena such as intensified intercapitalist competition (1994, p. 88). B-phases are certainly associated with a reorganization of production, and they may or may not be associated with a shift in hegemonic dominance. Even when the hegemonic leader retains global leadership, the character of that hegemon will change. Thusly, the United States may retain its hegemonic control, but it must capitalize on new technologies and organizational forms to do so. In some cycles of decline, hegemonic leaders are unable to maintain their monopoly and fall behind new countries that are in a better position to exploit new economic opportunities. Bergesen describes, for example, how the hegemonic shift from England to the United States at the end of the nineteenth century was tied to a shift from the British organization of economic production in family firms to the US organization in corporations (1983). Poulantzas also placed his analysis on top of a hegemonic shift from the United States to Western Europe. While world-system cycle analysts are divided about whether a hegemonic shift is occurring, they do agree that the exit from the current cycle of stagnation will require new forms of economic organization. Furthermore, they link the contemporary Third Wave of democratization to the current economic contraction. This assertion diverges radically from that of Huntington and others who argue that "[T]he wave of democratizations that began in 1974 was the product of the economic growth of the previous two decades" (1991, p. 61).

While the shifts to democracy have taken place around the globe, they are not found at all levels of the global hierarchy. Democratization in the Third Wave has found more fertile grounds in the semiperiphery. Why democracy in the semiperiphery? Semiperipheral countries are hardest hit by the shock waves of the B-Phase. At the same time, periods of instability and intracore competition give nations in the semiperiphery opportunities to increase their relative power. Bergesen argues that democracy is a preferable national strategy because it is enabling. "The pressure of the downturn generates social and political crises, and...semi-peripheral states turn on themselves and reconstitute internally in the hope of better dealing with the crisis of slow growth, inflation, unemployment, and staggering debt payments" (1992, p. 144).

But why should instability in the semiperiphery lead to democracy rather than fascism or bureaucratic authoritarianism? We know that one of the domestic manifestations of a semiperipheral position can be a disarticulated economy, which in turn has detrimental effects on democratic stability (Schwartzman 1989). We also have an extensive scholarship that illustrates the necessity and efficacy of "developmental dictatorships" in the semiperiphery [Gerschenkron (1966) on late developers in Western Europe, Gregor (1979) on Mussolini, O'Donnell on Latin America, and Wallerstein (1979) on the world-system, to name a few]. According to these authors, aggressive nondemocratic states historically have offered advantages over democratic ones. By restricting consumption and directing resources toward savings and investment, nations such as South Korea, Chile, and Brazil used nondemocratic regimes to improve their standing in the world-system hierarchy. We need to acknowledge the empirical fact that semiperipheral nations, which historically counted less frequently among democratic nations, now seem to make up the bulk of the Third Wave. Furthermore, we have to concede that while there were many authors who showed how developmental dictatorships were the natural response to a world crisis, there are now many more who are complacent to describe democracy as the natural response to a world shift. A world-system analysis sheds some light on this dilemma. The question must be revised to read: "Why were late developers more receptive to nondemocratic regimes in the B-phase of the free trade cycle and to democratic regimes in the B-phase of the global convergence cycle? Why is democracy now the way to negotiate the new global linkages?" Or, the even stronger version, which synthesizes aspects of core-semiperipheral relations and cyclical trends, "Why has democratic rule replaced authoritarian rule as the superior handmaiden of foreign capital penetration?"

One answer can be quickly deduced from the literatures that describe the relationship between the form of state and world-system location. Wallerstein argued that semiperipheral countries were more likely to have "interventionist" states because of the particular system of labor control found there. Authoritarian states were more successful in guaranteeing the semifeudal forms of labor control (tenancy or sharecropping) which were more prevalent in the semiperiphery (1984). Therefore, these semiperiphery nations, by virtue of global economic convergence, have lost their quality of "semiperipheralness" and taken on some qualities of the core, such as an enlarged working class and an industrial bourgeoisie that can contest the power of the landed aristocracy. Growth of these new sectors reduced the level of economic "disarticulation," thereby removing the obstructions to democracy. Thus, as countries develop and move into this zone, "they become prospects for democratization" (Huntington 1991, p. 60). One shortcoming of this deduction is that it reduces the world-system component to the "global convergence" argument and is silent about the world-system shifts and their repercussions for non-core countries. Furthermore, it doesn't speak to the dilemma of why the United States was an enthusiastic supporter of nondemocratic regimes some fifteen years earlier.

We need a model that speaks directly to aspects of this particular downturn, how it affects core-semiperipheral economic relations, and how this, in turn, contributes to democratization. By incorporating the global crisis into her analysis of Poland, Verdery takes one step in this direction. Core nations had two reactions to the crisis in the early 1970s: First, they earned money by lending abroad, and second, they shifted from Fordist production to flexible specialty production. These factors constituted the environment for socialist economies, which were equally affected by the global crisis. Governments first tried to salvage socialism without transforming it. "Instead of reforming the system from within, most Party leadership opted to meet their problems by...importing western capital and using it to buy advanced technology (or, as in Poland, to subsidize consumption)" (1993, p. 14). The world market was unable to absorb the increased volume of exported manufactured goods coming out of the socialist economies, and therefore, borrowers were unable to repay their debts. This debt crisis increased the power of that fraction of the ruling elite (within the Communist Party) that had advocated structural reforms, including markets and profits. Bureaucrats themselves created private companies at the interstices of the socialist state and the capitalist economy: They mediated export trade, and they imported computers for the state.

They also embarked on the new capitalist form of flexible specialization. Here, Verdery links the global cycle to democratization by contending that if the capitalist world still had been pursuing the Fordist conception of growth, it might have been more receptive to state organized "large-scale heroic production..." (1993, p. 16). Having moved to small-scale flexible specialization, however, core nations were less sympathetic to state directed growth (Figure 1, path A,B,C,G3,G4). Komlosy and Hofbauer add that the core nations were also less sympathetic to helping the East catch up to the West. Core nations followed the old Cold War regulations forbidding the export of advanced technology to Eastern Europe (1994, p. 135). As we have already seen in the discussion of Mexico and Brazil, the core response to the economic crisis created a new capitalism that struck at the heart of centralized control, undermining a host of state functions. Reformers invited foreign capital into their domain, but they also invited in privatization and other conditions that accompany such capital. In this way socialism was undermined by a government that had launched a venture to save it.

Cardoso also builds aspects of this particular B-phase into his work on Brazil. He posits that the global contraction led core nations to adopt economic policies toward non-core nations that not only created conflict between the state and fractions of the capitalist class, but also undermined the regime's stability.

> [T]he evolution of the international economic crisis and the pressure from international partners to place their equipment in Brazil's industrial projects...made it difficult for the Geisel government to keep its promise to sustain the national capital goods sector. Worsening foreign debt, fueled by the importation of foreign equipment...left the government even less room for maneuver in maintaining the goals of autonomy... [and] the local capital goods manufacturing sector" (1986, p. 144). "...It was against this background that the private sector discovered 'democracy' and some industrialists even rediscovered the constitution. (1986, p. 143)

In distancing themselves from the state, industrialists rediscovered democracy—"renewal of party-political activity and the emergence of pressure groups and social classes" (1986, p. 139), and then they discovered that the masses could be partners in this anti-government coalition. At the 1977 assembly of the National Manufacturing Sector Congress, entrepreneurs defended the workers' right to strike and asked for unqualified democracy and qualified economical liberalism (1986, p. 142). In 1978 they issued a public declaration which read "We wish to express our view of the path to economic development, based on social justice and promoted by democratic political institutions..." (1986, p. 145). For Cardoso, it was clearly the integration of the national development program into a "crisis-ridden" "free-enterprise" global economy that led the elite to withdraw legitimacy and demand a political opening.

The above B-phase answers link the nature of the current cycle of capitalist accumulation to core economic policies in less developed countries. In short, they give meaning to the notion of globalization of production. Having established this connection, we can draw from Seidman and others who demonstrate how this new globalization has transformed the working classes and led to new social movements, which the nondemocratic regimes found difficult to contain. In addition, drawing on the work of Poulantzas and others mentioned above, we see why the new technocratic and globally integrated elite may not have required total repression of the class conflict that was accompanying globalization. But why democratization? Democratization can actually decrease levels of mobilization and participation. By transforming a contentious and organized working class into a citizenry, democracy can more peacefully guide developing countries through the painful process of global integration. Because democracy encourages individuals to participate on the basis of unlimited collective identities (Catholics, Greens, Bavarians, etc), it fosters the individualization of class relations, particularly at the level of politics and ideology (Przeworski 1985, p. 12–13). Synthesizing many of these linkages, Robinson argues "All over the world, the Unites States is now promoting its version of 'democracy' as a way to relieve pressure from subordinate groups for more fundamental political, social, and economic change" (1996, p. 6) (Figure 1, path G1,A,C,F,G3,G4). This B-phase world-system perspective seems to offer the greatest insights in deciphering the deeper significance of the Third Wave of democratization.

CONCLUSION

The literature contains many informed works that focus in one way or another upon the global-civil society connection. What do we know? The majority (albeit not unanimous) conclude that the transitions were not simply popular uprisings. Many conclude that fractions of the capitalist classes played a significant part in preferring and achieving an alternative state form—democracy. Others stress that domestic transformations are situated in a world-system in which core trajectories have inescapable ramifications for the economic and political regimes of non-core nations. Our greatest insights, it seems to me, come from those works that identify class conflict as the social mechanism linking world-system processes to national political dynamics. In this framework, domestic political structures become part of the evolving transnational fabric of economic relations.

While the culturally distinct and event-specific accounts of transitions to democracy give us invaluable insight into the unfolding of the transitions, they keep us from an understanding of the global networks in which nations have been embedded for ages. The historical clustering and its companion wave paradigm leave case-study researchers little option but to seek conversations with comparativists. Inversely, the macro accounts give us invaluable insight into deep structures but withhold from us understanding of individual actors and questions of agency. The cross-national variation and its companion "voice" literature leave macro researchers little choice but to seek conversations with area-study researchers. "They desired freedom" is as deficient of an explanatory model as "the B-phase made them do it."

Such is a tall order. Specialization means that most researchers are unprepared to operate both multiple regression and ethnographic vehicles. For methodological and epistemological reasons, no one researcher is likely simultaneously to arrive at both "they desired freedom" and "the B-phase made them do it" conclusions. In fact these two perspectives rarely meet. Yet it is in that meeting that we have the most to gain. On the one hand, we have to avoid excessive fine-tuning of the hermetically sealed literatures of social movements or world-systems which stress single factor dynamics. On the other hand, we have to beware the false unions that substitute eclectic aggregation for theoretical synthesis. The excitement and frustrations of citizens in newly democratized nations have their counterparts in sociology. It is momentous.

ACKNOWLEDGMENTS

The author would like to thank anonymous reviews for their helpful suggestions.

Literature Cited

Arrighi G. 1985. Fascism to Democratic Socialism. In *Semiperipheral Development*, ed. G. Arrighi, pp. 243–79. Beverly Hills, CA: Sage

Arright G. 1994. *The Long Twentieth Century*. New York: Verso

Bergesen A. 1983. Economic crisis and merger movements: 1880's Britain and 1980's Unites States. In *Ascent and Decline in the World-System*, ed. E Friedman, pp. 27–39. Beverly Hills: Sage

Bergesen A. 1992. Communism's collapse: a world-system explanation. *J. Polit. Milit. Sociol.* 20(Summer):133–51

Bollen KA, Jackman RW. 1985. Economic and noneconomic determinants of political democracy in the 1960s. In *Research in Political Sociology*, pp. 27–48. New York: JAI

Bollen KA, Jackman RW. 1989. Democracy, stability, dichotomies. *Am. Sociol. Rev.* 54(Aug):612–21

Bunce V. 1993. Leaving socialism: a transition to democracy?. *Contention* 3(1): 35–47

Cardoso FH. 1986. *Entrepreneurs and the Transition Process: The Brazilian Case In Transitions from Authoritarian Rule: Comparative Perspectives*. ed. G O'Donnell, PC Schmitter, L Whitehead, pp. 137–53. Baltimore, MD: Johns Hopkins Univ. Press

Castells M, Laserna R. 1994. The new dependency: technological change and socioeconomic restructuring in Latin America. In *Comparative National Development*, ed. AD Kincaid, A Portes, pp. 57–83. Chapel Hill: Univ. N. Carolina

Chalmers D. 1990. *Dilemmas of Latin American Democratization: Dealing with International Forces. Inst. Latin Am. Iberian Stud. No. 18*. New York: Columbia Univ.

Conaghan CM, Espinal R. 1990. Unlikely transitions to uncertain regimes? Democracy without compromise in the Dominican Republic and Ecuador. *J. Latin Am. Stud.* 22(3):553–74

Crenshaw EM. 1995. Democracy and demographic inheritance: the influence of modernity and proto-modernity on political and civil rights, 1965-1980. *Am. Sociol. Rev.* 60(Oct):702–18

Chirot D. 1991. What happened in Eastern Europe in 1989? In *The Crisis of Leninism and the Decline of the Left*, ed. D Chirot, pp. 3–31. Seattle, WA: Univ. Wash. Press

Diamandouros PN. 1986. Regime change and the prospects for democracy in Greece: 1974–1983. In *Transitions from Authoritarian Rule: Southern Europe*, ed. G O'Donnell, PC Schmitter, L Whitehead, pp. 138–64. Baltimore, MD: Johns Hopkins Univ. Press

Draper T. 1992. Who killed Soviet Communism? *NY Rev. Books*. June 11:7–14

Evans P. 1979. *Dependent Development*. Princeton, NJ: Princeton Univ. Press

Fishman RM. 1990. Rethinking state and regime: Southern Europe's transition to democracy. *World Polit.* 42(3):422–40

Frieden J. 1991. *Debt, Development, and Democracy*. Princeton, NJ: Princeton Univ. Press

Fukuyama F. 1992. *The End of History and the Last Man*. New York: Oxford

Goldfarb J. 1992. *After the Fall: The Pursuit of Democracy in Eastern Europe*. NY: Basic Books

Gerschenkron A. 1966. *Economic Backwardness in Historical Perspective*. Cambridge, MA: Belknap

Gregor J. 1979. *Italian Fascism and Developmental Dictatorship*. Princeton, NJ: Princeton Univ. Press

Hobsbawm E. 1967. Peasants and rural migrants in politics. In *The Politics of Conformity in Latin America*, ed. C Veliz, pp. 43–65. London: Oxford Univ. Press

Holmes L. 1997. *Post-Communism*. Oxford: Polity

Huntington S. 1991. *The Third Wave: Democratization in the Late Twentieth Century.* Norman: Univ. Okla. Press

Kincaid AD, Portes A, eds. 1994. *Comparative National Development.* Chapel Hill: Univ. N. Carolina Press

Komlosy A, Hofbauer H. 1994. Eastern Europe: From Second World to First or Third World. *Contention* 3(2):129–43

Linz JJ, Stepan A, eds. 1978. *The Breakdown of Democratic Regimes.* Baltimore, MD: Johns Hopkins Univ. Press

Lipset SM. 1960. *Political Man.* Garden City, NJ: Anchor

Logan J. 1985. *Democracy From Above In Semiperipheral Development*, ed. G Arrighi, pp. 149–78. Beverly Hills, CA: Sage

Maravall JM, Santamaria J. 1986. Political change in Spain and the prospects for democracy. In *Transitions from Authoritarian Rule: Southern Europe,* ed. G O'Donnell, PC Schmitter, L Whitehead, pp. 71–108. Baltimore, MD: Johns Hopkins Univ. Press

Markoff J. 1996. *Waves of Democracy.* Thousand Oaks, CA: Pine Forge

Martins L. 1986. The "liberalization" of authoritarian rule in Brazil. In *Transitions from Authoritarian Rule: Latin America,* ed. G O'Donnell, PC Schmitter, L Whitehead, pp. 72–94. Baltimore, MD: Johns Hopkins Univ. Press

Marx K. 1964. *Class Struggles in France: 1848–1850.* New York: Int. Publ.

Moon CI. 1996. *Democratization and globalization as ideological and political foundations of economic policy.* Presented at Hoover Inst. Workshop. July, 1996. Stanford, CA

Moon CI, Kim YC. 1996. A circle of paradox: development, politics and democracy in South Korea. In *Development and Democracy,* ed. A Leftwich. Cambridge, UK: Polity

Munck GL. 1994. Democratic transitions in comparative perspective. *Compar. Polit.* April:355–75

O'Donnell G. 1973. *Modernization and Bureaucratic Authoritarianism.* Berkeley: Inst. Int. Stud., Univ. Calif.

O'Donnell G, Schmitter PC, Whitehead L. 1996. *Transitions from Authoritarian Rule.* Baltimore, MD: Johns Hopkins Univ. Press

Poulantzas N. 1976. *The Crisis of Dictatorships.* London: NLB

Przeworksi A. 1991. *Democracy and the Market.* Cambridge, UK: Cambridge Univ. Press

Przeworksi A. 1985. *Capitalism and Social Democracy.* Cambridge, UK: Cambridge Univ. Press

Przeworksi A. 1986. Some problems in the study of the transition to democracy. In *Transitions from Authoritarian Rule: Comparative Perspectives*, ed. G O'Donnell, PC Schmitter, L Whitehead, pp. 47–63. Baltimore, MD: Johns Hopkins Univ. Press

Robinson WI. 1996. *Promoting Polyarchy: Globalization, US Intervention, and Hegemony.* Cambridge, UK: Cambridge Univ. Press

Rouquie A. 1986. Demilitarization and the institutionalization of military-dominated polities in Latin America. In *Transitions from Authoritarian Rule: Comparative Perspectives,* ed. G O'Donnell, PC Schmitter, L Whitehead, pp. 108–36. Baltimore, MD: Johns Hopkins Univ. Press:

Rueschemeyer D, Stephens EH, Stephens J. 1992. *Capitalist Development and Democracy.* Chicago: Univ. Chicago Press

Schwartzman K. 1989. *The Social Origins of Democratic Collapse: The First Portuguese Republic in the Global Economy.* Lawrence: Univ. Press of Kans.

Seidman G. 1994. *Manufacturing Militancy.* Berkeley: Univ. Calif. Press

Shannon TR. 1989. *An Introduction to the World-System Perspective.* Boulder, CO: Westview

Steinmetz S. 1994. *Democratic Transition and Human Rights.* Albany: State Univ. New York

Therborn G. 1977. The rule of capital and the rise of democracy. *New Left Rev.* 103:3–42

Verdery K. 1993. What was socialism and why did it fall? *Contention* 3(1):1–23

Wall Street Journal. 1996. More Nations Embrace Democracy. June 25, p. 1

Wallerstein I. 1984. *The Modern World System.* New York: Academic

Wallerstein I. 1979. *The Capitalist World Economy.* Cambridge, UK: Cambridge Univ. Press

Wallerstein I. 1984. *The Politics of the World Economy.* Cambridge, UK: Cambridge Univ. Press

Wallerstein I. 1991. *Geopolitics and Geoculture.* Cambridge, UK: Cambridge Univ. Press

Whitehead L. 1986. International aspects of democratization. In *Transitions from Authoritarian Rule: Comparative Perspectives*, ed. G ODonnell, PC Schmitter, L Whitehead, pp. 3–46. Baltimore, MD: Johns Hopkins Univ. Press:

Zubeck V, Gentleman J. 1994. Economic crisis and the movement toward pluralism in Poland and Mexico. *Polit. Sci. Q.* 109(2): 335–59

Annu. Rev. Sociol. 1998. 24:183–214

SOCIAL DILEMMAS: The Anatomy of Cooperation

Peter Kollock

Department of Sociology, University of California at Los Angeles, Los Angeles, California 90095-1551; e-mail: KOLLOCK@UCLA.EDU

KEY WORDS: prisoner's dilemma, public good, commons, collective action

ABSTRACT

The study of social dilemmas is the study of the tension between individual and collective rationality. In a social dilemma, individually reasonable behavior leads to a situation in which everyone is worse off. The first part of this review is a discussion of categories of social dilemmas and how they are modeled. The key two-person social dilemmas (Prisoner's Dilemma, Assurance, Chicken) and multiple-person social dilemmas (public goods dilemmas and commons dilemmas) are examined. The second part is an extended treatment of possible solutions for social dilemmas. These solutions are organized into three broad categories based on whether the solutions assume egoistic actors and whether the structure of the situation can be changed: Motivational solutions assume actors are not completely egoistic and so give some weight to the outcomes of their partners. Strategic solutions assume egoistic actors, and neither of these categories of solutions involve changing the fundamental structure of the situation. Solutions that do involve changing the rules of the game are considered in the section on structural solutions. I conclude the review with a discussion of current research and directions for future work.

THE QUESTION OF COOPERATION

Social dilemmas are situations in which individual rationality leads to collective irrationality. That is, individually reasonable behavior leads to a situation in which everyone is worse off than they might have been otherwise. Many of the most challenging problems we face, from the interpersonal to the international, are at their core social dilemmas.

0360-0572/98/0815-0215/$0.800

As individuals we are each better off when we make use of a public resource, such as public television, without making any contribution, but if everyone acted on this conclusion, the public resource would not be provided and we would all be hurt. Each farmer does best by taking as much irrigation water as possible, and each fisher benefits from catching as many fish as possible, but the aggregate outcome of these individually reasonable decisions can be disaster—groundwater exhausted and fish species depleted to the point of extinction.

This review of the literature on social dilemmas is divided into two major sections. The first is a discussion of categories of social dilemmas and how they are modeled. The second is an extended treatment of possible solutions for social dilemmas. I conclude with a discussion of current research and directions for future work.

Any review of this length is necessarily selective. I have focused mainly but not exclusively on research since 1980 and on behavioral studies that use either experimental methods or field research. Even with these filters, the work I discuss is still a small sample; my goal is to provide a structure for understanding this area of research and a set of pointers to useful resources. For further information I would suggest other reviews by Komorita & Parks (1995, 1996), Ledyard (1995), Yamagishi (1995), van Lange et al (1992), Messick & Brewer (1983), Stroebe & Frey (1982), Orbell & Dawes (1981), Dawes (1980), Edney & Harper (1978a). A number of edited volumes are useful general resources, in particular the volumes that have come out of the biannual International Conference on Social Dilemmas: Liebrand & Messick (1996), Schulz et al (1994), Liebrand et al (1992), Wilke et al (1986). Other useful edited volumes include Schroeder (1995) and Hinde & Groebel (1991). An important set of field studies on social dilemmas can be found in Ostrom et al (1994), Bromley et al (1992), Ostrom (1990), McCay & Acheson (1987), Hardin & Baden (1977). There is even a popular press account of these issues in Poundstone (1992). Finally, a variety of resources are now available on the World Wide Web. I have collected a number of these sources at a Web page devoted to this review: www.sscnet.ucla.edu/soc/faculty/kollock/dilemmas (1998b).

MODELING SOCIAL DILEMMAS

All social dilemmas are marked by at least one *deficient equilibrium*. It is deficient in that there is at least one other outcome in which everyone is better off. It is an equilibrium in that no one has an incentive to change their behavior. Thus, at their worst, social dilemmas exemplify the true meaning of tragedy: "The essence of dramatic tragedy," wrote Whitehead, "is not unhappiness. It resides in the solemnity of the remorseless working of things" (quoted in Stroebe & Frey 1982). A group of people facing a social dilemma may completely understand the situation, may appreciate how each of their actions contribute to a disastrous outcome, and still be unable to do anything about it.

The most severe social dilemmas are also characterized by a *dominating strategy* that leads to a deficient equilibrium. A dominating strategy is a strategy that yields the best outcome for an individual regardless of what anyone else does. The compelling, and perverse, feature of these dilemmas is that there is no ambiguity about what one should do to benefit oneself, yet all are hurt if all follow this "rational" decision. However, not all social dilemmas involve dominating strategies, as we see below.

Necessary, Dangerous Metaphors

The literature in social dilemmas has revolved around three metaphorical stories that have assumed mythic proportions. These stories—the Prisoner's Dilemma, the problem of providing Public Goods, and the Tragedy of the Commons—have served as catalysts facilitating and structuring research. They have also served as blinders. The hegemony of these models has at times led researchers—or worse, policy makers—to believe mistakenly that these metaphors capture the whole range of social dilemmas or accurately model all empirical social dilemmas.

I deal with each of these models and their limitations below as well as with other models of social dilemmas that have traditionally received less attention. In categorizing social dilemmas, I make the first cut in distinguishing dilemmas that involve only two actors (known as dyadic or two-person dilemmas) from social dilemmas involving multiple actors (known as *N*-person dilemmas, where *N* is some number greater than two).

Two-Person Dilemmas

In 1950 Merrill Flood and Melvin Dresher—scientists at RAND Corporation in Santa Monica, California—carried out an informal experiment using a new game they had developed. The game was the simplest possible example of a social dilemma in that it involved only two people, each of whom faced a single choice between two options (termed cooperation and defection). Albert Tucker, a mathematician who was a colleague of theirs, created a story to go along with the game that involved two prisoners, which subsequently became known as the *Prisoner's Dilemma*—the game that launched a thousand studies (actually, several thousand).

The original story involves two prisoners who are separately given the choice between testifying against the other or keeping silent (see e.g. Luce & Raifa 1957). In my classroom I offer a simple example of the game: Two students are asked to take $1 out of their wallets. Each, in secret, decides whether to place the money in an envelope (cooperate) or to keep the money in one's pocket (defect). Each envelope is then given to the other person, and I double whatever money has been given. The possible outcomes (in dollars) are seen in Figure 1*a*. The game is marked by the fact that whatever choice one's partner makes, one is better off defecting (i.e. defecting is a dominating strategy): If Player II cooperates, Player I's defection brings a payoff of $3 for Player I, and $0 for Player II. If Player II defects, Player I is still better off defecting, which yields a payoff of $1 for both. Since the payoff structure is identical for both actors, they converge on mutual defection even though both would be better off if they had cooperated, a move that gives both actors a payoff of $2. In other words, it is a deficient equilibrium. This dilemma is at the heart of unsecured transactions. For example, when I buy something through the mail, I may be tempted to not send a check and the other person may be tempted to not send the goods, but if we both defect, we are each worse off than if we had consummated the exchange.

What defines the Prisoner's Dilemma is the relative value of the four outcomes. The best possible outcome is defecting while one's partner cooperates (designated DC). The next best outcome is mutual cooperation (CC) followed by mutual defection (DD), with the worst outcome being the case in which one cooperates while one's partner defects (CD). Thus, in a Prisoner's Dilemma, DC > CC > DD > CD.[1]

Two other important games can be created by switching the relative value of the outcomes. If mutual cooperation leads to a better outcome than unilateral defection (CC > DC > DD > CD), the situation is known as an *Assurance Game*; an example of this game is shown in Figure 1*b*. The name comes from the fact that a person would be willing to cooperate as long as that person were assured that the partner would cooperate as well. A common misunderstanding is that an Assurance Game presents no dilemma and leads inevitably to mutual cooperation. In fact, cooperation is not a dominating strategy, and if the person believes the partner will defect, the best the person can do is to defect as well. In other words, the Assurance Game has two equilibria: mutual cooperation, which is an optimal equilibrium, and mutual defection, which is a deficient equilibrium.[2] I may be happy to work with you on preparing a joint report, and a report to which we have both contributed may be the best possible outcome for me, but if I cannot prepare the report myself and I do not believe you will cooperate, I am best off defecting as well. The key issue in the Assurance

[1]There is a second inequality that is also often included as part of the definition: CC > (CD + DC)/2. This inequality states that mutual cooperation is more profitable that alternating exploitation of self with exploitation of other.

[2]Technically, the equilibria I discuss in this section are known as Nash equilibria. A Nash equilibrium is "any pair of strategies with the property that each player maximizes his or her payoff given what the other player does" (Ostrom et al 1994, p. 54).

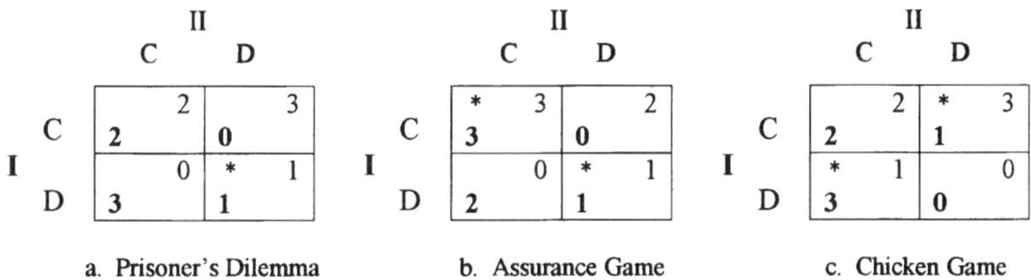

Figure 1 Three two-person games in their ordinal form: I and II designate Players I and II; C and D designate cooperation and defection. Player I's outcomes are shown in bold. Nash equilibria are designated with asterisks.

Game is whether we can trust each other. This game has received much less attention than the Prisoner's Dilemma Game, although I argue below that it is a more accurate model than the Prisoner's Dilemma Game of many social dilemma situations.

The third game discussed here is created by switching a different pair of outcomes in the Prisoner's Dilemma Game. If mutual defection yields a worse outcome than unilateral cooperation (DC > CC > CD > DD), we create the game of *Chicken*, which can be seen in Figure 1*c*. It is named after a game of dare that was made famous in the 1955 film *Rebel Without a Cause*. Two youths drive their cars toward each other (or in the case of the film, toward a cliff). The first youth to turn away is "chicken" and loses face, while the other youth basks in the glory of his courage. However, if neither youth turns away, they both end by dying—the worst outcome. If both turn away, the sting of being chicken is not as great since both drivers lost their nerve. There are two equilibria in the Chicken Game—unilateral defection and unilateral cooperation. If driving toward each other, you are sure the other person will lose their nerve and swerve, you are best off driving straight ahead, but if you believe the other person will not swerve, you are better off swerving and losing face rather than your life. In this sense, you have an advantage in this game if you can convince the other person that you are crazy, irrational, suicidal, or otherwise incapable or unwilling to change course. In such a setting the other driver will swerve and you will obtain the best possible outcome.

An alternate interpretation of the Chicken Game is a situation in which each person individually has the ability to produce an outcome that will benefit both parties, although providing the benefit involves some cost. Whereas mutual cooperation is the unambiguous goal for the Prisoner's Dilemma Game and the Assurance Game, that is not necessarily the case for the Chicken Game. If one person can provide a joint benefit, then it may make no sense for the second person to duplicate the effort. The problem comes when each person attempts to "stare the other down," each refusing to budge and hoping the other will give in and cooperate. The key problem then is avoiding a stalemate that results in the worst possible outcome.[3]

Note that unlike the Prisoner's Dilemma Game, neither the Assurance Game nor the Chicken Game has a dominating strategy. In the latter two games the partner's choice is crucial in determining one's best outcome—one wants to match the partner's choice in the Assurance Game and to make the opposite choice in the Chicken Game.

Multiple-Person Dilemmas

The first cut in categorizing social dilemmas was distinguishing between two-person and *N*-person dilemmas. Within *N*-person dilemmas we make the next cut, distinguishing between two broad types of multiple-person dilemmas in terms of how the costs and benefits are arranged for each individual (Cross & Guyer 1980). In the first type, known as a social fence, the individual is faced with an immediate cost that generates a benefit that is shared by all. The individual has an incentive to avoid the cost, but if all do so each is worse off than if they had managed to "scale the fence." In the second type, termed a social trap, the individual is tempted with an immediate benefit that produces a cost shared by all. If all succumb to the temptation, the outcome is a collective disaster.[4] Within each of these broad categories lies a richly developed metaphor that has driven research in the area: (*a*) the provision of public goods (a social fence) and (*b*) the tragedy of the commons (a social trap).[5] The potentially noxious outcomes of both types of social dilemmas stem from what economists refer to as externalities, which are present "whenever the behavior of a person affects the situation of other persons without the explicit agreement of that person or persons" (Buchanan 1971, p. 7). Broadly speaking, externalities are uncompensated interdependencies (Cornes & Sandler 1996).

PUBLIC GOODS DILEMMAS A public good is a resource from which all may benefit, regardless of whether they have helped provide the good—I can enjoy public television whether or not I contribute any money, and I can enjoy the parks in my city even if I do not pay municipal taxes. This is to say that public

[3]Poundstone (1992, p. 203) reports an anecdote by Anatol Rapoport that "the Fuegian language of the natives of Tierra del Fuego contains the word *mamihlapinatapai*, meaning, 'looking at each other hoping that either will offer to do something that both parties desire but are unwilling to do.'"

[4]Note that this general formulation of social dilemmas rests on learning models rather than on any assumption of more complex strategic decision-making, as is common in the economic models to be discussed.

[5]Other important dimensions along which social dilemmas can be categorized include the temporal lag between the original action and the eventual disaster (e.g. Messick & Brewer 1983) and whether the actors in a social dilemma each face an identical incentive structure or not (e.g. Marwell & Oliver 1993).

goods are *non-excludable* and as a result there is the temptation to enjoy the good without contributing to its creation or maintenance. Those who do so are termed free-riders, and while it is individually rational to free-ride, if all do so the public good is not provided and all are worse off. This decision is based on greed, i.e., the simple desire to obtain the best possible outcome for oneself. There is also a second reason that can lead to defection—a person may be willing to cooperate but fear that not enough others will do so to actually provide a public good. Rather than greed, the concern here is the fear of being a sucker, i.e., throwing away one's efforts on a lost cause.

Public goods are also distinguished by the fact that they are *nonrival* (Cornes & Sandler 1996) in that one person's use of the good does not diminish its availability to another person—my enjoyment of public television does not make less of it available to anyone else. A pure public good is completely nonexcludable and nonrival, but many public goods exhibit these two qualities only to a varying degree. The basic problem was described at least as early as 1739 by Hume, articulated by Samuelson in 1954, and made famous by Olson in 1965 with the publication of *The Logic of Collective Action*.

A key characteristic of public goods dilemmas is the relationship between the level of resources contributed toward the production of a public good and the level of the public good that is provided. This relationship is known as the production function (Marwell & Oliver 1993, Heckathorn 1996). Production functions can take on any number of forms, but the four basic production functions shown in Figure 2 can be used to model many of the most important dynamics in public goods dilemmas.[6]

With a decelerating production function (Figure 2*a*), initial contributions have the greatest effect, with additional contributions generating increasingly diminishing returns. With a linear production function (Figure 2*b*), each unit of resource contributed produces the same return. An accelerating production function (Figure 2*c*) produces few returns for the initial contributions but brings increasing returns as the contributions increase. Finally, discontinuities in the production function, such as the step-level function in Figure 2*d*, create thresholds (also known as provision points). In these cases little or no amount of the public good is produced until a certain level is reached, at which point a small increase in the level of contributions returns a large and discontinuous amount of the public good. In the analysis of public goods, one of the most important distinctions is whether there are threshold points in the production function (Ledyard 1995).

A common misunderstanding is the assumption that all N-person dilemmas have the structure of an N-person Prisoner's Dilemma Game. That is, that there

[6]Some production functions are combinations of these basic forms. A third-order S-shaped curve, for example, is composed of accelerating, linear, and decelerating components.

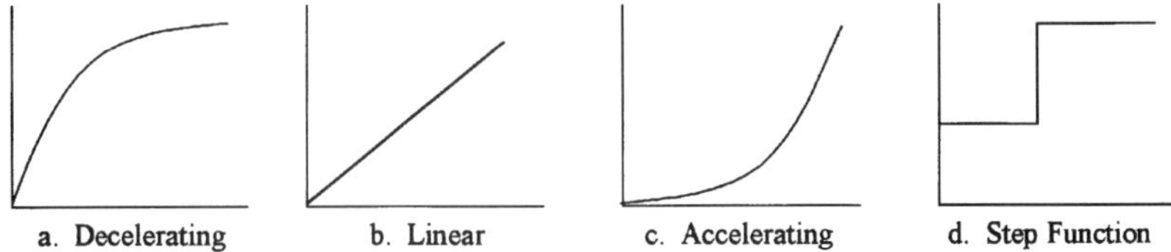

Figure 2 Four production functions (*a*) Decelerating, (*b*) Linear, (*c*) Accelerating, (*d*) Step Function

is a dominating strategy that leads to a deficient equilibrium in which no one cooperates.[7] In fact, various production functions can yield *N*-person versions of the Assurance Game and Chicken Game as well as the Prisoner's Dilemma Game.[8] Note that if a situation has the structure of an Assurance Game, there is no temptation to free-ride—the only concern is whether one will be a "sucker." In a Chicken Game, however, the incentive to free-ride can be even more severe than in the Prisoner's Dilemma Game (Yamagishi 1995).

COMMONS DILEMMAS The second mythic story commonly used in describing *N*-person dilemmas is the tragedy of the commons. Early statements of the basic problem can be found in Aristotle (*Politics*, Book II, Chapter 3).[9] The dilemma in its modern form was carefully described by Lloyd in 1832 and made famous by Hardin in 1968 when he published his article in *Science* on the topic. Hardin described a group of herders having open access to a common parcel of land on which they could let their cows graze. It is in each herder's interest to put as many cows as possible onto the land, even if the commons is damaged as a result. The herder receives all the benefits from the additional cows, and the damage to the commons is shared by the entire group. Yet if all herders make this individually reasonable decision, the commons is destroyed and all will suffer. When timber is harvested faster than it can grow or when fish are caught in greater numbers than their reproductive capacity, we face tragedies of the commons. Here again the problem is the non-excludability of a joint resource, but unlike public goods, a key feature of commons dilemmas is

[7]This belief has led to some misguided critiques of the game theoretic models underlying work on social dilemmas. For a rejoinder to these flawed criticisms as well as an honest discussion of the limits of game theoretic models, see Lohmann (1995).

[8]Heckathorn (1996) has written a very useful general analysis of different types of games and how they are the result of various production functions in combination with the relative value of the public good (note that this analysis concerns dyadic games). See also Schelling (1978) for an influential discussion and method of modeling different social dilemmas.

[9]And later in traditional rhymes: "They hang the man and flog the woman, That steal the goose from off the common, But let the greater villain loose, That steals the common from the goose" (quoted in Fairlie et al 1994).

the *subtractability* of the benefits (the opposite of being nonrival): The tree I cut, the fish I catch, and the water I use are not available for others.

For commons dilemmas, the issue is not the production function but the carrying capacity of the commons, which is a function of its replenishment rate. Different resource pools will be renewed at different rates—the reproduction rate of a species of fish, the yearly rainfall that adds to groundwater reserves, the rate at which pollutants dissipate in the air; this will determine the rate at which the subtractable joint resource can be appropriated without exhausting the commons.

In sum, public goods dilemmas concern the production of, and commons dilemmas involve the use of, a joint good from which it is difficult to exclude others. There are many reasons why excluding others might be costly (Ostrom et al 1994): the physical nature of the resource (it is difficult to fence in ocean fish or exclude tax scofflaws from the benefits of secure national borders); the available technology (enclosing huge range lands used to be prohibitively expensive—until the introduction of barbed wire); or existing laws and traditional norms (which might prohibit anyone being excluded from a commons or public good). These two basic forms of *N*-person dilemmas are further distinguished by the fact that public goods are significantly nonrival, whereas commons dilemmas involve a subtractable resource.[10]

The move from two-person to *N*-person dilemmas involves a number of profound shifts that affect the dynamics of the game. Dawes (1980) described three important ways in which the two-person Prisoner's Dilemma Game differed from the *N*-person version: First, in an *N*-person dilemma, one's actions are not necessarily revealed to others—anonymity becomes possible and an individual can free-ride without others noticing her or his actions. In the two-person case, each player "knows with certainty how the other has behaved" (Dawes 1980, p. 51). Second, the cost one imposes on others from defecting is focused completely on one's partner in the case of a two-person dilemma, whereas it is diffused throughout the group in an *N*-person dilemma. Finally, in a two-person dilemma, each person has significant control over one's partner's outcomes and so can shape the partner's behavior in important ways. In contrast, in an *N*-person dilemma, one may have little or no direct control over the outcomes others receive.

This list of distinguishing features is a useful starting point, but as we think about the whole range of social dilemmas, it is important to keep in mind two significant qualifications. First, anonymity, the diffusion of the harm of defection, and the inability to significantly impact others' outcomes are possible

[10]A nonrival good from which it is easy to exclude people is known as a club good (see Cornes & Sandler 1996 for an extended discussion of club goods). Goods that exhibit both subtractability and excludability are termed private goods.

though not inevitable features of N-person dilemmas. Kollock & Smith (1996), for example, discuss large-scale dilemmas that do not exhibit all of these features. Second, some of the features identified as characteristic of N-person dilemmas can be found in two-person dilemmas. For example, in the Prisoner's Dilemma Game as it is traditionally played in the experimental lab, each player knows with certainty how the partner has acted, but this is not the case for many of the two-person dilemmas in our empirical lives. I may promise my partner that I will run an errand for her while I am out, decide to take care only of my needs, and then claim upon returning that heavy traffic prevented me from fulfilling her request.

SOLVING SOCIAL DILEMMAS

In this section possible solutions to social dilemmas are considered. These solutions are divided into three broad categories based on whether the solutions assume egoistic actors and whether the structure of the situation ("the rules of the game") can be changed. Motivational solutions assume actors are not completely egoistic and so give some weight to the outcomes of their partners. Strategic solutions assume egoistic actors, and neither of these categories of solutions involves changing the fundamental structure of the situation. Solutions that do involve changing the rules of the game are considered in the third section on structural solutions. I have grouped together both structural solutions that assume egoistic actors and structural solutions that assume some weight is given to what others receive.

Motivational Solutions

Do individuals take their partners' outcomes into account when making a decision? Many of the models in the literature on social dilemmas assume actors who are focused only on their own outcomes, but it seems clear that many of us do give some weight to what our partner receives. As Dawes (1980, p. 176) commented, "Few of us would accept $500 with nothing for our friend in lieu of $495 for each of us."

SOCIAL VALUE ORIENTATIONS Research on social value orientations (e.g. Kuhlman & Marshello 1975, McClintock & Liebrand 1988) has sought to determine if there are stable individual differences in "preferences for particular distributions of outcomes to oneself and others" (van Lange et al 1992, p. 17). Many different social value orientations are theoretically possible, but most work has concentrated on various linear combinations of individuals' concern for the outcomes for themselves and their partners. One possibility is that an individual might behave so as to maximize joint outcomes (this is described as a cooperative orientation in this literature). An individual might also desire to maximize the relative difference between self and partner (a competitive orientation). Other orientations include maximizing the partner's outcome without regard for own outcome (altruism) or maximizing own outcome without any concern for the partner's outcome (individualism).[11] Research in numerous countries has found that most individuals can be classified as either cooperators, competitors, or individualists.

This work has shown that individuals with different social value orientations behave differently when faced with the same objective game (McClintock & Liebrand 1988, Liebrand et al 1986, Kramer et al 1986, Liebrand 1984). The researchers in this area have also shown that these orientations are relatively stable over time (Kuhlman et al 1986).[12] These studies make use of work by Kelley & Thibaut (1978) and Kelley (1979) on matrix transformations. Kelly & Thibaut argue that individuals often subjectively transform a given game and play it as if it were another game. There is, after all, no guarantee that subjects play an experimental game as intended by the researcher—for any of a variety of different reasons people might value particular outcomes more or less than the immediate objective payoff they receive.

Work on social value orientations has concentrated on assessing transformations that are the results of personality traits. Understanding that some individuals routinely give different weights to their own and partner's outcomes is an important piece of information in explaining the observed rates of cooperation in social dilemma situations. However, this knowledge is not very useful as a solution to dilemmas—this research does not tell us how to increase the level of cooperation.

One possibility would be to study how social value orientations are formed. A group of researchers (McClintock & Keil 1983, Toda et al 1978, McClintock 1974) have studied the development of cooperative and competitive orientations in children in several countries. Among other results, they have found that competition seems to be learned significantly earlier than cooperation and that overall levels of competitiveness can vary from country to country. But until the actual mechanisms are identified by which social orientations are learned, these insights still do not provide the basis for intervention in a social dilemma. Along these lines, a few studies (Frank et al 1993, Marwell & Ames 1981) have examined the effects of education later in life, examining whether

[11]Other more exotic orientations are also possible, such as martyrdom and sadism. Note that not all orientations can be modeled within this framework—another important social value orientation is minimizing the difference between own and partner's outcomes; this is related to issues such as equality and justice.

[12]Research has also found that stable individual differences exist in how trusting a person is and that this affects cooperation levels in social dilemma situations (e.g. Yamagishi 1986). Another individual difference that is noteworthy is the finding that people who cooperate are more likely to expect others to cooperate as well (Orbell & Dawes 1993).

students in different majors are more or less likely to cooperate. The amusing outcome is that some evidence suggests that people who study economics are more likely to free-ride. However, there are questions (mostly by economists) about how this result should be interpreted and how robust the finding is.

COMMUNICATION Another approach is to ask what features in the situation or environment (rather than in an individual's personality) affect the weight individuals give others' outcomes. One of the most robust findings in the literature is the positive effects of communication on rates of cooperation. Across a wide variety of studies, when individuals are given the chance to talk with each other, cooperation increases significantly (e.g. Orbell et al 1990, Orbell et al 1988, Liebrand 1984, Edney & Harper 1978b, Dawes et al 1977, Jerdee & Rosen 1974). While the effect is readily observed, explaining it has been more of a challenge. Messick & Brewer (1983) suggested four reasons (which touch on both motivational and strategic factors) why communication might increase cooperation. First, individuals may be able to gather information about the choices others are likely to make. This information, however, can have ambiguous effects. If I believe that most other people will cooperate in an *N*-person dilemma, does that give me a reason to cooperate or a greater temptation to defect? In part the decision will depend on the structure of the dilemma (in an Assurance Game, I will be happy to cooperate if others do) and on one's social value orientation. Second, communication gives group members the chance to make explicit commitments and promises about what they will do. However, research has been inconclusive about whether such commitments have an effect on cooperation rates (Orbell et al 1990, Dawes et al 1977). Third, communication offers an opportunity for moral suasion, i.e., appeals to what is the "right" or "proper" thing to do. The effects of moralizing have been the subject of very little research, although there are at least some indications that it can have a salutary effect on cooperation (Orbell & Dawes 1981). Finally, communication may create or reinforce a sense of group identity. This last point seems especially important, and the opinion of one of the key researchers in this area (Dawes 1991) is that the key effects of communication come from eliciting group identity.

GROUP IDENTITY The impact of group identity is manifold and profound, having effects across all three categories of solutions: motivational, strategic, and structural. Indeed, group identity can have such a powerful effect that it can influence rates of cooperation even in the absence of communication. Kramer & Brewer (1984, 1986; Brewer & Kramer 1986) have demonstrated that subjects are more willing to exhibit personal restraint in a commons dilemma simply as a result of being identified as members of a common group. Intergroup competition can have even more striking effects. In a study involving naturally occurring groups, Kollock (1998a,b) uncovered evidence of consistent transformations of a social dilemma situation, such that a Prisoner's Dilemma was treated as an Assurance Game when the partner was an in-group member and as a Prisoner's Dilemma Game when the partner was an out-group member. Experimental work by Bornstein and Rapoport (Bornstein et al 1990; Rapoport et al 1989; Rapoport & Bornstein 1987, 1989; Bornstein & Rapoport 1982) and the classic field experiments of Sherif et al (1961) have shown the powerful effect of intergroup competition in promoting cooperation within groups. However, this solution can be double-edged. Encouraging or creating group competition can serve the needs of group members (and leaders and politicians), but the social costs of the conflicts that result between groups can be severe.

Why are individuals more willing to cooperate if they feel part of a group? One possibility is that a collective social identity increases the altruism of the members. This is certainly a possibility, but something more strategic may be happening as well. Indeed, it can be difficult to distinguish apparent altruism from subtle long-term strategic considerations. This issue is taken up in the next section.[13]

Strategic Solutions

Strategic solutions assume egoistic actors and no changes to the structure of the game. These approaches rely on the ability of actors to shape the outcomes and hence behavior of other actors. For this reason, many of these strategic solutions are limited to repeated two-person dilemmas.

RECIPROCITY Far and away the most influential study on strategic solutions to social dilemmas is Axelrod's *The Evolution of Cooperation* (1984), in which he reports the results of a series of computer tournaments investigating the two-person Prisoner's Dilemma Game. While research on the Prisoner's Dilemma Game had gone on for many years prior to Axelrod's book, it was distinguished by its intriguing method, a provocative set of conclusions and recommendations, and arresting examples taken from such diverse areas as biology and the history of trench warfare. The study centered on two tournaments in which prominent game theorists (and in the second tournament, computer hobbyists) were invited to submit strategies for playing the Prisoner's Dilemma in a round-robin contest.

Axelrod identified three requirements in this environment for there to be even the possibility of the emergence of cooperation. First, it was essential that

[13]Note also that Kuhlman et al (1986) have argued that social value orientations themselves might be explained as different strategic responses to the problem of how to maximize one's own outcomes.

individuals be involved in an ongoing relationship. If individuals met only once, or equivalently, if this was the last time they would meet, the dominating strategy to defect in the Prisoner's Dilemma Game would make the pursuit of cooperation hopeless.[14] If the partners would meet again in the future, cooperation at least has a chance. The second condition is that individuals must be able to identify each other. The third condition is that individuals must have information about how the other person has behaved in the past. If identity is unknown or unstable and if there is no recollection or record of past interactions, individuals will be motivated to behave selfishly because they will not be accountable for their actions.

It was surprising to many at the time that the winner of Axelrod's two tournaments was the simplest strategy that had been submitted. This strategy, named Tit-for-Tat, cooperates on the first interaction and thereafter simply does whatever its partner did on the previous round. It has proven to be an effective strategy in many different environments, and it has the effect, in essence, of transforming a repeated Prisoner's Dilemma Game into a repeated Assurance Game (Yamagishi 1995; cf. Rapoport 1967). Playing against an individual using Tit-for-Tat means that the only long-term possibilities are mutual cooperation and mutual defection—there is no hope of exploiting this strategy in any kind of sustained way. In this sense it can provide a route to sustained mutual cooperation in a two-person Prisoner's Dilemma Game.

After studying the most successful strategies in the tournaments, Axelrod (1984, p. 110) distilled four pieces of advice that he would offer an individual playing an iterated Prisoner's Dilemma Game: (*a*) Don't be envious; (*b*) don't be the first to defect; (*c*) reciprocate both cooperation and defection; and (*d*) don't be too clever. The key point in his fourth piece of advice was that it was important for one's partner to clearly understand what strategy one was using. His first piece of advice is essentially an admonition against playing the Prisoner's Dilemma Game as if it were a zero-sum game, that is, a game in which one's interests were completely opposed to one's partner's (e.g. chess, competitive sports, mortal combat). In a zero-sum game, using one's partner as a standard of comparison is useful, as anything that works against one's partner necessarily helps oneself. However, trying to beat one's partner or being envious of their success[15] can lead to trouble in a mixed-motive situation such as the Prisoner's Dilemma. Trying to beat your partner can be self-defeating if it results in mutual defection.

[14]Axelrod's analysis is based on the logic of game theory. Empirically, one does sometimes observe cooperation in a one-shot Prisoner's Dilemma Game (e.g. Orbell & Dawes 1993, Hayashi et al 1997).

[15]This can be thought of as negatively weighting one's partner's outcomes, as is the case with the competitive social orientation discussed above.

A very important lesson from the tournaments was that Tit-for-Tat won not by beating its partners (indeed, it can only tie or do slightly worse than its partners), but by doing well on average, encouraging mutual cooperation with many of its partners. This seems to be one of the hardest lessons for individuals to learn, perhaps because of the dominance of the competitive game as a model in many cultures—if the only metaphor you have is the zero-sum game, you tend to treat everything as if it were a war. The book spawned a cottage industry of hundreds of studies that supported, extended, or critiqued the original work. Two very useful reviews of research that make use of Axelrod's studies are Axelrod & Dion (1988) and Axelrod & D'Ambrosio (1994).

The success of Tit-for-Tat led some commentators to suggest that this strategy be used as the basis of everything from childhood education to international relations. Here again we see the dangers of taking a useful metaphor too literally, assuming it accurately modeled any situation that even vaguely resembled a Prisoner's Dilemma. As Axelrod himself appreciated, the results of his tournaments depended on both the particular sample of strategies that were submitted and the assumptions underlying his study. One of the most important scope conditions of Axelrod's simulations was the assumption of perfect information. In a world in which mistakes, misperceptions, and accidents can occur, Tit-for-Tat can turn out to be an unsuccessful strategy because it retaliates immediately (Kollock 1993). Strategies that are more generous or forgiving than Tit-for-Tat can have important advantages in such settings because they avoid the danger of cycles of recrimination that can occur with Tit-for-Tat.

CHOICE OF PARTNERS Another key assumption of Axelrod's model was the network structure of the interacting strategies. In a sense it represented a very unusual social structure in which each actor was forced to interact each round and to interact with every other possible partner (as this was a round-robin tournament). Not playing the game or choosing only some partners with whom to interact were not options. One of the most important recent developments has been studies that permit players to exit a current relationship and/or choose alternative partners. Computer simulations by Schuessler (1989), Vanberg & Congleton (1992), and Hayashi and associates (Hayashi 1993, Yamagishi et al 1994) all found that a very successful strategy in these situations was to cooperate on the first interaction and continue cooperating until the first defection from one's partner, at which point the strategy exited the relationship. Hayashi (1993) also discovered that a version of this strategy (called Out-for-Tat), which incorporated some degree of forgiveness (i.e. a willingness to give a partner who had defected before a second chance), was even more successful. The conclusion of this work is that the strategy used in selecting one's partner can be more important than the strategy that is used in actually playing the

Prisoner's Dilemma Game. Experimental work by the same researchers (Yamagishi et al 1994) suggests that subjects follow something like an Out-for-Tat strategy in which the response to defection is not defection, but desertion.

GRIM TRIGGERS All of these studies involved two-person social dilemmas. Strategic solutions for *N*-person dilemmas are much more of a challenge because one's own actions may have little or no influence on what others do. One possibility that has been explored is the adoption of a "grim trigger" strategy, in which each individual agrees to cooperate only on the condition that all others in the group cooperate. In theory, if all adopt this strategy then each person's decision is decisive and free-riding is impossible. However, experimental work by Watabe (1992; Watabe & Yamagishi 1994) found subjects were leery of adopting such a risky strategy, and field studies by Ostrom and her colleagues (Ostrom et al 1994) uncovered no instances of groups actually using a trigger strategy in their community.

SOCIAL LEARNING A different approach to solving *N*-person dilemmas has been investigated by Macy (e.g. 1993, 1991). His model of decision-making does not assume that actors calculate marginal rates of return or work out dominating strategies. Basing his work on the principles of social learning theory, he assumes reward-seeking, penalty-aversive actors and asks under what conditions such cognitively modest actors might escape social dilemmas. In a series of computer simulations, he isolates a number of factors that can promote cooperation, including the presence of thresholds and the tendency for actors to imitate those around them.

GROUP RECIPROCITY Finally, we return to the issue of group identity and its effects. Making group identity salient has been shown to increase cooperation. While work in social identity theory (Tajfel 1981) argues that simply categorizing individuals into a common group is enough to increase their altruism toward the group, research by Karp et al (1993; see also Jin et al 1996) contests this conclusion. The effects of group identity stem, they argue, not from an altruism born of categorization, but from a belief in the interdependencies of group members and expectations of reciprocity among the members. In a series of studies they carefully removed any possibility or connotation of interdependency and found that simple categorization was not enough to create in-group favoritism.

It is the belief in future reciprocal exchanges between members, they argue, that moderates the temptation to defect and encourages cooperation. The expectation of in-group reciprocity seems to serve as a very deep heuristic that shapes our strategic decisions (Jin & Yamagishi 1997, Brewer 1981). The expectation of reciprocity appears to be so great that it sometimes manifests itself even in situations in which reciprocity is not logically possible (Watabe et al 1996, Hayashi et al 1997, Karp et al 1993). Further, this heuristic means that many Prisoner's Dilemma situations will be transformed into Assurance Games. Evidence for this transformation can be found in Watabe et al (1996) and Hayashi et al (1997).

Structural Solutions

In this section I relax the assumption that the rules of the game cannot be changed. Here I examine structural changes to social dilemmas that either modify the dilemma or eliminate it entirely. An important issue discussed below is how these structural changes are provided.

ITERATION AND IDENTIFIABILITY One approach to structural solutions is to create or reinforce those features of the environment that are prerequisites for strategic solutions. Returning to Axelrod (1984), this approach suggests three changes: (*a*) Make interaction more durable or frequent; (*b*) increase identifiability; and (*c*) increase information about individuals' actions. If individuals will not interact in the future, if identity is unknown or unstable, and if there is no recollection or record of past interactions, individuals will be motivated to behave selfishly because they will not be accountable for their actions. Knowing the identity and history of a person allows one to respond in an appropriate manner. If information about individuals and their actions is shared among the group, this also encourages the development of reputations, which can be a vital source of social information and control. These features will be important not just for facilitating strategic solutions but also as prerequisites for some of the other structural solutions discussed below, notably the use of monitoring and sanctioning systems. Along these lines, several studies have found that anonymity (the absence of identifiability) lowers rates of cooperation (Fox & Guyer 1978, Jerdee & Rosen 1974, Kahan 1973).[16]

However, it is important to note that ongoing interaction may not always have a salutary effect on social dilemmas. Axelrod was concerned with two-person Prisoner's Dilemmas, and in *N*-person Prisoner's Dilemmas (with no thresholds), there is a stronger temptation to move toward the equilibrium of zero cooperation, as defection has a smaller effect and one may not be able to impact others' outcomes and so encourage cooperation. Ledyard (1995) discusses this general issue and points to a number of studies that have found significant declines in cooperation over time in *N*-person dilemmas with no

[16]Note that anonymity in and of itself may not always have an effect (Kerr 1997). For example, if individuals do not understand the situation or do not care about the sanctions others impose, whether one is identifiable or not may not matter.

thresholds (e.g. Andreoni 1988, Banks et al 1988, Isaac et al 1985, Isaac et al 1984, Kim & Walker 1984).

PAYOFF STRUCTURE As one would expect, numerous studies have demonstrated that the greater the personal return from cooperation and the lower the return from defecting, the higher the levels of cooperation (Isaac & Walker 1988, Issac et al 1984, Komorita et al 1980, Bonacich et al 1976, Kelley & Grzelak 1972). Perhaps more surprising is the finding that cooperation rates increase significantly as the benefits to *others* from one's cooperation increase (Bonacich et al 1976, Kelley & Grzelak 1972, Komorita et al 1980). This argues that many people are positively weighting the outcomes of others.

The nature of the public good and how it is distributed can also have an effect. Alfano & Marwell (1980) found that cooperation levels were much greater when group members were asked to contribute to a public good that was nondivisible. That is, rather than each person getting an individual return, the group would receive a lump sum that had to be spent on a group activity. The very fact that the public good was indivisible may have helped reinforce a sense of group identity and interdependence among the subjects.

EFFICACY Many researchers have argued that one of the key reasons people do not cooperate in an *N*-person dilemma is the fact that a single person's actions may have no discernable effect on the situation. No one will be fired and no program will go off the air if I do not send in a $30 contribution to public television, and even if I do conserve water in a drought, it will have no measurable impact on the overall situation.

If a dilemma is structured in such a way that individuals can have a noticeable effect on the outcome—that is, they can make an efficacious contribution—cooperation rates can be increased. One way in which this can occur is if a public good has a step-level production function. If an individual believes the group is close to the threshold, then adding one's own contribution can be enough to put the group "over the top" and provide the good. One study (van de Kragt et al 1983) found that groups who were attempting to provide a public good with a threshold designated a subgroup of contributors (via lottery or volunteering) who would be just enough to provide the good. In this situation each person within the minimally contributing set knew that the provision of the public good was critically dependent on each of their actions. Free-riding was impossible, and each knew that their actions were necessary for the success of the group.[17]

[17]Other work has shown that increasing the level of the threshold can increase the amount of cooperation, although this also decreases the probability that the threshold will be met (Isaac et al 1988, Suleiman & Rapoport 1992).

Another experimental study by Bornstein et al (1990) demonstrates the joint effects of a step-level production function and group identity. The key innovation in these studies (see also Rapoport et al 1989; Rapoport & Bornstein 1987, 1989; Bornstein & Rapoport 1982) is that two groups are set up in competition against each other, with a prize going to the group that demonstrates the higher level of cooperation; the prize is then distributed equally to the winning group's members. This changes the structure of what was originally a Prisoner's Dilemma into a step-level public goods problem in which defection is no longer a dominating strategy. The creation of a step-level function (which is to say, a threshold point) shifts the structure of the game into an N-person version of the Chicken Game.

Work by Kerr (e.g. 1992) has also shown that cooperation in a public goods dilemma is more likely the larger the impact of a person's contribution. A similar strategy is used by public television and charities when they create "matching grants" in which someone agrees to double the contributions that others make.

The perception of efficacy can be enough to affect cooperation. Kerr (1989) and Rapoport et al (1989) found a significant relationship between perceived efficacy and contributions to a public good. Survey and field research have also found that most individuals involved in collective action believed that their actions had a significant effect on the provision of the public good, even if the size of the group was very large (Klandermans 1986, Mueller & Opp 1986, Moe 1980).

The creation of efficacy, real or perceived, can be an art. Consider the difficulties of a charity trying to raise money to feed poor children. A potential contributor may fear that her or his contribution will be wasted or wonder what good one person can do for an organization that raises millions of dollars. The response of at least one charity has been to assign each contributor a specific child. The contributor receives a photo and personal information about the child they are sponsoring and even an occasional letter from the child or one of the parents. The sense of personal responsibility it creates ("what happens if I stop contributing?") profoundly changes the decision of whether to cooperate.

GROUP SIZE Numerous studies have found that cooperation declines as group size increases (e.g. Komorita & Lapworth 1982, Fox & Guyer 1977, Bonacich et al 1976, Hamburger et al 1975). The possible reasons for this effect are many. Returning to Dawes's (1980) points about differences between two-person and N-person games, increasing group size may spread the harm caused by defection, make it harder to shape others' behavior, and make it easier to defect anonymously. The costs of organizing can also increase as group size grows (Olson 1965)—groups can find it harder to communicate and coordinate their actions. The efficacy and visibility of one's actions can also be diluted, and monitoring and sanctioning the behavior of others (see below) can become more of a challenge. This general effect has led some commentators to argue in favor of anarchistic social systems in which communities are organized as networks of small groups (Fox 1985).

However, none of these effects are inevitable as groups grow in size (Udehn 1993, Kollock & Smith 1996). Interestingly, some experimental work has found that the decrease in cooperation as group size increases tapers off quickly (Fox & Guyer 1977, Liebrand 1984), and other work has actually shown an increase in cooperation with larger groups (Yamagishi & Cook 1993, Isaac et al 1990). Part of the problem in reaching any precise conclusion about the effects of group size is that so many elements can vary as group size increases. It is in the end impossible to control for all possible parameters in order to study a "pure" group size effect (Orbell & Dawes 1981, Ledyard 1995). Researchers must decide which parameters are most important and carefully control them. Another difficulty with researching this effect thoroughly is that one must examine groups of varying sizes, including large groups, and running experiments with large groups creates extraordinary logistical difficulties and costs.

One explanation for why larger groups may be more likely to solve social dilemmas comes from Marwell & Oliver (1993). They argue that if a public good is highly nonrival, a large group is more likely to contain a critical mass of individuals whose interests are served by providing the good. One feature of a group that encourages the formation of a critical mass is the heterogeneity of the group in terms of the diversity of group members' interests and resources. The importance of group heterogeneity in solving social dilemmas is also explored by Glance & Huberman (1994).

BOUNDARIES This set of structural solutions deals with a core characteristic of social dilemmas—the nonexcludability of a joint good. Each of these solutions attempts to draw some kind of boundary around the collective good.

One of the first solutions proposed for commons dilemmas is the establishment of an external authority to regulate who had access to the commons or how people were to withdraw resources from the commons. This is, in a broad sense, Hobbes' classic solution of Leviathan: People give up some part of their personal freedom to an authority in return for some measure of social order. This is also the solution Hardin proposed in his famous article (1968) when he concluded that "freedom in a commons brings ruin to all." Hardin fully acknowledged that the outcome might be grossly unfair to some people, but given the global tragedy he felt was inevitable, he declared that "injustice is preferable to total ruin" (1968). This echoed Lloyd's (1832) grim conclusion that "To a plank in the sea, which cannot support all, all have not an equal right." A direct example of this strategy can be seen in the establishment of fish and game authorities that set strict limits on what can be caught and the length of the season. A similar approach can be taken in public goods dilemmas, where an external authority compels individuals to contribute money (as when a government collects taxes to provide public services) or labor, such as in the case of military conscription.

The willingness to hand over personal choice to a leader has been shown in some experimental studies. Messick et al (1983) and Samuelson & Messick (1986a) found that a group that was overusing a commons was willing to change the structure of the situation by electing a leader who would manage the harvesting of the commons for the group. Interestingly, subjects did not usually vote for themselves, instead electing a person who counteracted the group's performance to that point in time: someone who harvested few resources from the commons if the group had overharvested, and someone who harvested substantial resources if the group had underharvested to that point (Messick et al 1983, Samuelson et al 1984). However, Samuelson & Messick (1986b) and Rutte & Wilke (1985) found that subjects preferred not to create a leader if other structural changes were possible.

Severe problems can arise in establishing such an authority, as Crowe (1969) commented soon after the publication of Hardin's article. According to Crowe, Hardin assumes (*a*) that the global community can come to an agreement about what to value and how to rank those values, (*b*) that authorities will have sufficient coercive force to compel people to obey, and (*c*) that authorities can be trusted to remain free of corruption and to resist the influence of special interest groups. Crowe vigorously questions each of these assumptions and argues that even if Hardin's basic presumptions are correct, his solution is unworkable on a broad scale.

Another commonly suggested solution to the tragedy of the commons is to privatize the commons, that is, to break the commons up into private parcels on the assumption that individuals will take better care of their own property than common property. Two experimental studies (Cass & Edney 1978, Messick & McClelland 1983) indicate that individuals did better at managing their own "private commons" than they did harvesting as a group. However, there are a number of difficulties with this solution. First, not all goods can be privatized—it may be easy to divide up an actual meadow,[18] but how does one divide up schools of fish in the ocean, clean air, or many public goods such as national defense? Second, even if it is possible to divide up the common good, doing so raises grave questions about social justice: Who gets the newly privatized commons, and how are the parcels allocated? To the highest bidder? In a lottery? Third, while it may be reasonable to expect people to take good care

[18]Assuming the meadow is homogenous; see Ostrom 1990, p. 13.

of their own property, empirically there is no question that individuals routinely destroy their own property. Some have argued that there are "tragedies of enclosure" (Bromely 1991) just as there are tragedies of the commons. Finally, private property rights require a great deal of institutional support so that these rights can be enforced.

Some of the other assumptions in Hardin's original analysis have also been criticized. Notably, he assumes that commons are always open-access, that is, that there are no restrictions as to who may use the commons. However, this assumption is neither necessary nor historically accurate (Fairlie et al 1994, McCay & Acheson 1987). In fact, commons are often surrounded by local rules of access and enforcement mechanisms. One of the key findings of field research done on how communities manage common property is that groups often do find ways to regulate their own actions, and some of these arrangements have proven to be remarkably robust, lasting across several generations (McCay & Acheson 1987, Ostrom 1990, 1992, Ostrom et al 1994).

Thus, Ostrom (1990) proposes a third route away from the tragedy of the commons: the local regulation of access to and use of common property by those who actually use and have local knowledge of the resource. Ostrom isolated a number of design characteristics that were shared by communities that had a long history of successfully managing common resources. The first characteristic she discusses deals explicitly with the issue of excludability: Successful communities are marked by clearly defined boundaries—"Individuals or households who have rights to withdraw resource units from the [commons] must be clearly defined, as must the boundaries of the [commons] itself" (1990, p. 91).[19]

This is not to say that local communities inevitably solve their social dilemmas—there is no shortage of true tragedies as well as victories—but it does make the essential point that it is inappropriate to conclude that the only way out of a commons dilemma is through the use of some form of Leviathan or privatization. This has been the conclusion of a number of commentators who took Hardin's parable too literally. It is also the case that misguided intervention by an outside authority can take a bad situation and make it much worse (McCay & Acheson 1987).

SANCTIONS As Dawes (1980) pointed out, one of the great challenges of *N*-person dilemmas is that it is often not possible to directly affect others' outcomes and so shape their behavior. If the cooperators could be rewarded for their action and defectors punished, even large-scale dilemmas might be solved.

[19]Other design features identified by Ostrom are discussed in subsequent sections. Many of these characteristics are applicable to public goods dilemmas as well.

Indeed, one of Olson's (1965) key conclusions was the necessity of using selective incentives in encouraging cooperation. A selective incentive is a private good given as an inducement to contributing toward a public good. Anyone can watch public television, but only subscribers receive program guides, discount cards, and other rewards for subscribing. We may all have access to a common pool of blood at the blood bank, but at the University of California at Los Angeles, only those who do contribute blood receive a half day off with pay, food and drink, and occasionally even the chance to win more substantial prizes in a lottery. Field research on conservation behavior (Maki et al 1978, Winett et al 1978) has shown that selective incentives in the form of monetary rewards are effective in decreasing the consumption of water and electricity.

If carrots work, so do sticks. Experimental studies have shown that cooperation is more likely if individuals have the ability to punish defectors (Caldwell 1976, Komorita 1987). Such negative sanctions are the complement of the positive sanctions used in selective incentive systems—the target in this case is the defector rather than the cooperator.

However, implementing sanctioning systems raises two important problems. First, there are often significant costs to providing these systems. In order to reward or punish individuals, one must first be able to monitor their behavior (Hechter 1984). This may be trivially easy if we are working next to each other building an irrigation system, or essentially impossible, as when individuals in a large city decide to leave the water running in the privacy of their home. Even if one is able to keep track of individuals' actions, there are still costs in administering rewards or punishments. The rewards themselves can be costly, and administering negative sanctions can require the support of large and expensive institutions (e.g. a police force, an internal revenue service). Thus, it will sometimes be the case that the costs to monitor and sanction individuals will be greater than the benefits that come in terms of higher cooperation.

While monitoring and sanctioning costs can be very great, some situations exist in which the costs can be made very small through the right institutional arrangements (Ostrom 1990). In general, these costs can also be quite modest in small groups.[20] Ostrom (1990) in particular documents the many ways face-to-face communities create local monitoring and sanctioning systems. The presence of a monitoring and sanctioning system run by the community members themselves (as opposed to an external authority) was one of the design features Ostrom found in each of the successful communities she studied. Another common element Ostrom identified was that cooperative communities

[20]While this is true in many cases, secret defection is possible in even the smallest group, and there are some situations where monitoring is easily accomplished even in very large groups (e.g. Kollock & Smith 1996).

employed a graduated system of sanctions. While sanctions could be as severe as banishment from the group, the initial sanction for breaking a rule was often very low. Community members realized that even a well-intentioned person might break the rules when facing an unusual situation or extreme hardship. Severely punishing such a person might alienate him or her from the community, causing greater problems. Ostrom also found that even with a well-designed internal monitoring and sanctioning system, some conflict was inevitable. Thus, it was important that community members had access to low-cost conflict resolution mechanisms.

The second key problem in implementing sanctioning systems is that these systems are themselves public goods because one can enjoy the benefits of a sanctioning system without contributing to its provision or maintenance. Whether the sanctions are provided by an external authority or locally, there is the temptation to free ride. The police and judicial system continue to work even if I avoid paying taxes, and if everyone else in my community takes on the task of informally admonishing and criticizing defectors, I can avoid the costs of such actions and still enjoy the benefits they bring. This raises the question of when people will cooperate in providing this second-order public good (i.e. a public good designed to be a solution to an underlying social dilemma).

The most extensive set of experimental studies on the provision and use of sanctioning systems has been by Yamagishi (1992, 1988, 1986). While one might expect that people's decisions when faced with a second-order dilemma mirror their actions when faced with a first-order dilemma, this turns out not to be the case. Yamagishi found that trusting individuals (as measured via a scale administered prior to the experiment) were likely to cooperate in a first order-dilemma, but when they were given the opportunity to contribute toward the provision of a sanctioning system, relatively few did so. In contrast, a group of distrustful individuals exhibited low levels of cooperation in the first-order dilemma but were more willing to cooperate in the creation of a sanctioning system. The existence of a sanctioning system led to cooperation rates in the end that were similar to those of the trusting individuals.

Why people might be willing to cooperate in a second-order dilemma is an area ripe for research. Studies by Heckathorn (1996, 1989, 1988), Axelrod (1986), and Yamagishi & Takahashi (1994) provide some initial investigations based on computer simulations that examine the effect of collective sanctioning, "hypocritical" sanctioning (i.e. sanctions by actors who defect in the first-order dilemma), and the evolution of traits that encourage sanctioning.

CONCLUSIONS

The study of social dilemmas is the study of the tension between individual and collective rationality. It is the study of tragic (deficient) equilibria caused by externalities, that is, uncompensated interdependencies. Social dilemmas are also a sensitive research domain, in that a great many variables can affect cooperation rates, and small changes in these variables can sometimes have large effects (Ledyard 1995).

Studying Social Dilemmas

One of the great advantages of doing research in social dilemmas is that a well-specified set of models exists that allows one to capture the key dynamics in a simple and tractable way in the laboratory. This is also one of the downfalls of research in the area—it is perhaps too easy to set up a social dilemma and vary any one of an infinite number of variables rather than thinking strategically about which situations and which parameters are most important. The Prisoner's Dilemma Game in particular has served as a kind of readily available thermometer of cooperation that can be stuck into any situation. There is nothing to keep a researcher from examining the effects of eye color or pounds of meat consumed on cooperation rates, and some studies have come close to such esoterica. As Messick & Brewer (1983, p. 40) warned us at the end of their influential review, "There are more experiments that can be done than are worth doing and it is as important as it is tricky to determine which are which."

Current experimental work has introduced a number of important innovations in the design of studies. In particular, a number of researchers have increasingly relaxed the constrained designs of early work. One can now find research in which actors have the option of leaving the interaction, of choosing new partners, and even of choosing the game structures (Kakiuchi & Yamagishi 1997). Other researchers have developed designs that highlight the importance of the group, examining the effects of inter-group competition or the use of exclusion from the group (ostracism) as a sanction (Kerr 1997).

There are some chronic problems, however, in the manner in which experimental research is being conducted. Many experiments in this area have used trivially small incentives. "It makes no sense," said Orbell & Dawes (1981), "to spend large amounts of money for summer salaries, secretaries, computer terminals, and research assistants, and then motivate the subjects with microscopic amounts of money or course credits." The generalizability of our results is limited to the extent we use small incentives, and it is entirely possible that many of the inconclusive or contradictory results that are reported in the literature are due in part to subjects being faced with outcomes that are trivial. It is also the case that with few exceptions, most of these studies have involved very small groups. Our results are thus limited again to the extent that a 10-person group is defined as a "large" group.

Turning briefly to other methodologies, experimental work has been bolstered by studies based on computer simulations that allow one to investigate models involving very large groups, explore the logical terrain of one's theories, study problems that do not lend themselves to analytical solutions, and develop tenable models that can guide behavioral experiments (for recent collections, see Liebrand & Messick 1996, Axelrod 1997). Also important in recent years has been the emergence of a great many field studies based on the logic of social dilemmas. These include many studies on resource management as well as fascinating accounts on such topics as the Sicilian Mafia (Gambetta 1993) and a study of trespass disputes among ranchers in northern California (Ellickson 1991). While one gives up the careful control of experimental work by moving into the field, one can examine situations involving truly large groups and significant (even life-threatening) outcomes. I believe the strongest work combines multiple methodologies. Yamagishi and his colleagues (Yamagishi et al 1994, Yamagishi & Takahashi 1994, Yamagishi & Yamagishi 1994), for example, have combined simulations, survey research, and experimental studies in their research on trust and social dilemmas. Ostrom and her colleagues (Ostrom et al 1994) also have a long history of using multiple methods, combining field studies with experimental work.

Future Directions

In addition to the advances in research design and issues mentioned above, I believe especially promising directions for research in the future include work on the expectations and effects of generalized reciprocity within groups, the transformation of incentive structures, and a greater focus on the Assurance Game as a core model in understanding social dilemmas.

A great deal of attention has focused on how dilemmas might be structurally changed to reduce or eliminate the temptations to defect. But additional studies on how the incentive structure in dilemmas can be transformed via motivational or strategic means are also crucial. We have seen that there appear to be stable personality traits that result in distinct transformations of objective payoffs, and work on group identity provides evidence of transformation of payoffs depending on group membership. The robust effects of group identity and the expectation of reciprocity imply that such issues as the construction of group boundaries and the signaling of group membership will be of fundamental importance to the study of social dilemmas. Incentive structures can also be transformed via strategic mechanisms such as the adoption of a Tit-for-Tat strategy in a repeated Prisoner's Dilemma Game.

It is noteworthy that the result of many of these transformations is the framing of the social dilemma as an Assurance Game. Working within an Assurance Game does not eliminate the challenge of cooperation, but it does change our focus in many ways. Trustworthiness, trustfulness, and all those factors that influence these concepts become even more important (cf Yamagishi &

Yamagishi 1994). Further, because the key issue in these dilemmas is the assurance that others will cooperate, attempts to signal and advertise one's commitment to cooperate will be critical. This might be as simple as a public pledge to cooperate or an act that is more symbolic.[21] In this sense, signs that one is committed to a group or to a particular goal would be important in encouraging others to cooperate (e.g. wearing a crucifix, a lapel pin from a fraternal organization, gang colors, a union pin). More broadly, using the Assurance Game as one's model makes signaling and signal detection (or in the language of social psychology, dramaturgy and attribution) centrally relevant to a study of human cooperation.[22]

Transformations can also be important because they provide another potential path to solving social dilemmas. Rather than trying to solve the dilemma as it exists, it may be easier to work to transform the dilemma to, e.g., an Assurance Game and then use another set of more viable strategies to encourage cooperation (Kollock 1998a, Yamagishi 1995). Bornstein et al's (1990) research in which an *N*-person Prisoner's Dilemma Game is transformed into a Chicken Game via inter-group competition is an example of such an approach.

Ideally, we should pursue experimental designs that permit large groups, sizable incentives, and diverse populations. One possible approach to these challenges is to move away from physical group laboratories to experimental systems that are designed to make use of the many advantages of the Internet (Macy et al 1997). An experimental system based on the World Wide Web would make it much easier to run studies involving very large groups that are composed of more than just college undergraduates. Such a Web-based lab would also permit cross-national experiments, which would enable studies of cross-cultural interactions. One could even make use of monetary exchange rates in order to run experiments in countries where the incentives offered would be truly significant.

Uniting all of these studies is a core set of social dilemmas that can be explicitly and precisely modeled. This core set of models can serve as a kind of lingua franca for communication between disciplines. Researchers with very different goals and methodologies can map the results of each other's work onto their own through the use of these models. However, this potential is often not realized, and it is often the case that scholars in different disciplines remain unaware of each other's work. One of the most important goals for future work is for researchers to become more aware of related literatures in neigh-

[21]An excellent example of these processes is given by Fantasia (1988) in his case study of a wildcat strike.

[22]Note that dramaturgical issues are very important in a Chicken Game as well as in an Assurance Game, but for different reasons. In a Chicken Game one can try to convince the other that one will certainly not cooperate in hopes of forcing the partner to do so.

boring disciplines. In particular, I would encourage closer ties with experimental economists, who have produced a very useful body of work on social dilemmas (for a starting point, see Kagel & Roth 1995). We should work toward the integration of these various research traditions and the future collaboration of experimental social scientists across the disciplines of sociology, psychology, economics, political science, and anthropology.

ACKNOWLEDGMENTS

I owe a particular debt to Toshio Yamagishi, Marilynn Brewer, David Messick, Robyn Dawes, and John Orbell for their work and for the conversations I have had with them. I also thank Motoki Watabe for comments on an earlier draft.

Literature Cited

Alfano G, Marwell G. 1980. Experiments on the provisions of public goods by groups. III. Nondivisibility and free riding in real groups. *Soc. Psychol. Q.* 43(3):300–9

Andreoni J. 1988. Why free ride? Strategies and learning in public goods experiments. *J. Public Econ.* 37:291–304

Axelrod R. 1984. *The Evolution of Cooperation.* New York: Basic Books

Axelrod R. 1986. An evolutionary approach to norms. *Am. Polit. Sci. Rev.* 80:1095–1111

Axelrod R. 1997. *The Complexity of Cooperation.* Princeton, NJ: Princeton Univ. Press

Axelrod R, D'Ambrosio L. 1994. Annotated bibliography of the evolution of cooperation. Online document: http://ippsweb.ipps.lsa.umich.edu:70/1/ipps/papers/coop

Axelrod R, Dion D. 1988. The further evolution of cooperation. *Science* 242:1385–90

Banks J, Plott C, Porter D. 1988. An experimental analysis of unanimity in public goods provision mechanisms. *Rev. Econ. Stud.* 55:301–22

Bonacich P, Shure G, Kahan J, Meeker R. 1976. Cooperation and group size in the n-person prisoner's dilemma. *J. Conflict Resolution* 20:687–706

Bornstein G, Erev I, Rosen O. 1990. Intergroup competition as a structural solution to social dilemmas. *Soc. Behav.* 5(4): 247–60

Bornstein G, Rapoport A. 1982. Intergroup competition for the provision of step-level public goods: effects of preplay communication. *Eur. J. Soc. Psychol.* 18:125–42

Brewer MB. 1981. Ethnocentrism and its role in interpersonal trust. In *Scientific Inquiry and the Social Sciences*, ed. M Brewer, B Collins, pp. 345–60. San Francisco: Jossey-Bass

Brewer MB, Kramer RM. 1986. Choice behavior in social dilemmas: effects of social identity, group size, and decision framing. *J. Pers. Soc. Psychol.* 50:543–49

Bromley DW. 1991. *Environment and Economy: Property Rights and Public Policy.* Oxford, UK: Blackwell

Bromley DW, Feeny D, McKean M, Peters P, Gilles J, et al, eds. 1992. *Making the Commons Work: Theory, Practice, and Policy.* San Francisco: Inst. Contemp. Stud.

Buchanan JM. 1971. *The Bases for Collective Action.* New York: General Learning

Caldwell MD. 1976. Communication and sex effects in a five-person prisoner's dilemma game. *J. Pers. Soc. Psychol.* 33:273–80

Cass RC, Edney JJ. 1978. The commons dilemma: a simulation testing the effects of resource visibility and territorial division. *Hum. Ecol.* 6(4):371–86

Cornes R, Sandler T. 1996. *The Theory of Externalities, Public Goods, and Club Goods.* Cambridge: Cambridge Univ. Press. 2nd ed.

Cross J, Guyer M. 1980. *Social Traps*. Ann Arbor: Univ. Mich. Press

Crowe BL. 1969. The tragedy of the commons revisited. *Science* 166:1103–7

Dawes R. 1980. Social dilemmas. *Annu. Rev. Psychol.* 31:169–93

Dawes R. 1991. Social dilemmas, economic self-interest, and evolutionary theory. In *Frontiers of Mathematical Psychology: Essays in Honor of Clyde Coombs*, ed. DR Brown, JEK Smith, pp. 53–79. New York: Springer-Verlag

Dawes R, McTavish J, Shaklee H. 1977. Behavior, communication, and assumptions about other people's behavior in a commons dilemma situation. *J. Pers. Soc. Psychol.* 35:1–11

Edney JJ, Harper CS. 1978a. The commons dilemma: a review. *Contrib. Psychol. Environ. Manage.* 2:491–507

Edney JJ, Harper CS. 1978b. The effects of information in a resource management problem: a social trap analog. *Hum. Ecol.* 6: 387–95

Ellickson RC. 1991. *Order Without Law: How Neighbors Settle Disputes*. Cambridge, MA: Harvard Univ. Press

Fairlie S, Hildyard N, Lohmann N, Sexton S, et al. 1994. Whose common future: reclaiming the commons. *Environ. Urbanization* 6(1):106–30

Fantasia R. 1988. *Cultures of Solidarity: Consciousness, Action, and Contemporary American Workers*. Berkeley: Univ. Calif. Press

Fox DR. 1985. Psychology, ideology, utopia, and the commons. *Am. Psychol.* 40(1): 48–58

Fox J, Guyer M. 1977. Group size and others' strategy in an n-person game. *J. Conflict Resolut.* 21:323–38

Fox J, Guyer M. 1978. 'Public' choice and cooperation in n-person prisoner's dilemma. *J. Conflict Resolut.* 22:469–81

Frank R, Gilovich T, Regan D. 1993. Does studying economics inhibit cooperation? *J. Econ. Perpsect.* 7(2):159–71

Gambetta D. 1993. *The Sicilian Mafia: The Business of Private Protection*. Cambridge, MA: Harvard Univ. Press

Glance NS, Huberman BA. 1994. The dynamics of social dilemmas. *Sci. Am.* (Mar.): 76–81

Hamburger H, Guyer M, Fox J. 1975. Group size and cooperation. *J. Conflict Resolut.* 19:503–31

Hardin G. 1968. The tragedy of the commons. *Science* 162:1243–48

Hardin G, Baden J. 1977. *Managing the Commons*. San Francisco: Freeman

Hayashi N. 1993. From tit-for-tat to out-for-tat: the dilemma of the prisoner's network. *Sociol. Theory Methods* 8(1)(13):19–32 (in Japanese)

Hayashi N, Ostrom E, Walker J, Yamagishi T. 1997. *Reciprocity, trust and the illusion of control: a cross-societal study*. Work. Pap. Indiana Univ.

Hechter M. 1984. When actors comply: monitoring costs and the production of social order. *Acta Sociol.* 27:161–83

Heckathorn DD. 1988. Collective sanctions and the creation of prisoner's dilemma norms. *Am. J. Sociol.* 94(3):535–62

Heckathorn DD. 1989. Collective action and the second-order free-rider problem. *Rationality Soc.* 1(1):78–100

Heckathorn DD. 1996. The dynamics and dilemmas of collective action. *Am. Sociol. Rev.* 61:250–77

Hinde RA, Groebel J. 1991. *Cooperation and Prosocial Behaviour*. Cambridge, UK: Cambridge Univ. Press

Hume D. 1739/1976. *A Treatise of Human Nature*. Oxford, UK: Oxford Univ. Press

Isaac RM, McCue K, Plott C. 1985. Public goods provision in an experimental environment. *J. Public Econ.* 26:51–74

Isaac RM, Schmidtz D, Walker J. 1988. The assurance problem in a laboratory market. *Public Choice* 62(3):217–36

Isaac RM, Walker J. 1988. Group size effects in public goods provision: the voluntary contribution mechanism. *Q. J. Econ.* 103: 179–99

Isaac RM, Walker J, Thomas S. 1984. Divergent evidence on free riding: an experimental examination of possible explanations. *Public Choice* 43:113–49

Isaac RM, Walker J, Williams A. 1990. *Group size and the voluntary provision of public goods: experimental evidence utilizing very large groups*. Work. Pap. Indiana Univ.

Jerdee TH, Rosen B. 1974. Effects of opportunity to communicate and visibility of individual decisions on behavior in the common interest. *J. Appl. Soc. Psychol.* 59: 712–16

Jin N, Yamagishi T. 1997. Group heuristics in social dilemmas. *Jpn. J. Soc. Psychol.* 12: 190–98 (in Japanese with English summary)

Jin N, Yamagishi T, Kiyonari T. 1996. Bilateral dependency and the minimal group paradigm. *Jpn. J. Psychol.* 67:77–85 (in Japanese with English summary)

Kagel J, Roth A. 1995. *The Handbook of Experimental Economics*. Princeton, NJ: Princeton Univ. Press

Kahan JP. 1973. Noninteraction in an anonymous three-person prisoner's dilemma game. *Behav. Sci.* 18(2):124–27

Kakiuchi R, Yamagishi T. 1997. *The dilemma of trust*. Seventh Int. Conf. on Soc. Dilemmas, Cairns, Australia

Karp D, Jin N, Yamagishi T, Shinotsuka H. 1993. Raising the minimum in the minimal group paradigm. *Jpn. J. Exp. Soc. Psychol.* 32:231–40

Kelley HH. 1979. *Personal Relationships: Their Structures and Processes*. Hillsdale, NJ: Lawrence Erlbaum

Kelley HH, Grzelak J. 1972. Conflict between individual and common interest in an N-person relationship. *J. Pers. Soc. Psychol.* 21:190–97

Kelley HH, Thibaut JW. 1978. *Interpersonal Relations: A Theory of Interdependence*. New York: Wiley & Sons

Kerr N. 1989. Illusions of efficacy: the effects of group size on perceived efficacy in social dilemmas. *J. Exp. Soc. Psychol.* 25: 287–313

Kerr N. 1992. Efficacy as a causal and moderating variable in social dilemmas. In *Social Dilemmas: Theoretical Issues and Research Findings*, ed. WBG Liebrand, DM Messick, HAM Wilke, pp. 59–80. Oxford: Pergamon

Kerr N. 1997. *Anonymity and social control in social dilemmas*. Seventh Int. Conf. on Soc. Dilemmas, Cairns, Australia

Kim O, Walker M. 1984. The free rider problem: experimental evidence. *Public Choice* 43:3–24

Klandermans B. 1986. Individual behavior in real life social dilemmas: a theory and some research results. In *Experimental Social Dilemmas,* ed. HAM Wilke, DM Messick, C Rutte, pp. 87–111. Frankfurt: Verlag Peter Lang

Kollock P. 1993. 'An eye for an eye leaves everyone blind': cooperation and accounting systems. *Am. Sociol. Rev.* 58(6):768–86

Kollock P. 1998a. Transforming social dilemmas: group identity and cooperation. In *Modeling Rational and Moral Agents,* ed. P Danielson, pp. 186–210. Oxford, UK: Oxford Univ. Press

Kollock P. 1988b. Social Dilemmas: Online Resources. www.sscnet.ucla.edu/ soc/faculty/kollock/dilemmas

Kollock P, Smith M. 1996. Managing the virtual commons: cooperation and conflict in computer communities. In *Computer-Mediated Communication: Linguistic, Social, and Cross-Cultural Perspectives*, ed. S Herring, pp. 109–28. Amsterdam: John Benjamins

Komorita SS. 1987. Cooperative choice in decomposed social dilemmas. *Pers. Soc. Psychol. Bull.* 13:53–63

Komorita SS, Lapworth CW. 1982. Cooperative choice among individuals versus groups in an n-person dilemma situation. *J. Pers. Soc. Psychol.* 42:487–96

Komorita SS, Parks CD. 1995. Interpersonal relations: mixed-motive interaction. *Annu. Rev. Psychol.* 46:183–207

Komorita SS, Parks CD. 1996. *Social Dilemmas.* Boulder, CO: Westview

Komorita SS, Sweeney J, Kravitz DA. 1980. Cooperative choice in the n-person dilemma situation. *J. Pers. Soc. Psychol.* 38: 504–16

Kramer RM, Brewer MB. 1984. Effects of group identity on resource use in a simulated commons dilemma. *J. Pers. Soc. Psychol.* 46:1044–56

Kramer RM, Brewer MB. 1986. Social group identity and the emergence of cooperation in resource conservation dilemmas. In *Experimental Social Dilemmas,* ed. HAM Wilke, DM Messick, C Rutte, pp. 205–34. Frankfurt: Verlag Peter Lang

Kramer RM, McClintock CG, Messick DM. 1986. Social values and cooperative response to a simulated resource conservation crisis. *J. Pers.* 54:576–91

Kuhlman DM, Camac CR, Cunha DA. 1986. Individual differences in social orientation. In *Experimental Social Dilemmas,* ed. HAM Wilke, DM Messick, C Rutte, pp. 151–74. Frankfurt: Verlag Peter Lang

Kuhlman DM, Marshello AFJ. 1975. Individual differences in game motivation as moderators of preprogrammed strategy effects in prisoner's dilemma. *J. Pers. Soc. Psychol.* 32(5):922–31

Ledyard JO. 1995. Public goods: a survey of experimental research. In *The Handbook of Experimental Economics,* ed. JH Kagel, AE Roth, pp. 111–94. Princeton, NJ: Princeton Univ. Press

Liebrand WBG. 1984. The effect of social motives, communication and group size on behavior in an n-person multi-stage mixed-motive game. *Eur. J. Soc. Psychol.* 14:239–64

Liebrand WBG, Messick DM, eds. 1996. *Frontiers in Social Dilemmas Research.* Berlin: Springer Verlag

Liebrand WBG, Messick DM, Wilke HAM, eds. 1992. *Social Dilemmas: Theoretical Issues and Research Findings*. New York: Pergamon

Liebrand WBG, Wilke HAM, Vogel R, Wolters FJM. 1986. Value orientation and conformity in three types of social dilemma games. *J. Conflict Resolut.* 30:77–97

Lloyd WF. [1832] 1977. On the checks to population. Reprinted in *Managing the Commons,* ed. G Hardin, J Baden. San Francisco: Freeman

Lohmann S. 1995. The poverty of Green and Shapiro. *Crit. Rev.* 9(1–2):127–300
Luce D, Raifa H. 1957. *Games and Decisions*. New York: Wiley
Macy MW. 1991. Chains of cooperation: threshold effects in collective action. *Am. Sociol. Rev.* 56(12):730–47
Macy MW. 1993. Social learning and the structure of collective action. In *Advances in Group Processes,* ed. E Lawler et al, 10:1–36. Greenwich, CT: JAI
Macy MW, Kollock P, Yamagishi T. 1997. *The 'Tiger's Cave' experiments: a proposal for a web-based laboratory for cross-cultural research on trust in social dilemmas.* Work. Pap. Cornell Univ.
Maki JE, Hoffman DM, Berk RA. 1978. A time series analysis of the impact of a water conservation campaign. *Eval. Q.* 2: 107–18
Marwell G, Ames R. 1981. Economists free ride, does anyone else? Experiments on the provision of public goods, IV. *J. Public Econ.* 15:295–310
Marwel G, Oliver P. 1993. *The Critical Mass in Collective Action: A Micro-Social Theory.* Cambridge, MA: Cambridge Univ. Press
McCay BJ, Acheson JM, eds. 1987. *The Question of the Commons: The Culture and Ecology of Communal Resources*. Tucson: Univ. Ariz. Press
McClintock CG. 1974. Development of social motives in Anglo-American and Mexican-American children. *J. Pers. Soc. Psychol.* 29:348–54
McClintock CG, Keil LJ. 1983. Social values: their definition, their development, and their impact upon human decision making in settings of outcome interdependence. In *Small Groups and Social Interaction*, ed. H Blumberg, A Hare, V Kent, M Davies, 2:123–43. London: Wiley
McClintock CG, Liebrand WBG. 1988. Role of interdependence structure, individual value orientation, and another's strategy in social decision making: a transformational analysis. *J. Pers. Soc. Psychol.* 55(3): 396–409
Messick DM, Brewer MB. 1983. Solving social dilemmas. In *Review of Personality and Social Psychology,* ed. L Wheeler, P Shaver, 4:11–44. Beverly Hills, CA: Sage
Messick DM, McClelland CL. 1983. Social traps and temporal traps. *Soc. Psychol. Bull.* 9:105–10
Messick DM, Wilke HAM, Brewer MB, Kramer RM, Zemke P, Lui L. 1983. Individual adaptations and structural change as solutions to social dilemmas. *J. Pers. Soc. Psychol.* 44:294–309
Moe TM. 1980. *The Organization of Interests: Incentives and Internal Dynamics of Political Interest Groups.* Chicago, IL: Univ. Chicago Press
Mueller EN, Opp KD. 1986. Rational choice and rebellious collective action. *Am. Polit. Sci. Rev.* 80:471–87
Olson M. 1965. *The Logic of Collective Action: Public Goods and the Theory of Groups*. Cambridge, MA: Harvard Univ. Press
Orbell J, Dawes R. 1981. Social dilemmas. In *Progress in Applied Social Psychology*, ed. GM Stephenson, JM Davis, 1:37–65. New York: Wiley
Orbell J, Dawes R. 1993. Social welfare, cooperators' advantage, and the option of not playing the game. *Am. Sociol. Rev.* 58(6): 787–800
Orbell J, Dawes R, van de Kragt A. 1990. The limits of multilateral promising. *Ethics* 100:616–27
Orbell J, van de Kragt A, Dawes R. 1988. Explaining discussion-induced cooperation. *J. Pers. Soc. Psychol.* 54:811–19
Ostrom E. 1990. *Governing the Commons: The Evolution of Institutions for Collective Action*. Cambridge, UK: Cambridge Univ. Press
Ostrom E. 1992. *Crafting Institutions for Self-Governing Irrigation Systems*. San Francisco: ICS
Ostrom E, Gardner R, Walker J. 1994. *Rules, Games, and Common-Pool Resources*. Ann Arbor: Univ. Mich. Press
Poundstone W. 1992. *Prisoner's Dilemma.* New York: Doubleday
Rapoport A. 1967. Optimal policies for the prisoner's dilemma. *Psychol. Rev.* 75: 136–48
Rapoport A, Bornstein G. 1987. Intergroup competition for the provision of binary public goods. *Psychol. Rev.* 94:291–99
Rapoport A, Bornstein G. 1989. Solving public good problems in competition between equal and unequal size groups. *J. Conflict Resolut.* 33:460–79
Rapoport A, Bornstein G, Erev I. 1989. Intergroup competition for public goods: effects of unequal resource and relative group size. *J. Pers. Soc. Psychol.* 56: 748–56
Rutte CG, Wilke HAM. 1985. Preferences for decision structures in a social dilemma situation. *Eur. J. Soc. Psychol.* 15:367–70
Samuelson CD, Messick DM. 1986a. Alternative structural solutions to resource dilemmas. *Organ. Behav. Hum. Decision Processes* 37:139–55
Samuelson CD, Messick DM. 1986b. Inequities in access to and use of shared re-

sources in social dilemmas. *J. Pers. Soc. Psychol.* 51:960–67
Samuelson CD, Messick DM, Rutte CG, Wilke HAM. 1984. Individual and structural solutions to resource dilemmas in two cultures. *J. Pers. Soc. Psychol.* 47:94–104
Samuelson P. 1954. The pure theory of public expenditure. *Rev. Econ. Statist.* 36:387–89
Schelling TC. 1978. *Micromotives and Macrobehavior*. New York: Norton
Schroeder DA, ed. 1995. *Social Dilemmas: Perspectives on Individuals and Groups*. Westport, CT: Praeger
Schuessler R. 1989. Exit threats and cooperation under anonymity. *J. Conflict Resolut.* 33:728–49
Schulz U, Albers W, Mueller U, eds. 1994. *Social Dilemmas and Cooperation*. New York: Springer-Verlag
Sherif M, Harvey O, White B, Hood W, Sherif C. 1961. *Intergroup Conflict and Cooperation: The Robber's Cave Experiment*. Norman, OK: Inst. Group Relat., Univ. Oklahoma
Stroebe W, Frey BS. 1982. Self-interest and collective action: the economics and psychology of public goods. *Br. J. Soc. Psychol.* 21:121–37
Suleiman R, Rapoport A. 1992. Provision of step-level public goods with continuous contribution. *J. Behav. Decision Making* 5(2):133–53
Tajfel H. 1981. *Human Groups and Social Categories*. Cambridge, UK: Cambridge Univ. Press
Toda M, Shinotsuka H, McClintock CG, Stech F. 1978. Development of competitive behavior as a function of culture, age, and social comparison. *J. Pers. Soc. Psychol.* 36: 835–39
Udehn L. 1993. Twenty-five years with *The Logic of Collective Action*. *Acta Sociol.* 36:239–61
van de Kragt A, Orbell J, Dawes R. 1983. The minimal contributing set as a solution to public goods problems. *Am. Polit. Sci. Rev.* 77:112–22
van Lange PAM, Liebrand WBG, Messick DM, Wilke HAM. 1992. Social dilemmas: the state of the art—introduction and literature review. In *Social Dilemmas: Theoretical Issues and Research Findings*, ed. WBG Liebrand, DM Messick, HAM Wilke, pp. 3–28. Oxford: Pergamon
Vanberg VJ, Congleton RD. 1992. Rationality, morality, and exit. *Am. Polit. Sci. Rev.* 86:418–31
Watabe M. 1992. Choice of strategies in a social dilemma. *Jpn. J. Exp. Soc. Psychol.* 32:171–82 (in Japanese with English summary)
Watabe M, Terai S, Hayashi N, Yamagishi T. 1996. Cooperation in the one-shot Prisoner's Dilemma based on expectations of reciprocity. *Jpn. J. Exp. Soc. Psychol.* 36: 183–96 (in Japanese with English summary)
Watabe M, Yamagishi T. 1994. Choice of strategies in social dilemma supergames. In *Social Dilemmas and Cooperation,* ed. U Schulz, W Albers, U Mueller, pp. 251–67. New York: Springer-Verlag
Wilke HAM, Messick DM, Rutte CG, eds. 1986. *Experimental Social Dilemmas*. Frankfurt: Verlag Peter Lang
Winett RA, Kagel JH, Battalio RC, Winkler RC. 1978. The effects of monetary rebates, feedback, and information on residential energy conservation. *J. Appl. Psychol.* 63: 73–80
Yamagishi T. 1986. The provision of a sanctioning system as a public good. *J. Pers. Soc. Psychol.* 51:110–16
Yamagishi T. 1988. Seriousness of social dilemmas and the provision of a sanctioning system. *Soc. Psychol. Q.* 51(1):32–42
Yamagishi T. 1992. Group size and the provision of a sanctioning system in a social dilemma. In *Social Dilemmas: Theoretical Issues and Research Findings,* ed. WBG Liebrand, DM Messick, HAM Wilke, pp. 267–87. Oxford: Pergamon
Yamagishi T. 1995. Social dilemmas. In *Sociological Perspectives on Social Psychology*, ed. K Cook, GA Fine, JS House, pp. 311–35. Boston: Allyn & Bacon
Yamagishi T, Cook K. 1993. Generalized exchange and social dilemmas. *Soc. Psychol. Q.* 56(4):235–48
Yamagishi T, Hayashi N, Jin N. 1994. Prisoner's dilemma networks: selection strategy versus action strategy. In *Social Dilemmas and Cooperation,* ed. U Schulz, W Albers, U Mueller, pp. 233–50. New York: Springer-Verlag
Yamagishi T, Takahashi N. 1994. Evolution of norms without metanorms. In *Social Dilemmas and Cooperation,* ed. U Schulz, W Albers, U Mueller, pp. 311–26. New York: Springer-Verlag
Yamagishi T, Yamagishi M. 1994. Trust and commitment in the United States and Japan. *Motivation Emotion* 18(2):129–66

Annu. Rev. Sociol. 1998. 24:215–38

BREAKDOWN THEORIES OF COLLECTIVE ACTION

Bert Useem

Department of Sociology, University of New Mexico, Albuquerque, New Mexico 87131

KEY WORDS: riots, collective violence, disorganization, solidarity, aggression

ABSTRACT

Historically, breakdown theory dominated the sociological study of collective action. In the 1970s, this theory was found to be increasingly unable to account for contemporaneous events and newly discovered historical facts. Resource mobilization theory displaced breakdown theory as the dominant paradigm. Yet the evidence against breakdown theory is weak once a distinction is made between routine and nonroutine collective action. Several recent contributions affirm the explanatory power of breakdown theory for nonroutine collective action. Breakdown theory also contributes to an understanding of the use of governmental force against protest and of the moral features of collective action. Breakdown and resource mobilization theories explain different types of phenomena, and both are needed to help account for the full range of forms of collective action.

INTRODUCTION

Breakdown theory is the classic sociological explanation of contentious forms of collective action such as riots, rebellion, and civil violence. The crux of the theory is that these sorts of events occur when the mechanisms of social control lose their restraining power. Breakdown theory was expressed in the mainstream of sociology by its standard-bearers: Comte through Durkheim, Gustave LeBon, and Gabriel Tarde in the European tradition; Robert Park and his student Herbert Blumer, Talcott Parsons and his student Neil Smelser in the American tradition.

0360-0572/98/0815-0215/$08.00

Breakdown theory's dominance ended during the 1970s. Researchers claimed that breakdown theory could not account for societal events as they were then unfolding—the social movements and collective violence of the 1960s and 1970s, nor for newly collected historical data. A new theory emerged to explain the anomalies. Resource mobilization (RM) theorists posited that collective action flows not from breakdown but from groups vying for political position and advantages. Rebellion is "simply politics by other means," stated William Gamson (1990 [1975], p. 139).

Resource mobilization theory gained quick acceptance, becoming by 1980 the dominant paradigm (Zald 1992, p. 327). Breakdown theory fell so far that a study could be criticized by merely pointing out that it left variation to be explained by breakdown processes. As an example, Anthony Oberschall (1973, p. 120) classified collectivities to greatly emphasize organizational ties within a community: whether they are organized along traditional/communal lines, or have little or no organization of any kind. He argued that in a segmented social structure (that is, the lower orders are not effectively integrated with the elite), collective action may arise under all three forms of horizontal organization. However, when the horizontal ties are weak or nonexistent, we should expect "short-lived, but violent... outbursts devoid of leadership, organization, and explicitly articulated goals" (Oberschall 1973, pp. 122–23).

Charles Tilly (1978, p. 83), one of the architects of resource mobilization theory, portrayed this as an escape clause and implied that Oberschall had not emphasized strongly enough the influence of prior organization. Tilly would later affirm that

> solidarity, rather than insufficient integration, provides the necessary conditions of collective action, and... rebellions, protest, collective violence, and related forms of action result from rational pursuit of shared interests (1984: 51–52).

As used by Tilly and others, solidarity refers to dense social networks and a strong collective identity. Breakdown (malintegration) refers to weak networks and a diffuse collective identity often created by chronic unemployment, family instability, and disruptive migration.

Recent scholarship, however, suggests a need to reconsider RM theorists' monopoly over the field. The thesis of this essay is that breakdown theory and RM theory analyze different phenomena, and that the sociological terrain needs to be opened up for breakdown theorists' insights.

RM RESEARCH: THE NEGATION OF THE NEGATION?

Few resource mobilization theorists have backed away from the claim that breakdown theory has been falsified by the evidence. The key research said to refute breakdown theory can divided into (*a*) the work by Charles Tilly and his collaborators on collective action in a European setting; (*b*) studies of the organizational bases of social movements; (*c*) analyses of the urban disorders of the 1960s; and (*d*) work on the connection between collective action and crime.

Collective Action In European Setting

The work of Charles Tilly and his colleagues has been pivotal in the swing away from breakdown theory. Tilly's group undertook a daunting task. They counted the incidence of collective action in several European countries over a 100-year period, against which they sought to test breakdown and RM models. Few would challenge the enormous contributions (methodological, historical, and theoretical) made by this impressive body of research. Yet *pace* Tilly, the refutation of the breakdown theory is not one of them.

That Tilly's research is not a crucial test of breakdown theory has been argued by Frances Piven and Richard Cloward (1992). To back up for a moment, in his theoretical work, Tilly (1978, pp. 14-15, 23) recognizes that the heart of breakdown theory is a distinction between "routine collective action" (e.g. electoral rallies, peaceful protest) and "nonroutine collective" action (e.g. rebellion, collective violence, riots). The difference, to expand on this point, is not so much that participants in riots and rebellion injure people and destroy property. Boxers, armies, and wrecking crews are paid to do physically similar things. Rather, it is that participants must free themselves from the restraints on behavior, both moral and physical, that society normally makes strongest and is most concerned about. Breakdown theory posits that only nonroutine collective action flows out of breakdown processes; routine collective action is said to arise from and reinforce solidarity.

Yet when Tilly and associates measured the incidence of collective action, the routine/nonroutine distinction was lost. In one study, Shorter & Tilly (1974) sought to explain the timing of strikes in France over the period 1865–1965. Piven & Cloward (1992, p. 306) point out that strikes became legal in France in 1865 and thus presumably were more akin to routine collective than nonroutine action. Shorter & Tilly made no additional effort to distinguish between "routine" and "nonroutine" strike activity. The same problem occurs in the other key studies claiming to disprove breakdown theory, including those by Lodhi & Tilly (1973) and Snyder & Tilly (1972).

Piven & Cloward (1992, p. 306) maintain that the flaw is fatal: "Taken as a whole, this corpus of research does not answer the question of the conditions under which ordinary people do in fact resort to violence or defiance, and the findings cannot be taken to refute the [breakdown] perspective." This criticism has gone unrebutted and is, in my opinion, fair.

Furthermore, the empirical case in favor of resource mobilization as a replacement for breakdown theory is also problematic. I focus on one study because it raises a theoretical issue discussed below. In building the RM model, Snyder & Tilly (1972) argue that high levels of governmental repression should increase the cost of collective action and thus reduce the likelihood that groups will be able to mobilize and make demands. To test this hypothesis, they regressed the number of collective action participants for each year in France between 1830 and 1960 on three separate indicators of repression: (*a*) size of the national budget, measuring the "bulk" of the government; (*b*) person-days in jails for each year, including for ordinary crime; and (*c*) "excess arrests," a five-year lagged variable measuring whether, in a given year, there were more arrests than would otherwise be expected from the number of collective action participants in that year and the overall pattern of arrest/participants for the entire 131-year period.

The regression coefficient for the national budget is in the predicted direction; the one for person-days in jails is also in the predicted direction but weak; and the one for excess arrests is in the opposite of the predicted direction and weak. One could argue (although Snyder & Tilly do not) that excess arrests is the only direct measure of governmental repression; the other two are so distant from government repression as to be irrelevant. If so, the results seem to suggest not only that repression does not work, but that it may slightly increase collective action. In fairness, though, Snyder & Tilly note that the three measures of repression are less than ideal, each presenting "some difficulties" (1972, pp. 527–28).

The point here is the tenuous nature of evidence assembled by the Tilly group with regard to the causes of nonroutine collective action. The point is not trivial, given the impact of the research on the field.

Secondary Groups and Social Movements

RM theorists argue that preexisting organization, both formal and informal, facilitates collective action. Organization provides resources, such as pooled labor and leadership; it schools participants in civic cooperation and public mindedness, and extends the interpersonal bonds through which recruitment takes place. Resources, public spiritedness, and social bonds, in turn, help make possible the hard work often needed to sustain collective action. Organization also permits the "bloc" mobilization of preexisting groups directly into movements.

The finding of a positive association between organization and collective action has been replicated in dozens of studies and is irrefutable—at least in regard to certain forms of collective action. These forms include (*a*) community-based protest movements, such as those over abortion (Luker 1984, Staggenborg 1991), property taxes (Lo 1990), and school busing to achieve racial integration (Useem 1980); (*b*) elite-supported protest movements, such as Mothers Against Drunk Driving (McCarthy et al 1988, Weed 1987), and social movements employing disciplined civil disobedience, such as the US civil rights movement (McAdam 1986, Morris 1984). Yet this research contradicts breakdown theory only if the collective action being studied falls into the nonroutine category.

While no one has been able to define exactly what "routine" and "nonroutine" mean, some cases are easily classified. By almost anyone's standard, the riots that occurred in US cities in the 1960s were nonroutine. They entailed massive looting, widespread violence, and direct defiance of orders by law enforcement agencies to disperse. If the evidence on these disturbances runs against breakdown theory, the position is damaged. (This evidence is reviewed in the next section.)

Other collective action noted above just as clearly belongs to the routine category. Mothers Against Drunk Driving, for example, looks a lot like the other pluralist interest groups that routinely vie for political influence. MADD's tactics include public and youth education, lobbying for tougher laws against drunk driving, assisting victims of drunk drivers, and urging police to beef up their enforcement efforts. Breakdown and RM theorists alike would anticipate that MADD would be a product of something other than social breakdown. The evidence bears this out. For example, Frank Weed (1987, p. 264–65) reports that, based on a 1985 survey of local chapter officers, the typical MADD activist was 41 years of age, married, had attended college, held a high-status job, and was involved in one or more other community organizations. John McCarthy and colleagues (1988) found that counties with more affluent and highly educated residents were more likely to have MADD chapters than counties with less affluent, less educated residents.

There are also hard cases. Eric Hirsch (1990) tested breakdown and resource mobilization theory against data on student involvement in a 1985 anti-apartheid protest movement at Columbia University. On the one hand, the students' defiant tactics—they blockaded the administration building for three weeks demanding that the University sell its stock in companies doing business in South Africa—suggest nonroutine collective action. On the other hand, these were students at one of the country's elite universities, far from the sort of setting or population that breakdown theorists have in mind.

Indeed, Hirsch's quantitative data, derived from a survey of undergraduates, seem to support a middle-case interpretation. Hirsch regressed a measure of protest participation on ten independent variables. Five of the ten measured either general ideological orientation or attitudes specific to the situation itself, such as the belief that divestment would influence the South African government. None of these five variables appears to have a direct bearing on the breakdown and RM positions. The other five independent variables do. They include membership in campus political action organizations, membership in other types of campus organizations, and a dummy variable for freshman status.

All five of the general variables have a significant impact on participation, together explaining 59% of the variance. None of the five breakdown/RM variables has significant regression coefficients. In other words, student protestors were neither more nor less likely than other students to be a member of a campus political action organization, any other type of campus organization, or a member of the freshman class. If the results can be interpreted as failing to support the breakdown theory, as Hirsch (1990, p. 251) argues, so too for the RM position.

In sum, resource mobilization theorists have demonstrated that prior organization has a great deal to do with the ability of a group to act. Intuitively it makes sense that routine social movements draw on the resources embedded in their communities such as trust, information, and skills in civic participation. But that does not exhaust the question of what conditions generate nonroutine collective action.

Revisionist Studies of Urban Riots of the 1960s

Resource mobilization theorists commonly assert that the same forces that generate social movements are also responsible for the outbreak of urban collective violence. The Tillys (1975, p. 290) state that "no matter where we look, we should rarely find uprooted, marginal, disorganized people heavily involved in collective action." This expectation, they continue, is borne out by the evidence on the urban riots of the 1960s (1975, p. 291–94). If this assessment holds up, the breakdown position is damaged.

Research on the urban riots of the 1960s took one of two approaches. Some studies explained riot participation by determining the characteristics that distinguished rioters from nonrioters. Other studies compared cities that had riots to those that did not.

STUDIES USING INDIVIDUAL-LEVEL DATA The most important individual-level data were collected in connection with the National Advisory Commission on Civil Disorders (NACCD 1968a,b). The data sources included: (*a*) a survey conducted in the first three months of 1968 in 15 cities under the direction of Angus Campbell and Howard Schuman; (*b*) surveys conducted in Newark and Detroit after major riots in those cities in 1967; (*c*) police records of individuals arrested during the riots in a number of cities.

The Campbell/Schuman (NACCD 1968b, p. 12) survey obtained data from 2800 African Americans in 15 cities. While too few respondents admitted to riot participation to allow for analysis (1968b, p. 54), the questionnaire did include a number of items concerning attitudes toward rioting and other types of collective action. Abraham Miller and colleagues (1976) have reanalyzed these data in a way that is particularly useful for present purposes.

Miller distinguished among four groups: apathetics, nonviolent protestors, violence-prone protestors, and the riot prone. He found that "violent protestors" were a "hybrid" group, with very mixed attitudes and demographic characteristic. For this reason, Miller focused on two "pure" groups: nonviolent protestors (seemingly akin to actors engaged in routine collective action) and the riot prone (seemingly akin to actors engaged in nonroutine collective action).

The data indicate that riot-prone respondents, compared to the nonviolent protestors, tended to have relatively low levels of education and income, to be socialized in a broken home, to be unmarried, and to be relatively young (Miller et al 1976, p. 361). For example, 71% of the respondents at least 44 years of age and in the highest occupational category were protestors, but less than 3% of the same group were rioters. In contrast, 22% of the 16–19-year olds who had unskilled occupations were rioters, but only 15% of this group were protestors (Miller et al 1976, p. 362-363). Miller concludes,

> If such measures as being married, being reared in an intact family, and attaining the relatively upper rungs of occupation, income, and education ladder can be justifiably considered as measures of social integration then it is clear that rioters... emerged from the least socially integrated and lower elements of the community (Miller et al 1976, p. 361).

These findings are consistent with a breakdown explanation of nonroutine collective action.

The results of the surveys conducted of residents in Detroit and Newark yielded results less favorable to breakdown theory. The Detroit sample were interviewed two weeks after a major riot in that city; the Newark sample about six months after the riot there. From these data, the National Advisory Commission reported that "there are no substantial differences in unemployment between the rioters and the noninvolved" (NACCD 1968a, p. 75).

While this finding continues to be widely cited as evidence against breakdown theory (e.g. Skolnick & Fyfe 1993, p. 76), it should be regarded cautiously. First, the tables have small N's: 154 and 189 for the Detroit and Newark samples, respectively. For the Detroit sample, there were only 27 rioters interviewed, to be distributed into the employed or unemployed cells; for the Newark sample, 84 rioters were distributed to the two cells.

Second, the Newark respondents (but not the Detroit respondents) were asked if they had been unemployed for at least a month during the previous year. Fifty-four percent of the rioters, compared to 37% of the nonrioters, stated that they had been so unemployed, a difference that is statistically significant. If the rioters were more likely than nonrioters to have been unemployed in the previous year, it is not clear why this is not reflected in rates of current unemployment.

Third, the overall levels of unemployment were "extremely high" (NACCD 1968a, p. 75)—about a third of both samples. Apparently, Detroit and Newark were communities in which work had already begun to "disappear" (Wilson 1996). One could argue that these high levels of unemployment made rioting more likely in those communities, compared to communities with full employment, even if unemployed individuals were no more likely to riot than were employed individuals. This community-wide effect of unemployment should show up in city-level data. It does, as we see in the next section.

The Commission (NACCD 1968b, p. 247) also reports data from nine cities on the proportion of riot arrestees who had been previously arrested. This proportion ranged from 39% (Buffalo, New York) to 100% in two cities (New Brunswick and Elizabeth, New Jersey). The Commission discounts the significance of these findings, pointing out that "50 to 90 percent of the Negro males in the urban ghettos have criminal records" (1968b, p. 237). From this and other considerations, the Commission concludes that "the criminal element is not over-represented among the rioters" (1968b, p. 237). This conclusion has also been widely cited by resource mobiliation theorists as part of the readily available evidence against breakdown theory.

Still, these findings can be reconciled with breakdown theory. If there is any realism to the upper-end figure of 90%, this would suggest that prior criminality could not predict which inner-city residents rioted (because there is little variation), but it might still be able to explain why riots occurred there and not elsewhere. One could argue that in areas in which the arrest rates are as high as 90%, the stigma of arrest losses its inhibiting effect, including for the criminal act of rioting. This remains speculative.

STUDIES USING CITY-LEVEL DATA The most influential research using the city as the unit of observation was reported in a series of papers by Seymour Spilerman (1970, 1971, 1976). Spilerman found that only two city-level characteristics were significantly related to riot occurrence and intensity: (*a*) the numerical size of the African-American population, and (*b*) location outside of the South. All other community characteristics, including unemployment, education, and income, had no independent effect. Spilerman argues that the factor most responsible for riots, overshadowing any effects of community conditions, was the "widespread availability of television and its network news structure" (1976, p. 790). Television brought scenes of the civil rights movements into "every ghetto." This, in turn, "contributed in a fundamental way to the creation of a black solidarity that would transcend the boundaries of community."

The theoretical significance of these findings for breakdown theory, as well as the findings themselves, remain open to challenge. First, with regard to the region effect, Piven & Cloward (1992, p. 312) argue that rioting may have occurred outside the South because "northern ghettos were less cohesive than southern black communities." This does not show up in the analysis because "cohesiveness" is not measured directly by Spilerman. The same point could be made about the effect of black community size: large black communities, compared to smaller ones, may have had weaker social controls, especially under conditions of high unemployment. Additional evidence on these points is needed.

Second, Spilerman adduces no evidence that television had the impact he said it had, that is, to create greater solidarity among inner-city African Americans. His argument is plausible, but not self-evident, especially in the absence of an independent measure of solidarity. An indirect measure is the crime rate. If black solidarity was increasing in this period, there should have been a corresponding decline in the crime rate. Yet the crime rate for African Americans increased rapidly in this period (LaFree & Drass 1996, p. 622). Even if we were to assume that television was a key independent variable, the causal mechanism may differ from the one Spilerman identifies. Robert Putnam (1995) argues that television viewing (which is concentrated among the less educated sectors) fragments communities and reduces solidarity. Perhaps that effect was present too, or instead.

Finally, Spilerman's key empirical finding—that community conditions were irrelevant to the outbreak of violence—has been challenged. In one study, Susan Olzak and Suzanne Shanahan (1996, p. 946) found that "cities with higher rates of unemployment for blacks had significantly higher rates of unrest," at least under conditions of heightened inter-minority competition. In another study, Daniel Myers (1997, p. 110) reported that the number of nonwhites unemployed in a given city had a strong effect on riot rates, although he cautions that further research is needed to determine "exactly how unemployment contributes to civil unrest." These two studies, relying on data that are more complete than were available to Spilerman, help shift the burden back to the critics of breakdown theory.

Collective Action, Crime, and Age

From its founding, breakdown theory has hypothesized links between riots/rebellion and other signs of breakdown, such as crime. One strategy to test this link has been to examine whether rates of collective action and rates of crime track together over time. The Tillys (1975) found that crime and collective action varied independently in France, Italy, and Germany from 1830 to 1930. In contrast, Ted Gurr (1976) established that crime waves tended to occur during periods of high levels of civil strife in the four areas he studied (London, Stockholm, New South Wales, and Calcutta).

In a more recent study, Gary LaFree and Kriss Drass (1997) examined the covariation between rates of crime and collective action in the United States over the period 1955 to 1991. They found that crime rates and collective action rose in tandem from 1955 to the early 1970s but, after that, crime rates and collective action were negatively related.

LaFree & Drass (1997, p. 849) argue that the first half of the time series supports breakdown theory: Crime and collective action seem to "spring in part from the same social forces." The second half of the time series, though, is more consistent with RM theory, the authors maintain. They argue that the two rates departed because collective action, but not crime, requires organizational resources, which ostensibly became tighter in the post-1974 period. Also, beefed-up law enforcement had a stronger effect on riots than on crime. Additional work needs to be done on the first point, because LaFree & Drass do not show there was an actual decrease of resources. "Resources," of course, must be measured independently of the incidence of collective action.

Another strategy would be to examine the pattern of correlations between (*a*) crime and collective action (routine and nonroutine) and (*b*) other relevant variables such as age. The premise here is that like phenomena correlate in like ways.

It is ancient criminological wisdom (supported by a large body of evidence) that young people commit crime at relatively high rates. For most crimes, rates of commission peak in the late teen years and then fall to half their peak level by the mid-twenties (Blumstein 1995, Gottfredson & Hirschi 1990, p. 123–126). If crime shares properties with rioting, but not routine collective action, we would anticipate that age would correlate with rioting in a similar way but not with routine collective action. This is what we find.

From its multiple data sources, the 1968 National Advisory Commission on Civil Disorders concluded that rioters were predominantly "late teenagers or young adults" (NACCD 1968b, p. 74). For example, in the Detroit survey noted above, 61% of the self-reported rioters were between the ages of 15 and 24, and 86% were between 15 and 35. Moreover, this correlation appears to be stable over time. A study of the rioters arrested in the 1992 Los Angeles riots found that their age distribution was almost identical to the age distribution of those arrested in the 1965 Los Angeles riot (Petersilia & Abrahamse 1994, p. 140–144). This suggests that the impact of age on rioting is a life-cycle effect (that is, rioting is something that people do when they are young but not older) rather than a period or generational effect.

In contrast, a similar pattern of correlations is not found between age and participation in routine forms of collective action such as voluntary organizations and voting. Affiliation with voluntary organizations is greatest among the group between the ages of 30 and 49, somewhat lower for those over 50, and much lower for the group 17–29 (Verba & Nie 1972, p. 181). And, controlling for additional demographic variables, age increases the likelihood of voting (Wolfinger & Rosenstone 1980, p. 47). Of course, many phenomena are correlated with age (playing volleyball, for example) but have nothing to do with crime. Still, the point is that crime and nonroutine collective action seem to share a similar place in the life-cycle, one not shared by routine collective action.

RECENT ADVANCES

The resource mobilization consensus notwithstanding, a number of recent studies have contributed to the development of the breakdown position. The most fully developed of these, by Frances Piven and Richard Cloward (1977), argues that the leading social movements of the 1930s and the 1960s were products of social breakdown: for the former, the dislocations produced by the Great Depression; for the latter, the uprooting migration and modernization that followed World War II. Along the same lines, Jack Goldstone (1980) found that protest groups being active during periods of social crisis or breakdown is a better predictor of success than their organizational strength or tactics. Finally, Useem and colleagues link breakdown in institutional effectiveness to the spread of the 1992 riot in Los Angeles (Useem 1997) and to the occurrence of the US prison riots (Useem 1985, Useem & Kimball 1989, Useem et al 1996). Here I highlight several additional recent contributions.

Spiral of Ethnic Conflict

Two recent studies of ethnic collective violence come to similar conclusions, which in turn are broadly consistent with a breakdown model. Psychoanalyst Sudhir Kakar (1996a) examined collective violence between Muslims and Hindus in the Indian city of Hyderabad. Sociologist Anthony Oberschall (1997) analyzed the collective violence that followed the breakup of the Yugoslav state. In both studies, the explanadum is not ethnic conflict per se, but its form of unrestrained violence. In Hyderabad, the Hindu-Muslim riots took anything but a ritualized form. Rather, they were infused with deadly intent, accompanied by the destruction of temples, mosques, and shrines and the burning of houses. The vocabulary, on both sides, was victory with honor and defeat with humiliation and deep emotional wounds. In the former Yugoslavia, the conflict entailed the expulsion of a quarter of the population from their homelands ("ethnic cleansing"), torture, mass executions and rape, and the sniper-killings of civilians.

Both Kakar and Oberschall argue that extreme collective violence emerges out of a spiral of conflict, polarization, and ultimately bloody, mutual recriminations. In both case studies, breakdown elements permitted the polarization to begin and to continue.

In Oberschall's account, the fall of the Yugoslav state was followed by a disintegration of the other institutions, including the economy. In the void, extremist leaders formed militias, targeted moderates for refusing to go along with them, and recruited members from large pools of unskilled men. As the economy further deteriorated with the start of the war, a criminal economy took its place, fueled by widespread looting, ransom of captured civilians, and seizure of property from those expelled from their homes and homeland.

On a theoretical level, Oberschall's analysis is instructive for two reasons. First, classic breakdown theory pictures collective violence as a by-product of impersonal, structural change. But Oberschall shows that, in this case, human agents were causing the breakdown, decisively and purposefully. Breakdown of the social order was part of the strategy of conflict escalation, which then fed on itself.

Second, Oberschall's analysis suggests that the distinction between breakdown and solidarity is too simplistic. Much depends on the kinds of groups that are breaking down and the kinds that are forming. The place, timing, and mood of these processes are also important. Francis Fukuyama (1996, p. 15) makes a relevant point: "It is as if there is a natural, universal human impulse toward sociability, which, if blocked from expressing itself through social structures like the family or voluntary organizations, appears in the forms like criminal gangs." In Bosnia, social decomposition was a precursor to the solidaristic groups that came to dominate the situation. These groups, moreover, appear to have been closer to Fukuyama's "criminal gangs" than the sorts of community groups and networks of solidarity that RM theorists have in mind.

In explaining Hindu-Muslim violence, Kakar (1996a,b) distinguishes community identification from communalism. The latter as used in the Indian context refers to a dominating sense of community identification, in which a sense of "we-ness" is replaced by "we are." This exclusive attachment to one's community is accompanied by hostility toward those communities that share a political and geographic space. Riots originate not only in the minds of men and women, according to Kakar, but early in their childhoods. Drawing on the work of Erik Erickson, Kakar finds that communalism becomes imprinted during the same developmental stages in which a child acquires a sense of self.

For ethnic/religious conflict within limits to turn to murderous ethnic conflict without limits, two shifts have to occur. At the cognitive level, the communal identity must take on overwhelming salience in a large number of people at the same time. Social identity comes to dominate if not to displace personal identity. At the affective level, love for one's group and hatred toward out-groups must be rekindled from feelings first developed in childhood. Drawing on psychoanalytic theory, Karkar (1996a, p. 43) refers to the preoccupation with minor differences, which cause greater hostility than do wide differences, as a key source of hateful representations of the other side. In Hyderabad, an initial attack by one side triggered fears of group annihilation in the other. Fueled by rumor and stoked by religious extremists, these fears generated a spiral of attacks and counterattacks.

Kakar's analysis is particularly instructive because he contrasts it with an explanation more consistent with the resource mobilization position: The Hindu-Muslim riots flowed out of group struggle over territorial control and political power (1996a, pp. 21–23, 194–196). The problem with this explanation is that it cannot account for the extraordinary nature of the riots: people, often neighbors, killing and maiming one another, rarely experiencing shame or guilt for the violence inflicted.

Disruption of Quotidian

David Snow and colleagues (1998) have recently advanced a version of the breakdown model that incorporates two other sets of theoretical insights into the model: prospect theory, as developed by Kahneman & Tversky (1979), and cultural theory, as developed by Bourdieu (1975), Schutz (1962), and Snow & Benford (1992). Prospect theory maintains that people frame their decisions in terms of gains or losses from their status quo or zero point, and losses loom larger than corresponding gains. The relevant element of cultural theory is the concept of "quotidian," the taken-for-granted attitude of everyday life and habituated routines. The quotidian normally keeps life stable and operating on an even keel. Examples of the quotidian include middle-class people going to work and making mortgage payments and homeless people making do with a meager but steady supply of provisions.

The synthesis of prospect and cultural theories is this. Social breakdown both (*a*) generates losses which, in turn, are experienced as highly salient deprivations (prospect theory), and (*b*) undercuts actors' confidence that their accustomed routines can continue to provide a satisfying future (cultural theory). It is this conjuncture of suddenly imposed deprivations and an uncertain future that gives rise to anger, indignation, and revolt. Snow and colleagues flesh-out (and to a degree, test) their position with several case studies, including work on homeless mobilization in eight cities, the mobilization of citizens following the 1979 accident at the Three-Mile Island nuclear power plant, peasant rebellions, and a prison riot.

In sum, even if one were to agree that breakdown theory has been an intellectual "straightjacket" (Gamson 1990, p. 130), this impressive paper by Snow and colleagues demonstrates that this need not be the case. It shows that breakdown theory can be stretched in different directions, here to incorporate recent advances in phenomenology and cognitive psychology. The key argument—that the collapse of everyday routines changes the cognitive and affective content of actors' minds, setting the stage for rebellion—seems plausible, if unproven. This refreshing analysis should open up new avenues of research.

GOVERNMENTAL "REPRESSION"

The reader might suspect that the wedge between breakdown and resource mobilization theories runs deeper than the causes of collective action per se. One issue concerns the properties of governmental force against protestors and rioters. A second issue, contrasting moral sentiments, is discussed in the next section.

As is often the case, Tilly provides the clearest explication of the logic of the RM position. He challenges the breakdown position that there exists a meaningful distinction between "legitimate" and "illegitimate" force.

> The very same acts, indeed, switch from illegitimate to legitimate if a constituted authority performs them. Killing appears in both columns, but with very different values. The values depend on whether the killer is a soldier, a policeman, an executioner, or a private person. (1984, p. 56)

Tilly adds that, as a practical matter, he would call the police if someone stole his wallet. Still, he believes that the distinction between legitimate and illegitimate force "should never have entered the world of systematic explanation" (1984, p. 56). Finally, Tilly seems to discount the possibility that riots are genuinely frightening to the public. The term "riot" itself, Tilly argues, is merely a "legal device" that authorities use to justify the use of force against assembled citizens.

These arguments, in turn, permit Tilly to define "governmental repression" as any governmental action that raises the "costs" of collective action. As noted earlier, Tilly used this definition of repression in his work on European collective action, and it has been adapted widely by others in the resource mobilization tradition (Opp & Roehl 1990, Tarrow 1994, p. 92–93, McAdam 1982, p. 218–229). RM analysts now routinely refer to the "repression works" hypothesis.

Breakdown theorists believe that the distinction between legitimate and illegitimate force is valid even, indeed especially, in regard to governmental use of force. In this view, "repression" is reserved for governmental action that violates legal rights and/or political norms. The supposition is the existence of a set of stable political standards (*a*) against which public officials are held accountable, (*b*) from which departures are exceptional rather than routine, and (*c*) that permit citizens to know, with some certitude, the circumstances in which the government will use force against collective action (Allen 1996, Hayek 1944). At the extremes, cases are easily distinguished: police shooting peaceful protestors (repression) versus police arresting looters or even using deadly force when needed to protect an innocent third party from a murderous assault (lawful exercise of state authority).

Furthermore, breakdown theorists would insist that government action against rebellion may involve more than an attempt to "raise its costs." Fundamental to virtually all legal systems—modern and premodern, East and West—is a distinction between criminal and civil law (Cooter 1984, Robinson 1996). Civil law "prices" or raises the costs of certain behavior, either to dissuade it, provide a remedy to an injured party, or facilitate an equitable distribution of losses. The priced behavior may warrant reproval, but its wrongfulness does not rise to the level of a criminal act. Criminal law, in contrast, entails more than raising the costs of certain behavior. It attempts to convey society's moral condemnation for the prohibited behavior, sometimes in the most unequivocal and dramatic manner possible: imprisonment or even death.

RM theorists use the vocabulary of civil law, rather than criminal law, as if to assume away the possibility that government action against rioters/protestors represents a moral consensus within a community. Breakdown theorists would look for variation across situations. The concept of a general state of fear and the rights of potential riot victims provides a normative basis for government action against rioters. From the point of view of breakdown theory, "repression" cannot be measured by counting the number of protestors arrested and shot by police. One must determine, as well, the existence of a moral consensus and/or legal justification behind those arrests and shootings. While this makes governmental repression hard to isolate and measure, it also argues against supposing that all governmental action against rebellion is repression.

These arguments are open to empirical testing. To illustrate, one sort of evidence would be effects of riots on handgun ownership. By way of background, criminologists have found that handgun purchases and crime rates covary over time. While in principle the causal direction could go either way, the bulk of evidence supports the "fear and loathing" hypothesis: when crime rates rise, people buy handguns out of fear (McDowall 1995). Thus, if riots have the effect of generating handgun purchases, then it could be reasonably inferred that they strike fear into the public.

The evidence supports this argument. David McDowall and Colin Loftin (1983) found that requests for handgun permits rose dramatically after major riots in Detroit in the mid-1960s. Charles Clotfelter (1981) found the same effect in the six states that he studied. By Clotfelter's calculation, a 50% increase in civil disorders increased handgun purchases by 5%.

Figure 1 extends these analyses. It plots handgun production for domestic sales, homicide rates, and a measure of total riot activity per annum in the United States between 1964 and 1994.[1]

A visual inspection of the graph suggests, first, that homicide rates and handgun rates track together closely, per the fear-and-loathing hypothesis. Second, in certain years, handgun production jumps above what would be anticipated from homicide rates alone; these years, in turn, seem to correspond to periods in which there are upsurges in rioting.

Both observations are confirmed by regression analyses, in which riot intensity and homicide rates in one year were used to predict handgun production in the subsequent year. Riot intensity per annum was recoded to a dummy variable: Each year was coded as one of, or not one of, the top fifth of the riot-intense years. Results from standard OLS regression indicated (via the Durbin-Watson statistic) significant autocorrelation. Further investigation suggested that the error structure could be characterized by a first-order autoregressive process. In a subsequent regression both coefficients were statistically significant ($p < .001$) and in the predicted direction.

In sum, both increased homicides and widespread rioting appear to strike fear into others at a level sufficient to generate gun purchases. This speaks to the variable role that collective action plays in democratic societies, depending on its form. Ronald Dworkin (1985, p. 104–116) has argued that civil disobedience has earned a legitimate if informal role in the US political system. Few now regret nor condemn the Civil Rights movement and its most celebrated uses of civil disobedience, for example. Yet if civil disobedience is no longer a "frightening idea in the United States," as Dworkin (1985, p. 105) argues, the evidence above suggests the same is not true for urban riots.

MORAL SENTIMENTS AND COLLECTIVE ACTION

Breakdown and resource mobilization theorists also differ on moral features of collective action. Useful in describing these differences is Peter Gay's (1993) point that aggression implies "attack" which, in ordinary language, has two meanings. Attack may refer to a setting upon another in a hostile way. Examples include a criminal attack, an attack from ambush in warfare, or a scathing attack by a literary critic. But attack can also refer to an adaptive mastery: A scientist may attack a puzzling problem of nature; an orchestra can attack a challenging composition; or a university may aggressively pursue a program of equal employment opportunity. In Gay's account, the aggressiveness of the

[1]The data sources for Figure 1 are described in Appendix A. Riot activity was measured by transforming into z-scores the per annum number of arrests, injuries, deaths, days rioted and arsons, and then summing those scores for each year. A year could have a negative intensity score if it fell below the mean on one or more of these measures.

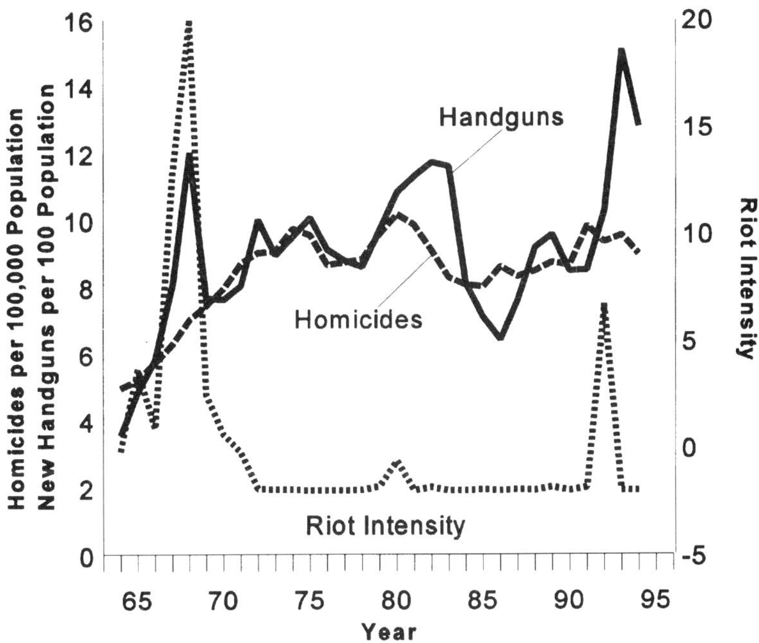

Figure 1 Homicides, new handguns, and riot intensity, United States, 1964–1994.

bourgeoisie of the nineteenth century exacted grievous costs, in the form of abused natives, exploited laborers, and discarded artisans, but it also permitted people to transform and shape their environment in ways unprecedented (1993, p. 6). Attack can, as well, be counteraggression: One can fight back against bullies, parry insults, and assert oneself against cutthroat competition.

Few would challenge that collective action is aggression. The disagreement is over the kind of aggression, or attack, it is. Resource mobilization theorists are mainly creatures of the 1960s and 1970s and, as such, tend to emphasize aggression's positive dimensions. Collective action is ordinary people taking control over their lives, in this view. For example, Charles Tilly (1978, p. 2) opens *From Mobilization to Revolution* by describing an attempt by English villagers in 1765 to pull down a workhouse, and he is at pains to point out that in the sense of "frenzy, confusion, or wanton destruction" the event was "not a riot"; on the contrary, both sides "knew what they were doing" and "did as best they could." These events, Tilly makes clear, were constructive aggression.

Breakdown theorists are more likely to see collective action as hostile aggression. They concede that collective action may secure immediate concessions and may even plant the seeds of a new social order. But they are far more inclined than RM theorists to worry that collective action has another side. This concern permits James Q. Wilson (1993, p. 229–230) to refer to the events in Los Angeles in April 1992 not as a rebellion, but as the "terrible riots" that "racked the city I love."

Indeed, only the most rigid and unreconstructed resource mobilization theorists would fail to see hostile aggressiveness when, during both the 1980 Miami riot and 1992 Los Angeles riot, passing motorists were pulled from their vehicles to be beaten, maimed, or even killed. Portes & Stepick (1993, p. 48–49) describe Miami's "nightmarish" experience: "Whites were doused with gasoline and set afire in their cars; others were dragged out and beaten repeatedly with chunks of concrete and bricks, run over by cars, stabbed with screwdrivers, and shot. One was left dying in the street, a red rose in his mouth."

But how is one to know if, in any particular instance of aggression, constructive or destructive impulses predominate? One problem is that the answer will depend upon whether one relies on statements by the aggressor or the party whose ox is gored. During the April 1992 riots, Korean businesses were targeted for looting and arson (Ong & Hee 1993, Tierney 1994). From the Korean merchants' point of view, the riot was driven by destructive impulses, at best, by a mean-spirited revenge for perceived slights of honor and disrespect. But what target of aggression would agree that the blows against them are warranted?

Moreover, to continue with the example, what struck James Q. Wilson (1993, p. 230) most about the April 1992 riots was that the rioters felt an obligation to justify their behavior. From this Wilson makes an interesting observation: Individuals inevitably offer a moral justification whenever their actions, however destructive and purely self-interested, violate a moral principle. Thus, the fact that the Los Angeles rioters offered a moral justification for their action is not informative.

Yet how does Wilson know that the rioters' complaints of injustice and discrimination were disingenuous, that their explanations of their own behavior were mere rationalizations, and that the firebombs and looting were not warranted by abuses of the past? There were plenty of observers willing to accept these justifications, who insisted that the events were a rebellion and not a riot (e.g. Johnson et al 1992).

The problem is that human complexity is not suspended when people pour onto the streets. Collective behavior is behavior. Certainly Kakar's work on Hindu-Muslim violence suggests that surface discourse may imperfectly reflect underlying concerns. What actuates aggressors may be obscured by the defensive stratagems that Peter Gay calls "alibis for aggression": beliefs, principles, and comforting bromides used to rationalize verbal or physical militancy against others (1993, p. 1–8, 35–38). Perhaps alibis for aggression are what Wilson heard expressed by the Los Angeles rioters, although I know of no evidence that would prove this. The best we can do is carefully tease out the evidence, case by case. We are far from the last chapter on urban riots, far from even knowing what they are about.

FUTURE DIRECTIONS

To recapitulate, breakdown theorists argue that defiant or "nonroutine" forms of collective action occur when the mechanisms of social control falter or everyday routines are disrupted. If this stance is accepted as plausible, future work should identify different ways in which breakdown processes may generate collective disorders. Possible formulations include these:

Social Capital/Breakdown Theory

Social capital theorists argue that economic prosperity requires strong networks of cooperation among people and high levels of interpersonal trust associated with such networks (Coleman 1990, Putnam 1993, Fukuyama 1995). For students of collective behavior, the social capital perspective puts two distinct causal arguments on the agenda.

One concerns the connection, if any, between social capital and rebellion. Fukuyama (1995, p. 295–306; 1996) asserts that US urban riots, both in the 1960s and 1990s, were an outcome of low levels of social capital in the African-American community: a predominance of single-parent families and weak larger groups. This lack of cohesion is a legacy of slavery, Fukuyama argues.

A second key question concerns the connection among state intervention, social capital, and rebellion. Here the analysis is complicated by the fact that social capital theorists are divided between those who argue that state intervention crowds out social capital and those who imply a synergistic relationship (Evans 1996). The former position is that state intervention, including law, tends to destroy social trust and norms of cooperation (Coleman 1990, Pildes 1996, Cover 1983). The latter position is that effective state intervention promotes civic engagement and reshapes norms in a positive direction and, conversely, that high levels of civic engagement nourish state effectiveness (Putnam 1993, Sunstein 1996, Posner 1996).

While no resolution to this debate is in sight, adding rebellion to the equation is intriguing. The crowd-out theorist would argue that state intervention might have short-run benefits, such as the amelioration of specific grievances, but long-run costs: a decline of productive cooperation, pervasive cynicism, and disaffection that presage urban crime and disturbances. The synergists would argue that state intervention, when practiced skillfully and strategically, would increase a population's attachment to society. Collective action would take primarily "routine" forms rather than "nonroutine" forms.

Routine-Disorder/Breakdown Theory

James Q. Wilson (1968) observed that, for every person, there is a public space in which his or her sense of safety, propriety, and self-worth are either affirmed or jeopardized by the events and people encountered. Hence, Wilson goes on to argue, routine disorders—vandalism, public drinking, graffiti, and corner gangs—corrode community morale, stimulate people and commerce to move away, and cause crime. Wesley Skogan (1990) verified key elements of Wilson's argument, based on data collected on crime, disorder, and residents' perceptions of disorder in 40 urban neighborhoods. He shows, first, that urban residents, regardless of racial, ethnic, or economic background, agree about what constitutes order and how much there is in their neighborhood; second, disorder both spawns serious crime and plays a key role in neighborhood decline. Subsequent researchers have also verified the routine-disorders argument as well as amplified theoretical aspects of it (Bursik & Grasmick 1993, Kelling & Coles 1996, Sampson 1995).

Wilson's insight and its verification suggest the possibility that routine disorders may also contribute to nonroutine collective action. For example, one would like to see if Skogan's objective and subjective indices of disorder could also be used to predict the occurrence of US urban riots. If this were shown to be true, the findings would fit nicely with the breakdown position.

Clash of Civilizations/Breakdown Theory

Samuel Huntington (1996a, 1996b) has argued that, with the end of the Cold War, the world is becoming increasingly divided along the lines of culture and religion rather than economics or ideology. Accordingly, the clash between the world's seven or eight major civilizations will be the basis of the most hostile conflicts, which pose the greatest risk of escalating into collective violence. Huntington goes on to predict that non-Western countries formerly united by ideology or historical circumstance but divided by civilization will tend to fall apart with a high potential for collective violence. In the Western context, countries that fall prey to multiculturalism and uncontrolled immigration will experience a disuniting of society, followed by decay and disintegration. Huntington's argument fits squarely within the breakdown tradition: Nonroutine collective action erupts when a mechanism of integration—in this formulation, a cultural core—is weakened.

In sum, social-capital, routine-disorder, and clash-of-civilizations perspectives may each serve as a launching pad to rethink the sources and dynamics of collective action. To the extent that these routes are taken, they will require us to relax the assumption that the nation state is the unit around which collective action revolves in all cases, to distinguish more clearly the causes of routine and nonroutine collective action, and to look to cultural differences as sources of conflict.

CONCLUSION

Rebellion would be easier to understand, our theories of it more parsimonious and powerful, if it flowed out of one condition and toward one purpose: power politics. To be sure, much collective action does involve political contention and constitutes politics by other means. But to breakdown theorists, this does not exhaust the range of possibilities.

Ethnic and racial groups may attack one another in a spiral of hatred and revenge. From time to time, collective action appears to serve as the vehicle through which the dispossessed and those detached from and unconcerned about the welfare of society express their hostility, vent their rage, or secure short-term material advantages. While these goals are not irrational (nothing is more individually rational than crime), neither are they politics by other means.

The breakdown position is not an "intellectual weapon" concocted to "discredit mass movements of which one is critical," as Gamson (1990, p. 133) alleges; nor is it cynicism. Rather, it is a recognition of the complexity and diversity of social life. To argue that all collective action is part and parcel of political struggle is to exaggerate the centrality of power and impute an ideology of social change where none may exist.

In my view, efforts to replace breakdown theory with resource mobilization theory are ill-founded. Both logic and evidence seem to suggest that the breakdown and RM theories explain different kinds of collective action. Each approach deserves recognition. Also, much of interest appears to occur in a middle ground, in some sort of amalgam between breakdown and RM processes.

In sum, breakdown theory was developed to explain collective action that involves a basic rupture of the social order. Breakdown processes do not destroy a community root and branch, producing a mass of atomized individuals, but they can cripple a community's ability to perform key functions. Such ruptures are rare. But they do happen.

ACKNOWLEDGEMENTS

I thank Jack Goldstone, Gary LaFree, Anthony Oberschall, John Roberts, David Snow, and Richard Wood for their helpful comments. Gregg Lee Carter generously provided his data on US urban riots. David McDowall helped make available ATF data on handguns. Aki Takeuchi assisted with the data analysis.

Appendix A

The data on riot intensity are from three sources: a data set provided by Gregg Lee Carter, covering the period 1964 to 1971; three major indexed papers (*New*

York Times, Washington Post, Chicago Tribune), for the period 1972 to 1985; and the Westlaw Inc. newspaper database, for the period 1986 to 1994. Carter collected his data from five key sources, including published and unpublished data from the Lemberg Center for the Study of Violence at Brandeis University, the *New York Times* and *Washington Post*, and compilations made by the staff of a US Senate commitee (for a detailed discussion, see Carter, 1983, ch. 2). The Westlaw database permits a key-word computer search of 150 US newspapers.

In general, it would be preferable to use a single data source for the entire period. The problem is that the only data source that covers the entire period is the major indexed newspapers. A decision not to use the Carter and Westlaw data would have resulted in a significant loss of information for the periods they cover. Balancing the tradeoffs, I decided to make use of the data from Carter and Westlaw. Carter (1983, p. 75–78) argues, with supporting evidence, that a riot severity index is best constructed using five indices (arrests, injuries, deaths, arsons, and days rioted). I accepted this argument. The five indices for each riot were transformed to Z-scores, which were then summed for each year. The data on homicides are from the *Bureau of Justice Statistics* (1996). The handgun data are from annual reports of the Bureau of Alcohol, Tobacco and Firearms (1991, 1995).

Literature Cited

Allen FA. 1996. *The Habits of Legality: Criminal Justice and the Rule of Law*. New York: Oxford Univ. Press

Baldassare M, ed. 1994. *The Los Angeles Riots: Lessons for the Urban Future.* Boulder, CO: Westview

Blumstein A. 1995. Violence by young people: Why the deadly nexus. *Natl. Inst. Justice J.* Aug:2–9

Bourdieu P. 1975. *Outline of a Theory of Practice.* Cambridge, UK: Cambridge Univ. Press

Bureau of Alcohol, Tobacco and Firearms. (BATF). 1991. How many guns? *ATF News,* May 22

Bureau of Alcohol, Tobacco and Firearms. (BATF). 1996. *1995 Factbook.* Washington, DC: BATF, Off. Enforce.

Bureau of Justice Statistics (BJS). 1996. *Sourcebook of Criminal Justice Statistics, 1995.* Albany, NY: Hindelang Criminal Justice Res. Cent.

Bursik R Jr, Grasmick HG. 1993. *Neighborhoods and Crime: The Dimensions of Effective Community Control.* New York: Lexington

Carter GL. 1983. *Explaining the severity of the 1960's Black rioting: a city level investigation of curvilinear and structural break hypothesis.* PhD thesis. Columbia Univ., New York

Clotfelter CT. 1981. Crime, disorders, and the demand for handguns: an empirical analysis. *Law Policy Q.* 3:425–41

Coleman JS. 1990. *Foundations of Social Theory.* Cambridge, MA: Harvard Univ. Press

Cooter R. 1984. Prices and sanctions. *Columbia Law Rev.* 84:1523–60

Cover RM. 1983. The Supreme Court, 1982 term—foreword: nomos and narrative. *Harv. Law Rev.* 97:4–68

Dworkin R. 1985. *A Matter of Principle.* Cambridge, MA: Harvard Univ. Press

Evans P. 1996. Introduction: development

strategies across the public-private divide. *World Dev.* 24(6):1033–37

Fukuyama F. 1995. *Trust: The Social Virtues and the Creation of Prosperity.* New York: Free Press

Fukuyama F. 1996. Trust: social capital and the global economy. *Current* 379:12–18

Gamson WA. 1990. (1975). *The Strategy of Social Protest.* Belmont, CA: Wadsworth

Gay P. 1993. *The Cultivation of Hatred: The Bourgeois Experience, Victoria to Freud.* New York: Norton

Goldstone JA. 1980. The weakness of organization: a new look at Gamson's The Strategy of Social Protest. *Am. J. Sociol.* 85: 1017–42

Gottfredson MR, Hirschi T. 1990. *A General Theory of Crime.* Stanford, CA: Stanford Univ. Press

Gurr TR. 1976. *Rogues, Rebels, and Reformers.* Beverly Hills, CA: Sage

Hirsch EL. 1990. Sacrifice for the cause: group processes, recruitment, and commitment in a student social movement. *Am. Sociol. Rev.* 55:243–54

Huntington SP. 1996a. Modernity is not enough. *Foreign Aff.* 75(6):28–46

Huntington SP. 1996b. *The Clash of Civilizations and the Remaking of the World Order.* New York: Simon & Schuster

Johnson JH Jr, Jones CK, Farrell W Jr, Oliver ML. 1992. The Los Angeles rebellion: a retrospective view. *Econ. Dev. Q.* 6: 356–72

Kahneman D, Tversky A. 1979. Prospect theory: an analysis of decision under risk. *Econometrica* 47:263–97

Kakar S. 1996a. *The Colors of Violence: Cultural Identities, Religion, and Conflict.* Chicago, IL: Univ. Chicago Press

Kakar S. 1996b. Religious conflict in the modern world. *Soc. Sci. Info.* 35:447–58

Kelling GL, Coles CM. 1996. *Fixing Broken Windows: Restoring Order and Reducing Crime in Our Communities.* New York: Free Press

LaFree G, Drass K. 1996. The effect of changes in intraracial income inequality and educational attainment on changes in arrest rates for African Americans and whites, 1957 to 1990. *Am. Sociol. Rev.* 61:614–34

LaFree G, Drass K. 1997. African American collective action and crime, 1955–91. *Soc. Forces* 75:835–53

Lo CYH. 1990. *Small Property versus Big Government: Social Origins of the Property Tax Revolt.* Berkeley: Univ. Calif. Press

Lodhi AQ, Tilly C. 1973. Urbanization, criminality and collective violence in nineteenth-century France. *Am. J. Sociol.* 79: 296–318

Luker K. 1984. *Abortion and the Politics of Motherhood.* Berkeley: Univ. Calif. Press

McAdam D. 1982. *Political Process and the Development of Black Insurgency, 1930–1970.* Chicago: Univ. Chicago Press

McAdam D. 1986. Recruitment to high risk activism: the case of freedom summer. *Am. J. Sociol.* 92:64–90

McCarthy JD, Wolfson M, Baker DP, Mosakowski E. 1988. The founding of social movement organizations: local citizens' groups opposing drunk driving. In *Ecological Models of Organizations,* ed. GR Carroll, pp. 71–84. Cambridge, MA: Ballinger

McDowall D. 1995. Firearms and self defense. *Ann. Am. Acad. Polit. Soc. Sci.* 539:130–41

McDowall D, Loftin C. 1983. Collective security and the demand for legal handguns. *Am. J. Sociol.* 88:1146–61

Miller AH, Bolce LH, Halligan MR. 1976. The new urban blacks. *Ethnicity* 3:338–67

Morris A. 1984. *The Origins of Civil Rights Movement.* New York: Free Press

Morris AD, Mueller CM, eds. 1992. *Frontiers in Social Movement Theory.* New Haven, CT: Yale Univ. Press

Myers D. 1997. Racial rioting in the 1960s: an event history analysis of local conditions. *Am. Sociol. Rev.*62:94–112

National Advisory Commission on Civil Disorders (NACCD). 1968a. *Report of the National Advisory Commission on Civil Disorders.* Washington, DC: USGPO

National Advisory Commission on Civil Disorders (NACCD). 1968b. *Supplemental Studies for the National Advisory Commission on Civil Disorders.* Washington, DC: USGPO

Oberschall A. 1973. *Social Conflict and Social Movements.* Englewood Cliffs, NJ: Prentice Hall

Oberschall A. 1997. *Bosnia: civil war, ethnic cleansing, atrocities.* Presented at Mellon Semin. New Nationalism, New Identities, New Perspect., Duke Univ., Durham, NC

Olzak S, Shanahan S. 1996. Deprivation and race riots: an extension of Spilerman's analysis. *Soc. Forces* 74:931–61

Ong P, Hee S. 1993. *Losses in the Los Angeles Civil Unrest, April 29–May 1, 1992.* Los Angeles: Cent. Pac. Rim Stud., UCLA

Opp K-D, Roehl W. 1990. Repression, micromobilization, and political protest. *Soc. Forces* 69:521–48

Petersilia J, Abrahamse A. 1994. A profile of those arrested. See Baldassare 1994, pp. 135–47

Pildes RH. 1996. The destruction of social

capital through law. *Univ. Penn. Law Rev.* 144:2055–77

Piven FF, Cloward RA. 1977. *Poor People's Movements: Why They Succeed, How They Fail*. New York: Pantheon

Piven FF, Cloward RA. 1992. Normalizing collective protest. See Morris & Mueller 1992, pp. 301–25

Portes A, Stepick A. 1993. *City on the Edge: The Transformation of Miami*. Berkeley: Univ. Calif. Press

Posner E. 1996. The regulation of groups: the influence of legal and nonlegal sanctions on collective action. *Univ. Chicago Law Rev.* 63:133–97

Putnam RD. 1993. *Making Democracy Work: Civic Traditions in Modern Italy*. Princeton, NJ: Princeton Univ. Press

Putnam RD. 1995. Tuning in, tuning out: the strange disappearance of social capital in America. *PS: Polit. Sci. Polit.* 24:664–83

Robinson PH. 1996. The criminal-civil distinction and the utility of desert. *Boston Univ. Law Rev.* 76:201–14

Sampson RJ. 1995. The community. In *Crime*, ed. JQ Wilson, J Petersilia, pp. 193–216. San Francisco: Inst. Contemp. Stud.

Schutz A. 1962. *The Problem of Social Reality*. The Hague: Nijhoff

Shorter E, Tilly C. 1974. *Strikes in France, 1830 to 1968*. New York: Cambridge Univ. Press

Skogan WG. 1990. *Disorder and Decline: Crime and the Spiral of Decay in American Neighborhoods*. New York: Free Press

Skolnick JH, Fyfe JF. 1993. *Above the Law: Police and the Excessive Use of Force*. New York: Free Press

Snow D, Benford RD. 1992. Master frames and cycles of protest. See Morris & Mueller 1992, pp. 133–55

Snow DA, Cress DM, Downey L, Jones AW. 1998. Disrupting the quotidian: reconceptualizing the relationship between breakdown and the emergence of collective action. *Mobilization* 3:1–20

Snyder D, Tilly C. 1972. Hardship and collective violence in France: 1830 to 1960. *Am. Sociol. Rev.* 37:520–32

Spilerman S. 1970. The causes of racial disturbances: a comparison of alternative explanations. *Am. Sociol. Rev.* 35:627–49

Spilerman S. 1971. The causes of racial disturbances: tests of an explanation. *Am. Sociol. Rev.* 36:427–42

Spilerman S. 1976. Structural characteristics of cities and the severity of racial disorders. *Am. Sociol. Rev.* 41:771–93

Staggenborg S. 1991. *The Pro-Choice Movement: Organization and Activism in the Abortion Conflict*. New York: Oxford Univ. Press

Sunstein CR. 1996. On the expressive functions of the law. *Univ. Penn. Law Rev.* 144:2021–53

Tarrow S. 1994. *Power in Movement: Social Movements, Collective Action and Politics*. Cambridge, UK: Cambridge Univ. Press

Tierney K. 1994. Property damage and violence: a collective behavior analysis. See Baldassare 1994, pp. 149–73

Tilly C. 1978. *From Mobilization to Revolution*. Reading, MA: Addison-Wesley

Tilly C. 1984. *Big Structures, Large Processes, Huge Comparisons*. New York: Russell Sage Found.

Tilly C, Tilly L, Tilly R. 1975. *The Rebellious Century 1830–1930*. Cambridge, MA: Harvard Univ. Press

Useem B. 1980. Solidarity model, breakdown model, and the Boston anti-busing movement. *Am. Sociol. Rev.* 45:357–69

Useem B. 1985. Disorganization and the New Mexico prison riot of 1980. *Am. Sociol. Rev.* 50:667–88

Useem B. 1997. The state and collective disorders: the Los Angeles riot/protest of April, 1992. *Soc. Forces* 76:357–77

Useem B, Camp C, Camp G. 1996. *Resolution of Prison Riots: Strategies and Policies*. New York: Oxford Univ. Press

Useem B, Kimball PA. 1989. *States of Siege: U.S. Prison Riots, 1971–1986*. New York: Oxford Univ. Press

Verba S, Nie N. 1972. *Participation in America: Political Democracy and Social Equality*. New York: Harper & Row

von Hayek FA. 1944. *The Road to Serfdom*. Chicago, IL: Univ. Chicago Press

Weed FJ. 1987. Grass roots activism and drunk driving issues: a survey of MADD chapters. *Law Policy* 31:259–78

Wilson JQ. 1968. *Thinking About Crime*. New York: Basic Books. Rev. ed.

Wilson JQ. 1993. *The Moral Sense*. New York: Free Press

Wilson WJ. 1996. *When Work Disappears: The World of the New Urban Poor*. New York: Knopf

Wolfinger RE, Rosenstone SJ. 1980. *Who Votes?* New Haven, CT: Yale Univ. Press

Zald MN. 1992. Looking backward to look forward: reflections on the past and future of the resource mobilization research perspective. See Morris & Mueller 1992, pp. 326–48

Annu. Rev. Sociol. 1998. 24:239–64

WARMER AND MORE SOCIAL: Recent Developments in Cognitive Social Psychology

Norbert Schwarz

Institute for Social Research and Department of Psychology, University of Michigan, Ann Arbor, Michigan 48106-1248; e-mail: nschwarz@umich.edu

KEY WORDS: social judgment, social cognition, communication, mood, motivation

ABSTRACT

Since the late 1970s, theorizing in psychological social psychology has been dominated by the computer metaphor of information processing models, which fostered an emphasis on "cold" cognition and the conceptualization of individuals as isolated information processors. More recent research shows a renewed interest in the interplay of feeling and thinking in social judgment and in the role of unconscious processes in reasoning and behavior. Moreover, research into socially situated cognition and the interplay of communication and cognition highlights the role of conversational norms, social interdependence, and power in social judgment. Experimental research into these issues is reviewed. The emerging picture is compatible with social psychology's latest metaphor, humans as motivated tacticians who pragmatically adapt their reasoning strategies to the requirements at hand.

INTRODUCTION

Independent of their theoretical orientations, social psychologists agree on two basic tenets (Taylor 1997, p. 3):

> The first is that individual behavior is strongly influenced by the environment, especially the social environment. The person does not function in an individualistic vacuum, but in a social context that influences thought, feeling, and action. The second point of consensus is that the individual actively construes social situations. We do not respond to environments as they are, but as we interpret them to be.

0360-0572/98/0815-0239$08.00

For the past two decades, psychological social psychologists have largely focused on the latter tenet, emphasizing inside-the-head phenomena, and have left the former tenet to sociological social psychologists. As Markus & Zajonc (1985) observed, [psychological] "social psychology and cognitive social psychology are today nearly synonymous. The cognitive approach is now clearly the dominant approach among social psychologists, having virtually no competitors" (1985, p. 137). Moreover, the nature of cognitive theorizing shifted from an emphasis on "warm" cognition and motivated reasoning to an emphasis on "cold" cognition. Consequently, memory processes, logical inference, and cognitive biases became key topics of interest in cognitive social psychology. This shift reflected the advent of information processing models in cognitive psychology in the late 1960s (Neisser 1967; for an introduction see Lachman et al 1979) and their rapid adoption by social psychologists in the 1970s, documented in a seminal volume on "person memory" (Hastie et al 1980). The resulting theoretical approach, known as social cognition, has been characterized as social psychology under the paradigm of information processing (Strack 1988). It emphasized information encoding, storage, and retrieval and drew heavily on computer metaphors (see Wyer & Srull 1989).

On the positive side, the information processing approach has rapidly advanced our understanding of the cognitive processes underlying many social phenomena (for reviews, see Devine et al 1994). Moreover, its emphasis on detailed process models has changed the field's standards for what counts as appropriate evidence: "It was no longer enough to detail a theoretical model and use the results as confirmation of the model. If one stated what one thought the process was, one had to demonstrate the intervening steps" (Taylor 1998, p. 74). To obtain relevant "process data," social psychologists now include response latencies, recall and recognition tests, think-aloud protocols, and similar measures in their experiments (for reviews, see the contributions in Schwarz & Sudman 1996), and they increasingly employ mediational analyses (Baron & Kenny 1986) to test the theoretically specified process assumptions.

Yet the adoption of the information processing paradigm was not without its drawbacks. Most importantly, the computer metaphor, around which models of information processing are built, constrained the range of phenomena addressed by cognitive social psychologists in several ways. First, this metaphor does not easily lend itself to investigations of emotional and motivational influences on human cognition and behavior and hence fostered a neglect of "warm" cognition in favor of an emphasis on "cold" cognition. Consequently, the complex treatment of perceivers' goals and needs that characterized the New Look (e.g. Bruner 1957) was reduced to simpler processing goals, such as forming an accurate impression versus remembering the material presented in the experiment (e.g. Hamilton et al 1980; for a critical discussion, see Hilton & Darley 1991). Similarly, the role of affective states in cognition and behavior was largely ignored (Zajonc 1980). Second, reliance on the computer metaphor as a guiding framework also fostered an exclusive concentration on individuals as isolated information processors. This focus resulted in a neglect of the social context in which humans do much of their thinking, prompting Schneider (1991, p. 553) to wonder, "Where, oh where, is the social in social cognition?"

Finally, investigations of overt social behavior became a rare event. As Forgas (1981, p. 3) observed early on, "social psychology found itself transformed into a field now mainly concerned not with human social action, but with human beings as thinkers and information processors about social stimuli." And whatever these "thinkers and information processors" thought about, they seemed likely to get it wrong, as a long list of biases and shortcomings in social judgment illustrated (Nisbett & Ross 1980, Ross 1977).

More recently, however, the field has moved beyond these constraints. Cognitive social psychologists have turned to explorations of the role of moods, emotions, goals, and motivations in human reasoning, with "warm" cognition receiving considerable attention, as illustrated in the three volumes of the *Handbook of Motivation and Cognition* (Sorrentino & Higgins 1986, 1995; Higgins & Sorrentino 1990). Moreover, they have rediscovered that humans do much of their thinking in a social context and have turned to the exploration of socially situated cognition (for a review, see Levine et al 1993) and the interplay of cognition and communication in human reasoning (for reviews, see Hilton 1990, 1991, 1995; Krauss & Fussell 1996; Schwarz 1996). Complementing these developments, they reconsidered the fallibility of human judgment from a pragmatic perspective, emphasizing William James's (1890, p. 333) credo that "my thinking is first and last and always for the sake of my doing." From this perspective, many violations of normative models seem less detrimental than earlier discussions implied, leading some observers to conclude that "people are good enough perceivers" (Fiske 1992). Although human social action is still not a common topic in cognitive social psychology, its cognitive and motivational underpinnings have received renewed attention (see the contributions in Gollwitzer & Bargh 1996).

I review these developments by highlighting representative lines of research. The first section of the review illustrates the renewed interest in "warm" cognition by addressing one theme of this development, namely the interplay of feeling and thinking in social judgment, stereotyping, and persuasion (for a broader coverage of "warm" cognition, see the contributions in Sorrentino & Higgins 1986, Higgins & Sorrentino 1990). The second section addresses socially situated cognition and emphasizes the influence of the immediate social context on individuals' judgment strategies. Research in this domain has highlighted the role of social interdependence, power, and accountability and has drawn attention to the influence of conversational processes on human reasoning.

The picture that emerges from this work is consistent with cognitive social psychology's latest metaphor, the person as a *motivated tactician* (Fiske & Taylor 1991). "The motivated tactician is viewed as having multiple information processing strategies available, selecting among them on the basis of goals, motives, needs, and forces in the environment. As such, the motivated tactician exemplifies the pragmatic tradition in social psychology" (Taylor 1998, p. 75). As becomes apparent in this review, the choice of processing strategies is highly sensitive to a wide range of relevant information, provided by the immediate social context, internal states, and long-term goals. The motivated tactician metaphor is compatible with a growing number of dual-process models that distinguish between heuristic and systematic processing strategies in person perception (e.g. Brewer 1988, Fiske & Neuberg 1990), persuasion (e.g. Bohner et al 1995, Eagly & Chaiken 1993, Petty & Cacioppo 1986), and decision making (e.g. Payne et al 1993) and identify the conditions under which different strategies are likely to be employed (for reviews, see the contributions in Chaiken & Trope 1998). At present, this metaphor promises to replace its predecessors—which captured earlier research themes by portraying persons either as consistency seekers, wishful thinkers, lay scientists, or cognitive misers—by suggesting that all of them apply under some specific conditions. Yet, the motivated tactician's ability to flexibly adjust his or her cognitive processes to situational requirements is not without limits, as an increasing body of research into unconscious processes and the limits of mental control indicates. Selected aspects of this research are addressed in the final section of this review.

THE INTERPLAY OF FEELING AND THINKING

Cognitive social psychologists' interest in the interplay of feeling and thinking has mostly focused on global happy and sad moods rather than on specific emotions, like anger or fear. Whereas emotions have a specific referent (i.e. we are angry "about something") and draw attention to the eliciting event, moods lack a specific referent (i.e. we are "in" a happy mood) and are of a more diffuse and less intense nature, usually not capturing individuals' attention (see Clore et al 1994, Morris 1989). As an important consequence, moods may function in the background of other activities, influencing a wide range of cognitive processes and overt behaviors. Of particular interest has been their influence on memory, judgment, and the choice of information processing strategies.

Memory and Judgment

Numerous studies demonstrated that people evaluate nearly everything—ranging from consumer goods and the state of the economy to the quality of their lives—more positively when in a good than in a bad mood (for reviews, see Clore et al 1994, Forgas 1995, Schwarz & Clore 1996). Moreover, these influences translate into overt behavior (for a review, see Isen 1984), including weather-induced mood effects on the stock market (Saunders 1993). In most studies, moods have been experimentally induced, either by minor events (e.g. finding a dime or receiving a cookie), exposure to valenced material (e.g. watching a sad video or recalling a happy event from one's past), or natural circumstances (e.g. sunny or rainy weather), with similar results across different manipulations. The impact of moods on judgment has been traced to two different processes, namely differential recall of material from memory and the use of one's feelings as a source of information.

MEMORY Individuals are more likely to recall positive material from memory when they are in a happy rather than sad mood. Following initial suggestions by Isen et al (1978), Bower (1981, 1991) conceptualized these effects in an associative network model of memory. Moods are thought to function as central nodes in an associative network, which are linked to related ideas, events of corresponding valence, autonomic activity, and muscular and expressive patterns. When new material is learned, it is associated with the nodes that are active at learning. Accordingly, material acquired while in a particular mood is linked to the respective mood node. When the person is in the same mood later on, activation spreads from the mood node along the pathways, increasing the activation of other nodes, which represent the related material. When the activation exceeds a certain threshold, the represented material comes into consciousness. This model makes two key predictions: First, memory is enhanced when the affective state at the time of encoding matches the affective state at the time of retrieval (*state-dependent learning*). Thus, we are more likely to recall material acquired in a particular mood when we are in the same, rather than a different, mood at the time of recall. Second, any given material is more likely to be retrieved when its affective tone matches the individual's mood at the time of recall (*mood-congruent memory*). Thus, information of a positive valence is more likely to come to mind when we are in a happy rather than sad mood.

Although both predictions received considerable empirical support in experimental and clinical research, this research also revealed a number of complications that are beyond the scope of this chapter (see Blaney 1986, Clore et al 1994, Morris 1989, Singer & Salovey 1988). In general, mood-congruent recall is most likely to be obtained for self-referenced material, such as autobiographical events, that meets the conditions of both of the above hypotheses: When something good (bad) happens to us, it puts us in a positive (negative) affective state, and its subsequent recall is facilitated when we are again in a similar affective state. Note that this situation simultaneously provides for matching mood states at learning and recall, thus satisfying the conditions of state-dependent learning, as well as for matches between the valence of the material and the mood at recall, thus satisfying the conditions of mood-congruent memory.

From this perspective, mood effects on judgment are mediated by mood-congruent recall from memory: When asked how satisfied we are with our life, for example, we recall relevant information from memory. However, positive (negative) material is more likely to come to mind when we are in a happy (sad) mood, resulting in a mood-congruent sample of relevant information and hence a mood-congruent judgment.

FEELINGS AS INFORMATION As an alternative approach, Schwarz & Clore (1983, 1996) suggested that our feelings themselves may serve as a source of information in making a judgment. Specifically, individuals may simplify the judgmental task by asking themselves, "How do I feel about it?" Some evaluative judgments refer, by definition, to one's affective reaction to the target (e.g. feelings of liking), and one's current feelings may indeed be elicited by the target. However, due to the undifferentiated and unfocused nature of moods, it is often difficult to distinguish between one's affective reaction to the object of judgment and one's preexisting mood state. Accordingly, individuals may misread their preexisting feelings as a reaction to the target, resulting in more positive evaluations under happy rather than sad moods.

If so, mood effects should be eliminated when the informational value of one's current feelings for the judgment at hand is called into question. Empirically, this is the case. For example, respondents reported lower life-satisfaction in telephone interviews when called on rainy rather than sunny days, reflecting the impact of the weather on their current mood. This effect was eliminated, however, when the interviewer inquired about the weather, thus drawing respondents' attention to this extraneous source of their mood (Schwarz & Clore 1983). Such a discounting effect would not be expected if the impact of mood were mediated by mood-congruent recall: Attributing one's sad mood to the rainy weather only discredits the informational value of the sad mood as a reflection of one's life in general; it does not discredit the implications of actually experienced negative life events that may come to mind.

These and related findings indicate that moods, emotions (e.g. Keltner et al 1993), bodily states (e.g. Stepper & Strack 1993, Zillman 1978), and phenomenal experiences (e.g. Clore 1992) may themselves serve as a source of information that individuals draw on according to a "How-do-I-feel-about-it?"

heuristic (for reviews, see Schwarz & Clore 1996). Accordingly, feelings may influence judgments either directly, by serving as a source of information, or indirectly, by influencing what comes to mind. Consequently, the motivated tactician's judgments are likely to be tainted by current moods independent of whether the person engages in heuristic judgment strategies or engages in more elaborate recall of relevant information from memory (Forgas 1995). Complementing this focus on cognitive processes, other researchers have attempted to illuminate the physiological and brain mechanisms underlying affective influences on human reasoning, a topic that is beyond the scope of this chapter (for reviews, see Damasio 1994, LeDoux 1996, Cacioppo et al 1996).

Moods and Processing Strategies

In addition to influencing memory and judgment, moods have also been found to influence performance on a wide variety of cognitive tasks (for reviews and different theoretical perspectives, see Clore et al 1994, Fiedler 1988, Forgas 1995, Isen 1987, Schwarz & Clore 1996). While the findings bearing on formal reasoning tasks (such as syllogistic reasoning, puzzles, or anagrams) are complex and inconsistent (see Clore et al 1994), the findings bearing on social reasoning tasks (most notably, impression formation, stereotyping, and persuasion) show a more coherent pattern. In general, individuals in a sad mood are more likely to use a systematic, data-driven strategy of information processing, with considerable attention to detail. In contrast, individuals in a happy mood are more likely to rely on preexisting general knowledge structures, using a top-down, heuristic strategy of information processing, with less attention to detail.

Consistent with the motivated tactician metaphor, these differences can again be traced to the informative functions of feelings (Bless et al 1996, Schwarz 1990, Schwarz & Clore 1996). We usually feel bad when we encounter a threat of negative or a lack of positive outcomes, and feel good when we obtain positive outcomes and are not threatened by negative ones. Hence, our moods reflect the state of our environment, and being in a bad mood signals a problematic situation, whereas being in a good mood signals a benign situation. If so, we may expect that the motivated tactician's thought processes are tuned to meet the situational requirements signaled by these feelings. When negative feelings signal a problematic situation, the individual is likely to attend to the details at hand, investing the effort necessary for a careful analysis. In contrast, when positive feelings signal a benign situation, the individual may see little need to engage in cognitive effort, unless this is required by other current goals. Hence, the individual may rely on preexisting knowledge structures, which have worked well in the past, and may prefer simple heuristics over more effortful, detail-oriented judgmental strategies.

Numerous studies are compatible with this general perspective, as illustrated below. Importantly, mood effects on processing style are eliminated when the informational value of the mood is undermined (Sinclair et al 1994), paralleling the findings in the judgment domain discussed above. This finding supports the informative functions logic and is incompatible with competing approaches that attempted to trace mood effects on processing style to differential influences of happy and sad moods on individuals' cognitive capacity (e.g. Mackie & Worth 1989; for a detailed discussion, see Schwarz & Clore 1996).

IMPRESSION FORMATION AND STEREOTYPING In forming an impression of others, we can rely on detailed information about the target person or can simplify the task by drawing on preexisting knowledge structures, such as stereotypes pertaining to the target's social category (Brewer 1988, Bodenhausen 1990, Fiske & Neuberg 1990, Macrae et al 1994b). Consistent with the above perspective, being in a good mood has consistently been found to increase stereotyping (e.g. Bodenhausen et al 1994a,b), unless the target person is clearly inconsistent with the stereotype, thus undermining the applicability of the general knowledge structure (e.g. Bless et al 1996c). In contrast, being in a sad mood reliably decreases stereotyping and increases the use of individuating information (for a review, see Bless et al 1996b). Across many person perception tasks, individuals in a chronic or temporary sad mood have been found to make more use of detailed individuating information, to show less halo effect, to be less influenced by the order of information presentation, and to be more accurate in performance appraisals than individuals in a happy mood, with individuals in a neutral mood falling in between (e.g. Edwards & Weary 1993, Hildebrandt-Saints & Weary 1989, Sinclair 1988, Sinclair & Marks 1992). Similar findings have been obtained for individuals' reliance on scripts pertaining to typical situations (such as having dinner in a restaurant) versus their reliance on what actually transpired in the situation (Bless et al 1996a). Throughout, individuals in a good mood are more likely to rely on preexisting general knowledge structures, proceeding on a "business-as-usual" routine, whereas individuals in a sad mood are more likely to pay close attention to the specifics at hand, much as one would expect when negative feelings provide the motivated tactician with a problem signal.

PERSUASION Research into mood and persuasion parallels these findings. In general, a message that presents strong arguments is more persuasive than a message that presents weak arguments, provided that recipients are motivated to process the content of the message and to elaborate on the arguments. If recipients do not engage in message elaboration, the advantage of strong over weak arguments is eliminated (for reviews, see Eagly & Chaiken 1993, Petty

& Cacioppo 1986). Numerous studies demonstrated that sad individuals are more likely to engage in spontaneous message elaboration than happy individuals, with individuals in a neutral mood falling in between (for reviews, see Mackie et al 1992, Schwarz et al 1991a). Consequently, sad individuals are strongly influenced by compelling arguments and not influenced by weak arguments, whereas happy individuals are moderately, but equally, influenced by both. Hence, a strong message fares better with a sad than with a happy audience, but if communicators have nothing compelling to say they had better put recipients into a good mood.

Importantly, happy individuals' spontaneous tendency not to think about the arguments in much detail can be overridden by other goals (e.g. Wegener et al 1995) or explicit task instructions (e.g. Bless et al 1990, Martin et al 1993). What characterizes the information processing of happy individuals is not a general cognitive or motivational impairment, but a tendency to spontaneously rely on simplifying heuristics and general knowledge structures in the absence of goals that require otherwise, again consistent with the metaphor of the motivated tactician.

Summary

In summary, social cognition researchers have complemented the emphasis on "cold" cognition that characterized initial research under the information processing paradigm by exploring the interplay of feeling and thinking. This research revealed pervasive effects of temporary feelings on memory, judgment, and reasoning strategies across a wide range of content domains. The emerging findings highlight that our feelings serve informative functions in judgment and in the self-regulation of cognitive activity, thus linking affect, cognition, and motivation. To date, this work has disproportionately focused on global moods at the expense of more specific emotions (but see Mathews & MacLeod 1994). Moreover, it has not addressed how the social context in which a given feeling is experienced may moderate its impact on cognitive and motivational processes.

SOCIALLY SITUATED COGNITION

The increased attention to "warm" cognition remained true to cognitive (social) psychology's focus on "inside-the-head" phenomena, while filling some of the more glaring gaps fostered by the computer metaphor of information processing models. Complementing this richer picture of inside-the-head phenomena, cognitive social psychologists have recently rediscovered that humans do much of their thinking in a social context. Consistent with the motivated tactician metaphor, researchers explored how characteristics of the social situation influence cognition and information processing strategies, paying attention to variables such as the accountability of the actors (e.g. Tetlock 1992), their anticipation of audience reactions (e.g. McCann & Higgins 1992), and their interdependence and position in a power hierarchy (e.g. Fiske & Depret 1996). A related line of work emphasized the impact of conversational processes on human reasoning and traced many cognitive biases and apparent shortcomings of judgment documented in the laboratory to the specific nature of communication in research situations, suggesting that the observed biases may be less powerful under more natural conditions (e.g. Hilton 1995, Schwarz 1996). In addition, cognitive social psychologists turned to collaborative cognition and extended previous research into group problem solving by exploring how people collaborate on reasoning and memory tasks (e.g. Resnick et al 1991, Wegner 1987). Finally, the field has developed an increased interest in cultural influences on cognitive processes and human behavior (e.g. Markus & Kitayama 1991, Nisbett & Cohen 1996, Goldberger & Veroff 1995; for a comprehensive review, see Fiske et al 1998.

The next two sections review selected aspects of cognitive social psychologists' interest in situated cognition and highlight that thought processes are tuned to meet situational requirements, consistent with the motivated tactician metaphor.

The Motivated Tactician in Social Situations

As noted previously, dual-process models of judgment (Chaiken & Trope 1998) emphasize that individuals can rely on systematic processing strategies that involve considerable effort and attention to detail or can rely on heuristic processing strategies that simplify the task at hand. As implied by the motivated tactician metaphor, the choice of processing strategies is highly sensitive to individuals' goals (for reviews, see Gollwitzer 1990, Hilton & Darley 1991) and features of the social situation, as some exemplary lines of research may illustrate.

INTERDEPENDENCE AND POWER In the domain of person perception, individuals are most likely to simplify impression formation by drawing on the target person's category membership at the expense of more detailed individuating information when little is at stake. Hence, stereotyping is the rule under standard laboratory conditions, but the impact of stereotypes is attenuated when participants expect future interactions with the target person under conditions of interdependence (e.g. Berscheid et al 1976, Neuberg & Fiske 1987, Neuberg 1989), independent of whether the interdependence is cooperative or competitive in nature. Fiske & Neuberg (1990; see also Brewer 1988) proposed a continuum model of impression formation that assigns a crucial role to perceivers' goals: When the relationship is important to the perceiver, the perceiver will allocate sufficient cognitive resources to form an individuated impression based on specific information about the target person; when the relationship is unimportant, the perceiver will simplify the judgmental task by drawing on the target's category membership, resulting in a stereotypic judgment.

Extending this work, Fiske and colleagues (for a review, see Fiske & Depret 1996) have recently addressed the role of power in person perception. They observed that powerless individuals, whose outcomes depend on a more powerful other's actions, are particularly likely to seek the most diagnostic information available about the powerful other. In contrast, powerful individuals not only fail to seek complex information about their subordinates but have been found to attend more to stereotype-confirming than to stereotype-disconfirming information, thus further increasing the impact of stereotypes. "Whereas powerlessness demands vigilance, power allows people to ignore the most informative cues about others," as Fiske & Depret (1996, p. 34) concluded—at least as long as they are not dependent on the powerless other's actions.

ACCOUNTABILITY AND AUDIENCE EFFECTS Much as research into impression formation has typically ignored the interdependence of judge and target, research into social judgment and decision making has typically studied individuals' thought processes in a social vacuum. Consequently, participants in judgment studies "do not need to worry about the interpersonal consequences of their conduct ('How will others react if I do this? How effectively can I justify my views if challenged?')," as Tetlock (1992, p. 335) observed. Extending earlier work into audience effects on cognitive processes (e.g. Zajonc 1960), Tetlock and his colleagues explored the impact of judges' accountability on their choice of information processing strategies and conceptualized the findings in a *social contingency model* of judgment, which makes three key predictions (for a comprehensive review, see Tetlock 1992).

First, when individuals have no prior commitment to a position, are accountable for their conduct, and know their constituency's attitudes and preferences, "they simply adopt positions likely to gain the favor of those to whom they feel accountable" (Tetlock 1992, p. 340), essentially following an acceptability heuristic. For example, individuals who have to justify their views to a liberal audience report more liberal opinions than those who have to justify them to a conservative audience. When these reports pertain to a well-known attitude object, the observed conformity effects at the reporting stage are usually short lived and do not result in enduring attitude change on private measures (e.g. Tetlock et al 1989). This is not the case, however, when the reports pertain to a previously unknown attitude object, such as a target person described by the experimenter (e.g. Higgins & Rholes 1978). In this case, tailoring one's judgments to an audience that is assumed to like (or dislike) the person has been found to result in private attitude change as well as biased recall (for reviews, see Higgins 1981, McCann & Higgins 1992). In Higgins &

Rholes's (1978) study, for example, participants were asked to reproduce the original information about the target person, and these recall data indicated positive or negative distortions, respectively, after participants described the person to a positively or negatively predisposed audience. Such modifications of the mental representation of the attitude object are most likely when the respective representation is not well formed at the time the individual tailors the report to an audience. When such modifications of the mental representation occur, they are likely to result in lasting effects on subsequent judgments.

Second, when individuals have no prior commitment to a position and do *not* know their constituency's attitudes and preferences, accountability motivates them "to abandon their cognitive miserly ways and to become relatively flexible, self-critical and multidimensional thinkers" (Tetlock 1992, p. 340). Under these conditions, content analyses of confidential thought protocols reveal considerable thought complexity, a weighting of arguments on both sides and preparation for possible critical challenges, resulting in changes in the mental representation of the topic (e.g. Tetlock et al 1989).

Finally, "when people have irrevocably committed themselves to a course of action, accountability will again motivate cognitive effort." Yet, in this case, "the result will be rigid, defensive, and evaluatively consistent thought. Accountability will prompt people to generate as many reasons as they can why they are right and potential critics wrong" (Tetlock 1992, p. 340), an observation that is consistent with earlier work into the effects of commitment on attitude change (Kiesler 1971).

These predictions have received considerable support across a wide range of judgment and decision tasks in laboratory experiments and field studies (see Tetlock 1992). Importantly, this research also demonstrated that the more careful and deliberate processing evoked by being accountable to an audience with unknown preferences can increase as well as decrease cognitive biases (e.g. Tetlock & Boettger 1996), an issue addressed in more detail in the section on judgmental biases.

MINORITY AND MAJORITY INFLUENCE In light of the motivated tactician's sensitivity to the social nature of the judgment situation, we may further expect that perceptions of the majority or minority status of a communicator influence how the communicator's message is processed. Historically, social psychological research into influence processes has typically focused on individuals' compliance and conformity with a perceived majority, consistent with the pioneering work of Sherif (1936) and Asch (1955). Moscovici (1976, 1980) challenged this tradition by drawing attention to key differences in majority and minority influence. According to his conversion theory, opinion majorities exert influence by eliciting public compliance and conformity, whereas opinion minorities may elicit private attitude change via informational routes, provided that they argue their point consistently and without compromise. The empirical support for Moscovici's (1980) original proposal and its refinements (Mugny & Perez 1991) is mixed (for a meta-analysis, see Wood et al 1994). One aspect that has received particular attention in recent research is whether perceived majority or minority support influences the extent to which recipients of a message engage in systematic or heuristic processing.

In general, people assume that their attitudes and opinions are widely shared by members of their group [a phenomenon known as the "false consensus" bias (Ross, Greene, & House 1977)], but not necessarily by others. When these assumptions are called into question, either through a counterattitudinal message from a majority or through a proattitudinal message from a minority, recipients are likely to think carefully about the message. Hence, they are influenced when the message presents strong arguments, but not when it presents weak arguments. Moreover, this attitude change is obtained on private measures (thus minimizing conformity pressures) and can be predicted on the basis of their thoughts about the arguments. In contrast, proattitudinal messages from a majority, or counterattitudinal messages from a minority, are consistent with recipients' expectations, receive less thought and are less likely to result in private attitude change (Baker & Petty 1994, Mackie 1987). Accordingly, the extent to which a message receives systematic elaboration and elicits private attitude change is not a function of its majority or minority support per se, in contrast to the assumptions of Moscovici's (1980) conversion theory, nor is it solely a function of message content. Instead, message processing depends on whether the combination of message content and source violates expectations and hence requires thought (for different perspectives, see Bohner et al 1996, De Vries et al 1996, Wood et al 1994).

Note, however, that conversion theory (Moscovici 1980) emphasizes that minorities need to argue their point consistently over extended periods to exert an influence, a condition that has not been met in persuasion experiments limited to one message presentation. Nevertheless, the conceptual framework of dual-process models of persuasion promises to further our understanding of the differential processes underlying majority and minority influence (see Mackie & Skelly 1994), although more realistic procedures will be required to capture the dynamics of actual confrontation with majorities and minorities in face-to-face settings.

SUMMARY As the selected lines of research illustrate, individuals' processing strategies are tuned to meet the requirements of the social situation. This work has extended the range of social cognition research from "thinking about social stimuli" to "thinking in a social context." Much of our thinking in social contexts, however, is intricately intertwined with conversational processes, to be addressed in the next section.

Cognition and Communication

As Krauss & Fussell (1996, p. 655) noted, "Communication is one of the primary means by which people affect one another, and, in light of this, one might expect the study of communication to be a core topic of social psychology, but historically that has not been the case." In fact, social psychologists not only have neglected communication as a key topic of inquiry, but also have failed to take into account how communicative processes shape thinking in a social context. Focusing on individuals as isolated information processors, cognitive (social) psychologists have documented a wide range of biases and shortcomings of judgment that violate common sense and basic logic, calling the rationality of human judgment into question (for reviews, see Fiske & Taylor 1991, Nisbett & Ross 1980, Ross 1977). Recent research suggests, however, that many of the well-known fallacies can be traced in part to the nature of communication in research settings and do not necessarily reflect inherent shortcomings of human judgment. To understand the underlying processes, we need to consider how the communication between researchers and research participants differs from communication in daily life.

As a large body of research documented (for reviews, see Clark 1985, Levinson 1983, Sperber & Wilson 1986), social discourse proceeds according to a "co-operative" principle (Grice 1975), which can be expressed in the form of four maxims. A maxim of quality enjoins speakers not to say anything they believe to be false or lack adequate evidence for, and a maxim of relation enjoins speakers to make their contribution relevant to the aims of the ongoing conversation. In addition, a maxim of quantity requires speakers to make their contribution as informative as is required, but not more informative than is required, while a maxim of manner holds that the contribution should be clear rather than obscure, ambiguous, or wordy. Accordingly, "communicated information comes with a guarantee of relevance" (Sperber & Wilson 1986, p. vi) and listeners are entitled to assume that speakers try "to be informative, truthful, relevant, and clear"—and listeners interpret speakers' utterances "on the assumption that they are trying to live up to these ideals" (Clark & Clark 1977, p. 122).

These tacit assumptions are routinely violated in research situations, and these violations contribute to a broad range of apparent biases of judgment and artifacts in survey measurement, as a few examples may illustrate (for extensive reviews, see Hilton 1995; Schwarz 1994, 1996).

THE CONVERSATIONAL RELEVANCE OF "IRRELEVANT" INFORMATION In judgment research, experimenters as social communicators often introduce information that is neither informative nor relevant. However, participants have no reason to doubt the relevance of information provided to them in a serious research setting and are "likely to seek relevance in any experimental message" (Kahneman & Tversky 1982, p. 502). As a consequence, they go beyond the literal meaning of the utterance and treat irrelevant information as relevant, resulting in judgmental errors relative to normative models that consider only the literal meaning of the utterance but not the implications of the communicative context. These errors are due to violations of conversational norms on the part of the experimenter and are obtained under circumstances that neither conform to conversational norms nor allow the insight that the usual conversational maxims do not apply.

For example, Kahneman & Tversky (1973) provided participants with a description of a target person who "shows no interest in political and social issues and spends most of his free time on his many hobbies which include home carpentry, sailing, and mathematical puzzles." This person was said to be randomly drawn from a sample of engineers and lawyers, and participants had to determine the person's profession. They predicted that the person is most likely an engineer, independent of whether the base-rate probability for any person in the sample being an engineer was .30 or .70. These predictions indicate that participants relied on individuating information of little diagnostic value at the expense of more diagnostic base-rate information, thus violating normative (Bayesian) models of judgment (for a review of related studies, see Nisbett & Ross 1980 and Ginossar & Trope 1987; for a critique of the normative assumptions, see Gigerenzer 1991). Does this imply, however, that they did not note that the personality sketch provided to them was uninformative? Or did they draw on this information because they inferred that the researcher wanted them to consider it—or else, why would it be presented to them in the first place? An extended replication of Kahneman & Tversky's (1973) study supports the latter possibility (Schwarz et al 1991c). When the personality description was provided as a narrative allegedly written by a psychologist, participants again concluded that the target person is an engineer, independent of the base-rate of lawyers and engineers in the sample. Yet, when the same description was presented as a random sample of information about this person, allegedly drawn by a computer from a larger file assembled by psychologists, participants relied on the more diagnostic base-rate information to make a prediction. This reflects that a narrative written by the researcher comes with the guarantee of relevance that characterizes cooperative communication, a guarantee that does not extend to a random sample of information drawn by a computer. Hence, participants tried to make sense of the personality information provided to them in the former case, but were happy to ignore it in the latter (see also Krosnick et al 1990).

Similar conversational analyses have been offered for other judgmental biases that reflect reliance on normatively irrelevant information, including the fundamental attribution error, i.e. dispositional attributions on the basis of nondiagnostic behavior (e.g. Wright & Wells 1988); the dilution effect, i.e. the observation that nondiagnostic information attenuates the impact of more diagnostic information in impression formation (e.g. Tetlock & Boettger 1996); the conjunction fallacy (e.g. Dulany & Hilton 1991); and misleading question effects in eyewitness testimony (e.g. Dodd & Bradshaw 1980). In fact, when explicitly asked, participants usually seem aware that the normatively irrelevant information is of little informational value (e.g. Miller et al 1984). Nevertheless, they typically proceed to use it in making a judgment because the sheer fact that it has been presented renders it conversationally relevant in the given context. Once the "guarantee of relevance" is undermined, participants are less inclined to see relevance in the information provided to them and the impact of normatively irrelevant information is attenuated (see Hilton 1995, Schwarz 1996). Moreover, increasing individuals' motivation to arrive at a defensible judgment, e.g. by making them accountable, does not attenuate reliance on normatively irrelevant information presented by the researcher. To the contrary, it increases their efforts to find meaning in the material presented to them (e.g. Tetlock & Boettger 1996).

In summary, the procedures typically used in psychological research are likely to result in an overestimation of the size and the pervasiveness of judgmental biases. Note, however, that a conversational analysis does *not* imply that violations of conversational norms are the *sole* source of judgmental biases. Like most robust phenomena, judgmental biases are likely to have many determinants. If we are to understand their operation in natural contexts, however, we need to ensure that their emergence in laboratory experiments does not reflect the operation of determinants that are unlikely to hold in other settings.

CONVERSATIONAL RELEVANCE AND RESPONSE EFFECTS IN SURVEY RESEARCH

These considerations of socially situated cognition in the research context extend beyond the psychological laboratory and apply as well to survey interviews. Like participants in an experiment, survey respondents draw on the researcher's contributions to the interview to determine the meaning of the questions posed to them. The researcher's contributions include the content of preceding questions as well as apparently formal characteristics of the questionnaire, such as the numeric values presented as part of a rating scale, as a few examples may illustrate (for reviews, see Clark & Schober 1992, Schwarz 1996, Strack 1994, Sudman et al 1996).

To survey researchers' concern, about 30% of the respondents of any sample are willing to provide opinions on highly obscure or even completely fictitious issues, such as the "Agricultural Trade Act of 1978" (e.g. Bishop et al 1986, Schuman & Presser 1981). Such findings apparently document that the fear of appearing uninformed may induce "many respondents to conjure up opinions even when they had not given the particular issue any thought prior to the interview" (Erikson et al 1988, p. 44; Converse 1964). Yet, the sheer fact that a question about some issue is asked presupposes that the issue exists—or else asking a question about it would violate every norm of conversational conduct. Having no reason to assume that the researcher would ask meaningless questions, respondents turn to the context of the ambiguous question to make sense of it, much as they would be expected to do in any other conversation. Once they assign a particular meaning to the issue, they may have no difficulty reporting a subjectively meaningful opinion. Supporting this reasoning, Strack et al (1991) observed that German university students favored the introduction of a fictitious "educational contribution" when a preceding question pertained to fellowships for students but opposed it when it pertained to tuition. Open-ended responses confirmed that they used the content of the preceding question to determine the nature of the fictitious issue. While findings of this type (see Schwarz 1996) provide the comforting assurance that respondents do not conjure up opinions to avoid appearing uninformed, they again highlight the extent to which insensitivity to conversational processes may foster misleading conclusions about human cognition and behavior.

In addition to drawing on the content of preceding questions, respondents make systematic use of apparently formal features of questionnaire design in determining question meaning. For example, when asked how successful they have been in life, on a scale ranging from "not at all successful" to "extremely successful," respondents have to determine what the researcher means by "not at all successful." Does this term refer to the absence of great achievements or to the presence of explicit failures? Empirically, they adopt the former interpretation when the numeric values of the rating scale run from 0 to 10, but the latter when the values run from -5 to +5, resulting in markedly different responses (Schwarz et al 1991b). In general, a scale format that runs from negative to positive numeric values indicates that the researcher has a bipolar dimension in mind (e.g. presence of failure to presence of success), whereas the use of only positive values indicates a unipolar dimension (e.g. different degrees of success). Similar considerations apply to the influence of other response formats, including differences between open and closed question formats, the use of "don't know" filters, and the impact of frequency scales on behavioral reports, all of which can be fruitfully conceptualized in a conversational inference framework (Clark & Schober 1992, Schwarz 1996). Throughout, what appear as artifacts of meaningless formal features of questionnaires can be traced to respondents' systematic use of contextual information in an attempt to determine the intended meaning of the question and the nature of their task.

SUMMARY As these examples illustrate, many apparent biases in social judgment and artifacts in survey measurement do not necessarily reflect inherent shortcomings of human judgmental processes. Instead, they reflect that research participants are cooperative communicators who draw on the researcher's contributions to the ongoing conversation in an attempt to provide useful information. Unfortunately, they miss one crucial point: Although the researchers are likely to observe conversational norms in all other situations, they may violate them in the research context by deliberately presenting information that is irrelevant to the task at hand or by inadvertently introducing features that carry information of which they are not aware. Unless we learn to take the information conveyed by our research procedures into account, we run the risk of painting an inappropriately negative picture of human judgment.

The Motivated Tactician's Limits: Automaticity, Implicit Cognition, and Mental Control

The research reviewed so far highlighted individuals' ability to flexibly tune their thought processes to the requirements at hand. Yet "you can't always think what you want" (Wegner 1992, p. 193), and a review of recent developments in cognitive social psychology would be incomplete without drawing attention to social psychologists' increasing interest in automatic, nonconscious influences on thought and behavior and the limits of mental control (for comprehensive reviews, see Bargh 1994, Greenwald & Banaji 1995, Wegner & Wenzlaff 1996, Wegner & Bargh 1998).

AUTOMATICITY AND IMPLICIT COGNITION Implicit cognitions are "introspectively unidentified (or inaccurately identified)" traces of past experiences that influence judgments or behaviors (Greenwald & Banaji 1995, p. 5). Predating interest in this domain by several decades, Zajonc (1968) demonstrated, for example, that repeated exposure to an unknown stimulus (e.g. a Chinese idiograph) increases liking for the stimulus. Importantly, effects of previous exposure on liking are obtained under conditions where participants cannot recognize the stimulus as having been previously presented (Kunst-Wilson & Zajonc 1980) and are eliminated when participants are aware of the previous exposure (Bornstein & D'Agostino 1992). Effects of this type reflect that previous exposure leaves memory traces that increase the fluency with which the stimulus can be processed later (Jacoby 1989), and that the experience of perceptual fluency can itself serve as a basis of judgment (e.g. Reber et al 1998). Such dissociations between "explicit memory" (what one is able to recall or recognize) and "implicit memory" (memory traces inferred from an impact of the learning experience on other measures) have received considerable attention in cognitive psychology (see Jacoby & Kelley 1987 and the contributions in Reder 1996). Extending this work, social psychologists have begun to explore the role of such unconscious influences in judgment and behavior (Greenwald & Banaji 1995).

An unconscious influence of particular interest is the automatic activation of stereotypes (e.g. Banaji et al 1993, Devine 1989), which may affect individuals' behavior outside of awareness. For example, Bargh et al (1996) asked participants to form meaningful sentences from strings of words that contained elements related to the elderly stereotype, like "forgetful," "Florida," or "bingo." Although none of these words was explicitly related to the concept of "slowness," this concept, which is part of the general elderly stereotype, was apparently activated and influenced participants' behavior: After ostensible completion of the experiment, participants primed with the elderly stereotype walked more slowly to the elevator than participants exposed to other concepts. A growing body of research illustrates the role of such automatic and unconscious influences in everyday life (for a review, see Bargh 1997) and their controllability and interplay with conscious cognition is the topic of considerable debate (see the contributions in Wyer 1997).

MENTAL CONTROL Importantly, research in this domain not only documented pervasive effects of automatically activated knowledge structures, but also suggested that attempts to avoid unwanted influences of knowledge activation may often backfire. Suppose that a person anticipates an interaction with a skinhead and wants to avoid any undue influences of stereotypic knowledge about the group on the impression formed of the exemplar. To accomplish this, the person may attempt to suppress the stereotype, essentially trying not to think "skinhead." Unfortunately, this effort is likely to be of limited success, as Macrae et al (1994a) demonstrated. Although we can suppress unwanted thoughts for a limited period, we are only successful at doing so when no other task taxes our cognitive resources. When we are distracted by another task, or terminate our efforts when no longer required, the unwanted thoughts bounce back with renewed vigor (for reviews, see Wegner & Wenzlaff 1996, Wegner & Bargh 1998, and the contributions in Wegner & Pennebaker 1993). These rebound effects reflect that thought suppression involves a monitoring process that checks if the unwanted thoughts intrude into consciousness. Ironically, this monitoring process increases the activation of the unwanted material in memory. Consequently, the unwanted material becomes highly accessible, and we may end up thinking, and doing, exactly what we wanted to avoid when the cognitive resources required for suppression are taxed.

SUMMARY As these examples illustrate, a growing body of research demonstrates pervasive unconscious influences of automatic knowledge activation on judgment and behavior and highlights the limits of intentional mental control. At present, the interplay of conscious and unconscious processes in social judgment and behavior is not well understood, but its exploration is likely to be a focal area of social cognition research in the near future.

CONCLUSIONS

In sum, cognitive social psychology complemented its previous emphasis on "cold" cognition and individuals as isolated information processors with a renewed interest in the interplay of feeling and thinking and the exploration of social influences on human cognition. The picture that emerges from these developments is compatible with social psychology's latest metaphor, humans as *motivated tacticians* (Fiske & Taylor 1991) who pragmatically adapt their processing strategies to the requirements of the situation at hand in an effort to get things done. Hence, they pay close attention to complex information and engage in systematic and effortful processing strategies when required, but rely on cognitive shortcuts, simple heuristics, and preexisting knowledge structures in the perceived absence of such requirements; and they engage in rigid and defensive processing once committed to a position or course of action (Gollwitzer 1990, Tetlock 1992). To determine the requirements at hand, they attend to a wide range of internal and external cues. They are more likely to pay attention to the details at hand when negative feelings signal a problematic situation and to rely on general knowledge structures and simple heuristics when positive feelings signal a benign situation (Schwarz & Clore 1996). Similarly, they attend to complex information about others when the other is powerful and may affect their outcomes, but not otherwise (Fiske & Depret 1996), and they consider the likely interpersonal consequences of their judgments and decisions when they are held accountable, but not otherwise (Tetlock 1992). The conditions under which the motivated tactician is most likely to get it wrong are conditions under which normally adaptive assumptions are thwarted, as is the case when researchers present irrelevant information under circumstances that suggest otherwise (Hilton 1995, Schwarz 1996). Yet, this emphasis on the pragmatic and adaptive nature of social thinking needs to be balanced by a recognition of the pervasive role of unconscious influences on social judgment and behavior (Bargh 1997, Greenwald & Banaji 1995), which are likely to be more fully understood in the near future.

Depending on the normative perspective taken, we may lament the errors that the motivated tactician makes or praise the flexible adaptation of processing strategies to the individual's goals. Over the past decades, social psychologists have embraced Bayesian probability theory and related normative models as the gold standard against which human judgment is to be evaluated, and found human judgment lacking (for different perspectives, see Nisbett & Ross 1980; Gigerenzer 1991, 1996; Kahneman & Tversky 1996). In recent years, the field has increasingly adopted a more pragmatic perspective (e.g. Fiske 1992, 1993; Funder 1987).

> Before labeling an effect a cognitive flaw, one should consider (1) the interpersonal, institutional, and political goals that people are trying to achieve by making judgments of a particular type (e.g. Do people seek to achieve causal understanding or to express their moral approval/disapproval? Do people attempt to maximize expected utility or to minimize risk of serious criticism?) and (2) whether cognitive strategies that serve people well in everyday life may lead them seriously astray in laboratory experiments on judgment and choice. (Tetlock 1992, p. 360)

The accumulating evidence indicates that the fallibility of human judgment is less detrimental than normative analyses would suggest and that people may be "good enough" (Fiske 1992) thinkers to get things done, true to William James's (1890, p. 333) credo that "my thinking is first and last and always for the sake of my doing."

ACKNOWLEDGMENTS

I thank Herbert Bless, James Hilton, James House, Richard Nisbett, and Daphna Oyserman for stimulating discussions and helpful comments.

Literature Cited

Abelson RP. 1994. A personal perspective on social cognition. See Devine et al 1994, pp. 15–40

Asch SE. 1955. Opinions and social pressure. *Sci. Am.* 193:31–35

Baker SM, Petty RE. 1994. Majority and minority influence: source-position imbalance as a determinant of message scrutiny. *J. Pers. Soc. Psychol.* 67:5–19

Banaji MR, Hardin C, Rothman AJ. 1993. Implicit stereotyping in person judgment. *J. Pers. Soc. Psychol.* 65:272–81

Bargh JA. 1994. The four horsemen of automaticity: awareness, intention, efficiency, and control in social cognition. See Wyer & Srull 1994, 1:1–40

Bargh JA. 1997. The automaticity of everyday life. See Wyer 1997, pp. 1—62

Bargh JA, Chen M, Burrows L. 1996. Automaticity of social behavior: direct effects of trait construct and stereotype activation on action. *J. Pers. Soc. Psychol.* 71:230–44

Baron RM, Kenny DA. 1986. The moderator-mediator variable distinction in social psychological research: conceptual, strategic, and statistical conssiderations. *J. Pers. Soc. Psychol.* 51:1173–82

Berscheid E, Graziano W, Monson T, Dermer M. 1976. Outcome dependency, attention, attribution, and attraction. *J. Pers. Soc. Psychol.* 34:978–89

Bishop GF, Oldendick RW, Tuchfarber AJ. 1986. Opinions on fictitious issues: the pressure to answer survey questions. *Public Opin. Q.* 50:240–50

Blaney PH. 1986. Affect and memory: a review. *Psychol. Bull.* 99:229–46

Bless H, Bohner G, Schwarz N, Strack F. 1990. Mood and persuasion: a cognitive response analysis. *Pers. Soc. Psychol. Bull.* 16:331–45

Bless H, Clore GL, Schwarz N, Golisano V, Rabe C, Wölk M. 1996a. Mood and the use of scripts: does being in a happy mood really lead to mindlessness? *J. Pers. Soc. Psychol.* 71:665–79

Bless H, Schwarz N, Kemmelmeier M. 1996b. Mood and stereotyping: the impact of moods on the use of general knowledge structures. *Eur. Rev. Soc. Psychol.* 7: 63–93

Bless H, Schwarz N, Wieland R. 1996c. Mood and stereotyping: the impact of category membership and individuating information. *Eur. J. Soc. Psychol.* 26:935–59

Bodenhausen GV. 1990. Stereotypes as judgmental heuristics. Evidence of circadian variations in discrimination. *Psychol. Sci.* 1:319–22

Bodenhausen GV, Kramer GP, Süsser K. 1994a. Happiness and stereotypic thinking in social judgment. *J. Pers. Soc. Psychol.* 66:621–32

Bodenhausen GV, Sheppard LA, Kramer GP. 1994b. Negative affect and social judgment: the differential impact of anger and sadness. *Eur. J. Soc. Psychol.* 24:45–62

Bohner G, Erb HP, Reinhard M, Frank E. 1996. Distinctiveness information in minority and majority influence. *Br. J. Soc. Psychol.* 35:27–46

Bohner G, Moskowitz G, Chaiken S. 1995. The interplay of heuristic and systematic processing of social information. *Eur. Rev. Soc. Psychol.* 6:33–68

Bornstein RF, D'Agostino PA. 1992. Stimulus recognition and the mere exposure effect. *J. Pers. Soc. Psychol.* 63:545–52

Bower GH. 1981. Mood and memory. *Am. Psychol.* 36:129–48

Bower GH. 1991. Mood congruity of social judgments. In *Emotion and Social Judgments,* ed. JP Forgas, pp. 31–53. Oxford: Pergamon

Brewer MB. 1988. A dual process model of impression formation. See Wyer & Srull, 1:1–36

Bruner JS. 1957. On perceptual readiness. *Psychol. Rev.* 64:123–52

Cacioppo JT, Berntson GG, Crites SL. 1996. Social neuroscience: principles of psychophysiological arousal and response. See Higgins & Kruglanski 1996, pp. 72–101

Chaiken S, Trope Y, eds. 1998. *Dual-Process Models in Social Psychology.* New York: Guilford. In press

Clark HH. 1985. Language use and language users. See Lindzey & Aronson 1985, 2: 179–232

Clark HH, Clark EV. 1977. *Psychology and Language.* New York: Harcourt Brace Jovanovich

Clark HH, Schober MF. 1992. Asking questions and influencing answers. In *Questions about Questions,* ed. JM Tanur, pp. 15–48. New York: Russel Sage

Clore GL. 1992. Cognitive phenomenology: feelings and the construction of judgment. See Martin & Tesser 1992, pp. 133–64

Clore GL, Schwarz N, Conway M. 1994. Affective causes and consequences of social information processing. See Wyer & Srull 1994, 1:323–418

Converse PE. 1964. The nature of belief systems in the mass public. In *Ideology and Discontent,* ed. DE Apter, pp. 206–61. New York: Free Press

Damasio AR. 1994. *Descartes' Error: Emotion, Reason and the Human Brain.* New York: Grosset/Putnam

Devine PG. 1989. Stereotypes and prejudice: their automatic and controlled components. *J. Pers. Soc. Psychol.* 56:5–18

Devine PG, Hamilton DL, Ostrom TM, eds. 1994. *Social Cognition: Impact on Social Psychology.* San Diego: Academic

De Vries NK, De Dreu CKW, Gordijn E, Schuurman M. 1996. Majority and minority influence: a dual role interpretation. *Eur. Rev. Soc. Psychol.* 7:145–72

Dodd DH, Bradshaw JM. 1980. Leading questions and memory: pragmatic constraints. *J. Verb. Learn. Verb. Behav.* 19:695–704

Dulany DE, Hilton DJ. 1991. Conversational implicature, conscious representation, and the conjunction fallacy. *Soc. Cogn.* 9: 85–110

Eagly AH, Chaiken S. 1993. *The Psychology of Attitudes.* Fort Worth, TX: Harcourt Brace Jovanovich

Edwards JA, Weary G. 1993. Depression and the impression-formation continuum: piecemeal processing despite the availability of category information. *J. Pers. Soc. Psychol.* 64:636–45

Erikson RS, Luttberg NR, Tedin KT. 1988. *American Public Opinion.* New York: Macmillan. 3rd ed.

Fiedler K. 1988. Emotional mood, cognitive style, and behavior regulation. In *Affect, Cognition, and Social Behavior,* ed. K Fiedler, J Forgas, pp. 100–19. Toronto: Hogrefe Int.

Fiske ST. 1992. Thinking is for doing: portraits of social cognition from daguerreotype to laserphoto. *J. Pers. Soc. Psychol.* 63:877–89

Fiske ST. 1993. Social cognition and social perception. *Annu. Rev. Psychol.* 44:155–94

Fiske ST, Depret E. 1996. Control, interdependence and power: understanding social cognition in its social context. *Eur. Rev. Soc. Psychol.* 7:31–62

Fiske AP, Kitayama S, Markus, Nisbett RE.

1998. The cultural matrix of social psychology. In *Handbook of Social Psychology,* ed. DT Gilbert, ST Fiske, G Lindzey, 2:915–81. New York: Random House

Fiske ST, Neuberg SL. 1990. A continuum of impression formation, from category-based to individuating processes: influences of information and motivation on attention and interpretation. *Adv. Exp. Soc. Psychol.* 23:1–74

Fiske ST, Taylor SE. 1991. *Social Cognition.* New York: McGraw-Hill. 2nd ed.

Forgas JP. 1981. What is social about social cognition? In *Social Cognition. Perspectives on Everyday Understanding,* ed. JP Forgas, pp. 1–26. New York: Academic

Forgas JP. 1995. Emotion in social judgments: review and a new affect infusion model (AIM). *Psychol. Bull.* 117:39–66

Funder DC. 1987. Errors and mistakes: evaluating the accuracy of social judgment. *Psychol. Bull.* 101:75–90

Gigerenzer G. 1991. How to make cognitive illusions disappear: beyond "heuristics and biases." *Eur. Rev. Soc. Psychol.* 2:83–116

Gigerenzer G. 1996. On narrow norms and vague heuristics: a reply to Kahneman and Tversky. *Psychol. Rev.* 103:592–96

Ginossar Z, Trope Y. 1987. Problem solving and judgment under uncertainty. *J. Pers. Soc. Psychol.* 52:464–74

Goldberger NR, Veroff JB, eds. 1995. *The Culture and Psychology Reader.* New York: NY Univ. Press

Gollwitzer PM. 1990. Action phases and mind-sets. In *Handbook of Motivation and Cognition,* ed. ET Higgins, RM Sorrentino, 2:53–92. New York: Guilford

Gollwitzer PM, Bargh JA, eds. 1996. *The Psychology of Action.* New York: Guilford

Greenwald AG, Banaji MR. 1995. Implicit social cognition: attitudes, self-esteem, and stereotypes. *Psychol. Rev.* 102:4–27

Grice HP. 1975. Logic and conversation. In *Syntax and Semantics: Speech Acts,* ed. P Cole, JL Morgan, 3:41–58. New York: Academic

Hamilton DL, Katz LB, Leirer VO. 1980. Organizational processes in impression formation. See Hastie et al 1980, pp. 121–53

Hastie R, Ostrom TM, Ebbesen EB, Wyer RS, Carlston DE, eds. 1980. *Person Memory: The Cognitive Basis of Social Perception.* Hillsdale, NJ: Erlbaum

Higgins ET. 1981. The communication game: implications for social cognition and persuasion. In *Social Cognition: The Ontario Symposium,* ed. ET Higgins, MP Zanna, CP Herman, 1:343–92. Hillsdale, NJ: Erlbaum

Higgins ET, Kruglanski A, eds. 1996. *Social Psychology: Handbook of Basic Principles.* New York: Guilford

Higgins ET, Rholes WS. 1978. Saying is believing: effects of message modification on memory and liking of the person described. *J. Exp. Soc. Psychol.* 14:363–78

Higgins ET, Sorrentino RM, eds. 1990. *Handbook of Motivation and Cognition, Vol 2.* New York: Guilford

Hildebrand-Saints L, Weary G. 1989. Depression and social information gathering. *Pers. Soc. Psychol. Bull.* 15:150–60

Hilton DJ. 1990. Conversational processes and causal explanation. *Psychol. Bull.* 107:65–81

Hilton DJ. 1991. A conversational model of causal explanation. *Eur. Rev. Soc. Psychol.* 2:31–50

Hilton DJ. 1995. The social context of reasoning: conversational inference and rational judgment. *Psychol. Bull.* 118:248–71

Hilton JL, Darley JM. 1991. The effects of interaction goals on person perception. *Adv. Exp. Soc. Psychol.* 24:235–67

Isen AM. 1984. Toward understanding the role of affect in cognition. See Wyer & Srull 1994, 3:179–236

Isen AM. 1987. Positive affect, cognitive processes, and social behavior. *Adv. Exp. Soc. Psychol.* 20:203–53

Isen AM, Shalker TE, Clark MS, Karp L. 1978. Affect, accessibility of material in memory, and behavior: a cognitive loop? *J. Pers. Soc. Psychol.* 36:1–12

Jacoby LL, Kelley CM. 1987. Unconscious influences of memory for a prior event. *Pers. Soc. Psychol. Bull.* 13:314–36

Jacoby LL, Kelley CM, Dywan J. 1989. Memory attributions. In *Varieties of Memory and Consciousness: Essays in Honour of Endel Tulving,* ed. HL Roediger, FIM Craik, pp. 391–422. Hillsdale, NJ: Erlbaum

James W. 1890. *The Principles of Psychology.* Vol. 2. New York: Holt

Kahneman D, Tversky A. 1973. On the psychology of prediction. *Psychol. Rev.* 80: 237–51

Kahneman D, Tversky A. 1982. On the study of statistical intuitions. In *Judgment Under Uncertainty: Heuristics and Biases,* ed. D Kahneman, P Slovic, A Tversky, pp. 493–508. Cambridge: Cambridge Univ. Press

Kahneman D, Tversky A. 1996. On the reality of cognitive illusions. *Psychol. Rev.* 103: 582–91

Keltner D, Ellsworth P, Edwards K. 1993. Beyond simple pessimism: effects of sadness and anger on social perception. *J. Pers. Soc. Psychol.* 64:740–52

Kiesler CA. 1971. *The Psychology of Commitment.* New York: Academic

Krauss RM, Fussel SR. 1996. Social psychological models of interpersonal communication. See Higgins & Kruglanski 1996, pp. 655–701

Krosnick JA, Li F, Lehman DR. 1990. Conversational conventions, order of information acquisition, and the effect of base rates and individuating information on social judgment. *J. Pers. Soc. Psychol.* 59:1140–52

Kunda Z. 1990. The case for motivated reasoning. *Psychol. Bull.* 108:331–50

Kunst-Wilson WR, Zajonc RB. 1980. Affective discrimination of stimuli that cannot be recognized. *Science* 207:557–58

Lachman R, Lachman JT, Butterfield EC. 1979. *Cognitive Psychology and Information Processing.* Hillsdale, NJ: Erlbaum

LeDoux J. 1996. *The Emotional Brain.* New York: Simon & Schuster

Levine JM, Resnick LB, Higgins ET. 1993. Social foundations of cognition. *Annu. Rev. Psychol.* 44:585–612

Levinson SC. 1983. *Pragmatics.* Cambridge: Cambridge Univ. Press

Lindzey G, Aronson E, eds. 1985. *Handbook of Social Psychology.* New York: Random House

Mackie DM. 1987. Systematic and nonsystematic processing of majority and minority persuasive communications. J. *Pers. Soc. Psychol.* 53:41–52

Mackie DM, Asuncion AG, Rosselli F. 1992. The impact of affective states on persuasion processes. In *Review of Personality and Social Psychology,* ed. M Clark, 14:247–70. Beverly Hills, CA: Sage

Mackie DM, Skelly JJ. 1994. The social cognition analysis of social influence: contributions to understanding persuasion and conformity. See Devine et al, pp. 259–90

Mackie DM, Worth LT. 1989. Cognitive deficits and the mediation of positive affect in persuasion. *J. Pers. Soc. Psychol.* 57: 27–40

Macrae CN, Bodenhausen GV, Milne AB, Jetten J. 1994a. Out of mind but back in sight: stereotypes on the rebound. *J. Pers. Soc. Psychol.* 67:808–17

Macrae CN, Milne AB, Bodenhausen GV. 1994b. Stereotypes as energy-saving devices: a peek inside the cognitive toolbox. *J. Pers. Soc. Psychol.* 66:37–47

Markus HR, Kitayama S. 1991. Culture and self: implications for cognition, emotion, and motivation. *Psychol. Rev.* 98:224–53

Markus HR, Zajonc RB. 1985. The cognitive perspective in social psychology. See Lindzey & Aronson 1985, 1:137–230

Martin LL, Tesser A, eds. 1992. *The Construction of Social Judgment.* Hillsdale, NJ: Erlbaum

Martin LL, Ward DW, Achée JW, Wyer RS. 1993. Mood as input: people have to interpret the motivational implications of their moods. *J. Pers. Soc. Psychol.* 64:317–26

Mathews A, MacLeod C. 1994. Cognitive approaches to emotion and emotional disorders. *Annu. Rev. Psychol.* 45:25–50

McCann CD, Higgins ET. 1992. Personal and contextual factors in communication: a review of the "communication game." In *Language, Interaction, and Social Cognition,* ed. GR Semin, K Fiedler, pp. 144–72. Newbury Park, CA: Sage

Miller AG, Schmidt D, Meyer C, Colella A. 1984. The perceived value of constrained behavior: pressures toward biased inference in the attitude attribution paradigm. *Soc. Psychol. Q.* 47:160–71

Morris WN. 1989. *Mood: The Frame of Mind.* New York: Springer-Verlag

Moscovici S. 1976. *Social Influence and Social Change.* London: Academic

Moscovici S. 1980. Toward a theory of conversion behavior. *Adv. Exp. Soc. Psychol.* 13:209–39

Mugny G, Perez JA. 1991. *The Social Psychology of Minority Influence.* Cambridge, UK: Cambridge Univ. Press

Neisser U. 1967. *Cognitive Psychology.* New York: Appleton-Century-Crofts

Neuberg SL, Fiske ST. 1987. Motivational influences on impression formation: outcome dependency, accuracy-driven attention, and individuating processes. *J. Pers. Soc. Psychol.* 53:431–41

Neuberg SL. 1989. The goal of forming accurate impressions during social interactions: attenuating the impact of negative expectancies. *J. Pers. Soc. Psychol.* 56: 374–86

Nisbett RE, Cohen D. 1996. *Culture of Honor: The Psychology of Violence in the South.* Boulder, CO: Westview

Nisbett RE, Ross L. 1980. *Human Inference: Strategies and Shortcomings of Social Judgment.* New York: Prentice Hall

Payne JW, Bettman JR, Johnson EJ, eds. 1993. *The Adaptive Decision Maker.* Cambridge: Cambridge Univ. Press

Petty R, Cacioppo J. 1986. *Communication and Persuasion: Central and Peripheral Routes to Attitude Change.* New York: Springer-Verlag

Reber R, Winkielman P, Schwarz N. 1998. Effects of perceptual fluency on affective judgments. *Psychol. Science* 9:45–48

Reder LM, ed. 1996. *Implicit Memory and Metacognition.* Mahwah, NJ: Erlbaum

Resnick LB, Levine JM, Teasly SD, eds. 1991.

Perspectives on Socially Shared Cognition. Washington, DC: Am. Psychol. Assoc.

Ross L. 1977. The intuitive psychologist and his shortcomings: distortions in the attribution process. *Adv. Exp. Soc. Psychol.* 10:173–220

Ross L, Greene D, House P. 1977. The false-consensus effect: an egocentric bias in social perception. *J. Exp. Soc. Psychol.* 13: 279–301

Saunders S. 1993. Stock prices and Wall Street weather. *Am. Econ. Rev.* 83:1337–45

Schneider D. 1991. Social cognition. *Annu. Rev. Psychol.* 42:527–61

Schuman H, Presser S. 1981. *Questions and Answers in Attitude Surveys.* New York: Academic

Schwarz N. 1990. Feelings as information: informational and motivational functions of affective states. See Higgins & Sorrentino 1990, 2:527–61

Schwarz N. 1994. Judgment in a social context: biases, shortcomings, and the logic of conversation. *Adv. Exp. Soc. Psychol.* 26: 123–62

Schwarz N. 1996. *Cognition and Communication: Judgmental Biases, Research Methods, and the Logic of Conversation.* Hillsdale, NJ: Erlbaum

Schwarz N, Bless H, Bohner G. 1991a. Mood and persuasion: affective states influence the processing of persuasive communications. *Adv. Exp. Soc. Psychol.* 24:161–99

Schwarz N, Clore GL. 1983. Mood, misattribution, and judgments of well-being: informative and directive functions of affective states. *J. Pers. Soc. Psychol.* 45: 513–23

Schwarz N, Clore GL. 1996. Feelings and phenomenal experiences. See Higgins & Kruglanski 1996, pp. 433–65

Schwarz N, Knäuper B, Hippler HJ, Noelle-Neumann E, Clark F. 1991b. Rating scales: numeric values may change the meaning of scale labels. *Public Opin. Q.* 55:570–82

Schwarz N, Strack F, Hilton DJ, Naderer G. 1991c. Judgmental biases and the logic of conversation: the contextual relevance of irrelevant information. *Soc. Cogn.* 9: 67–84

Schwarz N, Sudman S, eds. 1996. *Answering Questions: Methodology for Determining Cognitive and Communicative Processes in Survey Research.* San Francisco: Jossey-Bass

Sherif M. 1936. *The Psychology of Social Norms.* New York: Harper

Sinclair RC. 1988. Mood, categorization breadth, and performance appraisal: the effects of order of information acquisition and affective state on halo, accuracy, information retrieval, and evaluations. *Organ. Behav. Hum. Decis. Proc.* 42:22–46

Sinclair RC, Marks MM. 1992. The influence of mood state on judgment and action: effects on persuasion, categorization, social justice, person perception, and judgmental accuracy. See Martin & Tesser 1992, pp. 165–93

Sinclair RC, Marks MM, Clore GL. 1994. Mood-related persuasion depends on misattributions. *Soc. Cogn.* 12:309–26

Singer JA, Salovey P. 1988. Mood and memory: evaluating the network theory of affect. *Clin. Psychol. Rev.* 8:211–51

Sorrentino RM, Higgins ET, eds. 1986. *Handbook of Motivation and Cognition, Vol 1.* New York: Guilford

Sorrentino RM, Higgins ET, eds. 1995. *Handbook of Motivation and Cognition, Vol 3.* New York: Guilford

Sperber D, Wilson D. 1986. *Relevance: Communication and Cognition.* Cambridge, MA: Harvard Univ. Press

Stepper S, Strack F. 1993. Proprioceptive determinants of emotional and nonemotional feelings. *J. Pers. Soc. Psychol.* 64: 211–20

Strack F. 1988. Social Cognition: Sozialpsychologie innerhalb des Paradigmas der Informationsverarbeitung. [Social cognition: social psychology in the paradigm of information processing.] *Psychol. Rundschau* 39:72–82

Strack F. 1994. Response processes in social judgment. See Wyer & Srull 1994, 1: 287–322

Strack F, Schwarz N, Wänke M. 1991. Semantic and pragmatic aspects of context effects in social and psychological research. *Soc. Cogn.* 9:111–25

Sudman S, Bradburn NM, Schwarz N. 1996. *Thinking About Answers: The Application of Cognitive Processes to Survey Methodology.* San Francisco, CA: Jossey-Bass

Taylor SE. 1998. The social being in social psychology. In *Handbook of Social Psychology,* ed. D Gilbert, ST Fiske, G Lindzey, 1:58–98. New York: McGraw-Hill. 4th ed.

Tetlock PE. 1992. The impact of accountability on judgment and choice: toward a social contingency model. *Adv. Exp. Soc. Psychol.* 25:331–76

Tetlock PE, Boettger R. 1996. The dilution effect: judgmental bias, conversational convention, or a bit of both? *Eur. J. Soc. Psychol.* 26:915–34

Tetlock PE, Skitka L, Boettger R. 1989. Social and cognitive strategies of coping with accountability: conformity, complexity, and bolstering. *J. Pers. Soc. Psychol.* 57: 632–41

Wegener DT, Petty RE, Smith SM. 1995. Positive mood can increase or decrease message scrutiny: the hedonic contingency view of mood and message elaboration. *J. Pers. Soc. Psychol.* 69:5–15

Wegner DM. 1987. Transactive memory: a contemporary analysis of the group mind. In *Theories of Group Behavior,* ed. B Mullen, GR Goethals, pp. 185–208. New York: Springer-Verlag

Wegner DM. 1992. You can't always think what you want: problems in the suppression of unwanted thoughts. *Adv. Exp. Soc. Psychol.* 25:193–225

Wegner DM, Bargh JA. 1998. Control and automaticity in daily life. In *Handbook of Social Psychology,* ed. DT Gilbert, ST Fiske, G Lindzey, 1:446–96. New York: McGraw-Hill. 4th ed.

Wegner DM, Pennebaker JW, eds. 1993. *Handbook of Mental Control.* Englewood Cliffs, NJ: Prentice Hall

Wegner DM, Wenzlaff RM. 1996. Mental control. See Higgins & Kruglanski 1996, pp. 466–92

Wood W, Lundgren S, Ouellette JA, Busceme S, Blackstone T. 1994. Minority influence: a meta-analytic review of social influence processes. *Psychol. Bull.* 115:323–45

Wright EF. Wells GL. 1988. Is the attitude-attribution paradigm suitable for investigating the dispositional bias? *Pers. Soc. Psych. Bull.* 14:183–90

Wyer RS, ed. 1997. *Advances in Social Cognition,* 10. Mahwah, NJ: Erlbaum

Wyer RS, Srull TK. 1989. *Memory and Cognition in Its Social Context.* Hillsdale, NJ: Erlbaum

Wyer RS, Srull TK, eds. 1994. *Handbook of Social Cognition.* Hillsdale, NJ: Erlbaum. 2nd ed.

Zajonc RB. 1960. The process of cognitive tuning in communication. *J. Abnorm. Soc. Psychol.* 61:159–67

Zajonc RB. 1968. Attitudinal effects of mere exposure. *J. Pers. Soc. Psychol.* 9(Suppl. 2):1–27

Zajonc RB. 1980. Feeling and thinking. Preferences need no inferences. *Am. Psychol.* 35:151–75

Zillman D. 1978. Attribution and misattribution of excitatory reactions. In *New Directions in Attribution Research,* ed. JH Harvey, WI Ickes, RF Kidd, 2:335–68. Hillsdale, NJ: Erlbaum

Annu. Rev. Sociol. 1998. 24:265–90

DIFFUSION IN ORGANIZATIONS AND SOCIAL MOVEMENTS: From Hybrid Corn to Poison Pills

David Strang

Department of Sociology, Cornell University, Ithaca, New York 14853;
e-mail: ds20@cornell.edu

Sarah A. Soule

Department of Sociology, University of Arizona, Tucson, Arizona 85719;
e-mail: soule@U.arizona.edu

KEY WORDS: contagion, network analysis, discourse, protest, interorganizational relations

ABSTRACT

There has been rapid growth in the study of diffusion across organizations and social movements in recent years, fueled by interest in institutional arguments and in network and dynamic analysis. This research develops a sociologically grounded account of change emphasizing the channels along which practices flow. Our review focuses on characteristic lines of argument, emphasizing the structural and cultural logic of diffusion processes. We argue for closer theoretical attention to why practices diffuse at different rates and via different pathways in different settings. Three strategies for further development are proposed: broader comparative research designs, closer inspection of the content of social relations between collective actors, and more attention to diffusion industries run by the media and communities of experts.

What we really need is some new heroes in Engineering. I took that word from Deal's culture book, and I'm trying to identify the Engineering heroes.

Divisional Manager (Kunda 1992, p. 100)

They are making more out of this culture stuff than it's worth...I never read that stuff, maybe see it in passing. It's the same nauseating stuff they print in Business Week.

Group Manager (Kunda 1992, p. 180)

0360-0572/98/0815-0265$08.00

INTRODUCTION

As the above quotations suggest, skillful players in business and other arenas display a keen sense of fashions and movements within their spheres of action. Much as academics are aware of intellectual currents and exemplars in their fields, we may be confident that executives know what new developments are hot and which are not, and that political activists are attuned to successes and disappointments elsewhere. And as the quotes emphasize, individuals counter as well as endorse and employ the cultural materials provided by a larger system of discourse.

Diffusion studies work with this awareness and its consequences by examining how practices spread. They provide an opportunity to locate and document social structure, where we consider how patterns of apparent influence reflect durable social relations. And they provide an opportunity to observe the cultural construction of meaning, where we learn how practices are locally and globally interpreted, and ask why some practices flow while others languish.

This review treats contemporary uses of diffusion arguments within the fields of organizations and social movements. Diffusion imagery, models, and explanations are on the rise in both fields and with clearly productive effect. We seek to map the logic of these developments, emphasizing characteristic lines of argument, methods, and research designs. At the same time, we strike a cautionary note, arguing that theoretical advance requires closer attention to both structural and cultural bases of diffusion.

CONCEPTUAL OVERVIEW

Diffusion refers to the spread of something within a social system. The key term here is "spread," and it should be taken viscerally (as far as one's constructionism permits) to denote flow or movement from a source to an adopter, paradigmatically via communication and influence. We use the term "practice" to denote the diffusing item, which might be a behavior, strategy, belief, technology, or structure. Diffusion is the most general and abstract term we have for this sort of process, embracing contagion, mimicry, social learning, organized dissemination, and other family members.

The term "diffusion" is sometimes used in an alternative sense to denote increasing incidence: Something diffuses when more and more people do it. But treatment of diffusion as an outcome makes it uninteresting, since practices rise and fall in frequency for every possible reason. We thus focus on diffusion as a kind of causal process and seek to map some major lines of argument and important findings.

Diffusion arguments cannot be segregated easily from other causal dynamics. They verge on the one hand toward models of individual choice, since diffusion models often treat the adopter as a reflective decision-maker. They verge on the other hand toward a broader class of contextual and environmental processes, where conditions outside the actor shape behavior. While it is easy to see when one has strayed much too far (analyses of the diffusion of puberty or the diffusion effects of gender composition on job satisfaction), useful hard and fast rules are not readily apparent.

Rather than patrol the boundaries, we focus attention on lines of research with affinities to the core notions underlying diffusion. These include models that attend explicitly to flows of material along social relations, efforts of external change agents to promote adoption, and interpretive work aligning sources and adopters. The emphasis is on processes treated as involving meaningful behavior on the part of both source and adopter.[1]

Classical Diffusion Studies

All lines of argument have empirical fields of application to which they are particularly suited. The home territory of diffusion is the innovation. Innovations are novel (at least to the adopting community), making communication a necessary condition for adoption. Innovations are also culturally understood as progressive, strengthening the hand of change agents. And since innovations are risky and uncertain, adopters carefully weigh the experience of others before acting. The elective affinity between diffusion and innovation is so strong that we sometimes think of diffusion as the only causal process underlying the adoption pattern of innovations.

Diffusion studies thus generally investigate the introduction and adoption of an innovation. Classic studies include Ryan & Gross's (1943) analysis of the diffusion of hybrid corn, Hagerstrand's (1967) investigation of the diffusion of innovations such as the telephone and tests for tuberculosis involving the destruction of cattle in rural Sweden, and Coleman et al's (1966) analysis of the diffusion of a prescription drug in four Midwestern cities.

These studies focused directly on communication processes and channels, tracing the role of the mass media, professional change agents, and interpersonal interaction within the adopting community. Adoption patterns and self-reports pointed to the impact of external sources in introducing the innovation to cosmopolitans, and the cascading of adoption via relational networks within communities [most famously in Katz & Lazarsfeld's (1944) two-step flow of influence]. Relative innovativeness was explained largely by modern values and institutional markers of this orientation such as educational background, probably because the acceptance of modern, scientific practices was at issue. Rogers (1995) authoritatively reviews this literature.

[1]A quite different theoretical orientation would be "practice-centric," attending to the flow of resourceful practices across a landscape of carriers.

Contemporary "Macro" Diffusion Research

Diffusion arguments go in and out of style in sociology as in other disciplines. There is the greatest continuity in interpersonal studies of contagion and influence, but even here their fortunes are tied to relevance to empirical problems. For example, efforts to model the spread of HIV/AIDS has generated much important diffusion research (see the 1995 special issue of *Social Networks*). Interest in diffusion processes is also a function of broader intellectual movements, such as the role of social science in supporting the spread of modernizing innovation.

In this review we treat not the rich contemporary literature on interpersonal influence but instead the recent development of more "macro" diffusion analysis in two fields: social movements and organizations. In the study of social movements, views of contagion as the irrational, spontaneous transmission of antisocial behavior (LeBon 1897, Tarde 1903, Kornhauser 1959) have given way to nuanced studies of diffusion as reflecting "normal learning and influence processes as mediated by the network structures of everyday life" (McAdam 1995, p. 231). Diffusion processes play a central role in contemporary explanations of the incidence of collective action and the spread of protest symbols and tactics.[2]

Diffusion arguments also flourish when there is theoretical attention to the larger environment, to the way cultural models condition behavior, and to historical context and change rather than comparative statics. The new institutionalism (Powell & DiMaggio 1991) has precisely these emphases, and much diffusion research emerges in organizational studies where this school is most influential. Institutional lines of argument also appear in the social movement literature, as does network imagery in organizational research, so that diffusion studies in the two fields are fairly strongly connected.

Diffusion research in these fields differs in obvious ways both from the classics of the genre and from current work on interpersonal diffusion. Contemporary work on organizations and social movements typically examines the spread of behavioral strategies and structures rather than technical innovations, emphasizes adoptions by social collectivities more than individuals within those collectivities, works with a much larger historical and spatial canvas, and incorporates diffusion as one sort of explanation rather than as the overarching framework. As one example, Fligstein (1985) evaluates five theories of the rise of the multidivisional form across the nation's largest firms over the twentieth century, one of which involves imitation.

[2]The literature on recruitment to activism also emphasizes the effects of network ties. See Curtis & Zurcher (1973), Snow et al (1980), McAdam (1982, 1988), Morris (1984), McAdam & Paulsen (1993), and McCarthy (1996).

Given this context, contemporary diffusion research on social movements and organizations can learn from the classics but should not blindly copy them.

INITIAL ELEMENTS OF A DIFFUSION ARGUMENT

We briefly flag two important concerns that play a role in all kinds of diffusion arguments but that for present purposes are treated contextually rather than within our main story line.

What Is Observed?

While most diffusion research emphasizes that adopters are influenced by immediate or second-hand observation of the diffusing practice, there is often much ambiguity about what is actually observed. Sometimes we treat the potential adopter as exposed to the practice itself. This involves discovering that something is possible, witnessing it in action, or hearing secondhand about its objectives, rationale, and operation. For example, executives may come into contact with poison pills when they sit on the boards of other firms that have instituted them (Davis 1991), managers may learn which markets leading firms enter (Haveman 1993), and activists in Switzerland may hear about protests in the Netherlands (Kriesi et al 1995, Chapter 8).

A potential adopter may also observe the consequences of a practice. To continue the above examples, one might measure contact with companies that had successfully warded off takeovers by wielding the pill, or calculate rates of return for firms that enter various markets, or contrast situations in which protester demands were met to those in which they were not.

The contrast between observing practices and observing their outcomes is tied only loosely to a contrast between diffusion as mimicry and diffusion as social learning. One can readily motivate diffusion in rational choice-theoretic terms even when no information about consequences is provided (Banerjee 1992). And consequences may be implicit in descriptions of the practice or uninterpretable without close local knowledge or a good theory.

Research that directly measures the consequences of adoption elsewhere suggests that both are salient. Conell & Cohn (1995) find that French coal mining strikes were stimulated by other strikes in the same department but most strongly by victorious ones. And Holden (1986) shows that hijacking attempts were stimulated by prior hijackings, especially when a ransom was paid.

In most studies, however, these distinctions are not or cannot be made. We typically know that potential adopters are brought into contact with the diffusing practice but do not know quite what they see, particularly whether they observe results. This inability to specify what is observed produces some theoretical fuzziness about the microprocesses involved in diffusion.

Innovativeness

We also flag the issue of innovativeness, a topic that forms the flip-side of diffusion studies (see Kimberly 1981, Drazin & Schoonhoven 1996 for excellent discussions of the organizational literature). Innovation research asks what makes organizations capable of devising or adopting new technologies and practices.[3]

While some critics have regarded the literature as beyond interpretation (Downs & Mohr 1976), fairly consistent findings emerge (Damanpour 1991). Large, technically specialized organizations with low levels of formalization and centralization tend to innovate rapidly (Burns & Stalker 1961). Exposure to external competition and rapidly shrinking markets provide external spurs to innovation (for example, Osterman 1992, Studer-Ellis 1997). Internally, the adoption of new practices requires the active efforts of innovation champions and a robust coalition for change.

These lines of inquiry are relevant to diffusion analysis but ambiguously so, since they conflate openness to diffusion with internal inventiveness. In addition, diffusion studies tracking specific practices must attend to the congruence between adopter and practice at least as much as generalized innovativeness. Large, technically complex organizations may be quick to adopt innovations designed to handle information overload (Burns & Wholey 1993) but slow to adopt other practices such as "beer bash Fridays."

And while generalized innovativeness and particular congruences help us explain relative adoption rates of specific practices, neither contributes fundamentally to a theoretical analysis of diffusion. For that, we must examine communication and influence within the community where practices diffuse.

SOURCES AND STRUCTURAL MECHANISMS

Diffusion studies are rich in structural mechanisms: characteristic relations between source and adopter that promote diffusion. Conceptual work in the area tends to bring previously overlooked pathways and logics into sharp focus. Among the classics of this genre are Granovetter's "The Strength of Weak Ties" (1973) and DiMaggio & Powell's "The Iron Cage Revisited" (1983).[4]

The discussion builds from perhaps the most central opposition: diffusion into a population (external source or broadcast models) vs diffusion within a population (internal or contagion models). The two may operate in tandem, as

[3]The social movement literature has been much less concerned with variability in innovativeness, though Tilly (1978) and Tarrow (1994) emphasize a long historical evolution toward more flexible repertoires of contention.

[4]DiMaggio & Powell's discussion of homogenizing processes may be read as a conceptual mapping of diffusion mechanisms. Their account of coercive, mimetic, and normative sources of homogeneity intersects at many points with our discussion.

when people heard of John Kennedy's assassination on the radio and ran out into the streets to tell their neighbors. But internal and external sources often play different roles in a diffusion analysis and imply different adoption trajectories.

External Sources

The key external sources in classic diffusion research were mass media outlets like the newspaper, TV, and radio, and change agents such as the Farm Bureau's extension agent and the pharmaceutical company's detail man. Contemporary analyses of diffusion in organizations and social movements point to the same kinds of sources, often viewed more collectively (for example, effects of the national business press or the legal community).

MASS MEDIA The mass media plays a crucial role in amplifying and editing the diffusion of collective action, and much protest today is organized around that fact. Spilerman (1976) explains the temporal clustering of urban riots in the 1960s by arguing that television drew national attention to riots in Newark and Watts, creating a "black solidarity that transcended bounds of communities" (p. 790). Oberschall (1989) argues that the sit-in tactic diffused via the mass media: Students watched what other students were doing on the news and then staged their own sit-ins. Koopmans (1993) points out that the news media do much of the job of social movement organizers during periods of heightened mobilization and conflict.

The business media broadcast the stories of corporate heroes, depict best practice, and advertise managerial innovations and strategies. The business press introduces new innovations with glowing reports and later critiques both adopter and practice as faddish (Abrahamson & Fairchild 1997, Strang 1997). High levels of media attention speed the introduction of innovations like matrix management (Burns & Wholey 1993) and prompts mergers and acquisitions (Haunschild & Beckmann 1997) by providing information that complements that garnered via interorganizational ties.

CHANGE AGENTS Much recent organizational analysis treats the state and the professions as change agents that spread new practices and facilitate particular lines of innovative action. State policy instruments range from coercive mandates to cheerleading and often form a complex balance of the two. For example, Baron et al (1986) trace the diffusion of modern personnel practices to the mandates and infrastructure introduced by the state during World War II. Legislation on equal rights and affirmative action motivated personnel practices that build internal labor markets (Dobbin et al 1993), and weak federal sponsorship of HMOs precipitated state legislation and shifts in HMO population dynamics (Strang & Bradburn 1993).

The professions and other occupational communities form an allied source of new practices. They frequently mediate legal and policy imperatives: Lawyers construct recipes for meeting ambiguous mandates for affirmative action (Edelman 1990, 1992), which human resources professionals translate into standardized procedures (Sutton & Dobbin 1996). The accounting profession devises and disseminates organized responses to changing IRS regulations (Mezias 1990).

Other communities of experts operate more autonomously in the market for corporate efficiency. In the 1980s, organizational consultants and scholars interpreted Japanese business practice for the American manager (Ouchi 1981, Pascale & Athos 1981), and management faculty taught MBAs the virtues of the multidivisional form (Palmer et al 1993). Business consultants also devise and market innovations, from how to become personally effective (Covey 1989) to how to restructure organizations (Hammer & Champy 1994). Expert communities are internally organized and differentiated, most notably in the way academics enter the fray after the battle is over (Strang 1997) and move toward the arguments of practitioners (Barley et al 1988).

In social movements, experts cannot be distinguished so easily from adopters, as activists move seamlessly across the two roles. But it is clear that strategies and tactics are often imported into local settings. Morris (1981) and McAdam (1988) discuss the role of nonviolence workshops and training sessions conducted by outside activists in the civil rights movement. And many movements draw inspiration from social movement gurus such as Gandhi or Edward Abbey (whose book *The Monkey Wrench Gang* promoted controversial tactics like tree-spiking to halt the cutting of timber).

Internal Influence

Internal diffusion processes operate via information and influence flowing within the adopting population. Most often, especially in formal models, the flow is assumed to move grapevine-like from prior to potential adopters. This process focuses attention on interaction networks as the conduits of diffusion.

Classical formal models of intrapopulation diffusion also assume spatial homogeneity, where all members of the population have the same chance of affecting and being affected by each other. But few substantive arguments work this way. Instead, sociologists take advantage of intrapopulation diffusion to search for and document social structure.

COHESION THROUGH STRONG TIES The classic emphasis in analyses of face-to-face interaction treats influence as flowing along the lines of close social relations. Frequent interaction engenders much exchange of information about the character, motivations, and effects of diffusing practices. Particularly when organized by homophily, strong ties lead actors to take the perspective of the other and to exert powerful pressures for conformity.[5] Balance theoretic

[5]Some may recall the often stifling character of these pressures in the setting of the small town; others find a more compelling parallel in the atmosphere of the university department.

notions (Heider 1946) and their generalizations predict homogeneity within cliques (Davis 1967).

Some of these ideas surface in discussions of the benefits of strong, dense networks for organizing collective action. For example, Morris's (1981) account of the diffusion of protest tactics in the civil rights movement points to the strong and durable relationships linking black churches, colleges, and movement organizations such as the Southern Christian Leadership Conference). Mizruchi (1992) finds that corporations that constrain the profits of another firm also tend to influence the other firm's political behavior.

Analyses of organizational cultures and internal decision-making offer parallel accounts. In particular, Friedkin (1984, 1996) combines direct and short indirect paths to produce measures of structural cohesion. The social circles that emerge from this approach locate regions of consensus on controversial policy issues.

NEWS THROUGH WEAK TIES Granovetter (1973) suggests that new information may travel via weak ties rather than strong ones. The argument is that strongly related partners share many ties to third parties and so have little new to report to each other, while the social circles of weakly tied actors overlap less. Presumably the channel capacity of a weak tie is more restricted, however, making it a conduit for news rather than resocialization.

The well-documented role of interlocking directorates in organizational diffusion may perhaps be best understood as analogous to a weak interpersonal tie (though they are often discussed under the rubric of cohesion). These structures permit "business scan" (Useem 1984), as top managers gain a glimpse of what other firms do. For example, firms are more likely to adopt poison pill defenses against hostile takeover (Davis 1991), to adopt multidimensional forms (Palmer et al 1993), and to engage in takeover efforts (Haunschild 1993) if their managers sit on the boards of firms that have previously engaged in these activities.

The analogy to Granovetter's weak ties is not entirely apt, since board interlocks familiarize executives with novel strategies more than inform them of their existence (Davis 1991). But it seems implausible that board interlocks produce a parallel to the mutual socialization produced by cohesive interpersonal relations. Overall, board interlocks appear a relatively thin sort of linkage important for the flow of information about "high" corporate strategy (for example, mergers, CEO compensation, and prestigious innovations such as massive downsizing), but they are less relevant to other kinds of organizational innovations.

In the study of social movements, collective action often diffuses via weak ties carrying the news of what others have done. Rude (1964) points to the diffusion of collective action along transportation routes in England and France between 1730 and 1848, where travelers carried the news. Skinner (1964) details the intervillage networks facilitating peasant rebellions in China.

Bohstedt & Williams (1988) argue that market networks facilitated the spread of food riots across Devonshire in the late eighteenth century. And Gould (1991) shows how weak ties among Parisian neighborhoods helped mobilize support for the Paris Commune.

STRUCTURAL EQUIVALENCE AND COMPETITION Burt (1987) argues that structurally equivalent actors (those possessing similar ties to others) attend carefully to each other. He motivates the argument via a logic of competition: We keep up with the Joneses because we cannot afford to fall behind, most importantly in managing our mutual relation to the Smiths. As Friedkin (1984) observes, however, apparent diffusion via structural equivalence may represent the effects of similar patterns of contact with third parties.

Reanalyses of Coleman et al's *Medical Innovation* find that structurally equivalent doctors tend to adopt in tandem (Strang & Tuma 1993, Burt 1987). Galaskiewicz & Burt (1991) show that structurally equivalent pairs of corporate loan officers had closely aligned perspectives on local charities. And Mizruchi (1992) finds indirect interlocks to financial institutions a strong predictor of similar political contributions (though as Mizruchi notes, this may be interpreted as bank influence).

More prosaic forms of competition also generate mimicry. Much evidence suggests that firms in competition are highly responsive to each other's efforts at innovation. Japanese managerial and production practices diffused most quickly to firms exposed to external competition (Osterman 1992). Firms mimic those in their industry (Fligstein 1985, 1990), and states the policies of other states (Zhou 1993). In the social movements arena, Tarrow (1989a) argues that competition between protest organizations drives the diffusion of disruptive tactics as groups seek to outbid each other.

But these examples suggest that while competition often spurs imitation, it may also spur differentiation. Firms and social movements want to keep up with their competitors—but they also want to outdo them and to keep their distance. Thus Greve (1995, 1996) shows that radio stations do not imitate the strategic moves of stations in local markets (which would intensify competition). Instead, decisions are influenced by the behavior of sister stations in other markets and the behaviors that those sister stations come into contact with. Becker (1998) suggests that local congregations distance their programs and mission from other local congregations of the same denomination (with whom they most directly compete for adherents) while learning from congregations of other denominations.

PRESTIGE While the above social relations are all symmetric, adopters may be influenced strongly by prestigious, central actors in ways that are not reciprocated. Both social psychological and structural mechanisms are involved:

Lower ranking community members aspire to be like prestigious others, find it useful to resemble powerful leaders, and adoptions by central actors shift community norms or interaction patterns sufficiently that others find it hard not to go along.

For example, Fligstein (1990) argues that models of management diffuse from central firms to the larger business community as they prove their utility in responding to new politico-economic conditions. Haveman (1993) shows that deregulation led thrifts to follow large, financially profitable thrifts into new markets. And Han (1994) argues that mid-sized companies use the accounting firms that the largest firms in their industry employ, while large firms seek to differentiate themselves from each other.[6]

SPATIAL PROXIMITY Perhaps the most common finding in diffusion research is that spatially proximate actors influence each other. No distinctive logic can be proposed—rather, spatial proximity facilitates all kinds of interaction and influence. Where network relations are not mapped directly, proximity often provides the best summary of the likelihood of mutual awareness and interdependence.

In some work, spatial proximity is measured by pairwise distances. Knoke (1982) shows effects of geographic proximity on the spread of municipal reform. Hedstrom (1994) shows how the Swedish trade union movement expanded geographically. Petras & Zeitlin (1967) argue that radical ideology in Chile (measured by support for Allende) spread from mining communities to adjacent agricultural communities. And in a careful reanalysis of Spilerman's data using event history methods, Myers (1997) finds that the propensity to riot falls with distance from cities where riots have occurred.

Other studies examine contagion within spatially defined regions that may possess both high levels of interaction and a common sense of identity. For example, Davis & Greve (1997) point to the diffusion of golden parachutes via local business communities, while Burns & Wholey (1993) locate regional influences on the adoption of matrix management.[7]

CULTURAL CATEGORIES Finally, reference groups may be culturally constructed around common status and purpose rather than as dense webs of interaction. McAdam & Rucht (1993) point to the importance of cultural categories such as "activist" in promoting the spread of tactics where relational ties are thin. Chaves (1996) finds that the ordination of women was contagious within groups of denominations defined by shared theological orientations. And in a

[6]Like all other communities, organizations and social movements display prestige orderings (see Schrum & Wuthnow 1988, Fombrun & Shanley 1990).

[7]Tolnay et al (1996) find a surprising negative diffusion effect of geographic proximity on lynchings (and also exhaustion rather than contagion within counties). They argue that lynchings are a social control mechanism whose memory lingers in the local population.

direct comparison of a variety of diffusion channels, Soule (1997) shows that shantytown protests diffused between similar kinds of campuses (for example, between research universities) rather than within regions.

Culturally defined similarity may also inspire organizational arrangements that press for homogeneity. Strang & Chang (1993) show that the International Labor Organization has spurred the adoption and expansion of social security programs, particularly by the welfare laggards of the industrialized world (though the United States proved immune). Soule & Zylan (1997) find that AF(D)C reforms diffused within relevant administrative groupings rather than traditionally defined regions.

CULTURAL BASES OF DIFFUSION

Both theory and empirical work generally focus on the sorts of structural bases for diffusion catalogued above. But this is only part of the story. Structural opportunities for meaningful contact cannot tell us what sorts of practices are likely to diffuse, and such opportunities may lead to conflict or boundary formation as well as to diffusion.

An analysis of the cultural (in some usage, institutional) bases of diffusion speaks more directly to what spreads, replacing a theory of connections with a theory of connecting. We emphasize three lines of analysis: discussion of the interpretive work that catalyzes flow, inspection of the diffusion industries whose stock in trade is discourse, and examination of how empirical diffusion patterns are related to the cultural status of the diffusing item.

Interpretive Work as Mediating Diffusion

Cultural approaches emphasize that a self-consciously interpretive process underlies most adoption (though there is a place for unthinking mimicry and hysterical contagion; see Kerckhoff & Back 1968). Strang & Meyer (1993) discuss how practices are theorized in terms of general models and causal relationships. Snow & Benford (1992) apply Goffman's notion of a frame: an "interpretive schema that simplifies and condenses the 'world out there' by punctuating and encoding objects, situations, events, experiences, and sequences of action." (p. 137). Lillrank (1995) portrays the interpretive process as one of translating concrete practices into abstractions for export and then unpacking the abstraction into a (suitably modified) concrete practice upon arrival. Jointly, the argument is that practices diffuse as they are rendered salient, familiar, and compelling.[8]

Strang's (1997) inquiry into the American reception of quality circles explores theorization via a content analysis of public discourse. Articles in the

[8]Differences between these ideas have to do with the types of cultural materials viewed as most powerful (professional/scientific accounts vs cultural metaphors) and the patterns of diffusion anticipated (substantial homogeneity vs tailored differences).

business literature are coded for the claims they make about quality circles. The Japanese practice is found to have been theorized under two different frames, a dominant human relations interpretation and an undertheorized problem-solving one. These public discourses help us understand how and why American companies experimented with quality circles.

Snow (1993) examines framing in the importation of Nichiro Shoshu/Saka-gakkai (NSS), a Japanese-based Buddhist movement, into the United States. He emphasizes that the incorporation of American cultural symbols by the NSS has facilitated the movement's expansion and viability. The NSS displays national symbols such as the American flag in its ceremonies, directs members to be winners (a decidedly non-Buddhist ideal), and peppers its communiqués with American archetypes such as the pioneering spirit and town meetings.[9]

Perhaps the richest analysis of interpretation is Hirsch's (1986) discussion of the language associated with hostile takeovers. This imagery shifts dramatically over time, as initially stark portrayals of hostile takeovers as crimes committed by outsiders are replaced by a more complex, richer imagery of shootouts, Big Hat Boys, rescues, and Snow Whites. Hirsch treats this language as a cultural phenomenon that evolves along with takeover behavior and its social location within the business community, initially framing resistance and later framing acceptance.

In addition to generating interesting stories, attention to the interpretive work underlying diffusion has two main implications. It points out that practices do not flow: Theorized models and careful framings do. And it argues that interpretive work selects and transforms diffusing practices: Not all practices can be theorized or framed, and none come out of the process unmodified.

Fashion-Setting Communities

Interpretive work promoting diffusion is accomplished by both sources and adopters; sometimes the source, sometimes the adopter, and sometimes both play an active role (Snow & Benford 1995). But cultural approaches to diffusion direct particular attention to the external communities whose members make their living promulgating innovation and commenting on change. These others (Meyer 1995) have access and influence largely to the extent that their interpretive frames are compelling to decision makers, and so here we see much attention to the cultural conditions for diffusion.

Today, the management fashion industry is very big business. While the theorization and hyping of organizational action has always been fundamental to managing (Eccles & Nohria 1992), a strong trend toward the externalization

[9]Similarly, the shantytown tactic may have diffused rapidly in the college divestment movement because it provided a clear and compelling frame for the conflict emphasizing the living conditions of South African blacks. There is little evidence that use of the tactic prompted university divestment (Soule 1998).

of organizational analysis is apparent. The consultant, guru, and management scholar populations are on the rise, as are the output of the business press and the sales of business books (see Micklethwait & Wooldridge 1996).

Researchers have begun to probe the content of the business fashion-setting business. Barley & Kunda (1992) argue that managerial discourse oscillates between rational and normative models of organizing. Periods dominated by a master narrative of rationalism facilitate the construction, dissemination, and contagiousness of practices such as systems analysis, time and motion studies, and reengineering. Periods marked by a narrative of normative integration enhance the diffusion of human relations techniques and culture engineering.

These rhetorical frames appear to be the product of both local conditions and the cultural materials available in even wider societal frames. Barley & Kunda (1992) suggest that the rational-normative opposition reflects a deep antimony in Western culture that is regulated by temporal segregation. Shenhav (1995) links the rise of the Taylorist model to the professional mobility project of engineers, labor unrest, and the society-wide frame of Progressivism. And Abrahamson (1997) finds that turnover and labor union activity help explain the postemergence prevalence of normative rhetorics such as the human relations movement.

Collective discourses on narrower organizational practices also exhibit important regularities (Abrahamson 1996, Abrahamson & Fairchild 1997). Innovations have observable latency periods before bursting onto the scene and replace each other in quick succession. These dynamics seem to arise both from processes internal to the fashion industry and from exogenous drivers. Fashion setters must move on lest others catch up, and norms of progress mandate that old wine be placed in new bottles. Nor can fashions predicated on Japanese industrial superiority easily withstand a crash on the Nisei.

Discursive frames also arise in the social movement arena. Gamson & Mondigliani (1989) trace shifts in the discussions of nuclear power that enabled or disabled various forms of protest. The various media also apply characteristic modes of inquiry and representation. For example, newspapers editorialize while television is guided by a particular conception of balanced reporting where two sides of every issue are located and represented. Tarrow (1989) argues that the media's attention to the sensational produces spirals of more controversial action—an insight that might also be applied to organizational innovation.

The Cultural Status of the Diffusing Practice

Practices that accord with cultural understandings of appropriate and effective action tend to diffuse more quickly than those that do not. Strang (1990) shows that decolonization spread rapidly because it resonated with increasingly salient models of national community, popular sovereignty, and expanded participation. Hirsch (1986) notes that the frequency of hostile takeovers increased as the practice was symbolically legitimated, and Tolbert & Zucker (1983) find that the pace of civil service reform accelerated after professional groups came to consensus on its virtues.

Menzel (1960) organizes the results of much early diffusion research by observing that centrally placed actors are early adopters of culturally legitimate innovations, whereas illegitimate innovations are adopted by "marginal men" unconstrained by community norms. Contemporary research suggests similar patterns. For example, Kraatz & Zajac (1996) find that poor, failing liberal arts colleges adopt professional programs inconsistent with their larger identity. Leblebici et al (1991) note that fringe players were the carriers of innovations that challenged and repeatedly transformed the institutional structure of radio. Stearns & Allan (1996) argue that peripheral firms set off merger waves by responding quickly to changing political and economic conditions.

Strang & Meyer (1993) suggest that the more successfully theorized a diffusing practice is, the less its diffusion will be relationally structured. The notion is that an easily communicated, strongly legitimated innovation requires less local promotion and mutual sense-making than a practice that is hard to understand and motivate.[10] Davis & Greve (1997) make this point in a study of the diffusion of poison pill and golden parachute responses to the threat of hostile mergers. They find that the pill diffused rapidly via board interlocks, whereas parachutes spread slowly within local business communities. Davis & Greve argue that the public legitimacy of the poison pill permitted the relatively thin, information-carrying medium of corporate board contacts to channel adoption, while the scandalous parachute required mutual reassurance within business communities.

However, bandwagons are increasingly unlikely to form as illegitimacy rises in the eyes of adopters. For example, Kraatz & Zajac (1996) find no evidence of contagion in professional program adoption by liberal arts schools—colleges introducing these programs look more like defectors bowing to financial need than participants in a social movement for educational relevance. And Baker & Faulkner (1997) point to the extreme case of a real-estate swindle, whose perpetrators must minimize publicity and interaction.

A WIDER COMPARATIVE LENS

The most common design in diffusion research treats variability in the timing of adoption of a single practice across a single community (a relationally and culturally connected population). Almost all of the previously mentioned stud-

[10]In a convergent vein, Tarrow (1994) argues that modular forms of protest like the boycott and the mass petition supported more widespread action and faster diffusion because they could be flexibly utilized against different opponents and in service of different causes.

ies are of this type. Much less work compares rates, patterns, and causal mechanisms across settings. We emphasize work that promotes a broader comparative analysis.

Cycles of Protest and Innovation

Diffusion processes may play a role in more complex webs of action and reaction. For social movements, the tendency of diffusion dynamics to spread and amplify protest is opposed by increasingly strong responses by the state. Pitcher et al (1978) present an early formal model of the instigation and inhibition of collective violence as learning processes. Olzak (1992) models the dynamics of collective action as the combined result of contagion and exhaustion effects.

Tarrow (1989, 1994) points to a larger set of dynamics producing protest cycles like the American civil rights–to–antiwar cycle of the 1960s. Cycles are periods of heightened conflict when new ideas are developed rapidly and diffuse across movement organizations that support, compete, and learn from one another.[11] These cycles exhibit at least three kinds of diffusion: (*a*) Collective action spreads across space and sectors (class conflict might move from heavy to light industry). (*b*) New frames of meaning diffuse across as well as within movements (for example, the rubric of "rights" spread from the civil rights to the women's movement). And (*c*) novel tactics, such as the sit-in, are forged and diffuse within protest cycles.

McAdam (1995) elaborates this model in a discussion of relationships between initiator movements (such as Solidarity in Poland) and the spin-off movements that follow. Meyer & Whittier (1994) describe the strong influence of the women's movement on the ideas, tactics, and organizational structure of the 1980s peace movement.

Business communities display parallel dynamics in cycles of technological and managerial innovation. For example, the 1980s and 1990s have been a hotbed of efforts to transform organizations. Progressive firms such as Motorola, managerial consultants such as CSC Index, and gurus like Tom Peters are the carriers of a variety of strategies for enhancing quality, speeding innovation, downsizing, and empowering workers. These movements spread from firm to firm, often following a core-periphery pattern (from big manufacturing and high-tech to services to education and government). They compete but also learn from and build on each other, as opposing strategies such as TQM and reengineering become hard to distinguish in practice.

[11]Soule & Tarrow (1991) explore perhaps the first modern cycle of protest in the revolutions of 1848. Both spatial patterns in the temporal incidence of collective action and qualitative evidence make it clear that protest was diffusing across countries (mobs in Germany carried French flags and sang French songs). The rate of diffusion in this era of slower mass communications is startling.

Same Practice, Different Communities

A tale from a Korean village (Rogers & Kinkaid 1981) suggests the importance of cultural context. Family planning in the village of Oryu Li faced strong resistance from husbands, who beat their wives if they tried it. It spread only after a mother's club not only promoted contraception but restructured the distribution of power in the village. Led by the indefatigable Mrs. Choi, the club bought the local wineshop and fired its "chopstick girls," raised a pig, manufactured uniforms and sold them at a profit, and accumulated sufficient funds to buy much of the land surrounding the village. What would have occurred through contagious diffusion in a Midwestern town was in Oryu Li a saga of heroism, collective action, and changing gender roles.

In less dramatic fashion, explicit comparisons of diffusion processes across national societies demonstrate the operation of structural factors that would otherwise be missed. Cole (1985, 1989) argues that the diffusion patterns of small group activities in three countries were molded by national infrastructures for diffusion. In Japan and Sweden, central organizations bankrolled by industry promoted and oversaw the diffusion of best practice. The American business sector lacked such institutions, and instead business consultants operated in a free-for-all market for innovation.[12] Cole argues that the absence of a larger infrastructure led to tepid and faddish diffusion, where business consultants gained little access to top decision-makers and watered down their wares for mass promotion.

Guillen (1994) examines the reception of several major schools of management across four countries. He focuses on the impact of national cultural discourse, structures of state and occupational power, and business interests. For example, elite mentalities of modernism and a strong engineering profession hastened German use of scientific management techniques, while Spain's traditional humanism, labor unrest, and weak engineering profession led Taylorism to wilt on the vine.

Different Practices, Same Community

Comparisons of different practices diffusing in a single population or the same practice diffusing in different communities often highlight how cultural understandings shape adoption patterns. The work of Davis & Greve (1997) described above is very much in this line. Another example is Mizruchi & Fein's (1997) analysis of how authors have employed DiMaggio & Powell's (1983) concepts of coercive, mimetic, and normative mechanisms producing isomorphism. They find the greatest reference to mimetic processes, and argue that

[12]One does see a state-sponsored infrastructure in the American health sector, with its experiments, subsidized models, and regional innovation-diffusion centers (Fennell & Warnecke 1988).

this follows from the resonance of the idea of rational copying given the view that organizations are autonomous and are rational actors.

Rowan (1982) provides a more structural analysis of legitimation, arguing that innovations diffuse rapidly when core actors are in agreement and fizzle when they are not. For example, curriculum reform was adopted rapidly by school districts when the state legislature, the state educational agency, and the teacher's association supported the same model. School districts disregarded curricular innovations when this consensus fell apart (for example, when the legislature regarded new texts as too radical).

Shifts in Causal Effects During Diffusion

Finally, much research looks for shifts in causal processes as diffusion unfolds. The most influential such analysis is Tolbert & Zucker's (1983) discussion of how local rationality is replaced by conformity to institutional models. They argue that civil service reforms diffused slowly in the nineteenth century in ways consistent with relevant city characteristics. After 1915, when civil service practices had become widely legitimated in professional circles, reform diffused rapidly and indiscriminately.

A related logic of crescive institutionalization appears in organizational studies that examine the changing effect of prior adoptions (rather than conduct a separate discourse analysis). For example, Burns & Wholey (1993) find temporal decline in the effects of internal predictors and a growing effect of regional adoption in the diffusion of matrix management among hospitals. Budros (1997) shows that the internal precipitants of corporate downsizing weaken over time while the overall bandwagon effect grows.[13]

Much work on national educational and welfare policy finds similar dynamics. Welfare policy adoption early in the twentieth century was tied to economic transformations and development, whereas after World War II policies were adopted rapidly everywhere (Collier & Messick 1975). Educational systems were tied closely to national characteristics in the nineteenth century but spread in broadcast fashion in the twentieth century (Meyer et al 1992).

Westphal et al (1997) extend this well-documented institutionalization model in analysis of TQM practices across hospitals. Breaking with standard practice, they examine the relationship between the timing of adoption and what gets adopted, contrasting conventional implementation of TQM models (measured as closeness to average use and to theoretical models) with customization of TQM to local conditions. Early adopters are shown to customize while late adopters adopt conventional forms, and network ties to adopters en-

[13]Coefficient values for contagion are rather stable across the three historical periods of downsizing that Budros studies. But since the covariate (prior downsizing efforts) is rising continuously, the total effect of prior adoptions increases over time.

courage customization early and conventionality late. They further show that conformity to TQM standards is positively related to hospital legitimacy but negatively related to efficiency.

FORMAL MODELS AND ESTIMATION

Interest in diffusion has stimulated much attention to models and methods that capture the interdependence in outcomes central to contagion. This work builds upon the larger movement toward the dynamic analysis of longitudinal data. We briefly note the range of approaches and research strategies characteristic of quantitative analysis of diffusion.

Point-to-Point Processes

Early modeling work in diffusion arose out of attempts to fit curves to cumulative adoption patterns. The key theoretical discovery was that contagion implied the commonly observed S-shaped cumulative adoption curve. A standard mixed model combining both external and internal sources of diffusion (see Bartholomew 1982; Mahajan & Peterson 1985 for a review) gives

$$\lim_{\Delta t \to 0} \frac{\Pr[S(t+\Delta t)=s+1|S(t)=s]}{\Delta t} = [\alpha + \beta s(t)]n(t). \qquad 1.$$

Models of contagion have been pursued in two main directions. The first is to draw inferences about underlying mechanisms from the shape of the adoption curve. The classic example is Coleman et al's (1966) demonstration of differing temporal patterns of adoption for socially integrated and isolated doctors. Hernes (1972) and Diekmann (1989) find that marital rates resemble a diffusion process marked by increasing ardor but declining suitability. Yamaguchi (1994) shows that Hernes-type models provide a good fit to simple diffusion processes across simulated networks.

The more common strategy, however, is to model empirical diffusion processes at the individual level, writing event history formulations of Equation 1 that incorporate hypothesized interdependencies between adopters (Strang 1991, Morris 1993). For example, Davis (1992) analyzes the transmission of poison pill strategies by counting board interlocks with prior adopters; Zhou (1993) examines the diffusion of occupational licensing by counting the number of states with laws in place.

Strang & Tuma (1993) formalize and extend this strategy, proposing a heterogeneous diffusion framework that models the hazard as

$$r_n(t) = \exp\left[\alpha' \mathrm{x}_n + \sum_{s \in S(t)} \left(\beta' \mathrm{v}_n + \gamma' \mathrm{w}_s + \delta' \mathrm{z}_{ns}\right)\right]$$

for the multiplicative case and a related form for additive effects of contagion. This framework permits direct examination of intrinsic propensities to adopt, generalized susceptibility to influence, the infectiousness of prior adopters, and social proximity to be estimated via SAS macros (Strang 1995) or RATE (Tuma 1994). Simulation work (Greve et al 1995) indicates that heterogeneous diffusion models can be estimated robustly with complete data on populations and have some application when data is incomplete.

Spatial regression models (Doreian 1981, Marsden & Friedkin 1993) form a parallel strategy for estimating the effects of interdependence where outcomes are continuous—for example, if we studied the extensiveness of downsizing or the size of demonstrations. Models take the form

$$y = \rho W y + X\beta + \varepsilon \qquad 3.$$

where W represents the hypothesized structure of interdependence. While full information methods are unwieldy, Anselin (1988) and Land & Deane (1992) present estimation techniques that shortcut these problems and make spatial regression modeling widely accessible.

Few methods are available for recovering network structures of influence from data, as opposed to the hypothesis tests that heterogeneous diffusion and spatial regression models permit. Mantel (1967) develops a general permutation test for spatiotemporal clustering. This approach can be used to investigate network effects with a very general autocorrelation structure (Krackhardt 1988), though temporal ordering is sacrificed. Strang (1996) suggests the study of multiple adoption processes to identify network influence structures.

Threshold Processes

Models of threshold processes break with the notion of direct contagion to view potential adopters as responsive to the distribution of present adopters in the population (Granovetter 1978, Schelling 1978). For example, it seems plausible that white flight from cities is based on response to racial proportions rather than to direct encounters. Granovetter (1978) emphasizes the nonlinear dynamics produced by variation in individual thresholds, and Valente (1995) proposes local thresholds for reference groups based on direct network ties.

But thresholds have been difficult to establish empirically, with more use of revealed thresholds to describe adoption patterns (see Granovetter & Soong 1988, pp. 99–102; Valente 1995) than application of threshold models to predict behavior. Threshold processes are hard to identify if we need to locate both the reference group and the threshold. In the only explicit effort to locate thresholds of which we are aware, analysis of 85 policies diffusing across the United States provided no evidence of regional or national thresholds in state policy adoption (Strang 1996).

But other evidence does suggest that adopters often respond to combinations of signals. For example, Hagerstrand (1967) found that the spatial pattern of rural diffusion resembled that generated by simulations where two contacts with prior adopters led to adoption (simulations based on single contacts produced greater spatial scatter than was observed in empirical maps). And Asch (1951) demonstrated that nearly total opposition was required to induce most subjects to disbelieve their own eyes.

PIOUS HOPES FOR FUTURE RESEARCH

Design

While single-population, single-practice research designs will no doubt continue to dominate the diffusion literature, theoretical development would benefit from a larger comparative lens. Considerable insight has been developed on a case-by-case basis into the mechanisms behind the diffusion of a variety of important and interesting social practices. But insights are unlikely to be integrated, or analysts spurred to theorize more aggressively, without the challenges posed by comparative research.

Direct contrasts of diffusing practices can provide more nuanced views of the mechanisms involved, as the work of Davis & Greve (1997) illustrates. Independent studies of poison pills and golden parachutes would likely have asserted incompatible claims about the types of relational structures that underlie diffusion. Their joint analysis led to a deeper argument about how cultural meanings affect the strength of alternative diffusion mechanisms.

More attention to how innovations compete and support each other is also needed. In the social movement arena, many students of collective action are beginning to question the movement-centric focus that case studies reinforce. Attention to how tactics, strategies, symbols, and frames diffuse across movements produces a richer picture well worth the research investment. And studies of organizational diffusion would do well to place mutually evolving innovations in relation to each other rather than analyze them seriatim.

Finally, we call for examination of practices that fail to diffuse. There is a strong selection bias in diffusion research, where investigators choose ultimately popular practices as appropriate candidates for study. Investigation of practices that few adopt would provide a more balanced picture.

Study of practices that fail to diffuse would also shed light on those that do. For example, we noted above that the rapid diffusion of the shantytown tactic in the divestment movement may have flowed from its iconographic immediacy and symbolic power. Comparison to concrete tactics that were attempted but didn't diffuse (campus sleep-ins, for example) could examine this proposition, along with arguments about other attributes of tactics relevant to collective action (how they are repressed, how they build activist solidarity, how they appear on television, and whether they lead to desired results).

Substance

Relational analysis has been the backbone of diffusion research in sociology. But ideas based on interpersonal relations translate unclearly into situations where collective actors such as organizations are the adopters. The tendency to refer to the effect of any direct tie as cohesion is symptomatic (particularly since the ties under discussion often seem so weak). More important, the elaborate analyses of diffusion and diffusion-like dynamics mounted at the individual level (work such as that of Burt, Carley, Doreian, Friedkin, Macy, and Marsden) do far more with the network metaphor than analyses of collective actors seem able to pull off.

The problem is that collective actor parallels to face-to-face interaction are not as vivid or meaningful as the real thing. Valuable insights into diffusion trajectories have been garnered by analysis of interlocking directorates, geographic proximity, and culturally analyzed similarities as diffusion channels. But there is a need for close attention to what sort of information and influence flows through these channels. And it would be useful to develop models of interorganizational structure less colored by an analogy to direct interpersonal interaction.

Finally, the fashion setters who construct and disseminate new practices deserve renewed attention. Diffusion dynamics seem increasingly volatile, and diffusing practices increasingly constructed, as interpretive work is externalized in public discourse. Study of the media, consultants, and professional communities permits attention to cultural work and forms of agency that adopter-centric research overlooks. The impact of vibrant diffusion industries on the political and the business scene has hardly begun to be tapped.

ACKNOWLEDGMENTS

We thank Pam Haunschild, Heather Haveman, Woody Powell, and Sid Tarrow for their helpful suggestions.

Literature Cited

Abrahamson E. 1996. Management fashion. *Acad. Manage. Rev.* 21:254–85

Abrahamson E. 1997. The emergence and prevalence of employee management rhetorics: the effects of long waves, labor unions, and turnover, 1875 to 1992. *Acad. Manage. J.* 40:491–533

Abrahamson E, Fairchild G. 1997. *Manage-*

ment fashion: lifecycles, triggers, and collective learning processes. Paper presented at the Annu. Meet. Acad. Manage.

Anselin L. 1988. *Spatial Econometrics: Methods and Models*. Boston: Kluwer

Asch S. 1951. Effects of group pressure upon the modification and distortion of judgement. In *Groups, Leadership and Men*, ed. H. Guetzkow, pp. 177–96. Pittsburgh: Carnegie Press

Baker WE, Faulkner RR. 1997. *The diffusion of fraud.* Paper presented at the White Tie Event, San Diego, CA

Banerjee AV. 1992. A simple model of herd behavior. *Q. J. Econ.* 107:797–817

Barley SR, Kunda, G. 1992. Design and devotion: surges of rational and normative ideologies of control in managerial discourse. *Admin. Sci. Q.* 37:363–99

Barley SR, Meyer GW, Gash DC. 1988. Cultures of culture: academics, practitioners, and the pragmatics of normative control. *Admin. Sci. Q.* 33:24–57

Baron JN, Dobbin F, Jennings PD. 1986. War and peace: the evolution of modern personnel administration in US industry. *Am. J. Sociol.* 92:350–383

Becker PE. 1998. *Culture and Conflict: Institutions and the Moral Order of Local Religious Life*. New York: Cambridge Univ. Press

Bohstedt J, Williams D. 1988. The diffusion of riots: the patterns of 1766, 1795, and 1801 in Devonshire. *J. Interdisc. Hist.* 19:1–24

Budros A. 1997. *Historical analysis and the adoption of organizational innovations: the case of downsizing programs.* Paper presented at Annu. Meet. Am. Sociol. Assoc., Toronto

Burns LR, Wholey DR. 1993. Adoption and abandonment of matrix management programs: effects of organizational characteristics and interorganizational networks. *Acad. Manage. J.* 36:106–38

Burns T, Stalker GM. 1961. *The Management of Innovation*. London:Tavistock

Burt RS. 1987. Social contagion and innovation: cohesion versus structural equivalence. *Am. J. Sociol.* 92:1287–1335

Carley K. 1990. Structural constraints on communication: the diffusion of the homomorphic signal analysis technique through scientific fields. *J. Math. Sociol.* 15: 207–46

Chaves M. 1996. Ordaining women: the diffusion of an organizational innovation. *Am. J. Sociol.* 101:840–74

Cole RE. 1985. The macropolitics of organizational change: a comparative analysis of the spread of small-group activities. *Admin. Sci. Q.* 30:560–85

Cole RE. 1989. *Strategies for Learning*. Berkeley, CA: Univ. Calif. Press

Coleman JS, Katz E, Menzel H. 1966. *Medical Innovation*. New York: Bobbs-Merrill

Collier D, Messick R. 1975. Prerequisites versus diffusion: testing alternative explanations of social security adoption. *Am. Poli. Sci. Rev.* 69:1299–1315

Conell C, Cohn S. 1995. Learning from other people's actions: environmental variation and diffusion in French coal mining strikes, 1890–1935. *Am. J. Sociol.* 101: 366–403

Curtis RL, Zurcher LA. 1973. Stable resources of protest movement: the multi-organizational field. *Soc. Forces* 2:53–60

Damanpour F. 1991. Organizational innovation: a meta-analysis of effects of determinants and moderators. *Acad. Manage. J.* 34:555–90

Davis GF. 1991. Agents without principles? the spread of the Poison Pill through the intercorporate network. *Admin. Sci. Q.* 36: 583–613

Davis GF, Greve HR. 1997. Corporate elite networks and governance changes in the 1980s. *Am. J. Sociol.* 103:1–37

Davis JA. 1967. Clustering and structural balance in graphs. *Hum. Relat.* 20:131–7

Diekmann A. 1989. Diffusion and survival models for the process of entry into marriage. *J. Math. Sociol.* 14:31–44

DiMaggio PJ, Powell WW. 1983. The iron cage revisited: institutional isomorphism and collective rationality in organizational fields. *Am. Sociol. Rev.* 48: 147–160

Dobbin F, Sutton JR, Meyer JW, Scott WR. 1993. Equal opportunity law and the construction of internal labor markets. *Am. J. Sociol.* 99:396–427

Doreian P. 1981. Estimating linear models in spatially distributed data. In *Sociological Methodology*, ed. S Leinhardt, pp. 359–388. San Francisco: Jossey-Bass

Downs GW Jr, Mohr LB. 1976. Conceptual issues in the study of innovation. *Admin. Sci. Q.* 21:700–714

Drazin R, Schoonhoven CB. 1996. Community, population, and organizational effects on innovation: a multilevel perspective. *Acad. Manage. J.* 39:1065–83

Eccles RG, Nohria N. 1992. *Beyond the Hype.* Cambridge, MA: Harvard Bus. Sch. Press

Edelman LB. 1990. Legal environments and organizational governance: the expansion of due process in the American workplace. *Am. J. Sociol.* 95:1401–40

Edelman LB. 1992. Legal ambiguity and symbolic structures: organizational mediation of civil rights law. *Am. J. Sociol.* 97: 1531–76

Fligstein N. 1985. The spread of the multidivisional form. *Am. Sociol. Rev.* 50: 377–91

Fligstein N. 1990. *The Transformation of Corporate Control.* Cambridge, MA: Harvard Univ. Press

Fombrun C, Shanley M. 1990. What's in a name? Reputation building and corporate strategy. *Acad. Manage. J.* 33:233–58

Friedkin NE. 1984. Structural cohesion and equivalence explanations of social homogeneity. *Sociol. Meth. Res.* 12:235–61

Friedkin NE. 1996. A Structural Theory of Social Influence. Cambridge, UK: Cambridge Univ. Press

Galaskiewicz J, Burt RS. 1991. Interorganizational contagion in corporate philanthropy. *Admin. Sci. Q.* 36:88–105

Gamson WA, Mondigliani A. 1989. Media discourse and public opinion on nuclear power: a constructionist approach. *Am. J. Sociol.* 95:1–37

Granovetter MS. 1978. Threshold models of collective behavior. *Am. J. Sociol.* 836: 1420–43

Granovetter MS. 1973. The strength of weak ties. *Am. J. Sociol.* 78:1360–80

Granovetter MS, Soong R. 1988. Threshold models of diversity: Chinese restaurants, residential segregation, and the spiral of silence. In *Sociological Methodology,* ed. C Clogg, pp. 69–104. Washington, DC: Am. Sociol. Assoc.

Greve HR. 1995. Jumping ship: the diffusion of strategy abandonment. *Admin. Sci. Q.* 40:444–73

Greve HR. 1996. Patterns of competition: the diffusion of a market position in radio broadcasting. *Admin. Sci. Q.* 41:29–60

Greve HR, Strang D, Tuma NB. 1995. Specification and estimation of heterogeneous diffusion models. In *Sociological Methodology,* ed. PV Marsden, p. 377–420. New York: Blackwell

Guillen MF. 1994. *Models of Management: Work, Authority and Organization in Comparative Perspective.* Chicago, IL: Univ. Chicago Press

Hagerstrand T. 1967. *Innovation Diffusion as a Spatial Process.* Chicago, IL: Univ. Chicago Press

Han SK. 1994. Mimetic isomorphism and its effect on the Audit Services market. *Soc. Forces* 73:637–63

Haunschild PR. 1993. Interorganizational imitation: the impact of interlocks on corporate acquisition activity. *Admin. Sci. Q.* 38:564–92

Haunschild PR, Beckman C. 1997. When do interlocks matter? Alternative sources of information and interlock influence. Technical Report, Graduate School of Business, Stanford Univ.

Haveman HA. 1993. Follow the leader: mimetic isomorphism and entry into new markets. *Admin. Sci. Q.* 38:593–627

Hedstrom P. 1994. Contagious collectivities: on the spatial diffusion of Swedish trade unions, 1890–1940. *Am. J. Sociol.* 99: 1157–79

Heider F. 1946. Attitudes and cognitive organization. *J. Psychol.* 21:107–12

Hernes G. 1972. The process of entry into first marriage. *Am. Sociol. Rev.* 37:173–82

Hirsch PM. 1986. From ambushes to golden parachutes: corporate takeovers as an instance of cultural framing and institutional integration. *Am. J. Sociol.* 91:800–37

Holden RT. 1986. The contagiousness of aircraft hijacking. *Am. J. Sociol.* 91:874–904

Kerckhoff AC, Back KW. 1968. *The June Bug: A Study of Hysterical Contagion.* New York: Meredith

Kimberly JR. 1981. Managerial innovation. In *Handbook of Organizational Design,* ed. WH Starbuck, PC Nystrom, pp. 84–104. New York: Oxford Univ. Press

Knoke D. 1982. The spread of municipal reform: temporal, spatial, and social dynamics. *Am. J. Sociol.* 87:1314–39

Koopmans R. 1993. The dynamics of protest waves: West Germany, 1965 to 1989. *Am. Sociol. Rev.* 58:637–58

Kornhauser W. 1959. *The Politics of Mass Society.* New York: Free Press

Kraatz MS, Zajac EJ. 1996. Exploring the limits of the new institutionalism: the causes and consequences of illegitimate organizational change. *Am. Sociol. Rev.* 61:812–36

Krackhardt D. 1988. Predicting with networks: nonparametric multiple regression analysis of dyadic data. *Soc. Networks* 10:359–81

Kriesi HP, Koopmans R, Duyvendak JW, Guigni MG. 1995. *New Social Movements in Western Europe.* Minneapolis, MN: Univ. Minn. Press

Kunda G. 1992. *Engineering Culture.* Philadelphia, PA: Temple Univ. Press

Land KC, Deane G. 1992. On the large–sample estimation of regression models with spatial– or network–effects terms: a two-stage least squares approach. In *Sociological Methodology,* ed. PV Marsden, pp. 221–48. New York: Blackwell.

Lazarsfeld PF, Berelson BR, Gaudet H. 1944. *The People's Choice.* New York: Duell, Sloan & Pierce.

Leblebici H, Salancik GR, Copay A, King T. 1991. Institutional change and the transformation of interorganizational fields: an organizational history of the U.S. radio broadcasting industry. *Admin. Sci. Q.* 36: 333–63

LeBon G. 1897. *The Crowd.* London: Unwin

Lillrank P. 1995. The transfer of management innovations from Japan. *Org. Stud.* 16:971–89

Mantel N. 1967. The detection of disease clustering and a generalized regression strategy. *Cancer Res.* 27:209–20

Marsden PV, Podolny J. 1990. Dynamic analysis of network diffusion processes. In *Social Networks through Time,* ed. H Flap, J Weesie, pp. 197–214. Utrecht: ISOR

McAdam D. 1982. *Political Process and the Development of Black Insurgency, 1930-1970.* Chicago: Univ. Chicago Press

McAdam D. 1988. *Freedom Summer.* New York: Oxford Univ. Press

McAdam D. 1995. "Initiator" and "spin–off" movements: diffusion processes in protest cycles. In *Repertoires and Cycles of Collective Action,* ed. M Traugott, pp. 217–39. Durham, NC: Duke Univ. Press

McAdam D, Paulsen R. 1993. Specifying the relationship between social ties and activism. *Am. J. Sociol.* 99:640–67

McAdam D, Rucht D. 1993. The cross national diffusion of movement ideas. *Ann. Am. Acad. Polit. Soc. Sci.*

McCarthy JD. 1996. Constraints and opportunities in adopting, adapting, and inventing. In *Comparative Perspectives on Social Movements,* ed. JD McCarthy, D McAdam, MN Zald, pp. 141–51. Cambridge, UK: Cambridge Univ. Press

Menzel H. 1960. Innovation, integration, and marginality: a survey of physicians. *Am. Sociol. Rev.* 25:704–713

Meyer JW. 1994. Rationalized environments. In *Institutional Environments and Organizations,* ed. WR Scott, JW Meyer, pp. 28–54. San Francisco: Sage

Meyer JW, Ramirez F, Soysal Y. 1992. World expansion of mass education, 1870–1980. *Sociol. Educ.* 65:128–49

Mezias SJ. 1990. An institutional model of organizational practice: financial reporting at the Fortune 200. *Admin. Sci. Q.* 35: 431–57

Micklethwait J, Wooldridge A. 1996. *The Witch Doctors.* New York: Random

Mizruchi MS. 1992. *The Structure of Corporate Political Action.* Cambridge, MA: Harvard Univ. Press

Mizruchi MS, Fein L. 1997. Coercive, mimetic, and normative isomorphism: a study of the social construction of sociological knowledge. Paper presented at Annu. Meet. Am. Sociol. Assoc., Toronto

Morris A. 1981. Black Southern sit-in movement: an analysis of internal organization. *Am. Sociol. Rev.* 46:744–67

Morris M. 1993. Epidemiology and social networks: modeling structured diffusion. *Sociol. Meth. Res.* 22:99–126

Myers DJ. 1997. Racial rioting in the 1960s: an event history analysis of local conditions. *Am. Sociol. Rev.* 62:94–112

Oberschall A. 1989. The 1960s sit-ins: protest diffusion and movement takeoff. *Res. Soc. Movements, Conflict, Change* 11:31–33

Olzak S. 1992. *The Dynamics of Ethnic Competition and Conflict.* Stanford, CA: Stanford Univ. Press

Osterman P. 1994. How common is workplace transformation and who adopts it? *Industrial Labor Relat. Rev.* 47:173–88

Ouchi WG. 1981. *Theory Z.* Reading, MA: Addison-Wesley

Palmer DA, Jennings PD, Zhou X,. 1993. Late adoption of the multidivisional form by large U.S. corporations: institutional, political, and economic accounts. *Admin. Sci. Q.* 38:100–31

Pascale RT, Athos AG. 1981. *The Art of Japanese Management.* New York: Simon & Schuster

Petras J, Zeitlin M. 1967. Miners and agrarian radicalism. *Am. Sociol. Rev.* 32:578–86

Pfeffer J, Salancik GR. 1978. *The External Control of Organizations.* New York: Harper & Row

Pitcher BL, Hamblin RL, Miller JLL. 1978. The diffusion of collective violence. *Am. Sociol. Rev.* 431:23–35

Powell WW, DiMaggio PJ, eds. 1991. *The New Institutionalism in Organizational Analysis.* Chicago, IL: Univ. Chicago Press

Rogers EM. 1995. *Diffusion of Innovations.* New York: Free Press. 4th ed.

Rogers EM, Kincaid, DL. 1981. *Communication Networks: Toward a New Paradigm for Research.* New York: Free Press

Rowan B. 1982. Organizational structure and the institutional environment: the case of public schools. *Admin. Sci. Q.* 27:259–79

Rude G. 1964. *The Crowd in History,* 1730-1848. New York: Wiley

Ryan B, Gross NC. 1943. The diffusion of hybrid seed corn in two Iowa communities. *Rur. Sociol.* 8:15–24

Schelling TC. 1978. *Micromotives and Macrobehavior.* New York: Norton

Schrum W, Wuthnow R. 1988. Reputational status of organizations in technical systems. *Am. J. Sociol.* 93:882–912

Shenhav Y. 1995. From chaos to systems: the engineering foundations of organization theory, 1879–1932. *Admin. Sci. Q.* 40: 557–85

Snow DA. 1993. *Shakubaku: A Study of the Nichiren Shoshu Buddhist Movement in America, 1960-1975*. New York: Garland

Snow DA, Benford RD. 1995. *Alternative types of cross-national diffusion in the social movement arena*. Paper presented at the Conference on Cross–National Influences and Social Movement Research, Mont Pelerin, SW

Snow DA, Zurcher Jr. LA, Ekland-Olson S. 1980. Social networks and social movements: a microstructural approach to differential recruitment. *Am. Sociol. Rev.* 45: 878–901

Soule SA. 1997. The student divestment movement in the United States and tactical diffusion: the shantytown protest. *Soc. Forces* 75:855–83

Soule SA. 1998. Divestment by colleges and universities in the United States: institutional presssures toward isomorphism. In *Bending the Bars of the Iron Cage: Institutional Dynamics and Processes*, ed. WW Powell, DL Jones. Chicago: Univ. Chicago Press

Soule SA, Tarrow S. 1991. *Acting collectively, 1847-1849: how the repertoire of collective action changed and where it happened.* Paper presented at Annu. Conf. of Soc. Sci. Hist. Assoc., New Orleans

Soule SA, Zylan Y. 1997. Runaway train? the diffusion of state–level reform to AFDC eligibility requirements, 1950–1967. *Am. J. Sociol.* 103:733–62

Spilerman S. 1970. The causes of racial disturbances: a comparison of alternative explanations. *Am. Sociol. Rev.* 354:627–49

Stearns LB, Allan KD. 1996. Economic behavior in institutional environments: the corporate merger wave of the 1980s. *Am. Sociol. Rev.* 61:699–718

Strang D. 1990. From dependency to sovereignty: an event history analysis of decolonization. *Am. Sociol. Rev.* 55:846–60

Strang D. 1991. Adding social structure to diffusion models: an event history framework. *Sociol. Meth. Res.* 19:324–53

Strang D. 1995. mhdiff: SAS–IML procedures for estimating diffusion models. Technical Report 95–3a. Dep. Sociol., Cornell Univ.

Strang D. 1996. *Inducing a network influence structure from multiple diffusion processes*. Paper presented at Annu. Meet. of Am. Sociol. Assoc., New York

Strang D. 1997. *Cheap talk: managerial discourse on quality circles as an organizational innovation.* Paper presented at Annu. Meet. of Am. Sociol. Assoc., Toronto

Strang D, Bradburn EM. 1993. *Theorizing legitimacy or legitimating theory? competing institutional accounts of HMO policy, 1970-89.* Paper presented at Annu. Meet. of Am. Sociol. Assoc., Miami, FL

Strang D, Chang PM. 1993. The International Labour Organisation and the welfare state: institutional effects on national welfare spending, 1960–80. *Int. Org.* 47:235–62

Strang D, Meyer JW. 1993. Institutional conditions for diffusion. *Theory & Soc.* 22: 487–512

Strang D, Tuma NB. 1993. Spatial and temporal heterogeneity in diffusion. *Am. J. Sociol.* 99:614–39

Studer–Ellis E. 1997. *Organizational responses to adversity: evidence from higher educational organizations.* Paper presented at Annu. Meet. of Am. Sociol. Assoc., Toronto

Sutton JR, Dobbin F. 1996. The two faces of governance: responses to legal uncertainty in U.S. firms, 1955 to 1985. *Am. Sociol. Rev.* 61:794–811

Tarde G. 1903. *The Laws of Imitation.* New York: Holt

Tarrow S. 1989. *Democracy and Disorder: Protest and Politics in Italy, 1965-1975.* Oxford: Clarendon

Tarrow S. 1994. *Power in Movement.* New York: Cambridge Univ. Press

Tilly C. 1978. *From Mobilization to Revolution.* Boston, MA: Addison-Wesley

Tolbert PS, Zucker L. 1983. Institutional sources of change in the formal structure of organizations: the diffusion of Civil Service reform. *Admin. Sci. Q.* 28:22–39

Tuma NB. 1994. Invoking RATE, ver 3.0. Technical Report, Stanford Univ., Dept. Sociol.

Useem M. 1984. *The Inner Circle.* New York: Oxford Univ. Press

Valente TW. 1995. *Network Models of the Diffusion of Innovations.* Cresskill, NJ: Hampton

Westphal JD, Gulati R, Shortell SM. 1997. Customization or conformity? an institutional and network perspective on the content and consequences of TQM adoption. *Admin. Sci. Q.* 42:366–94

Yamaguchi K. 1994. Some accelerated failure–time regression models derived from diffusion process models: an application to a network diffusion analysis. In *Sociological Methodology*, ed. P Marsden, pp. 267–300. Washington, DC: Blackwell

Zhou X. 1993. Occupational power, state capacities, and the diffusion of licensing in the American states, 1890 to 1950. *Am. Sociol. Rev.* 58:536–52

Annu. Rev. Sociol. 1998. 24:291–311

ALCOHOL, DRUGS, AND VIOLENCE

Robert Nash Parker and Kathleen Auerhahn
Presley Center for Crime and Justice Studies, and Department of Sociology, University of California, Riverside, California 92521; e-mail: robnp@aol.com, auerhahn@wizard.ucr.edu

KEY WORDS: selective disinhibition, intoxication and aggression, tripartite framework, alcohol availability, psychopharmacological, economic compulsive, systemic

ABSTRACT

A review of the scientific literature on the relationship between alcohol and violence and that between drugs and violence is presented. A review and analysis of three major theoretical approaches to understanding these relationships are also presented. A number of conclusions are reached on the basis of these efforts. First, despite a number of published statements to the contrary, we find no significant evidence suggesting that drug use is associated with violence. Second, there is substantial evidence to suggest that alcohol use is significantly associated with violence of all kinds. Third, recent theoretical efforts reviewed here have, despite shortcomings, led to significant new understanding of how and why alcohol and drugs are related to violence. Fourth, these theoretical models and a growing number of empirical studies demonstrate the importance of social context for understanding violence and the ways in which alcohol and drugs are related to violence. Fifth, the shortcomings of these theoretical models and the lack of definitive empirical tests of these perspectives point to the major directions where future research on the relationship between alcohol and violence, and between drugs and violence, is needed.

INTRODUCTION

That the United States leads the industrialized nations in rates of interpersonal violence is a well-documented fact (National Research Council 1993). Examples of this can be seen in the extraordinarily high rates of violent crimes such

0360-0572/98/0815-0291$08.00

as homicide, robbery, and rape in the United States (National Research Council 1993, Parker & Rebhun 1995); an additional and disturbing fact that has come to light in recent years is the increasing rate of youth violence, particularly lethal violence (Blumstein 1995; Alaniz et al 1998).

During the last decade, interest has grown in the relationship between alcohol, drugs, and violence. In addition to the mostly misguided attention in mass media and in political circles to the relationship between illegal drugs and violence, a number of empirical studies have attempted to disentangle the associations between alcohol, drugs, and violence. Several studies have attempted to organize this knowledge into a comprehensive theoretical framework. This chapter synthesizes this body of work to assess the state of the art in thinking about the relationships between psychoactive substances and violent behavior.

Defining and understanding the complex relationships among alcohol, drugs, and violence require that we examine issues of pharmacology, settings, and larger social contexts to understand the mechanisms that associate substance use and violence in individuals. In addition to this, we must also consider not only the ways in which individuals are nested within larger social contexts, but also the ways in which these contexts themselves may create conditions in which violent behavior takes place, for example, the ways in which availability of substances, while itself conditioned to some degree by larger social forces, contributes to the spatial distribution of crime and violence.

We do not attempt to review the growing literature on the biological aspects of violence. Despite increased interest in this area of research, no credible scientific evidence currently exists that demonstrates any significant link between biological characteristics and violence (National Research Council 1993). Future research may reveal complex interactions among biological, pharmacological, psychological, and contextual aspects of alcohol- and drug-related violence, but no conclusive evidence exists to support this idea at present.

In addition to trying to understand the ways in which alcohol and drug use may contribute to violent behavior, it is also important to consider the ways that alcohol and other drugs relate to human behavior in general. Some advances have been made in the study of psychological expectancies concerning alcohol's effect on behavior (Brown 1993, Grube et al 1994), the relationship between alcohol and cognitive functioning (Pihl et al 1993), the impact of alcohol on aggressive behavior (Leonard & Taylor 1983), and the dynamic developmental effects of early exposure to alcohol and violence among young people (White et al 1993) and among women who have been victimized as children and as adults (Miller & Downs 1993, Widom & Ames 1994, Roesler & Dafler 1993).

Similar work has attempted to understand the links between illicit drugs and behavior, although due to the attention focused on the illegality of these substances, this body of work tends to be most concerned with illegal behaviors that might be associated with drugs. Examples from this literature include examinations of the links between drug use and delinquent behavior among juveniles (Watts & Wright 1990, Fagan 1993, Fagan et al 1990); relationships between substance use and domestic violence (Bennett 1995, Bennett et al 1994, Roberts 1987, Blount et al 1994); the ways in which the use and distribution of illicit drugs are related to all types of crime, particularly nonviolent property offenses (Ball et al 1982, Ball 1991, Baumer 1994, Greenberg 1976, Johnson et al 1994, Klein & Maxson 1985, McCoy et al 1995, Meiczkowski 1994, Feucht & Kyle 1996); and the impact of drug use on the ability to maintain interpersonal relationships (Joe 1996, Fishbein 1996, Lerner & Burns 1978).

A fairly common problem specific to theoretical and empirical investigations of the relationship between drugs and violence is the tendency—largely ideological—to lump all illicit drugs together, as if all drugs might be expected to have the same relationship to violent behavior. Different drugs certainly do have different pharmacological effects, which may or may not influence the user's tendency toward violence; this should be treated as a prominent empirical question, rather than as an afterthought usually addressed only when results are disaggregated by drug type. Another problem specific to the analysis of the impacts of illicit drugs on behavior that hinders our understanding of the relationship between drugs and violence in real-world (as opposed to laboratory) settings was cogently pointed out by one researcher—that the degree of both impurity and deception in the illicit drug market "makes any direct inferences between drug-taking and behavior seem almost ludicrous" (Greenberg 1976, p. 119; see also Johnson 1978). Evidence of the greater likelihood of polydrug use among more violent research subjects also confuses any causal inferences that can be made with respect to particular drugs (e.g. Spunt et al 1995, Inciardi & Pottieger 1994).

DRUGS, ALCOHOL, AND VIOLENCE AT THE INDIVIDUAL LEVEL

A rather fragmented research literature attempts to identify links between alcohol, drugs, and violence at the individual or pharmacological level. This work is discussed briefly below, mainly as a prelude to theoretical models developed in light of these empirical findings.

Evidence of an individual level association between alcohol and violence is widespread. For example, Collins (1981) reviewed a number of studies in which alcohol and violence were associated among individuals. Experimental studies have also shown a consistent relationship at the individual level between alcohol use and aggressive behavior, especially in the presence of social cues that would normally elicit an aggressive response; the consumption of alcohol increases the aggressiveness of this response (Taylor 1983, Gantner &

Taylor 1992, Pihl et al 1993). Roizen (1993, pp. 4–5) reports that in nearly 40 studies of violent offenders, and an equal number of studies of victims of violence, alcohol involvement was found in about 50% of the events and people examined. Although most individual-level studies assume that alcohol has a potentially causal role, an argument supported by the experimental studies cited here, some have argued variously that the relationship is spurious (Collins 1989), that both are caused by third factors (Jessor & Jessor 1977), or that aggression and violence precede alcohol and drug abuse (White et al 1987).

In general, little evidence suggests that illicit drugs are uniquely associated with the occurrence of violent crime. While respondents of the 1991 National Criminal Victimization Survey perceived more than one fourth of violent criminal assailants to be under the influence of alcohol, less than 10% of these assailants were reported by victims to be under the influence of illicit drugs. Of these, more than half were reported to be under the influence of both alcohol and drugs (Bureau of Justice Statistics 1992a). These percentages are supported by urinalysis data for persons arrested for violent offenses, which yield the finding that in 1990, only 5.6% of violent offenders were under the influence of illicit drugs at the time of their offense (US Bureau of Justice Statistics 1992b).

Studies of the drug and alcohol involvement of homicide offenders and victims also support the notion that alcohol is, overwhelmingly, the substance most frequently implicated in this particular form of violence (Abel 1987, Spunt et al 1994, 1995, Wieczorek et al 1990, Yarvis 1994, Fendrich et al 1995, Goldstein et al 1992). Interview studies with homicide offenders as well as toxicology studies of homicide victims consistently report that approximately half of all homicide offenders are intoxicated on drugs or alcohol at the time of the crime; similar percentages of homicide victims test positive for substance use as well (Abel 1987, Langevin et al 1982, Ray & Simons 1987, Fendrich et al 1995, Spunt et al 1994, 1995, Wieczorek et al 1990, Kratcoski 1990, Welte & Abel 1989, Garriott 1993, Tardiff et al 1995). Some evidence suggests that alcohol is the substance most frequently implicated in other violent events as well (Buss et al 1995, US Bureau of Justice Statistics 1992a).[1]

[1]Difficulties inherent in trying to assess the involvement of alcohol relative to other drugs in violent events are largely the result of the way in which the research agenda surrounding the relationship between drugs, alcohol, and violence has been constructed. The majority of data collection efforts seem to be focused either on one particular substance (e.g. cocaine) and its relationship to or involvement in violent episodes or on comparisons between alcohol and illicit drugs in general, thereby hindering comparisons not only between alcohol and other drugs, but between different illicit drugs as well. A recent example is the National Institute of Justice report entitled *Drugs, Alcohol, and Domestic Violence in Memphis* (1997), which details research conducted to determine the role of substance use in incidents of domestic violence. At no point in the report are alcohol and drug use separated into distinct phenomena, making it impossible to determine what substances may be associated with domestic violence.

A shortcoming common to much of the work that has attempted to disentangle the individual-level relationships between drugs, alcohol, and violence is that many researchers fail to make a theoretical and/or empirical distinction between different types of drugs. For this reason, a short review of the literature concerning the links between violence and specific types of illicit drugs is presented below in the hope that some general conclusions can be drawn about the nature and magnitude of the relationship between illicit drugs and violence.

Heroin

Evidence to support a link between heroin and violence is virtually nonexistent. While there is some evidence that heroin users participate in economically motivated property crimes (see Kaplan 1983, pp. 51–58 for a thoughtful and critical discussion of this issue), the work of Ball and his colleagues (Ball et al 1982, Ball 1991) fails to uncover persuasive evidence for a link between heroin use and violent crime. Although no specific measures for violent crime are reported in the analysis of self-reported criminality (validated by official records) from a sample of 243 heroin addicts in Baltimore, only 3% of the sample reported committing, on a daily basis, any crime other than theft; the figures for the weekly and "infrequent" commission of crimes other than theft are 3% and 9%, respectively (Ball et al 1982). A later, more comprehensive analysis undertaken to determine whether or not "common forces attributable to heroin addiction are of primary etiological importance with respect to crime" (Ball 1991, p. 413) compares addict samples from three major Eastern cities. Echoing the results of the 1982 study, involvement in violent crime was negligible, accounting for between 1.5% and 5.6% of all addict criminality across cities (Ball 1991, p. 419).

Amphetamines

Considerable investigation has been made into a possible pharmacological link between amphetamines and violence. Some evidence indicates that in rare cases, either sustained periods of heavy use or extremely high acute doses can induce what has variously been called "toxic psychosis" or "amphetamine-induced psychosis," a reaction that is virtually indistinguishable from schizophrenia (Ellinwood 1971, Fukushima 1994). Aside from these extremely rare cases, some evidence may speak to a link between violent behavior and amphetamine use in ethnographic samples (Joe 1996) and in case-study research (Ellinwood 1971). One researcher notes, however, that this link may result from situational influences: "several...subjects seem to have lost intellectual awareness because they lived alone and had little chance to cross-check their delusional thinking. A long-term solitary lifestyle seems particularly significant in fostering this effect" (Ellinwood 1971, p. 1173).

The importance of context and situation for the association between amphetamine use and violent behavior is supported by animal studies as well; Miczek & Tidey (1989) report that the social relationship between experimental animals significantly influences the level and type of violent behavior that they manifest when on amphetamines (Miczek & Tidey 1989, p. 75). Additionally, the baseline rate of violent or aggressive behavior prior to amphetamine administration was an important predictor of violent behavior after drug administration. The authors conclude from this review of animal studies that:

> Among the most important determinants of amphetamine effects on aggressive and defensive responses are the stimulus situation, species, prior experience with these types of behavior, and...dosage and chronicity of drug exposure. (Miczek & Tidey 1989, p. 71)

Cocaine

Some evidence suggests that cocaine use and violent behavior may be associated (Miller et al 1991, Budd 1989, Inciardi & Pottieger 1994); one of the most widely reported pharmacological effects of cocaine in users is feelings of paranoia (Goode 1993, Miller et al 1991). At least one group of researchers suggest that cocaine-associated violence "may in part be a defensive reaction to irrational fear" (Miller et al 1991, p. 1084).

The route of administration may influence the likelihood of violent behavior in users, with methods delivering the most intense and immediate effects being most closely associated with some forms of violent behavior. Users who smoked the drug in the form of "crack" were most likely to engage in violence proximate to cocaine use, followed by users taking the drug intravenously. Users who "snorted" the drug were found to be least likely to engage in violence (Giannini et al 1993).[2] However, these researchers also reported that forms of violence "requiring sustained activity" (defined by the authors to include such acts as rape and robbery) were not associated with route of administration of cocaine. Because of this, the authors conclude that "circumstance and situation may be as important as route of administration" (Giannini et al 1993, p. 69).

The greater influence of social rather than pharmacological factors on the cocaine-violence relationship has also been reported elsewhere. Goldstein et al (1991) found that the relationship of violence to volume of cocaine use varied according to gender, with only male "big users" of cocaine contributing disproportionately to the distribution of violent events reported by the sample as a

[2]Miller et al (1991) failed to find any such relationship between route of administration and violence; however, the authors point out that this lack of finding may be explained by the use of a treatment sample of users who were likely using cocaine in such high dosage and frequency as to blur any distinction between acute toxicity effects specific to route of administration (Miller et al 1991, p. 1084).

whole (Goldstein et al 1991, p. 354). Additional evidence for the importance of context can be found in ethnographic research, which reports that a great deal of violent behavior experienced by crack-using women arises as a result of their involvement in prostitution, which is related circumstantially, although not pharmacologically, to their drug use (Mieczkowski 1994, Johnson et al 1994).

An issue of research design has emerged in the extensive literature surrounding cocaine use and violence. Chitwood & Morningstar (1985) report systematic differences between samples of cocaine users in and out of treatment programs, with samples from those in treatment characterized by greater cocaine use in both frequency and volume. This difference has been reported elsewhere (e.g. Miller et al 1991); Inciardi & Pottieger (1994) also report that a comparison of cocaine users in treatment to users not in treatment reveals that treatment users were substantially more likely to be polydrug users and to engage in violence. These findings are important in that the type of sample used may, at least in the case of cocaine, greatly influence the findings about a drug-violence association.

Phencyclidine

Phencyclidine (PCP) is widely believed to be associated with violence; this conclusion is based almost exclusively on case study research, often of individuals with psychiatric disturbances (e.g. Lerner & Burns 1978, McCarron et al 1981). Ketamine, a drug pharmacologically quite similar to PCP, has enjoyed increasing popularity in recent years (Dotson et al 1995). PCP and Ketamine are classified as "dissociative anaesthetics" because they diminish awareness not only of pain but also of the environment in general. Delusions, paranoia, and (in rare cases) psychosis are among the most commonly reported effects of these drugs by users and clinicians (Marwah & Pitts 1986, Lerner & Burns 1978, McCarron 1986, Dotson et al 1995). However, one researcher concludes that "emotionally stable people under the influence of PCP probably will not act in a way very different from their normal behavior" (Siegel 1978, p. 285).

Official crime statistics fail to show conclusive evidence for a unique link between PCP use and violent crime; arrestees who were not under the influence of illicit drugs (according to urinalysis) were more likely to be charged with assault than were persons testing positive for PCP (Wish 1986). Among PCP-positive arrestees, the conditional distribution of offenses is influenced toward a greater likelihood of robbery charges, but Wish (1986) notes that this may be an artifact of demographic coincidence; PCP users tend to be younger than the average user of illicit drugs and thus coincide with the age group that dominates robbery arrests (Wish 1986, Maguire et al 1993).

Summary

This review of the evidence concerning the relationship between the use of various illicit drugs and violence makes it clear that support for such linkages is absent. At best, we can characterize the available results as inconclusive. The strongest evidence is for a link between cocaine use and violence; however, the conclusions of researchers whose findings support this idea universally highlight a social rather than a pharmacological basis for this link. At present, no compelling evidence exists to support an association between violence and amphetamines, Phencyclidine/Ketamine, or heroin. While there is some evidence that some of these drugs may induce psychosis, this reaction is exceedingly rare; virtually all research on this phenomenon consists of case studies, making it impossible to even estimate the frequency of such reactions in the population.

The most extensive research literature concerning drugs and violence is that of investigations of the relationship between cocaine use and violence. A search through *Sociological Abstracts* reveals that this literature has grown concurrently with concern about, if not use of, cocaine (see White House Office of National Drug Control Policy 1997 for use statistics). Between 1970 and 1980, only four articles with "cocaine" or "crack" in the title are indexed, while between 1980 and 1990 there are approximately 75; in the 1990s, this figure is at nearly 200 before the decade's end. However, even in the face of this profusion of research interest, we are still unable to say with any certainty that cocaine use and violent behavior are related. In part this may be attributable to the limitations inherent in ideologically driven research (e.g. Inciardi & Pottieger 1994); it may also indicate that such a link really does not exist, and that any amount of looking will continue to fail to uncover it. At this point in the state of our knowledge, it is clear that we must look beyond the level of the individual user in order to adequately understand and characterize the relationship (if any) between illicit drugs and violence.

THEORETICAL APPROACHES

We have identified four recent attempts to specify and/or explain the linkages among drugs, alcohol, and violence that are worthy of discussion, either for the fact of their prominence in the research literature or for the promise of greater understanding that they afford. Three of these four approaches have associated with them at least some empirical tests of the theories; these are discussed along with the explication of the theories. Each is discussed in turn, with attention then passing to the commonalities between these theories, to determine whether a useful synthesis can be made.

Fagan's Approach: Intoxication, Aggression, and the Functionality of Violence

Jeffrey Fagan has produced several attempts to formulate a comprehensive theory of the relationship between the use of psychoactive substances, violence, and aggression (Fagan 1990, 1993, Fagan et al 1990). In addition, he has also been part of a joint effort to further our understanding of youth violence in general (Fagan & Wilkinson 1998); this work is discussed here briefly vis-à-vis its complementarity with Fagan's formulations of the relationship of alcohol, drugs, and violence.

Above all, Fagan and his colleagues argue for the use of hierarchical or "nested contexts" models if we are to gain any understanding of the etiology of violence in general and of the relationships between substance use and violence (Fagan 1993, 1990). In his most recent work Fagan has argued for a "situated transactions" framework as the most promising way to understand youth violence (Luckenbill 1977).

In assessing the relationships between alcohol, drugs, and violence, Fagan (1990) has reviewed research and theoretical arguments from biological and physiological research, psychopharmacological studies, psychological and psychiatric approaches, and social and cultural perspectives in an attempt to present a comprehensive model of this relationship. He argues that the most important areas of consensus from these different perspectives are that intoxication has a significant impact on cognitive abilities and functioning, and that the nature of this impact varies according to the substance used but is, in the last instance, moderated by the context in which behavior takes place. For example, social and cultural meanings of how people function under the influence of alcohol, understandings about the impact of intoxication on judgment, the ability to perceive social cues, and the ability to focus on long- as well as short-term outcomes and desires are all extremely important factors in determining the outcome of a social situation in which drugs or alcohol are present and whether that situation will result in violence. The nature of the setting in which interaction takes place and the absence or presence of formal and informal means of social control are also important factors whereby intoxication influences aggression. Fagan also posits that intoxicated individuals tend to have limited response sets in situations of social interaction (1990, pp. 299–300); Fagan & Wilkinson (1998) extend this view to a general analysis of the etiology of youth violence.

To date, no empirical tests of this model exist. Fagan's approach leads to a very general theoretical model that would require substantial revision to permit empirical testing. For example, the outcome measure, aggression, is hardly the same thing as violence, although there is certainly some relationship between these concepts. Further theoretical explanation is needed to establish the transition from aggression to violence, as well as the linkages between the antecedents of aggression and aggression itself.

Fagan & Wilkinson propose a general model of youth violence that is relevant to this discussion. They propose that youth violence is "a functional, purposive behavior that serves definable goals within specific social contexts" (Fagan & Wilkinson 1998, p. 2). Fagan & Wilkinson argue that one of the most important benefits that accrue to youth from the use of violence is the attainment of status, something to which youths have limited access. The social world in which adolescents operate places an increasingly high premium on status and reputation; broader contextual influences such as technology (in the form of weapons) are important in "raising the stakes" of potentially violent situations, which may change the meanings attributed to different behaviors (Fagan & Wilkinson 1998). Another factor that may influence the meanings attributed to the actions of others is the consumption of drugs or alcohol, due to the behavioral expectancies that may be associated with them. These potentially violence-producing combinations in meaning-assignment may be particularly significant when considered in the context of the cognitive limitations of the developmental stage of adolescence (Leigh 1987). Dating violence may be a particularly relevant phenomenon to examine within this framework, given the highly charged adolescent expectancies surrounding alcohol consumption and sexuality (George et al 1988, Corcoran & Thomas 1991) as well as the heightened importance of sexuality to status attainment at this developmental stage (Fagan & Wilkinson 1998).

Selective Disinhibition: Parker's Approach

Parker (1993) and Parker & Rebhun (1995) attempt to specifically link alcohol and violence in an overall conceptual model, utilizing rates of homicide as the indicator of violent behavior. Parker & Rebhun (1995) advance a sociological approach to the relationship between alcohol and violence that is much different from earlier, biologically based formulations of this relationship (see Room & Collins 1983 for a review of that literature and the widespread criticisms applied to this notion). In these earlier conceptualizations, alcohol was conceived as a biochemical agent that had a universal effect on social behavior, despite substantial evidence from cross-cultural studies that alcohol has a differential impact on behavior depending on the social and cultural contexts in which it is consumed (see Marshall 1979 for a number of examples of this point).

Noting this limitation of previous formulations, Parker & Rebhun (1995) advance a social disinhibition approach, which tries to explain why normatively proscribed behavior is "disinhibited" in relatively few cases. Alcohol selectively disinhibits violence depending on contextual factors specific to the situation, the actors involved and their relationships to one another, and the impact of bystanders. In US society, norms about the appropriateness of violence in solving interpersonal disputes argue both for and against such behavior (Parker 1993). The theory proposes that individuals are constrained from engaging in certain behaviors in a social situation by the norms that they have internalized; however, people do violate norms and may have conflicting sets of norms to draw on in some situations. It is possible that norms that have the least institutional support are more likely to be disinhibited in a situation, all else being equal (Parker 1993, p. 118).

To explain how choices are made between these conflicting normative structures, Parker & Rebhun (1995, p. 34–35) introduce the tandem concepts of active and passive constraint. In potentially violent situations, it takes active constraint—a proactive and conscious decision not to use violence to "solve" the dispute—to preclude violence. In some of these cases, alcohol may disinhibit norms that usually prevent or constrain individuals from engaging in violent behavior. Thus, the selective nature of alcohol-related homicide is dependent upon the interaction of an impaired rationality and the nature of the social situation. The nature of the social situation, or the context in which behavior takes place, is of paramount importance in determining the outcome of a potentially violent situation. This is indicated by the fact that most alcohol-involved interpersonal disputes do not result in violence and homicide, but a few of these situations do (Parker & Rebhun 1995; see also Wilbanks 1984).

Parker & Rebhun (1995) further refined and specified their theoretical model of the ways in which alcohol consumption and homicide rates might be related at the aggregate level by incorporating into the model control variables suggested by previous literature on the etiology of homicide, such as subcultural theories (e.g. Wolfgang & Ferracuti 1976), social bonds theory (e.g. Hirschi 1969, Krohn 1991), deterrence theory, routine activities (Cohen & Felson 1979), and, taking a cue from strain and social disorganization theories (e.g. Merton 1949, also Wilson 1987), controls for economic inequality and poverty rates.

A test of this particular specification of the theory was reported by Parker (1995). Cross-sectional analysis of state-level data was undertaken for five different types of homicide, differentiated by circumstances of crime and/or victim-offender relationship (e.g. robbery homicide, family homicide). Alcohol consumption was a significant predictor of family intimate and primary nonintimate homicide, or those homicides involving the closest interpersonal relationships. These results suggest that norms prohibiting violence in resolving interpersonal disputes in close or intimate relationships may be weaker than such norms prescribed in other interactions; alcohol consumption would appear to contribute to the "selective disinhibition" of an already weak normative apparatus. Parker (1995, p. 27) also reported that the impact of poverty on robbery and other felony homicides was stronger in states with above average rates of alcohol consumption; the deterrent effect of capital punishment on homicide rates was strongest in states that had below average rates of alcohol consumption, providing further support for the importance of the interplay between alcohol consumption and contextual and social situational factors in the disinhibition of active constraint.

Parker & Rebhun (1995) also report the results of two tests of this approach that utilize longitudinal research designs. The first, using city-level data, yielded evidence that increases in alcohol availability help to explain why homicide nearly tripled in these cities between 1960 and 1980. This study also found some evidence for mediating effects of poverty, routine activities, and a lack of social bonds on the relationship between homicide and alcohol availability at the city level.

In an examination of the general hypothesis that alcohol has a causal impact on homicide, Parker & Rebhun (1995, p. 102–17) conducted a dynamic test of the impact of increases in the minimum drinking age on youth homicide at the state level. Using data from 1976 through 1983, Parker & Rebhun (1995) estimated a pooled cross-section and time series model in which two general types of homicide, primary and nonprimary (based on the prior relationship between victim and offender), in three age categories (15–18, 19–20, and 21–24) were analyzed. In the presence of a number of important predictors, the rate of beer consumption was found to be a significant predictor of homicide rates in five of the six age-homicide type combinations, and increases in the minimum drinking age had a negative and significant impact on primary homicides in all age categories.

Violence Across Time and Space: The Cultural Consequences of Availability

In another theoretical formulation that attempts to explain the links between alcohol availability and violence, Maria Luisa Alaniz, Robert Nash Parker, and others (1998, 1999) propose some mechanisms by which the spatial distribution of alcohol outlets and the targeted advertising of alcohol to particular communities—in both the spatial and demographic sense—may mediate this relationship.

The work of Alaniz et al (1998, 1999) focuses on the relationship of youth violence to alcohol availability. Given the recent increases in youth violence, including the increasing proportional contribution to overall rates of lethal violence (Blumstein 1995), this appears to be a very fruitful line of research to pursue, if one of the ultimate goals of such research is the prevention and reduction of the incidence of violence. Additionally, these authors propose that due to the differences in cultural and legal status for alcohol and drugs (even taking into account the illegality of alcohol to minors), the relationship between illicit drugs and violence is more likely to stem from properties of the illicit distribution system (see Goldstein 1985), while the relationship between alcohol and violence would be expected to be more related to ingestion of the substance, whether due to the effects of pharmacology, cultural expectancies surrounding alcohol's use, or both (Parker 1995, Alaniz et al 1998).

The authors propose two pathways by which alcohol availability may be related to youth violence. The first of these is largely grounded in Parker & Rebhun's (1995) selective disinhibition approach, in specifying the ways in which norms proscribing violence may be overcome (disinhibited) given the particular characteristics of a social situation, including the presence of alcohol. The second considers the distribution of alcohol outlets in physical space and the ways in which this distribution may produce "great attractors" (Alaniz et al 1998, p. 14), areas where social controls of all kind are diminished, if not completely absent; such areas have also been conceptualized as "hot spots" (Sherman et al 1989, Roncek & Maier 1991) and "deviance service centers" (Clairmont & Magill 1974). Alaniz et al theorize that in this kind of "anything-goes" atmosphere (1998, p. 15), active constraint may be more likely to become disabled. Add to this the kinds of circumstances in which youths usually drink; due to the illegal status of alcohol for minors, youths must usually consume alcohol in "semi-private" spaces, such as cars or deserted public parks, "thus [further] limiting the effectiveness of most external forms of social control" (Alaniz et al 1998, p. 13)

Alaniz et al (1999) also highlight the role of advertising in helping to articulate the link between outlet density and youth violence that is particularly relevant in minority communities, which bear a disproportionate share of all types of violence, including youth violence. This aspect of the theory is further explicated by Alaniz & Wilkes (1995), who undertook a semiotic analysis of alcohol advertising targeted at Latino communities. The authors argue that such attempts to target minority communities are very effective because, for minority groups in the United States,

> ...the state exhibits indifference or hostility to claims of citizenship; the market openly embraces the same people...components of Latino cultural armature are appropriated by advertisers, reinvented, and returned...[;] this form of reinvention constructs a symbolic system that builds alcohol consumption into an idealized lifeworld of its constituents. (Alaniz & Wilkes 1995, p. 433)

While this process of transforming cultural symbols into the commodity form is relevant for all sorts of products and services, it is especially relevant in the case of alcohol, given the highly charged nature of cultural expectancies surrounding its use (Brown et al 1987). In support of this thesis, Alaniz et al (1999) found that the density of alcohol advertising using sexist and demeaning images of minority women was associated, at the neighborhood level, with rates of sexual violence against females aged 12–18.

The importance of context and the cultural effects of advertising on youths is demonstrated particularly well by the findings of researchers who initially set out to study links between illicit drugs and delinquency among Latino youth populations; these researchers found that tobacco use was significantly related to violent delinquency, while the use of alcohol and illicit drugs was not found to be so related. The authors explain this finding thus:

> Youngsters who use tobacco act out tobacco-associated identities available in the media and popular culture. They express a range of symbols about themselves that suggest being independent, adult, adventuresome, and tough. These values are also associated with drug use and violent delinquency. (Watts & Wright 1990, p. 152)[3]

Goldstein's Tripartite Framework

In 1985, Paul J Goldstein made an explicit attempt to develop a theoretical framework to describe and explain the relationship between drugs and violence. Goldstein developed a typology of three ways in which drug use and drug trafficking may be causally related to violence.

"Psychopharmacological violence" is violence that stems from properties of the drug itself. In Goldstein's framework, this can be violence associated with drug ingestion by the victim, the perpetrator, or both. "Economic compulsive violence" is violence associated with the high costs of illicit drug use. This type of violence does not stem directly from the physiological effects of drugs but is motivated by the need or desire to obtain drugs. Based on the capacity to induce physical dependency, the drugs one would expect to be most often associated with economic compulsive violence would be opiates (particularly heroin) and cocaine, due to the capacity of these to produce strong physical and psychological dependencies in users. "Systemic violence" is defined by Goldstein as that type of violence associated with "traditionally aggressive patterns of interaction within the system of drug distribution and use" (Goldstein 1985, p. 497). Goldstein maintains that the risks of violence are greater to those involved in distribution than to those who are only users (Goldstein et al 1989).

In the years since Goldstein's original formulation, a fairly large number of empirical studies have been undertaken using this framework. Nearly all of them have been produced by researchers associated with Narcotic and Drug Research, Inc. as part of one of two major research initiatives; these are the

[3]It should be pointed out that the majority of the variance in violent delinquency is explained by prior incarceration; however, tobacco use also emerges as a significant, albeit weaker, predictor of violent delinquency, thus highlighting the importance of social context in the links between substance use and violent behavior.

Drug Relationships in Murder (DREIM) and the Drug Related Involvement in Violent Episodes/Female Drug Related Involvement in Violent Episodes (DRIVE/FEMDRIVE) projects.

The DREIM project involved extensive interviews with 268 homicide offenders incarcerated in New York State correctional facilities. One of the purposes of this project was to gain a more extensive understanding than that afforded by official police records of the role that drugs and alcohol play in homicide.

The DREIM project data indicated that the substance most likely to be used by homicide offenders on a regular basis as well as during the 24 hours directly preceding the crime was, overwhelmingly, alcohol. Marijuana and cocaine were the second and third most frequently implicated drugs in the lives of homicide offenders as well as in the offense itself (Spunt et al 1994, 1995).

Other empirical investigations that rely on the Goldstein framework have attempted to classify the relationship between drugs and all types of violence, under the auspices of the DRIVE/FEMDRIVE research initiative. The data collection for this project consisted of interviews with 152 male and 133 female subjects concerning both drug and alcohol use and also their participation in violent events, over an eight week period. In one analysis, Spunt et al (1990) reported that violent events are drug-related if any of the participants report drug use proximate to the incident; similarly, if there is no link to drug distribution or robbery, these "drug-related events" are classified as psychopharmacological. These researchers fail to identify any mechanism by which these psychopharmacological effects of drugs manifest themselves in violent behavior. For example, they conclude that "heroin and methadone were the [illicit] drugs most likely to be associated with psychopharmacological violence" (Spunt et al 1990, p. 299), despite the fact that virtually no evidence exists to support individual-level associations between opiate use and violence (Kaplan 1983, Ball et al 1982, Ball 1991).

Goldstein et al (1989) reported the results of research that was concerned primarily with the effect of the "crack epidemic" on homicide. Utilizing data from official police reports of homicides supplemented by an observational instrument designed by Goldstein and his research team, the authors concluded that slightly over half of the 414 New York City homicides sampled were drug-related. Evidence from official records indicated that 65% of these drug-related homicides involved crack cocaine as the primary substance, while another 22% were related to other forms of cocaine; combined, nearly 90% of drug-related homicides in the sample involved cocaine. Of these, the overwhelming majority (74.3% of all drug-related homicides) were classified as "systemic" by the researchers. Interestingly, all homicides in which alcohol was the primary substance involved were classified as psychopharmacological.

Another example of the use of the Goldstein typology is the analysis of nine female homicide offenders, reported by Brownstein et al (1994). This analysis provides further evidence that alcohol is the substance most commonly associated with homicide. The authors also conclude from these data that the use of alcohol or drugs by either perpetrator or victim proximate to the homicide makes the homicide primarily drug- or alcohol-related (Brownstein et al 1994, p. 110) despite the fact that the authors report, in some cases, long histories of spousal abuse on the part of the homicide victim, which another researcher might consider at least as important a causal factor as the fact of drug or alcohol consumption in leading up to the homicide.

A central problem that characterizes all the work that utilizes the Goldstein tripartite framework is that it is not treated as a set of testable propositions but rather as a set of assumptions about the nature of drug- and alcohol-related violence. Because of this, studies guided by this set of assumptions do not address the task of explaining mechanisms by which violent events might be related to the presence or use of drugs or alcohol; additionally, all of these studies fail to provide a detailed explanation of the way in which study events come to be classified into one type or another. Another problem with Goldstein's classificatory scheme is that the categories are not mutually exclusive. For example, many of the situations coded by researchers as events of systemic violence are economic in nature. Robbery of a drug dealer would seem to be an economically motivated crime but is classified as systemic in this framework, based on drug trafficking involvement of the victim and/or perpetrator. In short, the Goldstein framework seems biased toward support of the systemic model of drug-effected violence, which also limits the utility of the framework for explaining the relationship between alcohol—the substance most frequently implicated in violent events of all kinds—and violence. Additionally, the rigidity and inherently descriptive nature of the classification scheme fails to take into account the possibility of interactions between social context, individuals, and pharmacology.

CONCLUSIONS

Several clear conclusions can be drawn from this extensive review of the literature concerning drugs, alcohol, and violence. One is the overwhelming importance of context in any relationship that may exist between substance use and violent behavior. Our review of the literature finds a great deal of evidence that the social environment is a much more powerful contributor to the outcome of violent behavior than are pharmacological factors associated with any of the substances reviewed here.

The other consistent finding that we can report from this review of the empirical evidence is that when violent behavior is associated with a substance, that substance is, overwhelmingly, alcohol. Study after study indicates that, even in samples containing relatively high baseline rates of illicit drug use, violent events are overwhelmingly more likely to be associated with the consumption of alcohol than with any other substance. In fact, a review of the literature concerning rates of co-occurrence of violent crimes with the use of illicit substance fails to provide any support whatsoever for a link. The 1991 Criminal Victimization Survey indicates that less than 5% of violent assailants were perceived by their victims to be under the influence of illicit drugs; the corresponding figure for alcohol is more than four times that.

The consensus among the authors of previous reviews of research on alcohol, drugs, and violence (Roizen 1993, Collins 1981, Pernanen 1991) was that evidence existed for an association especially between alcohol and violence, but that the research base would not support any stronger conclusions. These and other reviews would invariably end with a call for more and better research to address the issue of whether evidence about a causal relationship between alcohol, drugs, and violence could be found. What was missing from those reviews, however, was a full recognition of the importance of theoretical development in the search for evidence about causality. Until the last ten years, such efforts were largely absent; a number of the studies cited here would replicate associational findings and end with this same lament about the absence of causal evidence. However, recent developments, especially the work of Goldstein and colleagues, Fagan, and Parker and colleagues, have led to an increased conceptual and theoretical base from which questions of causality can be better assessed. None of these approaches has succeeded in fully theorizing the potential relationships among alcohol, drugs, and violence, and none of these perspectives has provided definitive empirical tests of these theoretical models. Indeed, all of these approaches need more theoretical development as well as better data and methodological approaches to advance the state of knowledge about these relationships. However, at least it is reasonable to claim that research on alcohol, drugs, and violence demonstrates some promising theoretical approaches and some useful empirical studies based on those approaches. Much work is yet to be done, but the prospects for greater understanding of how and why alcohol and drugs contribute to violence have never been brighter.

ACKNOWLEDGMENTS

We would like to acknowledge the support of the University of California, Riverside; Raymond Orbach, Chancellor; David Warren, Vice Chancellor; Carlos Velez-Ibanez, Dean of the College of Humanities, Arts and Social Sciences; Linda Brewster Stearns, Chair, Sociology Department; as well as the State of California, for their support of the Presley Center for Crime and Justice Studies, which supported the authors during the completion of this article.

Literature Cited

Abel EL. 1987. Drugs and homicide in Erie County, New York. *Int. J. Addictions* 22(2):195–200

Alaniz ML, Parker RN, Gallegos A, Cartmill RS. 1998. Immigrants and violence: the importance of context. *Hispanic J. Behav. Sci.*. 20(2): In press

Alaniz ML, Parker RN, Gallegos A, Cartmill RS. 1999. Ethnic targeting and the objectification of women: alcohol advertising and violence against young Latinas. In *Currents in Criminology*, ed. RN Parker.

Alaniz ML, Wilkes C. 1995. Reinterpreting Latino culture in the commodity form: the case of alcohol advertising in the Mexican American community. *Hispanic J. Behav. Sci.* 17(4):430–51

Ball JC, Rosen L, Flueck JA, Nurco DN. 1982. Lifetime criminality of heroin addicts in the United States. *J. Drug Issues* 12: 225–39

Ball JC. 1991. The similarity of crime rates among male heroin addicts in New York City, Philadelphia, Baltimore. *J. Drug Issues* 21:413–27

Baumer E. 1994. Poverty, crack, crime: a cross-city analysis. *J. Res. Crime Delinq.* 31:311–27

Bennett LW. 1995. Substance abuse and the domestic assault of women. *Soc. Work* 40: 760–71

Bennett LW, Tolman RM, Rogalski CJ, Srinivasaraghavan J. 1994. Domestic abuse by male alcohol and drug addicts. *Violence Victims* 9:359–68

Blount WR, Silverman IJ, Sellers CS, Seese RA. 1994. Alcohol and drug use among abused women who kill, abused women who don't, their abusers. *J. Drug Issues* 24(2):165–77

Blumstein A. 1995. Youth violence, guns, the illicit drug industry. *J. Crim. Law Criminol.* 86(1):10–36

Brown SA. 1993. Drug effect expectancies and addictive behavior change. *Exp. Clin. Psychopharmacol.* 1(Oct):55–67

Brown SA, Christiansen BA, Goldman MS. 1987. The alcohol expectancy questionnaire: an instrument for the assessment of adolescent and adult alcohol expectancies. *J. Stud. Alcohol* 48(5):483–91

Brownstein HH, Spunt BJ, Crimmins S, Goldstein PJ, Langley S. 1994. Changing patterns of lethal violence by women: a research note. *Women Crim. Justice* 5: 99–118

Budd RD. 1989. Cocaine abuse and violent death. *Am. J. Drug Alcohol Abuse* 15: 375–82

Bureau of Justice Statistics. 1992a. *Drugs and Crime Facts. 1992.* Washington, DC: USGPO

Bureau of Justice Statistics. 1992b. *Drugs, Crime, the Justice System.* Washington, DC: USGPO

Buss TF, Abdu R, Walker JR. 1995. Alcohol, drugs, violence in a small city trauma center. *J. Substance Abuse Treat.* 12:75–83

Chitwood DD, Morningstar PC. 1985. Factors which differentiate cocaine users in treatment from nontreatment users. *Int. J. Addictions* 20:449–59

Clairmont DH, Magill D. 1974. *Africville: The Life and Death of a Canadian Black Community.* Toronto: McClelland & Stewart

Cohen LE, Felson M. 1979. Social change and crime rate trends: a routine activities approach. *Am. Sociol. Rev.* 44:588–607

Collins JJ Jr. 1981. Alcohol use and criminal behavior: an empirical, theoretical, methodological overview. In *Drinking and Crime: Perspectives on the Relationship between Alcohol Consumption and Criminal Behavior,* ed. JJ Collins Jr, pp. 288–316. New York: Guilford

Collins JJ Jr. 1989. Alcohol and interpersonal violence: less than meets the eye. In *Pathways to Criminal Violence,* ed. NA Weiner, ME Wolfgang, pp. 49–67. Newbury Park, CA: Sage

Corcoran KJ, Thomas LR. 1991. The influence of observed alcohol consumption on perceptions of initiation of sexual activity in a college dating situation. *J. Appl. Soc. Psychol.* 21:6:500–7

Dotson JW, Ackerman DL, West LJ. 1995. Ketamine abuse. *J. Drug Issues* 25:751–57

Ellinwood EH Jr. 1971. Assault and homicide associated with amphetamine abuse. *Am. J. Psychiatry* 127:1170–75

Fagan J. 1993. Interactions among drugs, alcohol, violence. *Health Affairs* 12(4):65–79

Fagan J. 1990. Intoxication and aggression in drugs and crime. In *Crime and Justice: A Review of Research*, ed. M. Tonry, JQ Wilson, 13:241–320. Chicago: Univ. Chicago Press

Fagan J, Wilkinson DL. 1998. The functions of adolescent violence. In *Violence in American Schools,* ed. DS Elliott, KR Williams, B Hamburg. Cambridge Univ. Press

Fagan J, Weis JG, Cheng Y. 1990. Delinquency and substance use among inner-city students. *J. Drug Issues* 20(3): 351–402

Fendrich M, Mackesy-Amiti ME, Goldstein P, Spunt B, Brownstein H. 1995. Substance involvement among juvenile murderers: comparisons with older offenders based on interviews with prison inmates. *Int. J. Addictions* 30(11):1363–82

Feucht TE, Kyle GM. 1996. *Methamphetamine Use Among Adult Arrestees: Findings from the Drug Use Forecasting (DUF) Program.* Washington, DC: Natl. Inst. Justice

Fishbein DH. 1996. Female PCP-using jail detainees: proneness to violence and gender differences. *Addictive Behav.* 21(2): 1:55–172

Fukushima A. 1994. Criminal responsibility in amphetamine psychosis. *Jpn. J. Psychiatr. Neurol.* 48(Suppl.):1–4

Gantner AB, Taylor SP. 1992. Human physical aggression as a function of alcohol and threat of harm. *Aggressive Behav.* 18:(1) 29–36

Garriott JC. 1993. Drug use among homicide victims: changing patterns. *Am. J. Forensic Med. Pathol.* 14(3):234–37

George WH, Gournic SJ, McAfee MP. 1988. Perceptions of postdrinking female sexuality: effects of gender, beverage choice, drink payment. *J. Appl. Soc. Psychol.* 18(15):1295–1317

Giannini AJ, Miller NS, Loiselle RH, Turner CE. 1993. Cocaine-associated violence and relationship to route of administration. *J. Substance Abuse Treatment* 10:67–69

Goldstein PJ. 1985. The drugs/violence nexus: a tripartite conceptual framework. *J. Drug Issues* 15:493–506

Goldstein P, Brownstein HH, Ryan PJ, Belluci PA. 1989. Crack and homicide in New York City 1988: a conceptually based event analysis. *Contemp. Drug Problems* Winter: 651–87

Goldstein P, Brownstein HH, Ryan PJ. 1992. Drug-related homicide in New York: 1984 and 1988. *Crime Delinq.* 38(4):459–76

Goldstein PJ, Bellucci PA, Spunt BJ, Miller T. 1991. Volume of cocaine use and violence: a comparison between men and women. *J. Drug Issues* 21:345–67

Goode E. 1993. *Drugs in American Society.* New York: McGraw-Hill. 4th ed.

Greenberg SW. 1976. The relationship between crime and amphetamine abuse: an empirical review of the literature. *Contemp. Drug Probl.* 5:101–30

Grube J, Ames GM, Delaney W. 1994. Alcohol expectancies and workplace drinking. *J. Appl. Soc. Psychol.* 24(7):646–60

Hirschi T. 1969. *Causes of Delinquency.* Berkeley: Univ. Calif. Press

Inciardi JA, Pottieger AE. 1994. Crack-cocaine use and street crime. *J. Drug Issues* 24:273–92

Jessor R, Jessor SL. 1977. *Problem Behavior and Psychosocial Development: A Longitudinal Study of Youth.* New York: Academic

Joe KA. 1996. The lives and times of Asian-Pacific American women drug users: an ethnographic study of their methamphetamine use. *J. Drug Issues* 26:199–218

Johnson BD, Natarajan M, Dunlap E, Elmoghazy E. 1994. Crack abusers and noncrack abusers: profiles of drug use, drug sales, nondrug criminality. *J. Drug Issues* 24: 117–41

Johnson KM. 1978. Neurochemical Pharmacology of Phencyclidine. In *Phencyclidine (PCP) Abuse: an Appraisal, NIDI Research Monograph No. 21,* ed. RC Petersen, RC Stillman, pp. 44–52. Rockville, MD: Dep. Health Human Serv.

Kaplan J. 1983. *The Hardest Drug: Heroin and Public Policy.* Chicago: Univ. Chicago Press

Klein MW, Maxson CL. 1985. 'Rock' sales in central Los Angeles. *Sociol. Soc. Res.* 69: 561–65

Kratcoski PC. 1990. Circumstances surrounding homicides by older offenders. *Criminal Justice Behav.* 17(4):420–30

Krohn MD. 1991. Control and deterrence theories. In *Criminology: A Contemporary Handbook,* ed. J Sheley, pp. 295–314. Belmont, CA: Wadsworth

Langevin R, Paitich D, Orchard B, Handy L, Russon A. 1982. The role of alcohol, drugs, suicide attempts, situational strains in homicide committed by offenders seen for psychiatric assessment. *Acta Psychiatr. Scand.* 66(3):229–42

Leigh BC. 1987. *Drinking and unsafe sex: background and issues.* NIMH/NIDA Workshop, Women and AIDS: Promoting Healthy Behaviors. Washington, DC

Leonard KE, Taylor SP. 1983. Exposure to pornography, permissive and nonpermissive cues, male aggression toward females. *Motivation Emotion* 7(3):291–99

Lerner SE, Burns RS. 1978. Phencyclidine use

among youth: history, epidemiology, and acute and chronic intoxication. See Johnson 1978, pp. 66–118

Luckenbill DF. 1977. Criminal homicide as a situated transaction. *Social Probl.* 25: 176–86

Maguire K, Pastore AL, Flanagan TJ, eds. 1993. *Sourcebook of Criminal Justice Statistics 1992.* US Dep. Justice, Bur. Justice Statist. Washington, DC: USGPO

Marshall M, ed. 1979. *Beliefs, Behaviors, Alcoholic Beverages: A Cross-Cultural Survey.* Ann Arbor: Univ. Mich. Press

Marwah J, Pitts DK. 1986. Psychopharmacology of phencyclidine. In *Phencyclidine: An Update, NIDA Res. Monogr. No. 64,* ed. DH Clout, pp. 127–35. Rockville, MD: Dep. Health Human Serv.

McCoy HV, Inciardi JA, Metsch LR, Pottieger AE. 1995. Women, crack, crime: gender comparisons of criminal activity among crack cocaine users. *Contemp. Drug Probl.* 22:435–51

McCarron M. 1986. *Phencyclidine intoxication.* In *Phencyclidine: an Update, NIDA Res. Monogr. No. 64,* ed. DH Clout, pp. 209–217. Rockville, MD: Dep. Health Human Serv.

Merton RK. 1949. *Social Theory and Social Structure.* Glencoe, IL: Free

Miczek KA, Tidey JW. 1989. Amphetamines: aggressive and social behavior. In *Pharmacology and Toxicology of Amphetamine and Related Designer Drugs,* ed. K Asghar, E Souza, pp. 68–100. Washington, DC: USGPO

Mieczkowski T. 1994. The experiences of women who sell crack: some descriptive data from the Detroit Crack Ethnography Project. *J. Drug Issues* 24:227–48

Miller BA, Downs WR. 1993. The impact of family violence on the use of alcohol by women: research indicates that women with alcohol problems have experienced high rates of violence during their childhoods and as adults. *Alcohol Health Res. World* 17(2):137–42

Miller NS, Gold MS, Mahler JC. 1991. Violent behaviors associated with cocaine use—possible pharmacological mechanisms. *Int. J. Addictions* 21:1077–88

National Institute of Justice. 1997. *Drugs, Alcohol, Domestic Violence in Memphis: Research Preview.* Natl. Criminal Justice Ref. Serv.

Parker RN. 1995. Bringing 'booze' back in: the relationship between alcohol and homicide. *J. Res. Crime Delinquency* 32 (1):3–38

Parker RN. 1993. Alcohol and theories of homicide. In *Advances in Criminological Theory,* ed. F Adler, W Laufer, 4:113–42. New Brunswick, NJ: Transaction

Parker RN, with LA Rebhun. 1995. *Alcohol and Homicide: A Deadly Combination of Two American Traditions.* Albany: State Univ. NY Press

Pernanen K. 1991. *Alcohol in Human Violence.* New York: Guilford

Pihl RO, Peterson JB, Lau MA. 1993. A biosocial model of the alcohol-aggression relationship. *J. Stud. Alcohol* 11(Sept):128–39 (Suppl.)

Ray MC, Simons RL. 1987. Convicted murderers' accounts of their crimes: a study of homicide in small communities. *Symbolic Interact.* 10(1):57–70

Reiss AJ Jr, Roth JA, eds. 1993. *Understanding and Preventing Violence.* Washington, DC: Natl. Acad. Press

Roberts AR. 1987. Psychosocial characteristics of batterers: a study of 234 men charged with domestic violence offenses. *J. Family Violence* 2:81–93

Roesler TA, Dafler CE. 1993. Chemical dissociation in adults sexually victimized as children: alcohol and drug use in adult survivors. *J. Substance Abuse Treatment* 10: 537–43

Roizen J. 1993. *Issues in the Epidemiology of Alcohol and Violence in Alcohol and Interpersonal Violence: Fostering Multidisciplinary Perspectives, Natl. Inst. on Alcohol Abuse and Alcoholism Res. Monogr. No. 24,* ed. SE Martin. Washington, DC: Natl. Inst. Health

Roncek DW, Maier PA. 1991. Bars, blocks, crimes revisited: linking the theory of routine activities to the empiricism of 'hot spots'. *Criminology* 29:725–54

Room R, Collins G, eds. 1983. *Alcohol and Disinhibition: Nature and Meaning of the Link.* Washington, DC: *Natl. Inst. Alcohol Abuse and Alcoholism, Res. Monogr. No. 2.*

Sherman LW, Gartin PR, Buerger ME. 1989. Hot spots of predatory crime: routine activities and the criminology of place. *Criminology* Vols. 27–56

Siegel RK. 1978. Phencyclidine, criminal behavior, the defence of diminished capacity. In *Phencyclidine (PCP) Abuse: An Appraisal,* ed. RC Petersen, RC Stillman, pp. 272–88. Rockville, MD: Dep. Health Human Serv.

Spunt B, Brownstein H, Goldstein P, Fendrich M, Liberty HJ. 1995. Drug use by homicide offenders. *J. Psychoactive Drugs* 27(2):125–34

Spunt B, Goldstein P, Brownstein HH, Fendrich M, Langley S. 1994. Alcohol and homicide: interviews with prison inmates. *J. Drug Issues* 24(1):143–63

Spunt BJ, Goldstein PJ, Belluci PA, Miller T. 1990. Race, ethnicity and gender differences in the drugs-violence relationship. *J. Psychoactive Drugs* 22:293–303

Stets JE. 1990. Verbal and physical aggression in marriage. *J. Marriage Family* 43: 721–32

Tardiff K, Marzuk PM, Leon AC, Hirsch CS, Stajik M, et al. 1995. Cocaine, opiates, ethanol in homicides in New York City: 1990 and 1991. *J. Forensic Sci.* 40(3): 387–90

Taylor SP. 1983. Alcohol and human physical aggression. In *Alcohol, Drug Abuse, Aggression,* ed. E Gottheil, KA Druley, TE Skoloda, HM Waxman. Springfield, IL: Thomas

Watts WD, Wright LS. 1990. The drug use–violent delinquency link among adolescent Mexican-Americans. In *Drugs and Violence: Causes, Correlates, Consequences, NIDA Res. Monogr. No. 103,* ed. M De La Rosa, EY Lambert, B Gropper, pp. 136–159. Washington, DC: USGPO

Welte JW, Abel EL. 1989. Homicide: drinking by the victim. *J. Stud. Alcohol* 50(3): 197–201

White HR, Hansell S, Brick J. 1993. Alcohol use and aggression among youth. *Alcohol Health Res. World* 17(2):144–50

White HR, Pandina RJ, LaGrange RL. 1987. Longitudinal predictors of serious substance abuse and delinquency. *Criminology* 25(3):715–40

White House Office of National Drug Control Policy. 1997. *Fact Sheet: Drug Use Trends. National Criminal Justice Reference Service.* Available online at http://www.ncjrs.org

Widom CS, Ames MA. 1994. Criminal consequences of childhood sexual victimization. *Child Abuse Neglect* 18(4):303–18

Wieczorek W, Welte J, Abel E. 1990. Alcohol, drugs, murder: a study of convicted homicide offenders. *J. Criminal Justice* 18: 217–27

Wilbanks W. 1984. *Murder in Miami.* Lantham, MD: Univ. Press Am.

Wilson WJ. 1987. *The Truly Disadvantaged: The Inner City, the Underclass, Public Policy.* Chicago: Univ. Chicago Press

Wish ED. 1986. PCP and crime: just another illicit drug? In *Phencyclidine: An Update. NIDA Res. Monogr. No. 64*, ed. DH Clout, pp. 174–89. Rockville, MD: Dep. Health Human Serv.

Wolfgang ME, Ferracuti F. 1976. *The Subculture of Violence: Towards an Integrated Theory in Criminology.* London: Tavistock

Yarvis RM. 1994. Patterns of substance abuse and intoxication among murderers. *Bull. Am. Acad. Psychiatry Law* 22(1):133–44

Annu. Rev. Sociol. 1998. 24:313–43

COMMENSURATION AS A SOCIAL PROCESS

Wendy Nelson Espeland
Department of Sociology, Northwestern University, Evanston, Illinois 60208-1330; e-mail: wne741@nwu.edu

Mitchell L. Stevens
Department of Sociology, Hamilton College, Clinton, New York 13323; e-mail: mstevens@hamilton.edu

KEY WORDS: commodification, quantification, measurement

ABSTRACT

Although it is evident in routine decision-making and a crucial vehicle of rationalization, commensuration as a general social process has been given little consideration by sociologists. This article defines commensuration as the comparison of different entities according to a common metric, notes commensuration's long history as an instrument of social thought, analyzes commensuration as a mode of power, and discusses the cognitive and political stakes inherent in calling something incommensurable. We provide a framework for future empirical study of commensuration and demonstrate how this analytic focus can inform established fields of sociological inquiry.

INTRODUCTION

Consider three examples. Faculty at a well-regarded liberal arts college recently received unexpected, generous raises. Some, concerned over the disparity between their comfortable salaries and those of the college's arguably underpaid staff, offered to share their raises with staff members. Their offers were rejected by administrators, who explained that their raises were "not about them." Faculty salaries are one criterion magazines use to rank colleges. Administrators, mindful of how fateful these rankings are, wished to protect

0360-0572/98/0815-0313$08.00

their favorable ranking with preemptive faculty raises. Partly because college raters pay closest attention to professors' incomes, faculty and staff compensation plans are not considered comparable.

Several working mothers recently described their strategy for managing their anxiety about the amount of time they spend away from their young children. Each week, they calculate a ratio of mom-to-caregiver hours. If the ratio is close, or favors mom, they feel better. One woman admitted to "fudging" her numbers to produce a guilt-ameliorating figure. An opposite appeasement strategy involves the invention of "quality time," when harried parents try to convince themselves that what matters is the richness, rather than the volume, of time spent with their children. The emergence of "quality time" as a way to mark the specialness of parental involvement corresponded to the large influx of mothers moving into the paid work force. But some mothers who embrace traditional roles, or who sacrifice careers and income to stay home with their children, sniff at the self-serving aroma of "quality time" (Hays 1996, Berger 1995:43–44).

An economist evaluating a proposed dam faced the problem of how to estimate the value of tubing down the river, an activity that the proposed dam would eliminate. Committed to including in his analysis the "cost" of losing this recreation enjoyed by thousands each warm weekend, he tried to synthesize a demand curve for tubing. Despite valiant efforts and sizable expenditures, his efforts to derive a robust price for tubing failed. As is common with characteristics that are hard to measure, the value of tubing was excluded from the analysis of the dam (Espeland 1998).

Commensuration—the transformation of different qualities into a common metric—is central in each of these examples. Whether it takes the form of rankings, ratios, or elusive prices, whether it is used to inform consumers and judge competitors, assuage a guilty conscience, or represent disparate forms of value, commensuration is crucial to how we categorize and make sense of the world.

The consequences of commensuration are complex and varied. Commensuration can render some aspects of life invisible or irrelevant, as the failure to price river tubing illustrates. The expansion of commensuration can be a political response to exclusion or inequality. This tactic is embraced by some lawmakers, environmentalists, and bureaucrats (including the economist just described) who wish to expand what is considered relevant in bureaucratic decisions (Taylor 1984, Espeland 1998), by women advocating comparable worth as a means for redressing pay inequity (Nelson & Bridges forthcoming, England 1992), or by economists grappling with problems of externalities (Baumol & Oates 1979). For the working mothers, commensuration can be a deeply personal way to negotiate difficult contradictions. But rejecting commensuration as an appropriate expression of value can also be a political response for those, like some homemakers, who see their identities jeopardized by the commodification of their work and the quantification of their investments.

We argue that commensuration is no mere technical process but a fundamental feature of social life. Commensuration as a practical task requires enormous organization and discipline that has become largely invisible to us. Commensuration is often so taken for granted that we forget the work it requires and the assumptions that surround its use. It seems natural that things have prices, that temporality is standardized, and that social phenomena can be measured. Our theories presume that we commensurate when choosing and that values can be expressed quantitatively. Commensuration changes the terms of what can be talked about, how we value, and how we treat what we value. It is symbolic, inherently interpretive, deeply political, and too important to be left implicit in sociological work.

Commensuration warrants more sustained and systematic treatment. (Scholars working toward this project include Porter 1995; Radin 1996; Anderson 1993; Espeland 1992, 1998; Hurley 1989; Sunstein 1994; Desrosières 1990; and Zelizer 1994.) We need to explain variation in what motivates people to commensurate, the forms they use to do so, commensuration's practical and political effects, and how people resist commensuration. This is possible only when commensuration is investigated as a field. Our neglect of commensuration as a general phenomenon and our failure to provide a framework for its investigation as such have kept us from appreciating its social and theoretical significance. Our goal is to begin building such a framework. We start by defining commensuration, describing its long intellectual history, and explaining its significance. We then discuss the cognitive and political stakes inherent in calling something incommensurable, we offer guidelines for future empirical studies, and we illustrate how this focus can illuminate current sociological research.

WHAT IS COMMENSURATION?

Commensuration is the expression or measurement of characteristics normally represented by different units according to a common metric. Utility, price, and cost-benefit ratios are common examples of commensuration, although the logic of commensuration is implicit in a very wide range of valuing systems: college rankings that numerically compare organizations; censuses and social statistics that make cities and nations numerically comparable; actuarial projects that attempt to quantify and compare vastly different kinds of risks; commodity futures that make uniform units out of products that may not yet exist; voting, and the pork-barrel trading of diverse interests that often lies behind it; calculation of different kinds of work in terms of labor costs; and the ad hoc calculations of trade-offs among such potentially incomparable values as career and family, breadth and depth in scholarship, and freedom and commitment in love.

Commensuration transforms qualities into quantities, difference into magnitude. It is a way to reduce and simplify disparate information into numbers that can easily be compared. This transformation allows people to quickly grasp, represent, and compare differences. One virtue of commensuration is that it offers standardized ways of constructing proxies for uncertain and elusive qualities. Another virtue is that it condenses and reduces the amount of information people have to process, which is useful for representing value and simplifying decision-making. The complexity of decisions has propelled the spread of commensuration in decision-making (Stokey & Zeckhauser 1978); so too has our growing appreciation of people's cognitive limitations (Tversky & Kahneman 1974, 1981; Thaler 1983; for a good review see Heimer 1988). Commensuration makes possible more mechanized decision-making. Computer programs that calculate utility functions, elicit and measure values, and identify alternatives that maximize people's utility can assure the consistency that people lack; in some cases, they mechanically tell people what to do. The technical advantages of commensuration can be enormous, but sometimes its symbolic and political advantages are paramount (Feldman & March 1981).

Commensuration sometimes responds to murky motives. It may be prompted by a desire to look rational, limit discretion, or conform to powerful expectations. Commensuration may be spurred by a desire to expand democratization (Cohen 1982, Espeland 1998), or by a wish to hide behind numbers, impose order, or shore up weak authority (Porter 1995). Commensuration can provide a robust defense for controversial decisions, expand a group's organizational or professional turf, or even be a means to appease God (Carruthers & Espeland 1991).

Our desire to manage uncertainty, impose control, or secure legitimacy propels us to create a dazzling array of strategies to use when we standardize. The scripts delivered by salespeople, the forms we use when we enroll our children in kindergarten or visit the doctor, and the practiced smiles of flight attendants are all forms of standardization. What distinguishes commensuration from other forms of standardization is the common metric it provides. When commensuration is used in decision-making, the procedure for deriving this metric amounts to a series of aggregations.

Most quantification can be understood as commensuration because quantification creates relations between different entities through a common metric. Commensuration is noticed most when it creates relations among things that seem fundamentally different ; quantification seems distinct from commensuration when the objects linked by numbers already seem alike. When we assume the unity conferred by numbers, when the homogeneity among things appears to be a property of the object rather than something produced by quantification, then we imagine we are simply counting or measuring something rather than commensurating disparate entities. For example, the census appears to be a method for counting people rather than a mechanism for constructing and evaluating relations among citizens of a state or region. This is because implicit in the act of counting is a conception of citizenship or identity that renders unproblematic the coherence of the relations among diverse people. As Theodore Porter (1986:24) put it, "It makes no sense to count people if their common personhood is not seen as somehow more significant than their differences."[1]

Commensuration is fundamentally relative. It creates relations between attributes or dimensions where value is revealed in the comparison. When used to make decisions, commensurated value is derived from the trade-offs made among the different aspects of a choice. Value emerges from comparisons that are framed in terms of how much of one thing is needed to compensate for something else. In complex choices, commensuration often occurs at several levels of analysis. For example, before building a dam, analysts want to know how the dam would affect the quality of water. Water quality has many dimensions (e.g. temperature, the amount and nature of dissolved solids, turbidity, pH), and even though these dimensions are already quantified, they are measured with different scales. Aggregating these attributes according to some broader metric creates "water quality."

The structure of value rooted in trade-offs is like that of an analogy: Its unity is based on the common relationship that two things have with a third thing, a metric. How difficult or controversial commensuration is depends partly on whether it is used routinely to express the value of something, on whether people accept it as a legitimate expression of value, and on how disparate-seeming are the entities being commensurated. For example, commodification has become so naturalized that it is hard to construe the value of some goods in forms apart from price.

Commensuration can be understood as a system for discarding information and organizing what remains into new forms. In abstracting and reducing information, the link between what is represented and the empirical world is obscured and uncertainty is absorbed (March & Simon 1958:138–39, 150–51). Everyday experience, practical reasoning, and empathetic identification become increasingly irrelevant bases for judgment as context is stripped away and relationships become more abstractly represented by numbers.

[1]Counting and measuring may be controversial if the likeness or comparability of the units being counted is disputed. For example, during the Constitutional Convention of 1787, Southerners who rejected slaves' citizenship rights nevertheless wished to expand their political clout in the House of Representatives. For the purposes of apportioning representatives, they agreed that slaves should count as "three-fifths of all other persons."

As we demonstrate below, the forms commensuration takes vary on several dimensions. First, modes of commensuration vary in how technologically elaborated they are. Some are highly elaborated, as in the cost-benefit analyses first developed by government bureaucrats and then elaborated by economists and decision theorists to adjudicate between diverse and often costly social policies (Porter 1992, 1995:148–89). Other modes are only marginally elaborated, such as the often ad hoc calculations made by spouses to determine the relative equitability of household chores (e.g. Hochschild 1989). Second, modes of commensuration vary in how visible or explicit they seem. There is some correlation between elaborateness of a mode of commensuration and explicitness of the project. For an economist trying to synthesize a demand curve for river tubing, the labor involved in commensuration is both deliberate and apparent; for spouses trying to equalize household contributions, the process may seem as natural as it does commonsensical. But performing some highly elaborated modes of commensuration, such as generating identical units of value in stocks or commodities futures (Cronon 1991:97–147; Porter 1995: 45–48), are complex technical feats that seem "natural" to traders and stockholders nevertheless. This suggests a third dimension of variation in modes of commensuration—institutionalization—which we address in further detail below. Finally, modes of commensuration vary according to who their agents are. Some modes are the jealously guarded turf of distinct professional bodies; actuary work in insurance is a prime example (Porter 1995:101–13). Other modes are made routine and then embedded in complex divisions of labor, as in the lower-level diagnostic and charting work done by nurses and physican residents, who standardize patients in part by transforming vital signs into discrete numerical measures (Bosk 1979, Chambliss 1996). Still other modes are common features of everyday social experience, as in consumers' efforts to locate bargains at the grocery store or make trade-offs among purchases.

HISTORICAL LEGACIES

The linking of rationality to commensurability, and irrationality to incommensurability, are old ideas that appealed to some of our deepest thinkers. As Martha Nussbaum wrote (1984:56–57; 1986), the pairing of numbering, measurement, and commensuration with order, the pairing of comprehension with control, and obversely, the pairing of incommensurability with chaos, anxiety, and threat are characteristic of Greek writing in the fifth and early fourth centuries BCE. Nussbaum argues that commensuration was crucial to Plato's understanding of the Good, since Plato believed that we need to make our ethical values commensurate in order to prioritize them. Complex ethical concerns, if left incommensurate, would create conflict, confusion, and pain.

As others would argue much later, Plato believed that commensuration as a mode of perceiving the world would also change those who used it. Commensuration would make us more rational and render human values more stable and less vulnerable to passion, luck, and fate. One of the great virtues of commensurability for Socrates and for Plato was that it could help us eliminate *akrasia* by structuring our choices in ways that make it obvious what we should do; commensuration would make our ethical or practical problems easy to solve in the same way that it is easy to choose between \$50 and \$200 (Nussbaum 1986:114).

But for Plato, an equally important feature of commensuration is that this willful elimination of the heterogeneity of values also stabilizes our emotions and attachments by removing motives for irrational behavior, motives such as commitment to passionate, singular love. If in using a general concept of value we can frame our choices as between more or less of the same quantity, we no longer feel the same way toward those things. If we understand our lover not as a uniquely compelling person but rather as one who provides us with some specific amount of general pleasure, we value our lover not only differently, but less. The more interchangeable our lover is with someone nearly as beautiful or more clever, the less vulnerable we are, and the less likely we are to pursue our lover with reckless abandon.

Plato's claim is powerful. He understood that in making us more stable and less passionate, commensuration was both appealing and frightening. For Aristotle, Nussbaum argues, eliminating our vulnerability, and therefore our passion, was a prospect too disturbing. He believed our sense of beauty depends precisely on its ephemeral qualities, that our ethics require us to invest in the singularity of others. Investing in what is unique is risky, but the loss of vulnerability is even more threatening, for goodness requires ethical risks, valuing things for their own sake, passion. For Aristotle, the fragility of goodness is undermined by understanding value as general and homogeneous (Nussbaum 1986, p. 235–354).

Commensuration can change our relations to what we value and alter how we invest in things and people. Commensuration makes the world more predictable, but at what cost? For Aristotle, a price too high; for Plato, an essential sacrifice. The homogeneity commensuration produces simultaneously diminishes risk and threatens the intensity and integrity of what we value. These two important themes found in Plato's and Aristotle's view of ethics reemerge in our most compelling critiques of modernity: in Karl Marx's critique of capitalism, where commodification distorts human relations by turning people into means and things into ends; in Max Weber's analysis of the constraints of the iron cage and the disenchantment attending rationalization; and in Georg Simmel's analysis of money, where the objectification of value inserts distance between us and what is valued, fostering intellectualization and detachment.

Commensuration is crucial for capitalism and so is a prominent theme in Karl Marx's work. For Marx, commensuration is key for understanding the central social categories of capitalism: labor, value, commodity, and money. Marx argued that under capitalism, labor is the great commensurator. Value is derived from labor, and the commensuration of value is also accomplished through labor. Value exists in precise quantities in all commodities but is not measured according to the particular products of various kinds of labor. Rather, value is expressed in terms of what these have in common: the general experience of labor, what Marx (1976 [1867]:992) calls abstract labor, which is measured as labor-time.[2]

Labor has dual qualities. Concrete labor is the distinctive labor process shaped by the particular things it produces, things that have specific uses for people, such as food to eat or clothes to wear. Concrete labor produces use-value, but it does not produce value in the general sense. Abstract labor, on the other hand, is the "socially necessary general labor" that produces undifferentiated value. It is the peculiar way we obtain goods under capitalism, where what we produce has no intrinsic relation to the products we ultimately acquire through our labor (Postone 1996, p. 149). Value, as an expression of abstract labor, commensurates because it abstracts away the distinctiveness of the particular forms of work, objects of work, and practical uses of these objects. The concrete labor that produces use-value and the abstract labor that constitutes value are not two separate kinds of labor but rather two aspects of labor under capitalism (Postone 1996:144).

The theoretical commensuration implicit in Marx's conception of abstract value is in turn crucial for his conception of commodity—the basic social form of capitalism. Abstract labor is what is common to all commodities. A commodity possesses both use-value and exchange value: It is both a product and a social relation that embodies exchange value. For use-value, labor matters qualitatively; for exchange-value, it matters quantitatively (Marx 1976 [1867]:136). The tension between qualitative expressiveness and use of labor, and its quantitative expressiveness (between what is incommensurate and what is commensurate), is part of the dual and contradictory nature of commodities. One way that commodification debases human life is that qualitative differences become quantitative differences: People become means, things become ends.

Money, for Marx, is not what makes commodities commensurate. This is an illusion (Marx 1976 [1867]:188); instead, money is an expression of the commensuration already embodied in abstract labor. But money is powerful, partly for the illusions that it helps sustain. As a means of circulating com-

[2]This discussion of abstract labor is indebted to Postone (1996, pp. 123–85).

modities, money obscures the social relations behind them. Because it allows us to buy anything, money becomes the universal object of possession. The ultimate "pimp," money mediates between our needs and the object of our needs, between life and the means of life, between my life and others (Marx 1976 [1867]:102). Money appears to us more real than the relations behind it, an end rather than a means to an end. Under capitalism, qualities are quantified, and all qualitative needs that cannot be expressed quantitatively, or bought, are inhibited (Heller 1976:55).

Commensuration and its limits are central themes in Max Weber's investigations of rationalization, which often parallel the dialogue between Plato and Aristotle on the virtues and threat of reason based on calculation. Weber's ambivalence did not allow him to choose sides. For Weber, the expanding role of calculation as a strategy to manage uncertainty was a central feature of Western rationalism and crucial for the development of capitalism. The growing importance of knowledge and technical expertise in everyday life, the increasing depersonalization of structures of power and authority, and our expanding control over material objects, social relations, and self are unifying characteristics of Western rationalism (Brubaker 1984:29–35). Calculation and standardization were crucial in each of these processes.

To take one example, Weber (1981:276) argued that rational capital accounting, a sophisticated form of commensuration, was essential to the development of modern capitalism. Accounting allows capitalists to rationally evaluate the outcomes of past investments, to calculate exactly the resources available to them and project future income, and to assess and compare future investments. Accounting reconceptualizes and depersonalizes business relations and fosters an objective stance toward business. But as Weber shows us, efforts to rationalize can be hard-fought battles. Those who benefit from an existing system of authority often resist mightily the intrusion of commensuration that threatens their privilege (Swetz 1987:181–82; Weber 1981:224).

The efficiency of bureaucracies and economic transactions depends on their growing depersonalization and objectification. The impersonality of economic and bureaucratic rationality is vastly enhanced by commensuration, because it standardizes relations between disparate things and reduces the relevance of context. This impersonality is hostile to ethical systems that depend on personal ties, which explains why religious elites often have aligned with aristocrats to protect patriarchal relations.

One way to think about the tension between ethical systems and formal rationality is to conceptualize it as a contest over the limits of commensuration. Ethical and political systems based on personal relations often emphasize the uniqueness of individuals or the distinctive relations between certain categories of individuals. But rational systems depend on numerous forms of commensuration, on bureaucracies that strictly separate offices from their incumbents, and on the elaborate rules that define offices. One might interpret formal rationality as rendering offices unique and the people who hold the offices commensurable. In this way, the incommensurability of individuals that is basic to much ethics confronts the radical commensuration of formal rationality. Conflicts generated by such confrontations are irreconcilable.

Where Weber emphasized the technical superiority of rational forms, Simmel was attentive to their symbolic and constitutive power. He investigated how our collaboration with social forms changes us. Simmel's (1978) extended analysis of money offers a brilliant analysis of commensuration. Simmel sees money as largely responsible for the increasing divergence between the objective and subjective culture that characterizes modern life. Money speeds up the pace of the production of cultural forms, making it harder for individuals to assimilate them. Money advances the development of people's intellectual faculties over their emotional faculties because of its vibrant instrumentality, its character as the "perfect tool." This quality extends the causal connections we make between things to such an extent that the end point, the ultimate value, becomes obscure. This is what accounts for the "calculating character of modern times," where people become obsessed with "measuring, weighing, and calculating"(Simmel 1978:443–44).

When a form becomes taken for granted as a means of understanding relationships and values, things that are hard to assimilate to the form seem increasingly unreal. Money also contributes to the transformation of substantive values into money values; this homogenizes life, but it also offers autonomy, even freedom. Simmel concludes his analysis with a profound point: Over time, money increasingly approximates a pure symbol of the relativity of value and of the relativistic character of existence more generally—a character that money helped to define (Simmel 1978:512).

Simmel's insights about money can be usefully extended to other forms of commensuration. Utility, for example, is an even more enveloping form of relativity because it embodies the relativity of all value, even of those things without prices. Utility can precisely convey any value and its relation to any other value, whether it is fresh air, children, or even death.[3]

The compulsion to create forms stems from our need to make sense of the world, but as Simmel understood, forms may possess a force that seems to adhere to them independent of their users. Forms create expectations as well as coherence, and a form's familiarity encourages our complicity. This complic-

[3]One important difference between money and other forms of commensuration is that some commensurated forms are even more abstract than money, having no tangible existence that makes their symbolic expression less distant. Utility cannot be inscribed with the faces of queens, so perhaps this makes it a less effective symbol. Because some forms of commensuration, including money, are so closely tied to our notions of rationality, these forms can symbolize rationality.

ity enhances the rhetorical appeal of forms and is one reason we find them compelling (see Burke 1969:58–59). Commensuration encourages us to believe that we can integrate all our values, unify our compartmentalized worlds, and measure our longings.

Fundamental to classical critiques of modernity, commensuration is also central to many contemporary versions of rational choice theory. Rational choice theory varies in its assumptions, goals, and applications, but many versions make commensuration a prerequisite for rationality. Steinbrunner (1974:25–46) characterizes rational choice theory as deriving from three key assumptions: First, that separate dimensions of values are integrated via tradeoffs in a deliberate balancing of competing claims of values. Integration is accomplished by creating some metric that gives the worth of one value in terms comparable to the other, and this commensuration of values must occur in advance of the final analysis of outcomes. Utility conceptually integrates values; it is a measure of absolute value, an ideal measure that would subsume all dimensions of value and provide a basis for making comparisons between choices. Second, alternative outcomes are evaluated and analyzed based on predictions about their consequences. Third, people adjust their expectations as more is known about how alternatives will perform, but these new expected outcomes are evaluated by the same metric.

WHY COMMENSURATION MATTERS

Investigating commensuration is important because it is ubiquitous and demands vast resources, discipline, and organization. Commensuration can radically transform the world by creating new social categories and backing them with the weight of powerful institutions. Commensuration is political: It reconstructs relations of authority, creates new political entities, and establishes new interpretive frameworks. Despite some advocates' claims, it is not a neutral or merely technical process.

Commensuration is everywhere, and we are more likely to notice failures of commensuration than its widespread, varied success. Our faith in price as a measure of value is so naturalized that we now routinely simulate markets for elusive and intangible qualities. Although efforts to price tubing might have failed, there are well-established procedures for attaching prices to everything from corporate goodwill to surrogate pregnancies.

Where markets do not exist they are often invented. Corporations routinely create internal markets for the goods and services produced by subunits, and these fictive prices matter enormously in people's jobs (Eccles 1985). Some business schools require students to bid for their courses. Economists advocate creating markets in pollution to help curtail both pollution and theoretically unsavory externalities (Baumol & Oates 1979). Insurers work to quantify such consequential uncertainties as the professional reputations of their clients (Heimer 1985).

Economists have developed dazzling techniques for measuring utility, and its conceptual and practical influence is hard to overstate. There is hardly an issue in government that is not framed by the logic of cost-benefit analysis; its deployment in matters of health care and safety (Jasanoff 1989, Weisbrod 1961), education and environment (Smith 1984), and program evaluation (Kee 1994:456–88) is routine. Social science is often synonymous with measurement and model-building. Commensuration is fundamental to management, regardless of whether its object is art or widgets. Bureaucrats and analysts use sophisticated decision models requiring commensurated values when making decisions on everything from welfare to warfare. We devote enormous resources to commensuration. We have industries, agencies, and disciplines dedicated to measuring and managing risk (Heimer 1985, Jasanoff 1986, Clark 1989), measuring public opinion, quantifying intelligence (Carson 1993), simulating prices (Portney 1994), assessing values, and making decisions—all of which depend on our capacity to commensurate anything.

Commensuration is a radical social form, partly because of the assumptions that inform its use. Its long associations with rationality make it ideologically potent. Assuming that values can be made commensurate and that commensuration is a prerequisite to rationality are powerful ideas. Embedded in this logic is another assumption: that all value is relative and that the value of something can be expressed only in terms of its relation to something else. This form of valuing denies the possibility of intrinsic value, pricelessness, or any absolute category of value. Commensuration presupposes that widely disparate or even idiosyncratic values can be expressed in standardized ways and that these expressions do not alter meanings relevant to decisions.

Commensuration is radically inclusive. It offers an abstract form of unity that can potentially encompass any valued thing. Whether commensuration is accomplished in a price, utility curve, cost-benefit ratio, or multi-attribute trade-off scheme, any value or preference can be made commensurate with any other. The capacity to create relationships between virtually anything is extraordinary in that it simultaneously overcomes distance (by creating ties between things where none before had existed) and imposes distance (by expressing value in such abstract, remote ways). In doing so, commensuration creates new things, new relations among disparate and remote things, and changes the meanings of old things (Goody 1986).

According to Hacking (1990:181–95), from 1820 to 1840, unprecedented and nearly universal numerical enthusiasm produced an "avalanche of numbers." One result was the discovery of an astonishing number of regularities: in worker illness, suicide, crime, epidemics, and childbearing. Determinism was a casualty of the exponential growth in the production of numbers, as quests for "exactness" gave way to relentless efforts to understand and tame chance. Another consequence was the rapid proliferation of categories—categories invented to name and sort the newfound regularities, categories that then became constitutive.

The category of "society," Porter argues, is largely a statistical construct (1995:37, 1986:156–57). The regularities revealed in suicide and crime could not be attributed to individuals. A broader category was needed to account for them, and beginning around 1830, they were designated properties of society. Such regularities were powerful evidence of the autonomous existence of society, of "collective forces," as Durkheim famously argued (1951:297–325; Hacking 1990:182). Society was soon understood as an aspect of life even more basic than state (Collini 1980:203). Interpreted as statistical laws that governed naturally, these regularities helped buttress laissez-faire liberalism. But the invention of crime rates in the 1830s and of unemployment rates some 70 years later as societal characteristics helped define these as collective responsibilities worthy of reform, rather than the just desserts of unworthy persons (Himmelfarb 1991:41).

Even controversial or artificial-seeming products of commensuration, once backed by powerful institutions, become real, fateful, and autonomous. As Porter notes (1995:41–42), bureaucrats and activists have turned Americans of Puerto Rican, Mexican, Cuban, Iberian, and Central and South American descent into "Hispanics." Once such statistical categories become routinized in bureaucracies or written into law, they became increasingly real and fateful. Deployed by bureaucrats and politicians, distributed by media, and analyzed by social scientists, their use gives them meaning, consequence, and objectivity. Official statistics become, in Latour & Woolgar's term (1986), "black boxes" that are hard to discredit or even to open.

Economic integration requires commensuration. The capacity to commensurate time, labor, product, monies, and securities has helped create a world where a powerful, if invisible, relationship exists between the unemployed factory worker in the United States and the child laborer in Malaysia.[4] Commensuration makes possible precise comparisons across vast cultural and geographical distances that allow transactions fundamental to global markets. The worldwide ascendancy of finance and service industries has propelled commensuration, one by-product of which is an increasing polarization of wealth.

[4]Commensuration was central to Taylor's (1947) efforts to control labor. Armed with stopwatches and calculations, scientific management would reduce work to its most elemental, standardized forms; Taylor wished to make management a scientific endeavor governed by rules and calculations and to transform relations between workers and managers by depersonalizing authority (Bendix 1956:274–81). The wages and perks of many Americans who talk on phones for a living are linked to performance evaluations performed by computers that track the volume and length of their calls and the seconds between them (Schwartz 1994:240–41).

The development of an international property market means that real estate prices in Manhattan are linked to those in London or Paris and are shaped by flows of capital from Japan or Hong Kong (Sassen 1994:5–6, 99–117). Japanese investors' forays into New York real estate, for example, drove up prices and squeezed many small businesses out of the market.

When built into large institutions, commensurative practices are powerful means for coordinating human action and making possible automated decision-making. Sophisticated forms of commensuration have transformed our financial markets. Computer programs that continually search for discrepancies between stock prices, futures, and options prices have generated new investment strategies and have mechanized a broad array of investment decision-making. Now, distinctions are made between "discretionary" traders, who rely on their own judgment and "system" traders, who rely on mechanically produced signals to make decisions (Lucas & Schwartz 1989).

Techniques for commensurating are not evenly distributed. These patterns may reflect longstanding interests in commensuration, where those with the most to gain from commensuration have become its most sophisticated practitioners. Not surprisingly, water development agencies had sophisticated methods for calculating the benefits of dams long before they devised these for costs (Espeland 1993). Other biases exist. Units of analyses are often used that obscure the distributional effects of policies. Cost-benefit analyses that "discount the future" favor immediate benefits and distant costs over long-term benefits and immediate costs. This spurs development at the expense of environmental costs (Schnaiberg 1980:334–44). Even more fundamentally, presuppositions for commensuration often reflect assumptions about commodification that are inherently political and asymmetrical (Radin 1996, Sunstein 1994).

And finally, efforts to translate incommensurable values into commensurated value not only can distort the character of people's investments but can repudiate identities that are closely linked to incommensurable values.

INCOMMENSURABLES

Commensuration sometimes transgresses deeply significant moral and cultural boundaries. Defining something as incommensurate is a special form of valuing. Incommensurables preclude trade-offs. An incommensurable category encompasses things that are defined as socially unique in a specific way: They are not to be expressed in terms of some other category of value. Following Raz (1986:326–29), we broadly define something as incommensurable when we deny that the value of two things is comparable. An incommensurable involves a "failure of transitivity," where neither of two valuable options is better than the other and there could exist some other option that is better than one but not the other. [Anderson (1995) and Sunstein (1994) offer slightly different definitions.]

The importance of incommensurable categories will vary, partly because the significance of this symbolic boundary varies. Their salience depends on how passionate we feel about them, on their centrality in defining our roles and identities, and on how much effort is required to breach them. Their importance also depends, as Simmel would argue, on the relative status of their oppositional form, commensuration. The extension of commensuration into more spheres of life may make incommensurable categories more meaningful, their defense more necessary. This extension may produce paradoxical effects, as when "pricing" children in law, labor, and insurance shifted the terms of their value from primarily economic to moral and emotional. Children became priceless (Zelizer 1985).

Sometimes trivial things are incommensurable. If I cannot choose between chocolate cake and lemon pie, and adding whipped cream to the cake doesn't make it better or worse, these desserts are formally incommensurable but hardly significant for how I understand myself or how I treat others. Sometimes incommensurables are expressed for purely strategic reasons, as a bargaining position. One way to get more leverage or a better price during negotiations is to assert the incommensurability of something. Labeling something as bargaining in order to discredit claims can also be a political response (Espeland 1998).

But incommensurables can be vital expressions of core values, signaling to people how they should act toward those things. Identities and crucial roles are often defined with incommensurable categories. Believing that something is incommensurable can qualify one for some kinds of relationships. When incommensurable categories are important for defining how to "be," Raz calls them "constitutive incommensurables" (Raz 1986:345–57). People facing a choice involving a constitutive incommensurable will often refuse to participate; for some, the idea of such a choice is abhorrent.

For Yavapai residents whose ancestral land was threatened by a proposed dam, land was a constitutive incommensurable (Espeland 1998). The Yavapai understood themselves in relation to this specific land. Valuing land as an incommensurable was closely tied to what it means to be Yavapai. The rational decision models used by bureaucrats to evaluate the proposed dam required that the various components of the decision be made commensurate, including the cost and consequences associated with the forced resettlement of the Yavapai community. This way of representing Yavapai interests and expressing the value of their land was a contradiction of those values and of Yavapai identity.

There are many other, common examples of constitutive incommensurables. Two of Raz's examples are children and friends. Believing that the value of children is not comparable to money and that the very idea of exchanging a child for money is repugnant is fundamental to being a good parent. The inappropriateness of using commercial means for valuing children is one way we define good parenting. Likewise, believing that friendship cannot be bought or that what we derive from our friendship with a person is distinctive and cannot be had with any other person is basic to what it means to be a good friend. Thinking that our friends were somehow interchangeable could keep us from having genuine friendships. The pain of selling a childhood home, the reluctance some feel about selling their blood, our disapproval of sex for profit, or even faculty qualms over ranking graduate students or evaluating subordinates compared to "benchmarks" are examples of people grappling with incommensurable categories. Believing in incommensurables is a way to limit what can be rationally chosen, and this can be an important social relationship.

Just as commensuration is a considerable social accomplishment, so too the creation of incommensurables requires work. Some party must draw boundaries around the thing whose value is to be kept, or made, distinctive and then defend the boundaries from encroachment. Sometimes these tasks are the purview of experts: art critics and museum professionals who certify some objects as masterworks or as especially worth exhibiting (Becker 1982, Alexander 1996); attending physicians who invoke clinical wisdom and professional privilege to designate some medical cases extraordinary (Bosk 1979). Sometimes these tasks are the purview of intimate others: the mothers and fathers of premature newborns, for example, who are encouraged by hospital staff to name their babies, dress them in clothes brought from home, personalize their ward cribs with toys and photographs, and otherwise mark their infants as unique (Heimer & Staffen 1998). In still other instances the production of incommensurables is the main business of entire organizations, even bureaucratic ones: preservation agencies, for example, that designate official historic sites, landmark neighborhoods, and wildlife habitats, as well as the organizations that do the grunt work of enforcing the rules. Whether they are priceless artworks, national treasures, or precious children, incommensurable things are often regarded as somehow sacred, and like all sacred objects, their distinctiveness is defined through symbols and ritual. This marking can be elaborate, or mundane: For example, the sequestering of certain cash in a special jar or drawer can define it as money for distinctive purposes and thus incommensurable with other savings (Zelizer 1994).

STUDYING COMMENSURATION

Commensuration is a general social process, it is political, and it is capable of transforming social relations. It deserves closer, systematic scrutiny. We next offer core guiding questions that help reveal variation in how naturalized, how fateful, and how resisted commensuration can be.

How Institutionalized Is the Commensurative Act?

Instances of commensuration vary by how institutionalized they are, that is, they vary in how automatically commensuration gets done and in how natural the process seems to involved parties. [This conception of institutionalization is indebted to Garfinkel 1967, Berger & Luckmann 1966, and the work of John Meyer and his colleagues (e.g. Meyer 1971, Zucker 1977, Jepperson 1991).] Attending to institutionalization enables us to appreciate the extent to which commensuration constructs what it measures.

Some instances of commensuration are so deeply institutionalized that they help to constitute what they purport to measure. For example, futures traders buy and sell agricultural commodities by virtue of standardized grading systems that constitute products for entire industries. Grading systems create explicit categories of relative quality, and hence relative value, that make possible trade in products that may not yet exist (Cronon 1991:97–147; Porter 1995:45–48). Rankings of academic institutions, which purport to measure relative quality according to some common metric of excellence, sometimes prompt members to reevaluate their perceptions of their own schools (Elsbach & Kramer 1996). As our earlier example suggests, institutions often respond directly to raters' criteria; even if members dispute the accuracy or legitimacy of rankings, they are too fateful to ignore.

Some commensurative practices exist only in theory, such as comparable-worth wage programs. Intended to improve chronic income disparities between women and men, comparable-worth programs commensurate skill and pay levels between traditionally female and traditionally male occupations (England 1992). But comparable-worth advocates have met with very little success in implementing such policies or even in securing judicial approval of them (Nelson & Bridges 1998). Such instances of commensuration are weakly institutionalized because so few parties use them. Little more than an argument (however good a one), this commensuration effectively exists only on paper.

But what determines the extent to which a commensurative act gets institutionalized? Phenomenological sociology suggests a preliminary answer. Berger & Luckmann argue that socially constructed meaning becomes more fact-like when it is objectivated or reified, that is, when social practices are organized to sustain the appearance that meaning stands outside of individual subjectivity, as part of the world (1966:47–92; Berger 1967:3–24). In keeping with this insight, we argue that as commensuration gets built into practical organizations of labor and resources, it becomes more taken for granted and more constitutive of what it measures. Thus, however arbitrary, the Chicago Board of Trade's standardized grades of grain quality became ever more constitutive of what they measured as the number of parties who used the measures grew: not only farmers and merchants, but also elevator operators, banks, the trade press, and ultimately the state legislature. In time, Chicago businessmen could make or lose fortunes trading in futures—commodities that exist only by virtue of a commensuration system (Cronon 1991:97–147).

Institutionalization as reification enables us to make predictions about the potential trajectory of other commensurative practices. We might expect, for example, that college rankings will become more constitutive of what they measure as their audiences expand: parents considering where to send their tuition dollars, faculty plotting careers at prestigious schools, and foundations whose grant-giving attends to such measures of institutional quality. On the other hand, commensurative acts that fail to get etched into practice, such as comparable-worth policies, will remain the purview of academic specialists and disappointed reformers.

How Does Commensuration Refract Power Relations?

Some proponents see commensuration as a technology of inclusion. This makes it especially valuable in democratic, pluralistic societies (Stokey & Zeckhauser 1978). Commensuration offers an adaptive, broadly legitimate device for conferring a formal parity in an unequal world; for pragmatic reformers, this is a hopeful beginning (Espeland 1998, Brown 1984). In decisions characterized by disparate values, diverse forms of knowledge, and the wish to incorporate people's preferences, commensuration offers a rigorous method for democratizing decisions and sharing power.

For supporters, the discipline of commensuration creates robust, "objective" knowledge that can constrain power. For example, Marx used the "moral statistics" of his day as essential weapons in his indictment of capitalism; Weber (1978:225) saw commensuration facilitating the leveling effects of bureaucratic rationality by providing sturdy mechanisms for challenging old forms of privilege; today, discrimination is often fought most effectively with numbers, by lawyers girded with statistics; and when standardized tests are used in hiring decisions, the odds for minorities can improve (Neckerman & Kirschenman 1991).

Critics of commensuration come from both the right and left. Conservatives disdain its equalizing effects, the loss of elite discretion that it fosters. Left-leaning critics see commensuration as another conduit of power that mystifies power relations, partly by emphasizing results at the expense of process and distribution (e.g. Tribe 1971, 1972). Commensuration, in propelling "decisionism," helps sustain the pretense that facts and values can be separated, that politics can be rendered technical (Habermas 1973:253–82).

But commensuration is not merely a tool of the powerful, a way to wage interest politics numerically. Porter (1995) argues that recourse to quantitative methods evinces weak authority. The spread of quantitative expertise represents a quest for "mechanical objectivity"—knowledge whose authority is based on close adherence to quantitative rules. Mechanical objectivity is most valued when decision-making is dispersed, when it incorporates diverse groups, when powerful outsiders must be accounted to, when decisions are public and politicized, and when decision-makers are distrusted. The legitimacy offered by numbers diminishes autonomy, because discretion is replaced by disciplined methods. This is why quantitative technologies are the province of weak elites and why they are resisted by those whose authority depends on expert judgment, character, or informal knowledge.

Understanding commensuration as a calculus of power requires that we appreciate the various guises of power, whether these are obvious or opaque, strategic or constitutive. While examples of numbers malleable enough to conform to powerful interests are easy to find (e.g. Delaney 1994), commensuration, once launched, can become hard to control. Strategic commensuration, our capacity to create numbers that reflect our will, is perhaps greatest when commensuration is less public and less accessible and when methods are new or not grounded in academic theory (which creates new partisans). Those who think they can manipulate numbers at will are often proved wrong in the long run.

Commensuration's constitutive power is perhaps an even more formidable force, altering the people and places where it intrudes. The capacity to create new categories and enforce mechanical objectivity are consequential powers, ones often associated with states or firms. Official statistics may be more important for the subjects they create ("Hispanics," "the unemployed," "gifted children") than for the technical advantage this knowledge confers. Once the categories are in place, people's behavior increasingly conforms to them. This is not the obvious power of coercion but the more elusive, passive power of discipline, increasingly self-inflicted. The validity of censuses, test scores, or public opinion polls requires complicity from their subjects. Individuals are made governable (Foucault 1991:87–104) and numbers become self-vindicating (Porter 1995:45) when measures guide the activities being measured or shape the images of those whose characteristics they measure.

Commensuration produces depersonalized, public forms of knowledge that are often deemed superior to private, particularistic forms of knowing (Reddy 1984). The authority of those who know most about something can be undermined by the rigorous methods of distant, if less informed, officials. For example, before measures were standardized by states, regions and villages often had their own distinctive measures. Such heterogeneity in measurement enhanced the salience of local knowledge and facilitated negotiability. A "just price" for a unit of grain could be accomplished by peasant strategies for manipulating how densely packed it was. This flexibility favored local interests over state powers; hence rulers often eagerly imposed new, standardized measures (Kula 1986).

Commensuration refracts power in many ways. It can enlarge decision-making or legitimate preordained decisions. It can be cynically manipulated by elites or it can limit their discretion. It can create disciplined subjectivities or arm dissenters. This variety makes commensuration a useful lens for investigating the multiple forms of power.

When Are Claims about Incommensurables Made?

Perhaps because of their ability to constitute value and alter power relations, some instances of commensuration generate discontent. Claims that some values are incommensurable—that they cannot or should not be ordinarily compared with other values—are not uncommon. Nor are they random. We hypothesize that the most frequent and most durable claims about incommensurability occur at the borderlands between institutional spheres, where different modes of valuing overlap and conflict. We suspect also that claims about incommensurables are likely when commensuration threatens some cherished identity.

Friedland & Alford (1991:232) define institutions as both supraorganizational patterns of activity and symbolic systems through which we give meaning to activity. Because societies are complexes of multiple institutions, they are characterized by multiple modes of valuing. We value monetarily when we enter a labor or commodity market; emotionally when espousing friendship or love for children or a mate; and bureaucratically when we gauge merit or fault by reference to formal rules. These different modes of valuing are not necessarily consistent with one another. A job that pays well may estrange us from loved ones if it requires a move to another city. Meticulous devotion to formal rules may make us adequate bureaucrats but horrible friends (Heimer 1992).

Institutional theorists argue that inconsistency and contradiction between institutions can be opportunities for social innovation and change (Orren & Skowronek 1994, Clemens 1997) but also sites of deep struggle as different modes of behaving, cognizing, and valuing conflict (Friedland & Alford 1991). We suspect that claims about incommensurables are likely to arise at the borderlands between institutions, where what counts as an ideal or normal mode of valuing is uncertain, and where proponents of a particular mode are entrepreneurial.

Debate surrounding commercial surrogate motherhood provides a clear example of dispute about incommensurables at the borderlands between institutions. Sometimes called contract pregnancy, commercial surrogate motherhood is a reproductive arrangement in which, for a fee, a woman agrees to become pregnant, carry the child, and relinquish her parental rights after delivery (see Anderson 1993:168–69). The practice has generated considerable controversy among feminists and legal scholars (e.g. Moody-Adams 1991, Satz 1992, Radin 1996). For its critics, commercial surrogate motherhood is an encroachment of market modes of valuing into intimate spheres of life. To combat the encroachment, some argue that "[w]omen's labor is *not* a commodity" (Anderson 1995:189, original emphasis), nor are the children born of that labor (Radin 1996:136–53).

What makes commercial surrogate motherhood a locus of claims about incommensurables? The practice exists in a social space where neither intimate nor market modes of valuing are hegemonic. As the legal scholar Margaret Radin notes, the distinction between the baby-selling of commercial surrogate motherhood and the baby-giving of traditional adoption arrangements—in which adoptive parents often wait for a child of a particular race or age and pay many costs associated with pregnancy—is a fragile one (Radin 1996:136–53). In such uncertain terrain we are likely to find vocal advocates for one or another mode of valuing, and claims about incommensurables can be viable weapons in the struggle to control the contested turf.

Incommensurables will also be claimed where entrepreneurs of one mode of valuing wish to move in to novel terrain. Radin's careful bid for the market incommensurability of children (1996), for example, is a direct response to celebrated arguments for a market in them (Posner 1992:150–54; Landes & Posner 1978; Becker 1981).

Claims about incommensurables are also likely when commensuration threatens a cherished identity. When commensuration seems to discount some component of the self, the short-changed may disavow the implicating mode of valuing. Like their forbearers in the alternative-school movement (Swidler 1979), many parents who home school their children are suspicious of letter grading and formal achievement tests that enable their children's skills to be compared quantitatively with those of other children. Deeply protective of the individuality of their children, home schoolers fear that standardized performance measures at best prevent, at worst erode, a conception of children as uniquely gifted persons (Stevens 1996).

Because collective identities are often defined symbolically, efforts to commensurate symbolic objects with other valuables can meet with fierce resistance. Because geographic territory is often deeply symbolic of national identity, for example, disputes over territorial sovereignty are often long and bitter. The impassioned territorial commitments of Israeli and Palestinian peoples have confounded countless efforts to commensurate territorial interests at diplomatic bargaining tables (Friedland & Hecht 1996).

That claims about incommensurables are sometimes made by parties who may risk loss suggests that such claims may be more strategic than constitutive. It is tempting to infer that claims of incommensurability are themselves a kind of bargaining strategy, akin to bluffing in a poker game to cover a bad hand or to up an opponent's ante. Surely some claims of incommensurability are strategic in this way. But claims about incommensurables may also simultaneously reflect deeply held convictions and clever bet-hedging. People who lose their community to an industrial disaster may find the symbolic void irreplaceable but will also use that loss as grounds for material compensation (Erikson 1976). Disentangling the constitutive from the strategic in claims about incommensurables requires careful empirical work and recognition that people often have multiple and even contradictory incentives.

COMMENSURATION IN ACTION

We believe that attention to commensuration provides novel insights into established fields of sociological inquiry. To conclude, we illustrate how such an analytic focus might inform work in three broad substantive areas: gender and work, politics and social movements, and institutional sociology. Our goal is to sketch the potential utility of this way of theorizing in order to encourage further and more systematic efforts.

Feminist Commensuration and Its Discontents

That commensuration has the potential to transform what it measures is demonstrated in the repeated efforts of feminists to value household work in metrics used to quantify paid labor. Nineteenth-century reformers (Siegel 1994), twentieth-century feminists, and social scientists have sought to re-value the typically unpaid cooking, cleaning, child-rearing, and household management tasks women do for their families in metrics of time and output. The goals of such efforts have been multiple: to implicate housework in broader critiques of capitalism (Luxton 1980, Hartmann 1981); to quantify unequal distributions of domestic work between men and women (e.g. Walker & Woods 1976, Hochschild 1989); to argue for paid housework (Oakley 1976:226); and to emphasize how much of housework is a low-status chore (Mainardi 1970). However, some women have been reluctant to commensurate their own home work with paid labor, which suggests both a symbolic boundary around domestic relationships and a fissure between feminist and "pro-family" women that the analytic lens of commensuration can help to define.

Central to "modern" conceptions of family (see Stacey 1990:3–19) is the belief that family relations are of a fundamentally different character than those of the marketplace: Families are havens partly because relations among family members are governed by something more than self-interested individual calculation (Lasch 1977). If families are partly defined by their nonmarket exchanges, then attempts to commensurate these exchanges with labor market transactions may undermine the distinctiveness of familial relations. If household work is made formally commensurate with other forms of paid labor, then families appear more like the nodes of resource agglomeration, consumption, and social reproduction that some economic theory imagines (Becker 1981) and less like the havens envisioned by "pro-family" movements both historical and contemporary (e.g. Ryan 1981, Martin 1996).

The transformative potential of commensurating housework with other kinds of labor is double-edged. Feminists who have advocated direct comparisons have done so in order to alter women's relationships to other family members and to the broader labor force. By encouraging housewives to think of themselves as workers, laboring under oppressive conditions, early liberal and radical feminists sought to change women's appraisals of their household situations in ways that would incite them to domestic activism: At least, men would do more and women less at home than the modern-traditional rules prescribed (Hole & Levine 1971:85); at most, more equitable allocations of housework and childrearing would allow radical new models of family (Firestone 1970). The commensuration of housework with other kinds of labor has helped feminists to argue convincingly that gender asymmetries in the division of domestic work unjustly constrain women's lives.

Other women have resisted workplace modes of valuing at home. Opponents of the Equal Rights Amendment (ERA) resisted the legislation partly because of how its advocates conceived of housework. The domestic arrangements that feminists found so impoverishing were a way of life for millions of women. Commensurating housewifery with other occupations and declaring it wanting further undermined the already eroding status of angry homemakers (Mansbridge 1986:90–117). Within the abortion controversy, many pro-life activists object to the commensuration of motherhood with paid-work occupations. Many full-time homemakers believe that workplace logic diminishes them, that their lives measured poorly on metrics of income, occupational attainment, and personal autonomy (Luker 1984:158–215).

By commensurating housework with paid labor, feminists sought to transform both social appraisals and the social organization of domestic work. By most accounts, however, their efforts are only weakly institutionalized. Feminists have succeeded in demonstrating the low status of housework and in altering the life expectations of many women. But as Hochschild (1989:12) states succinctly, "There has been a real change in women without much change in anything else": Men contribute only minimally more to household duties, workplaces only reluctantly accommodate employees' family demands, and childcare remains a domestic, not a public or corporate, obligation.[5] And as the ERA and abortion battles make clear, feminist efforts to com-

[5]In childcare, commensuration has also directed attention to other sorts of distinctions: quality vs quantity time; individualized attention vs group socialization; daycare or preschool; a nearby relative, a certified caregiver, or an imported au pair. With housework less emotionally loaded than childcare, fewer distinctions seem necessary. Nevertheless, commensuration remains contested in both arenas.

mensurate domesticity have generated concerted arguments about incommensurables. Women invested in domesticity have found some of the feminist equations deep threats to their identities.

Politics and Social Movements

Commensuration makes possible modern politics. Opinion polls, in eliciting and organizing attitudes, create the object we call public opinion (Herbst 1998). Politics, as the art of compromise, is a broad instance of commensuration. Political negotiation entails seeing one's own interests as comparable to the interests of others. Our conception of interests as a basic unit of political analysis implies commensuration. When political disputes are framed as a contest over interests, parties are granted a formal, categorical equality among those with a political stake. Interest-group politics portrays outcomes as if differences were a matter of magnitude—of how much something matters, or of whose interests were served—rather than as disparate modes of investment in the decision. Voting is one way to commensurate interests. Trading—of campaign dollars for a sympathetic ear in office, of my vote on your project for yours on mine (the essence of pork-barrel politics), of tit for tat at the bargaining tables where multiple interest groups attempt to forge mutually advantageous coalitions—requires that traders evaluate diverse interests along some shared order of magnitude. Such commensurative acts are at the heart of normal politics, explaining puzzles such as why we have so many dams (Reisner 1986) or why tax reform requires sports stadiums (Birnbaum & Murray 1987). Making qualitatively unlike interests comparable can be a formidable cognitive achievement; that politicians, campaign contributors, and rank-and-file voters do such commensurating all the time is testament to the extent to which the equation of diverse values is commonplace in modern life. (Of course, the mode of commensuration matters here: Trading votes is regarded as acceptable political behavior; buying and selling them is not.)

But as many social-movement activists discovered, commensurative politics brings its own quandaries. Many New Left student activists of the 1960s and 1970s avoided participation in normal party and electoral politics because they believed that the structures of those institutions were morally flawed. Some New Left activists equated negotiation and trading of interests with moral compromise. For them, conventional political activism was suspect precisely because it required trade-offs among inviolable interests and illegitimate ones. The New Left's "great refusal" to participate in the commensurative art of normal politics has been cited both as its greatest moral accomplishment (Breines 1989) and as a cause of its ultimate political weakness (e.g. Gitlin 1987).

The recent history of the Religious Right indicates just how consequential choices to commensurate interests can be. Although a few conservative Christian leaders have long advocated translating the faith into political activism (Ribuffo 1983), only relatively recently did large numbers of rank-and-file believers begin to conceive of themselves as distinctive players in the realm of normal politics (Himmelstein 1990). A great accomplishment of conservative Christian leaders since the 1970s has been convincing many rank-and-file Christians to enact their faith in the political arena: Doing so has obliged believers to consider the comparability of their faith-based interests with the more secular agendas of other conservative factions (e.g. Klatch 1987, Rozell & Wilcox 1996). Typically cultural-traditionalists, conservative Christians cooperated with libertarian and economic conservatives to win three consecutive Republican presidencies (e.g. Himmelstein 1990, Martin 1996). But the believers were dismayed when their unequivocal stances on abortion, school prayer, and homosexuality became compromisable interests at Washington bargaining tables (Diamond 1995, Martin 1996). The powerful Christian Coalition has recently confronted a difficult choice: holding close to policy positions dear to conservative Christians or becoming more flexible in its stances on abortion, homosexuality, and other divisive issues in order to cooperate with other interest groups and a wider array of politicians (e.g. Reed 1993). Throughout its recent past, then, the Religious Right has wrestled with whether, and how, to commensurate its faith-based commitments with the secular parties and profane interests it encounters in the broader political arena.

That some movement activists from left to right have been wary of the compromises normal politics requires suggests their awareness of the transformative potential inherent in commensurating disparate values.[6] When we opt to negotiate with parties who do not share our vision of the world (e.g. members of the "Establishment," those not born again), we risk alienation of our interests. Negotiation requires commensurating with the enemy: It requires comparing the cherished with the reprehensible in ways that make the former less distinctive, less incomparably valuable than it once was. Not surprisingly, movements that stake their identities on incommensurables—radical democracy, heavenly truths, and native lands, for examples—face a dilemma even coming to the bargaining table.

(Of course, sometimes social movements embrace commensuration as a legitimating device. For women's reform organizations during the Progressive Era, the substitution of money for personal service was a way for women to

[6]Just as commensuration creates new social relations, so too does creating incommensurables. Not all incommensurables carry the same cultural weight, but some things defined as incommensurable may be subject to distinct rules of conduct. For example, family heirlooms bestowed on particular persons are often subject to special uses and, except under extraordinary conditions, are removed from markets.

signal that theirs were serious, modern organizations. As Clemens (1997: 209–10) argues, these women understood that citizenship required cash.)

Institutional Sociology

The ability of commensuration to create new social relations and even new social entities is clear in recent work by institutional sociologists. Studies of the elaboration and worldwide diffusion of census activity (Ventresca 1995) and of formal accounting procedures (Meyer 1986, Miller & O'Leary 1987, Carruthers & Espeland 1991) show how particular measuring, recording, and ranking processes help to make and remake phenomena they ostensibly describe.

Ventresca (1995) argues that the worldwide diffusion of relatively standardized modes of census administration helped render different parts of the world formally comparable. Shared counting procedures help shape how different populations make sense of one another and of themselves. With similar censuses, societies with wildly disparate histories, cultures, and economic and political structures are made to seem easily comparable. Vital statistics on scores of nations can be aggregated, summarized, and ordinally ranked—on a single page—facilitating charitable, diplomatic, and market linkages across vast stretches of social and geographic space.

Studies of accountancy offer parallel pictures of commensuration practices that make qualitative unlikes quantitatively comparable. Standardized accounting procedures make a firm's varied assets and liabilities, from raw materials to workers, uniformly calculable in monetary terms (Miller & O'Leary 1987) so as to produce values like "net worth." Like census figures, net worth is easily compared across firms (Carruthers & Espeland 1991). Such comparability permits us to understand firms as financial portfolios rather than as productive units. With accountants busy creating comparable bottom lines, executives can buy and sell firms while focusing on their profitability rather than on what they produce (Espeland & Hirsch 1990, Fligstein 1991).

But commensuration does more than produce new relations. It can also produce new entities. Common to these quite different studies of censuses and accounting procedures is the notion, informed in part by the work of Foucault (1973, 1977, 1978), that preponderant administrative practices create what they purport to describe. For example, Ventresca argues that modern census procedures help to create the nation-states they quantify. Censuses define the boundaries of state sovereignty by specifying just who is within those boundaries and who is not. The very structure of a census as an official count of persons assumes an aggregate relationship between nation and individual—the nation-state is the individuals it counts. Censuses also reify these individuals, marking them as non-, quasi-, or full citizens of a particular state and lending broad cultural salience to those facets of individual identity about which census counters, and their questionnaires, query (Ventresca 1995). In rendering nation-states more comparable, censuses also constitute what they compare (Desrosières 1990).

Conceptually similar processes characterize the rise of formal accounting procedures. Accountants, promising information that will improve efficiency, have historically sought ever more elaborate means of measuring labor output and labor costs; such measurements enable designation of modal and optimal levels of productivity against which many workers can be ranked and compared. Accounts thus help to construct such organizationally consequential beings as the average worker, the ideal worker, and the suboptimal worker (Miller & O'Leary 1987).

Social critics from Simmel to Foucault have sought to portray how modernization reconstitutes human subjectivity and transforms long-established social relations. Examining particular instances of commensuration may enable institutional scholars to better discern the mechanics of those changes. Recent theoretical work underscores this potential. Neoinstitutionalists operationalize modernity as a "Western cultural account," global in scope, that among other things assumes the calculability of all social values. In that modern story, human progress is incremental: Only by measuring can individuals or nation-states know how they are faring in personal or global history (Meyer et al 1994). Acts of commensuration facilitate comparative measurement across vast differences of sentiment, person, kind, culture, and nation. Rationalist, imperialist, and at times transformative, they may be key ways that we make ourselves modern.

ACKNOWLEDGMENTS

This research was supported in part by the Hamilton College Dean of Faculty. Thanks to Michael Burawoy, Bruce Carruthers, Dennis Gilbert, Peter Levin, Michael Lounsbury, Philip Klinkner, Kirk Pillow, and Marc Ventresca for scholarly assistance. Detailed comments by an anonymous reviewer greatly improved the effort.

Literature Cited

Alexander VD. 1996. Pictures at an exhibition: conflicting pressures in museums and the display of art. *Am. J. Sociol.* 101: 797–839

Anderson E. 1993.*Value in Ethics and Economics.* Cambridge, UK: Harvard Univ. Press

Baumol W, Oates W. 1979. *Economics, Environmental Policy, and the Quality of Life.* Englewood Cliffs, NJ: Prentice-Hall

Becker GS. 1981. *A Treatise on the Family.* Cambridge, MA: Harvard Univ. Press

Becker HS. 1982. *Art Worlds.* Berkeley: Univ. Calif. Press

Bendix R. 1956. *Work and Authority in Industry.* New York: Wiley

Berger BM. 1995. *An Essay on Culture.* Berkeley: Univ. Calif. Press

Berger PL. 1967. *The Sacred Canopy: Elements of a Sociological Theory of Religion.* New York: Doubleday

Berger PL, Luckmann T. 1966. *The Social Construction of Reality: A Treatise in the Sociology of Knowledge.* New York: Doubleday

Birnbaum JH, Murray AS. 1987. *Showdown at Gucci Gulch: Lawmakers, Lobbyists, and the Unlikely Triumph of Tax Reform.* New York: Vintage Books

Bosk CL. 1979. *Forgive and Remember: Managing Medical Failure.* Chicago: Univ. Chicago Press

Breines W. 1989. *Community and Organization in the New Left, 1962–1968: The Great Refusal.* New Brunswick, NJ: Rutgers Univ. Press

Brown CA. 1984. The Central Arizona Water Control Study: a case for multiobjective planning and public involvement. *Water Resour. Bull.* 20:331–37

Brubaker R. 1984. *The Limits of Rationality: An Essay on the Social and Moral Thought of Max Weber.* London: Allen & Unwin

Burke K. 1969. *A Rhetoric of Motives.* Berkeley: Univ. Calif. Press

Carruthers BG, Espeland WN. 1991. Accounting for rationality: double-entry bookkeeping and the rhetoric of economic rationality. *Am. J. Soc.* 91:31–96

Carson J. 1993. Army alpha, Army brass, and the search for Army intelligence. *Isis* 84: 279–309

Chambliss DF. 1996. *Beyond Caring: Hospitals, Nurses, and the Social Organization of Ethics.* Chicago: Univ. Chicago Press

Clark L. 1989. *Acceptable Risk? Making Decisions in a Toxic Environment.* Berkeley: Univ. Calif. Press

Clemens ES. 1997. *The People's Lobby: Organizational Innovation and the Rise of Interest Group Politics in the United States, 1890–1925.* Chicago: Univ. Chicago Press

Cohen PC. 1982. *A Calculating People: The Spread of Numeracy in Early America.* Chicago: Univ. Chicago Press

Collini S. 1980. Political theory and the science of society in Victorian Britain. *Hist. J.* 23:203–31

Cronon W. 1991. *Nature's Metropolis: Chicago and the Great West.* New York: Norton

Delaney K. 1994. The organizational construction of the bottom line. *Soc. Probl.* 41:201–22

Desrosières A. 1990. How to make things which hold together: social science, statistics and the state. In *Discourses on Society,* ed. P Wagner, B Wittrock, R Whitley, 15:195–218

Diamond S. 1995. *Roads to Dominion: Right-Wing Movements and Political Power in the United States.* New York: Guilford

Durkheim E. 1951. *Suicide: A Study in Sociology.* Transl. JA Spaulding, G Simpson, 1951. New York: Free Press

Eccles RG. 1985. *The Transfer Pricing Problem: A Theory for Practice.* Lexington: Lexington Books

Elsbach KD, Kramer RM. 1996. Members' responses to organizational identity threats: encountering and countering the *Business Week* rankings. *Admin. Sci. Q.* 41:442–76

England P. 1992. *Comparable Worth: Theories and Evidence.* New York: Aldine de Gruyter

Erikson KT. 1976. *Everything in Its Path: Destruction of Community in the Buffalo Creek Flood.* New York: Simon & Schuster

Espeland WN. 1992. *Contested rationalities: commensuration and the representation of value in public choice.* PhD thesis. Univ. Chicago, Chicago. 367 pp.

Espeland WN. 1993. Power, policy and paperwork: the bureaucratic representation of interests. *Qual. Soc.* 16:297–317

Espeland WN. 1998. *The Struggle for Water: Politics, Rationality and Identity in the American Southwest.* Chicago: Univ. Chicago Press

Espeland WN, Hirsch P. 1990. Ownership changes, accounting practices and the redefinition of the corporation. *Account. Organ. Soc.* 15:77–96

Feldman M, March JG. 1981. Information in

organizations as signal and symbol. *Adm. Sci. Q.* 26:171–86
Firestone S. 1970. *The Dialectic of Sex.* New York: Bantam Books
Fligstein N. 1991. *The Transformation of Corporate Control.* Cambridge, MA: Harvard Univ. Press
Foucault M. 1973. *The Birth of the Clinic.* Transl. A Sheridan. London: Tavistock
Foucault M. 1977. *Discipline and Punish.* Transl. A Sheridan. New York: Pantheon
Foucault M. 1978. *The History of Sexuality.* Transl. R Hurley. New York: Pantheon
Foucault M. 1991. On governmentality. In *The Foucault Effect,* ed. G Burchell, C Gordon, P Miller, pp. 87–104. Chicago: Univ. Chicago Press
Friedland R, Alford RR. 1991. Bringing society back in: symbols, practices, and institutional contradictions. In *The New Institutionalism in Organizational Analysis,* ed. WW Powell, PJ DiMaggio, pp. 232–63. Chicago: Univ. Chicago Press
Friedland R, Hecht R. 1996. *To Rule Jerusalem.* New York: Cambridge Univ. Press
Garfinkel H. 1967. *Studies in Ethnomethodology.* Englewood Cliffs, NJ: Prentice-Hall
Gitlin T. 1987. *The Sixties: Years of Hope, Days of Rage.* New York: Bantam Books
Goody J. 1986. *The Logic of Writing and the Organization of Society.* Cambridge, UK: Cambridge Univ. Press
Habermas J. 1973. *Theory and Practice.* Transl. J Viertel. Boston: Beacon
Hacking I. 1990. *The Taming of Chance.* Cambridge, UK: Cambridge Univ. Press
Hartmann HI. 1981. The family as the locus of gender, class, and political struggle: the example of housework. *Signs* 6:366–94
Hays S. 1996. *The Cultural Contradictions of Motherhood.* New Haven; Yale Univ. Press
Heimer CA. 1985. *Reactive Risk and Rational Action.* Berkeley: Univ. Calif. Press
Heimer CA. 1988. Social structure, psychology, and the estimation of risk. *Annu. Rev. Sociol.* 14:491–519
Heimer CA. 1992. Doing your job and helping your friends: universalistic norms about obligations to particular others in networks. In *Networks and Organizations: Structure, Form, and Action,* ed. N Nohria, RG Eccles, pp. 143–64. Boston: Harvard Bus. Sch. Press
Heimer CA, Staffen LR. 1998. *For the Sake of the Children: The Social Organization of Responsibility in the Hospital and Home.* Chicago: Univ. Chicago Press
Heller A. 1976. *The Theory of Need in Marx.* London: Allison & Busby
Herbst S. 1998. *Reading Public Opinion: How Political Actors View the Democratic Process.* Chicago: Univ. Chicago Press
Himmelfarb G. 1991. *Poverty and Compassion: The Moral Imagination of the Late Victorians.* New York: Knopf
Himmelstein JL. 1990. *To the Right: The Transformation of American Conservatism.* Berkeley: Univ. Calif. Press
Hochschild A. 1989. *The Second Shift: Working Mothers and the Revolution at Home.* New York: Viking
Hole J, Levine E. 1971. *Rebirth of Feminism.* New York: Quadrangle Books
Hurley S. 1989. *Natural Reasons.* New York: Cambridge Univ. Press
Jasanoff S. 1986. *Risk Management and Political Culture.* New York: Russell Sage Found.
Jasanoff S. 1989. The problem of rationality in American health and safety regulations. In *Expert Evidence: Interpreting Science in the Law,* ed. R Smith, B Wynne, pp. 151–83. London: Routledge
Jepperson RL. 1991. Institutions, institutional effects, and institutionalism. In *The New Institutionalism in Organizational Analysis,* ed. WW Powell, PJ DiMaggio, pp. 143–63. Chicago: Univ. Chicago Press
Kee JE. 1994. *Handbook of Practical Program Evaluation.* San Francisco: Jossey-Bass
Klatch RE. 1987. *Women of the New Right.* Philadelphia: Temple Univ. Press
Kula W. 1986. *Men Who Measure.* Princeton: Princeton Univ. Press
Landes EM, Posner RA. 1978. The economics of the baby shortage. *J. Legal Stud.* 7: 323–48
Lasch C. 1977. *Haven in a Heartless World.* New York: Pantheon
Latour B, Woolgar S. 1986. *Laboratory Life: The Construction of Scientific Facts.* Princeton: Princeton Univ. Press
Lave J. 1988. *Cognition in Practice.* Cambridge, UK: Cambridge Univ. Press
Lucas HC, Schwartz RA, eds. 1989. *The Challenge of Information Technology for the Securities Markets.* Homewood, IL: Dow Jones-Irwin
Luker K. 1984. *Abortion and the Politics of Motherhood.* Berkeley: Univ. Calif. Press
Luxton M. 1980. *More Than a Labor of Love.* Toronto: Women's Press
March JG, Simon HA. 1958. *Organizations.* New York: Wiley
Mainardi P. 1970. The politics of housework. In *Sisterhood is Powerful,* ed. R Morgan, pp. 446–54. New York: Random House
Mansbridge J. 1986. *Why We Lost the ERA.* Chicago: Univ. Chicago Press
Martin W. 1996. *With God on Our Side: The*

Rise of the Religious Right in America. New York: Broadway Books

Marx K. 1976 (1867). *Capital: A Critique of Political Economy,* Vol. 1. New York: Vintage

Meyer JW. 1986. Social environments and organizational accounting. *Account. Organ. Soc.* 11:345–56

Meyer JW, Boli J, Thomas GM. 1994. Ontology and rationalization in the western cultural account. In *Institutional Environments and Organizations,* ed. R Scott, JW Meyer, et al, pp. 9–27. Thousand Oaks: Sage

Miller P, O'Leary T. 1987. Accounting and the construction of the governable person. *Account.Organ.Soc.* 12:235–65

Moody-Adams M. 1991. On surrogacy: morality, markets, and motherhood. *Public Aff. Q.* 5:175–90

Neckerman K, Kirschenman J. 1991. We'd love to hire them, but...: the meaning of race for employers. In *The Urban Underclass,* ed. C Jencks, P Peterson, pp. 203–32. Washington, DC: Brookings Inst.

Nelson RL, Bridges WP. Forthcoming. *Legalizing Gender Inequality: Courts, Markets, and Unequal Pay for Women in the United States.* Cambridge, UK: Cambridge Univ. Press

Nussbaum MC. 1984. Plato on commensurability and desire. *Proc. Aristotelian Soc.* 58:55–80 (Suppl. vol.)

Nussbaum MC. 1986. *The Fragility of Goodness: Luck and Ethics in Greek Tragedy and Philosophy.* Cambridge, UK: Cambridge Univ. Press

Oakley A. 1976. *Woman's Work: The Housewife, Past and Present.* New York: Vintage Books

Orren K, Skowronek S. 1994. Beyond the iconography of order: notes for a new institutionalism. In *The Dynamics of American Politics: Approaches and Interpretations,* ed. L Dodd, C Jillson, pp. 311–30. Boulder, CO: Westview

Porter TM. 1986. *The Rise of Statistical Thinking, 1820–1900.* Princeton: Princeton Univ. Press

Porter TM. 1992. Objectivity as standardization: the rhetoric of impersonality in measurement, statistics, and cost-benefit analysis. In *Rethinking Objectivity,* ed. A Megill. *Ann. Scholarsh.* 9:19–59.

Porter TM. 1995. *Trust in Numbers.* Princeton: Princeton Univ. Press

Portney PR. 1994. The contingent valuation debate: why economists should care. *J. Econ. Perspect.* 8:3–17

Posner RA. 1992. *Economic Analysis of Law.* Boston: Little, Brown. 4th ed.

Postone M. 1996.. *Time, Labor, and Social Domination.* Cambridge, UK: Cambridge Univ. Press

Radin MJ. 1996. *Contested Commodities.* Cambridge, MA: Harvard Univ. Press

Raz J. 1986. *The Morality of Freedom.* Oxford: Oxford Univ. Press

Reddy WM. 1984. *The Rise of Market Culture: The Textile Trade and French Society, 1750–1900.* Cambridge, UK: Cambridge Univ. Press

Reed R Jr. 1993. Casting a wider net. *Policy Rev.* Summer; pp. 31–35

Reisner M. 1986. *Cadillac Desert: The American West and Its Disappearing Water.* New York: Penguin

Ribuffo LR. 1983. *The Old Christian Right: The Protestant Far Right from the Great Depression to the Cold War.* Philadelphia: Temple Univ. Press

Rozell MJ, Wilcox C. 1996. Second coming: the strategies of the new Christian right. *Poli. Sci. Q.* 111:271–94

Ryan MP. 1981. *Cradle of the Middle Class: The Family in Oneida County, New York, 1790–1865.* New York: Cambridge Univ. Press

Sassen S. 1994. *Cities in the World Economy.* Thousand Oaks, CA: Pine Forge

Satz D. 1992. Markets in women's reproductive labor. *Philos. Public. Aff.* 21:107–31

Schnaiberg A. 1980. *The Environment from Surplus to Scarcity.* Oxford: Oxford Univ. Press

Schwartz B. 1994. *The Costs of Living: How Market Freedom Erodes the Best Things in Life.* New York: Norton

Siegel R. 1994. Home as work: the first women's rights claims concerning wives' household labor, 1850–1880. *Yale Law J.* 105:1073–217

Simmel G. 1978 (1907) *The Philosophy of Money.* Transl. T Bottomore, D Frisby. Boston: Routledge & Kegan Paul

Smith K, ed. 1984. *Environmental Policy under Reagan's Executive Order: The Role of Cost-Benefit Analysis.* Chapel Hill: Univ. NC Press

Stacey J. 1990. *Brave New Families: Stories of Domestic Upheaval in Late Twentieth Century America.* New York: Basic Books

Steinbrunner JD. 1974. *The Cybernetic Theory of Decision.* Princeton: Princeton Univ. Press

Stevens ML. 1996. *Kingdom and coalition: hierarchy and autonomy in the home education movement.* PhD thesis. Northwestern Univ., Evanston, IL

Stokey E, Zeckhauser R. 1978. *A Primer for Policy Analysis.* New York: Norton

Sunstein CR. 1994. Incommensurability and

valuation in law. *Mich. Law Rev.* 92: 779–861

Swetz FJ. 1987. *Capitalism and Arithmetic: The New Math of the 15th Century.* La Salle, IL: Open Court

Swidler A. 1979. *Organization Without Authority: Dilemmas of Social Control in Free Schools.* Cambridge, MA: Harvard Univ. Press

Taylor FW. 1947. *Scientific Management.* New York: Harper

Taylor S. 1984. *Making Bureaucracies Think.* Palo Alto, CA: Stanford Univ. Press

Thaler RH. 1983. Illusions and mirages in public policy. *Public Interest* 73:60–74

Tribe L. 1971. Trial by mathematics: precision and ritual in the legal process. *Harv. Law Rev.* 84:1329–92

Tribe L. 1972. Policy science: analysis or ideology? *Philos. Public Aff.* 2:66–110

Tversky A, Kahneman D. 1974. Judgment under uncertainty: heuristics and biases. *Science* 185:1124–31

Tversky A, Kahneman D. 1981. The framing of decisions and the psychology of choice. *Science* 211:453–58

Ventresca M. 1995. *When states count: institutional and political dynamics in modern census establishment, 1800–1993.* PhD thesis. Stanford Univ., Stanford, CA

Walker KE, Woods ME. 1976. *Time Use: A Measure of Household Production of Goods and Services.* Washington, DC: Am. Home Econ. Assoc.

Weber M. 1978 (1913). *Economy and Society*, eds. G Roth, C Wittich. Berkeley: Univ. Calif. Press

Weber M. 1981 (1927). *General Economic History.* Transl. FY Knight. New Brunswick, NJ: Transaction Books

Weisbrod B. 1961. *Economics of Public Health: Measuring the Economic Impact of Diseases.* Philadelphia: Univ. Penn. Press

Zelizer V. 1985. *Pricing the Priceless Child.* New York: Basic Books

Zelizer V. 1994. *The Social Meaning of Money.* Princeton: Princeton Univ. Press

Zucker LG. 1977. The role of institutionalization in cultural persistence. *Am. Sociol. Rev.* 42:726–43

Annu. Rev. Sociol. 1998. 24:345–70

Measuring Meaning Structures

John W. Mohr

Department of Sociology, University of California, Santa Barbara, California 93106-9430; e-mail: mohr@sscf.ucsb.edu

KEY WORDS: culture, meaning, network, structuralism, institutions

ABSTRACT

The recent cultural turn in American sociology has inspired a number of more scientifically oriented scholars to study the meanings that are embedded within institutions, practices, and cultural artifacts. I focus here on research that (*a*) emphasizes institutional (rather than individual) meanings, (*b*) uses a structural approach to interpretation, and (*c*) employs formal algorithms or quantitative procedures for reducing the complexity of meanings to simpler structural principles. I discuss two core methodological issues—the assessment of similarities and differences between items in a cultural system and the process by which structure-preserving simplifications are found in the data. I also highlight the importance of two-mode analytic procedures and I review some of the perceived benefits and criticisms of this style of research.

INTRODUCTION

The cultural turn that has recently swept through much of American sociology has meant that sociologists are ever more frequently focusing on the role of symbols, meanings, texts, cultural frames, and cognitive schemas in their theorizations of social processes and institutions. Although this resurgence of interest in cultural phenomena is often associated with the shift towards more humanistic and interpretative methodologies, an increasing number of quantitatively oriented scholars have also begun to turn their attention to the study of cultural meanings. In the process a new body of research has begun to emerge in which social practices, classificatory distinctions, and cultural artifacts of various sorts are being formally analyzed in order to reveal underlying structures of meaning.

0360-0572/98/0815-0345$08.00

This work is scattered across many substantive areas of research. It has no coherent center or easily definable boundaries. There is, as yet, no clearly articulated core methodology or statement of theoretical intent. As a consequence, I adopt a somewhat idiosyncratic set of inclusion rules for the material covered in this review. My focus emphasizes studies that measure institutional (or cultural) rather than individual meanings. I pay special attention to those projects that have (if only implicitly) adopted some variant of a structuralist approach to interpretation. And I devote particular attention to describing the ways in which formal analytic methodologies are being employed to reduce complex collections of cultural data to simpler, more easily intelligible structures of meaning.

I begin with a short discussion of how the measurement of meaning developed in American sociology up to and including recent attempts to study institutional processes through the formal analysis of meaning structures. I then highlight the main elements of a structural approach to meaning and describe two methodological issues that are involved in conducting this type of research—the measurement of similarities and differences, and the reduction of complexity through various types of formal analyses. I focus next on one particularly promising class of analytical methods that seems to me to hold out the greatest promise for future progress. I end with a brief discussion of some of the advantages and disadvantages of formal approaches to interpreting meanings.

MEANING AND MEASUREMENT IN CONTEXT

Formal analysis of meaning structures is not new to the social sciences. Much important research has been done by scholars in other disciplines, including the pioneering work on semantic differential techniques by the psychologist Charles Osgood and his colleagues (Snider & Osgood 1969). Cognitive psychologists have carried this trajectory forward in a myriad of ways. Applications and extensions of this work have been pursued by linguists, political scientists, market researchers, and anthropologists. The latter group in particular, and especially cognitive anthropologists such as Roy D'Andrade (D'Andrade 1995), have been especially instrumental in developing the theory and method of meaning analysis as a formal endeavor.

Formal analysis of meaning has also had a long-standing home in at least two areas of American sociology. Meaning measurement has been a central concern of sociologists who use survey methods to study opinions, attitudes, and beliefs (Sudman et al 1996). Content analysis of meanings in textual data is a second area that has been systematically developed since the early work of Bernard Berelson (Berelson 1952). However, with the exception of a few subfields such as political sociology, where opinion research continues to be important, both of these methodological projects have become isolated from the core research traditions of sociological work. This is partly because the data sources (opinion surveys and coded texts) have been difficult to acquire and are generally limited to specialized areas of investigation. Many quantitative sociologists also seem to believe that the dynamics of social structure (formal organizations, social movements, processes of social mobility and status attainment, and the like) can be measured, but that the more ephemeral aspects of cultural meanings cannot. Thus, the meaningful character of social action (and of institutional life more generally) has appeared as part of the broader theoretical context which frames these research programs rather than as something that is measured directly.

Recent work has begun to bridge the divide between culture and social structure. The flourishing of symbolic interactionism and ethnomethodology during the sixties contributed to an enduring and widespread appreciation of the socially constructed character of the social world (Berger & Luckman 1967). Subsequent theoretical statements almost universally emphasized the dialectical or dualistic relationship between cultural meanings and social structures (Bauman 1973, Sahlins 1976, Bourdieu 1977, Giddens 1984, Swidler 1986, Sewell 1992). Slowly, these insights have come to be incorporated into the empirical projects that characterize core regions of the discipline. Culture was first linked to the logic of the production process in popular culture industries (Peterson & Berger 1975, Peterson 1976). It was shown to be an important and measurable factor in the prediction of status attainment outcomes (DiMaggio 1982, DiMaggio & Mohr 1985, Mohr & DiMaggio 1995). Institutionalists demonstrated the significance of symbols and cultural processes in the study of organizations and their environments (Meyer & Rowan 1977, DiMaggio & Powell 1991). Social movement theorists showed the importance of cognitive frames (Snow et al 1986, Eyerman & Jamison 1991) and cultural processes of identity formation (Darnovsky et al 1995). Many other examples could be pointed to.

However, the study of cultural phenomena is not the same as the analysis of meaning. As Wendy Griswold has persistently complained, most of the research continues to sidestep the problem of meaning analysis altogether. The distribution of genres has been mapped, elements of cultural production have been counted, levels of cultural knowledge have been measured, increases of organizational homogeneity have been demonstrated, but the meanings that are constitutive of these cultural phenomena have largely been left aside. Griswold has sought to develop methodological approaches that incorporate sociology's empirical rigor and sophisticated understanding of social structure while also taking the meanings embedded within literary and other cultural texts as a critical element of the analysis (Griswold 1987a,b, 1992, 1993). While she has been instrumental in focusing attention on this problem, Griswold's own work has largely been directed toward the study of literature and, although she is rigorously empirical, the formal measurement of meaning has not been her goal.

ACTORS, ACTIONS, AND OBJECTS OF ACTION: A NEWER INSTITUTIONALISM

In this essay, I review many examples of sociological work that seeks to directly measure cultural meanings. My focus will be largely methodological in that I will organize the discussion around the question of how this type of research is conducted. But I begin with three recent examples that demonstrate the potential contributions of meaning measurement for the empirical investigation of core sociological questions. What sets this work apart is the folding together of cultural meanings and social structures as primary elements within the same research design. Such an approach much more faithfully reflects theorists' contention that social structures and cultural structures are mutually constitutive. Thus, in the following examples, meanings are measured in order to show how social structures are created. All three examples concern historical changes in institutional forms, a reflectioin of the fact that historical sociology has been an especially fertile terrain for this style of research because researchers are constrained, by necessity, to analyzing meanings embedded within texts (Franzosi & Mohr 1997).

Charles Tilly has been a long-standing leader in this style of research. His recent work is especially instructive. Tilly (1997) seeks to explain the parliamentarization of British politics, that is, how the structure of political influence shifted from the local to the national level while the nature of collective claim-making was transformed from a reliance on spontaneous acts of (often violent) protest toward the more formalized grievance mechanisms of political parties and organized social movements. Though this might be viewed as a problem of organizational change or of the formal transformation of political structure, Tilly sees this as an occasion for cultural analysis. He emphasizes the need to understand how the popular meaning of politics changed during these years, and especially how conceptions of social rights shifted along with ideas about how to make a collective claim in defense of one's rights. His analysis relies on textual data, especially verbatim summaries of contemporary newspaper articles reporting on some 8,000 "contentious gatherings" that occurred between 1758 and 1834.

Tilly argues that shifting relations between claim-makers and claimants defines the character of political institutions. For his analysis, Tilly divides 12,000 or so different contentious groups into 64 social categories (farmers, friendly societies, workers, masters, constables, militia, parishioners, gentlemen, local officials, and so on). He then looks for claim-making relationships among these groups by analyzing his data on contentious gatherings to see what actors made what kinds of claims (attacking, donkeying, petitioning, arresting, applauding, addressing, and other similar efforts) against what other actors. A blockmodel analysis, divided by time periods, shows how the meaning and structure of political action changed dramatically during these years.

DiMaggio & Mullen (1993) provide a second example. Their study concerns how American communities went about celebrating National Music Week in 1924. Like Tilly, DiMaggio & Mullen are interested in the way power and influence are organized and, also like Tilly, they see the social structure of community politics as being built up out of shifting systems of meaning. The events studied here are not contentious gatherings, however, but formally organized community rituals. They collected data on 833 events occurring in 419 different communities, focusing on the actors, actions, and objects of action in each event. In this case, the actors were the event participants (clubs, churches, ethnic associations, employee groups, and the like). The catalogue of actions included the various types of musical events that were planned—those that tended to reinforce status group boundaries (e.g. religious or classical music concerts) and those that had a more inclusive focus (band and patriotic music, group sings, and so forth). The objects of action were the types of audiences that were encouraged to participate: Were they general admission events or events that were staged in such a way as to assemble people who were defined as members of specific associations, congregations, or as residents of particular institutions?

Once again, it is the relations between these three sets of elements—participants, performances, and audiences—that DiMaggio & Mullen use to construct a measure of the shifting institutional logics of community political structure. What they discover are four relatively distinct modes of organizing community rituals that they then link to the foundations of political authority in each community. They identify these as (*a*) "rituals of ratification" that tend to reaffirm traditional arrangements of the social order; (*b*) "rituals of communitas" that constitute community members as individuals who are unmediated by private associations but, nonetheless, members of a collective unity; (*c*) "rituals of civic unity" that constitute people as individual consumers and participants in a local economy that all have a vested interest in supporting; and (*d*) "rituals of incorporation" that identify community members as workers, members of ethnic groups, and other diverse collectivities that must be somehow integrated into a whole.

The third example is a study by Mohr & Guerra-Pearson (1998) of community social welfare agencies in New York City during the Progressive Era. Here the question is how particular kinds of organizational forms come to be institutionalized. Like much work in the organizational ecology tradition, Mohr & Guerra-Pearson focus on the ways in which different types of organizations compete for resource niches by making jurisdictional claims over specific regions of institutional space. Unlike work in this tradition, however, the focus is explicitly shifted to the interpretations that organizational actors propose about the meaning of institutional activities. As before, three sorts of foundational elements are studied. Using written descriptions of organizational activities for some 600 organizations, Mohr & Guerra-Pearson collected information at four different times about status categories that were used to describe relief recipients (men, women, boys, girls, children, sailors, travelers, the working, able-bodied, and so on); classes of social problems (criminality, delinquency, disability, immorality, and the like); and technologies of organizational action (such as general relief, employment assistance, vocational training, and character-building).

In this study, it is the structure of the organizational environment that is mapped. Relations between organizations are measured according to the similarities of their claims about the region of institutional space in which they seek to operate. Similarity among claims is defined by the extent to which organizations apply the same technologies to the same status identities, afflicted by the same types of social problems. Differences of interpretation arise when alternative combinations are invoked (as when different technologies are purported to be effective for treating the same classes of problems). Multidimensional scaling enables the organizations' niche locations to be mapped out on the basis of the claims that were made about how poverty problems should be interpreted and addressed. Using this approach, Mohr & Guerra-Pearson demonstrate how settlement houses waged a (losing) battle with social work bureaucracies and other more rationalized organizational forms in their bid to become the primary institution for delivering community social welfare services during these years.

I have begun with these examples for several reasons. First, all three employ structural methods for measuring meanings. In Tilly's case, the meanings concern collective actors' sense of public rights and their conceptions about the appropriate means for securing those rights. DiMaggio & Mullen study the meanings of community and sets of emergent norms about how to symbolically consecrate the social order. Mohr & Guerra-Pearson analyze organizational interpretations of community social problems and contesting claims about appropriate solutions to those problems. In each case, the relevant systems of meanings are studied empirically through an analysis of the relationships that actors impose on various primitive institutional elements (actors, actions and objects of action). Finally, all of these studies make explicit linkages between the systems of meanings that are investigated and the social structures in which they are embedded. Indeed, the point of each project is to demonstrate the ways in which enduring social institutions are explicitly constructed out of a complex process of negotiation and contestation over cultural meanings.

THE STRUCTURAL APPROACH TO INTERPRETATION

The key methodological maneuver in these projects can be traced to the structural method of interpretation, generally associated with the semiotic, structuralist, and poststructuralist intellectual projects that thrived in Europe beginning in the 1960s. Although diverse in both methods and goals, most of this work is either in the tradition of or in response to the work of the French linguist, Ferdinand de Saussure [(1916) 1959]. Structuralism (in this Saussurian tradition) was founded on the argument that meaning was constituted through the systematic distinctions that differentiate words (or sounds, or signs) from one another. A number of analytic principles follow from this. Content is seen as being fundamentally arbitrary. Patterns of differences within a broader system of cultural objects become the focus of analysis. The interpretation of meaning is seen to be connected to the analysis of the system of relations that link cultural objects. As developed most famously in the writings of the anthropologist Claude Lévi-Strauss (1963), much of the work of interpretation comes to be directed toward the identification of underlying (deep) structural principles that serve to organize the larger complexity of relational patterns.

There is an enormous literature that discusses, evaluates, and critiques these intellectual projects. Useful introductions are provided by Hawkes (1977), Pettit (1977), Kurzweil (1980), Wuthnow (1987), and Caws (1988). Moreover, as the discussion in Caws (1988), D'Andrade (1995), and Emirbayer (1998) make clear, the developments of the Saussurian structural tradition paralleled a broad variety of other intellectual movements that were also shifting toward a relational mode of analysis during the same period. The research that I review here is (for the most part) only loosely coupled to these literatures and I will not spend the time to develop these connections in any detail. I will simply point out that most of the work that I discuss in this review adopts (if only implicitly) some type of structural approach to the problem of interpreting meaning.

As an example of this mode of analysis, consider Karen Cerulo's (1988, 1995) research on national anthems. Cerulo shows that national anthems can be analyzed as cultural meaning systems and that the structures that are identified in the process can be used for comparative analysis. She accomplishes this by treating music as a series of symbolic codes: "melodic codes, phrase codes, harmonic codes, form codes, dynamic codes, rhythmic codes, and orchestral codes." Musical notes are the elements that, when combined, generate these code systems. Hence, it is the pattern of relations between the notes that is relevant; the musical notes themselves lack any specific intrinsic value, rather they "derive their meaning according to their placement within a larger system" (1988, p. 319). Through a complex and ingenious series of measurements devoted to assessing the relational patterns of the notes, Cerulo maps out the musical structure of over 150 national anthems. The "meaning" of the music is thus represented by these structural mappings which, as Cerulo demonstrates, closely correspond to the sorts of genre distinctions (e.g. between a march and a hymn) that musicologists employ to differentiate these styles of music. See Timothy Dowd (1992) for a similar approach to analyzing American popular songs.

Cerulo (1995) proceeds to show that several basic social processes very effectively predict the type of musical composition that a specific country is likely to adopt. In particular, she shows that position within the world political economic system, relationship to neighboring countries, to a specific colonial power, and to a cohort of other nations, all influence the character of the musical composition that is chosen for a national anthem. She uses a similar type of analysis to map out the basic structural characteristics of national flags (by looking at how color, pattern, and images are arrayed relationally within the flag). Her analysis demonstrates that the same factors influenced the selection of these sorts of national symbols as well.

Cerulo's work illustrates the core principles of the type of structural analysis that is the focus of this review: (*a*) basic elements within a cultural system are identified, (*b*) the pattern of relations between these elements is recorded, (*c*) a structural organization is identified by applying a pattern-preserving set of reductive principles to the system of relations, and (*d*) the resulting structure (which now can be used as a representation for the meaning embedded in the cultural system) is reconnected to the institutional context that is being investigated. To begin such an analysis, three problems need to be solved. First, basic elements of the cultural system have to be identified. Second, a relevant system of relations must be identified. Third, the pattern of relations must be recorded. These are not trivial tasks.

Initial decisions regarding what will count as the cultural elements whose relational arrangement will be analyzed is critical to determining the significance of the meaning structures that can be uncovered. Because Cerulo was interested in identifying aesthetic structures, she turned to expert literatures in graphic design and music theory for guidance in selecting relevant elements for inclusion. This illustration is generalizable. Every structural analysis must begin with the identification of a relevant set of cultural items, and these items are never simply available in an immediate fashion. An informed cultural or institutional theory is necessary to enable us to notice and to be able to make relevant distinctions between the constituent elements.

The same cautionary note applies to the selection of relational measures. Elements of a cultural system can be similar or different in any number of ways; the trick is to identify those relations that matter. Some of the most important criticisms of the French structuralists were that they frequently got lost in their own overly formalistic models of structure. This is what Philip Pettit described as the dangers of mere "pattern-picking" (Pettit 1977, p. 41). When one reads, for example, Clifford Geertz's (1973) criticisms of Lévi-Strauss, it is hard not to be persuaded by his complaints that the structuralists were wrong to focus solely on the cultural phenomena in isolation from what we might describe as the institutional contexts of culture. This was manifested in their tendency to treat cultural codes as closed systems. For the structuralists, the logic of culture was all too often presumed to lie within the cultural system itself (or, as in the case of Lévi-Strauss, within some intrinsic ordering properties of the human mind).

There is a solution to this dilemma, however; relations of elements within a cultural system should be determined on the basis of how the elements are linked to the practical demands of the institutional system of which they are a part. This is an argument that goes under the general heading of practice theory. Classic statements of this perspective include Bourdieu (1977), Geertz (1973), and Giddens (1984). Useful summaries and commentaries can be found in Ortner (1994) and Friedland & Alford (1991). The argument is that any cultural system is structured as an embodiment of the range of activities, social conflicts, and moral dilemmas that individuals are compelled to engage with as they go about negotiating the sorts of everyday events that confront them in their lives. This insight has direct implications for the measuring of meaning structures. It suggests that when we think about identifying a set of cultural items, asking how they are related to one another, and assessing the type of structural model that might be relevant, it is important to begin with the question of what type of practical utility such a cultural system plays within a concrete institutional setting. Ideally, relations between the cultural elements should be assessed by looking at how actors, organizations, or institutions make practical use of the cultural distinctions being investigated.

MEASURING RELATIONS

Once the relevant elements and relational contexts of a cultural system have been identified, measurement can begin. The first task is to compare each element in the cultural system with every other element in terms of the identified relationship. Four types of measurement strategies can be distinguished. Similarities and differences among cultural items can be assessed according to (*a*) subjective judgements, (*b*) common attributes, (*c*) relations to others, and (*d*) structural-functional profiles.

Subjective Similarity

Two cultural items can be said to be similar to one another to the extent that individuals make a cognitive judgement that they are of "the same sort." Because they often are faced with the need of collecting data in different language situations or from nonliterate respondents, cognitive anthropologists have been especially innovative in devising a great many alternative methods for collecting these kinds of data (see Hays 1976, Weller & Romney 1988, D'Andrade 1995). For example, respondents are asked to judge the similarity of pairs of cultural items directly, or they are asked to select which two out of three items are most similar to one another. A third method is to ask the respondent to sort cards referring to cultural items into piles of things that "go together." Scores can then be aggregated across a number of respondents to derive a set of average measures of inter-item similarities. Richard Shweder used these techniques to investigate how individuals in different cultures understand the concept of the person (Shweder & Bourne 1991). For example, he used pile sort techniques to assess how individuals in India organize their understanding of 81 different personality traits. Included here were terms translated as "crooked," "lazy," "obstinate," "brutally frank," "loyal," "harmless," "fickle," "contemplative," and so on. The resulting 81 x 81 matrix was used by Shweder & Bourne to demonstrate that the respondents' cultural understanding of these terms was structured around generalized dimensions of power and social desirability.

Attribute Similarity

Items within a cultural system can also be compared on the basis of the sets of selected attributes that they share. This type of technique can also be used in collecting interview data. Csikszentmihalyi & Rochberg-Halton (1981) employed this strategy in their study of the meaning of household possessions among Chicago families. A list of items was first elicited by asking respondents "What are the things in your home that are special for you?" Interviewers then asked about the meanings that were attached to each of these items. This resulted in a listing of 1694 objects (collapsed for analysis into 41 types). The respondent's meaningful associations were classified into 37 categories of value, such as, the object is special because it is a memento, or because it is part of a collection, or because it belonged to a specific relative, or because it reflects a specific achievement, etc. The 41 types of cultural items were then compared to one another in terms of the types of valuations associated with each. The same general method was used by Mohr & Guerra-Pearson (1998) to assess the discursive similarity of community social welfare organizations in the article discussed earlier. In this case organizations were compared to one another on the basis of the similarity of the claims that they made about the types of solution technologies that were seen to be appropriate for classes of persons and types of problems.

Relational Similarity

Similarity among items within a cultural system can also be assessed by looking for the presence or absence of various types of social relationships that link cultural objects together. Thomas Schweizer (1993) also studied household possessions (in an urban neighborhood in French Polynesia, a group of hunter-gatherers in Zaire, and a peasant community in Java). In Schweizer's study, however, categories of possessions were seen to be similar or different from one another depending upon which individuals in the community possessed the same sets of items. So, for example, on the basis of who owned what in Papeete, a refrigerator was more like a radio and a bicycle was more like a kerosene stove. Thus, Schweizer interprets the status meaning of various material possessions by understanding what members of the community possess what types of goods. Also important are measures of similarity based on relationships that directly connect the cultural items (or elements) to one another. Boorman & Levitt (1983) used this method to study how meanings were organized in federal bankruptcy law. They coded the internal citation references of the 55 subsections of Article 9 of the Uniform Commercial Code. Thus, rather than asking individuals to sort cultural items that went together, Boorman & Levitt asked which subsections of legal code were "substitutable" in the sense that they were similarly referenced by other subsections of the legal code. This is the same type of measure that was used by Tilly (1997) in his parliamentarization article to measure similarities among categories of collective actors. Those groups that had similar profiles of relationships to all other groups were linked together in the blockmodel analysis as being structurally equivalent.

Similarity of Structural Function

In some situations the measurement of similarities and differences has to incorporate more complex information. To assess the structural meaning of cultural items embedded within sequences and narratives, it is necessary to preserve more than pairwise information on similarities. It is also necessary to know how items are located within the broader context of the narrative or sequential ordering of events (Abbott 1983, 1990). For example, most contemporary approaches to content analysis require that words be compared on the basis of their syntactic or narrative function within the text. How one should gather this data is very much under debate (see Roberts 1989, Franzosi 1989, 1990, Carley 1993, Carley & Kaufer 1993). In general, however, most strategies call for the preservation of two types of information—the semantic function of a word within a field of meaning (e.g. within a sentence) and the specific relationships that occur within that field to other (functionally defined) words. For example, Roberto Franzosi proposes that similarities of words within a text be recorded in such a way that their functions within a localized semantic grammar are preserved. This is an important extension (and formalization) of Tilly's methods. In his study of contentious gatherings in Italy between 1919 and 1922, Franzosi (1997) coded newspaper stories so that various categories of agents (labor unionists, owners, brownshirts, police, and various others) are compared to one another according to the extent to which they fulfilled the same institutional function (instigators of violence, recipients of violence, and so on). To get at this kind of information it is necessary to record who does what to whom, and in what sequence.

FINDING STRUCTURE

Having collected information regarding the relations of similarity (or difference) among a set of items within a cultural or institutional system, the next task is to find structure-preserving simplifications that may allow the complexity of the system to be more easily understood. Ideally, one hopes to identify some deeper, simpler, structural logic—that is, a principle or set of principles that account for the arrangement of parts within the cultural system (Ortner 1994). The relations between cultural items are the key to such an investigation. The analytical task is to discover how these relations are related to one another. Structuralist methods are geared toward the identification of transformations that allow the relations among the relations to be reduced to more easily understandable and or visible patterns. I discuss four general classes of methods for accomplishing this: (*a*) multidimensional scaling and clustering, (*b*) network analysis, (*c*) Boolean algebra, and (*d*) sequence analysis. Each of these approaches makes use of the relational information in different ways in order to highlight various qualities of the meaning structure.

Multidimensional Scaling and Clustering

Multidimensional scaling analysis (MDS) is one of the oldest and most widely used methods for mapping out the relational system of differences in the measurement of meanings. Simply stated, an MDS analysis reads in a square matrix of similarities or differences (actually half of a square matrix is usually used because the input data are often symmetrical) and produces a transformation of the data that seeks to locate all of the objects in a common (two- or more dimensional) space in such a way that the similarities in the input matrix are transformed into Euclidean distances. An MDS space would thus represent a series of objects in such a way that (generally speaking) if two items are similar to one another (in the input matrix) then they are located near one another in the space. If they are dissimilar, they are located far apart. When analyzed in two (or three) dimensions, the items can then be easily plotted in such a way as to visually convey the relational structure in which they are embedded.

Clustering methods have also been used for studying cultural meanings. There are a great variety of clustering methods, but all seek to group items together according to some algorithmic principle for deciding which are most alike given the input matrix of item by item similarities. One of the primary differences between clustering methods and MDS is that the latter locates items in a way that takes into account the totality of all relational similarities in each iteration, whereas clustering methods tend to connect items to clusters that are deemed (by some criteria) to be most similar in a localized (or pairwise) sense. The two methods are often used together (as when the coordinates of an MDS space are submitted to a cluster analysis in order to more clearly designate subregions within the space). The Sage books on these topics are both excellent and still quite useful (Kruskal & Wish 1978, Aldenderfer & Blashfield 1984).

These techniques have been widely used by cognitive anthropologists for studying meaning systems. As D'Andrade (1995) explains, the 1970s were a time when basic theories about culture as knowledge systems were connected to formal methods of analysis. It was during these years that many of the classic applications of these techniques to understanding the structure of cultural meaning systems were pioneered. For example, Burton & Kirk (1977, 1979) used MDS to model gender assumptions in Maasai culture. They asked their respondents to think about the personality characteristics of various social identities differentiated by age and gender (small boy, older boy, warrior, adult male, small girl, older girl, and young adult woman). Using triad tests, they collected information on similarities among 13 personality traits (disobedient, brave, frank, hardworking, socially competent, playful, lazy, respectful, fickle, suspicious, clever, skittish, and stingy).

Their findings showed that small boys were expected to be playful, successful, brave, respectful, clever, and disobedient, but as they aged, they were expected to also become hardworking and to no longer be disobedient. Once they became warriors, however, expectations shifted so that they were expected to be realistic and, once again, disobedient, while stinginess was frowned upon. Burton & Kirk relate these shifts in cultural beliefs to changes in males' roles within the community. For example, as warriors, young men are often on raiding parties away from home where they are expected to use their own initiative and, when appropriate, to disobey the commands that had been given them by the elders in the village. They are also expected to work together as a group, relying on one another for survival, making stinginess a significant liability. The analyses show a very different pattern for women. Young adult women are expected to be lazy and stingy and they are expected not to be successful, clever, or brave. Kirk & Burton note that the shift in normative expectations for men and women that occurs after circumcision is striking. For men, the change marks a time of ascendant authority and autonomy. For women it marks a clear acceleration of negative stereotyping and formal disempowerment. They conclude that a primary function of circumcision rituals in Maasai culture is to dramatize and institutionalize differences in power between men and women. Numerous other examples from this period of anthropological research could be pointed to. Another classic example is the study by Roy D'Andrade and his colleagues in which they used MDS to model the structure of meanings regarding disease categories among English and Spanish speaking students (D'Andrade et al 1972).

Sociologists have traditionally used MDS techniques to study social networks or social organizational structures, such as in Laumann & Knoke's (1987) study of the structure of policy domains. More recently, sociologists have begun employing MDS analyses to map out cultural meaning structures in a fashion that is more reminiscent of the work of anthropologists. For example, Ennis (1992) and Cappell & Guterbock (1992) used MDS techniques to model the structure of American sociological specialties. Ventresca & Yin (1997) used MDS to analyze the meaning of social categories in a broad historical sample of national census surveys. Mohr (1998) uses MDS techniques to analyze gendered assumptions in the structure of poverty classifications used by Progressive Era social reformers.

Network Analysis

The one subfield within American sociology that has always been thoroughly structuralist (in the relational sense) is social network analysis. Typically in this research tradition, individuals are the nodes, and various types of social relationships that link individuals to one another (friendship, kinship, social exchanges of various sorts) constitute the "ties" out of which a pattern of social organization is constructed. Over the years, network scholars have developed an enormous array of conceptual and methodological tools for thinking about the structural properties of social networks. The methods can be divided into two general types—those emphasizing connectivity and those focusing on structural equivalence (Burt 1978, Wasserman & Faust 1994). The former are largely concerned with how the relationships between individuals in a social network are mediated by the structure of ties that directly connects them. Concepts like network centrality, between-ness, and adjacency are especially important here. The latter approach focuses on ways in which individuals stand in structurally equivalent positions because they share common patterns of relationships to all others in the network. The key concept here is the idea of a structural role (White et al 1976). While most of the empirical work has been directed to understanding the properties of social networks, these methods can also be extremely useful in the study of cultural meaning structures.

Kathleen Carley has been one of the pioneers in applying network methodologies to the study of cultural phenomena, especially in her work on textual analysis (Carley 1986, 1993, Carley & Kaufer 1993). Carley uses network analysis techniques to map out the structure of meanings within narratives. Like Cerulo, Carley then proceeds to use these structural representations of meanings to compare cultural phenomena. For example, Carley (1994) uses these techniques to map the structure of meaning in 30 science-fiction novels written during different periods of history. She codes information on ways in which the authors describe the features, actions, and other characters' perceptions of robots. By studying the relationships between the features that were attributed to robots by the novels' authors as a network of concepts, Carley is able to represent changes in the meaning structure of how robots were portrayed over time. Prior to 1950 they were described as dangerous nonmetallic humanoids composed of batteries, electron tubes, and human parts that inspired fear, anger, hatred, and pity in others. By the 1980s they were instead being described as clever, loyal, curious, and capable of sarcasm, being embarrassed, making love, programming computers, and dreaming.

A very different example can be found in Hammond's (1972) analysis of the ruins of Mayan architecture. He employed network models of connectivity (between plazas) as a way of studying how public space was used. On the basis of these models, Hammond was able to deduce which plaza served as the central marketplace and to postulate that the Mayan ballcourt game was, initially at least, a sport reserved for an elite audience.

Structural equivalence approaches to network analysis have also be used to understand cultural phenomena. Mohr (1994) uses this method to map the structure of moral discourse within which poverty relief agencies differentiated among various classes of gendered status identities (mothers, soldiers, widows, working men, the blind, and various others) during the Progressive Era. Here, it is the status identities themselves that are the items within the cultural system. Relations among identities were measured by assessing the profile of relief practices that were applied to each (58 different practices were investigated, e.g. some classes of the poor were given money by the state, others were placed in the poorhouse, some were given counseling by the church, others were given job training by private agencies, and so on). A block-model analysis showed that it was possible to identify different role positions within the system of moral discourse that closely corresponded to Theda Skocpol's (1992) arguments about American welfare politics during these years. The discourse role analysis was also shown to be an effective predictor of the likelihood that any given status category would be described with morally coded terms.

Other examples can also be pointed to. Peter Bearman (1993) uses structural equivalence to show how changes in the social organization of elites in 16th-century England led to the emergence of abstract religious and constitutionalist rhetorics. Anheier & Gerhards (1991a) use structural equivalence measures of the role structure of German writers to explain the development of cultural myths about writers—the myth of the writer as a "notorious loner," as "a poor poet," as "the misunderstood genius," and member of a "romantic literary circle" are all shown to correspond to the social organization of German writers. Finally, Patrick Doreian (1987) uses structural equivalence measures to reanalyze Hammond's data on Mayan architecture.

Boolean Algebra

Boolean algebra is an increasingly popular method for formally analyzing qualitative data. Charles Ragin (1987) has been instrumental in bringing these methods to the attention of sociologists in recent years. This approach (also known as qualitative comparative analysis, or QCA) begins with a set number of cases that vary in terms of the presence or absence of some outcome (or product). Cases are grouped according to their profile of features. Boolean algebra is then applied to identify logically irreducible and nonredundant combinations of features that are associated with certain outcomes. As in network methods, the method presumes a finite number of cases within a system (rather than a sample from a population), and the focus is on qualities (presence and absence rather than measured quantities) of the features. Unlike the methods discussed above, the usual goal of a Boolean analysis is to ascertain which features of a set of cases have a causal relationship with some other feature (or outcome) that is being explained. In this sense, QCA is similar to logistic regression analysis, although as Ragin explains (1995), there are variety of reasons why one might prefer using QCA, including the fact that it can be applied with many fewer cases.

Because of the emphasis on hypothesis-testing, QCA has generally not been applied to the analysis of meaning structures in the same manner as MDS or network techniques. There are some exceptions. Degenne & Lebeaux (1996) use Boolean techniques to analyze the structure of belief systems. Using French survey data they show a causal ordering of religious beliefs and practices (respondents who pray regularly also go to church regularly or they "believe in paradise, purgatory, hell," both of which imply that their children will be given a religious education, and so on). More generally, however, applications of Boolean analysis tend to be very much in the spirit of the work described in this review, and to resonate especially well with those works in which meanings are seen to be a constituent element of institutional patterns. For example, John Foran (1997) uses QCA to analyze the role that five factors (dependent development, economic crisis, repressive/personalist state, world system opportunity, and political cultures of resistance) have played in the success, failure, or quiescence of a dozen recent revolutionary situations. Foran demonstrates that all factors must be present for success, and that the last three of these factors, including a particular cultural orientation, are especially salient.

Sequence Analysis

Sequence analysis is another qualitatively oriented methodology that is increasingly being employed by sociologists. These methods are used for finding reduced form patterns in the sequencing of events through time. Andrew Abbott (1988, 1992) has been instrumental in bringing these methods into mainstream sociology. This is another methodological approach in which elements within a system are compared on the basis of their similarities to one another. These kinds of methods can also be used for identifying certain types of cultural meaning structures.

Abbott & Forrest (1986) used these methods to understand cultural diffusion among communities of English Morris Dancers. By studying the sequencing of dance steps, Abbott & Forrest were able to identify common dance traditions that they used to analyze the diffusion of cultural forms among nineteenth-century rural English communities. Other methods have also been suggested for analyzing narrative structures. Peter Abell's (1987) work emphasizes the comparison of sequences in multiple narratives. David Heise (1988, 1989) has developed Event Structure Analysis (ESA) and a computer program, ETHNO, for its implementation which has been applied by Larry Griffin (1993) to studying the unfolding of historical event logics. Here again, a structural representation is created of a particular institutional (meaning) system that can then be used as a formal basis for comparative analysis.

MEASURING THE DUALITY OF SOCIAL AND CULTURAL STRUCTURES

I started this review by noting that theorists have emphasized the duality of social and cultural structures and I suggested that one important reason for measuring meaning is that doing so allows us to take this theoretical mandate seriously. The three examples of institutional analysis with which I began were selected to illustrate how the measurement of meaning can be used to analyze the cultural construction of social structures. It should be apparent, however, that we also need to attend to the ways in which social structures produce cultural meaning systems. Indeed, my earlier discussion of practice theory would suggest that such an approach is critical for cultural analysis. My focus until now has been to suggest some ways in which meaning structures can be measured. In this section, I discuss several methods that can be employed to focus attention on the duality that inheres between cultural and social structures. These are the class of methods that are described as two-mode data analytic strategies because they simultaneously order both columns and rows of a data matrix. Several methods are available.

Correspondence Analysis

Probably the most familiar example of this kind of approach is correspondence analysis (Weller & Romney 1990). Like MDS, correspondence analysis can be used to represent a set of cultural items in a dimensional space, thereby allowing their underlying structural patterns to be represented visually. At the same time, correspondence analysis enables the relational foundations of the cultural system to be treated as a set of (social-structural) elements that are themselves ordered in terms of their relations to the cultural domain. Thus, this methodology allows both the social and the cultural dimensions to be plotted within the same measurement space.

As an early proponent of practice theory, Pierre Bourdieu was naturally drawn toward this methodology and he has used it extensively in his research. In *Distinction* (1984), Bourdieu uses data on the cultural tastes of different class fractions to identify the class based logic of cultural goods. Thus, Bourdieu shows that taste in music, film, painting, recreational activities, and other cultural domains is organized according to the structure of social classes in France, and using correspondence analysis, he is able to simultaneously plot the various social locations (e.g. the determinants of class structure) according to their relative location within the space of cultural distinctions. These analyses have been central to Bourdieu's theoretical goal of measuring the relationship between social and cultural domains, and he used them to demonstrate that, for example, class locations are ordered according to two salient dimensions—the total volume and relative composition of cultural and economic capital.

Because of its ability to represent the duality of mutually constituted structures, correspondence analysis is beginning to be used more frequently by American sociologists as well (although other approaches have also begun to be developed, such as the proposal of Borgatti & Everett 1997 for using MDS to analyze two-mode data). Ann Mische (1998), for example, uses correspondence analysis to analyze how youth movements in Brazil were structured by the types of political beliefs which they held at the same time that the political discourse itself was structured by the groups who were constituting it.

Lattice Analysis

Galois lattices are another approach that is explicitly oriented toward the representation of the dual ordering of rows and columns. Whereas correspondence analysis can be viewed as a two-mode extension of MDS techniques, lattice analysis provides a dual mapping of rows and columns based on Boolean set theory.

Mohr & Duquenne (1997) use lattices to analyze the changing institutional logics of poverty relief during the Progressive Era. Here the duality between cultural meanings and social practices is operationalized explicitly. Reformers' classifications of the poor (distressed, destitute, fallen, deserving, homeless, indigent, misfortunate, needy, poor, stranger, and worthy) are shown to be embedded within a hierarchically ordered meaning system by the structuring of organizational practices (giving advice, giving food, giving money, paying a person to chop wood, placing a relief applicant in an asylum, and so on).

The use of lattices demonstrates how it was that the cultural and practical logics were mutually constitutive. In other words, the ordering of the poverty classifications is shown to be determined by the ordering of the relief activities and vice versa. By mapping the changes in this dualistic structure through time, Mohr and Duquenne demonstrate how the institutional logic of the nineteenth century poorhouse system was replaced by a far more progressive system founded in the rhetoric and practice of social work professionals.

The paper by Thomas Schweizer (1993) discussed earlier provides another example. Recall that Schweizer analyzes the relationship that inheres between the status logic of material possessions and the social ranking of individuals. He shows that the meaning of possessions can be interpreted by understanding what members of the community possess what types of goods. Simultaneously (and dually), Schweizer assesses the ranking of individual community members in the social order by observing what material goods they possess. The structural duality of these two orders (the individual members of the community and the material possessions that they hold) consists in the fact that the ordering of one is simultaneously dependent upon the ordering of the other. Vincent Duquenne (1995) provides an additional example of the use of lattices to analyze status orders and material wealth.

Hierarchical Classification Models

A final example of two-mode analytic techniques is the hierarchical classification model developed by Paul de Boeck and Seymour Rosenberg, which is implemented in the software program HICLAS (Rosenberg et al 1995). This is an interative algorithm that accomplishes the same goal as a lattice analysis by employing set theoretical principles to cluster items in the rows (objects) and the columns (attributes) of a two-way two-mode binary matrix such that equivalent items are classed together, the classes of objects are hierarchically ordered, the classes of attributes are hierarchically ordered, and the two hierarchical orders are relatd to one another.

This technique has been employed to measure several types of cultural meaning systems. Anheier & Gerhards (1991b) use this method to understand how famous writers (Ernest Hemingway, William Shakespeare, and others) were organized into a field of literary influence by comparing which contemporary German writers cite them as having been inspirational in their own work. The results allow Anheier & Gerhards to describe the dual mapping of blocks of contemporary writers onto a clustering of literary influences in much the same way as Bourdieu's analysis maps social classes and cultural tastes in the same measurement space. Rosenberg (1989) uses HICLAS to analyze meaning structures in Thomas Wolfe's autobiographical novel, *Look Homeward, Angel*. In this case the set structure of various attributes of individuals is dually mapped onto the set structure of characters within the novel. Rosenberg shows with this method that members of Wolfe's family are organized in clear subsets of attributes (his brother Fred is a subset of his sister Mabel, who is a subset of his mother). Rosenberg also demonstrates that Wolfe's description of his own identity at different ages is hierarchically nested, and that Wolfe's description of his self shifts through life to being more and less like various members of his family.

ADVANTAGES AND DISADVANTAGES OF FORMAL ANALYSIS

Precisely because the measurement of meanings lies at the boundaries of the more scientistic and the more humanistic approaches to analyzing social phenomena, it is guaranteed to create controversy. Norman Denzin (1991), for example, complains that scientifically oriented studies of culture have a tendency to reify and reduce the intrinsic complexities of cultural meanings. There is no doubt that he is right about this. All measurement projects end up reifying reality to some extent. Moreover, it is clear that there are other more hermeneutic and post-structuralist approaches to the problem of interpretation that proceed along very different pathways and have a great deal to offer. It would be a mistake to presume that the type of structuralist models of meaning that have been reviewed here are in any sense exhaustive or even that they should be ceded some sort of empirical primacy.

Measuring meaning structures does have its benefits, however. As Robert Merton (1957) suggested in his classic essay regarding the advantages of empirical research, the use of formal methods brings a pressure for the clarification of one's concepts and may lead to the discovery of anomalous findings that call theoretical assumptions into question. Moreover, as Hage & Harary (1983, p. 9) argued in their attempt to persuade anthropologists of the advantages of graph theory, the shift toward quantitative relational methodologies also has a number of more specific advantages. While my focus in this review has been somewhat different, I think Hage & Harary's list is applicable here as well. In somewhat more generalized form, these advantages are the following:

1. Structural models are iconic. They look like what they represent. Whether one uses MDS techniques to generate a picture of the similarity relationships between cultural items or one employs a lattice to map out the hierarchical duality of cultural items and actions, these techniques allow us to see the patterns of difference out of which meanings are constructed. Once we see these patterns, we can begin to understand them.
2. Structural models provide us with a rich conceptual vocabulary for thinking about meanings. Simplicity, complexity, centrality, duality, permutations, and transformations are ideas that have a natural foundation in structural

models. As we try to grapple with understanding phenomena such as cultural boundaries, cultural identities, cultural differentiation, and cultural narrativity, I suspect that these kinds of structural concepts will be of much use to us.

3. Structural models provide us with the tools for quantifying aspects of meaning structures. As I have tried to indicate here, we can quantify meanings without reducing them to some artificially linear metric. Instead we can build structural models that simply represent relationships of similarity and difference that are embedded within practices. Once we have found a way of measuring these kinds of phenomena, however, we (and others) are in a position to be able to replicate our interpretations and to subject our ideas to various kinds of formal tests to help assess the validity of our interpretation.

CONCLUSION

While I will be pleased if qualitatively oriented scholars are persuaded by the merits of these arguments and the utility of these techniques, my primary goal has been to convince sociologists who already use quantitative methods to embrace the measurement of meaning and to incorporate these measures into a more balanced approach to social research that recognizes the duality of cultural and social structures. In this regard I fully agree with Harrison White when he argues that "interpretive approaches are central to achieving a next level of adequacy in social data" (1997:57–58). I also agree with Jepperson and Swidler's (1994) contention that culture is no more intrinsically difficult to measure than other social phenomena and that the greatest impediments to the formal analysis of culture are conceptual rather than methodological.

I have focused here on one very basic level of conceptualization. I have argued that cultural meanings are built up out of structures of difference and that by attending to the patterns of relations that link items within a cultural system, we can use formal methodologies to measure and analyze meaning structures. I have also suggested that a critical componenet of any such endeavor is determining the linkage between meanings and practices and that relations between the former should be determined by their embeddedness within the latter, and vice versa. Beyond this, I have said very little here about what purposes these measurements should be put to or how cultural analysis should proceed. I have done this quite intentionally because I believe that these are general purpose methods that can be employed to accomplish a great variety of things. This should not be taken to indicate that a theoretical context for their use is unnecessary or undesirable. On the contrary, to use these methods without a theoretical goal in mind is unlikely to yield much that is of sociological interest.

In this review I have provided a sampling of the types of research projects that are beginning to appear in the sociological literature that seek to analyze the structure of institutional meanings. As I suggested earlier, there is as yet no coherent body of literature or collection of scholars identified with this project. There is, however, tremendous enthusiasm and opportunity for research of this sort. Before closing, it seems appropriate to offer a small list of suggestions for scholars who have an interest in this style of research. In summary form, my advice is to first, get the text, second, find the use, and third, map the meaning.

Get the Text

Meanings are complex things. Any attempt to model them or subject them to formal analysis invariably involves a gross simplification of the cultural material. As a consequence, it behooves us to postpone this simplification process as long as is feasible. If we can wait until the third step—the stage at which we are consciously trying to reduce the data according to some structural principles—we have much greater control over the way in which we simplify the cultural material. In practical terms, this means that we should always try to gather data as unobtrusively as possible. It is best to avoid imposing an arbitrary coding scheme on the data if it can be avoided. Instead, we should try to find a way to get the entire "text" into a computer (or to come as close as possible to this ideal).

In this regard it is probably worth pointing out that we are just now entering what must surely be the golden age of textual analysis. What sets this moment in history apart is the incredible proliferation of on-line and on-disk textual materials. Previously, scholars who were interested in doing some form of content analysis were compelled to spend huge amounts of time readying their texts for analysis. Now one can easily sit at one's desk and more or less instantaneously summon up a fantastic array of cultural texts in electronic form. This includes software editions of many contemporary novels (currently being marketed for use in laptop computers) for about the same price as a hardbound book, newspaper and magazine articles (published on the Internet), annual reports of corporations (available on CD-Rom), full transcripts of free-form conversations and other types of social exchanges (occurring in virtual "chatrooms" and user interest groups on the Internet), to name but a few.

Find the Use

As I argued earlier, the most critical component of the meaning measurement process is the identification of the systems of relations that will be used to generate the assessment of similarities and differences among cultural items. Because there are invariably any number of ways in which these relations might be assessed, it is essential that a theoretically informed metric be applied at this stage of the analysis. The best rule of thumb in this situation is to locate and evaluate the relevant domain of practical activity in which the identified system of cultural meanings is embedded. Differences in practice produce (and are produced by) differences in meaning. Therefore the goal of an empirical analysis should be to assess how the various cultural elements are differentially implicated in alternative forms of practice.

Map the Meaning

Not all of the examples of cultural interpretation that I've described in this review use structural models as a way of representing cultural meanings. Clearly situations exist wherein this kind of formal approach simply isn't feasible or desirable. Nonetheless, part of what I've tried to suggest here is that the project of finding meaning structures is not really different from the project of measuring meaning structures, or rather, that there is a difference in the degree of formality rather than in the type of endeavor. But, having said that much, I do think that we can profitably make greater use of formal methods and especially the sorts of two-mode modeling techniques that I discussed earlier.

Finally, the techniques that I have referred to are readily available and usually quite simple to use. Scaling and correspondence analysis programs are included in most major statistical packages. Boolean algebras and sequence analysis programs are easily obtainable and geared to run on most microcomputers. Network analysis packages are likewise widely available and, nowadays at least, quite user-friendly and intelligible.

Of course, as anyone who has employed these methods will readily testify, there is nothing simple or determinate about the interpretive work that one must perform after having completed a structural analysis. In a sense, once one has mapped the meaning structure of a given institutional practice, one is in the same position as a scholar who has just emerged from an intensive field study, chock full of ideas and images. Any visual representation of a meaning structure is still largely a Rorschach test upon which one must seek to project an interpretation. But, to the extent that one has carefully thought about the linkage between culture and practice and how it informs one's data selection, measures of differentiation, and structural modeling, so too one should have little difficulty in interpreting the meaning structures that have been identified.

ACKNOWLEDGMENTS

I would like to thank Ann Swidler for originally inviting me to write up a version of this review for the ASA Culture Section Conference on Meaning and Measurement, held at George Mason University in August 1995. Bill Bielby, Paul DiMaggio, Mustafa Emirbayer, Noah Friedkin, Roger Friedland, John Martin, Pep Rodriguez, Bruce Straits, John Sutton, and an anonymous reviewer provided valuable comments and advice.

Literature Cited

Abbott A. 1983. Sequences of social events: concepts and methods for the analysis of order in social processes. *Hist. Methods* 16(4):129–47

Abbott A. 1988. Transcending general linear reality. *Sociol. Theory* 6:169–86

Abbott A. 1990. Primer on sequence methods. *Org. Sci.* 1:373–92

Abbott A. 1992. From causes to events: notes on narrative positivism. *Sociol. Methods Res.* 20(4):428–55

Abbott A, Forrest J. 1986. Optimal matching methods for historical sequences. *J. Interdiscip. Hist.* 26(3):471–94

Abell P. 1987. *The Syntax of Social Life: The Theory and Method of Comparative Narratives*. Oxford: Clarendon

Aldenderfer MS, Blashfield RK. 1984. *Cluster Analysis*. Beverly Hills, CA: Sage

Anheier H, Gerhards J. 1991a. Literary myths and social structure. *Soc. Forces* 69: 811–30

Anheier H, Gerhards J. 1991b. The acknowledgment of literary influence: a structural analysis of a German literary network. *Sociol. Forum* 6(1):137–56

Bauman Z. 1973. *Culture as Praxis*. London: Routledge and Kegan Paul

Bearman P. 1993. *Relations into Rhetorics*. New Brunswick, NJ: Rutgers Univ. Press

Berelson B. 1952. *Content Analysis in Communication Research*. Glencoe, IL: Free Press

Berger PL, Luckmann T. 1967. *The Social Construction of Reality*. New York: Doubleday

Boorman SA, Levitt PR. 1983. Blockmodeling complex statutes: mapping techniques based on combinatorial optimization for analyzing economic legislation and its stress points over time. *Econ. Letters* 13: 1–9

Borgatti SP, Everett MG. 1997. Network analysis of 2-mode data. *Soc. Networks* 19:243–69

Bourdieu P. 1977. *Outline of a Theory of Practice*. Cambridge, UK: Cambridge Univ. Press

Bourdieu P. 1984. *Distinction: A Social Critique of the Judgement of Taste*. Cambridge, MA: Harvard Univ. Press

Burt RS. 1978. Cohesion versus structural equivalence as a basis for network subgroups. *Sociol. Methods Res.* 7:189–212

Burton M, Kirk L. 1979. Sex differences in Maasai cognition of personality and social identity. *Am. Anthro.* 81:841–73

Cappell CL, Guterbock TM. 1992. Visible colleges: the social and conceptual structure of sociology specialties. *Am. Sociol. Rev.* 57:266–73

Carley K. 1986. An approach for relating social structure to cognitive structure. *J. Math. Soc.* 12:137–89

Carley KM. 1994. Extracting culture through textual analysis. *Poetics* 22:291–312

Carley KM. 1993. Coding choices for textual analysis: a comparison of content analysis and map analysis. *Sociol. Methodol.* 23: 75–126

Carley KM, Kaufer DS. 1993. Semantic connectivity: an approach for analyzing symbols in semantic networks. *Comm. Theory* 3:183–213

Caws P. 1988. *Structuralism: The Art of the Intelligible*. Atlantic Highlands, NJ: Humanities Press Int.

Cerulo K. 1988. Analyzing cultural products: a new method of measurement. *Soc. Sci. Res.* 17:317–52

Cerulo K. 1995. *Identity Designs: The Sights and Sounds of a Nation*. New Brunswick, NJ: Rutgers Univ. Press

Csikszentmihalyi M, Rochberg-Halton E. 1981. *The Meaning of Things: Domestic Symbols and the Self*. Cambridge, UK: Cambridge Univ. Press

D'Andrade RG. 1995. *The Development of Cognitive Anthropology*. Cambridge, UK: Cambridge Univ. Press

D'Andrade RG, Quinn N, Nerlove S, Romney AK. 1972. Categories of disease in American-English and Mexican-Spanish. In *Multidimensional Scaling*, Vol. 2, ed. AK Romney, R Shepard, SB Nerlove. New York: Seminar

Darnovsky M, Epstein B, Flacks R. 1995. *Cultural Politics and Social Movements*. Philadelphia: Temple Univ. Press

Degenne A, Lebeaux M-O. 1996. Boolean analysis of questionnaire data. *Soc. Networks* 18:231–45

Denzin NK. 1991. Empiricist cultural studies in America: a deconstructive reading. *Curr. Persp. Social Theory* 11:17–39

de Saussure F. [1916] 1959. *Course in General Linguistics*. New York: McGraw-Hill

DiMaggio PJ. 1992. Cultural capital and school success: the impact of status-culture participation on the grades of U.S. high school students. *Am. Sociol. Rev.* 47: 189–201

DiMaggio PJ, Mohr J. 1985. Cultural capital, educational attainment and marital selection. *Amer. J. Sociol.* 90(6):1231–61

DiMaggio PJ, Mullen A. 1993. *Organizing*

communities: models of collective action in national music week, 1924. Presented at Am. Sociol. Assoc. Meet., 88th, Miami

Doreian P. 1987. Equivalence in a social network. *J. Math. Soc.* 13:243–82

Dowd TJ. 1992. The musical structure and social context of number one songs, 1955 to 1988: an exploratory analysis. In *Vocabularies of Public Life: Empirical Essays in Symbolic Structure,* ed. R Wuthnow. New York. Routledge

Duquenne V. 1995. Models of possessions and lattice analysis. *Soc. Sci. Info.* 34(2): 253–67

Duquenne V, Mohr JW, Le Pape A. 1998. Comparison of dual orderings in time. *Soc. Sci. Info.* 37:(2):227–53

Emirbayer M. 1997. Manifesto for a relational sociology. *Amer. J. Sociol.* 103(2): 281–317

Ennis JG. 1992. The social organization of sociological knowledge: modeling the intersection of specialties. *Am. Sociol. Rev.* 57: 259–65

Eyerman R, Jamison A. 1991. *Social Movements: A Cognitive Approach.* University Park, PA: Penn. State Univ. Press

Foran J. 1997. The future of revolutions at the *fin-de-siècle. Third World Q.* 18(5): 791–820.

Franzosi R. 1989. From words to numbers: a generalized and linguistics-based coding procedure for collecting textual data. *Sociol. Methodol.* 19:263–98

Franzosi R. 1990. Computer-assisted coding of textual data. *Sociol. Meth. Res.* 19(2): 225–57

Franzosi R. 1997. Mobilization and countermobilization processes: from the "Red Years" (1919–20) to the "Black Years" (1921–22) in Italy. *Theory Soc.* 26(2-3): 275–304

Franzosi R, Mohr JW. 1997. New directions in formalization and historical analysis. *Theory Soc.* 26(2-3):133–60

Friedland R, Alford RR. 1991. Bringing society back in: symbols, practices and institutional contradictions. In *The New Institutionalism in Organizational Analysis*, ed. WW Powell, P DiMaggio, pp. 232–63. Chicago: Univ. Chicago Press

Geertz C. 1973. *The Interpretation of Cultures*. New York: Basic Books

Giddens A. 1984. *The Constitution of Society: Outline of a Theory of Structuration.* Berkeley: Univ. Calif. Press

Griffin LJ. 1993. Narrative, event-structure analysis, and causal interpretation in historical sociology. *Am. J. Sociol.* 98: 1094–1133

Griswold W. 1987a. A methodological framework for the sociology of culture. *Sociol. Methodol.* 17:1–35

Griswold W. 1987b. The fabrication of meaning: literary interpretation in the United States, Great Britain, and the West Indies. *Am. J. Sociol.* 92(5):1077–1117

Griswold W. 1992. The writing on the mud wall: Nigerian novels and the imaginary village. *Am. Sociol. Rev.* 57:709–24

Griswold W. 1993. Recent moves in the sociology of literature. *Annu. Rev. Sociol.* 19: 455–67

Hage P, Harary F. 1983. *Structural Models in Anthropology.* Cambridge, UK: Cambridge Univ. Press

Hammond NDC. 1972. The planning of a Maya ceremonial center. *Scientific Am.* 226:83–91

Hawkes T. 1977. *Structuralism and Semiotics.* Berkeley, CA: Univ. Calif. Press

Hays TE. 1976. An empirical method for the identification of covert categories in ethnobiology. *Am. Ethnol.* 3(3)489–507

Heise D. 1988. Computer analysis of cultural structures. *Soc. Sci. Computer Rev.* 6: 183–96

Heise D. 1989. Modeling event structures. *J. Math. Soc.* 14:139–69

Kirk L, Burton M. 1977. Meaning and context: a study of contextual shifts in meaning of Maasai personality descriptors. *Am. Ethnol.* 4:734–61

Kruskal JB, Wish M. 1978. *Multidimensional Scaling*. Beverly Hills, CA: Sage

Kurzweil E. 1980. *The Age of Structuralism: Lévi-Strauss to Foucault.* New York: Columbia Univ. Press

Laumann EO, Knoke D. 1987. *Organization State: Social Change in National Policy Domains.* Madison: Univ. Wisc. Press

Lévi-Strauss C. 1963. *Structural Anthropology.* New York: Basic Books

Merton RK, ed. 1957. The bearing of empirical research on sociological theory. In *Social Theory and Social Structure.* Glencoe, IL: Free Press

Meyer J, Rowan B. 1977. Institutionalized organizations: formal structure as myth and ceremony. *Amer. J. Sociol.* 83:340–63

Mische A. 1998. *Projects, identities. and social networks: Brazilian youth mobilization and the making of civic culture.* Presented at Am. Sociol. Assoc. Meet., 93, San Francisco

Mohr JW. 1994. Soldiers, mothers, tramps and others: discourse roles in the 1907 New York City Charity Directory. *Poetics* 22: 327–57

Mohr JW. 1998. The classificatory logics of state welfare systems: towards a formal analysis. In *Public Rights, Public Rules:*

Constituting Citizens in the World Polity and National Policy, ed. C McNeely. NY: Garland. In press

Mohr JW, DiMaggio P. 1995. The intergenerational transmission of cultural capital. *Res. Soc. Strat. Mob.* 14:169–200

Mohr JW, Duquenne V. 1997. The duality of culture and practice: poverty relief in New York City, 1888–1917. *Theory Soc.* 26(2-3):305–56

Mohr JW, Guerra-Pearson F. 1998. The differentiation of institutional space: organizational forms in the New York social welfare sector, 1888–1917. In *Bending the Bars of the Iron Cage,* ed. W Powell, D Jones. Chicago: Univ. Chicago Press. In press

Ortner S. 1994. Theory in anthropology since the sixties. In *Culture/Power/History: A Reader in Contemporary Social Theory*, ed. NB Dirks, G Eley, SB Ortner, pp. 372–411. Princeton, NJ: Princeton Univ. Press

Peterson RA. 1976. The production of culture. *Am. Behav. Sci.* 19:669–83

Peterson RA, Berger DG. 1975. Cycles in symbol production: the case of popular music. *Am. Sociol. Rev.* 40:158–73

Pettit P. 1977. *The Concept of Structuralism: A Critical Analysis.* Berkeley: Univ. Calif. Press

Powell WW, DiMaggio PJ. 1991. *The New Institutionalism in Organizational Analysis.* Chicago: Univ. Chicago Press

Ragin C. 1987. *The Comparative Method: Moving Beyond Qualitative and Quantitative Strategies.* Berkeley: Univ. Calif. Press

Ragin C. 1995. Using qualitative comparative analysis to study configurations. In *Computer-Aided Qualitative Data Analysis*, ed. U Kelle, pp. 177–89. Thousand Oaks, CA: Sage

Roberts CW. 1989. Other than counting words: a linguistic approach to content analysis. *Soc. Forces* 68(1):147–77

Rosenberg S. 1989. A study of personality in literary autobiography: an analysis of Thomas Wolfe's *Look Homeward Angel. J. Pers. Soc. Psy.* 56:416–30

Rosenberg S, Mechelen I, De Boeck P. 1995. A hierarchical classes model: theory and method with applications in psychology and psychopathology. In *Clustering and Classification*, ed. P Arabie, L Hubert, G DeSoete. Teaneck, NJ: World Scientific

Sahlins M. 1976. *Culture and Practical Reason.* Chicago: Univ. Chicago Press

Schweizer T. 1993. The dual ordering of people and possessions. *Curr. Anthro.* 34: 469–83

Sewell WH Jr. 1992. A theory of structure: duality, agency and transformation. *Amer. J. Sociol.* 98 (Jul):1–29

Shweder RA, Bourne EJ. 1991. Does the concept of the person vary cross-culturally? In *Thinking Through Cultures: Expeditions in Cultural Psychology*, ed. RA Shweder, pp. 113–55. Cambridge, MA: Harvard Univ. Press

Skocpol T. 1992. *Protecting Soldiers and Mothers: The Political Origins of Social Policy in the United States.* Cambridge, MA: Harvard Univ. Press.

Snider JG, Osgood CE. 1969. *Semantic Differential Technique: A Sourcebook.* Chicago: Aldine

Snow DA, Rochford EB Jr, Worden SK, Benford RD. 1986. Frame alignment processes, micromobilization, and movement participation. *Am. Sociol. Rev.* 51:464–81

Sudman S, Bradburn NM, Schwarz N. 1996. *Thinking About Answers: The Application of Cognitive Processes to Survey Methodology.* San Francisco: Jossey-Bass

Swidler A. 1986. Culture in action: symbols and strategies. *Am. Sociol. Rev.* 51:273–86

Tilly C. 1997. Parliamentarization of popular contention in Great Britain, 1758–1834. *Theory Soc.* 26(2-3):245–73

Ventresca M, Yin X. 1997. *Representing economy and society: comparative trends in what states count, 1800–1970.* Presented at Am. Sociol. Assoc. Meet., 92nd, Toronto

Wasserman S, Faust K. 1994. *Social Network Analysis: Methods and Applications.* Cambridge, UK: Cambridge Univ. Press

Weller SC, Romney AK. 1988. *Systematic Data Collection.* Newbury Park, CA: Sage

Weller SC, Romney AK. 1990. *Metric Scaling: Correspondence Analysis.* Newbury Park, CA: Sage

White HC, Boorman SA, Breiger RL. 1976. Social structure from multiple networks. I: Blockmodels of roles and positions. *Amer. J. Sociol.* 81:730–80

Wuthnow R. 1987. *Meaning and Moral Order: Explorations in Cultural Analysis.* Berkeley: Univ. Calif. Press

Annu. Rev. Sociol. 1998. 98:371–93

WAS IT WORTH THE EFFORT? The Outcomes and Consequences of Social Movements

Marco G. Giugni
Department of Political Science, University of Geneva, Switzerland,
e-mail: marco.giugni@politic.unige.ch

KEY WORDS: disruption, organization, public opinion, political opportunity structures, social change

ABSTRACT

Research on social movements has usually addressed issues of movement emergence and mobilization, yet has paid less attention to their outcomes and consequences. Although there exists a considerable amount of work on this aspect, little systematic research has been done so far. Most existing work focuses on political and policy outcomes of movements, whereas few studies address their broader cultural and institutional effects. Furthermore, we still know little about the indirect and unintended consequences produced by movements. Early studies have dealt with the effectiveness of disruptive and violent actions and with the role of several organizational variables for movement success. More recently, scholars have begun to analyze movement outcomes in their political context by looking at the role of public opinion, allies, and state structures. A comparative perspective promises to be a fruitful avenue of research in this regard.

INTRODUCTION

If we trust our intuitions, the last big European cycle of protest caused such fundamental changes in the social and political structures that we are still wondering about the kind of world we are now living in. In the eyes of a neutral observer, the democracy movements that shook Eastern Europe in 1989 were

0360-0572/98/0815-0371$08.00

clearly instrumental in bringing about the new order. Mass actions and street demonstrations in Czechoslovakia, East Germany, Hungary, Poland, and Romania have brought about the fall of the Communist regimes in those countries and, together with popular mobilizations in the Baltic Republics later on, the collapse of the Soviet Union in 1991. That the movements must have played a significant role can be seen in the impressive growth of popular mobilizations in those countries. Take the example of East Germany. Oberschall (1996) reports an impressive increase in the number of participants in protests and demonstrations in Leipzig, where the key events took place during 1989. Whereas the celebration of the anniversary of Karl Liebknecht and Rosa Luxemburg on January 15 saw the presence of 150–200 participants, the protest marches from Nikolai church to the center, which (starting from October 16) took place every Monday until Christmas, mobilized from 110,000 to 450,000 people. Yet even the most relentless optimists would concede that, without major changes in the structures of power, the protests and mass demonstrations would hardly have had such dramatic consequences. In fact, one can argue that in the absence of such changes the movements themselves would not take on such a big scale. Two major transformations in the states' structures gave a big boost to the democracy movements in Easter Europe and helped them change our world: Gorbachev's perestroïka and the cracks in the Communist states' alliance system. Movement mobilization and state breakdown combined in a complex way to bring about a revolutionary outcome.

Another example: During the summer of 1995 the Dutch oil company Shell announced plans to destroy the Brent Spar offshore oil rig located in the North Sea because it became unusable. This decision provoked the immediate reaction by outraged environmentalist groups, especially Greenpeace, which foresaw an ecological disaster and called for a boycott of Shell products worldwide. Many consumers took the boycott seriously and the company's sales went down considerably in the days following the appeal. Particularly in Germany, drivers avoided Shell's gas stations in favor of other companies. Worried by the fall of sales and the bad public image it was receiving, the oil company abandoned the project of destroying the oil rig, thus conceding a significant victory to Greenpeace and the environmental movement.

This example is very different from the previous one. For one thing, the events were much more limited in time, space, and scope. While the revolutions in Eastern Europe lasted several months (indeed, a very short time for a revolution), involved thousands of participants, and had dramatic social and political repercussions for the entire world, the Greenpeace boycott was called by a single organization and was successful within a few weeks, but this certainly did not alter the foundations of contemporary society. Another difference is that Greenpeace activists had seemingly expected—or at least hoped—that Shell would withdraw from its decision, whereas no one could have foreseen the fundamental changes brought about by the opposition to the Communist regimes. Despite these differences, the two examples taken together illustrate several problems and difficulties inherent in the study of the consequences of social movements. The principal difficulty is how to establish a causal relationship between a series of events that we can reasonably classify as social movement actions and an observed change in society, be it minor or fundamental, durable or temporary. Both our examples display social movement activities and were followed by changes that the movements had asked for, although the scope of those changes, in one case, went well beyond any possible anticipation. But the problem of causal attribution remains the same. Even for the apparently more obvious effect in the Brent Spar case, we cannot a priori exclude the intervention of a third party (a member of the political elite, for example) which may have caused the withdrawal of Shell's decision. In addition, both the protest cycle for democracy and Greenpeace's call for a boycott might have had a series of long-term consequences that neither the populations of Eastern Europe nor Greenpeace activists had planned. As I hope it will become clear by the end of the paper, these methodological problems can only be resolved theoretically.

Social scientists often have a hard time finding consensus on many aspects of their collective enterprise. Students of social movements are certainly no exception to this rule. They often disagree on the causes of protest, its development over time, its fate, and the methods of analysis. Yet they all seem to agree that the study of the effects of social movements has largely been neglected, and it has become common sense to cite this state of affairs (e.g. Berkowitz 1974, Gurr 1980, McAdam et al 1988, Tarrow 1993). Such neglect is quite astonishing, for the ultimate end of movements is to bring about change. The field, however, is not as empty as several observers have maintained.[1] Nevertheless, we still lack systematic empirical analyses that would add to our knowledge of the conditions under which movements produce certain effects. Furthermore, a striking disparity exists between the large body of work on political and policy outcomes and the sporadic studies on the cultural and institutional effects of social movements. This review reflects this state of affairs. (For previous reviews see Amenta et al 1992, Burstein et al 1995, Gurr 1980, Jenkins 1981, McAdam et al 1988, Mirowsky & Ross 1981, Schumaker 1978.) I first address the two main axes of early research: the moderation/disruption

[1]The fact that, due to lack of space, I had to leave out a great many existing works is a clear indication that there is a large body of literature on movement consequences. I have provided a more exhaustive overview of the extant literature in another paper (Giugni 1994), on which the present one is partly based. It should also be noted that studies of social revolutions, insofar as the latter are the product of social movements or coalitions between movements and oppositional elites, may be considered as the most dramatic effect of movements. Again, for space reasons I will not deal with this aspect.

axis and the organization/disorder axis. Second, I review work that has attempted to put movements and their outcomes in their larger social and political context. Third, I point to some logical as well as methodological problems of existing work that have prevented the cumulative gathering of systematic knowledge. In the end, I hope to be able to show that, while there exists a considerable amount of work on this topic, little systematic research has been done. This is especially true when it comes to comparisons across countries and across movements to specify the conditions that foster certain types of impact, an approach that I view as one of the most promising avenues for future research.

THE POWER OF MOVEMENTS

Most research so far has focused on the intended effects of social movements. Early work has looked in particular at the impact of movement-controlled variables by attempting to single out the characteristics of movements that are most conducive to success or, more generally, that help certain outcomes to occur. In this respect, one can discern two closely interrelated lines of investigation. The first line concerns the impact, mostly on policy, of various organizational variables and has brought researchers to ask whether strongly organized movements are more successful than loosely organized movements. The second line of inquiry has looked at the effects of disruptive and violent protest behavior and has opened a debate in the literature about whether the use of disruptive tactics by social movements is more likely to lead to policy changes than moderate tactics. This debate has largely dealt with the effectiveness of violence. Let us briefly discuss each of these two aspects.

The Impact of Organization

Resource mobilization theory has dominated the study of social movements and contentious politics for at least three decades. It is therefore little surprising that research on movement outcomes has paid a lot of attention to the role of the organizational characteristics of movements. There is a fair amount of theoretical and empirical work that links various movement-controlled variables to their alleged impact. While early theoretical work has speculated over the link between government responsiveness and the nature of movement demands, organizational size and stability, leadership, and strategies (e.g. Etzioni 1970, Lipsky & Levi 1972), other authors have tried to show it empirically. Brill's (1971) finding (based on a case study of rent strikes) that success is not likely to result if the movement leaders are unable to build an effective organization is typical in this respect. Relevant work includes Shorter & Tilly's (1974) examination of the effect of organizational variables on the outcomes of strikes in France, Staggenborg's (1988) inquiry into the consequences of professionalization and formalization in the pro-choice movement, and Clemens' (1993) investigation of the impact of organizational repertoires on institutional change. We also have a substantial body of literature on the effects of lobbying strategies on governmental decisions and congressional action (e.g. Fowler & Shaiko 1987, Milbrath 1970, Metz 1986). However, these studies often are more concerned with interest-group politics than social movements themselves.

Important evidence about the relationship between various organizational variables and the success of social movements comes from Gamson's *The Strategy of Social Protest* (1990), which after more than two decades remains perhaps the most systematic attempt to inquire into the impact and effectiveness of social movements. The author's comprehensive analysis of the careers of 53 American challenging groups active between 1800 and 1945 led him to conclude that (*a*) groups with single-issue demands were more successful than groups with multiple-issue demands, (*b*) the use of selective incentives was positively correlated with success, (*c*) the use of violence and generally disruptive tactics was associated with success, while being the objects of violence made it more difficult (as we will see in more detail below) and (*d*) successful groups tended to be more bureaucratized, centralized, and unfactionalized, which is the most important point for the present purpose. Finally, he tested the role of context variables and found that times (quiet or turbulent) did not matter much, whereas political crises seemed to have an effect on the outcomes of the challenging groups examined.

Gamson's work has raised a number of criticisms, mostly methodological (Goldstone 1980, Gurr 1980, Snyder & Kelly 1976, Webb et al 1983, Zelditch 1978), but also a series of reanalyses of his data, which the author had appended to the book (Frey et al 1992, Goldstone 1980, Mirowsky & Ross 1981, Steedly & Foley 1979).[2] As in the case of the role of disruptive tactics, most of these works have confirmed Gamson's principal findings, at least in part. For example, Steedly & Foley (1979), using more sophisticated techniques, found group success related, in order of relative importance, to the nondisplacement nature of the goals, the number of alliances, the absence of factionalism, the existence of specific and limited goals, and the willingness to use sanctions. Similarly, Mirowsky and Ross (1981), aiming at finding the locus of control over movement success, found protester-controlled factors more important than the support of third parties or the situation for a successful outcome. Of these protester-controlled factors, the organization and, above all, the beliefs and goals were seen as crucial for success. More recently, Frey et al (1992)

[2]These reanalyses have been included in the book's second edition (Gamson 1990).

pointed to the importance of not having displacement goals and group factionalism to obtain new advantages. Thus, Gamson's central argument stressing internal variables and resource mobilization as determinants of group success found further support. However, Piven and Cloward's (1979) thesis that movements have a chance to succeed to the extent that they avoid building a strong organization brought a fundamental criticism to Gamson's stress on the effectiveness of organization, a criticism that has triggered a debate in both scholarly and general audience journals. In addition, Goldstone's (1980) reanalysis of Gamson's data cast serious doubts over his findings and pointed to a perspective on social movement outcomes that takes into account their broader political context. Before I return to this aspect, I would like to discuss the second main axis of existing research: the impact of disruption.

The Effectiveness of Disruptive and Violent Protest

Overall, the use by social movements of disruptive tactics and violence seems to increase their potential for change. Several authors have argued that, contrary to the pluralist claim that moderation in politics is more effective than disruption, the use of force by social movements increases the chances that they reach their goals (Astin et al 1975, McAdam 1983, Tarrow 1994, Tilly et al 1975). Again, Gamson's (1990) study provides empirical evidence of the effectiveness of violence and the use of constraints. He found that the use of violence and, more generally, disruptive tactics by challenging groups was positively correlated to his two measures of success: the acceptance of challengers as legitimate claimants and the obtaining of new advantages for constituents. These findings are backed up by some of the aforementioned reanalyses of his data, in particular those by Mirowsky & Ross (1981) and Steedly & Foley (1979). Yet there is no consensus on this point, nor on the implications of this for movements.

Much evidence on the relationship between disruptive or violent movement tactics and their impact comes from two important strands of research: the study of strikes and the many analyses of the wave of urban riots that occurred in several American cities at the end of the sixties. As far as strike activity is concerned, Taft & Ross (1969), on the basis of a study of violent labor conflicts in the United States through 1968, found little evidence that violence would help unions to reach their goals. A similar conclusion has been reached by Snyder and Kelly (1976). By analyzing quantitative data on strikes that occurred in Italy between 1878 and 1903, Snyder and Kelly were able to show that violent strikes were less successful than peaceful ones. These results contradict those obtained by Shorter & Tilly (1971) in their study of strikes in France, who found a positive correlation between the use of violence and strike outcomes. Research on strike activity, however, has gone beyond the specific question of disruption or violence to examine broader issues related to the industrial conflict (Cohn 1993, Franzosi 1994, Hicks & Swank 1984, Swank 1983, Shorter & Tilly 1974, Snyder & Kelly 1976).

The effectiveness of disruptive protest and movements has been analyzed thoroughly in the aftermath of the urban riots of the 1960s in the United States (for reviews see Gurr 1980, Isaac & Kelly 1981, Piven & Cloward 1993). To be sure, rioting behavior and social movements are not equivalent, though they are both instances of contentious politics, defined as "collective activity on the part of claimants—or those who claim to represent them—relying at least in part on noninstitutionalized forms of interaction with elites, opponents, or the state" (Tarrow 1996:874). Social movements, on the other hand, may be defined as "sustained challenges to powerholders in the name of a disadvantaged population living under the jurisdiction or influence of those powerholders" (Tarrow 1996:874; see also Tarrow 1994, Tilly 1984). However, studying riots can yield important insights on the effectiveness of disruption and violent protest by social movements. In addition, the American riots of the sixties have sparked the interest on the latter aspect among students of social movements. Some authors, including Hahn (1970), McClurg Mueller (1978), Isaac & Kelly (1981), Kelly & Snyder (1980), and Sears & McConahay (1973), have focused explicitly on the effects of violence. In general, the evidence gathered does not allow for a definitive answer to the question whether rioting is beneficial or detrimental to the population involved. Kelly & Snyder (1980), for example, suggested that there is no causal relationship between the frequency and severity of violence displayed in American cities during the 1960s and the distribution of black socioeconomic gains at the local level, either by income level or by employment and occupational changes. Feagin & Hahn (1973), in a monograph on ghetto riots, maintain that the latter led at best to limited reform and mostly to changes in police policies. Nevertheless, the authors did not provide systematic evidence for their argument. Berkowitz (1974), who looked at socioeconomic changes at the neighborhood level brought about by ghetto riots between 1960 and 1970, found no differential improvement for riot tracts, arguing against a positive effect of the riots (see also Levitan et al 1975). Even more pessimistically, Welch (1975) showed that the riots led to an increase in urban expenditures for control and punishment of rioters, and much less in their favor. However, Colby's (1975) findings in a way contradict Welch's, because he found that the riots had a positive influence on redistribution policy, though no influence on regulatory policy at the state level. On the other hand, Jennings (1979), also through a comparison of states but over time as well, found some support for a positive correlation between the number of riots and the increase in AFDC recipients.

Many studies of the urban riots in American cities are directly related to Piven & Cloward's (1993) well-known thesis about the regulating functions of public welfare (for reviews see Piven & Cloward 1993, Trattner 1983). As it is known, these authors provocatively argued that welfare systems serve two principal functions: to maintain a supply of low-wage labor and to restore order in periods of civil turmoil. According to this thesis, hence, turmoil and disruptive actions do provoke policy change, but this can hardly be seen as success, for such concessions are usually withdrawn once the turmoil subsides. A series of studies carried out during the 1970s and 1980s attempted to reexamine this thesis (e.g. Albritton 1979, Betz 1974, Colby 1982, Hicks & Swank 1983, Isaac & Kelly 1981, Jennings 1979, 1980, 1983, Schramm & Turbott 1983, Sharp & Maynard-Moody 1991). In addition, other authors have addressed Piven and Cloward's argument, but focusing on the relief expansion of the thirties (e.g. Jenkins & Brents 1989, Kerbo & Shaffer 1992; see further Valocchi 1990). Again, although much of the disagreement with Piven and Cloward's thesis bears not so much on the results in themselves, but rather their interpretation, in the whole it is difficult out of this impressive amount of empirical work to provide a clear-cut answer to the question whether disruption can produce policy changes and, if so, what this means for the movements.

Such uncertainty of results calls for a conditional analysis that singles out the circumstances under which violence matters. This task was accomplished by Button (1978), among others, in one of the most comprehensive empirical studies of the political impact of the 1960s riots. He maintained that violence is conducive to political and social change under five general conditions: 1. when powerholders have enough public resources to meet the demands of the movement, 2. when violent actions and events are neither too frequent as to cause massive societal and political instability nor severe enough to be noticed and to represent a threat, 3. when a relevant share of powerholders and the public are sympathetic to the goals of the movement and the violence is not so severe as to undermine this sympathy, 4. when the aims and demands of the movement are relatively limited, specific, and clear, and 5. when violence is adopted in combination with peaceful and conventional strategies (Button 1978). Button's approach has the advantage of avoiding the formulation of a too-simple causal relationship between the use of violence and its outcomes. On the other hand, it seems so broad as to run the risk of leading to trivial results. A narrower argument in this respect has been put forth by Schumaker (1978), who has looked at the conditions under which disruptive tactics work. His results suggest that the use of constraints is more effective when the conflict is limited to the protest group and their target (i.e. when the scope of conflict is narrow). In contrast, when the public becomes involved in the conflict (i.e. when the scope of conflict is broad), the use of constraints tends to reduce the chances of a successful outcome. Other analyses based on the 1960s urban riots, however, suggest that militancy is generally not conducive to success (Schumaker 1975). Similarly, a study of official responses to 60 protest incidents that occurred in the Philippines, Malaysia, and Thailand between 1960 and 1977 showed that the use of violent constraints (i.e. militancy), except when the group of protesters was large, had negative effects on the protest's outcomes because repression was more likely to occur (O'Keefe & Schumaker 1983).

MOVEMENT OUTCOMES IN CONTEXT

To summarize the paper so far, existing research on the impact of several internal characteristics of social movements, such as the use of disruptive tactics and actions, seems to yield contradictory findings. Nevertheless, this contradiction may well be more apparent than real. The puzzle may be solved once we acknowledge the crucial role of the broader political context in facilitating or constraining both the mobilization and the potential outcomes of movements. Strategies that work in a given context may simply be ineffective in other political settings and vice versa. Thus, more recent work has shifted away from the study of the effectiveness of disruption and the organizational characteristics of social movements toward the environmental conditions that channel their consequences. This has been done in two distinct directions. First, the role of public opinion in facilitating or preventing movements to make an impact has been thoroughly investigated, particularly in the United States. A major turn in the study of movement outcomes, however, has secondly come from comparative analyses that attempt to link them to the movements' political context. Next I briefly consider these two avenues of research.

Public Opinion

Social movements, particularly when they express themselves through their most typical form of action, public demonstrations, address their message simultaneously to two distinct targets: the powerholders and the general public. On the one hand, they press the political authorities for recognition as well as to get their demands met, at least in part. On the other hand, they seek public support and try to sensitize the population to their cause. At the same time, the most common political targets of contemporary movements, namely local or national governments, pay particular attention to public opinion and fluctuations therein. All this makes a strong case for taking public opinion into account as an important external factor in the study of the outcomes of social movements. This has been done above all in the United States. Public opinion has entered the study of movement outcomes both as explanatory variable and explanandum. In the former case, one examines how and to what extent movements produce changes in the perceptions people have of a given issue (e.g. Gusfield 1981, Lawson 1976, Oberschall 1973, Orfield 1975). However, while it seems rather obvious that protest activities raise the awareness of the population over certain political issues, changes in public opinion can also help movements to reach their goals by making decision-makers more responsive to their demands. Hence, several authors have stressed the role of public opinion for legislative change (e.g. Burstein 1979a–c, 1985, Burstein & Freudenburg 1978, Costain & Majstorovic 1994, Page & Shapiro 1983, Weissberg 1976), though not always related to the impact of social movements.

Paul Burstein is certainly among those who have paid most attention to this aspect. In his analysis of the struggle for equal employment opportunity in the United States, he showed that "equal employment opportunity legislation was adopted as the result of social changes that were manifested in public opinion, crystallized in the civil rights and women's movements, and transformed into public policy by political leaders" (Burstein 1985:125), thus pointing to the interconnections of public opinion, movement activities, and congressional action in bringing about policy changes for discriminated-against groups. In similar fashion, Costain and Majstorovic (1994) studied the multiple origins of women's rights legislation by stressing the same three sets of factors. As they argue, there are several views of the relationship between public opinion and legislative action. They see four prevailing interpretations: 1. a public opinion interpretation, stating a direct relationship between public opinion and legislative change, 2. an interpretation that sees public opinion as filtering the impact of outside events on legislative action, 3. an elite behavior interpretation, according to which public opinion is affected by legislative elites, and 4. a social movement interpretation, whereby legislation results from the joint action of social movements, public opinion, and media coverage. The latter appears as the most plausible interpretation, for not only does it take into account both movement actions and changes in public opinion, but it also acknowledges the fundamental role of the media for movement mobilization and outcomes. The way in which the media cover, frame, and interpret social movements has largely been neglected in the existing literature. Together with the analysis of the role of political opportunty structures for movement outcomes, this is a promising avenue for future research (e.g. Gamson and Wolfsfeld 1993).

Political Opportunity Structures

As our initial example about the fall of the Communist regimes of Eastern Europe illustrates, and as Goldstone's (1980) reanalysis of Gamson's data made clear, the study of the outcomes of social movements cannot avoid taking into account the political context in which they operate. On the basis of a series of methodological criticisms, Goldstone challenged both Gamson's main conclusions and his basic theoretical tenet. He found that the organizational and tactical characteristics had no effect on group success. The timing of success, he maintained, is independent of the challengers' organization and tactics. What is most important, he suggested, is that the resource mobilization model be replaced by a model that stresses the crucial role of broad, system-wide national crises for the success of social movements. We have a name for it: the political-process model. By looking at how external political factors affect protest behavior, this approach also stresses the importance of the movements' larger environment for their outcomes (e.g. Kitschelt 1986, Kriesi et al 1995, McAdam 1982, Rochon & Mazmanian 1993, Tarrow 1994). This, I think, is a clear theoretical advance and a way to follow.

The central concept in the political process model is that of political opportunity structure. In spite of various conceptualizations, two aspects appear to be crucial for the understanding of the relation between social movements and their political environment: the system of alliances and oppositions and the structure of the state. The importance of having powerful allies both within and without the institutional arena has been stressed on several occasions. Early work focused in particular on the context of social support and conceived of alliances as a political resource that movements can use to become more successful, since movements were considered as powerless challengers. One of the first systematic statements in this respect was made by Lipsky (1968; see also Lipsky 1970, Lipsky & Olson 1977), who saw movements as strongly dependent on the activation of third parties to be successful in the long run. Schumaker (1975) arrived at a similar conclusion in his study of the responsiveness of political authorities to racial riots. On the other hand, third parties also include opponents, which might influence the oversimplified relationship between movements and the state and either prevent or facilitate their outcomes. Yet few authors have looked at the role of opponents (e.g. Barkan 1984, Jasper & Poulsen 1993, McAdam 1982, Turk & Zucker 1984). Following this perspective, the effectiveness of social movements depends on their capability to engage in bargaining activities with allies and opponents (Burstein et al 1995).

The importance of political resources and institutions for movement outcomes has also been stressed by Jenkins & Perrow (1977), who have suggested a link between changes in the political environment that offer social resources, on the one hand, and the rise and success of farm-worker insurgents, on the other hand. The conducive environment in their study is represented by the government and a coalition of liberal support organizations. Ultimately, they argue, the success of powerless insurgents is due to a combination of sustained outside support, the disunity of the political elites, and their tolerance, which provided the movement with crucial resources. Similarly, Piven and Cloward (1979) point to the important constraining role of institutions, which shape opportunities for action, model its forms, and limit its impact. They maintain that protest is more likely to have a real impact when challengers have a central role in institutions and when powerful allies have a stake in those institutions. Specifically, they view the electoral-representative system as a major factor mediating the political impact of institutional disruptions.

In line with this emphasis on political institutions, more recent work has begun to follow what I see as the most promising avenue of research on the outcomes of social movements: to carry on cross-national comparisons of movements and to examine one or more instances of a various array of their potential consequences in order to formulate plausible causal theories about the link between movement actions and those consequences. In so doing, one can assess the filtering role of the political context on movement outcomes. Following this perspective, Amenta et al (1992) have shown for the case of early social policy in the United States that the political mediation model, which places political opportunity structure as a mediating factor between social movements and their success, offers the best explanation. Ultimately, therefore, the state and the political party system determine whether social movements can win acceptance and new advantages.

Although attempts at comparing movement outcomes across countries are not new (e.g. Gurr 1983, Kitschelt 1986, Kowalewski & Schumaker 1981, Midttun & Rucht 1994, Rüdig 1990), there is still a huge void in the literature as opposed to case studies of single movements or countries. The best known of these cross-national studies is probably that of Kitschelt. In his influential comparison of the antinuclear movement in four western democracies (Kitschelt 1986), he makes a strong case for the structural determinants of social movement outcomes, arguing that the success of the antinuclear movement is strongly dependent on political opportunity structures. A more recent contribution elaborates on Kitschelt's model to show the crucial role of political opportunities in shaping the outcomes of Western European new social movements (Giugni 1995). Hopefully, other scholars will soon join these efforts and carry on comparative studies on the outcomes and consequences of social movements.

SUCCESS, FAILURE, OUTCOMES, CONSEQUENCES

At this point, there is need for clarification of certain terms of our discussion. So far, we have seen that a first strand of research has inquired into the internal and organizational characteristics of social movements that may help them to bring about (policy) outcomes and hence to become successful. A second strand has tried to put the movements in their larger social and political environment, in particular by examining the role of public opinion and political opportunity structures as intervening factors mediating the movement-outcome nexus. To do so, scholars have relied on various typologies of outcomes. The best known is certainly the one proposed by Gamson (1990), who has defined success as a set of outcomes that fall into two basic clusters: the acceptance of a challenging group by its antagonists as a valid spokesman for a legitimate set of interests, and the gain of new advantages by the group's beneficiary during the challenge and its aftermath. By combining these two dimensions, the author has defined four possible outcomes of a challenge: 1. full response, 2. preemption, 3. co-optation, and 4. collapse. Unfortunately, this typology is not fully exploited in the empirical analyses, which remain for the most part confined to the two-fold distinction between acceptance and new advantages. I have lingered on Gamson's main findings earlier. What matters here is to see how his simple typology has influenced much subsequent research. In some way, on the other hand, it has also put some limits to research, for it brought the focus on the organizations instead of on the broader cycles of protest, which may include various movements whose combined effect might be more important than the impact of a single challenging group (Tarrow 1994).

Several authors have adopted the distinction between acceptance and new advantages or have given a revised version of it. Among the former are obviously those who have reanalyzed Gamson's original data (Frey et al 1992, Goldstone 1980, Mirowsky & Ross 1981, Steedly & Foley 1979). Webb and several collaborators also built on Gamson's typology and work, but used a different dataset (Webb et al 1983). Amenta et al (1992), on the other hand, defined three levels of success in an attempt to elaborate on Gamson's typology: co-optation or the recognition from opponents or the state, gains in policies that aid the group, and the transformation of challengers into a member of the polity. Within each type, in addition, there are various degrees of success. Here, however, we begin to see the dangers entailed in the use of the notions of success and failure. First, such a perspective assumes that social movements are homogeneous and hence tends to attribute success or failure to an entire movement, unless one focuses on single organizations as Gamson did. Yet often there is little agreement among movement leaders and participants, even within a given organization, regarding which goal must be pursued. Second, as it is not always uniformly evaluated by everyone, success raises the question of subjectivity. Movement participants and external observers may have different perceptions of what counts as success, and the same action may be judged as successful by some participants and as failed by others. Finally, the notion of success is problematic because it overstates the intention of participants. Once again, while social movements are rational efforts to bring about change, many of their consequences are unintended and often unrelated to their claims.

These ambiguities notwithstanding, numerous scholars have looked at the determinants of movement success or failure (e.g. Amenta et al 1992, Banaszak 1996, Brill 1971, Burstein et al 1995, Frey et al 1992, Gamson 1990, Goldstone 1980, Mirowsky & Ross 1987, Nichols 1987, Perrot 1987, Piven & Cloward 1979, Shorter & Tilly 1971, Steedly & Foley 1979). Therefore, most of the existing typologies are framed, explicitly or implicitly, in terms of success.

Here are only a few examples. (*a*) Rochon & Mazmanian (1993) added a third type of impact to Gamson's distinction, thus defining three arenas of movement success: policy changes (new advantages in Gamson's terminology), changes in the policy process (Gamson's acceptance), and changes in social values. (*b*) Drawing both from the social-problems literature and the public-policy literature, Schumaker (1975) defined five criteria of government responsiveness to movement demands: access, agenda, policy, output, and impact. (*c*) Rüdig (1990) used this typology in his comprehensive study of the antinuclear movement worldwide. (*d*) Burstein et al (1995) also relied on this typology, pointing out correctly that it addresses several aspects of the political process that had previously been left out. However, they added structural effects as a sixth type of government responsiveness, thus acknowledging that movement can provoke alterations in the institutional arrangements of society. (*e*) Kitschelt (1986) also stressed structural effects, i.e. a transformation of the political structures, in addition to procedural effects (Gamson's acceptance) and substantive effects (Gamson's new advantages). This typology allows for a link between the outcomes of social movements and their political context. (*f*) In quite a similar way, Gurr (1980) had previously defined three types of outcomes of violent conflicts: effects on the group fate, policy changes, and societal or systemic effects. The advantage of this typology is that it makes a clear distinction between internal effects on the movement and external effects on policy or the larger society. (*g*) Kriesi (1995) added a further distinction to Kitschelt's typology by defining two types of substantive impact: reactive effects, i.e. the prevention of "new disadvantages," and proactive effects, i.e. the introduction of "new advantages." This distinction is relevant with regard to political opportunity structures, for it allows us to link social movement outcomes to the strength of the state and has been used to investigate the outcomes of Western European new social movements (Giugni 1995). (*h*) Finally, Rucht (1992) acknowledged the need to distinguish between goal-related outcomes and broader consequences by classifying the effects of social movements according to two dimensions: internal vs external and intended vs unintended.

Gurr's and Rochon & Mazmanian's typologies present a further advantage: They acknowledge the possibility that different types of outcomes be related to each other. This is an important point. Gurr (1980), for example, suggested that group changes and systemic changes be seen as ultimate outcomes that take place through policy changes, which, in turn, are the proximate result of violent conflicts (Gurr 1980). Rochon & Mazmanian (1993) maintain that substantial gains may be more easily obtained once a challenging group has reached some degree of acceptance. Other authors have similarly explored how social movements can make a greater impact by pursuing goals in administrative agencies and courts once they have achieved policy responsiveness (e.g. Burstein 1985, 1991, Handler 1978, Sabatier 1975). A recent interesting variant has been proposed by Diani (1997), who claims that when movements are able to facilitate the emergence of new social networks they will be more influential in processes of political and cultural change. Here, we abandon the classificatory terrain to begin to reason in terms of relationships between variables. In other words, it is the beginning of a theory of movement outcomes. Unfortunately, very little research has been done to show how a certain type of impact can help to bring about another type. In this, however, we have another interesting avenue for future research.

Several authors have stressed the methodological problems that have been preventing social scientists from systematically analyzing the consequences of the presence and action of social movements, including the problem of causal attribution, the problem of time reference and effect stability, the problem of movement goal adaptation, the problem of interrelated effects, and the problem of unintended and perverse effects (Rucht 1992 see further Giugni 1994, Gurr 1980, Snyder & Kelly 1979). Although this is not the place to propose solutions to these and related methodological problems, it would perhaps help to point out a logical puzzle that lies uphill, the recognition of which would make the task of setting research agenda easier. It has to do with the blurring of some fundamental distinctions between types of potential effects of movements. The vast majority of the existing studies deal with effects that are related to the movements' stated programs and ends. The Brent Spar case mentioned at the outset is a good example: A declared goal by a challenging group is reached, allegedly as a result (at least in part) of the group's actions. But only under exceptional circumstances do movement actions have such an immediate and successful impact. Most of the time, movements promote their programs cumulatively over months and even years of claim-making (C Tilly, 1998a). This makes the analysis much more complicated. Yet most research has focused on *outcomes* of social movements, which we may define as a special case of the more general set of their *consequences*: those that relate directly to the goals and ends of challengers.

Even more narrowly, work on outcomes has usually looked at the impact of movements on government policy or legislation (e.g. Amenta et al 1992; Banaszak 1996; Burstein 1979a, 1985; Burstein & Freudenburg 1978; Button 1978, 1989; Costain & Majstorovic 1994; Gelb 1989; Gelb and Palley 1987; Huberts 1989; MacDougal et al 1995). Three only partly correct assumptions are perhaps at the origin of this strong focus on policy outcomes. First, the view held by the political process approach that social movements are essentially targeting political authorities and institutions and, hence, they are mainly aimed at provoking political change. While such a definition covers a crucial aspect of the national social movement and is widely adopted in the literature (McAdam et al 1996, Tarrow 1994, Tilly 1984), contemporary movements often address the larger public, aiming, for example, to change attitudes and opinions on a given matter. In addition, other authors have warned us about the dangers of restricting our attention to the political side of new social movements, as they have identity-related goals that do not necessarily require a political target (Melucci 1996). Second, and related to the first point, the eagerness to find the causes of movement success or failure, an attitude facilitated by the activist past of many scholars and by a sympathetic stand toward many contemporary movements. Third, the conviction that policy changes are more easily measured than cultural changes. The latter reason would explain why we still have rather few studies on the cultural aspects of movements except for the individual-level consequences of participation in social movements and activism, on which there is a considerable body of literature (e.g. Abramowitz & Nassi 1981, Demerath et al 1971, Fendrich 1974, 1977, Fendrich & Krauss 1978, Fendrich & Lovoy 1988, Fendrich & Tarlau 1973, Jennings 1987, Jennings & Niemi 1981, Marwell et al 1987, McAdam 1988, 1989, 1998a, Nassi & Abramowitz 1979, Whalen & Flacks 1980).

To be sure, there is work on what may be seen as instances of the cultural impact of movements, such as their spillover effects from one movement to the other (Meyer & Whittier 1994), their capacity to generate social capitals (Diani 1997), their impact on the media (Gamson & Wolfsfeld 1993), and so forth, but these are rather sporadic in comparison to the huge amount of works on policy outcomes. Other authors, on the other hand, have looked at the cultural determinants of movement success as measured through policy or legislative change (e.g. Banaszak 1996), thus reversing the causal arrow.

Studying the ways in which social movements have their demands met is, of course, a legitimate endeavor that will help improve our knowledge of the causal processes involved in social and political change. Yet, like all kinds of actions, the effects of social movements are often indirect, unintended, and sometimes even in contradiction to their goals (on the unintended consequences of social action, see Tilly 1996). Increased repression, for example, is often an immediate effect of protest, but the long-term consequences may be differenct (della Porta 1995). Tarrow (1989, 1993, 1994) goes precisely in this direction when he looks at the broad repercussions of cycles of protest, including cycles of reform. In his study of the Italian protest cycle of the 1960s and 1970s (Tarrow 1989), the author shows that this period of disorder made a crucial impact and left a positive legacy for Italian democracy by promoting reform, expanding the political arena, giving autonomy to Italian voters, and, above all, expanding the repertoire of the legitimate forms of political participation. By analyzing social movements at the macro level, Tarrow established a link between two broad phenomena: the emergence, development, and decline of a cycle of protest, on the one hand, and political, institutional, and cultural changes, on the other hand, whereby the former plays a crucial role in bringing about the latter. The lesson to be drawn here is that both the short-term and the long-term consequences of movement actions must be examined (Andrews 1997).

Empirical work that focuses explicitly on the unintended consequences of social movements is quite rare (e.g. Deng 1997, Paul et al 1997). Yet, as Charles

Tilly (1998a) has put it, "this range of effects far surpasses the explicit demands made by activists in the course of social movements, and sometimes negates them. By any standard, 'success' and 'failure' hardly describe most of the effects." In addition, he maintains, third parties can act and produce changes in the zone of a movement's activities and interests. According to Tilly, the difficulties of analyzing the consequences of social movements arise precisely from this logical situation, which he has schematized as three overlapping circles. Analysts should take into consideration three sets of variables: 1. all movement claims, 2. all effects of movements' actions, and 3. all effects of outside events and actions. The overlapping of these three variables creates four situations that must be analytically distinguished. As Figure 1 shows, what I defined as outcomes, i.e. effects of movement actions that bear directly on movement claims, result from the overlapping of set 1 and 2. If the effects can be completely attributed to the movement's action, we can speak of success when they are positive and failure when they are negative (intersection A), although the problem of the differential evaluation of success remains. But at least a part of outcomes are produced as joint effects of movement actions and outside influences (intersection B). Furthermore, sometimes external events and actions may produce effects that satisfy movement claims (intersection C). Finally, we must take into account the possibility of joint effects of movement actions and outside influences that do not bear directly on movement claims, i.e. unintended consequences. Once we have posed the fundamental logical problem so nicely illustrated by Tilly, we will be in a better position to build causal theories about social movements, their success or failure, their outcomes, and the broader consequences of their actions.

CONCLUSION

As the review of the relevant literature reveals, much work on the impact of social movements and protest behavior was done during the seventies. The spark was provided by the wave of student and antiwar protest as well as the riots that occurred in American cities during the sixties. The latter, in particular, incited American scholars to inquire not only into the causes, but also the consequences of violent political behavior. European scholars, on the other hand, have usually privileged the broad processes that have led to the emergence of the new social movements, hence paying only little attention to their repercussions on society, especially in empirical research. Subsequently, the interest in the effects of movements has somewhat waned. It resurfaced recently, however. Two forthcoming collective volumes (M Giugni et al 1998a,b) and recently published works and ongoing studies, testify to this renewed interest in the consequences of social movements, which stems less from the need to understand current practices in society, such as riot behavior in urban settings, than from the willingness to fill an important gap in the social movement lit-

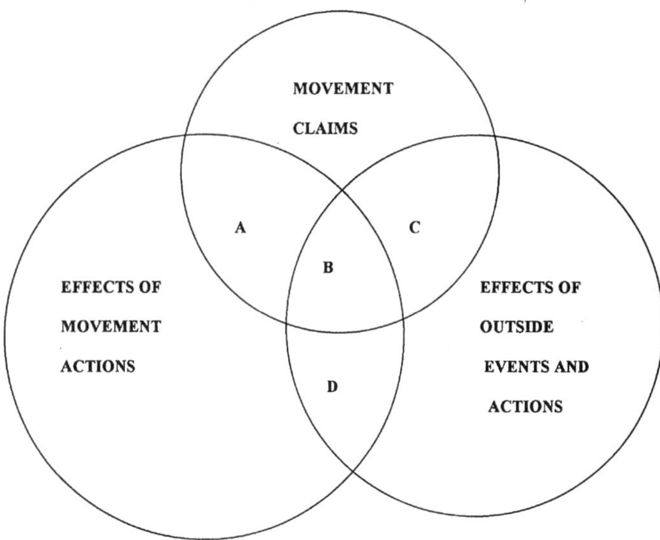

A = EFFECTS OF MOVEMENT ACTIONS THAT BEAR DIRECTLY ON MOVEMENT CLAIMS

B = JOINT EFFECTS OF MOVEMENT ACTIONS AND OUTSIDE INFLUENCES THAT BEAR DIRECTLY ON MOVEMENT CLAIMS

C = EFFECTS OF OUTSIDE INFLUENCES (BUT NOT OF MOVEMENT ACTIONS)THAT BEAR DIRECTLY ON MOVEMENT CLAIMS

D = JOINT EFFECTS OF MOVEMENT ACTIONS AND OUTSIDE INFLUENCES THAT **DON'T** BEAR ON MOVEMENT CLAIMS

Source: Tilly (1998)

Figure 1 The problem of identifying social movement outcomes

erature. As such, it is less focused on those characteristics and features shown by the phenomena currently under way and more genuinely aimed at unveiling the processes and dynamics that allow movements to make an impact on different aspects of society. This alone gives us some reassurances that more attention will be paid in the future to crucial consequences of social movements previously neglected. I am referring in particular to their potential for influencing processes of broader cultural and institutional change.

An agenda for future research should focus on the comparative study of the outcomes and consequences of social movements. Comparisons between different political contexts, different movements, and different periods will shed light over the causal dynamics involved in processes of social and political change. A promising way to do so is to adopt a historical comparative design aimed at analyzing concordances and differences in order to generate explanations. Specifically, we would have much to gain from conducting in-depth comparisons of different national cases and different movements over a relatively long period, thereby comparing interactions that allow distinct movements to have a given type of consequence in different countries. By analyzing movement consequences following a comparative design, in addition, we will be able to avoid the formulation of invariant models that serve so badly the need of social sciences (Tilly 1995). In addition, as Tilly (1998a) has correctly put it, the study of the outcomes and consequences of social movements implies, and indeed requires, the analysis of movement interactions and dynamics. If we do not pay careful attention to such interactions and dynamics, the methodological problems I have pointed out will always render our analyses weak and our conclusions shaky. If we do not first clarify the dynamics that have led hundreds of thousands of people to challenge the Communist regimes in Eastern Europe, we will hardly be able to establish whether those protests were instrumental in the dramatic changes that occurred and how. Similarly, if we do not first shed light on the interactions between Greenpeace activists, political elites and institutions, public opinion, and Shell's leaders, we will find it difficult to attribute the company's decision to destroy the Brent Spar oil rig to the environmentalists' outraged call for a boycott. After all, without interactions there are simply no outcomes or consequences.

ACKNOWLEDGMENTS

Research for this paper has been made possible by a grant of the Swiss National Science Foundation.

Literature Cited

Abramowitz SI, Nassi AJ. 1981. Keeping the faith: psychological correlates of activism persistence into middle adulthood. *J. Youth Adolesc.* 10:507–23

Albritton RB. 1979. Social amelioration through mass insurgency? A reexamination of the Piven and Cloward thesis. *Am. Polit. Sci. Rev.* 73:1003–11

Amenta E, Carruthers BG, Zylan Y. 1992. A hero for the aged? The Townsend movement, the political mediation model, and U.S. old-age policy, 1934–1950. *Am. J. Sociol.* 98:308–39

Andrews KT. 1997. The impact of social movements on the political process: the civil rights movement and black election politics in Mississippi. *Am. Sociol. Rev.* 62:800–19

Astin AW, Astin HS, Bayer AE, Bisconti AD. 1975. *The Power of Protest*. San Francisco: Jossey-Bass

Banaszak LA. 1996. *Why Movements Succeed or Fail*. Princeton, NJ: Princeton Univ. Press

Barkan SA. 1984. Legal control of the southern civil rights movement. *Am. Sociol. Rev.* 49:552–65

Berkowitz WR. 1974. Socioeconomic indicator changes in ghetto riot tracts. *Urban Aff. Q.* 10:69–94

Betz M. 1974. Riots and welfare: are they related? *Soc. Probl.* 21:345–55

Brill H. 1971. *Why Organizers Fail*. Berkeley, CA: Univ. Calif. Press

Burstein P. 1979a. Public opinion, demonstrations, and the passage of anti-discrimination legislation. *Public Opin. Q.* 43:157–72

Burstein P. 1979b. Equal employment opportunity legislation and the incomes of women and nonwhites. *Am. Sociol. Rev.* 44:367–91

Burstein P. 1979c. Senate voting on the Vietnam war, 1964–1973. *J. Polit. Mil. Sociol.* 7:271–82

Burstein P. 1985. *Discrimination, Jobs, and Politics*. Chicago: Univ. Chicago Press

Burstein P. 1991. Legal mobilization as a social movement tactic: the struggle for equal employment opportunity. *Am. J. Sociol.* 96:1201–25

Burstein P, Einwohner RL, Hollander JA. 1995. The success of political movements: a bargaining perspective. In *The Politics of Social Protest*, ed. J Craig Jenkins, B Klandermans, pp. 275–95. Minneapolis: Univ. Minn. Press

Burstein P, Freudenburg P. 1978. Changing public policy: the impact of public opinion, anti-war demonstrations and war costs on senate voting on Vietnam war motions. *Am. J. Sociol.* 84:99–122

Button JW. 1978. *Black Violence*. Princeton, NJ: Princeton Univ. Press

Button JW. 1989. *Blacks and Social Change*. Princeton, NJ: Princeton Univ. Press

Clemens ES. 1993. Organizational repertoires and institutional change: women's groups and the transformation of U.S. politics, 1890–1920. *Am. J. Sociol.* 98:755–98

Cohn S. 1993. *When Strikes Make Sense—and Why*. New York: Plenum

Colby D. 1975. The effects of riots on public policy: exploratory note. *Int. J. Group Tens.* 5:156–62

Colby D. 1982. A test of the relative efficacy of political tactics. *Am. J. Polit. Sci.* 26: 741–53

Costain AN, Majstorovic S. 1994. Congress, social movements and public opinion: multiple origins of women's rights legislation. *Polit. Res. Q.* 47:111–35

della Porta D. 1995. *Social Movements, Political Violence, and the State*. Cambridge, UK: Cambridge Univ. Press

Demerath NJ, Marwell G, Aiken M. 1971. *Dynamics of Idealism*. San Francisco: Jossey-Bass

Deng F. 1997. Information gaps and uninteded outcomes of social movements: the 1989 Chinese student movement. *Am. J. Sociol.* 102:1085–1112

Diani M. 1997. Social movements and social capital: a network perspective on movement outcomes. Mobilization 2:129–47

Etzioni A. 1970. *Demonstration Democracy*. New York: Gordon & Breach

Feagin JR, Hahn H. 1973. *Ghetto Revolts*. New York: Macmillan

Fendrich JM. 1974. Activists ten years later: a test of generational unit continuity. *J. Soc. Issues* 30:95–118

Fendrich JM. 1977. Keeping the faith or pursuing the good life: a study of the consequences of participation in the civil rights movement. *Am. Sociol. Rev.* 42:144–57

Fendrich JM, Krauss EM. 1978. Student activism and adult left-wing politics: a causal model of political socialization for black, white and Japanese students of the 1960s generation. *Res. Soc. Mov. Confl. Change* 1:231–56

Fendrich JM, Lovoy KL. 1988. Back to the future: adult political behavior of former political activists. *Am. Sociol. Rev.* 53: 780–84

Fendrich JM, Tarleau AT. 1973. Marching to a different drummer: occupational and political correlates of former student activists. *Soc. Forces* 52:245–53

Fowler LL, Shaiko RG. 1987. The grass roots connection: environmental activists and senate roll calls. *Am. J. Polit. Sci.* 31: 484–510

Franzosi R. 1994. *The Puzzle of Strikes*. Cambridge, UK: Cambridge Univ. Press

Frey RS, Dietz T, Kalof L. 1992. Characteristics of successful American protest groups: another look at Gamson's *Strategy of Social Protest*. *Am. J. Sociol.* 98:368–87

Gamson WA. 1990. *The Strategy of Social Protest*. Belmont, CA: Wadsworth. 2nd ed.

Gamson WA, Wolfsfeld G. 1993. Movements and media as interacting systems. *Ann. Am. Acad. Polit. Soc. Sci.* 528:114–25

Gelb J. 1989. *Feminism and Politics*. Berkeley, CA: Univ. Calif. Press

Gelb J, Lief Palley M. 1987. *Women and Public Policies*. Princeton, NJ: Princeton Univ. Press. 2nd ed.

Giugni MG. 1994. *The outcomes of social movements: a review of the literature*. Working Pap. 197. New York: Cent. Stud. Soc. Change, New Sch. Soc. Res.

Giugni MG. 1995. Outcomes of new social movements. See Kriesi et al 1995:207–37

Giugni M, McAdam D, Tilly C, eds. 1998a. *How Movements Matter*. Minneapolis, MN: Univ. Minn. Press. In press

Giugni M, McAdam D, Tilly C, eds. 1998b. *From Contention to Democracy*. Boulder, CO: Rowman & Littlefield. In press

Goldstone JA. 1980. The weakness of organization: a new look at Gamson's *The Strategy of Social Protest*. *Am. J. Sociol.* 85: 1017–42, 1426–32

Gurr TR. 1980. On the outcomes of violent conflict. In *Handbook of Political Conflict, Theory and Research*, ed. TR Gurr, pp. 238–94. New York: Free Press

Gurr TR, ed. 1983. Group protest and policy responses: new cross-national perspectives. *Am. Behav.* 26: Entire issue

Gusfield JR. 1981. *The Culture of Public Problems*. Chicago: Univ. Chicago Press

Hahn H. 1970. Civic responses to riots: a reappraisal of Kerner Commission data. *Publ. Opin. Q.* 34:101–7

Handler J. 1978. *Social Movements and the Legal System*. New York: Academic

Hicks A, Swank DH. 1983. Civil disorder, relief mobilization, and AFDC caseloads: a reexamination of the Piven and Cloward thesis. *Am. J. Polit. Sci.* 27:695–716

Hicks A, Swank DH. 1984. On the political economy of welfare expansion: a comparative analysis of 18 advanced capitalist democracies, 1960–1977. *Compar. Polit. Sci.* 17:87–119

Huberts LW. 1989. The influence of social movements on government policy. *Int. Soc. Mov. Res.* 1:395–426

Isaac L, Kelly WR. 1981. Racial insurgency, the state, and welfare expansion: local and national level evidence from the postwar United States. *Am. J. Sociol.* 86:1348–86

Jasper JM, Poulsen J. 1993. Fighting back: vulnerabilities, blunders, and countermobilization by the targets in three animal rights campaigns. *Sociol. Forum* 8: 639–57

Jenkins JC. 1981. Sociopolitical movements. In *The Handbook of Political Behavior*, Vol. 4, ed. SL Long, pp. 81–153. New York: Plenum

Jenkins JC, Brents B. 1989. Social protest, hegemonic competition, and social reform: a political struggle interpretation of the origins of the American welfare state. *Am. Sociol. Rev.* 54:891–909

Jenkins JC, Perrow C. 1977. Insurgency of the powerless: farm worker movements (1946–1972). *Am. Sociol. Rev.* 42:249–68

Jennings ET. 1979. Civil turmoil and the growth of welfare rolls: a comparative state policy analysis. *Policy Stud. J.* 7:739–45

Jennings ET. 1980. Urban riots and welfare policy change: a test of the Piven-Cloward theory. In *Why Policies Succeed or Fail*, ed. HM Ingram, DE Mann, pp. 59–82. Beverly Hills, CA: Sage

Jennings ET. 1983. Racial insurgency, the state, and welfare expansion: a critical comment and reanalysis. *Am. J. Sociol.* 88:1220–36

Jennings MK. 1987. Residues of a movement: the aging of the American protest generation. *Am. Polit. Sci. Rev.* 81:367–82

Jennings MK, Niemi RG. 1981. *Generations and Politics*. Princeton, NJ: Princeton Univ. Press

Joppke C. 1993. *Mobilizing Against Nuclear Energy*. Berkeley, CA: Univ. Calif. Press

Kelly WR, Snyder D. 1980. Racial violence and socioeconomic changes among blacks in the United States. *Soc. Forces* 58: 739–60

Kerbo HR, Shaffer RA. 1992. Lower class insurgency and the political process: the response of the U.S. unemployed, 1890–1940. *Soc. Probl.* 39:139–54

Kitschelt H. 1986. Political opportunity structures and political protest: anti-nuclear movements in four democracies. *Brit. J. Polit. Sci.* 16:57–85

Kowalewski D, Schumaker P. 1981. Protest outcomes in the Soviet Union. *Sociol. Q.* 22:57–68

Kriesi H. 1995. *The political opportunity structure of new social movements: its impact on their mobilization*. In *The Politics of Social Protest*, ed. JC Jenkins, B Klandermans, pp. 167–98. Minneapolis: Univ. Minn. Press

Kriesi H, Koopmans R, Duyvendak JW, Giugni MG. 1995. *New social movements in Western Europe*. Minneapolis: Univ. Minn. Press

Lawson SF. 1976. *Black Ballots*. New York: Columbia Univ. Press

Levitan SA, Johnston WB, Taggart R. 1975. *Still a Dream*. Cambridge, MA: Harvard Univ. Press

Lipsky M. 1968. Protest as a political resource. *Am. Polit. Sci. Rev.* 62:1144–58

Lipsky M. 1970. *Protest in City Politics*. Chicago: Rand McNally

Lipsky M, Levi M. 1972. Community organization as a political resource. In *People and Politics in Urban Society*, ed. H Hahn. Beverly Hills, CA: Sage

Lipsky M, Olson DJ. 1977. *Commission Poli-*

tics. New Brunswick, NJ: Transaction Books

MacDougal J, Minicucci SD, Myers D. 1995. The House of Representatives' vote on the Gulf War, 1991: measuring peace movement impact. *Res. Soc. Mov. Confl. Change* 18:255–84

Marwel G, Aiken M, Demerath NJ. 1987. The persistence of political attitudes among 1960s civil rights activists. *Publ. Opin. Q.* 51:359–75

McAdam D. 1982. *Political Process and the Development of Black Insurgency, 1930–1970*. Chicago: Univ. Chicago Press

McAdam D. 1983. Tactical innovation and the pace of insurgency. *Am. Sociol. Rev.* 48: 735–54

McAdam D. 1988. *Freedom Summer*. New York: Oxford Univ. Press

McAdam D. 1989. The biographical consequences of actvism. *Am. Sociol. Rev.* 54: 744–60

McAdam D. 1998a. The biographical impact of activism. See Giugni et al 1998a

McAdam D, McCarthy JD, Zald MN. 1988. Social movements. In *Handbook of Sociology*, ed. NJ Smelser, pp. 695–737. Beverly Hills, CA: Sage

McAdam D, McCarthy JD, Zald MN, eds. 1996. *Comparative Perspectives on Social Movements*. Cambridge, UK: Cambridge Univ. Press

McClurg Mueller C. 1978. Riot violence and protest outcomes. *J. Polit. Mil. Sociol.* 6: 49–63

Melucci A. 1996. *Challenging Codes*. Cambridge, UK: Cambridge Univ. Press

Metz S. 1986. The anti-apartheid movement and populist instinct in American politics. *Polit. Sci. Q.* 101:379–95

Meyer DS, Whittier N. 1994. Social movement spillover. *Soc. Probl.* 41:277–98

Midttun A, Rucht D. 1994. Comparing policy outcomes of conflicts over nuclear power: description and explanation. In *States and Anti-Nuclear Movements*, ed. H Flam, pp. 383–415. Edinburgh: Edinburgh Univ. Press

Milbrath L. 1970. The impact of lobbying on governmental decisions. In *Policy Analysis in Political Science*, ed. I Sharkansky, pp. 360–81. Chicago: Markham

Mirowsky J, Ross C. 1981. Protest group success: the impact of group characteristics, social control, and context. *Sociol. Focus* 14:177–92

Nassi AJ, Abramowitz SI. 1979. Transition or transformation? Personal and political development of former Berkeley free speech movement activists. *J. Youth Adolesc.* 8: 21–35

Nichols E. 1987. U.S. nuclear power and the success of the American anti-nuclear movement. *Berkeley J. Sociol.* 32:167–92

Oberschall A. 1973. *Social Conflict and Social Movements*. Englewood-Cliffs, NJ: Prentice-Hall

Oberschall A. 1996. Opportunities and framing in the Eastern European revolts of 1989. See McAdam et al 1996:93–121

O'Keefe M, Schumaker PD. 1983. Protest effectiveness in Southeast Asia. *Am. Behav. Sci.* 26:375–94

Orfield G. 1975. *Congressional Power*. New York: Harcourt Brace Jovanovich

Page B, Shapiro RY. 1983. Effects of public opinion on policy. *Am. Polit. Sci. Rev.* 77: 175–90

Paul S, Mahler S, Schwartz M. 1997. Mass action and social structure. *Polit. Power Soc. Theory* 11:45–99

Perrot M. 1987. *Workers on Strike*. Leamington Spa, UK: Berg

Piven F Fox, Cloward RA. 1979. *Poor People's Movements*. New York: Vintage

Piven F Fox, Cloward RA. 1993. *Regulating the Poor*. New York: Vintage. 2nd ed.

Rochon T, Mazmanian DA. 1993. Social movements and the policy process. *Ann. Am. Acad. Polit. Soc. Sci.* 528:75–87

Rucht D. 1992. *Studying the effects of social movements: conceptualization and problems*. Presented at ECPR Joint Session, Limerick, Ireland

Rüdig W. 1990. *Anti-Nuclear Movements*. Harlow, UK: Longman

Sabatier P. 1975. Social movements and regulatory agencies. *Policy Sci.* 6:301–42

Schramm SF, Turbott JP. 1983. Civil disorder and the welfare explosion: a two-step process. *Am. Sociol. Rev.* 48:408–14

Schumaker PD. 1975. Policy responsiveness to protest-group demands. *J. Polit.* 37: 488–521

Schumaker PD. 1978. The scope of political conflict and the effectiveness of constraints in contemporary urban protest. *Sociol. Q.* 19:168–84

Sears D, McConahay J. 1973. *The Politics of Violence*. Boston: Houghton Mifflin

Sharp EB, Maynard-Moody S. 1991. Theories of the local welfare role. *Am. J. Polit. Sci.* 35:934–50

Shorter E, Tilly C. 1971. Le déclin de la grève violente en France de 1890 à 1935. *Mouv. Soc.* 79:95–118

Shorter E, Tilly C. 1974. *Strikes in France 1830–1968*. Cambridge: Harvard Univ. Press

Snyder D, Kelly WR. 1976. Industrial violence in Italy, 1878–1903. *Am. J. Sociol.* 82:131–62

Snyder D, Kelly WR. 1979. Strategies for investigating violence and social change: illustrations from analyses of racial disorders and implications for mobilization research. In *The Dynamics of Social Movements*, ed. MN Zald, JD McCarthy. Cambridge, MA: Winthrop

Staggenborg S. 1988. The consequences of professionalization and formalization in the pro-choice movement. *Am. Sociol. Rev.* 53:585–605

Steedly HR, Foley JW. 1979. The success of protest groups: multivariate analyses. *Soc. Sci. Res.* 8:1–15

Swank DH. 1983. Between incrementalism and revolution: group protest and the welfare state. *Am. Behav. Sci.* 26:291–310

Taft D, Ross P. 1969. American labor violence: its causes, character, and outcome. In *Violence in America*, ed. HD Graham, TR Gurr. New York: Praeger

Tarrow S. 1989. *Democracy and Disorder*. Oxford: Clarendon

Tarrow S. 1993. Social protest and policy reform: May 1968 and the Loi d'Orientation in France. *Comp. Polit. Stud.* 25:579–607

Tarrow S. 1994. *Power in Movement*. Cambridge, UK: Cambridge Univ. Press

Tarrow S. 1996. Social movements in contentious politics: a review article. *Am. Polit. Sci. Rev.* 90:874–83

Tilly C. 1984. Social movements and national politics. In *Statemaking and Social Movements*, ed. C Bright, S Harding, pp. 297–317. Ann Arbor, MI: Univ. Mich. Press

Tilly C. 1996. Invisible elbow. *Sociol. Forum* 11:589–601

Tilly C. 1998a. From interactions to outcomes in social movements. See Giugni et al 1998a

Tilly C, Tilly L, Tilly R. 1975. *The Rebellious Century, 1830–1930*. Cambridge, MA: Harvard Univ. Press

Trattner WI, ed. 1983. *Social Welfare or Social Control*. Knoxville, TN: Univ. Tenn. Press

Turk H, Zucker LG. 1984. Majority and organized opposition: on effects of social movements. *Res. Soc. Mov. Confl. Change* 7: 249–69

Valocchi S. 1990. The unemployed workers movement: a reexamination of the Piven and Cloward thesis. *Soc. Probl.* 37: 191–205

Webb K, Zimmermann E, Marsh M, Aish A-M, Mironesco C, et al. 1983. Etiology and outcomes of protest: new European perspectives. *Am. Behav. Sci.* 26:311–31

Weissberg R. 1976. *Public Opinion and American Democracy*. Englewood Cliffs, NJ: Prentice-Hall

Welch S. 1975. The impact of urban riots on urban expenditures. *Am. J. Polit. Sci.* 29: 741–60

Whalen J, Flacks R. 1980. The Isla Vista "bank burners" ten years later: notes on the fate of student activists. *Sociol. Focus* 13: 215–36

Zelditch M. 1978. Review essay: outsiders' politics. *Am. J. Sociol.* 83:1514–20

Annu. Rev. Sociol. 1998. 24:395–421

INTERMARRIAGE AND HOMOGAMY: Causes, Patterns, Trends

Matthijs Kalmijn

Department of Sociology, Utrecht University, Utrecht, The Netherlands; e-mail: m.kalmijn@fsw.ruu.nl

KEY WORDS: marriage markets, marriage, mate selection, assortative mating, endogamy

ABSTRACT

People have a tendency to marry within their social group or to marry a person who is close to them in status. Although many characteristics play a role in the choice of a spouse, sociologists have most often examined endogamy and homogamy with respect to race/ethnicity, religion, and socioeconomic status. I first give an overview of hypotheses on the causes of endogamy and homogamy. The various hypotheses that have been suggested in the literature can be distinguished as arguments about three more general factors: (*a*) the preferences of marriage candidates for certain characteristics in a spouse, (*b*) the interference of "third parties" in the selection process, and (*c*) the constraints of the marriage market in which candidates are searching for a spouse. Second, I summarize empirical research by answering four questions: (*a*) To what extent are groups endogamous and how do groups differ in this respect? (*b*) How has endogamy changed over time? (*c*) Which factors are related to endogamy? (*d*) How do various dimensions of partner choice coincide? Third, I discuss strengths and weaknesses of past research. Strengths include the mass of descriptive work that has been done and the development of a multifaceted theoretical perspective which gives sociological theorizing an edge over psychological and economic theories of partner choice. Weaknesses include the lack of standardization of methods in describing patterns and trends and the relatively weak integration of empirical and theoretical work.

0360-0572/98/0815-0395$08.00

INTRODUCTION

Since the beginning of this century, sociologists have described patterns of partner choice and have tried to explain why people marry within their group (endogamy) and why people marry persons close in status (homogamy). The research literature can be divided into three traditions, depending on which type of characteristic is considered. Research on ethnic and racial intermarriage originated in immigrant countries such as the United States and is motivated by the question of whether the various nationality groups would integrate with one another and with the original population (Drachsler 1920; Wirth & Goldhamer 1944). Research on religious intermarriage has been done both in and outside the United States and has been concerned with the extent to which churches control the life choices of their members and the degree to which religious involvement translates into the membership of "communal groups" (Kennedy 1944). Research on socioeconomic homogamy was developed by stratification researchers who used marriage patterns in conjunction with mobility patterns to describe how open stratification systems are (Glass 1954).

Although the underlying issues are diverse, one common theme is that all traditions characterize social differentiation by describing patterns of social interaction. Building on the Weberian notion of status group closure, students have argued that interaction between social groups provides a fundamental way to describe the group boundaries that make up the social structure. Because marriage is an intimate and often long-term relationship, intermarriage or heterogamy not only reveals the existence of interaction across group boundaries, it also shows that members of different groups accept each other as social equals. Intermarriage can thus be regarded as an intimate link between social groups; conversely, endogamy or homogamy can be regarded as a form of group closure.

Another common theme lies in the consequences of intermarriage. First, intermarriage decreases the salience of cultural distinctions in future generations because the children of mixed marriages are less likely to identify themselves with a single group. Although mixed couples may socialize their children into the culture of a single group, these children are less likely to identify with that group when intermarriage in society is common. Second, by intermarrying, individuals may lose the negative attitudes they have toward other groups. Although personal interaction between groups sometimes fosters conflicts by making economic and cultural differences more apparent, if the relationship is intimate, interaction gives people an opportunity to realize the individual variety among the members of another group and, in doing so, may ultimately weaken their prejudices and stereotypes. Because intermarriage often connects the social networks of the two spouses, this applies to a range of outgroup members and not just to the immediate partners.

In short, what makes intermarriage sociologically relevant lies in its inherent dynamic: It is not just a reflection of the boundaries that currently separate groups in society, it also bears the potential of cultural and socioeconomic change. While marriage patterns are in this sense telling social indicators, they do not tell us everything. First, if members of two groups do not marry one another, it does not necessarily mean that both groups are closed. It takes two to marry, and if one group is closed while the other is open, endogamy may still prevail. Research on marriage is less informative in this respect than, for instance, research on individual racial prejudice. In a similar vein, homogamy tells a somewhat ambiguous story about the preferences and prejudices of status groups. Homogamy will occur if people prefer to marry into high-status groups, but it will also occur when people prefer to marry status-equals. In high-status groups, preferences for high-status spouses and preferences for status-equals are similar, but in lower-status groups, these are different.

Second, marriage patterns result from both preference and opportunity. Opportunity to marry within the group depends on many factors, such as residential segregation, the composition of local marriage markets, group size, and so on. As a result, endogamy does not necessarily point to a personally felt social distance toward a certain outgroup. Such preferences play a role, but to what extent they determine the actual choices people make is an empirical question. Marriage patterns simply tell us which groups interact with whom, and while this is an important piece of information, they do not tell us why.

A third and final limitation of marriage patterns lies in demographic trends. Declining marriage rates, the rise of cohabitation, and the increase in divorce suggest that it is not always valid to treat marriage patterns as indicators of differentiation in society as a whole. Some of these problems can be solved more easily than others. The rise of cohabitation poses no real problem because one can often include cohabiting couples in the analysis. Declining marriage rates are also less of a problem because they are largely the result of marriage delays; the vast majority of a given birth cohort eventually marries. The rise of divorce is more problematic, because intermarriage and divorce are often positively related. A high rate of ethnic intermarriage may point to open social groups, but if mixed marriages are more likely to break up, such a conclusion would need further study.

In the past decades, researchers have described patterns of intermarriage, examined individual variations in intermarriage, and assessed changes in intermarriage over time. In addition, both theoretical and empirical studies have developed hypotheses about why people marry within their group and why some do while others do not. Because such hypotheses are often not tested directly, I divide my review into a theoretical and an empirical section. The goal of the theoretical section is to review micro- and macro-level hypotheses about the causes of intermarriage and homogamy and to put these into a general theoretical framework. The goal of the empirical section is to summarize patterns, variations, and trends in intermarriage. I focus on the three main sociological group characteristics (i.e. race and ethnicity, religion, and socioeconomic status), I limit myself to Western societies, and I discuss studies conducted in the last decade.

THEORETICAL WORK ON INTERMARRIAGE AND HOMOGAMY

Marriage patterns arise from the interplay between three social forces: the preferences of individuals for certain characteristics in a spouse, the influence of the social group of which they are members, and the constraints of the marriage market in which they are searching for a spouse (Kalmijn 1991b). Although these factors represent analytically distinct hypotheses, they have most often been regarded as complementary elements of a single theory, and that is what distinguishes the sociological perspective from economic or psychological theories on partner choice (e.g. Winch 1958).

Preferences of Marriage Candidates

To understand aggregate patterns of marriage selection, researchers use the concept of a marriage market. Unmarried men and women operate within a marriage market where each individual considers a set of potential spouses. Potential spouses are evaluated on the basis of the resources they have to offer and individuals compete with each other for the spouse they want most by offering their own resources in return. Several kinds of resources obviously play a role in the choice of a spouse, but sociologists have mostly focused on socioeconomic and cultural resources. When married, spouses pool these resources to produce family goods, such as economic well-being, status, social confirmation, and affection.

SOCIOECONOMIC RESOURCES Socioeconomic resources are defined as resources that produce economic well-being and status. Economic well-being is shared by the family members and status is granted to the family as a unit rather than to its individual members. As a result, the income and status of one spouse contribute to the income and status of the other by raising the income and status of the family. People maximize their income and status by searching for a spouse with attractive socioeconomic resources. The outcome of this competition is that the most attractive candidates select among themselves while the least attractive candidates have to rely on one another. Competition for socioeconomic resources on the marriage market thus leads to an aggregate pattern of homogamy.

The nature of this competition varies with the role women play in society. When marriage is based on the benefits that stem from the division of paid and domestic labor in the household, prevailing gender differences in earnings give men a comparative advantage in productive labor so that the wife's time is used more productively when it is spent on household labor. As a result, men and women exchange paid and domestic labor resources. Similar arguments have been made with regard to status and prestige. When the status of the family depends primarily on the occupation of the husband, there will be an exchange of male prestige and female qualities in other respects, such as class background, physical attractiveness, and cultural participation (Jacobs & Furstenberg 1986; Stevens et al 1990; Uunk 1996).

Both types of exchange suggest that men, unlike women, do not compete among themselves for female socioeconomic resources in the marriage market. There are good reasons to believe that this has changed. An increasing number of married women participate in the labor market and married women's work is now less often motivated by temporary economic needs of the family. Several authors believe that these changes have made women's socioeconomic resources increasingly attractive to men. The wife's human capital may facilitate the husband's access to networks that are helpful in his career, her earnings may subsidize his human capital investments, and the economic security she provides may lessen his need to settle for short-term career benefits, thus increasing his opportunity to choose more attractive, long-term career objectives. Because female labor is now often the reflection of women's desire to work outside the home, rather than a reflection of the economic needs of the family, the wife's socioeconomic resources may also become increasingly important for the status of the family (Davis 1984).

CULTURAL RESOURCES While the importance of socioeconomic resources is based on a preference to marry a resourceful spouse, independent of one's own resources, the role of cultural resources is based on a preference to marry someone who is similar. Preferences for cultural similarity have been addressed most extensively in the social psychological literature on personal attraction (Byrne 1971). Similarity of values and opinions leads to mutual confirmation of each other's behavior and worldviews, similarity of taste is attractive because it enlarges opportunities to participate in joint activities, and similarity of knowledge creates a common basis for conversation, which enhances mutual understanding.

Although originally developed to explain attraction between strangers in day-to-day interaction, these notions have also been applied to marriage (DiMaggio & Mohr 1985; Kalmijn 1994). Because cultural similarity leads to personal attraction, it is a prerequisite for getting involved with someone. Because of its instrumental effects, cultural similarity also encourages people to establish a long-term relationship. Since many activities in marriage are joint, such as the raising of children, the purchase of a house and other consumer durables, and the spending of leisure time, dissimilarity in taste would complicate these shared activities. More generally, people prefer to marry someone who has similar cultural resources because this enables them to develop a common lifestyle in marriage that produces social confirmation and affection.

PREFERENCES AND HOMOGAMY Preferences for socioeconomic and cultural resources do not by themselves translate into homogamy and endogamy with respect to social characteristics. Some authors argue that social characteristics are correlated with such resources, and that homogamy or endogamy is the unintended by-product of individual preferences for resources in a partner. This argument has often been made for educational homogamy, because education is not only strongly related to income and status, but also to taste, values, and lifestyles (Kalmijn 1991a). Similar arguments can be made for horizontally differentiated groups, such as ethnic groups, although in this case, endogamy is probably more the result of preferences for cultural similarity and not so much the result of competition for economically attractive spouses.

Other authors argue that social characteristics are more than simply correlates of the resources partners bring to the marriage market. Characteristics such as education, occupation, race, and ethnicity are also seen as badges that individuals wear to show others what kind of person they are. In this perspective, spouse selection is regarded as a filter process. In the first step, people develop a network of friends, acquaintances, and possibly marriage candidates with whom they share some objective social characteristic. In the second step, people find their spouse by interacting within these homogeneous networks. The second step is also the phase in which psychological characteristics come into play, but at that time, homogamy with respect to objective social characteristics is already insured (Murstein 1976).

Third Parties

A second hypothesis about why people marry within their group focuses on people who are not directly involved in the marriage. Because mixed marriages may threaten the internal cohesion and homogeneity of the group, "third parties" have an incentive to keep new generations from marrying exogamously. There are two ways in which third parties prevent exogamy: by group identification and by group sanctions.

GROUP IDENTIFICATION Children are typically brought up with a sense of group identification. Identification either takes the form of an awareness of a common social history, what is sometimes called a "sense of peoplehood" (Gordon 1964), or it can take the form of a more psychological sense of being different from others. The stronger such feelings of group identification, the more people have internalized norms of endogamy, and the more likely it is that they marry homogamously or endogamously. The notion of group identification has been especially important for racial and ethnic groups, where norms of endogamy are believed to be firmly internalized (Merton 1941). Such norms, however, may also apply to other kinds of groups such as social classes and educational groups.

How strongly younger generations identify themselves with the group depends to a great extent on the homogeneity of the networks in which they are embedded. When adolescents live in neighborhoods that are homogeneous with respect to the social and cultural characteristics of their parents, they are more likely to develop a sense of belonging to that group. While residential segregation in urban areas hampers opportunities to intermarry directly, as is discussed later, it also reduced exogamy by intensifying feelings of group solidarity. Identification with the origin group is believed to be weakened by higher education. Owing to the emphasis on individual achievement and universalistic principles in higher education, the college-educated may be less likely to identify themselves with their social and cultural roots (Hwang et al 1995).

GROUP SANCTIONS Even if people have not internalized norms of endogamy, they may still refrain from marrying exogamously because of the sanctions third parties apply. The three most important examples of parties that sanction intermarriage are the family, the church, and the state. Although in Western societies parental control over children's marriage decisions is limited, there are still ways in which parents can interfere. They set up meetings with potential spouses, they play the role of matchmaker, they give advice and opinions about the candidates, and they may withdraw support in the early years of the child's marriage. Nevertheless, they do not have strong sanctions when children decide against their will.

Somewhat stronger sanctions are provided by the church. Both the Catholic church and various Protestant denominations have denounced interfaith marriages for centuries, although the nature and strength of their disapproval have changed over time. Religious institutions attempt to control intermarriage in part because they are competing for members. Religious intermarriage entails the risk of losing members and may weaken church attachment in future generations. If interfaith marriages occur anyway, it is not always in the interest of the church to apply sanctions because the competing church may accept the marriage and hence gain members. This helps explain why the Roman Catholic church, for example, has often accepted interfaith marriages on the condition that the children be raised as Catholics. Because of competing pressures, however, spouses in interfaith marriages often decide not to raise their children in a religious fashion. If this occurs, both religious institutions stand to lose strength in society.

The strongest sanctions against intermarriage have been provided by the state. Laws on racial intermarriage in the United States—abolished in

1967—are a well-known example (Davis 1991). When slavery was abolished, the gradual decline in formal inequality of blacks and whites went hand-in-hand with a growing anxiety about the social boundary between the races, and this anxiety was stronger when contacts were more intimate. Interracial dating and marriage were condemned with great vigor, and strong social norms emerged against interracial contacts with possible sexual undertones, such as interracial dancing and swimming. The emerging doctrine of no social equality was formalized in legislation that segregated the races in public facilities (Jim Crow laws) and legislation that controlled their sexual and marital contacts (antimiscegenation laws).

Marriage Markets

Endogamy and homogamy are not only governed by individual- and group-level factors, but also by structural arrangements. The chances to marry endogamously are higher the more often one meets people within the group and the more often one interacts with group members on a day-to-day basis. Contact opportunities are shaped by several structural arrangements. Some studies focus on the demographic composition of the population as a whole, other studies examine regional distributions of groups, and yet other studies analyze smaller, functional settings, such as the school and the workplace.

THE LOGIC OF NUMBERS When interaction occurs randomly, the chance that a woman in a certain group marries someone in her own group equals the proportion of men who are in that group. As a result, members of a small group will have lower chances of marrying endogamously than members of a larger group. The effect of group size implies that endogamy is negatively related to the degree of heterogeneity of a population (Blau & Schwartz 1984). To explain this, one can think of two populations, each consisting of two groups. One population is heterogeneous and has 50% in each group (e.g. 100 in group A, 100 in group B), while the other is homogeneous and has 90% in one group and 10% in the other (e.g. 180 in group A, 20 in group B). Both populations have equal numbers of males and females in each group. In the heterogeneous population, the number of women expected to marry within the group will be 0.5 x 50 = 25 for A and 0.5 x 50 = 25 for B, which boils down to 50% marrying within the group. In the homogeneous population, the number of women expected to marry within the group will be 0.9 x 90 = 81 for A and 0.1 x 10 = 1 for B, which boils down to 82%. This shows that in a heterogeneous population, endogamy is lower than in a homogeneous population, provided that marriage is random.

THE GEOGRAPHY OF GROUPS The chance to encounter a member of one's own group does not depend on group size alone but also on the way a group is dispersed geographically (Blau & Schwartz 1984). Groups that are concentrated in specific regions of the country generally have more opportunity to marry endogamously than groups that are not (Lieberson & Waters 1988). Examples are common in the literature on ethnic groups, e.g. Asian-Americans in California, Jewish-Americans in New York City, or Catholics and Protestants separated in the southern and northern parts of the Netherlands. An additional reason why it is important to consider the geography of groups is that isolation may be correlated with group size. Smaller groups are often more isolated. Jewish-Americans, for example, may have partly overcome the constraints of their small group size through geographic concentration. They are a small group in a large country, but a large group in a small region.

Although relaxing the assumption of an even geographic distribution is more realistic, it also leads to new problems. If one controls for geographic segregation—by calculating endogamy rates for specific regions, for instance—one implicitly assumes that people base their decision to live in a given area on factors that are independent of ingroup preferences. This is not always realistic. For instance, there is much regional concentration of Italian-Americans in the United States, but even though this can in part be attributed to their particular immigration history and occupational opportunities, the preferences of Italian-Americans play a role as well (Lieberson 1980). While it is difficult to make a precise distinction between preferences and constraints, it is generally true that the smaller the marriage market one studies, the more the structure of the market is affected by preferences and the less by constraints.

LOCAL MARRIAGE MARKETS Unmarried people do not just wander around a region looking for a spouse; they spend most of their life in small and functional places, such as neighborhoods, schools, workplaces, bars, and clubs. Such "local marriage markets" are often socially segregated, and that is why they are important for explaining marriage patterns. In the sociological literature, three local markets have been considered most frequently: the school, the neighborhood, and the workplace. Of these three, schools are considered the most efficient markets because they are homogeneous with respect to age and heterogeneous with respect to sex. Workplaces are considered less efficient, but increased participation of women in the labor market and declining occupational sex segregation suggest that this may have changed (Davis 1984). Although it has not often been studied where couples meet, a French study shows that the settings sociologists analyze are not the most common meeting places. Among young French couples, fewer than 5% met in the neighborhood, fewer than 10% met at school, and just over 10% met at work (Bozon & Heran 1989).

To clarify how local marriage markets affect homogamy, authors have looked at the composition of these markets with respect to social characteristics. What distinguishes the neighborhood from the school and the workplace is that it is homogeneous with respect to factors such as ethnicity, race, religion, and family background, i.e. characteristics transmitted by parents (Lieberson 1980). Schools are less homogeneous in ascribed characteristics, although there are exceptions, e.g. Catholic colleges and black colleges. At the same time, schools are not necessarily homogeneous with respect to educational attainment. Differences in ultimate educational attainment are larger in high schools, for example, than in universities, simply because the educational system works like a funnel, particularly in the United States (Mare 1991). In general, however, it is expected that colleges promote educational homogamy more than neighborhoods do, while neighborhoods promote ethnic endogamy and homogamy of family background more than schools. Whether workplaces encourage homogamy highly depends on the type of work, but on average, they probably do not encourage socioeconomic homogamy as much as schools.

EMPIRICAL WORK ON INTERMARRIAGE AND HOMOGAMY

Empirical work has addressed four questions: (*a*) To what extent are groups endogamous or homogamous, and how do groups differ in these respects? (*b*) How have endogamy and homogamy changed over time? (*c*) Which factors are related to endogamy and homogamy, and in particular, what is the role of gender, education, and geographic regions and local marriage markets? (*d*) How do various dimensions of partner choice coincide? Before I summarize the main findings, I discuss how researchers have tackled these issues methodologically.

Measures and Models

Intermarriage can be calculated for the stock of marriages at a given point in time (prevalence measures) or for people who marry in a given period of time (incidence measures). Incidence measures are generally preferable, in particular if one analyzes trends. If the stock of marriages is used, one can analyze characteristics at the time of survey or characteristics at the time of marriage. The latter measures are more suitable than the former because some characteristics change after marriage. Because partners may become more alike during marriage—they may switch faith, for example, or influence each other's occupational career—current measures of homogamy tend to be biased upwardly. To describe intermarriage, various measures have been used. To explain these, it is helpful to consider the following marriage table.

MEASURES The most general measure is the percentage of couples intermarrying: $(C_{BA}+C_{AB})/N$. When calculating group-specific measures, it makes a difference if one considers couples or individuals. The percentage of A-type

		FEMALES		
		Group A	*Group B*	*Total married*
	Group A	C_{AA}	C_{AB}	M_A
MALES	*Group B*	C_{BA}	C_{BB}	M_B
	Total married	F_A	F_B	N

couples intermarrying is $(C_{BA}+C_{AB})/(C_{BA}+C_{AB}+C_{AA})$, while the percentage of A-type married persons intermarrying is C_{AB}/M_A for males and C_{BA}/F_A for females. While percentages are simple and informative measures to describe intermarriage, they provide little information about the strength of endogamy because they lack a reference point. If 40% of a group marries endogamously, is this evidence for a preference to marry within rather than outside the group? Percentages are also less useful for comparing groups because when selection is random, small groups are less likely to marry within their group than large groups.

These problems are overcome by a more recent measure, the odds ratio. The odds ratio is defined as the odds that an A-type male marries an A-type female (rather than a B-type female), divided by the odds that a B-type male marries an A-type female, i.e. $(C_{AA}/C_{AB})/(C_{BA}/C_{BB})$. The odds ratio for women is equivalent, i.e. $(C_{AA}/C_{BA})/(C_{AB}/C_{BB})$. If there are more than two groups in the marriage table, one can calculate odds ratios for each group separately. If C_{AX} and C_{XA} are marriages of A-type males and females with all other groups, and C_{XX} are marriages that do not involve A-type males or females, the odds ratio can be defined as $(C_{AA}/C_{AX})/(C_{XA}/C_{XX})$. Odds ratios have two important advantages. First, they provide a reference point: Odds ratios greater than one indicate that there is more endogamy than one would expect, and the larger the ratio, the greater the degree of endogamy. Second, odds ratios are useful for comparing endogamy across groups because they are independent of the relative sizes of the groups in the marriage table.

A disadvantage of the measures discussed above is that they are based on the married or marrying population. A measure of intermarriage that takes into account that not everyone marries is the intermarriage index Z, which is based on so-called harmonic mean models developed by Schoen (1988). If M_P and F_P refer to the total number of males and females in the respective groups (married and unmarried), Z is defined as $(C_{AB}/M_{PA}+C_{BA}/F_{PA}+C_{BA}/M_{PB}+C_{AB}/F_{PB})/(M_A/M_{PA}+M_B/M_{PB}+F_A/F_{PA}+F_B/F_{PB})$. This intermarriage index ranges from zero for minimum intermarriage to one for maximum intermarriage. When selection is random, the index takes the value of 0.5 (Schoen 1988).

Percentages, odds ratios, and the intermarriage index can be applied to both ordered and nonordered characteristics. For ordered characteristics, another common measure is the Pearsonian correlation between spouses' traits. A positive correlation means that high-status men marry higher-status women than low-status men; it does not necessarily mean that people marry within their group. The correlation between the ages of husband and wife, for example, is strongly positive, even though most men marry somewhat younger women.

MODELS Second to measures of intermarriage, loglinear models have been used to describe patterns of marriage selection. These models assume that the expected counts in the marriage table are a multiplicative function of sample size, the number of males in a group, the number of females in a group, and an interaction parameter, which measures marriage selection independent of the marginal row and column distributions. Many ways to model the interaction parameter exist, but most authors present parameters for the tendency to marry within the group (endogamy) and parameters for the tendency to avoid intermarrying when controlling for the tendency to marry within the group (intermarriage). The latter parameters are often equivalent to odds ratios and have been described by the metaphors of distances or boundaries between groups (Mare 1991; Kalmijn 1991b). When characteristics are ordered, loglinear models also provide single measures of association that are comparable to correlations but independent of the marginal distributions, i.e. uniform association models (Hout 1982). When characteristics are not ordered, special types of loglinear models exist that provide measures of the distances between groups as revealed by the marriage frequencies in the table, i.e. logmultiplicative models (Johnson 1980; Kalmijn 1993a).

Patterns of Intermarriage and Homogamy

In describing patterns of intermarriage and homogamy, researchers have addressed three questions: (*a*) To what extent do subgroups marry endogamously? (*b*) If subgroups marry out, with what groups are they most likely to intermarry? and (*c*) How do subgroups compare in their degree of endogamy?

RACE/ETHNICITY Most American studies of ethnic intermarriage analyze data from the perspective of the minority group and focus on specific types of subgroups. Several decades ago, interest largely focused on European immigrant subgroups and their children. More recently, new immigrant subgroups such as Asian- and Hispanic-Americans are being studied, though there is a resurgent interest in the descendants of the older immigrants, sometimes referred to as white ethnic groups. Intermarriage of blacks has always been studied frequently. Research on intermarriage of American Indians, in contrast, is scarce.

Recent national estimates of the percentage of persons who are married endogamously vary around 95% for blacks (Sweet & Bumpass 1987), 75% for Asian subgroups (Lee & Yamanaka 1990), 65% for Hispanic subgroups (U.S. Bureau of the Census 1985), 45% for American Indians (Snipp 1989), and

25% for (unmixed) European subgroups (Alba & Golden 1986). Although these percentages are high, they do not indicate whether groups are endogamous. Loglinear models and harmonic mean analyses are more informative in this respect and show that virtually all ethnic subgroups marry within their group more often than can be expected under random mating (Jiobu 1988; Schoen & Thomas 1989; Sandefur & McKinnell 1986; Alba & Golden 1986).

A low degree of endogamy does not necessarily imply integration; this also depends on patterns of outmarriage. When Hispanic subgroups marry exogamously, for example, they often marry with other Hispanic subgroups and hence keep a distance from the non-Hispanic white majority (Gurak & Fitzpatrick 1982). Asian-Americans who marry out, in contrast, rarely marry other Asian subgroups and instead marry with whites (Lee & Yamanaka 1990). Intermarriage between European subgroups also reveals meaningful patterns. In the first half of this century, marriage selection was characterized by a large distance between Western and Northern Europeans on the one hand and Southern, Central, and Eastern Europeans on the other (Pagnini & Morgan 1990; Kalmijn 1993a). This finding has been interpreted as evidence of a boundary between the "old" and "new" European immigrants to the United States.

How do subgroups compare in their degree of endogamy? Unfortunately, most studies focus on one type of subgroup at a time without analyzing other types. A broader focus is provided by Lieberson and Water, who present a list of odds ratios for more than 20 groups (1988). European subgroups and American Indians appear to have the lowest rates of endogamy, Hispanic and Asian subgroups have intermediate levels of endogamy, and blacks have the highest rates. There are also differences among European subgroups—for instance, endogamy is lower for "old" than for "new" European groups—but these are small when considering the range in the list. The main conclusion of Lieberson and Water's analysis is that groups who are more recent to the host society have higher degrees of closure, a regularity that fits well into assimilation theories. Blacks are the prime exception to this pattern. A similar relationship between the newness of a group and its level of endogamy is found in Australia (Jones & Luijkx 1996).

RELIGION Religious intermarriage has primarily been studied in religiously heterogeneous societies. Some authors use current religious affiliation to measure intermarriage, while others use the religion in which spouses were raised. Endogamy is higher when current affiliation is used, because spouses often switch faith or lose their religion after entering a mixed marriage (Glenn 1982). Estimates for the United States that use parental religion show that in the late 1970s, 62% of Catholics were married within their group, 84% of Protestants were married endogamously, and 80% of Jews were married endogamously (Glenn 1982). Loglinear analyses further show that both Catholics and Protestants have a tendency to marry within rather than outside their group; this is found in the United States (Kalmijn 1991b), the Netherlands (Hendrickx et al 1991), Germany (Hendrickx et al 1994), Australia (Hayes 1991), and Switzerland (Schoen & Thomas 1990). Comparisons between countries using odds ratios show that endogamy is strongest in Ireland and Northern Ireland, as one would expect, and that Catholic endogamy is stronger in the United States than in most European countries (Klein & Wunder 1996).

Which religious groups are most endogamous? Loglinear analyses in the United States indicate that Catholics are somewhat more closed than Protestants (Johnson 1980). Loglinear analyses have not included Jews, but it is safe to say that American Jews are more endogamous than Catholics because their intermarriage percentage is comparable to that of Catholics, while they are a much smaller group. Detailed loglinear analyses of Protestant denominations show that more-conservative Protestant denominations, such as the Rereformed in the Netherlands (Hendrickx et al 1994) and Baptists in the United States and Australia (Johnson 1980; Hayes 1991) are more endogamous than liberal denominations. These findings are consistent with the notion of third-party control: Denominations and religions that are more traditional in religious doctrine and have higher degrees of church involvement among their members also have the highest degree of endogamy.

When analyzing marriages between religious groups, authors have used the concept of social distance and have developed loglinear models providing such measures. In the United States, such analyses point to the following order of groups: Baptists, Methodists, liberal Protestants, Lutherans, and Catholics (Johnson 1980). These distances have been interpreted in terms of ritual and regional dimensions. Groups on the left side of the continuum are more democratic in their organization, have less detailed prescriptions of ritual, and emphasize more spontaneous forms of worshiping than groups on the right side of the continuum. Regional patterns play a role here as well. Baptists and Methodists are concentrated in the South, for example, while Catholics are concentrated in the Northeast.

SOCIOECONOMIC STATUS The literature on socioeconomic homogamy can be distinguished into studies of ascribed status and studies of achieved status. Ascribed status positions are measured by the occupational class of the father and the father-in-law. Achieved status positions are measured by education and occupation. Education is used more often because it is a convenient status indicator of women and changes little after marriage. In most countries, educational homogamy is quite strong (about 0.55), occupational homogamy is somewhat weaker (about 0.40), while the correlation between husbands' and wives' class origins is the weakest, about 0.30 (Kalmijn 1991a; Uunk 1996).

Loglinear analyses provide additional insights in the association between partners' status positions. Such analyses first show that people marry within rather than outside socioeconomic groups, although some groups are more closed than others. Groups at the top and the bottom of the educational hierarchy are more closed than groups in the middle (Uunk et al 1996; Hendrickx 1994). These tendencies may be due to the role of opportunity: If people at the bottom prefer to marry out, they can only choose higher groups and if people at the top prefer to marry out, they can only choose lower groups. People from farm background have an exceptionally high rate of endogamy, a finding that can probably be explained in terms of the social and geographic isolation of the rural population (Kalmijn 1991a; Uunk et al 1996; Jones & Davis 1988).

Next to a tendency to marry within the group, there is a tendency for marriage to become less common the farther away the two status positions are. Some status boundaries are harder to cross than others, however. For education, the strongest boundary is that between college graduates and lesser-educated persons (Mare 1991; Kalmijn 1991a). A common interpretation of this finding is that colleges function as local marriage markets that are physically separated from settings in which lesser-educated persons are involved. Patterns of occupational homogamy, like patterns of intergenerational occupational mobility, are dominated by the line that divides blue-collar and white-collar occupations (Hout 1982; Hayes 1993). More detailed analyses of occupational homogamy have shown that there is more homogamy with respect to the cultural status of occupations than with respect to the economic status of occupations (Kalmijn 1994). This suggests that preferences for cultural similarity are stronger than preferences for economically attractive spouses.

Trends in Intermarriage and Homogamy

Trends have been analyzed in three ways. (*a*) Some researchers compare marriage or birth cohorts at a single point in time. Such synthetic cohort studies are potentially biased because older cohorts have been married longer than younger cohorts. Cohorts differ in their rate of attrition, and this attrition may be selective because the likelihood of divorce is inversely related to homogamy. (*b*) Other studies compare the stock of intact marriages at different points in time. This design has the disadvantage of containing much overlap of marriages in the points of comparison, which leads to an underestimation of linear trends. (*c*) Others, finally, compare recently formed marriages in different periods, either through annual marriage licenses or through comparisons of newlyweds in multiple surveys or censuses. This method is most suitable for analyzing trends because it gives a picture of the changing incidence of intermarriage.

RACE/ETHNICITY Analyses of marriage records generally reveal an increase in intermarriage of new ethnic groups in the last decades; this applies to Hispanic intermarriage in New York City (Gilbertson et al 1996), to Asian intermarriage in Hawaii (Schoen & Thomas 1989), and to Asian intermarriage of males—not females—in New York City (Sung 1990). The trend in black-white intermarriage has been documented for a longer time period and in more states. Annual marriage records in 33 states reveal that black-white intermarriage has increased significantly in both northern and southern states since the legal ban on intermarriage was lifted, although it remains exceptionally low (Kalmijn 1993b). Comparisons of the 1980 and 1990 American censuses confirm this conclusion (Qian 1997). Ethnic characteristics that are not included in marriage licenses have primarily been analyzed through synthetic cohort analyses. Such studies reveal growing outmarriage across birth cohorts for European-American groups (Alba & Golden 1986; Lieberson & Waters 1988), for American Indians (Eschbach 1995), and for ethnic groups in Australia (Jones & Luijkx 1996).

The decline in ethnic endogamy has typically been interpreted from an assimilation perspective: Through generational replacement, national origin groups gradually integrate in the host society. Consistent with this perspective, most analyses find that the children of immigrants marry out more often than the immigrants themselves (Gilbertson et al 1996; Lee & Yamanaka 1990; Alba 1976). Because trends also occur within generations of immigrants, individual assimilation to the host society is not a sufficient explanation (Gilbertson et al 1996; Sung 1990). An additional interpretation is that assimilation is a process at the macro level: When more and more members of an ethnic group are of the second or third generation—when an ethnic group becomes "older"—all generations find it easier to adapt to the host society. Another interpretation is more general in nature and points to the weakening influence of third parties in marriage choice and the declining importance of ascription as a basis of evaluating other people.

RELIGION In the United States, trends in religious homogamy have primarily been assessed through surveys, largely because few places report religion on their marriage licenses and because the census is not allowed to ask questions on religious affiliation. By analyzing national surveys conducted between 1955 and 1989 and using a design that separates the effects of period and duration of marriage, Kalmijn (1991b) shows that intermarriage between Catholics and Protestants has increased in a linear fashion between 1920 and 1980. Trends in intermarriage between Jews and non-Jews have been documented by comparing subsequent surveys (Lazerwitz 1995) and by comparing marriage cohorts within a single survey (Kosmin et al 1991). Both types of analyses show that Jewish-Gentile intermarriage has increased considerably over the last decades. An exception to these trends are conservative Christian groups, who appeared to have stable endogamy rates over time (McCutcheon 1988).

In many other Western societies, questions on religion are included in marriage records so that long-term trends can be documented there more easily. A loglinear trend analysis of annual Dutch marriage records since the 1930s shows that religious endogamy of Catholics and the conservative Re-Reformed Protestants has declined (Hendrickx et al 1991). The more liberal Dutch Reformed Protestants experienced no decline, but they had low levels of endogamy to begin with. Marriage records in Switzerland (Schoen & Thomas 1990) and Germany (Hendrickx et al 1994) also reveal a decline in the level of endogamy of Catholics and Protestants. That the boundaries between religious groups in Europe and the United States have weakened during the twentieth century is consistent with the notion of declining third-party control and matches long-term processes such as secularization and depillarization.

SOCIOECONOMIC STATUS Trends in socioeconomic homogamy are most frequently studied by analyzing class background and education. In most industrialized countries, there has been a decline in the importance of social background for marriage choice. This has been found for the United States (Kalmijn 1991a), the Netherlands (Uunk 1996), Hungary (Uunk et al 1996), and France (Forsé & Chauvel 1995). The most common interpretation of this trend lies in the role of third parties and opportunity. Young adults have become increasingly independent of parents so that parents have less direct or indirect control over the choices their children make. People also spend more time in school settings, which are more heterogeneous with respect to social class background than the parental neighborhood.

Trends in educational homogamy do not point in one direction. A loglinear analysis of 18 postwar industrial nations by Ultee & Luijkx (1990) reveals that five countries experienced a decline in educational homogamy, three countries experienced an increase, while the remaining ten revealed no meaningful trend. Country-specific loglinear analyses also reveal a mixed pattern, although they do not reveal a decline in homogamy: (*a*) a strong increase in the United States (Mare 1991; Kalmijn 1991a), Hungary (Uunk et al 1996), and Germany (Blossfeld & Timm 1997); (*b*) a slight increase in the Netherlands (Hendrickx 1994); and (*c*) stability in Australia (Jones 1987) and France (Forsé & Chauvel 1995).

Several hypotheses have been suggested to explain these trends. Some authors argue that opportunities for making a match on education have increased. People marry later and spend more time in school, but the time interval between leaving school and marriage has narrowed. As a result, it is now more likely that unmarried people, especially the college educated, meet their spouse in school (Mare 1991). Others point to the role of preferences. Education has become an increasingly important proxy for both cultural taste and socioeconomic success, and competition among men for socioeconomic resources in women may have increased (Kalmijn 1991a; Schoen & Wooldredge 1989). There are also hypotheses predicting a decrease in educational homogamy. Some authors argue that marriage choice has become increasingly based on emotional or affective considerations. Because romantic considerations often overrule status concerns, one would expect a decline in all forms of status homogamy (Ultee & Luijkx 1990).

An attempt to reconcile these hypotheses is made by Smits et al (1998), who argue that educational homogamy will initially increase with levels of industrialization because in this phase, education becomes the dominant criterion for socioeconomic success and cultural norms and values. Romantic considerations and individualism gain importance in later stages of the industrialization process when high standards of living are guaranteed for everyone. As a result, educational homogamy will first increase with levels of industrialization, but will eventually decrease. A comparison of 64 countries provides indirect support for this claim: The relationship between educational homogamy and the level of industrialization follows an inverted "U."

Variations in Intermarriage and Homogamy

Next to describing patterns and trends, authors have analyzed variations in intermarriage and have examined what factors contribute to outmarriage. Recurring themes in the literature are differences by sex, by education, and by region. Although these factors are generally studied in an exploratory fashion, they also give us clues about the causes of endogamy.

SEX DIFFERENCES Sex differences have most often been studied in the literature on racial and ethnic intermarriage. Studies on black-white intermarriage in the United States consistently show that black men marry whites more often than black women (Kalmijn 1993b; Schoen & Wooldredge 1989). A traditional interpretation of this finding is that minority men are able to compensate for their lower "ethnic prestige" by offering white women a high occupational status or income. Although in principle one could reverse the exchange—high-status minority women could marry white men of lower status—under conditions of traditional sex-roles, this type of marriage is believed to be uncommon because the status of the family is largely dependent on the status of the husband.

Although the interpretation is plausible, findings for other ethnic groups provide a counterpoint. Asian-American women, for example, and in particular Japanese-American women, marry whites more often than their male counterparts (Sung 1990). A speculative interpretation of this exception is that Asian-American women are attractive marriage candidates for white men because of their physical appearance and presumed acceptance of more traditional power relationships in marriage. A more-plausible interpretation lies in the role of opportunity: the presence of American soldiers in Japan and Korea. A recent analysis shows that excluding such war brides leads to a substantial reduction in the sex differential in Asian-American intermarriage (JJ Jacobs & T Labov, unpublished manuscript).

Sex differences have also been studied in the analysis of socioeconomic homogamy. A common finding is that highly educated men and men in professional and technical occupations marry down more often than up (Mare 1991; Kalmijn 1994). Laymen generally interpret downmarrying as evidence of a reluctance on the part of men to marry high-status women, but most of the asymmetry is due to differences in the composition of men's and women's characteristics. On average, women have traditionally been less educated and less often have had high-status occupations than men. Once such differences are taken into account through loglinear analyses, researchers generally find little evidence of asymmetry (Mare 1991). Similar conclusions apply to trends: Educational downmarrying among men has become less common, but this is largely due to the increased educational attainment of women (Mare 1991).

EDUCATIONAL EFFECTS Another frequently examined factor in intermarriage is education. Many studies have found that more highly-educated members of ethnic or racial minority groups marry exogamously more often than their lesser-educated peers. This applies to white ethnic groups (Lieberson & Waters 1988), blacks (Kalmijn 1993b; Schoen & Wooldredge 1989), and American Indians (Sandefur & McKinnell 1986). Less consistent evidence is found for outmarriage of Asian-Americans (Hwang et al 1995; Wong 1989; Schoen & Thomas 1989).

Educational effects have been interpreted in terms of both opportunity and preference. The former interpretation states that better educated minority members are more often exposed to settings such as colleges and high-status occupations where they form a relatively smaller group than in the population at large. Another interpretation states that more highly educated persons—of both majority and minority groups—have a more individualistic attitude, are less attached to their family and community of origin, and have a more universalistic view on life than lesser-educated persons. As a result, they would find ascribed characteristics less relevant in deciding whom to marry.

DIFFERENCES BETWEEN REGIONS AND SETTINGS Virtually all studies find large regional differences in intermarriage. Asian-Americans marry out less often in California, where they are concentrated, than in the rest of the United States (Wong 1989), Indian-Americans are more endogamous in so-called Indian States (Sandefur & McKinnell 1986), and blacks marry more endogamously in states where the percentage of blacks in the population is larger, a relationship that is observed both in and outside the South (Kalmijn 1993b). Such patterns undoubtedly point to the role of opportunity: The smaller the group, the more difficult it is to marry within the group. Hypotheses about group size and its corollary, heterogeneity, have also been examined by analyzing (Standard) Metropolitan Statistical Areas [(S)MSAs) or states through correlational analyses. These studies find that relative group size is negatively correlated with black outmarriage and ethnic outmarriage; similarly, racial, ethnic, and occupational heterogeneity have positive effects on the respective types of intermarriage (Blau et al 1982; Hwang et al 1994).

The role of opportunity has also been analyzed by considering local marriage markets. In a classic study, Ramsøy (1966) analyzed marriage licenses in a Norwegian city and found that husbands and wives lived close to each other before marriage, and in fact closer than one would expect under conditions of random mating in a city. While this confirms that neighborhoods are marriage markets, Ramsøy also showed that people who lived close to one another before marriage did not marry more homogamously with respect to occupation than people who lived far apart. Hence, it appeared that the neighborhood did not by itself promote occupational homogamy. Ramsøy's analysis was criticized on methodological grounds by Peach (1974), but later, more elaborate analyses of newlyweds in a New Zealand city by Morgan (1981) found no clear link between spatial and status proximity either. Analyses of ethnic endogamy yield a more promising conclusion. Anderson & Saenz (1994), for example, find that MSAs in which Mexican-Americans are residentially segregated from non-Hispanic whites have lower degrees of Mexican-American outmarriage, even when other group characteristics such as mean educational level are controlled for.

The school is another local marriage market, but its role in promoting educational homogamy has only been studied indirectly. Mare (1991) found that people who marry closer to finishing school, or while in school, marry people who are more similar in education than people who marry long after finishing school. This relationship was found to be present only for higher levels of education. A similar relationship is found in Germany, although there, a decline in educational homogamy is only observed when comparing couples who married a few years after leaving school with couples who married much later (Blossfeld & Timm 1997). These findings provide indirect evidence that schools function as marriage markets that favor educational homogamy. Schools, and in particular colleges, are educationally homogeneous, while the settings people face when they search for a partner at a later stage, such as work settings and public places, tend to be less homogeneous. Further evidence on the role of schools is provided by Uunk & Kalmijn (1996), who show that the college-educated in the Netherlands have a tendency to marry someone who has the same college major. In the Netherlands, fields of study can be regarded as local marriage markets within the university because students choose a major when they first enroll and do not follow courses in other fields.

Multiple Dimensions

Most early studies analyzed a single sociological characteristic at a time or analyzed several characteristics one-by-one. Since partners choose each other on the basis of multiple characteristics, it is important to analyze more than one factor in marriage choice. In the last decades, several such multidimensional analyses have been done, although most are limited to two dimensions. Research on multiple dimensions has been guided by two hypotheses: the by-product hypothesis and the exchange hypothesis.

BY-PRODUCT HYPOTHESES There is a considerable overlap between social groups in society. Ethnic groups, for example, differ in educational level, religion and ethnicity often coincide, and education and social background are correlated. Because the various social dimensions on which individuals select one another are correlated, and because people are believed to take all these dimensions into account when choosing a spouse, the question arises if and to what extent homogamy in one group dimension is the by-product of selection in another group dimension.

An early attempt to examine this issue empirically was done by Warren (1966; see also Blau and Duncan 1967:354–59), who showed that the correlation between the spouses' fathers' occupations is reduced substantially when controlling for spouses' education. This result led Warren to conclude that social class homogamy is largely a by-product of educational homogamy. More recent analyses confirm this and show in addition that educational homogamy is in part a by-product of matching of social origins (Kalmijn 1991a; Uunk 1996). Hence, both forms of homogamy appear to be weaker when a multidimensional analysis is used, although even then, educational homogamy remains stronger than homogamy of social origins.

The by-product hypothesis has also been a theme in the study of ethnic intermarriage. A classic study of New Haven in the first half of this century by Kennedy (1944) showed that intermarriage is more common between groups who have the same faith, such as between Italians and Poles on the one hand (both largely Catholic) and between Hungarians and Russians on the other (both largely Jewish). Kennedy used the now classic term "triple melting pot" to describe this pattern. Kennedy's triple melting pot confirms the by-product hypothesis because it reveals that marriage boundaries between certain ethnic groups are in part the result of differences with respect to religion. Recent, more sophisticated loglinear analyses confirm that there are strong marriage boundaries between ethnic groups who have a dissimilar faith (Alba & Golden

1986), but no studies have simultaneously analyzed individual ethnic and religious characteristics of husbands and wives.

EXCHANGE HYPOTHESES A second theme in multidimensional analyses is the question of whether people trade characteristics when choosing a spouse. Several examples of exchange have been considered, but the most debated case was introduced by Davis (1941) and Merton (1941), who argued that members of ethnic groups whose prestige in society is low would have better chances of marrying outside their group if they offered a high socioeconomic status in return.

The Davis-Merton hypothesis is most frequently examined in research on ethnic and racial intermarriage. Loglinear and harmonic mean analyses of black-white intermarriage by Kalmijn (1993a) and Schoen & Wooldredge (1989) show that with respect to education, white women marry up more often when marrying a black man than when marrying a white man; similarly, black men marry down more often when marrying a white woman than when marrying a black woman. Similar conclusions apply when examining the marriage choices of white men and black women. White men marry down less often when marrying exogenously and black women marry up less often in mixed marriages. These asymmetries in spouses' educational characteristics are assessed after controlling for the marginal educational distributions of race-sex groups and thereby support the hypothesis that majority men and women marry a minority spouse in part under the condition of socioeconomic status gains.

While the pattern of black-white marriage provides support for the Davis-Merton hypothesis, studies of other types of ethnic homogamy are less consistent. In a harmonic mean analysis of Asian intermarriage in Hawaii, Schoen & Thomas (1989) show that after controlling for differences in educational distributions, white women marry up more often when they marry Filipino and Japanese males, consistent with the notion of exchange. The reverse is true, however, when white women marry Hawaiian or Chinese males.

The exchange hypothesis has also been applied to other dimensions of partner choice, such as physical attractiveness and cultural participation. To examine exchanges, studies generally rely on correlational analyses in which socioeconomic characteristics of the husband are regressed on socioeconomic and noneconomic characteristics of the wife. Effects of the wife's noneconomic characteristics on the husband's socioeconomic characteristics are usually called crossing effects and are considered evidence for exchange.

In an early analysis of physical attractiveness of women and occupational prestige of men, Taylor & Glenn (1976) show that female attractiveness has a positive effect on the occupational prestige of the man she marries, even when controlling for her own socioeconomic characteristics. A drawback of this analysis is that husband's attractiveness was not included in the model. If occupational prestige and attractiveness are correlated within individuals, and if people match in attractiveness, part of the effect of female attractiveness on male prestige may be spurious. A more recent analysis, which also controls for the physical attractiveness of the husband, confirms this. Stevens et al (1990) find no effect of female attractiveness on husbands' education, suggesting that no exchanges are being made.

Another example of exchange is that between socioeconomic status and participation in high culture. DiMaggio & Mohr (1985) find that participation of the wife in high culture has a positive effect on the educational level of the husband, net of the educational level of the wife. Because no measures of the husband's cultural participation were included in this model, the exchange effect might again be due to homogamy with respect to cultural participation. An analysis for the Netherlands, however, shows that this is not the case. Uunk (1996) analyzes the correlation between the wife's cultural participation and the husband's educational level while controlling not only for the wife's educational level but also for the husband's cultural participation. Uunk finds a significant partial association between female high culture and male education, providing support for the exchange hypothesis.

CONCLUSION

Sociological research on marriage choices has generated many insights in how modern society is differentiated. In general, social groups in society appear closed, in the sense that men and women more often choose partners within their group than one would expect under random mating. Although some groups are more closed than others, examples of social groups who marry exogamously have not (yet) been found. Research on intermarriage also reveals how societies change. Overall, ascribed bases of group membership have become less important, while achieved bases of group membership, and especially those governed by education, have not lost salience. This is not to say that ascribed groups are mixing freely now. Ethnic, religious, and particularly racial boundaries still exist, but they are weaker than they used to be.

The focus of the literature has largely been descriptive. Researchers have scrutinized a mass of data—coming from censuses, surveys, and marriage licenses—and have studied many groups, several countries, and long periods of time. Because marriage patterns are telling indicators of how closed groups in a society are, the descriptive focus of the literature has much to say for it. Monitoring such a social indicator also requires a certain degree of standardization, and in this respect, the literature has its shortcomings. Some studies are limited to percentages, which are heavily affected by relative group size, making it difficult to compare endogamy across groups. Other studies use loglinear models, and while these are an advance from a methodological point of view, they have probably made the literature less accessible to a general audience than it deserves to be. In carrying on its descriptive mission, the literature would gain by using simple odds ratios next to percentages or loglinear models when describing the degree of endogamy of groups. A good example of such an approach is provided in Lieberson & Waters (1988). In describing trends, it would also be useful to focus on recently formed marriages rather than on the stock of marriages at a given point in time, largely because the aim is to present social indicators for a clearly defined period in time.

In a theoretical sense, there has also been progress in the field. There are many theories about partner choice, and such notions provide important clues about the causes of intermarriage and homogamy. In general, marriage patterns arise from three social forces: the preferences of individuals for resources in a partner, the influence of the social group, and the constraints of the marriage market. The multifaceted perspective that has been developed over the years gives sociological theorizing an edge over competing theories of marriage choice such as those developed by psychologists and economists.

Considerable empirical evidence exists for these theoretical notions, but the integration of empirical and theoretical work is less than perfect. There are two basic problems in empirical work. First, many hypotheses are tested in an indirect fashion. The role of third-party control, for example, is documented by comparing ethnic groups or religious denominations, but little information is available on what these parties in fact are doing. Similarly, the trend towards increasing educational homogamy may point to heightened competition for economic resources on the marriage market, but this is an interpretation, not a test. A second and related problem in empirical work is that many of the observed regularities and relationships can be attributed to all three types of causes, while little is yet known about the relative strengths of these factors. That more highly educated members of minority groups are less endogamous, for example, may be attributed to a universalistic attitude brought about by higher education, but can also be explained in terms of greater opportunities to meet outgroup members. In a similar fashion, residential segregation may foster endogamy by lowering opportunities, but its effect may also be explained by different socialization practices in segregated areas.

While it is clear that progress can be made in integrating theoretical and empirical work, this is not a straightforward task either. One possible solution is to shift the focus from the aggregate to the individual level. In the past, most studies have compared countries, groups, or time periods, but few studies have analyzed individual differences in intermarriage. The main advantage of an individual approach is that it facilitates the inclusion of a range of covariates for each of the three elements of the theory. For example, one can focus on socialization practices and characteristics of the parental home to test hypotheses about third-party control. One can also include sex-role attitudes or expectations regarding paid and domestic labor later in life to examine the role of preferences. Finally, one can include contextual variables, such as characteristics of the settings in which young adults are embedded (schools, workplaces, neighborhoods) to assess the effects of local marriage markets on intermarriage.

While an individual design would facilitate the multivariate analyses that are needed to test hypotheses more directly and to compare the strength of alternative explanations, such a design has its problems as well. Because multivariate analyses of marriage choices use individuals as the unit of analysis, they provide a one-sided view of marriage. It takes two to marry, and for that reason most authors have used loglinear or harmonic mean models. Such models correctly use marriages as the unit of analysis, rather than individuals, but make it difficult to include multiple covariates in the model. From a methodological point of view, such models are preferable, but if the prime concern is to test theories, their advantage is not so obvious.

Literature Cited

Alba RD. 1976. Social assimilation among American Catholic national-origin groups. *Am. Sociol. Rev.* 41:1030–46

Alba RD, Golden RM. 1986. Patterns of ethnic marriage in the United States. *Soc. Forces* 65:202–23

Anderson RN, Saenz R. 1994. Structural determinants of Mexican American intermarriage, 1975–1980. *Soc. Sci. Q.* 75: 414–30

Blau PM, Blum TC, Schwartz JE. 1982. Heterogeneity and intermarriage. *Am. Sociol. Rev.* 47:45–62

Blau PM, Duncan OD. 1967. *The American Occupational Structure.* New York: Wiley

Blau PM, Schwartz JE. 1984. *Crosscutting Social Circles.* London: Academic

Blossfeld H-P, Timm A. 1997. Der Einfluß des Bildungssystems auf den Heiratsmarkt: ein längsschnittanalyse der Wahl von Heiratspartnerern im Lebenslaub. *Kölner Z. Soziol. Sozialpsychol.* 49:440–76

Bozon M, Heran F. 1989. Finding a spouse: a survey of how French couples meet. *Population* 44:91–121

Byrne D. 1971. *The Attraction Paradigm.* New York: Academic

Davis FJ. 1991. *Who Is Black? One Nation's Definition.* University Park: Penn. State Univ. Press

Davis K. 1941. Intermarriage in caste societies. *Am. Anthropol.* 43:388–95

Davis K. 1984. Wives and work: consequences of the sex-role revolution. *Popul. Dev. Rev.* 10:397–417

DiMaggio P, Mohr J. 1985. Cultural capital, educational attainment, and marital selection. *Am. J. Sociol.* 90:1231–61

Drachsler J. 1920. *Democracy and Assimilation: The Blending of Immigrant Heritages in America.* New York: Macmillan

Eschbach K. 1995. The enduring and vanishing American Indian: American Indian population growth and intermarriage in 1990. *Ethn. Racial Stud.* 18:89–108

Forsé M, Chauvel L. 1995. L'évolution de l'homogamie en France. *Rev. Fr. Sociol.* 36:123–42

Gilbertson GA, Fitzpatrick JP, Lijun Y. 1996. Hispanic intermarriage in New York City:

new evidence from 1991. *Int. Migr. Rev.* 30:445–59

Glass D. 1954. *Social Mobility in Britain.* London: Routledge & Kegan Paul

Glenn ND. 1982. Interreligious marriage in the United States: patterns and recent trends. *J. Marriage Fam.* 44:555–66

Gordon MM. 1964. *Assimilation in American Life.* New York: Oxford Univ. Press

Gurak DT, Fitzpatrick JP. 1982. Intermarriage among Hispanic groups in New York City. *Am. J. Sociol.* 87:921–34

Hayes BC. 1991. Religious identification and marriage patterns in Australia. *J. Sci. Study Relig.* 30:469–78

Hayes BC. 1993. Occupational homogamy within Northern Ireland and the Republic of Ireland: a loglinear analysis. *Int. J. Sociol. Soc. Policy* 13:99–117

Hendrickx J. 1994. *The analysis of religious assortative mating: an application of design techniques for categorical models.* PhD thesis. Nijmegen Univ., Netherlands. 312 pp.

Hendrickx J, Lammers J, Ultee WC. 1991. Religious assortative marriage in the Netherlands, 1938–1983. *Rev. Relig. Res.* 33: 123–45

Hendrickx J, Schreuder O, Ultee WC. 1994. Die konfessionelle Mischehe in Deutschland (1901–1986) und den Niederlanden (1914–1986). *Kölner Z. Soziol. Sozialpsychol.* 46:619–45

Hout M. 1982. The association between husbands' and wives' occupations in two-earner families. *Am. J. Sociol.* 88:397–409

Hwang SS, Saenz R, Aguirre BE. 1994. Structural and individual determinants of outmarriage among Chinese, Filipino, and Japanese Americans in California. *Sociol. Inq.* 64:396–414

Hwang SS, Saenz R, Aguirre BE. 1995. The SES-selectivity of interracially married Asians. *Int. Migr. Rev.* 29:469–91

Jacobs JJ, Furstenberg FF. 1986. Changing places, conjugal careers, and women's marital mobility. *Soc. Forces* 64:714–32

Jiobu RM. 1988. *Ethnicity and Assimilation.* Albany: State Univ. NY Press

Johnson RA. 1980. *Religious Assortative Marriage in the United States.* New York: Academic

Jones FL. 1987. Marriage patterns and the stratification system: trends in educational homogamy since the 1930s. *Aust. NZ J. Sociol.* 23:185–98

Jones FL, Davis P. 1988. Class structuration and patterns of social closure in Australia and New Zealand. *Sociology* 22:271–91

Jones FL, Luijkx R. 1996. Post-war patterns of intermarriage in Australia: the Mediterranean experience. *Eur. Sociol. Rev.* 12: 67–86

Kalmijn M. 1991a. Status homogamy in the United States. *Am. J. Sociol.* 97:496–523

Kalmijn M. 1991b. Shifting boundaries: trends in religious and educational homogamy. *Am. Sociol. Rev.* 56:786–800

Kalmijn M. 1993a. Spouse selection among the children of European immigrants: a comparison of marriage cohorts in the 1960 census. *Int. Migr. Rev.* 27:51–78

Kalmijn M. 1993b. Trends in black/white intermarriage. *Soc. Forces* 72:119–46

Kalmijn M. 1994. Assortative mating by cultural and economic occupational status. *Am. J. Sociol.* 100:422–52

Kennedy RJR. 1944. Single or triple melting pot? Intermarriage trends in New Haven, 1870–1940. *Am. J. Sociol.* 49:331–39

Klein T, Wunder E. 1996. Regionale Disparitaten und Konfessionswechsel als Ursache konfessioneller Homogamie. *Kölner Z. Soziol. Sozialpsychol.* 48:96–125

Kosmin BA, Goldstein S, Waksberg J, Lerer N, Keysar A, Scheckner J. 1991. *Highlights of the 1990 National Jewish Population Survey.* New York: Counc. Jewish Fed.

Lazerwitz B. 1995. Jewish-Christian marriages and conversions, 1971 and 1990. *Sociol. Relig.* 56:433–43

Lee SM, Yamanaka K. 1990. Patterns of Asian American intermarriage and marital assimilation. *J. Comp. Fam. Stud.* 21: 287–305

Lieberson S. 1980. *A Piece of the Pie: Blacks and White Immigrants Since 1880.* Berkeley: Univ. Calif. Press

Lieberson S, Waters MC. 1988. *From Many Strands: Ethnic and Racial Groups in Contemporary America.* New York: Russell Sage Found.

Mare RD. 1991. Five decades of educational assortative mating. *Am. Sociol. Rev.* 56: 15–32

McCutcheon AL. 1988. Denominations and religious intermarriage: trends among white Americans in the twentieth century. *Rev. Relig. Res.* 29:213–27

Merton RK. 1941. Intermarriage and the social structure. *Psychiatry* 4:361–74

Morgan BS. 1981. A contribution to the debate on homogamy, propinquity, and segregation. *J. Marriage Fam.* 43:909–21

Murstein BI. 1976. *Who Will Marry Whom: Theories and Research in Marital Choice.* New York: Springer

Pagnini DL, Morgan PS. 1990. Intermarriage and social distance among U.S. immigrants at the turn of the century. *Am. J. Sociol.* 96:405–32

Peach C. 1974. Homogamy, propinquity, and segregation: a re-evaluation. *Am. Sociol. Rev.* 39:636–41

Qian Z. 1997. Breaking the racial barriers: variations in interracial marriage between 1980 and 1990. *Demography* 34:263–76

Ramsøy NR. 1966. Assortative mating and the structure of cities. *Am. Sociol. Rev.* 31: 773–86

Sandefur GD, McKinnell T. 1986. American Indian intermarriage. *Soc. Sci. Res.* 15: 347–71

Schoen R. 1988. *Modeling Multigroup Populations*. New York: Plenum

Schoen R, Thomas B. 1989. Intergroup marriage in Hawaii, 1969–1971 and 1979–1981. *Sociol. Perspect.* 32:365–82

Schoen R, Thomas B. 1990. Religious intermarriage in Switzerland, 1969–72 and 1979–82. *Eur. J. Popul.* 6:359–76

Schoen R, Wooldredge J. 1989. Marriage choices in North Carolina and Virginia, 1969–71 and 1979–81. *J. Marriage Fam.* 51:465–81

Smits J, Ultee W, Lammers J. 1998. Educational homogamy in 65 countries: the explanation of differences in openness with country-level explanatory variables. *Am. Sociol. Rev.* In press

Snipp CM. 1989. *American Judians: the first of this land.* New York: Russell Sage

Stevens G, Owens D, Schaefer EC. 1990. Education and attractiveness in marriage choices. *Soc. Psychol. Q.* 53:62–70

Sung BL. 1990. Chinese American intermarriage. *J. Comp. Fam. Stud.* 21:337–52

Sweet JA, Bumpass LL. 1987. *American Families and Households*. New York: Russell Sage

Taylor PA, Glenn ND. 1976. The utility of education and attractiveness for females' status attainment through marriage. *Am. Sociol. Rev.* 41:484–98

Ultee WC, Luijkx R. 1990. Educational heterogamy and father to son occupational mobility in 23 industrial nations: general societal openness or compensatory strategies of reproduction? *Eur. Sociol. Rev.* 6: 125–49

US Bureau of the Census. 1985. Marital characteristics. 1980 Census of Population, Subject Report, PC80-2-4C. Washington, DC: US Gov. Printing Off.

Uunk WJG. 1996. *Who marries whom? The role of social origins, education and high culture in mate selection of industrial societies during the twentieth century.* PhD thesis. Nijmegen Univ., Netherlands. 181 pp.

Uunk WJG, Ganzeboom HBG, Róbert P. 1996. Bivariate and multivariate scaled association models: an application to homogamy of social origin and education in Hungary between 1930 and 1979. *Qual. Quant.* 30:323–43

Uunk WJG, Kalmijn M. 1996. Wie trouwt met wie binnen de opleidingselite: de invloed van studierichting en onderwijsniveau. *Sociol. Gids* 43:183–200

Warren BL. 1966. A multiple variable approach to the assortative mating phenomenon. *Eugen. Q.* 13:285–90

Winch RF. 1958. *Mate Selection: A Study of Complementary Needs.* New York: Harper

Wirth L, Goldhamer H. 1944. The hybrid and the problem of miscegenation. In *Characteristics of the American Negro*, ed. O Klineberg, pp. 251–369. New York: Harper

Wong MG. 1989. A look at intermarriage among the Chinese in the United States in 1980. *Sociol. Perspect.* 32:87–107

Annu. Rev. Sociol. 1998. 24:423–52

ETHNIC AND NATIONALIST VIOLENCE

Rogers Brubaker
Department of Sociology, University of California, Los Angeles, 264 Haines Hall, Los Angeles, California 90095-1551; e-mail: brubaker@soc.ucla.edu

David D. Laitin
Department of Political Science, University of Chicago, 5828 S. University Avenue, Chicago, IL 60637; e-mail: d-laitin@uchicago.edu

KEY WORDS: ethnicity, nationalism, conflict

ABSTRACT

Work on ethnic and nationalist violence has emerged from two largely non-intersecting literatures: studies of ethnic conflict and studies of political violence. Only recently have the former begun to attend to the dynamics of violence and the latter to the dynamics of ethnicization. Since the emergent literature on ethnic violence is not structured by clearly defined theoretical oppositions, we organize our review by broad similarities of methodological approach: (*a*) Inductive work at various levels of aggregation seeks to identify the patterns, mechanisms, and recurrent processes implicated in ethnic violence. (*b*) Theory-driven work employs models of rational action drawn from international relations theory, game theory, and general rational action theory. (*c*) Culturalist work highlights the discursive, symbolic, and ritualistic aspects of ethnic violence. We conclude with a plea for the disaggregated analysis of the heterogeneous phenomena we too casually lump together as "ethnic violence."

INTRODUCTION

The bloody dissolution of Yugoslavia, intermittently violent ethnonational conflicts on the southern periphery of the former Soviet Union, the ghastly

0360-0572/9X/0815-0423$08.00

butchery in Rwanda, and Hindu-Muslim riots in parts of India, among other dispiriting events, have focused renewed public attention in recent years on ethnic and nationalist violence as a striking symptom of the "new world disorder."

To be sure, measured against the universe of possible instances, actual instances of ethnic and nationalist violence remain rare. This crucial point is obscured in the literature, much of which samples on the dependent variable (Fearon & Laitin 1996) or metaphorically mischaracterizes vast regions (such as post-communist Eastern Europe and Eurasia in its entirety or all of sub-Saharan Africa) as a seething cauldron on the verge of boiling over or as a tinderbox, which a single careless spark could ignite into an inferno of ethnonational violence (Bowen 1996, Brubaker 1998). Ethnic violence warrants our attention because it is appalling, not because it is ubiquitous.

Nonetheless, although measurement and coding problems prevent confident calculations, two general features of the late modern, post–Cold War world—in addition to the particular traumas of state collapse in the Soviet and Yugoslav cases—have probably contributed to a recent increase in the incidence of ethnic and nationalist violence and have certainly contributed to an increase in the share of ethnic and nationalist violence in all political violence—that is, to what might be called the ethnicization of political violence. The first could be called "the decay of the Weberian state": the decline (uneven, to be sure) in states' capacities to maintain order by monopolizing the legitimate use of violence in their territories and the emergence in some regions—most strikingly in sub-Saharan Africa—of so-called quasi-states (Jackson 1990, Jackson & Rosberg 1982), organizations formally acknowledged and recognized as states yet lacking (or possessing only in small degree) the empirical attributes of stateness.

The end of the Cold War has further weakened many third world states as superpowers have curtailed their commitments of military and other state-strengthening resources, while the citizenries—and even, it could be argued, the neighbors—of Soviet successor states are more threatened by state weakness than by state strength (Holmes 1997). Such weakly Weberian states or quasi-states are more susceptible to—and are by definition less capable of repressing, though not, alas, of committing—violence of all kinds, including ethnic violence (Desjarlais & Kleinman 1994). Meanwhile, the stronger states of the West are increasingly reluctant to use military force—especially unilaterally, without a broad consensus among allied states—to intervene in conflicts outside their boundaries (Haas 1997). As a result, weakly Weberian third world states can no longer rely on an external patron to maintain peace as they could during the Cold War era.

The second contextual aspect of the post–Cold War world to highlight is the eclipse of the left-right ideological axis that has defined the grand lines of much political conflict—and many civil wars—since the French Revolution. From the 1950s through the early 1980s, violence-wielding opponents of existing regimes could best mobilize resources—money, weapons, and political and logistical support—by framing their opposition to incumbents in the language of the grand ideological confrontation between capitalism and communism. Incumbents mobilized resources in the same way. Today, these incentives to frame conflicts in grand ideological terms have disappeared. Even without direct positive incentives to frame conflicts in ethnic terms, this has led to a marked ethnicization of violent challenger-incumbent contests as the major non-ethnic framing for such contests has become less plausible and profitable.

Moreover, there may be positive incentives to frame such contests in ethnic terms. With the increasing significance worldwide of diasporic social formations (Clifford 1994, Appadurai 1997), for example, both challengers and incumbents may increasingly seek resources from dispersed transborder ethnic kin (Tambiah 1986, Anderson 1992). And a thickening web of international and nongovernmental organizations has provided greater international legitimacy, visibility, and support for ethnic group claims (normatively buttressed by culturalist extensions and transformations of the initially strongly individualist human rights language that prevailed in the decades immediately following World War II). This institutional and normative transformation at the level of what Meyer (1987) calls the "world polity" provides a further incentive for the ethnic framing of challenges to incumbent regimes. To foreshadow a theme we underscore later: Ethnicity is not the ultimate, irreducible source of violent conflict in such cases. Rather, conflicts driven by struggles for power between challengers and incumbents are newly ethnicized, newly framed in ethnic terms.

Ethnicity, Violence, and Ethnic Violence

Attempts to theorize ethnic and nationalist violence have grown from the soil of two largely nonintersecting literatures: studies of ethnicity, ethnic conflict, and nationalism on the one hand, and studies of collective or political violence on the other. Within each of these large and loosely integrated literatures, ethnic and nationalist violence has only recently become a distinct subject of inquiry in its own right.

In the study of ethnicity, ethnic conflict, and nationalism, accounts of *conflict* have not been distinguished sharply from accounts of *violence*. Violence has generally been conceptualized—if only tacitly—as a *degree* of conflict rather than as a *form* of conflict, or indeed as a form of social or political action in its own right. Most discussions of violence in the former Yugoslavia, for example, are embedded in richly contextual narratives of the breakup of the state

(Glenny 1992, Cohen 1993, Woodward 1995). Violence as such has seldom been made an explicit and sustained theoretical or analytical focus in studies of ethnic conflict [though this has begun to change with Lemarchand's (1996) work on Burundi, and Tambiah's (1996), Brass's (1997) and Horowitz's (forthcoming) work on ethnic riots].

In the study of collective or political violence, on the other hand, ethnicity figured (until recently) only incidentally and peripherally. In a number of influential studies (e.g. Gurr 1970, Tilly 1978) ethnicity figured scarcely at all. Revealingly, Gurr used the general term "dissidents" to describe nongovernmental participants in civil strife. Although the empirical significance of ethnicity was recognized, its theoretical significance was seldom addressed explicitly; it was as if there was nothing analytically distinctive about ethnic (or ethnically conditioned or framed) violence. Ethnicity thus remained theoretically exogenous rather than being integrated into key analytical or theoretical concepts.

In recent years, to be sure, a pronounced "ethnic turn" has occurred in the study of political violence, paralleling the ethnic turn in international relations, security studies, and other precincts of the post–Cold War academic world. But this sudden turn to ethnicity and nationality too often has been external and mechanical (Brubaker 1998). Although ethnicity now occupies a central place in the study of collective and political violence, it remains a "foreign body" deriving from other theoretical traditions. It has yet to be theoretically digested, or theorized in a subtle or sophisticated manner.

This suggests two opportunities for theoretical advance today—and in fact significant work is beginning to emerge in these areas. On the one hand, it is important to take violence as such more seriously in studies of ethnic and nationalist conflict. It is important, that is, to ask specific questions about, and seek specific explanations for, the occurrence—and nonoccurrence (Fearon & Laitin 1996)—of violence in conflictual situations. These questions and explanations should be distinguished from questions and explanations of the existence, and even the intensity, of conflict. We lack strong evidence showing that higher levels of conflict (measured independently of violence) lead to higher levels of violence. Even where violence is clearly rooted in preexisting conflict, it should not be treated as a natural, self-explanatory outgrowth of such conflict, something that occurs automatically when the conflict reaches a certain intensity, a certain "temperature." Violence is not a quantitative degree of conflict but a qualitative form of conflict, with its own dynamics. The shift from nonviolent to violent modes of conflict is a phase shift (Williams 1994:62, Tambiah 1996:292) that requires particular theoretical attention.

The study of violence should be emancipated from the study of conflict and treated as an autonomous phenomenon in its own right. For example, to the extent that ethnic entrepreneurs recruit young men who are already inclined toward or practiced in other forms of violence, and help bestow meaning on that violence and honor and social status on its perpetrators, we may have as much to learn about the sources and dynamics of ethnic violence from the literature on criminology (Katz 1988) as from the literature on ethnicity or ethnic conflict.

At the same time, the strand of the literature that grows out of work on political violence and collective violence should take ethnicity and nationality more seriously. This does not mean paying more attention to them; as noted above, there has already been a pronounced ethnic turn in the study of political violence and collective violence. *That* political violence can be ethnic is well established, indeed too well established; *how* it is ethnic remains obscure. The most fundamental questions—for example, how the adjective "ethnic" modifies the noun "violence"—remain unclear and largely unexamined. Sustained attention needs to be paid to the forms and dynamics of ethnicization, to the many and subtle ways in which violence—and conditions, processes, activities, and narratives linked to violence—can take on ethnic hues.

Defining the Domain

In reviewing emerging work in anthropology, political science, and to a lesser extent other disciplines as well as sociology, we immediately face the problem that there is no clearly demarcated field or subfield of social scientific inquiry addressing ethnic and nationalist violence, no well-defined body of literature on the subject, no agreed-upon set of key questions or problems, no established research programs (or set of competing research programs). The problem is not that there is no agreement on *how* things are to be explained; it is that there is no agreement on *what* is to be explained, or *whether* there is a single set of phenomena to be explained. Rather than confronting competing theories or explanations, we confront alternative ways of posing questions, alternative approaches to or "takes" on ethnic and nationalist violence, alternative ways of conceptualizing the phenomenon and of situating it in the context of wider theoretical debates. In consequence, this review specifies the contours and attempts a critical assessment of an emergent rather than a fully formed literature.

What are we talking about when we talk about ethnic or nationalist violence? The answer is by no means obvious. First, despite its seemingly palpable core, violence is itself an ambiguous and elastic concept (Tilly 1978:174), shading over from the direct use of force to cause bodily harm through the compelling or inducing of actions by direct threat of such force to partly or fully metaphorical notions of cultural or symbolic violence (Bourdieu & Wacquant 1992:167–74). But the difficulties and ambiguities involved in characterizing or classifying violence (which we shall understand here in a narrow sense) as ethnic or nationalist[1] are even greater. Although these difficulties have yet to receive—and cannot receive here—the full exploration they deserve, a few summary points can be made:

1. The coding of past, present, or feared future violence as ethnic is not only an analytical but a practical matter. Violence is regularly accompanied by social struggles to define its meaning and specify its causes, the outcome of which—for example, the labeling of an event as a pogrom, a riot, or a rebellion—may have important consequences (Brass 1996b).
2. Coding practices are influenced heavily by prevailing interpretive frames. Today, the ethnic frame is immediately and widely available and legitimate; it imposes itself on, or at least suggests itself to, actors and analysts alike. This generates a coding bias in the ethnic direction. A generation ago, the coding bias was in the opposite direction. Today, we—again, actors and analysts alike—are no longer blind *to* ethnicity, but we may be blinded *by* it. Our ethnic bias in framing may lead us to overestimate the incidence of ethnic violence by unjustifiably seeing ethnicity at work everywhere and thereby artifactually multiplying instances of "ethnic violence" (Bowen 1996). More soberingly, since coding or framing is partly constitutive of the phenomenon of ethnic violence, not simply an external way of registering and coming to terms with it intellectually, our coding bias may actually increase the incidence (and not simply the perceived incidence) of ethnic violence.
3. With these caveats in mind, we define ethnic violence on first approximation as violence perpetrated across ethnic lines, in which at least one party is not a state (or a representative of a state), and in which the putative ethnic difference is coded—by perpetrators, targets, influential third parties, or analysts—as having been integral rather than incidental to the violence, that is, in which the violence is coded as having been meaningfully oriented in some way to the different ethnicity of the target.

This preliminary definition allows us to exclude the violence between Germans and Frenchmen on the Marne in 1914. Similarly, it allows us to exclude the assassination of Robert F. Kennedy, since the shooting was not interpreted in ethnoreligious terms as a Catholic being shot by a Muslim. But the definition hardly allows us to define a focused domain of research. A great profusion of work—only a small fraction of which is engaged by most contemporary analysts of ethnic violence—is related in one way or another to ethnic vio-

[1]To avoid cumbersome repetition, we refer simply to "ethnic" rather than to "ethnic or nationalist." But we understand "ethnic" broadly as including "nationalist" (insofar as this latter term designates ethnic or ethnocultural forms of nationalism, as opposed to purely "civic" or state-centered forms of nationalism).

lence. The range and heterogeneity of this work compel us to be highly selective in our review. We have had to exclude many pertinent literatures, or at best touch on them only in passing. These include literatures on pogroms (Klier & Lambroza 1992) and genocides (Dobkowski & Wallimann 1992); on antisemitism (Langmuir 1990), Nazism (Burleigh & Wippermann 1991), fascism, and the radical right (Rogger & Weber 1965); on racial violence (Horowitz 1983), race riots (Grimshaw 1969), and policing in racially or ethnically mixed settings (Keith 1993); on slavery (Blackburn 1997), colonialism (Cooper & Stoler 1997), third-world nationalist revolutions (Chaliand 1977, Goldstone et al 1991), and state formation [especially in contexts of encounters with aboriginal populations (Bodley 1982, Ferguson & Whitehead 1992)]; on separatism (Heraclides 1990), irredentism (Horowitz 1991b), and the formation of new nation-states (Brubaker 1996); on xenophobia and anti-immigrant violence (Björgo & Witte 1993), "ethnic unmixing" (Brubaker 1995, Hayden 1996), forced migration (Marrus 1985), and refugee flows (Zolberg et al 1989); on religious violence (Davis 1973); on terrorism (Stohl 1983, Waldmann 1992), paramilitary formations (Fairbanks 1995), and state violence (van den Berghe 1990, Nagengast 1994); on conflict management (Azar & Burton 1986) and peace studies (Väyrynen et al 1987); on the phenomenology or experiential dimensions of violence (Nordstrom & Martin 1992); and on rage (Scheff & Retzinger 1991), humiliation (Miller 1993), fear (Green 1994), and other emotions and psychological mechanisms (e.g. projection, displacement, identification) implicated in ethnic and nationalist violence (Volkan 1991, Kakar 1990).[2] Clearly, this would be an unmanageable set of literatures to survey. Moreover, most of these are well-established, specialized literatures addressing particular historical forms and settings of ethnic or nationalist violence, whereas we have interpreted our task as that of bringing into focus a newly emerging literature addressing ethnic violence as such. For different reasons, we neglect the theoretically impoverished policy-oriented literature on conflict management, and for lack of professional competence, we neglect the psychological literature.

Since the emerging literature we survey is not structured around clearly defined theoretical oppositions, we organize our review not by theoretical position but by broad similarities of approach. We begin by considering a variety of inductive analyses of ethnic and nationalist violence that build on statistical analysis of large data sets, on the extraction of patterns from sets of broadly similar cases, on controlled comparisons, and on case studies. We next consider clusters of theory-driven work on ethnic violence deriving from the realist

[2]Citations here are merely illustrative; we have tried to cite relatively recent, wide-ranging, or otherwise exemplary works, in which ample citations to further pertinent literature can be found.

tradition in international relations, from game theory, and from rational choice theory. We conclude by examining culturalist analyses of ethnic violence.

We recognize the awkwardness of this organizing scheme. It is logically unsatisfactory, combining methodological and substantive criteria. It lumps theoretically and methodologically heterogeneous work under the loose rubric "inductive." It risks implying, incorrectly, that inductive work is not theoretically informed, and that culturalist approaches are neither inductive nor theory driven. We nonetheless adopt this scheme in an effort to mirror as best we can the emerging clusters of work.

INDUCTIVE APPROACHES

Without questioning the truism that all research—and all phases of research (including data collection)—is theoretically informed, we can characterize the work grouped under this heading as primarily data-driven rather than theory-driven. This work seeks to identify the regularities, patterns, mechanisms, and recurrent processes comprising the structure and texture of ethnic violence in inductive fashion through the systematic analysis of empirical data. The data in question range from large sets of highly aggregated data through small-*n* comparisons to single case studies. Methods of analysis range from statistical analysis and causal modeling to qualitative interpretation. We organize our discussion by level of aggregation.

Large Data Sets

Gurr has been a leading figure in the study of political violence for three decades and a pioneer in the statistical analysis of large data sets in this domain (1968). His first major work (1970) outlined an "integrated theory of political violence" as the product of the politicization and activation of discontent arising from relative deprivation. Although ethnicity played no role in his early work, it has become central to his recent work (1993a, 1993b, 1994, Harff & Gurr 1989, Gurr & Harff 1994). This work has been built on a large-scale data set surveying 233 "minorities at risk" that have (*a*) suffered (or benefited from) economic or political discrimination and/or (*b*) mobilized politically in defense of collective interests since 1945. For each of these "nonstate communal groups"—classified as ethnonationalists, indigenous peoples, ethnoclasses, militant sects, and communal contenders—Gurr and associates have assembled and coded on ordinal scales a wide array of data on background characteristics (such as group coherence and concentration), intergroup differentials and discrimination, and group grievances and collective action. They then seek to explain forms and magnitudes of nonviolent protest, violent protest, and rebellion through an eclectic synthesis of grievance and mobilization variables.

This work sensitizes us to the sharply differing dynamics, configurations, and magnitudes of ethnic violence across regions. This comparative perspective is crucial, since violence in Northern Ireland or in the Basque region, while unsettling in the context of post–World War II Europe, can be placed in more benign perspective when compared to Burundi, Rwanda, Sri Lanka, or post–Cold War Bosnia, where killing is measured not in the hundreds and thousands but in the tens or even hundreds of thousands (Heisler 1990). The standardized data set built by Gurr and associates gives us little reason to believe that the processes and mechanisms generating violence in Northern Ireland are the same as those that drive the violence in Sri Lanka. It is not even clear, as we shall suggest in the conclusion, that these are both instances of the same thing (i.e. ethnic violence).

If for Gurr the unit of analysis is the group, for Olzak (1992), Tarrow (1994), and Beissinger (1998), the unit is the event. Assembling data on ethnic and racial confrontations and protests in the United States in the late nineteenth and early twentieth century, Olzak uses event history analysis and ecological theories of competition and niche overlap to show that the breakdown of ethnic and racial segregation, by increasing economic and political competition, triggers exclusionary collective action, including ethnic and racial violence. Beissinger, constructing a database on violent collective events in the disintegrating Soviet Union and its incipient successor states, analyzes the highly clustered incidence of nationalist violence in the context of a larger cycle of nationalist contention. He shows that nationalist struggles turned increasingly violent (and increasingly assumed the form of sustained armed conflict) late in the mobilizational cycle, in connection with the contestation of republican (and incipient state) borders at a moment when effective authority (to the extent it existed at all) was passing from the collapsing center to the incipient successor states. In part, Beissinger echoes the findings of Tarrow (1994, Della Porta & Tarrow 1986) concerning the tendency for violence in Italy to occur toward the end of a mobilizational cycle. Although not directly concerned with ethnicity, Tarrow's work—notably his finding that violence does not map directly onto protest—has implications for the study of ethnic violence. In Italy, violence appears to increase when organized protest weakens. As mobilization wanes, violence is practiced by splinter groups as the only way to cause disruption. Although the dynamics of the two cases differ, both Beissinger and Tarrow analyze violence as a phase in a mobilizational cycle rather than as a natural expression of social conflict or social protest.

Case-Based Pattern Finding

For the analysis of ethnic conflict and violence in postcolonial Africa and Asia, Horowitz (1985) remains the classic text. Seeking to extract patterns from sets of broadly comparable cases, he stresses the social psychological and cognitive underpinnings as well as the richly elaborated symbolic dimensions of violent ethnic conflict, giving particular emphasis to comparative, anxiety-laden judgments of group worth and competing claims to group legitimacy.[3] At the same time, Horowitz has given systematic attention to the effects of institutions—notably electoral systems, armed forces, and federalist arrangements—in fostering or preventing violent ethnic conflict (1985:Parts 3–5, 1991c). His arguments concerning institutional design—notably the design of electoral systems—in the context of post-apartheid South Africa (1991a) have led to a lively debate with Lijphart (1990).

More recently, Horowitz (forthcoming) has returned to an earlier (1973, 1983) concern with ethnic riots. He analyzes the morphology and dynamics of the "deadly ethnic riot," building inductively from detailed reports on a hundred riots, mainly since 1965, in some 40 postcolonial countries. Arguing for a disaggregated approach to ethnic violence, Horowitz distinguishes the deadly ethnic riot—defined as mass civilian intergroup violence in which victims are chosen by their group membership—from other forms of ethnic (or more or less ethnicized) violence such as genocide, lynchings, gang assault, violent protest, feuds, terrorism, and internal warfare. The deadly ethnic riot is marked by highly uneven clustering in time and space, relatively spontaneous character (though not without elements of organization and planning), careful selection of victims by their categorical identity, passionate expression of intergroup antipathies, and seemingly gratuitous mutilation of victims.

Using broadly similar inductive approaches, other scholars have addressed ethnic riots in recent years, chiefly in the South Asian context (Freitag 1989; Das 1990a; Spencer 1990; Pandey 1992; Jaffrelot 1994; Brass 1996a, 1997). The most sustained contribution in this genre is Tambiah's (1996) richly textured, multilayered account. While distancing himself from a simplistic instrumentalist interpretation of ethnic riots as the joint product of political manipulation and organized thuggery, Tambiah devotes considerable attention to the routinization and ritualization of violence, to the "organized, anticipated, programmed, and recurring features and phases of seemingly spontaneous, chaotic, and orgiastic actions" (p. 230), the cultural repertory and social infrastructure [what Brass (1996b:12) calls "institutionalized riot systems"] through which riots are accomplished. At the same time, however, reworking Le Bon, Canetti, and Durkheim, Tambiah seeks to theorize the social psychological dynamics of volatile crowd behavior.

Other works in the pattern-finding mode address not particular forms of ethnic violence (such as the deadly ethnic riot) in their entirety but rather (like

[3]Working within a broadly similar theoretical tradition, Petersen (1998) argues that structurally induced resentment, linking individual emotion and group status, best accounts for ethnic violence in a broad range of East European cases.

Horowitz 1985) general mechanisms and processes that are implicated in ethnic violence. As Blalock (1989) notes in a different context, such mechanisms and processes, although not the immediate or underlying cause of violent conflicts, do causally shape their incidence and modalities. Here we restrict our attention to one class of such mechanisms and processes (albeit a large and important one): to the ways in which *inter*-ethnic violence is conditioned and fostered by *intra*-ethnic processes.[4]

One such mechanism involves in-group policing. As analyzed by Laitin (1995a), this involves the formal or informal administration of sanctions, even violent sanctions, within a group so as to enforce a certain line of action vis-à-vis outsiders (who may be defined not only in ethnic terms but in religious, ideological, class, or any other terms). Practices such as "necklacing" in South African townships, "kneecapping" by the IRA, the execution of Palestinians alleged to have sold land to Israelis, and the killing of alleged "collaborators" in many other settings have attracted notoriety as techniques used by ethnonationalist radicals to maintain control over in-group followers. Pfaffenberger (1994), for example, shows how members of the dominant Tamil separatist group in Sri Lanka, the Liberation Tigers, have prevented young male Tamils from leaving Jaffna and murdered leaders of rival Tamil groups, dissidents within their own ranks, and civilian Tamils suspected of helping the Sinhalese.

A second intragroup mechanism—and a classical theme in the sociology of conflict (Simmel 1955, Coser 1956)—involves the deliberate staging, instigation, provocation, dramatization, or intensification of violent or potentially violent confrontations with outsiders. Such instigative and provocative actions are ordinarily undertaken by vulnerable incumbents seeking to deflect within-group challenges to their position by redefining the fundamental lines of conflict as inter- rather than (as challengers would have it) intragroup; but they may also be undertaken by challengers seeking to discredit incumbents.

Gagnon's (1994/1995) analysis of the role of intra-Serbian struggles in driving the bloody breakup of Yugoslavia is the most theoretically explicit recent contribution along these lines. Gagnon argues that a conservative coalition of party leaders, local and regional elites, nationalist intellectuals, and segments of the military leadership, threatened in the mid-1980s by economic crisis and strong demands for market-oriented and democratic reforms, provoked violent ethnic confrontation—first in Kosovo and then, more fatefully, in the Serb-inhabited borderland regions of Croatia—in a successful attempt to define ethnicity (specifically the alleged threat to Serb ethnicity) as the most

[4]General mechanisms may, of course, be specified in a deductive as well as an inductive manner. Although most of the work cited in the rest of this subsection is broadly inductive, we also cite here for reasons of convenience a few deductive works. Deductive theorizing about general mechanisms implicated in ethnic violence is considered in more sustained fashion in the next section.

pressing political issue and thereby to defeat reformist challengers and retain their grip on power. Although Gagnon's empirical analysis is one-sided in its exclusive focus on the Serbian leadership (partially similar points could be made about the Croatian leadership), his theoretical argument on the within-group sources of intergroup conflict is valuable. In a broader study of nationalism and democratization, Snyder (1998) argues that such strategies of provocation are particularly likely to occur, and to succeed, in newly democratizing but institutionally weak regimes. Other instances of such cultivated confrontations arising from intragroup dynamics are found in Deng's (1995) study of the Sudan and Prunier's (1995) study of Rwanda.

A third important intragroup mechanism is ethnic outbidding (Rabushka & Shepsle 1972, Rothschild 1981, Horowitz 1985:Chapter 8, Kaufman 1996). This can occur in a context of competitive electoral politics when two or more parties identified with the same ethnic group compete for support, neither (in particular electoral configurations) having an incentive to cultivate voters of other ethnicities, each seeking to demonstrate to their constituencies that it is more nationalistic than the other, and each seeking to protect itself from the other's charges that it is "soft" on ethnic issues. The outbidding can "o'erleap itself" into violent confrontations, dismantling the very democratic institutions that gave rise to the outbidding. This is a powerful mechanism (and a general one, not confined to *ethnic* outbidding). *How* it works is theoretically clear, and *that* it sometimes works to intensify conflict and generate violence was classically, and tragically, illustrated in Sri Lanka (Horowitz 1991c, Pfaffenberger 1994).

Yet outbidding does not always occur, and it does not always pay off as a political strategy when it is attempted. Contrary to many interpretations, Gagnon (1996) argues that the violent collapse of Yugoslavia had nothing to do with ethnic outbidding. In his account, Serbian elites instigated violent conflict, and framed it in terms of ethnic antagonism, not to mobilize but to demobilize the population, to forestall challenges to the regime. When they needed to appeal for public support during election campaigns, elites engaged not in ethnic outbidding but in "ethnic underbidding," striving to appear more moderate rather than more radical than their opponents on ethnic issues. Further work needs to be done (following Horowitz 1985) in specifying the conditions (e.g. different types of electoral systems) in which such outbidding is more or less likely to occur, and more or less likely to pay off.

A fourth intragroup mechanism concerns the dynamics of recruitment into gangs, terrorist groups, or guerrilla armies organized for ethnic violence. Although most ethnic leaders are well educated and from middle-class backgrounds, the rank-and-file members of such organizations are more often poorly educated and from lower or working class backgrounds (Waldmann 1985, 1989; Clark 1984). Considerable attention has been focused on the intergroup dynamics that favor recruitment into such organizations. For example, interviewing IRA members, White (1993:Chapter 4) finds that many working-class Catholics joined the IRA after experiencing violence in their neighborhoods at the hands of British security forces and loyalist paramilitaries. We have little systematic knowledge, however, about the social and psychological processes within groups that govern the recruitment of young men (and, much more rarely, women) into disciplined, ethnically organized violence-wielding groups—processes such as the distribution of honor, the promising and provision of material and symbolic rewards for martyrs, rituals of manhood, the shaming of those who would shun violence, intergenerational tensions that may lead the impetuous young to challenge overcautious elders, and so on.

"Small-N" Comparisons

Controlled comparisons have been relatively few, especially those comparing regions suffering from ethnic violence with regions in which similar ethnic conflicts have not issued in violence. The Basque/Catalan comparison is a natural in this respect and has been explored by Laitin (1995b), who focuses on linguistic tipping phenomena and the differential availability of recruits for guerrilla activity from rural social groups governed by norms of honor, and by Díez Medrano (1995), who focuses on the social bases of the nationalist movements. Varshney (1997) compares Indian cities that have similar proportions of Muslim and Hindu inhabitants and that share other background variables, yet have strikingly divergent outcomes in terms of communal violence. He argues that high levels of "civic engagement" between communal groups explain low levels of violence between Muslims and Hindus. Waldmann (1985, 1989) compares the violent ethnic conflicts in the Basque region and Northern Ireland to the (largely) nonviolent conflicts in Catalonia and Quebec, and explains the transition from nonviolent nationalist protest to violent conflict in the former cases in terms of the loss of middle-class control over the nationalist movement. Friedland and Hecht (1998) compare the violent conflicts for control of sacred places in Jerusalem and the Indian city of Ayodhya. In both cases, they show, struggles over religious rights at sacred centers claimed by two religions—Jews and Muslims in Jerusalem, Hindus and Muslims in Ayodhya—have been closely bound up with struggles to establish, extend, or reconfigure nation-states.The comparison of Rwanda and Burundi is compelling because of stunning violence in both cases despite quite different historical conditions. This comparison has not been analyzed systematically, but Lemarchand (1996) suggestively discusses the multiple ways in which the two cases have become intertwined. To be sure, the idea of controlling all relevant variables through a "natural experiment" is illusory. But Laitin (1995b) defends the exercise as worthwhile because it compels us to focus on specific processes under differing conditions, setting limits to overgeneralized theory.

Case Studies

In this domain as in others, "cases" continue to be identified generally with countries. Thus substantial literatures have formed around key cases such as Northern Ireland (McGarry & O'Leary 1995; Feldman 1991; Bruce 1992; Bell 1993; White 1993; Aretxaga 1993, 1995); Yugoslavia (Woodward 1995, Cohen 1993, Glenny 1992, Denich 1994, Gagnon 1994/1995); Sri Lanka (Kapferer 1988; Tambiah 1986; Kemper 1991; Pfaffenberger 1991, 1994; Spencer 1990; Sabaratnam 1990); and Rwanda and Burundi (Lemarchand 1996, Prunier 1995, Malkki 1995). The identification of case with country, however, is a matter of convention, not logic. Ethnic or nationalist violence in a country is treated as a case when the violence is portrayed as a single processual whole. If the violence is instead construed as a set of separate (though perhaps interdependent) instances, then it becomes a case set, suitable for controlled comparison or even for a large-*n* study. In Olzak's (1992) study of confrontations and protests, for example, the United States is not a case but the location for a large-*n* study of events. The breakup of Yugoslavia has most often been treated as a single complex interconnected case, but if we had adequately disaggregated data, it could be studied as a set of cases (for example, of recruitment to unofficial or quasi-official violence-wielding nationalist militias or gangs).

Most case studies are organized around a core argumentative line. In Woodward's 1995 analysis of Yugoslavia, for example, the cumulative effect of economic crisis, a weakening central state, and external powers' recognition of constituent "nations" that were incapable of acting like states created a security dilemma for minorities in the newly recognized states. For Deng (1995), the attempt by the North to identify the Sudanese nation as an Arab one could lead only to rebellion from the South, which had been enslaved by Arabs but never assimilated into an Arab culture. For Kapferer (1988), Sinhalese Buddhist myths and rituals—rooted in an embracing cosmology and "ingrained in the practices of everyday life" (p. 34)—provided a crucial cultural underpinning for a radically nationalizing Sinhalese political agenda and for anti-Tamil violence in Sri Lanka. In Prunier's 1995 analysis of Rwanda, an externally imposed ideology of sharp difference between Hutus and Tutsis, and postcolonial claims to exclusive control of the state on both sides of this colonially reified group difference, created a security dilemma favoring preemptive violence.

At the same time, authors of these and other case studies recognize that the explanatory lines they highlight are partial, and they consequently embed these arguments in richly contextualized narratives specifying a web of intertwined supporting, subsidiary, or qualifying arguments. As a result, one cannot evaluate these works on the same metric as one would the statistical or even the small-*n* studies. The rhetorical weight in case studies tends to be carried by the richness and density of texture; although a major argumentative line is almost always identifiable, the argument takes the form of a seamless web rather than a distinct set of explanatory propositions. Attempts to extract precise propositions from such case studies often reduce the original argument to the point of caricature. [5] However, close reading of such works can yield rich material on microsocial processes at low levels of aggregation that macro theories miss.

THEORY-DRIVEN RATIONAL ACTION APPROACHES

The main clusters of theory-driven work on ethnic violence have employed models of rational action, drawing in particular from the realist tradition in international relations, from game theory, and from rational choice theory in general.[6] Although "rational action" (or "strategy," the preferred term of international relations and game theory) is understood differently in these traditions (referring in international relations to the grand designs of states engaged in power politics, in game theory to the fully specified plan for playing a particular game, and in rational choice theory in general to individual action oriented to the maximization of subjective expected utility), ethnic violence in all three traditions is seen as a product of rational action (rather than emotion or irrationality), though structural background conditions are seen as crucially shaping the contexts of choice.

International Relations Approaches

International relations scholars of the realist school (Jervis 1978) posit the existence of a "security dilemma" under conditions of anarchy in which even nonaggressive moves to enhance one's security, perceived as threatening by others, trigger countermoves that ultimately reduce one's own security. While formulated to explain interstate wars, the security dilemma has been applied to intrastate ethnic violence as well.

A line of argument initiated by Posen (1993) focuses on the windows of opportunity—and vulnerability—occasioned by the collapse of central authority in multiethnic empires (see also Carment et al 1997). In such circumstances, especially given an historical record of serious intergroup hostilities (amplified and distorted, of course, in the retelling), groups are likely to view one another's nationalist mobilization as threatening. These perceived threats may create incentives for preemptive attack (or at least for countermobilization that will in turn be perceived as threatening by the other group, engendering a mo-

[5]Blalock (1989:14) notes the degradation of propositional conflict that typically occurs once case studies get taken up in the literature and involved in theoretical controversy.

[6]These clusters are not, of course, mutually exclusive. For example, Lake & Rothchild (1996) draw on elements from all three.

bilization spiral that can lead to violence, especially since violent action can be undertaken autonomously, under conditions of state breakdown, by small bands of radicals outside the control of the weak, fledgling successor states).

To be sure, the international relations perspective on ethnic violence has its weaknesses. Ethnic conflict differs sharply from interstate conflict (Laitin 1995c). States are distinct and sharply bounded entities [though to treat them as unitary actors, as international relations scholars commonly do (Van Evera 1994), is problematic (Mann 1993:Chapters 3, 21)]. In contrast, ethnic groups are not "given" entities with unambiguous rules of membership, as is well known from a generation of research (Barth 1967, Young 1965). Rarely is a single leader recognized as authoritatively entitled to speak in the name of the group. As a result, ethnic groups generally lack what states ordinarily possess, namely, a leader or leaders capable of negotiating and enforcing settlements (Paden 1990, Podolefsky 1990). Moreover, ethnic group membership is fluid and context-dependent. Relatively high rates of intermarriage (as in the former Yugoslavia) mean that many people, faced with interethnic violence, are not sure where they belong. Boundary-strengthening, group-making projects *within* ethnic groups are almost always central to violent conflicts *between* groups, but these crucial intragroup processes are obscured by international relations–inspired approaches that treat ethnic groups as unitary actors.

Game Theoretic Approaches

In examining ethnic violence, game theorists subsume the issue as part of a general theory of social order (Kandori 1992, Landa 1994). With specific reference to ethnic violence, however, game theorists seek to understand the rationale for the choice to use violence, assuming that violence will be costly to both sides in any conflict (Fearon 1995). They are not satisfied with theories, especially psychological ones (Tajfel 1978), that can account for conflict or mistrust but not for violence. Game theorists seek to provide a specific account of violence rather than accept it as an unexplained and unintended byproduct of tense ethnic conflicts.

There is no unitary or complete game theory of ethnic violence. Rather, game theorists have identified certain general mechanisms that help account for particular aspects of the problem of ethnic violence. Here we review game-theoretic accounts of three such mechanisms, associated with problems of credible commitments, asymmetric information, and intragroup dynamics, respectively.

Fearon (1994) has developed a model of the problem of credible commitments and ethnic violence. In this model, the problem arises in a newly independent state dominated by one ethnic group but containing at least one powerful minority group as well. The model focuses on the inability of an ethnicized state leadership to "credibly commit" itself to protect the lives and property of subordinate ethnic groups, who, as a result, have an interest in fighting for independence immediately rather than waiting to see if the leadership honors its commitment to protect them. Once a war breaks out, as Walter (1994) shows, settlement is extremely difficult, because neither side will want to disarm without full confidence that the agreement will be adhered to; but no one will have such confidence unless the other side disarms. Weingast (1998) shows that individuals who are told by their group leaders that they are targets for extermination would rationally take up arms even if the probability is negligible that their leaders' prognostications are accurate, since a low probability event with drastic consequences has a high expected disutility. Therefore ethnic war can emerge from a commitment problem even if only vague suggestions of repression exist, or if only a maniacal wing of the ruling group has genocidal intentions. Weingast's work is sensitive to the importance of institutions such as the consociational ones described by Lijphart (1977) that enhance the credibility of commitments. In the absence of such institutions, ethnic violence is more likely to occur.

Some scholars discount the credible commitments problem, arguing that many states do not even seek to make such commitments to protect their minorities. Rothchild (1991) shows that ethnic violence in Africa is associated strongly with regimes that show no interest in bargaining with disaffected groups. In many cases violence results neither from fear nor from failed coordination but from deliberate policy. However, if violence of this type were not reciprocated, and carried few costs for its perpetrators, it would be, in game-theoretic terms, a dominant strategy for leaders of ethnocratic regimes; and researchers must then explain why this sort of violence is not more common than it is.

Concerning the problem of information asymmetry, Fearon & Laitin (1996) suggest, with Deutsch (1954), that ethnic solidarity results from high levels of communication. As a result, in everyday interaction within an ethnic group, if someone takes advantage of someone else, the victim will be able to identify the malfeasant and to refuse future cooperation with him or her. High levels of interaction and of information about past interaction make possible the "evolution of cooperation" (Axelrod 1984) within a community. Interethnic relations, however, are characterized by low levels of information; the past conduct of members of the other ethnic group, as individuals, is not known. Under such conditions, an ethnic incident can more easily spiral into sustained violence, if members of each group, not being able to identify particular culprits, punish any or all members of the other group. This unfortunate equilibrium, Fearon and Laitin show, is not unique. They describe an alternate equilibrium, one that helps explain why violent spiraling, although gruesome, is rare. They find that even under conditions of state weakness or breakdown, ethnic cooperation can be maintained by local institutions of in-group policing—where leaders of one group help identify and punish the instigators of the violence against members of the other group—and intergroup mediation. The in-group policing equilibrium is one in which interethnic violence can be cauterized quickly.

Concerning in-group dynamics, game theory can help to clarify the microfoundations for the intragroup processes discussed previously in the section on case-based pattern finding. Game theoretic approaches, attuned to the individual level of analysis, do not assume—as do many theorists of ethnic conflict—that members of ethnic groups share a common vision or common interests. Kuran (1998a, 1998b) assumes that people have distinct preferences for some combination of ethnically marked and generic, ethnically indifferent consumption (including not only goods but activities, modes of association, policies, and so on). Ethnic entrepreneurs, who will be more successful to the extent that their constituents favor ethnic over generic consumption, try to induce the former at the expense of the latter. Such pressures, and constituents' interdependent responses to them, can trigger ethnification cascades—sharp and self-sustaining shifts from ethnically neutral to ethnically marked activities that divide once integrated societies into separate ethnic segments between whom violence is much more likely to flare up, and spread, than between the same individuals before the "cascade." Laitin (1995b) uses a cascade model similar to that of Kuran. He assumes that ethnic activists, in the context of a national revival, will use tactics of humiliation to induce co-nationals to invest in the cultural repertoires of the dormant nation. But when humiliation fails, and when activists fear that no cascade toward the national revival is possible, they will consider the possibility of inducing both intra- and interethnic violence.

Rational Action Theory

Rational action perspectives on ethnicity and nationalism have proliferated in recent years (Rogowski 1985, Meadwell 1989, Banton 1994). Yet despite an abundance of informal observations concerning the strategic, calculated, or otherwise instrumental dimensions of ethnic or nationalist violence, few systematic attempts have been made (apart from the international relations and game-theoretic traditions mentioned above) to analyze ethnic and nationalist violence as such from a rational action perspective. One exception is Hechter (1995), who claims that "nationalist violence can best be explained instrumentally." Hechter argues that while the dispositions linked to emotional or expressive violence are distributed randomly in a population, and thus have no effect at the aggregate level, the dispositions underlying instrumental violence are clustered systematically and thus are decisive at the aggregate level. This argument presupposes that the dispositions underlying emotional or expressive violence are idiosyncratic individual characteristics, yet surely such powerful violence-fostering emotions as rage or panic-like fear may be clustered systematically at particular places and times and thus may be significant at the aggregate level. But Hechter does stake claim to territory into which rationalists—for all their expansionist inclinations—have so far hesitated to tread. He also clearly states a series of propositions about the relation between group solidarity, state strength and autonomy, and oppositional nationalist violence. Another exception is Hardin (1995), who applies broadly rational choice perspectives (following Olson 1975) to the formation of ethnic groups and their development of exclusionary norms and then relies on an informal game model to explain how groups with such norms can "tip" toward violence.

Blalock's general theory of power and conflict (1989), though not specifically addressed to ethnic or nationalist violence, analyzes structures, mechanisms, and processes that are often implicated in such violence. These include the small, disciplined "conflict groups" specifically organized to carry out violence and the mechanisms through which protracted conflicts are sustained or terminated. He adopts a modified rational-actor persepective—modified in emphasizing structures of power and dependency and allowing for noneconomic goals and the the role of misperception, deception, ideological bias, and so on in shaping the subjective probabilities on the basis of which action is undertaken.

CULTURALIST APPROACHES

Culturalist analyses of ethnic and nationalist violence reflect the broader "cultural turn" the social sciences have taken in the past 20 years. Although such analyses are extremely heterogeneous, they generally characterize ethnic violence as meaningful, culturally constructed, discursively mediated, symbolically saturated, and ritually regulated. Some culturalist analyses expressly reject causal analysis in favor of interpretive understanding (Zulaika 1988) or adopt a stance of epistemological skepticism (Pandey 1992, Brass 1997). Yet for the most part, culturalist accounts do advance explanatory claims, although the status and precise nature of the claims are not always clear. Here we sketch a few clusters of recurring themes in culturalist analyses.

The Cultural Construction of Fear

Like the rational action approaches just considered, culturalist approaches seek to show that even apparently senseless ethnic violence "makes sense" (Kapferer 1988) in certain contexts. Yet while they claim to discover a "logic" to ethnic and ethnoreligious violence (Spencer 1990, Zulaika 1988, Juergensmeyer 1988) and reject representations of it as chaotic, random, meaningless, irrational, or purely emotive, culturalists claim that such violence makes sense not in instrumental terms but in terms of its meaningful relation to or resonance with other elements of the culturally defined context.

Culturalist analyses construe the relevant context in different ways. One major focus of attention has been on the cultural construction of fear, on the rhetorical processes, symbolic resources, and representational forms through which a demonized, dehumanized, or otherwise threatening ethnically defined "other" has been constructed. The social construction of fear, to be sure, is not a new theme in analyses of ethnic violence. It was central to Horowitz (1985:175–184), who in turn drew on a generation of work in social psychology. Yet while Horowitz sought to elaborate a universal "positional group psychology" to account for cross-cultural regularities in patterns of ethnic antipathy and anxiety, recent culturalist accounts have tended to emphasize particular features of individual cultural contexts; they have emphasized the cultural and historical rather than social psychological grounding of ethnic fear. A literature has emerged on the construction of fearful Hindu beliefs about Muslims in India (in the context of opposed ethnoreligious idioms and practices, religiously justified social segregation, and the rise of militant Hindu nationalism) (Gaborieau 1985, Pandey 1992, Hansen 1996); of Sinhalese beliefs about Tamils in Sri Lanka (in the context of an ethnocratic Sinhalese state, Tamil terrorism, state repression, and unchecked rumor) (Spencer 1990); and of Serbian beliefs about Croats in disintegrating Yugoslavia (in the context of a nationalizing Croatian successor state symbolically linked to, and triggering memories of, the murderous wartime Ustasha regime) (Glenny 1992, Denich 1994). Once such ethnically focused fear is in place, ethnic violence no longer seems random or meaningless but all too horrifyingly meaningful.

Without using the term, culturalist analyses have thus been concerned with what we discussed above as the security dilemma—with the conditions under which preemptive attacks against an ethnically defined other may "make sense." Unlike the international relations approaches to the security dilemma, however—and unlike political and economic approaches to ethnic violence in general—culturalist approaches seek to specify the manner in which fears and threats are constructed through narratives, myths, rituals, commemorations, and other cultural representations (Atran 1990). Culturalist analyses thus see security dilemmas as subjective, not objective, and as located in the realm of meaning and discourse, not in the external world. Many cultural analyses (e.g. Tambiah 1996, Bowman 1994) acknowledge the crucial role of ethnic elites in engendering ethnic insecurity through highly selective and often distorted narratives and representations, the deliberate planting of rumors, and so on. But the success of such entrepreneurs of fear is seen as contingent on the historically conditioned cultural resonance of their inflammatory appeals; cultural "materials" are seen as having an inner logic or connectedness that makes them at least moderately refractory to willful manipulation by cynical politicians.

Although such accounts may be plausible, even compelling "on the level of meaning" (Weber 1968:11), they have two weaknesses. The first is evidentiary: It is difficult to know whether, when, where, to what extent, and in what manner the posited beliefs and fears were actually held. How do we know that, in India, the most "rabid and senseless Hindu propaganda," "the most outrageous suggestions" about the allegedly evil, dangerous, and threatening Muslim "other," have come to be "widely believed," and to constitute "a whole new 'common sense'" (Pandey 1992:42–43, Hansen 1996)? How do we know that, in Sri Lanka in 1983, Tamils were believed to be "superhumanly cruel and cunning and, like demons, ubiquitous" (Spencer 1990:619) or "agents of evil," to be rooted out through a kind of "gigantic exorcism" (Kapferer 1988:101)? How do we know that, in the Serb-populated borderlands of Croatia, Serbs really feared Croats as latter-day Ustashas? Lacking direct evidence (or possessing at best anecdotal evidence) of beliefs and fears, culturalist accounts often rely on nationalist propaganda tracts (Pandey 1992:43, Lemarchand 1996:Chapter 2) but are unable to gauge the extent to which or the manner in which such fearful propaganda has been internalized by its addressees. [Malkki (1995) has attempted to document the extent of such internalization in her fieldwork among Hutu refugees from Burundi, but because this work concerns the victims of near-genocidal violence, not the perpetrators, it speaks most directly to the consequences rather than to the causes of ethnic violence—although consequences of past violence can become causes of future violence in the course of a long-term cycle of intractable violent conflict (Lemarchand 1996, Atran 1990)].

The second problem is that such accounts (though culturalist accounts are not alone in this respect) tend to explain too much and to overpredict ethnic violence. They can not explain why violence occurs only at particular times and places, and why, even at such times and places, only some persons participate in it. Cultural contextualizations of ethnic violence, however vivid, are not themselves explanations of it.

Framing Conflict as Ethnic

In southern Slovakia in 1995, a pair of Hungarian youths were pushed from a train by Slovakian youths after a soccer match. Although one of the youths was seriously injured, and although the incident occurred after the Hungarians had been singing Hungarian nationalist songs, the violence was interpreted as drunken behavior by unruly soccer fans rather than as ethnic violence, and even the nationalist press in Hungary made no attempt to mobilize around the incident (Brubaker field notes). Similarly, the burning down of an Estonian secondary school in a predominantly Russian region of Estonia in 1995 was interpreted as a Mafia hit, even on the Estonian side, and no mobilization occurred, even though no one could suggest why the Mafia might have been interested in a secondary school (Laitin field notes). These incidents illustrate what we alluded to in the introduction as the constitutive significance of coding or framing processes in ethnic violence. The "ethnic" quality of ethnic violence is not intrinsic to the act itself; it emerges through after-the-fact interpretive claims. Such claims may be contested, generating what Horowitz (1991a:2) has called a metaconflict—a "conflict over the nature of the conflict" that may, in turn, feed back into the conflict in such a way as to generate (by furnishing advance legitimation for) future violence (Lemarchand 1996:Chapter 2, McGarry & O'Leary 1995). Such social struggles over the proper coding and interpretation of acts of violence are therefore worth studying in their own right (Brass 1996a, 1997; Abelmann & Lie 1995) as an important aspect of the phenomenon of ethnic violence.

Gender

Like other forms of violence and war, and like the phenomena of ethnicity and nationhood in general (Verdery 1994), ethnic and nationalist violence is strongly gendered. The Basque ETA and the Irish Republican Army (IRA), for example, are overwhelmingly male (Waldmann 1989:154, Zulaika 1988:182), although Aretxaga (1995:138) discusses women's efforts to be recognized as full members of the IRA rather than of its women's counterpart. As victims of ethnic violence, women are sometimes deliberately spared, at other times deliberately targeted [for example, in the notorious mass rapes of Bosnia Muslim women by Bosnian Serbs (Korać 1994)]. More research is needed on the specific roles that women may play in certain ethnic riots, not necessarily as direct perpetrators but, for example, in shaming men into participating (Hansen 1996:153). Katz (1988) argues that while women as well as men are susceptible to the "seductions of crime," the characteristic modalities of women's criminal activities are different; we might expect the same to be true of ethnic violence.

The representation of ethnic violence is also strongly gendered. Recent research on nationalism shows that in many settings, prospective threats to (as well as actual attacks on) "the nation" are construed as a feared or actual violation or rape of an "innocent, female nation" by a brutal male aggressor (Harris 1993:170, Verdery 1994:248–249). To defend or retaliate against such threats or attacks, conspicuously masculinist virtues may be asserted in compensatory or overcompensatory fashion. In India, for example, Hindu nationalist organizations offer a "way of recuperating masculinity" to their recruits, enabling them to "overcome the [stereotypically] 'effeminate' Hindu man and emulate the demonized enemy, the allegedly strong, aggressive, militarized, potent and masculine Muslim" (Hansen 1996:148, 153).

Ritual, Symbolism, Performance

A number of analysts—echoing themes from the Manchester school of social anthropology (Gluckman 1954, Turner 1969)—have underscored the ritualized aspects of ethnic violence. Gaborieau (1985) highlights "rituals of provocation," which he describes as "codified procedures" of deliberate disrespect, desecration, or violation of sacred or symbolically charged spaces, times, or objects—in India, for example, the killing of cows by Muslims, or the disturbance of Muslim worship by noisy Hindu processions (on noise as a cultural weapon in ethnoreligious struggles, see Roberts 1990). Marches and processions through space "owned" by another group have triggered violence in Northern Ireland and India with sufficient regularity and predictability to warrant calling these too rituals of provocation (Feldman 1991:29–30, Jaffrelot 1994, Tambiah 1996:240). Even without deliberate provocation, conflicting claims to the same sacred spaces (Ayodhya, Jerusalem) or sacred times (when ritual calendars overlap) may provide the occasion for ethnic violence (Van der Veer 1994; Tambiah 1996:Chapter 9; Das 1990b:9ff; Friedland & Hecht 1991, 1996). Freitag (1989) and Tambiah (1985:Chapter 4, 1996:Chapter 8) have applied what the latter calls a semiotic and performative perspective on rituals and public events to ethnic confrontations, disturbances, and riots in South Asia. Performance and ritual are also emphasized in Zulaika's (1988) study of the cultural context of violence in a Basque village. Van der Veer (1996) sees riots as a form of ritual antagonism expressing an opposition between the self and an impure, alien, or demonic "other." Following Davis's (1973) analysis of the "rites of violence" in the religious riots of sixteenth-century France, analysts of ethnic riots have called attention to the ritualized nature and symbolic resonance of the seemingly gratuitous forms of mutilation often involved (e.g. hacking off of body parts, desecration of corpses).

Feldman's (1991) study of Northern Ireland is the most sustained discussion of the symbolic dimension of ethnic violence. Feldman focuses on the ethnically charged symbolism of urban space in Belfast, the increasing ethnic partitioning of which is both a consequence of ethnic violence and a reinforcing cause of future violence. He also analyzes the equally charged symbolism of the body. Ironically, given his critique of instrumental analyses of ethnic violence, Feldman devotes a great deal of attention to the body as an instrument, as a weapon deployed by those (in his case, IRA prisoners) for whom it is the only resource. Of course, as he shows in rich detail, this instrumentalization of the body through the "dirty protest" (in which prisoners denied special political status refused to wear prison clothing and smeared feces on the walls) and the subsequent hunger strike (in which 10 prisoners died) was achieved in symbolically resonant form [analyzed also by Aretxaga (1993, 1995), the latter piece focusing on female prisoners' own "dirty protest," centered on the display of menstrual blood].

It should be emphasized that no serious culturalist theory today argues that violence flows directly from deeply encoded cultural propensities to violence or from the sheer fact of cultural difference. In this salutary sense, there are no purely culturalist explanations of ethnic violence; and it is difficult to simply classify as culturalist a work such as Tambiah (1996), in which cultural, economic, political, and psychological considerations are deftly interwoven. By considering separately culturalist approaches, we do not imply that they are or ought to be segregated from other approaches. We suggest, rather, that such approaches highlight aspects of ethnic violence—discursive, symbolic, and ritualistic aspects—that should ideally be addressed by other approaches as well.

CONCLUSION: A PLEA FOR DISAGGREGATION

The temptation to adopt currently fashionable terms of practice as terms of analysis is endemic to sociology and kindred disciplines. But it ought to be resisted. The notion of "ethnic violence" is a case in point—a category of practice, produced and reproduced by social actors such as journalists, politicians, foundation officers, and NGO representatives, that should not be (but often is) taken over uncritically as a category of analysis by social scientists. Despite sage counsel urging disaggregation (Snyder 1978, Williams 1994, Horowitz forthcoming), too much social scientific work in this domain (as in others) involves highly aggregated explananda, as if ethnic violence were a homogeneous substance varying only in magnitude. To build a research program around an aggregated notion of ethnic violence is to let public coding—often highly questionable, as when the Somali and Tadjikistani civil wars are coded as ethnic—drive sociological analysis.

The paradigmatic instances of ethnic and nationalist violence are large events, extended in space and time. Moreover, they are composite and causally heterogeneous, consisting not of an assemblage of causally identical unit instances of ethnic violence but of a number of different types of actions, processes, occurrences, and events. For example, it is evident from the case literature that in Sri Lanka "ethnic violence" consists of episodic riots on the one hand and more continuous low-level terrorism (and state violence in response to the terrorism) on the other, all occurring against the background of the "cultural violence" perpetrated by a series of ethnocratic Sinhalese governments. Not only do the riots, terrorism, and state violence involve sharply opposed mechanisms and dynamics (in terms of degree and mode of organization, mode of recruitment and involvement of participants, affective tone, symbolic significance, contagiousness, degree and modality of purposeful rationality, and so on), but within each category there is also a great deal of causal heterogeneity. Thus an ethnic riot typically involves at one level deliberate manipulation and organization by a small number of instigators but also, at other levels, turbulent currents of crowd behavior governed by powerful emotions and compelling collective representations requiring social psychological and cultural modes of analysis.

There is no reason to believe that these heterogeneous components of large-scale ethnic violence can be understood or explained through a single theoretical lens. Rather than aspire to construct a theory of ethnic and nationalist violence—a theory that would be vitiated by its lack of a meaningful explanandum—we should seek to identify, analyze, and explain the heterogeneous processes and mechanisms involved in generating the varied instances of what we all too casually lump together—given our prevailing ethnicizing interpretive frames—as "ethnic violence." This can be accomplished only through a research strategy firmly committed to disaggregation in both data collection and theory building.

ACKNOWLEDGMENTS

The authors wish to thank John Bowen, James Fearon, and Timur Kuran for their comments on earlier drafts and Joan Beth Wolf for her able assistance in compiling a preliminary bibliography.

Literature Cited

Abelmann N, Lie J. 1995. *Blue Dreams: Korean Americans and the Los Angeles Riots*. Cambridge, MA: Harvard Univ. Press

Anderson B. 1992. *Long-distance nationalism: world capitalism and the rise of identity politics*. Wertheim Lecture 1992, Center for Asian Studies, Amsterdam

Appadurai A. 1997. *Modernity at Large*. Minneapolis: Univ. Minn. Press

Aretxaga B. 1993. Striking with hunger: cultural meanings of political violence in Northern Ireland. In *The Violence Within: Cultural and Political Opposition in Divided Nations*, ed. KB Warren, pp. 219–53. Boulder, CO: Westview

Aretxaga B. 1995. Dirty protest: symbolic overdetermination and gender in Northern Ireland ethnic violence. *Ethos* 23(2): 123–48

Atran S. 1990. Stones against the iron fist, terror within the nation: alternating structures of violence and cultural identity in the Israeli-Palestinian conflict. *Polit. Soc.* 18(4):481–526

Axelrod R. 1984. *The Evolution of Cooperation*. New York: Basic

Azar EE, Burton JW, eds. 1986. *International Conflict Resolution: Theory and Practice*. Sussex and Boulder: Wheatsheaf and Lynne Rienner

Banton M. 1994. Modeling ethnic and national relations. *Ethnic Racial Stud.* 17(1): 1–19

Barth F, ed. 1967. *Ethnic Groups and Boundaries: The Social Organization of Cultural Difference*. Boston: Little Brown

Beissinger MR. 1998. Nationalist violence and the state: political authority and contentious repertoires in the former USSR. *Comp. Polit.* In press

Bell JB. 1993. *The Irish Troubles: A Generation of Violence 1967–1992*. New York: St. Martin's

Björgo T, Witte R, eds. 1993. *Racist Violence in Europe*. New York: St. Martin's

Blackburn R. 1997. *The Making of New World Slavery: From the Baroque to the Modern 1492–1800*. New York: Verso

Blalock HM Jr. 1989. *Power and Conflict: Toward a General Theory*. Newbury Park, CA: Sage

Bodley J, ed. 1982. *Victims of Progress*. Palo Alto, CA: Mayfield. 2nd ed

Bourdieu P, Wacquant LJD. 1992. *An Invita-*

tion to Reflexive Sociology. Chicago, IL: Univ. Chicago Press

Bowen JR. 1996. The myth of global ethnic conflict. *J. Democr.* 7(4):3–14

Bowman G. 1994. Ethnic violence and the phantasy of the antagonist: the mobilisation of national identity in former Yugoslavia. *Polish Sociol. Rev.* 106:133–53

Brass PR, ed. 1996a. *Riots and Pogroms*. New York: New York Univ. Press

Brass PR. 1996b. Introduction: discourse of ethnicity, communalism, and violence. See Brass 1996a, pp. 1–55

Brass PR. 1997. *Theft of an Idol: Text and Context in the Representation of Collective Violence*. Princeton, NJ: Princeton Univ. Press

Brubaker R. 1995. Aftermaths of empire and the unmixing of peoples: historical and comparative perspectives. *Ethnic Racial Stud.* 18(2):189–218

Brubaker R. 1996. *Nationalism Reframed: Nationhood and the National Question in the New Europe*. Cambridge and New York: Cambridge Univ. Press

Brubaker R. 1998. Myths and misconceptions in the study of nationalism. In *The State of the Nation: Ernest Gellner and the Theory of Nationalism*, ed. John Hall. Cambridge and New York: Cambridge Univ. Press. In press

Bruce S. 1992. *The Red Hand: Protestant Paramilitaries in Northern Ireland*. Oxford: Oxford Univ. Press

Burleigh M, Wippermann W. 1991. *The Racial State: Germany 1933–1945*. New York: Cambridge Univ. Press

Carment D, Rowlands D, James P. 1997. Ethnic conflict and third party intervention. In *Enforcing Cooperation: Risky States and Intergovernmental Management of Conflict,* ed. G Schneider, P Weitsman, pp. 104–32. New York: MacMillan

Chaliand G. 1977. *Revolution in the Third World*. New York: Viking

Clark R. 1984. *The Basque Insurgents: ETA, 1952–1980*. Madison: Univ. Wisc. Press

Clifford J. 1994. Diasporas. *Cult. Anthropol.* 9(3):302–38

Cohen L. 1993. *Broken Bonds: The Disintegration of Yugoslavia*. Boulder, CO: Westview

Cooper F, Stoler AL, eds. 1997. *Tensions of Empire: Colonial Cultures in a Bourgeois World*. Berkeley: Univ. Calif. Press

Coser L. 1956. *The Functions of Social Conflict*. New York: Free

Das V, ed. 1990a. *Mirrors of Violence: Communities, Riots, and Survivors in South Asia*. Oxford and New York: Oxford Univ. Press

Das V. 1990b. Introduction: communities, riots, survivors—the South Asian experience. See Das 1990a, pp. 1–36

Davis NZ. 1973. The rites of violence: religious riot in sixteenth-century France. *Past Present* (59):51–91

Della Porta D, Tarrow S. 1986. Unwanted children: political violence and the cycle of protest in Italy, 1966–1973. *Eur. J. Polit. Res.* 14:607–32

Deng FM. 1995. *War of Visions: Conflict of Identities in the Sudan*. Washington, DC: Brookings Inst.

Denich B. 1994. Dismembering Yugoslavia: nationalist ideologies and the symbolic revival of genocide. *Am. Ethnol.* 21(2): 367–90

Desjarlais R, Kleinman A. 1994. Violence and demoralization in the new world order. *Anthropol. Today* 10(5):9–12

Deutsch K. 1954. *Nationalism and Social Communication*. Cambridge, MA: MIT Press

Díez Medrano J. 1995. *Divided Nations*. Ithaca, NY: Cornell Univ. Press

Dobkowski MN, Wallimann I. 1992. *Genocide in Our Time: an Annotated Bibliography with Analytical Introductions*. Ann Arbor, MI: Pierian

Fairbanks CH Jr. 1995. The postcommunist wars. *J. Democr.* 6(4):18–34

Fearon JD. 1994. *Ethnic war as a commitment problem*. Paper presented at Annu. Meet. Am. Polit. Sci. Assoc., New York

Fearon JD.1995. Rationalist explanations for war. *Int. Organ.* 49:379–414

Fearon JD, Laitin DD. 1996. Explaining interethnic cooperation. *Am. Polit. Sci. Rev.* 90(4):715–35

Feldman A. 1991. *Formations of Violence: The Narrative of the Body and Political Terror in Northern Ireland*. Chicago, IL: Univ. Chicago Press

Ferguson RB, Whitehead NL, eds. 1992. *War in the Tribal Zone: Expanding States and Indigenous Warfare*. Santa Fe, NM: School Am. Res. Press

Freitag SB. 1989. *Collective Action and Community: Public Arenas and the Emergence of Communalism in North India*. Berkeley: Univ. Calif. Press

Friedland R, Hecht RD. 1991. The politics of sacred place: Jerusalem's Temple Mount/*al-haram al-sharif.* In *Sacred Places and Profane Spaces: Essays in the Geographics of Judaism, Christianity, and Islam*, ed. J Scott, P Simpson-Housley, pp. 21–61. New York: Greenwood

Friedland R, Hecht RD. 1996. Divisions at the center: the organization of political violence at Jerusalem's Temple Mount/*al-*

haram al-sharif—1929 and 1990. See Brass 1996a, pp. 114–53
Friedland R, Hecht RD. 1998. Profane violence at the sacred center: the case of Jerusalem and Ayodhya. Unpublished manuscript, Depts. of Sociology and Religious Studies, Univ. Calif., Santa Barbara
Gaborieau M. 1985. From Al-Beruni to Jinnah: idiom, ritual and ideology of the Hindu-Muslim confrontation in South Asia. *Anthropol. Today* 1(3):7–14
Gagnon VP. 1994–1995. Ethnic nationalism and international conflict: the case of Serbia. *Int. Secur.* 19(3):130–66
Gagnon VP. 1996. *Ethnic conflict as demobilizer: the case of Serbia. Inst. European Stud. Working Paper No. 96.1.* Inst. European Stud., Cornell Univ.
Glenny M. 1992. *The Fall of Yugoslavia: The Third Balkan War.* London: Penguin
Gluckman M. 1954. *Rituals of Rebellion in South-East Africa.* Manchester, UK: Manchester Univ. Press
Goldstone JA, Gurr TR, Moshiri F, eds. 1991. *Revolutions of the Late Twentieth Century.* Boulder, CO: Westview
Green L. 1994. Fear as a way of life. *Cult. Anthropol.* 9(2):227–56
Grimshaw A. 1969. *Racial Violence in the United States.* Chicago, IL: Aldine
Gurr TR. 1968. A casual model of civil strife: a comparative analysis using new indices. *Am. Polit. Sci. Rev.* 62(4):1104–24
Gurr TR. 1970. *Why Men Rebel.* Princeton, NJ: Princeton Univ. Press
Gurr TR. 1993a. *Minorities at Risk: A Global View of Ethnopolitical Conflicts.* Washington, DC: US Inst. Peace
Gurr TR. 1993b. Why minorities rebel: a global analysis of communal mobilization and conflict since 1945. *Int. Polit. Sci. Rev.* 14(2):161–201
Gurr TR. 1994. Peoples against states: ethnopolitical conflict and the changing world system. *Int. Stud. Q.* 38:347–77
Gurr TR, Harff B. 1994. *Ethnic Conflict in World Politics.* Boulder, CO: Westview
Haas EB. 1997. *Nationalism, Liberalism and Progress.* Ithaca, NY: Cornell Univ. Press
Hansen TB. 1996. Recuperating masculinity: Hindu nationalism, violence and the exorcism of the Muslim "Other." *Crit. Anthropol.* 16(2):137–72
Hardin R. 1995. *One for All: the Logic of Group Conflict.* Princeton, NJ: Princeton Univ. Press
Harff B, Gurr TR. 1989. Victims of the state: genocide, politicides and group repression since 1945. *Int. Rev. Victimol.* 1:23–41
Harris R. 1993. The "Child of the Barbarian": rape, race and nationalism in France during the First World War. *Past Present* 141: 170–206
Hayden RM. 1996. Imagined communities and real victims: self-determination and ethnic cleansing in Yugoslavia. *Am. Ethnol.* 23(4):783–801
Hechter M. 1995. Explaining nationalist violence. *Nations Natl.* 1(1):53–68
Heisler M. 1991. Ethnicity and ethnic relations in the modern West. See Montville 1991, pp. 21–52
Heraclides A. 1990. Secessionist minorities and external involvement. *Int. Organ.* 44(3):341–78
Holmes S. 1997. What Russia teaches us now: how weak states threaten freedom. *Am. Prospect* 33:30–39
Horowitz DL. 1973. Direct, displaced, and cumulative ethnic aggression. *Comp. Polit.* 6:1–16
Horowitz DL. 1983. Racial violence in the United States. In *Ethnic Pluralism and Public Policy: Achieving Equality in the United States and Britain*, ed. N Glazer, K Young, pp. 187–211. Lexington, MA: Lexington/Heinemann Educ.
Horowitz DL. 1985. *Ethnic Groups in Conflict.* Berkeley: Univ. Calif. Press
Horowitz DL. 1991a. *A Democratic South Africa?: Constitutional Engineering in a Divided Society.* Berkeley: Univ. Calif. Press
Horowitz DL. 1991b. Irredentas and secessions: adjacent phenomena, neglected considerations. In *Irredentism and International Politics*, ed. N Chazan. pp. 9–22. Boulder, CO: Lynne Rienner/Adamantine
Horowitz DL. 1991c. Making moderation pay: the comparative politics of ethnic conflict management. See Montville 1991, pp. 451–75
Horowitz DL. Forthcoming. *Deadly Ethnic Riots.*
Jackson RH. 1990. *Quasi-States: Sovereignty, International Relations and the Third World.* New York: Cambridge Univ. Press
Jackson RH, CG Rosberg. 1982. Why Africa's weak states persist: the empirical and juridical in statehood. *World Polit.* 35(1): 1–24
Jaffrelot C. 1994. *Processions Hindoues, stratégies politiques et émeutes entre Hindous et Musulmans.* In *Violences et Nonviolences en Inde,* ed. D Vidal, G Tarabout, E Meyer, pp. 261–87. Paris: École Hautes Étud. Sci. Soc.
Jervis R. 1978. Cooperation under the security dilemma. *World Polit.* 30(2):167–214
Juergensmeyer M. 1988. The logic of religious violence: the case of the Punjab. *Contrib. Indian Sociol.* 22(1):65–88
Kakar S. 1990. Some unconscious aspects of

ethnic violence in India. See Das 1990a, pp. 135–45
Kandori M. 1992. Social norms and community enforcement. *Rev. Econ. Stud.* 59:63–80
Kapferer B. 1988. *Legends of People, Myths of State: Violence, Intolerance, and Political Culture in Sri Lanka and Australia.* Washington, DC: Smithsonian Inst. Press
Katz J. 1988. *Seductions of Crime: Moral and Sensual Attractions in Doing Evil.* New York: Basic
Kaufman SJ. 1996. Spiraling to ethnic war: elites, masses, and Moscow in Moldova's civil war. *Int. Secur.* 21(2):108–38
Keith M. 1993. *Race, Riots and Policing: Lore and Disorder in a Multi-Racist Society.* London: UCL
Kemper S. 1991. *The Presence of the Past: Chronicles, Politics, and Culture in Sinhala Life.* Ithaca, NY: Cornell Univ. Press
Klier JD, Lambroza S, eds. 1992. *Pogroms: Anti-Jewish Violence in Modern Russian History.* New York: Cambridge Univ. Press
Korać M. 1994. Representation of mass rape in ethnic conflicts in what was Yugoslavia. *Sociologija* 36(4):495–514
Kuran T. 1998a. Ethnic dissimilation and its international diffusion. In *Ethnic Conflict: Fear, Diffusion, and Escalation*, ed. DA Lake, D Rothchild, pp. 35–60. Princeton, NJ: Princeton Univ. Press
Kuran T. 1998b. Ethnic norms and their transformation through reputational cascades. *J. Legal Stud.* 27: In press
Laitin DD. 1995a. Marginality: a microperspective. *Rational. Soc.* 7(1):31–57
Laitin DD. 1995b. National revivals and violence. *Arch. Eur. Sociol.* 36(1):3–43
Laitin DD. 1995c. *Ethnic cleansing, liberal style.* Paper presented to the Harvard-MIT Transnational Security Project seminar on Intergroup Conflict, Human Rights, and Refugees, November 20, 1995
Lake DA, Rothchild D. 1996. Containing fear: the origins and management of ethnic conflict. *Int. Secur.* 21(2):41–75
Landa JT. 1994. *Trust, Ethnicity and Identity.* Ann Arbor: Univ. Mich. Press
Langmuir GI. 1990. *Toward a Definition of Antisemitism.* Berkeley: Univ. Calif. Press
Lemarchand R. 1996. *Burundi: Ethnic Conflict and Genocide.* New York/Cambridge: Woodrow Wilson Center Press/Cambridge Univ. Press
Lijphart A. 1977. *Democracy in Plural Societies.* New Haven, CT: Yale Univ. Press
Lijphart A. 1990. The alternative vote: a realistic alternative for South Africa? *Politikon* 18(2):91–101
Malkki L. 1995. *Purity and Exile: Violence, Memory, and National Cosmology Among Hutu Refugees in Tanzania.* Chicago, IL: Univ. Chicago Press
Mann M. 1993. *The Sources of Social Power: The Rise of Classes and Nation-States, 1760–1914*, Vol. II. New York: Cambridge Univ. Press
Marrus MR. 1985. *The Unwanted: European Refugees in the Twentieth Century.* New York: Oxford Univ. Press
McGarry J, O'Leary B. 1995. *Explaining Northern Ireland: Broken Images.* Oxford: Blackwell
Meadwell H. 1989. Ethnic nationalism and collective choice theory. *Comp. Polit. Stud.* 22:139–54
Meyer JW. 1987. The world polity and the authority of the nation-state. In *Institutional Structure: Constituting State, Society, and the Individual*, ed. GM Thomas, JW Meyer, FO Ramirez, pp. 41–70. Newbury Park, CA: Sage
Miller WI. 1993. *Humiliation.* Ithaca, NY: Cornell Univ. Press
Montville J, ed. 1991. *Conflict and Peacemaking in Multiethnic Societies.* Lexington, MA: Lexington
Nagengast C. 1994. Violence, terror, and the crisis of the state. *Annu. Rev. Anthropol.* 23:109–36
Nordstrom C, Martin J, eds. 1992. *The Paths to Domination, Resistance, and Terror.* Berkeley: Univ. Calif. Press
Olson M. 1975. *The Logic of Collective Action: Public Goods and the Theory of Groups.* Cambridge, MA: Harvard Univ. Press
Olzak S. 1992. *The Dynamics of Ethnic Competition and Conflict.* Stanford, CA: Stanford Univ. Press
Paden JN. 1991. National system development and conflict resolution in Nigeria. See Montville 1991, pp. 411–32
Pandey G. 1992. In defense of the fragment: writing about Hindu-Muslim riots in India today. *Representations* 37:27–55
Petersen R. 1998. *Fear, Hatred, Resentment: Delineating Paths to Ethnic Violence in Eastern Europe.* Unpublished manuscript, Dept. of Political Science, Washington Univ., St. Louis
Pfaffenberger B. 1991. Ethnic conflict and youth insurgency in Sri Lanka: the social origins of Tamil separatism. See Montville 1991, pp. 241–58
Pfaffenberger B. 1994. The structure of protracted conflict: the case of Sri Lanka. *Humboldt J. Soc. Relat.* 20(2):121–47
Podolefsky A. 1990. Mediator roles in Simbu conflict management. *Ethnology* 29(1): 67–81

Posen BR. 1993. The security dilemma and ethnic conflict. *Survival* 35(1):27–47

Prunier G. 1995. *The Rwanda Crisis 1959–1994: History of a Genocide*. London: Hurst

Rabushka A, Shepsle KA. 1972. *Politics in Plural Societies: A Theory of Democratic Instability*. Columbus, OH: Merrill

Roberts M. 1990. Noise as cultural struggle: tom-tom beating, the British, and communal disturbances in Sri Lanka, 1880s–1930s. See Das 1990a, pp. 240–85

Rogger H, Weber E, eds. 1965. *The European Right: a Historical Profile*. Berkeley: Univ. Calif. Press

Rogowski R. 1985. Causes and varieties of nationalism—a rationalist account. In *New Nationalisms of the Developed West: Toward Explanation*, ed. EA Tiryakian, R Rogowski. pp. 87–108. Boston: Allen & Unwin

Rothchild D. 1991. An interactive model for state-ethnic relations. In *Conflict Resolution in Africa*, ed. FM Deng, IW Zartman. Washington, DC: Brookings Inst.

Rothschild J. 1981. *Ethnopolitics, a Conceptual Framework*. New York: Columbia Univ. Press

Sabaratnam L. 1990. Sri Lanka: the lion and the tiger in the ethnic archipelago. See van den Berghe 1990, pp. 187–220

Scheff TJ, Retzinger SM. 1991. *Emotions and Violence: Shame and Rage in Destructive Conflicts*. Lexington, MA: Lexington

Simmel G. 1955. "*Conflict" and "The Web of Group-Affiliations,"* trans. KH Wolff, R Bendix. New York: Free

Snyder D. 1978. Collective violence: a research agenda and some strategic considerations. *J. Confl. Resol.* 22(3):499–534

Snyder J. 1998. *Nationalist Conflict in the Age of Democracy*. New York: Norton. In press

Spencer J. 1990. Collective violence and everyday practice in Sri Lanka. *Mod. Asia Stud.* 24(3):603–23

Stohl M, ed. 1983. *The Politics of Terrorism*. 2nd ed. New York: Marcel Dekker

Tajfel H, ed. 1978. *Differentiation Between Social Groups*. London: Academic

Tambiah SJ. 1985. *Culture, Thought, and Social Action : An Anthropological Perspective* Cambridge, MA: Harvard Univ. Press

Tambiah SJ. 1986. *Sri Lanka: Ethnic Fratricide and the Dismantling of Democracy*. Chicago, IL: Univ. Chicago Press

Tambiah SJ. 1996. *Leveling Crowds: Ethnonationalist Conflicts and Collective Violence in South Asia*. Berkeley: Univ. Calif. Press

Tarrow S. 1994. *Power in Movement*. Cambridge, UK: Cambridge Univ. Press

Tilly C. 1978. *From Mobilization to Revolution*. Reading, MA: Addison-Wesley

Turner V. 1969. *The Ritual Process*. London: Routledge

Väyrynen R, Senghaas D, Schmidt C, eds. 1987. *The Quest for Peace: Transcending Collective Violence and War Among Societies, Cultures and States*. Beverly Hills, CA/London: Sage/Int. Soc. Sci. Counc.

van den Berghe PL, ed. 1990. *State Violence and Ethnicity*. Niwot, CO: Univ. Press Colo.

van der Veer P. 1994. *Religious Nationalism: Hindus and Muslims in India*. Berkeley: Univ. Calif. Press

van der Veer P. 1996. Riots and rituals: the construction of violence and public space in Hindu nationalism. See Brass 1996a, pp. 154–76

van Evera S. 1994. Hypotheses on nationalism and war. *Int. Secur.* 18(4):5–39

Varshney A. 1997. Postmodernism, civic engagement and ethnic conflict: a passage to India. *Comp. Polit.* 30(1):1–20

Verdery K. 1994. From parent-state to family patriarchs: gender and nation in contemporary Eastern Europe. *East Eur. Polit. Soc.* 8(2):225–55

Volkan V. 1991. Psychoanalytic aspects of ethnic conflicts. See Montville 1991, pp. 81–92

Waldmann P. 1985. Gewaltsamer Separatismus. Am Beispiel der Basken, Franko-Kanadier und Nordiren. *Kölner Z. Soziol. Sozialpsychol.* 37(2):203–29

Waldmann P. 1989. *Ethnischer Radikalismus: Ursachen und Folgen gewaltsamer Minderheitenkonflikte am Beispiel des Baskenlandes, Nordirlands und Quebecs*. Opladen: Wesdeutscher

Waldmann P.1992. Ethnic and sociorevolutionary terrorism: a comparison of structures. *Int. Soc. Mov. Res.* 4:237–357

Walter B. 1994. *The resolution of civil wars: why negotiations fail*. Ph.D thesis, Polit. Sci. Dept., Univ. Chicago

Weber M. 1968. *Economy and Society*, ed. G Roth, C Wittich. Berkeley: Univ. Calif. Press

Weingast B. 1998. Constructing trust: the politics and economics of ethnic and regional conflict. In *Institutions and Social Order*, ed. V Haufler, K Soltan, E Uslaner. Ann Arbor: Univ. Mich. Press. In press

White RW. 1993. *Provisional Irish Republicans: An Oral and Interpretive History*. Westport, CT: Greenwood

Williams RM Jr. 1994. The sociology of ethnic conflicts: comparative international perspectives. *Annu. Rev. Sociol.* 20:49–79

Woodward SL. 1995. *Balkan Tragedy: Chaos and Dissolution After the Cold War*. Washington, DC: Brookings Inst.

Young C. 1965. *Politics in the Congo*. Princeton, NJ: Princeton Univ. Press

Zolberg A, Suhrke A, Aguayo S. 1989. *Escape From Violence: Conflict and the Refugee Crisis in the Developing World*. New York: Oxford Univ. Press

Zulaika J. 1988. *Basque Violence: Metaphor and Sacrament*. Reno: Univ. Nevada Press

Annu. Rev. Sociol. 1998. 24:453–76

CONTEMPORARY DEVELOPMENTS IN SOCIOLOGICAL THEORY: Current Projects and Conditions of Possibility

Charles Camic and Neil Gross

Department of Sociology, University of Wisconsin-Madison, Madison, Wisconsin 53706; e-mail camic@ssc.wisc.edu, ngross@ssc.wisc.edu

KEYWORDS: social theory, history of sociology, sociology of science, fragmentation and synthesis

ABSTRACT

This paper characterizes the field of sociological theory since the mid-1980s as the site of eight active and diverse intellectual projects. These projects are (I) to construct general analytical tools for use in empirical social research, (II) to synthesize multiple theoretical approaches; (III) to refine existing theoretical research programs; (IV) to stimulate dialogue among different theoretical perspectives; (V) to enlarge and reconstruct current theoretical approaches conceptually, methodologically, socially, and politically; (VI) to analyze a range of past theoretical ideas; (VII) to offer a diagnosis of contemporary social conditions; and (VIII) to dissolve the enterprise of sociological theory. We discuss the contours of these projects and identify some of the major ideas and theorists associated with each. We conclude with a brief discussion of the organizational structure of the contemporary theory field, observing that most current theoretical projects are formulated with insufficient attention to their conditions of possibility.

INTRODUCTION

Sociological theory has a long history of taking stock of itself. It lies among those distinctive academic specialties where a general review of the existing literature is not an occasional undertaking but part of the routine activity of many members of the area, a feature of every required survey course on theory,

0360-0572/98/0815-0453$08.00

and a necessary component of every work purporting to be an original contribution to the field.

Under these circumstances there exists no shortage of recent articles, monographs, textbooks, and edited collections analyzing contemporary developments in the theory field, a subject also addressed in previous volumes of the *Annual Review of Sociology*. Among these various contributions, Giddens & J Turner (1987), Ritzer (1988c, 1990b), B Turner (1996b), J Turner (1991), and R Wallace & Wolf (1995) all discuss trends in the theory area; the theorists, texts, and intellectual currents making up these trends; and the substantive arguments and conceptual frameworks associated with these developments.

This chapter does not substitute for these detailed reviews. Its primary aim is not to resume the conceptual schemes and substantive arguments found in contemporary theories but to identify and briefly overview some of the major intellectual projects currently under way in the theory area. In research on earlier historical periods, we have shown that attention to a theorist's intellectual objectives and purposes increases understanding of the conceptual tools and empirical claims he or she articulated (e.g. Camic 1989, Gross 1997). In speaking in this chapter of "projects," we make a preliminary effort to extend this approach to the contemporary period by focusing on some principal tasks that those in the theory area are now seeking to accomplish, on the organizing programs or agenda that contributors to the field are developing their concepts and arguments in order to advance, and on the descriptive and evaluative assessments of the present state of the theory area that frequently accompany these programs.

We begin by identifying eight such projects and conclude with a discussion of their organizational conditions of possibility. All eight projects are contemporary, found in the theory literature in the period on which we concentrate, the mid-1980s to the present. Analysis of other periods would necessarily produce a different set of programs, whose degree of overlap with the following listing would be an empirical question. Throughout, we deal primarily with American developments, generally incorporating works by European theorists only insofar as these have appeared in English since the mid-1980s and have since then figured consequentially into American discussions. Even taking into account these restrictions, this survey of the literature is selective, and the eight projects do not provide an exhaustive charting of lines of current theoretical activity.

Furthermore, it should be recognized that these eight projects are not, as a rule, mutually exclusive of one another. There are theorists who have pursued more than one, both simultaneously and in different career stages, as we occasionally note, though it is not possible here to devote sufficient attention to particular individuals fully to characterize their projects over time or even in single works. We also emphasize that our eight project categories are internally heterogeneous and that they bring together theorists who differ in other respects while separating those often grouped as similar in other scholarly classifications. But this simply testifies to the value of multiple classification schemes: to the fact that thinkers with a common agenda for sociological theory may differ in the concepts and arguments they use to advance this agenda, just as theorists who converge in argument and concept may use these means to advance very different projects within the theory area.

In discussing contemporary sociological theory, we consider an area with notoriously fuzzy boundaries. In identifying what works fall within these boundaries, we borrow Wittgenstein's notion of "family resemblances." Wittgenstein (1953:31–33) analyzes groups of elements that "have no one thing in common which makes us use the same word for all" elements; just as there are "various resemblances between members of a family, build, features, colour of eyes, gait, temperament, etc. etc.," so there are "family resemblances" among the elements of these other groups, i.e. "a complicated network of similarities overlapping and criss-crossing: sometimes overall similarities, sometimes similarities of detail." It is such family resemblances that constitute the contemporary theory field: criss-crossing similarities in terms of analytical issues and problems, intellectual ancestory and points of departure, vocabulary and style of argument, self-identification (calling one's own work "theory"), institutional membership (belonging to theory sections of sociological associations), group adoption (having one's contribution embraced by theorists), and more. No fixed cluster of these traits defines a family member nor makes it possible to track down all the stepchildren, distant cousins, and black sheep. Nonetheless, after one has spent some time among family members, it is not difficult to recognize the different branches of the family tree.

EIGHT PROJECTS FOR CONTEMPORARY SOCIOLOGICAL THEORY

Project I: Construction of General Tools for Use in Empirical Analysis

For one group of contemporary theorists, the principal task of sociological theory is to build analytical tools—concepts, explanatory propositions, interpretive guidelines, etc—directly applicable in the study of empirical problems. This project, according to many of its recent proponents, is increasingly threatened by abstract, self-referential theorizing that distances itself from the substantive issues that arise in areas of empirical social research.

This is the position of Chafetz: "[S]ociological theory is integrally related to research" (1988:2) and "ghettoizes" itself when it retreats into "abstract epistemological and ontological [discussion of issues such as] agency/micro and structure/macro" (1993:60–62). Opposing this retreat, Chafetz sets for theory the task of developing a "diverse set of practical tools"—general explanatory statements and the concepts they contain—"from which one can select those most helpful in solving any given [empirical] problem." She carries this agenda forward by articulating a multivariable, "eclectic structural theory" of the causes of gender stratification (1988:1, 51–54).

Along similar lines, Rule (1997) objects that the theory field is now a "cacophony" of discordant approaches (rational choice, network analysis, etc), each of limited range, and has lost sight of the discipline's "perennial issues"—its substantive questions about deviance, economic growth, civil violence, etc. For Rule, "the development of analytical tools" that address such questions is the principal task for contemporary theory, a task he himself takes up by formulating general propositions about the sources of civil violence (1997:1, 5, 19, 261–17; see also Rule 1988, Skocpol 1986). Calhoun, too, calls for "more studies that seek to advance theory in the cause of contemporary sociological research and understanding, as distinct from those which aim mainly at clarifying what [theorists] have already said" (1997:2). His preference, however, is for theory to supply not a set of general propositions and concepts but culturally sensitive "guidelines" or "frameworks for interpretation" of changing social practices (Calhoun 1996b:86, 92; see also Calhoun 1995, 1996a).

Pierre Bourdieu's writings (1988, 1990a, 1990b, 1993a, 1993b, Bourdieu & Wacquant 1992) offer perhaps the most elaborate case for this project. Rejecting "empty theoreticism"—general "programmatic discourse that is its own end," focused on other abstract theories and unwilling "to sully [its] hands in empirical research"—Bourdieu's agenda is to develop a "set of conceptual tools and procedures for constructing objects and for transferring knowledge [from] one area of inquiry into another" (Bourdieu 1988:774, 777, Bourdieu 1993b:45, Bourdieu & Wacquant 1992:5). Unlike other advocates of this program, however, Bourdieu does not envision these tools as a broad, eclectic assemblage suited to piecemeal appropriation. He concentrates instead on a limited set of concepts: most famously, "habitus," the "ensemble of dispositions" toward action and perception that operates from within social agents; and "field," the configuration of relations between social positions, or the structured space where social struggles unfold (Bourdieu & Wacquant 1992: 16–19). Insisting on the "two-way relationship between habitus and field," Bourdieu seeks to transcend the hoary intellectual antinomy between objectivism and subjectivism by "integrating into a single model the analysis of the experience of social agents and the analysis of the objective structures that make this experience possible" (1988:782–84) and by then deploying this model in empirical studies of spheres ranging from art and science to the economy and law. But he does not propose this model as a general "systematization" or a universal "discourse on the social world"; it is a temporary "machine for research" that "accomplishes and abolishes itself in the scientific work it has helped produce" (1993b:29; Bourdieu & Wacquant 1992:159–61; for discussion, see Calhoun et al 1993, Swartz 1997).

In contrast, W Wallace believes it is at last time for the theorist to codify a general "metalanguage," "a single conceptual matrix"—consisting of eight basic descriptive and twelve explanatory variables—for use throughout sociology, the basis for a "discipline-wide consensus" (1988:60). With this program, he veers toward Project II, though Wallace makes no claims for a theoretical synthesis. He regards his matrix as furnishing only a general "nomenclature" for empirically oriented work, i.e. for the creation of "many kinds of descriptions and explanations" (1988:60, 1983:9).

Project II: Synthesis of Multiple Theoretical Approaches

The analysis of existing social theories that is often criticized by proponents of Project I actually animates a second contemporary project. This project rests on the conviction that it is now possible to achieve a comprehensive synthesis of previously divergent theoretical perspectives. According to some theorists, such a synthesis is well under way; for others, it is a vital opportunity now to be seized.

A decade ago, Ritzer (1988a, 1990a) forecast a coming era of theoretical synthesis, and today efforts toward synthesis can be found in various quarters: in Scheff's program to "assimilate [contending] theoretical proposals in the human sciences...within a much larger matrix" by use of a "micro-linguistic analysis of discourse" situated in "the context of larger wholes" (1997:7–10, see also 1990); in Runciman's macro-historical "theory of social relations, social structure, and social evolution," offered as a "general synthesis" aiming to "do for the study of societies what Darwin [did] for the study of species" (1989b:60, 449; 1989a:13; see also 1983); and in Emirbayer's recent "manifesto for a relational sociology" that tries to rework "micro" and "macro" and to forge a "unitary frame of reference" upon which diverse social thinkers are said to be "fast converging" (1997:311–12; Emirbayer & Goodwin 1994).

The project of theoretical synthesis has also been embraced by some of the most widely discussed figures in contemporary theory. Included here are those broadly sympathetic with the research focus of Project I. J Turner, for example, has urged that steps be taken to break down the barriers that divide theorists and to advance toward a "theoretical synthesis" at the macro, meso, and micro levels—especially the last, where he has developed a synthetic theory of social interaction (1987, 1988, 1991). Recognizing that a theory unifying all levels may be far off, Turner believes that, at each level, "existing theories have captured many of the operative dynamics of the social universe," bringing sociology near to empirically testable general theory of the type found in the natural sciences: i.e. to timeless principles that cut across substantive areas (1989:17, 1991:591). He fears, however, that this goal may be defeated by the "anti-positivism" of other theorists and by various organizational divisions within sociology (1990, 1992; S Turner & J Turner 1990). Somewhat more optimistic, R Collins envisions a "comprehensive theory [for] every arena of society"—theory in the form of "generalized explanatory models" of basic social processes—though this will not take shape immediately (1986a:1351, 1989: 124, 1981b, 1992). Given the discipline's current fragmentation, the theorist's present task is to promote "mutual confrontation" of available theoretical traditions and to bridge productive areas of substantive research in order "to compare, to synthesize, and to cumulate"—as Collins has done in identifying power and status as central dimensions of all interaction and in proposing "interaction ritual chains" as part of the micro-foundation of macrostructure (1994:295, 1986a:1355, 1981a; Kemper & R Collins 1990). (See also the program for a unified "comprehensive theory" proposed by Fararo 1989a, 1989b; Fararo & Skvoretz 1986; Skvoretz & Fararo 1996.)

Important variants of the synthesis project have also appeared among those for whom theory has greater autonomy from empirical research. Equating theory with general "presuppositions" about human action and social order, Alexander has argued for the imminent convergence at this level of all major—and hitherto one-sided—theories, classical and contemporary, announcing that "synthetic rather than polemical theorizing is now the order of the day" (1988d:77). As to the content of this "new movement," Alexander has variously predicted and promoted the following: a "multidimensional" synthesis of "normative and instrumental" views of action, "material and ideal" views of order (1982–1983); a Parsons-inspired "neofunctionalism" that "relink[s] theorizing about action and order, conflict and stability, structure and culture" (Alexander & Colomy 1990:57; Alexander 1985); a post-Parsonsian "micro-macro synthesis" integrating "action and structure, subjectivity and objectivity" (Alexander & Giesen 1987:4; Alexander 1987:376–77, 1988b,d); and a "new form of synthetic social theory" that moves beyond neofunctionalism and carries the micro-macro synthesis in the direction of "culturalist theories opened up to the model of culture-as-language" (Alexander 1998:288, 1988c, 1995). Along parallel lines, Münch's earlier call ([1982]1987, [1982]1988) for a "synthesis" based on Parsonsian action theory has become an agenda for a "new synthesis" connecting "Parsonian theory and competing theoretical approaches" that treat the economics, politics, and symbolics of action (1987:149, 1994).

Giddens (1984, 1987, 1995, 1996) has pursued a similar cause, forecasting a revolutionary "new synthesis"—open to work outside sociology and geared to the world society of the next century—to replace the competing theories of the past. Key to this change, in his view, is theoretical advance, seen not as cumulation of natural science–like generalizations but as "conceptual innovation." To this end, he faults structuralism and functionalism for overlooking that actors are "vastly skilled in the practical accomplishments of social activities," while also criticizing phenomenology and ethnomethodology for neglecting the "structural constraint" that affects such activities (1987:43, 1984: xxvii, 26). He proposes "structuration theory" as the alternative that both recognizes the "duality of structure"—the fact that "the structural properties of social systems [i.e. their rules and resources] are both medium and outcome of the practices they recursively organize"—and problematizes, for "specific historical circumstances, the relation between knowledgeable activity . . . and social reproduction brought about in an unintended fashion" (1984:25, 1996:72; for discussion, see Cohen 1989). More ambitiously still, Luhmann (1985, 1987, 1995), alarmed over sociology's "theory crisis," draws on work in biology and cybernetics to fashion what he sees as a unified theory of self-referential, or autopoietic, social systems. Conceiving such systems (societies, interactions) to be composed not of agents or actions but of communication, and analyzing how these systems evolve or adapt with respect to their environments through meaningful communication, Luhmann views this approach as providing the needed basis for a "comprehensive theory of the social," a theory of "*everything* social" (1995:xxxvii, xlvii).

The paradox of these diverse synthetic projects has not escaped notice. Unified though they are on a program of synthesis, they generally diverge on the substance of this program, each thereby undercutting the other's case for the reality of the particular synthesis in question. To be sure, there are terminological overlaps (agency/structure, micro/macro), and overcoming these divisions is a concern shared by several (though not all) projects, much the way calls to reconcile order/change or consensus/conflict were commonplace a generation ago. But even strong advocates of synthesis have conceded that current theories use terms like micro and macro very differently and may not "offer adequate bases for dealing with micro-macro integration" (Ritzer 1988b:705–6). Surveying the plurality of options, S Turner & J Turner (1990:170) flatly state that "recent synthetic theories...have not been successful" at theoretical unification, while Holmwood & Stewart (1994)—in a kind of reversion to Project I—take failed syntheses as an occasion to broach new explanatory problems.

Project III: Refinement of Theoretical Research Programs

For observers like B Turner (1989, 1996a), the heterogeneity of synthetic theories makes "fragmentation and division rather than successful accumulation [the] dominant trend in sociological theory," though there are exceptions to this pattern. They are found in pockets of the discipline once called "schools"—i.e. in areas committed to the ongoing elaboration of a single theoretical orientation closely tied to an empirical research tradition (B Turner 1996a:9–10). The continuing development of several of these "theoretical research programs" (to borrow a term from D Wagner and Berger 1985) constitutes a third major project in the field of contemporary theory.

Visible among these approaches has been rational-choice theory. The rubric encompasses different positions, some suggestive of the synthetic goals of Project II (see Abell 1996a, Coleman 1989, 1993, Lindenberg 1986). Typically, however, the approach offloads many topics onto other theories to concentrate on constructing formal models of the processes by which interdependent, utility-maximizing actors "combine to produce social outcomes"; it then seeks to elaborate these models and extend their empirical range (Coleman & Fararo 1992a:xi–xii; Coleman 1990; Hechter 1983; Abell 1996b). With this in view, rational-choice theorists are now working to incorporate "social structure into models of individual choice" (Macy & Flache 1995) and to use these models in areas where they would seem inapplicable, e.g. in studies of family, religion, and gender, and in research on social solidarity (Hechter 1983, 1987; Hechter & Kanazawa 1997; for criticism, see Barnes 1995, Coleman & Fararo 1992b, England & Kilbourne 1990, Smelser 1998). A similar theoretical project is also being cultivated within Analytical Marxism. Here formal rational-choice models are again embraced and elaborated, but now as part of a program to bring Marxism out of the nineteenth century, to clarify its core concepts, to place its "macro-structural" theses on "micro-foundations" that specify their causal mechanisms, and to apply this perspective in research on class structure, exploitation, etc (Wright 1989:47–49; Elster 1985; Mayer 1994; Roemer 1986; for critique, see Burawoy 1986, 1989).

Another current focus for the project of theoretical refinement is expectations-states theory, which has continued its effort to formulate concepts and general propositions to describe and explain the status structure of small groups, to extend these ideas to further aspects of group interaction processes, and to test these formulations empirically (Berger et al 1989, Berger & Zelditch 1993, Fisek et al 1995, D Wagner & Berger 1985). This program has spawned several major subprograms, plus active attempts to integrate these, each new step hailed as calling for "more explicit formalization of the theory" and "research to test its more subtle implications" (D Wagner & Berger 1993:48). In these ways, the expectations-states program mirrors developments in other formal approaches to the analysis of interaction, such as exchange theory, network analysis, and projects combining the two (see Burt 1992, Cook 1987, Cook & Whitmeyer 1992, White 1992; cf Blau 1994).

Other elaborative projects are under way in connection with less formal theoretical approaches. Rebounding from its relative quiescence during the 1960s and 1970s, symbolic interactionism, for example, is now in a state of "revitalization" and "ferment," retaining some of its traditional concern with the concrete interactional basis of meaning, identity, and self, but moving in new directions: on the one hand by diversifying and "turn[ing] increasingly toward power, history, and distinctive versions of social structure" as subjects for interactionist research and theorizing (Plummer 1996:236–38); and on the other hand by bridging outward (as more tightly knit approaches such as rational choice have yet to do) to connect with other contemporary perspectives, notably cultural studies and postmodernism (Denzin 1992, Fine 1993, Goffman 1983, Joas 1987, Becker & McCall 1990, Stryker 1987). In ethnomethodology, a diversifying but continually developing theoretical research program is also clearly in evidence (Maynard & Clayman 1991).

Project IV: Dialogue Among Multiple Theoretical Approaches

If the multitude of positions found within the theory area has led numbers of theorists to decry fragmentation and, as an alternative, either to seek shelter in empirical research or to envision an all-encompassing synthesis or to cleave to a particular theoretical approach, a different reaction animates a fourth project. In this case, the presence of multiple approaches is welcomed as a potential opportunity for fruitful theoretical dialogue.

This program has affinities with the pluralist agenda articulated a generation ago by theorists like Merton who held that "it is not so much the plurality of paradigms as the collective acceptance by practicing sociologists of a single paradigm proposed as a panacea that would constitute a deep crisis with ensuing stasis" (Merton 1975:29; cf Eisenstadt & Curelaru 1976, Rorty 1979). But current dialogic projects seek not only to emphasize the functions of theoretical diversity but also to recognize and promote combinations and interactions of different theoretical perspectives—an objective that may be understood in different ways.

In some contemporary projects, for example, theoretical dialogue is viewed as a means to other kinds of programmatic ends, including tool construction (Rule 1997), broad (or partial) theoretical synthesis (R Collins 1994, Münch 1994), and theoretical reconstruction (Calhoun 1995; see also Bauman 1992).

Beyond such instrumental uses of discourse, however, dialogue has also been recently elaborated into a project in and of itself by Mouzelis (1995), Wiley (1990), and most fully, Levine (1986, 1995). Believing that communication—calmly "grasping truly alternative points of view"—is "the healing response" to cries of fragmentation, Levine sets for theorists the task of cultivating the "spirit of dialogue," especially by "tak[ing] stock of our manifold forms of social knowledge" and thus building a "common vocabulary that social scientists can use to engage in constructive conversations about their differences" while "opening [themselves] to a wider range of options" (1995:2, 297, 305, 324, 329). This project underlies Levine's (1985, 1991) own efforts to examine the dialectic interplay between the ideas of Simmel and Parsons, and it can be seen as well in the work of scholars carrying forth the Marx-Weber dialogue (Antonio & Glassman 1985, Wiley 1987).

Project V: Enlargement/Reconstruction of Current Theoretical Approaches

For many contemporary theorists the range of options before them is, or until recently has been, severely limited in some fundamental respect. Their project is to identify and fill one or more conceptual, methodological, social, moral, or political lacunae in the theoretical perspectives available to them and then to work out the reconstructive implications of the resulting enlargement of sociological theory—implications that vary in scope and depth from theorist to theorist.

Proposals for conceptual augmentation have been numerous and diverse, spanning the distance from B Turner's program to encompass human corporeality and overcome sociological theory's neglect of "the most obvious fact of human existence, namely that human beings have… bodies" (1984:41), on the one side, to steps by Alexander (1988a), Archer (1988), Connor (1996), J Hall (1990b), Somers (1995), Swidler (1986), and Wuthnow (1987) to awaken contemporary theory to the structural, symbolic, and institutional dimensions of culture and to recent work in anthropology and cultural studies, on the other side. Elsewhere, S Turner (1994) and Camic (1986, 1989) have urged renewed attention to habitual action—Turner to combat the concept of social practices, Camic to defend a sociology of action forms or practices. Others have called for the theoretical incorporation of revised conceptions of the self (Seidler 1994, Wiley 1994, Wolfe 1991) and of emotion and the irrational (Campbell 1996, Scheff 1997, Sica 1988). (See also Urry 1996 on the "singular absence" of the topic of time and space in sociological theory prior to the early 1980s.)

The pioneering effort along these lines, published slightly earlier but widely discussed in the period under review, is Habermas's concept of communicative action. Brought forth to accommodate circumstances where "the actions of the agents involved are coordinated not through … calculations of success"—as assumed in theories that define action in instrumental, goal-directed, and related terms—"but through acts of reaching understanding [viewed as] a cooperative process of interpretation," communicative action provides Habermas with a "comprehensive counter-concept": a means of reconceptualizing rationality (as communicative rationality), the organization of the social world (as the relationship between the communicatively based "lifeworld" and instrumental "system" processes), and also the evolution and present condition of society (Habermas [1981]1984:101, 285–86, Joas 1991:99; see also Habermas [1981]1989, [1983]1990, [1985]1987, [1988]1992, [1992]1996, Calhoun 1992a, Honneth & Joas 1991a). More recently, Joas, who has criticized Habermas's formulations, has outlined an ambitious alternative to dominant action-theoretical approaches, one that seeks to focalize "the creativity of action"— the potentially creative dimension of all human activity (Honneth & Joas 1991b:4; Joas 1993, 1996). Faulting the tendency of modern theorists to squeeze social action into a dichotomy of rational versus normative action, Joas draws from the early American pragmatists to show that all action takes the form of an alternation between "unreflected habitual action" and the creation of "a new mode of acting, which can gradually take root and thus become itself an unreflected routine" (1996:129). He uses this reorientation as a foundation for reconstructing theories of contemporary culture, collective action, and social change.

Proposals to fill voids of a more methodological sort have also assumed various shapes. Often launched as critiques of "positivist" views of knowledge still felt to dominate the theory area, these programs—reviewed in detail elsewhere—have included efforts to predicate sociological theory on recent developments in realist and hermeneutic philosophies of science (Outhwaite 1987, 1996, Sayer 1992, Shapiro & Sica 1984) as well as on some of the diverse epistemological lessons of critical theory, feminist theory, poststructuralism, postmodernism, and the sociology of science (Agger 1991, DeVault 1996, Fuller 1988, J Hall 1990a). More prosaically, work in the theory area, as it was passed on by the previous generation of theorists, has been charged with a neglect of history, with applying "universal theoretical terms [to] all aspects of social life, regardless of times and places" (Skocpol 1984:2–3). In the last two decades, this critique has inspired numerous theoretical contributions sensitive to the specifics of time and location (for review, see Mandalios 1996), among them Mann's (1986, 1993) theory of social power and Sewell's (1992, 1996) efforts to reformulate Giddens's concept of social structure and to make "events" a viable "theoretical category" (see also Abbott 1995).

Perhaps the most distinctive current focus, however, has been on an omission brought to light by various contemporary social movements. This is the "reality of differences" (Lemert 1995): what Calhoun defines as the "basic and urgent project [of] developing ways to take seriously such fundamental categorical differences" as gender, race, ethnicity, sexuality, language, class, region, and nation (1995:xix–xxii). Among these differences, it is the neglect of gender that has received the widest treatment, as feminist scholars have attacked sociological theory for its restrictive assumptions about which aspects of social reality merit analysis, for its marginalization of feminist contributions, for its masculinist reliance on "logical dichotomies" and tendency to suppress the agency of subjects and "re-attribut[e it] to social phenomena" (Sprague 1997: 93; Smith 1989:49; see also Alway 1995, Lengermann & Niebrugge-Brantley 1990, Stacey & Thorne 1985, 1996, Wallace 1989). On such grounds, feminist theorists have proposed varying degrees of theoretical reconstruction: in some cases, the inclusion of gender into established theoretical approaches (Chafetz 1988, Walby 1988); in others, radical alterations of the aims and procedures of all existing approaches (e.g. Haraway 1985, Smith 1990, 1993; for review, see Chafetz 1997, Clough 1994, Lovell 1996). Related lines of argument have emerged elsewhere as well: in the demand for theories of oppression, struggle, motherhood, and community constructed from the neglected and "unique standpoint [of] Black womanhood, unavailable to other groups" (P Collins 1990: 33); in the critique of sociological theory for omitting the concerns and contributions of peoples of color in both the Western and post-colonial worlds (Connell 1997, S Hall 1996, Gilroy 1993); and in the claim that theory has also avoided questions of sexual identity, exhibiting both disinterest in gays, lesbians, bisexuals, and transsexuals and an unwillingness to rethink its basic terms from the perspective of sexual difference (Butler 1993, Clough 1994, Seidman 1996).

Amid these developments, sociological theory has also been widely indicted for its exclusion of moral issues, for having strayed from its origins to become a "detached enterprise of abstract problems [that lack] immediate implications for everyday schemes of moral and political action and belief" (Wardell & S Turner 1986:11; see also Levine 1995, B Turner 1989, 1996a). An interest in ending these exclusions forms a leitmotiv in many of the works already reviewed in this section, some of them explicitly advocating a renewal of "critical theory"—in Habermas's case from the standpoint of communicative rationality, in Calhoun's from the perspective of difference. But heightened concern with theory as a moral and political enterprise is evident in numerous other sources, including Selznick's (1992) sweeping program to build a "liberal communitarianism" on the foundations of pragmatist social theory (cf Bellah et al 1985, Etzioni 1996, Horowitz 1993, Wallerstein 1997, Wolfe 1989).

Project VI: Engagement with Past Theoretical Ideas

Proponents of the preceding projects differ markedly in their attitude toward a sixth line of theoretical activity. This is the analysis of various theoretically significant ideas found in the writings of social thinkers from the past—a program that brings together theorists working to advance some of these other contemporary projects and scholars who are relatively aloof from such efforts.

The range of work falling within this category is vast. Recent years have witnessed an outpouring of research on and reinterpretation of all the major classical theorists, Comte, Spencer, Marx, Durkheim, Weber, Simmel, and Mead (for a review, see the chapters in Camic 1997a), along with efforts to revitalize and critically extend their perspectives, as seen, for example, in various lines of "neo-Weberian" scholarship (R Collins 1986b, Eisenstadt 1987, 1992, 1996, Kalberg 1994, Lehman & Roth 1993, Scaff 1989, Schluchter 1989, Sica 1988, Whimster & Lash 1987). Increased interest has also been shown in the ideas of such latter-day figures as Parsons, Mannheim, Merton, and Garfinkel (Camic 1991, 1992, Crothers 1987, Heritage 1984, Hilbert 1992, Kettler et al 1984, Sztompka 1986) and in the work of earlier women thinkers (McDonald 1994), intellectuals of African descent (Lemert 1993, Seidman 1994a), and other "neglected theorists" (*Sociological Theory* 1994–1995), Norbert Elias perhaps chief among them (Fletcher 1997, Mennell 1989).

These studies cannot be separately reviewed here, but generally they locate themselves as projects integral to the theory area (rather than as contributions mainly to the history of sociology) on different grounds. These run the gamut from the utilitarian claim that works from the past contain concepts and generalizations "worth salvaging and using" in order to address contemporary research questions (R Collins 1986b:3) to the "noninstrumental" idea that "conversing with great minds," via "writings of unsurpassed scholarly texture," is a vital experience, "humbling and invigorating" (Poggi 1996:40–42; cf Alexander 1989). Between the extremes, scholars have also recently urged the careful application of hermeneutic methods to past theoretical works; instead of "cannibalizing classical statements in search of testable fragments," such methods strive for "a contextual or holistic understanding of [each] theorist's project" (Sica 1988:138). In this way, they expand the range of theoretical alternatives beyond the bounds of present possibilities and reveal the contingent historical processes by which some theoretical approaches were established at the expense of others (Camic 1997b; cf Calhoun 1995, S Turner 1996a).

Project VII: Diagnosis of Contemporary Social Conditions

Not past theoretical ideas but present social realities form the main focus of a seventh contemporary project. This sets for theory the task of providing for the late twentieth century what the classical theorists furnished for their era but now demands overhaul: an analysis of the nature and dynamics of modernity, of the social forces shaping human life in the current period.

This project is sometimes pursued in close conjunction with others we have identified. On the basis of his concept of communicative action, for example, Habermas ([1981]1989) examines the modern world (descriptively and normatively) in terms of the growing penetration, or "colonization," of the communicative processes of the "lifeworld," found in areas such as family and public discussion, by the instrumental processes of economic, political, and legal "systems." In turn, Luhmann draws on systems theory to argue that whereas "in modern society, functional systems...have the possibility of self-steering," there are inherent limits on the extent to which the political system can effectively regulate other social spheres (1997:45). In Luhmann's view, the contemporary world is unique in the intensity of its calls for such regulation; analysis of the limits of societal steering thus forms part of "the self-description of modern society" (1997:54). For his part Giddens mobilizes structuration theory to characterize the present age of "late modernity" as the "increasing interconnection" between two developments: the reflexive organization of "self-identity," as individuals confront distinctive forms of risk amid a "transformation of intimacy" and relationships of trust; and "globalization" in its economic, political, military, and cultural dimensions (Giddens 1991:1–6, see also 1987, 1994a,b, 1996).

This emphasis on globalization is not unique to Giddens. Albrow's comment that contemporary sociologists "are falling over themselves in their haste to re-thematize old topics in the light of globalizing processes" (1993: 732) perhaps reflects the particular perspective of British sociology (see, e.g., Featherstone 1990, Robertson 1992). But Albrow's (1997) own recent work on globalization, Sklair's (1995) attempt to transcend state-centered views of the global system with a theory of "transnational practices," and Meyer et al's (1997) analysis of the diffusion of the nation-state model in the context of "world society" are lines of thinking that all evidence growing concern with the dynamics and consequences of new patterns of interconnection among the world's societies, institutions, and peoples.

Efforts to theorize contemporary conditions have taken several other directions as well. For Touraine, "social life is constructed through struggles and negotiations around the implementation of...cultural orientations"—struggles that, "in today's post-industrial society...center upon… the production and mass distribution of representations, data and languages" and thus turn the analytical spotlight to contemporary social movements (1995:358, 1988; see also Eder 1993, Offe 1985). For Beck, the modern world has witnessed a "renaissance of political subjectivity" due to the emergence of a "risk society" beset with environmental hazards; here "socially recognized risks...contain a peculiar political explosive" that ignites activity outside conventional politics (1992:24, 1994:18). In other work, theorists have looked to the public sphere (Calhoun 1992a), identity politics (Calhoun 1994), the collapse of the Communist bloc (Offe 1997), the apparent waning of the ideology of liberal reformism (Wallerstein 1995), doubts about the "intelligibility" and "shapeability" of the social world (P Wagner 1994:176), citizenship debates (B Turner 1993, Laclau 1990), and the nature of contemporary capitalism (Lash & Urry 1987) and culture (Bauman 1992; see also the new afterword in Bell [1976] 1996)—all to advance the agenda of coming to intellectual terms with the distinctive characteristics of the current historical epoch.

Project VIII: Dissolution of Sociological Theory

As theorists have reckoned with the features of the present age, a very different project—an anti-project—has emerged in proposals to bring the enterprise of sociological theory to an end. Accepting in various degrees the post-modernist assault on the activity of social-scientific "theory" and on the reality of the "social," these proposals generally call for the multidisciplinary development of critical, non–social-scientistic narratives.

The challenge to "theory" has been raised by Lemert, who employs post-modernist epistemological critiques to argue that "whatever social theory today is or is not, it has few choices beyond accepting, getting around, or resisting the stance of radical and continuing doubt about the final vocabulary available for use in speaking about the social world" (1992:20). Given this, Lemert (1992, 1993, 1994a,b, 1995) holds that sociological theorists must relinquish their aspirations to be purveyors of abstract scientific truths, instead becoming what Rorty (1989) calls "ironists"—intellectuals who recognize that there exists no theoretical metalanguage for objectively arbitrating between competing truth claims. Drawing on thinkers like Foucault (1972) and Lyotard (1984), Seidman launches a similar attack on sociological theory for its generalizing, universalist ambitions, observing that "once the veil of epistemic privilege is torn away by post-modernists, [social-scientific theory] appears as a social force enmeshed in particular cultural and power struggles" (1994c:124). This kind of sociological theory should therefore be replaced by a diversity of "social theories" in the form of "broad social narratives [that] relate stories of origin and development, tales of crisis, decline, or progress," but that do not pretend "to discover the one true vocabulary that mirrors the social universe" (1994c:120). Moreover, because sociologists hold no monopoly over such narratives, theorists need to "move sociology away from its historic role as a discipline" and open themselves up to insights about the social from feminist theory, post-colonial studies, queer theory, and so on (Lemert 1994a:268; see also Seidman 1994c, B Turner 1990).

For other contemporary scholars, however, even the "social" itself is deeply problematic. This is so, in Game's (1991) view, because the writings of Barthes, Derrida, and Irigaray have shown that "the social is written, that there is no extra-discursive real outside cultural systems" (1991:4). For this reason, all forms of sociological theory that assume that theoretical terms are ideational representations of reality must give way to a "deconstructive sociology" that imagines and analyzes the social only as text, alert to the power interests that lie behind representationalist thinking (see also Brown 1990, Clough 1993). For Baudrillard (1983), in contrast, it is the present historical period itself that marks the "end of the perspective space of the social." As a result of the contemporary diffusion of various technologies of simulation, the activity of representation has itself become increasingly impossible, and the social, as a representation of the real, collapses: "[T]he social only exists in a perspective space, it dies in the space of simulation..." (1983:83). Under these conditions, sociological theory as a discourse on the social necessarily loses all viability (see Kellner 1994, Bogard 1990, Denzin 1986, Gane 1991; for critical discussion, see Bauman 1992, Seidman & D Wagner 1992, Seidman 1994b).

DISCUSSION AND CONCLUSION: CONDITIONS OF POSSIBILITY

There are areas in sociology where the presence of this number of active and diverse projects would generally be seen as evidence of intellectual vitality.

Among the majority in the theory area, however, this is not the prevailing sentiment. Pessimists, disillusioned over what they take to be the direction of the area, here greatly outnumber those who are now sanguine about the field or some particular contemporary project.

Expressions of this attitude are widespread, though efforts to get to its roots have been meager. Proponents of the theoretical projects described above often portray themselves in dismay, facing a hard battle on behalf of their cause. Rarely, however, do theorists provide a serious and constructive assessment of the forces arrayed against their particular agenda. To the contrary, most contemporary theory programs put themselves forth on exclusively intellectual grounds, giving minimal sociological attention to the organizational conditions that confront them—conditions these programs must reckon with realistically if they are to advance their aims. Four important conditions of possibility are discussed below.

OTHER PROJECTS With isolated exceptions, few contemporary projects evince awareness of the range of other projects with which they share the theory field. This situation precludes systematic consideration in the field of possible relationships among projects: of the different intellectual questions to which the various projects may be differentially applicable; of the points at which different programs might operate in collaborative, complementary, integrable, or cross-cutting modes, in contrast to points at which they are competitive or mutually irrelevant (on these options, see Levine 1986). Added to this problem is the tendency among several projects simply to lump the majority of alternative projects together in an undifferentiated mass. It is thus that advocates of tool-construction (Project I) are prone to regard all other theoretical efforts as little more than the exegesis of past ideas (Project VI?), overlooking in the process even a number of differently formulated variants of their own program—an oversight exhibited in other projects as well. By this kind of lumping, various projects misassess their relative position in the theory area: tool-constructors, for example, regularly, but wrongly, presenting their agenda as a beleagured minority stance; synthesizers (Project II) erring in the opposite direction by absorbing all other lines of theoretical work into their own program, thereby fostering the widely accepted but inaccurate view that this one project is contemporary sociological theory as such.

SOCIOLOGY AT LARGE Quantitative data on the organization of sociology document that, during the very period when these contemporary theory projects have been under way, not only did "new theoretical approaches [fail to] provide a unified perspective for the discipline as a whole," but contributions from the theory area ceased "to be closely connected to the sociology literature" at large (Crane & Small 1992:229–30). Historical evidence suggests that this is no recent development: that the impact of sociological theory on sociological research has long been tenuous, with theory an unwanted presence in many of the ever-changing speciality areas of the discipline (Sica 1989a,b). With occasional exceptions, however, theorists have been slow to think through the implications of this and to fashion suitable roles for themselves under these conditions. To the contrary, current theoretical projects often read like efforts to wish the conditions away, to deny that the strong "internal connectivity" between research areas that gives centrality to "theory" in a discipline like economics is simply not an institutional feature of sociology (Crane & Small 1992:208, 231).

EXTERNAL FORCES As a result of its own "fragile professional standing," the entire discipline of sociology has been buffeted during this same recent period by major changes in its social and institutional links to other academic disciplines, in its relations to its different patrons and publics, and in the size and composition of its student clienteles (Halliday 1992). Save for scattered commentary on the first of these points, however, theorists have rarely considered the bearing of these developments on the viability of their own projects. And even regarding the first point, their opinions are divided, with some theorists anticipating only minor adjustments in the disciplinary status quo and others expecting and calling for closer ties between sociological theory and everything from biology to all the social sciences as well as history and cultural studies. For those urging these ties, the common hope is that they will produce a "flourishing" back-and-forward exchange between these other fields and work in sociological theory (Calhoun 1992b); but theorists need also to recognize that reciprocated exchanges have been the exception—that theoretical projects inside sociology have drawn from without far more often than they have been elsewhere drawn upon (Crane & Small 1992:231–32).

HISTORICAL LEGACIES Almost invariably, contemporary theoretical projects rest on historical narratives, accounts of the theory field (and sometimes of sociology and forces external to it) at previous times—the 1940s and 1950s, the 1950s and 1960s, the 1960s and 1970s—different theorists choose different slices. But their historical narratives are ordinarily more than window dressing: for each narrative is the baseline for the particular project that the theorist seeks to put on the agenda for the future, an analysis of what the theory field thus far offers and does not offer, an inventory of its resources and lacunae, of its problems and possibilities. Take the historical narrative away and one removes much of the rationale for the project it accompanies. Yet, for all this, few theorists exhibit much historical care in constructing their narratives, in defining the intellectual and institutional legacies that the contemporary theory field actually confronts. Indeed, so lax are theorists in this respect that their historical claims tend not only to cancel one another out, but also to meet broad disconfirmation when subjected to direct historical investigation (see Platt 1996).

In the course of advancing their different projects, a few contemporary theorists have given serious attention to some of these organizational factors (Bourdieu & Wacquant 1992, Calhoun 1992b, R Collins 1986a, 1989, Levine 1995, Sica 1989b, S Turner & J Turner 1990). But systematic examination of the intellectual and institutional relations among the diverse projects that now constitute the theory field, of the field's complex historical legacies, and of its current position within sociology and in regard to various external forces has yet to crystallize into a program in its own right, a project that would problematize the form or forms appropriate to sociological theory under present conditions of possibility. If at least some current projects are to succeed, however, contemporary developments would seem to warrant also including this project square on the theorist's agenda.

ACKNOWLEDGMENTS

We would like to thank Craig Calhoun, Ira Cohen, Hans Joas, and Alan Sica for very helpful comments on this chapter.

Literature Cited

Abbott A. 1995. Sequence analysis: new methods for old ideas. *Annu. Rev. Sociol.* 21:93–113

Abell P. 1996a. Homo sociologicus: Do we need him/her? See SP Turner 1996b, pp. 229–34

Abell P. 1996b. Sociological theory and rational choice. See BS Turner 1996b, pp. 252–73

Agger B. 1991. Critical theory, poststructuralism, postmodernism: their sociological relevance. *Annu. Rev. Sociol.* 17:105–31

Albrow M. 1993. Review of *Globalization: Social Theory and Global Culture,* by R Robertson. *Sociology* 27:732–33

Albrow M. 1997. *The Global Age: State and Society Beyond Modernity.* Stanford, CA: Stanford Univ. Press

Alexander JC. 1982–1983. *Theoretical Logic in Sociology.* Berkeley: Univ. Calif. Press. 4 vols.

Alexander JC, ed. 1985. *Neofunctionalism.* Beverly Hills, CA: Sage

Alexander JC. 1987. *Twenty Lectures: Sociological Theory Since World War II.* New York: Columbia Univ. Press

Alexander JC, ed. 1988a. *Durkheimian Sociology: Cultural Studies.* Cambridge, UK: Cambridge Univ. Press

Alexander JC 1988b. *Action and Its Environments: Toward a New Synthesis.* New York: Columbia Univ. Press

Alexander JC 1988c. Durkheimian sociology and cultural studies today. See Alexander 1989, pp. 156–73

Alexander JC. 1988d. The new theoretical movement. In *Handbook of Sociology,* ed. N Smelser, pp. 77–101. Newbury Park, CA: Sage

Alexander JC. 1989. *Structure and Meaning: Relinking Classical Sociology.* New York: Columbia Univ. Press

Alexander JC. 1995. *Fin de Siècle Social Theory.* London: Verso

Alexander JC. 1998. *Neofunctionalism and After.* Cambridge, MA: Blackwell

Alexander JC, Colomy P. 1990. Neofunctionalism today: reconstructing a theoretical tradition. See Alexander 1998, pp. 53–91

Alexander JC, Giesen B. 1987. From reduction to linkage: the long view of the micro-macro link. In *The Micro-Macro Link,* ed. JC Alexander, B Giesen, R Münch, NJ Smelser, pp. 1–42. Berkeley: Univ. Calif. Press

Alway J. 1995. The trouble with gender: tales of the still-missing feminist revolution in sociological theory. *Soc. Theory* 13:209–28
Antonio RJ, Glassman RM, eds. 1985. *A Weber-Marx Dialogue.* Lawrence, KS: Univ. Kans. Press
Archer MS. 1988. *Culture and Agency: The Place of Culture in Social Theory.* Cambridge, UK: Cambridge Univ. Press
Barnes B. 1995. *The Elements of Social Theory.* Princeton, NJ: Princeton Univ. Press
Baudrillard J. 1983. *In the Shadow of the Silent Majorities . . . Or the End of the Social and Other Essays.* Transl. P Foss, P Patton, J Johnston. New York: Semiotext(e) (From French)
Bauman Z. 1992. *Intimations of Postmodernity.* London: Routledge
Beck U. 1992. *Risk Society: Towards a New Modernity.* Transl. M Ritter. London: Sage (From German)
Beck U. 1994. The reinvention of politics: towards a theory of reflexive modernization. In *Reflexive Modernization: Politics, Tradition and Aesthetics in the Modern Social Order,* ed. U Beck, A Giddens, S Lash, pp. 1–55. Transl. M Ritter. Stanford, CA: Stanford Univ. Press (From German)
Becker HS, McCall MM, eds. 1990. *Symbolic Interaction and Cultural Studies.* Chicago: Univ. Chicago Press
Bell D. [1976] 1996. *The Cultural Contradictions of Capitalism.* New York: Basic Books
Bellah RN, Madsen R, Sullivan WM, Swidler A, Tipton SM. 1985. *Habits of the Heart.* New York: Harper & Row
Berger J, Zelditch M Jr, eds. 1993. *Theoretical Research Programs: Studies in the Growth of Theory.* Stanford, CA: Stanford Univ. Press
Berger J, Zelditch M Jr, Anderson B, eds. 1989. *Sociological Theories in Progress.* Newbury Park, CA: Sage
Blau PM. 1994. *Structural Contexts of Opportunities.* Chicago: Univ. Chicago Press
Bogard W. 1990. Closing down the social: Baudrillard's challenge to contemporary sociology. *Soc. Theory* 8:1–15
Bourdieu P. 1988. Vive le crise! *Theory Soc.* 17:773–87
Bourdieu P. 1990a. *The Logic of Practice.* Transl. R Nice. Stanford, CA: Stanford Univ. Press (From French)
Bourdieu P. 1990b. *In Other Words: Essays Towards a Reflexive Sociology.* Transl. M Adamson. Stanford, CA: Stanford Univ. Press (From French)
Bourdieu P. 1993a. *The Field of Cultural Production.* New York: Columbia Univ. Press
Bourdieu P. 1993b. *Sociology in Question.* Transl. R Nice. London: Sage (From French)
Bourdieu P, Wacquant LJD. 1992. *An Invitation to Reflexive Sociology.* Chicago: Univ. Chicago Press
Brown RH. 1990. Rhetoric, textuality, and the postmodern turn in sociological theory. *Soc. Theory* 8:188–97
Burawoy M. 1986. Making nonsense of Marx. *Contemp. Soc.* 15:704–7
Burawoy M. 1989. Marxism without microfoundations. *Socialist Rev.* 19:53–86
Burt RS. 1992. *Structural Holes: The Social Structure of Competition.* Cambridge, MA: Harvard Univ. Press
Butler JP. 1993. *Bodies that Matter: On the Discursive Limits of "Sex."* New York: Routledge
Calhoun CJ, ed. 1992a. *Habermas and the Public Sphere.* Cambridge, MA: MIT Press
Calhoun CJ. 1992b. Sociology, other disciplines, and the project of a general understanding of social life. See Halliday & Janowitz 1992, pp. 137–95
Calhoun CJ, ed. 1994. *Social Theory and the Politics of Identity.* Oxford: Blackwell
Calhoun CJ. 1995. *Critical Social Theory.* Oxford: Blackwell
Calhoun CJ. 1996a. Editor's comment. *Soc. Theory* 14:1–2
Calhoun CJ. 1996b. Whose classics? Which readings? Interpretation and cultural difference in the canonization of sociological theory. See SP Turner 1996b, pp.70–96
Calhoun CJ. 1997. Editor's comments and call for papers. *Soc. Theory* 15:1–2
Calhoun CJ, LiPuma E, Postone M, eds. 1993. *Bourdieu: Critical Perspectives.* Chicago: Univ. Chicago Press
Camic C. 1986. The matter of habit. *Am. J. Sociol.* 91:1039–87
Camic C. 1989. *Structure* after 50 years. *Am. J. Sociol.* 95:38–107
Camic C, ed. 1991. *Talcott Parsons: The Early Essays.* Chicago: Univ. Chicago Press
Camic C. 1992. Reputation and predecessor selection. *Am. Sociol. Rev.* 57:421–45
Camic C, ed. 1997a. *Reclaiming the Sociological Classics: The State of the Scholarship.* Cambridge, MA: Blackwell
Camic C. 1997b. Uneven development in the history of sociology. *Swiss J. Sociol.* 23:227–33
Campbell C. 1996. *The Myth of Social Action.* Cambridge, UK: Cambridge Univ. Press
Chafetz JS. 1988. *Feminist Sociology.* Itasca, IL: Peacock
Chafetz JS. 1993. Sociological theory: a case of multiple personality disorder. *Am. Sociol.* 24:60–62
Chafetz JS. 1997. Feminist theory and sociol-

ogy: underutilized contributions to mainstream theory. *Annu. Rev. Sociol.* 23: 97–120

Clough PT. 1993. On the brink of deconstructing sociology: critical reading of Dorothy Smith's standpoint epistemology. *Sociol. Q.* 34:169–82

Clough PT. 1994. *Feminist Thought.* Oxford: Blackwell

Cohen IJ. 1989. *Structuration Theory: Anthony Giddens and the Constitution of Social Life.* London: MacMillan

Coleman JS. 1989. Rationality and society. *Ration. Soc.* 1:5–9

Coleman JS. 1990. *Foundations of Social Theory.* Cambridge, MA: Harvard Univ. Press

Coleman JS. 1993. The impact of Gary Becker's work on sociology. *Acta Sociol.* 36:169–78

Coleman JS, Fararo TJ. 1992a. Introduction. See Coleman & Fararo 1992b, pp. ix–xxii

Coleman JS, Fararo TJ, eds. 1992b. *Rational Choice Theory: Advocacy and Critique.* Newbury Park, CA: Sage

Collins PH. 1990. *Black Feminist Thought: Knowledge, Consciousness, and the Politics of Empowerment.* Boston: Unwin Hyman

Collins R. 1981a. On the microfoundations of macrosociology. *Am. J. Sociol.* 86: 984–1014

Collins R. 1981b. *Sociology Since Midcentury: Essays in Theory Cumulation.* New York: Academic Press

Collins R. 1986a. Is sociology in the doldrums? *Am. J. Sociol.* 91:1336–55

Collins R. 1986b. *Weberian Sociological Theory.* Cambridge, UK: Cambridge Univ. Press

Collins R. 1989. Sociology: proscience or antiscience? *Am. Sociol. Rev.* 54:124–39

Collins R. 1992. Three modes of sociology. See Seidman & D Wagner 1992, pp. 164–97

Collins R. 1994. *Four Sociological Traditions.* New York: Oxford Univ. Press

Connell RW. 1997. Why is classical theory classical? *Am. J. Sociol.* 102:1511–57

Conner S. 1996. Cultural sociology and cultural sciences. See BS Turner 1996b, pp. 340–68

Cook KS, ed. 1987. *Social Exchange Theory.* Newbury Park, CA: Sage

Cook KS, Whitmeyer JM. 1992. Two approaches to social structure: exchange theory and network analysis. *Annu. Rev. Sociol.* 22:29–50

Crane D, Small H. 1992. American sociology since the seventies: the emerging identity crisis in the discipline. See Halliday & Janowitz 1992, pp. 197–234

Crothers C. 1987. *Robert K. Merton.* London: Tavistock

Denzin NK. 1986. Postmodern social theory. *Soc. Theory* 4:194–204

Denzin NK. 1992. *Symbolic Interactionism and Cultural Studies.* Oxford: Blackwell

DeVault ML. 1996. Talking back to sociology: distinctive contributions of feminist methodology. *Annu. Rev. Sociol.* 22:29–50

Eder K. 1993. *The New Politics of Class: Social Movements and Cultural Dynamics in Advanced Societies.* London: Sage

Eisenstadt SN, ed. 1987. *Patterns of Modernity.* New York: New York Univ. Press

Eisenstadt SN, ed. 1992. *Democracy and Modernity.* New York: Brill

Eisenstadt SN. 1996. *Japanese Civilization.* Chicago: Univ. Chicago Press

Eisenstadt SN, Curelaru M. 1976. *The Form of Sociology.* New York: Wiley & Sons

Elster J. 1985. *Making Sense of Marx.* Cambridge, UK: Cambridge Univ. Press

Emirbayer M. 1997. Manifesto for a relational sociology. *Am. J. Sociol.* 103:281–317

Emirbayer M, Goodwin J. 1994. Network analysis, culture, and the problem of agency. *Am. J. Sociol.* 99:1411–54

England P, Kilbourne BS. 1990. Feminist critiques of the separative model of the self: implications for rational choice theory. *Ration. Soc.* 2: 156–71

Etzioni A. 1996. *The New Golden Rule: Community and Morality in a Democratic Society.* New York: Basic Books

Fararo TJ. 1989a. *The Meaning of General Theoretical Sociology.* Cambridge, UK: Cambridge Univ. Press

Fararo TJ. 1989b. The spirit of unification in sociological theory. *Soc. Theory* 7:175–90

Fararo TJ, Skvoretz J. 1986. E-state structuralism: a theoretical method. *Am. Sociol. Rev.* 51:591–602

Featherstone M, ed. 1990. *Global Culture: Nationalism, Globalization and Modernity.* London: Sage

Fine G. 1993. The sad demise, mysterious disappearance, and glorious triumph of symbolic interactionism. *Annu. Rev. Sociol.* 19:61–87

Fisek MH, Berger J, Norman RZ. 1995. Evaluations and the formation of expectations. *Am. J. Sociol.* 101:721–46

Fletcher J. 1997. *Violence and Civilization: An Introduction to the Work of Norbert Elias.* Cambridge, UK: Polity

Foucault M. 1972. *The Archaeology of Knowledge.* Transl. AM Sheridan Smith. New York: Pantheon (From French)

Fuller S. 1988. *Social Epistemology.* Bloomington: Indiana Univ. Press

Game A. 1991. *Undoing the Social: Towards*

a Deconstructive Sociology. Buckingham, UK: Open Univ. Press
Gane M. 1991. *Baudrillard: Critical and Fatal Theory*. London: Routledge
Giddens A. 1984. *The Constitution of Society*. Berkeley: Univ. Calif. Press
Giddens A. 1987. *Social Theory and Modern Sociology*. Stanford: Stanford Univ. Press
Giddens A. 1991. *Modernity and Self-Identity*. Stanford: Stanford Univ. Press
Giddens A. 1994a. *Beyond Left and Right: The Future of Radical Politics*. Stanford, CA: Stanford Univ. Press
Giddens A. 1994b. Living in a post-traditional society. See Beck 1994, pp. 56–109
Giddens A. 1995. *Politics, Sociology and Social Theory*. Stanford, CA: Stanford Univ. Press
Giddens A. 1996. *In Defense of Sociology*. Cambridge, UK: Polity
Giddens A, Turner JH, eds. 1987. *Social Theory Today*. Cambridge, UK: Polity
Gilroy P. 1993. *The Black Atlantic: Modernity and Double Consciousness*. Cambridge, MA: Harvard Univ. Press
Goffman E. 1983. The interaction order. *Am. Sociol. Rev.* 48:1–17
Gross N. 1997. Durkheim's pragmatism lectures: a contextual interpretation. *Soc. Theory* 15:126–49
Habermas J. [1981]1984. *The Theory of Communicative Action*, Vol. 1. Transl. T McCarthy. Boston: Beacon (From German)
Habermas J. [1981]1989. *The Theory of Communicative Action*, Vol. 2. Transl. T McCarthy. Boston: Beacon (From German)
Habermas J. [1983]1990. *Moral Consciousness and Communicative Action*. Transl. C Lenhardt, SW Nicholsen. Cambridge, MA: MIT Press (From German)
Habermas J. [1985]1987. *The Philosophical Discourse of Modernity*. Transl. FG Lawrence. Cambridge, MA: MIT Press (From German)
Habermas J. [1988]1992. *Postmetaphysical Thinking*. Transl. WM Hohengarten. Cambridge, MA: MIT Press (From German)
Habermas. J. [1992]1996. *Between Facts and Norms*. Transl. W Rehg. Cambridge, MA: MIT Press (From German)
Hall JR. 1990a. Epistemology and sociohistorical inquiry. *Annu. Rev. Sociol.* 16: 329–51
Hall JR. 1990b. Social interaction, culture, and historical studies. See Becker & McCall 1990, pp. 16–45
Hall S. 1996. Cultural studies and the politics of internationalization: an interview with Stuart Hall by Kuan-Hsing Chen, 1992. In *Stuart Hall: Critical Dialogues in Cultural Studies*, ed. D Morley, K Chen, pp. 392–408. London: Routledge
Halliday TC. 1992. Introduction: sociology's fragile professionalism. See Halliday & Janowitz 1992, pp. 3–42
Halliday TC, Janowitz M, eds. 1992. *Sociology and Its Publics: The Forms and Fates of Disciplinary Organization*. Chicago: Univ. Chicago Press
Haraway DJ. 1985. A manifesto for cyborgs: science, technology, and socialist feminism in the 1980s. *Social. Rev.* 15:65–108
Hechter M, ed. 1983. *The Microfoundations of Macrosociology*. Philadelphia: Temple Univ. Press
Hechter M. 1987. *Principles of Group Solidarity*. Berkeley: Univ. Calif. Press
Hechter M, Kanazawa S. 1997. Sociological rational choice theory. *Annu. Rev. Sociol.* 23:191–214
Heritage J. 1984. *Garfinkel and Ethnomethodology*. New York: Polity
Hilbert RA. 1992. *The Classical Roots of Ethnomethodology*. Chapel Hill: Univ. N. C. Press
Holmwood J, Stewart A. 1994. Synthesis and fragmentation in social theory. *Soc. Theory* 12:83–100
Honneth A, Joas H, eds. 1991a. *Communicative Action: Essays on Jürgen Habermas's The Theory of Communicative Action*. Transl. J Gaines, DL Jones. Cambridge, MA: MIT Press (From German)
Honneth A, Joas H. 1991b. Introduction. See Honneth & Joas 1991a, pp. 1–6
Horowitz IL. 1993. *The Decomposition of Sociology*. New York: Oxford Univ. Press
Joas H. 1987. Symbolic interactionism. See Giddens & JH Turner 1987, pp. 82–115
Joas H. 1991. The unhappy marriage of hermeneutics and functionalism. See Honneth & Joas 1991a. pp. 97–118
Joas H. 1993. *Pragmatism and Social Theory*. Transl. J Gaines, R Meyer, S Minner. Chicago: Univ. Chicago Press (From German)
Joas H. 1996. *The Creativity of Action*. Transl. J Gaines, P Keast. Chicago: Univ. Chicago Press (From German)
Kalberg S. 1994. *Max Weber's Comparative Historical Sociology*. Chicago: Univ. Chicago Press
Kellner D. 1994. Introduction: Jean Baudrillard in the fin-de-millennium. In *Baudrillard: A Critical Reader*, ed. D Kellner, pp. 1–23. Oxford: Blackwell
Kemper TD, Collins R. 1990. Dimensions of microinteraction. *Am. J. Sociol.* 96:32–68
Kettler D, Meja V, Stehr N. 1984. *Karl Mannheim*. London: Tavistock
Laclau E. 1990. *New Reflections on the Revolution of Our Time*. London: Verso
Lash S, Urry J. 1987. *The End of Organized Capitalism*. Madison: Univ. Wisc. Press

Lehmann H, Roth G, eds. 1993. *Weber's "Protestant Ethic."* Cambridge, UK: Cambridge Univ. Press

Lemert CC. 1992. General social theory, irony, postmodernism. See Seidman & D Wagner 1992, pp. 17–46

Lemert CC. 1993. Introduction: social theory: its uses and pleasures. In *Social Theory: The Multicultural and Classic Readings,* ed. C Lemert, pp.1–24. Boulder, CO: Westview

Lemert CC. 1994a. Post-structuralism and sociology. See Seidman 1994b, pp. 265–81

Lemert CC. 1994b. Social theory at the early end of a short century. *Soc. Theory* 12: 140–52

Lemert CC. 1995. *Sociology After the Crisis.* Boulder, CO: Westview

Lengermann PM, Niebrugge-Brantley J. 1990. Feminist sociological theory: the near future prospects. See Ritzer 1990b, pp. 316–44

Levine DN. 1985. *The Flight from Ambiguity.* Chicago: Univ. Chicago Press

Levine DN. 1986. The forms and functions of social knowledge. In *Metatheory in Social Science,* ed. DW Fiske, RA Shweder, pp. 271–83. Chicago: Univ. Chicago Press

Levine DN. 1991. Simmel and Parsons reconsidered. *Am. J. Sociol.* 96:1097–116

Levine DN. 1995. *Visions of the Sociological Tradition.* Chicago: Univ. Chicago Press

Lindenberg S. 1986. How sociological theory lost its central issue and what can be done about it. In *Approaches to Social Theory,* ed. S Lindenberg, JS Coleman, S Nowak, pp. 19–24. New York: Russell Sage Found.

Lovell T. 1996. Feminist social theory. See BS Turner 1996, pp. 307–39

Luhmann N. 1985. Society, meaning, religion—based on self-reference. *Sociol. Anal.* 46:5–20

Luhmann N. 1987. The evolutionary differentiation between society and interaction. In *The Micro-Macro Link,* ed. J Alexander et al, pp. 112–31. Berkeley: Univ. Calif. Press

Luhmann N. 1995. *Social Systems.* Transl. J. Bednarz. Stanford, CA: Stanford Univ. Press (From German)

Luhmann N. 1997. Limits of steering. *Theor. Cult. Soc.* 14:41–57

Lyotard J. 1984. *The Postmodern Condition: A Report on Knowledge.* Transl. G Bennington, B Massumi. Minneapolis: Univ. Minn. Press (From French)

Macy MW, Flache A. 1995. Beyond rationality in models of choice. *Annu. Rev. Sociol.* 21:73–91

Mandalios J. 1996. Historical sociology. See BS Turner 1996b, pp. 278–302

Mann M. 1986. *The Sources of Social Power,* Vol. 1. Cambridge, UK: Cambridge Univ. Press

Mann M. 1993. *The Sources of Social Power,* Vol. 2. Cambridge, UK: Cambridge Univ. Press

Mayer T. 1994. *Analytical Marxism.* Thousand Oaks, CA: Sage

Maynard DW, Clayman SE. 1991.The diversity of ethnomethodology. *Annu. Rev. Sociol.* 17:385–418

McDonald L. 1994. *The Women Founders of the Social Sciences.* Ottawa, Ont, Canada: Carleton Univ. Press

Mennell S. 1989. *Norbert Elias.* Oxford: Blackwell

Merton RK. 1975. Structural analysis in sociology. In *Approaches to the Study of Social Structure,* ed. PM Blau, pp. 21–52. New York: Free Press

Meyer JW, Boli J, Thomas GM, Ramirez F. 1997. World society and the nation-state. *Am. J. Sociol.* 103:144–81

Mouzelis NP. 1995. *Sociological Theory: What Went Wrong? Diagnosis and Remedies.* London: Routledge

Münch R. [1982]1987. *Theory of Action.* Transl. PJ Gudel, S Minner, N Johnson. London: Routledge (From German)

Münch R. [1982]1988. *Understanding Modernity.* Transl. S Minner, N Johnson, G Silverberg, R Schilling, S Kalberg. London: Routledge (From German)

Münch R. 1987. Parsonian theory today: in search of a new synthesis. See Giddens & JH Turner 1987, pp. 116–55

Münch R. 1994. *Sociological Theory from the 1850s to the Present.* Chicago: Nelson-Hall. 3 vols.

Offe C. 1985. New social movements: challenging the boundaries of institutional politics. *Soc. Res.* 52:817–68

Offe C. 1997. *Varieties of Transition: The East European and East German Experience.* Cambridge, MA: MIT Press

Outhwaite W. 1987. *New Philosophies of Science: Realism, Hermeneutics and Critical Theory.* New York: St. Martin's

Outhwaite W. 1996. The philosophy of science. See BS Turner 1996b, pp. 83–106

Platt J. 1996. *A History of Sociological Research Methods in America, 1920–1960.* Cambridge, UK: Cambridge Univ. Press

Plummer K. 1996. Symbolic interactionism in the twentieth century. See BS Turner 1996b, pp. 223–51

Poggi G. 1996. Lego quia inutile: an alternative justification for the classics. See SP Turner 1996b, pp. 39–47

Ritzer G. 1988a. Sociological metatheory: a

defense of a subfield by a delineation of its parameters. *Soc. Theory* 6:187–200
Ritzer G. 1988b. The micro-macro link: problems and propsects. *Contemp. Sociol.* 17: 703–6
Ritzer G. 1988c. *Sociological Theory.* New York: Knopf
Ritzer G. 1990a. The current status of sociology theory: the new syntheses. See Ritzer 1990b, pp. 1–30
Ritzer G, ed. 1990b. *Frontiers of Social Theory: The New Synthesis.* New York: Columbia Univ. Press
Robertson R. 1992. *Globalization: Social Theory and Global Culture.* Newbury Park, CA: Sage
Roemer J, ed. 1986. *Analytical Marxism.* Cambridge, UK: Cambridge Univ. Press
Rorty R. 1979. *Philosophy and the Mirror of Nature.* Princeton, NJ: Princeton Univ. Press
Rorty R. 1989. *Contingency, Irony, and Solidarity.* Cambridge, UK: Cambridge Univ. Press
Rule JB. 1988. *Theories of Civil Violence.* Berkeley: Univ. Calif. Press
Rule JB. 1997. *Theory and Progress in Social Science.* Cambridge, UK: Cambridge Univ. Press
Runciman WG. 1983. *A Treatise on Social Theory,* Vol. 1. Cambridge, UK: Cambridge Univ. Press
Runciman WG. 1989a. *Confessions of a Reluctant Theorist.* London: Harvester
Runciman WG. 1989b. *A Treatise on Social Theory,* Vol. 2. Cambridge, UK: Cambridge Univ. Press
Sayer A. 1992. *Method in Social Science.* London: Routledge
Scaff LA. 1989. *Fleeing the Iron Cage.* Berkeley: Univ. Calif. Press
Scheff TJ. 1990. *Microsociology: Discourse, Emotion, and Social Structure.* Chicago: Univ. Chicago Press
Scheff TJ. 1997. *Emotions, the Social Bond, and Human Reality.* Cambridge, UK: Cambridge Univ. Press
Schluchter W. 1989. *Rationalism, Religion, and Domination: A Weberian Perspective.* Transl. N Solomon. Berkeley: Univ. Calif. Press (From German)
Seidler VJ. 1994. *Recovering the Self.* London: Routledge
Seidman S. 1994a. *Contested Knowledge: Social Theory in the Postmodern Era.* Oxford: Blackwell
Seidman S, ed. 1994b. *The Postmodern Turn: New Perspectives on Social Theory.* Cambridge, UK: Cambridge Univ. Press
Seidman S. 1994c. The end of sociological theory. See Seidman 1994b, pp. 119–39
Seidman S, ed. 1996. *Queer Theory/Sociology.* Oxford: Blackwell
Seidman S, Wagner DG, eds. 1992. *Postmodernism and Social Theory.* Cambridge, MA: Blackwell
Selznick P. 1992. *The Moral Commonwealth: Social Theory and the Promise of Community.* Berkeley: Univ. Calif. Press
Sewell WH Jr. 1992. A theory of structure: duality, agency, and transformation. *Am. J. Sociol.* 98:1–29
Sewell WH Jr. 1996. Historical events as transformations of structures. *Theory Soc.* 25:841–81
Shapiro G, Sica A, eds. 1984. *Hermeneutics: Questions and Prospects.* Amherst: Univ. Mass. Press
Sica A. 1988. *Weber, Irrationality, and Social Order.* Berkeley: Univ. Calif. Press
Sica A. 1989a. Handbooks past and present. *Contemp. Soc.* 18:504–8
Sica A. 1989b. Social theory's "constituency." *Am. Sociol.* 20:227–41
Sklair L. 1995. *Sociology of the Global System.* Baltimore, MD: Johns Hopkins Univ. Press. 2nd ed.
Skocpol T, ed. 1984. *Vision and Method in Historical Sociology.* Cambridge, UK: Cambridge Univ. Press
Skocpol T. 1986. The dead end of metatheory. *Contemp. Soc.* 16:10–12
Skvoretz J, Fararo TJ. 1996. Status and participation in task groups. *Am. J. Sociol.* 101: 1366–414
Smelser NJ. 1998. The rational and the ambivalent in the social sciences. *Am. Sociol. Rev.* 63:1–16
Smith DE. 1989. Sociological theory: methods of writing patriarchy. See Wallace 1989, pp. 34–64
Smith DE. 1990. *The Conceptual Practices of Power: A Feminist Sociology of Knowledge.* Boston: Northeastern Univ. Press
Smith DE. 1993. High noon in textland: a critique of Clough. *Sociol. Q.* 34:183–92
Soc. Theory 1994–1995. Special issues on "Neglected Theorists." 12(3), 13(1)
Somers MR. 1995. What's political or cultural about political culture and the public sphere? *Soc. Theory* 13:113–44
Sprague J. 1997. Holy men and big guns: the can(n)on in social theory. *Gender Soc.* 11: 88–107
Stacey J, Thorne B. 1985. The missing feminist revolution in sociology. *Soc. Probl.* 32:301–16
Stacey J, Thorne B. 1996. The missing feminist revolution: ten years later. *Perspectives* (Newsl. Theory Sec. Am. Soc. Assoc.) 18(3):1–4

Stryker S. 1987. The vitalization of symbolic interactionism. *Soc. Psychol. Q.* 50:83–94

Swartz D. 1997. *Culture and Power: The Sociology of Pierre Bourdieu.* Chicago: Univ. Chicago Press

Swidler A. 1986. Culture in action: symbols and strategies. *Am. Sociol. Rev.* 51:273–86

Sztompka P. 1986. *Robert K. Merton.* New York: St. Martin's

Touraine A. 1988. *Return of the Actor: Social Theory in Postindustrial Society.* Transl. M Godzich. Minneapolis: Univ. Minn. Press (From French)

Touraine A. 1995. *Critique of Modernity.* Transl. D Macey. Oxford: Blackwell (From French)

Turner BS. 1984. *The Body and Society: Explorations in Social Theory.* Oxford: Blackwell

Turner BS. 1989. Reflections on cumulative theorizing in sociology. In *Theory Building in Sociology,* ed. JH Turner, pp. 131–47. Newbury Park, CA: Sage

Turner BS. 1990. Periodization and politics in the postmodern. In *Theories of Modernity and Postmodernity,* ed. B Turner, pp. 1–13. London: Sage

Turner BS, ed. 1993. *Citizenship and Social Theory.* London: Sage

Turner BS. 1996a. Introduction. See BS Turner 1996b, pp. 1–19

Turner BS, ed. 1996b. *The Blackwell Companion to Social Theory.* Oxford: Blackwell

Turner JH. 1987. Analytical theorizing. See Giddens & JH Turner 1987, pp. 156–94

Turner JH. 1988. *A Theory of Social Interaction.* Stanford, CA: Stanford Univ. Press

Turner JH. 1989. Introduction: can sociology be a cumulative science? In *Theory Building in Sociology,* ed. JH Turner, pp. 7–18. Newbury Park, CA: Sage

Turner JH. 1990. The past, present, and future of theory in American sociology. See Ritzer 1990b, pp. 347–70

Turner JH. 1991. *The Structure of Sociological Theory.* Belmont, CA: Wadsworth

Turner JH. 1992. The promise of positivism. See Seidman & D Wagner 1992, pp. 157–77

Turner SP. 1994. *The Social Theory of Practices: Tradition, Tacit Knowledge, and Presuppositions.* Chicago: Univ. Chicago Press

Turner SP. 1996a. Introduction: social theory and sociology. See SP Turner 1996b, pp. 1–16

Turner SP, ed. 1996b. *Social Theory and Sociology: The Classics and Beyond.* Cambridge, MA: Blackwell

Turner SP, Turner JH. 1990. *The Impossible Science.* Newbury Park, CA: Sage

Urry J. 1996. Sociology of time and space. See BS Turner 1996b, pp. 369–95

Wagner, DG, Berger J. 1985. Do sociological theories grow? *Am. J. Sociol.* 90:697–728

Wagner, DG, Berger J. 1993. Status characteristics theory: the growth of a program. See Berger & Zelditch 1993, pp. 23–63

Wagner P. 1994. *A Sociology of Modernity: Liberty and Discipline.* London: Routledge

Walby S. 1988. Gender politics and social theory. *Sociology* 22:215–32

Wallace RA, ed. 1989. *Feminism and Sociological Theory.* Newbury Park, CA: Sage

Wallace RA, Wolf A. 1995. *Contemporary Sociological Theory.* Englewood Cliffs, NJ: Prentice-Hall

Wallace WL. 1983. *Principles of Scientific Sociology.* New York: Aldine

Wallace WL. 1988. Towards a disciplinary matrix in sociology. In *Handbook of Sociology,* ed. N Smelser, pp. 23–76. Newbury Park, CA: Sage

Wallerstein IM. 1995. *After Liberalism.* New York: New Press

Wallerstein IM. 1997. Social science and the quest for a just society. *Am. J. Sociol.* 102: 1241–57

Wardell ML, Turner SP. 1986. Introduction: dissolution of the classical project. In *Sociological Theory in Transition,* ed. ML Wardell, SP Turner, pp. 11–18. Boston: Allen & Unwin

Whimster S, Lash S, eds. 1987. *Max Weber and Rationality.* London: Allen & Unwin

White HC. 1992. *Identity and Control: A Structural Theory of Social Action.* Princeton, NJ: Princeton Univ. Press

Wiley N, ed. 1987. *The Marx-Weber Debate.* Beverly Hills, CA: Sage

Wiley N. 1990. The history and politics of recent sociological theory. See Ritzer 1990b, pp. 392–415

Wiley N. 1994. *The Semiotic Self.* Chicago: Univ. Chicago Press

Wittgenstein L. 1953. *Philosophical Investigations.* Transl. GEM Anscombe. New York: Macmillan (From German)

Wolfe A. 1989. *Whose Keeper? Social Science and Moral Obligation.* Berkeley: Univ. Calif. Press

Wolfe A. 1991. Mind, self, society, and computer: artificial intelligence and the sociology of mind. *Am. J. Sociol.* 96:1073–96

Wright EO. 1989. What is analytical Marxism? *Social. Rev.* 19:35–56

Wuthnow R. 1987. *Meaning and Moral Order: Explorations in Cultural Analysis.* Berkeley: Univ. Calif. Press

Annu. Rev. Sociol. 1998. 24:477–98

USING COMPUTERS TO ANALYZE ETHNOGRAPHIC FIELD DATA: Theoretical and Practical Considerations

Daniel Dohan and Martín Sánchez-Jankowski

Robert Wood Johnson Foundation Scholars in Health Policy Research Program, School of Public Health, University of California, Berkeley, California 94720; e-mail: dohan@uclink.berkeley.edu

Department of Sociology, University of California, Berkeley, California 94720; e-mail: sanjan@socrates.berkeley.edu

KEY WORDS: qualitative methods, ethnography, computer software, data analysis

ABSTRACT

Computer-assisted data analysis is usually associated with the analysis of aggregate data according to the tenets of logical positivism. But there are more than twenty computer programs designed to assist researchers analyzing ethnographic data, and these programs may be used by researchers with a variety of epistemological orientations. Some computer-assisted qualitative data analysis (CAQDA) programs automate analysis procedures that have been used by generations of ethnographers. Others open up new directions through the use of linked coding schemes, hypertext, and case-based hypothesis testing. Ethnographers interested in computer assistance must acquaint themselves with the variety of capabilities and programs available because no one program dominates the CAQDA field. In this article, we provide an overview of the theoretical and practical considerations bearing on the choice of CAQDA software.

0360-0572/98/0815-0477$08.00

INTRODUCTION

Computer-assisted analysis in sociology is currently associated with the profession's constructed category of "quantitative research" rather than its constructed category of "qualitative research."[1] Statistical procedures available in mainstream software packages such as SAS and SPSS facilitate the analysis of aggregate data, and most sociologists using these data have adopted an orientation of logical positivism. Thus, computer-assisted analysis carries connotations of hard data, computation, and objectivity. On the other hand, sociologists associated with qualitative research have generally held that aggregate data analysis using statistical procedures either misses important sociological causes of social action or emphasizes explanation (the hallmark of logical positivism) at the expense of understanding. The general overstatement of the differences between quantitative and qualitative research has meant that qualitative researchers have shown a slowness, if not reluctance, to use computer assistance in data analysis.

Just as it can with aggregate data, computer assistance can facilitate systematic computational research with qualitative data. In addition, CAQDA (computer-assisted qualitative data analysis) technologies can be useful for researchers who place themselves outside the positivistic research tradition. For example, within participant-observation research, there are three epistemological traditions: positivism, symbolic-interactionism, and ethnomethodology. While symbolic-interactionism and ethnomethodology appear antithetical to the use of computer-assisted analysis, a close look at the capabilities of current CAQDA software suggests these packages could be useful for research in these traditions and could become even more useful in the near future.

Software for the analysis of qualitative data has appeared relatively recently, and although qualitative sociologists have been slow to adopt this software, at present there are more than twenty packages available. No one package dominates, however, so the qualitative analyst interested in computer assistance must decide which package to use. The amount and kind of ethnographic data on hand or to be collected, the purpose of the research, the epistemological framework of the researcher, and the goodness of fit between the research project and the capabilities of available software all figure into this decision. In the end, the analyst may decide that no CAQDA software is called for. A review of ethnographies in journals and books published in the last five years suggests that many ethnographers either do not use any CAQDA soft-

[1]The constructed categories of "quantitative" and "qualitative" research have led sociologists to misunderstand the fact that real differences in research method are due to adherence to different epistemologies and not to the use of quantitative or qualitative data. For ease of reading, we drop the use of quotation marks, but the constructed nature of the categories quantitative research and qualitative research should be borne in mind.

ware or consider their use of it so unobtrusive that they fail to mention it at all in their ethnographic reports.[2]

In this article, we discuss the capabilities and limitations of CAQDA in general, the factors that distinguish one CAQDA software package from another, and specific qualities of a number of software packages. We intend this discussion to serve as a theoretical and practical introduction to CAQDA use. In the article's conclusion, we return to the methodological issues broached above to consider if the gap between quantitative and qualitative research might be bridged by current and future CAQDA packages. We do not endorse any particular analytical strategy nor do we recommend or review any particular software package in this article.[3]

QUALITATIVE DATA ANALYSIS AND THE PERSONAL COMPUTER

From QDA to CAQDA

Ethnographers have been using computers for decades. Interviews and fieldnotes have been transcribed into word processors (Kirk 1981), and many ethnographers now carry portable lap-top computers into the field. The use of computers for the analysis (rather than the gathering) of ethnographic data is a more recent development.

Many CAQDA software packages facilitate data analysis from the grounded-theory perspective codified by Glaser & Strauss (Lonkila 1995). Grounded theorists advocate close contact with raw data, the emergence of analytical categories from the data through memo writing, and comparison as the primary analytical tool (Glaser & Strauss 1967). Elements of grounded theory are common in CAQDA in part because Glaser & Strauss are explicit about the principles and procedures involved in this kind of analysis (see especially Strauss 1987).

Several general approaches to qualitative data analysis (QDA) incorporate elements of grounded theory or are consistent with that perspective. For example, while Pfaffenberger does not explicitly embrace the grounded-theory method of analysis, his three fundamentals for the analysis of qualitative data

[2]With few exceptions, ethnographic works published in *Qualitative Sociology, Journal of Contemporary Ethnography,* and *Symbolic Interaction* as well as in the *American Sociological Review,* the *American Journal of Sociology, Social Forces,* and *Social Problems* make no mention of the use of CAQDA. Book-length ethnographies in our areas of expertise (gangs, poverty, urban and community studies) reviewed in the journals listed above (as well as in *Contemporary Sociology*), and those discussed in three recent overviews of qualitative research (Charmaz & Olesen 1997, Horowitz 1997, Morrill & Fine 1997) also rarely mention CAQDA.

[3]By way of full disclosure, Sánchez-Jankowski is now using the askSam package, and Dohan is using the Folio Views package.

(rewriting, coding, and comparison) are consistent with grounded-theory methods (Pfaffenberger 1988:26–30). Huberman & Miles propose a three-part conceptualization of the analysis process: data reduction, data display, and conclusion drawing/verification. As in grounded-theory approaches, data reduction, display, and conclusion drawing are causally and temporally intertwined (Huberman & Miles 1994:429). Huberman & Miles expand these abstract procedures into a concrete set of thirteen "tactics" for undertaking qualitative analysis (Huberman & Miles 1994:432). These range from noting patterns and themes, clustering, and counting to making contrasts and comparisons, shuttling between data and categories, building a logical chain of evidence, and making conceptual/theoretical coherence. Tesch distills ten "principles and practices" in the analysis of many types of qualitative data. While the principles (data analysis is concurrent with collection, analysis is not rigid, and the result of analysis is a higher-level synthesis) outnumber the practices (data are segmented, data are categorized, the main intellectual tool is comparison), Tesch's approach follows the general thrust of grounded-theory analysis (Tesch 1990:95–97).

QDA that is consistent with grounded theory uses a sequential style of analysis that is highly data-intensive. Advocates of these methods urge the analyst to begin data analysis while collection is under way, to reduce the data using codes or categories, to shuttle between data and codes, and to compare coded and raw data to make tentative and ultimate conclusions. This analytical strategy returns the analyst to the database over and over again, and each step of analysis is readily translated into computer modules and procedures. Because grounded-theory and similar analytical strategies are consistent with logical positivism, they present practical challenges to computer programs but few epistemological challenges.

Researchers relying on context-dependent methods of analysis such as the extended-case method (Burawoy 1998, Burawoy et al 1991), symbolic-interactionism (Blumer 1969:Ch. 1), and ethnomethodology (Garfinkel 1967) may also find software designed around the grounded-theory principles helpful. But they are less likely to be able to take advantage of all the built-in features of these packages. The analytical principles of these context-dependent methods are more difficult to codify than those of grounded theory. So, while grounded theorists may find themselves able to take advantage of a wide variety of computer resources as they move from QDA to CAQDA, ethnographers working in other traditions may find that computer assistance limits their analyses unless they limit the extent to which they make use of computers.

First Steps and Basic Capabilities of CAQDA

Fortunately for ethnographers working outside of the grounded-theory tradition, computer assistance is not an all-or-nothing affair. Some features of contemporary CAQDA may be used and others may be ignored. We organize our discussion of the practicalities of CAQDA analysis around seven tasks performed by the user of CAQDA software (Weitzman & Miles 1995:Ch. 3). Analysts, whether positivists or not, may find some of the tasks required by CAQDA to be theoretically or practically onerous. But different software packages require different tasks, so analysts can pick and choose software that facilitates the tasks they are interested in without requiring those they find objectionable.

ENTERING DATA Seemingly mundane decisions made early in the ethnographic project may have significant practical, methodological, and theoretical consequences. How to enter data into the computer is a seemingly mundane decision with enormous consequences. Which data are entered into the computer, how they are entered, and which remain outside the computer shape all further analyses of the data. Fischer notes that data can enter a computer in a myriad of forms, from the "beginning" methods of text processing on a word processor to "advanced" methods of digital signal processing of videotape (Fischer 1994:15–21). For the moment, we confine ourselves to issues related to the entry of text; we address audio, visual, and graphic forms of data in later sections of this article. A primary consideration for researchers entering text data into the personal computer is the size of the textual unit of analysis. Notes entered into a dedicated CAQDA package are divided into analysis "chunks"—which can be single words, lines of text, paragraphs, hypertext note cards, or larger files. Especially important is the size of chunks—the indivisible units that are de-contextualized and re-contextualized during the analysis process (Tesch 1991b). For example, larger chunks of text are more likely to contain data falling into several analytical categories, and this may complicate positive correlational analysis. But for analysts interested in context-dependence, smaller chunks may prove worthless unless the CAQDA software contains elaborate coding or linking procedures.

Practical issues also arise at the data-entry stage. Should the qualitative database include expanded and annotated fieldnotes, interview transcripts, and memos? Memos can be electronically linked to existing data via hypertext connections or in situ "pop-up" notes. What are the advantages of integrating memos into the qualitative database? Are the advantages of an all-inclusive database worth the costs of greater storage overhead and slower processing times? Removing memos from the CAQDA software environment may hamper the goal of comprehensive analyses of ethnographic data, but it may bolster a sociological imagination that extends beyond the parameters of a particular software package.

ORGANIZING DATA Cases and variables organize quantitative datasets. The organization of ethnographic data varies depending on the research project at hand. The number of ethnographers involved in the project, the number of field sites, the variety of data types, and the theoretical orientation of the researchers all influence how the ethnographic dataset is organized. Researchers should at least familiarize themselves with basic database-management principles (Tesch 1990:199–210; Winer & Carrière 1991) to be sure that early decisions about the structure of the qualitative database do not create insurmountable data-management problems later in the project.

SEARCHING FOR AND RETRIEVING DATA Computers increase the ethnographer's ability to search for and retrieve text. For some ethnographers, search and retrieval represents the end of the computer's usefulness as a qualitative data analyst assistant, and several CAQDA packages are designed for this kind of analysis. At the least, searching for and retrieving data involves the ability to find and display a string of text characters that has been entered into the database (Tesch 1990:181–94). CAQDA software usually allows ethnographers to search for root forms of words or synonyms, to use wildcard characters, and to mount combination searches such as those based on word proximity or word order. Boolean-defined searches for multiple items round out the menu for searches. Retrieval of searched-for items is governed, again, by the size of text chunks and the flexibility of the package in retrieving consecutive or proximate chunks.

CODING DATA Coding, also referred to as indexing (Richards & Richards 1991a, 1994:457) or content analysis (Berg 1995:Ch. 9), is a central feature of much CAQDA. The use of the computer need not affect the fundamentals of data coding. Weaver & Atkinson coded their illustrative fieldnote material manually before entering the data into their CAQDA package (1994:52–53). Most discussions of computer-assisted coding reinforce what Weaver & Atkinson learned through practical experience: The hard work in coding data is intellectual, not mechanical. Computer assistance does not relieve the ethnographer of the need to spend many hours devising, revising, and applying an indexing system that is reliable and valid (a general approach is Werner & Schoepfle 1987). Moreover, computer assistance can impose limitations or restrictions on the coding process that can create problems for ethnographers (Weaver & Atkinson 1994:38–42). Coding should be driven by the theoretical orientations that inspired the original research. Analysts must be confident that using the computer facilitates their work. They must remain alert to the possibility that coding data with a well-designed computer program can become an end unto itself; highlighting sections of text with combinations of on-screen colors or sorting and re-sorting half-coded notes can easily create the comforting appearance of progress.

ANALYZING CODES Analysis of codes begins as soon as the first data are coded. Codes are defined in relationship to each other, so their application to a set of data implies theory. CAQDA software can make this implicit theory explicit by generating a list or map of codes and their relationships. Some packages constrain the development of a coding scheme to encourage the analyst to make positive connections between codes, such as hierarchical connections between more and less inclusive ones (Richards & Richards 1995) or sequential connections between coded events (Carsaro & Heise 1990). Analyzing codes is thus simultaneous with the coding process.

Once sufficient data have been coded, other analytical possibilities develop. In most CAQDA packages, analysts search for codes as easily as they explore raw data. Boolean capabilities are useful here, particularly for analysts interested in computation, because they allow the ethnographer to count instances of codes or conjunctions of codes. Alternatively, packages that retrieve text associated with particular codes or conjunctions of code may be useful for analysts interested in interpretational analysis.

Aside from data entry, the analysis of codes is the area of the computer's greatest influence on theory and methods. Software design may force the analyst to consider the previously unexamined relationship between concepts in the research project. The flip side of the coin is that software may limit the ability of the analyst to develop theory in desired directions. The ability to mount comprehensive searches for codes and sets of codes means that ethnographic analysis may benefit from less bias. But large-scale searches can also bury the analyst in chaotic results. In short, the computer-assisted analysis of codes has theoretical and methodological implications surpassed only by those taken during the first steps of data entry.

LINKING DATA The most recent development in the analysis of qualitative data requires computer assistance (Coffey & Atkinson 1996:181–87). Software available in the last decade allows analysts to create hypertext links between combinations of data, codes, memos, and research reports. Graphics, sound, and video may also be incorporated into "hyperspace" databases; (Weaver & Atkinson 1994:Ch. 5). Analysis based on data linking may prove a boon for ethnographers who collect non-textual data, especially if hypertext moves out of the researcher's office and becomes a medium for the distribution of research reports. Even for ethnographers who rely exclusively on text, the metaphor and activity of creating links in the ethnographic database have potential for generating innovative results. For researchers working outside of the positivistic tradition, linking data may be particularly valuable. Hyperlinks concretize nonlinear data-analysis techniques and free the researcher from reliance on computation. Reports that incorporate graphics, sound, and video can more readily make the case for the significance of context.

But hypertext technology also imposes special limitations on analysts. At present, the incorporation of text into hypertext "spaces" is inevitably fraught with more burdensome formatting limitations than those imposed by traditional text databases. Integrating sound or video into an ethnographic database involves technological expertise beyond the use of the word processor. In addition, the publication of materials using sound or video technology may introduce new ethical considerations, such as the protection of research subjects' confidentiality.

ANALYZING LINKS Analyzing links within the database is a more general form of analyzing codes. As in the analysis of codes, links may be analyzed only after a certain number have been established in the data. Once established, the links may be abstracted from the original data and analyzed as a system or network of their own. Compared to the analysis of codes, the analysis of links is more flexible and general. Greater complexity is possible in hypertext links than in coding schemes, so the representation of linked data may consequently be more complicated. At the same time, the ability to grasp at a glance a properly abstracted set of links allows analysts to bring "right brain" analysis to ethnographic analysis even when coding and linking have produced a complex data structure (Agar 1991). Similar to linking technologies, the computer's ability to analyze links may be especially appreciated by those working in symbolic-interactionist, ethnomethodological, and other nonpositivist traditions. The challenges and drawbacks of linking data, codes, and memos apply equally to their analysis.

Summary

Computer-assisted qualitative data analysis does not differ fundamentally, for the most part, from the nonmechanical qualitative analysis traditions from which it has developed. Most computers ease the labor burden and broaden the scope of common analysis tasks such as typing up field data and memos, searching for text, coding data, and sorting and comparing codes. Hypermedia is an unique contribution of computer technology to the analysis of qualitative data. Linking text, analysis, and non-text materials (graphics, sound, and video) in a single analytical space outside of the mind's eye is not possible manually.

Computer assistance is not free—theoretically or methodologically. The design of most CAQDA software after the metaphors and practices of grounded-theory analysis means that ethnographers who are working outside of that tradition may have to coax a recalcitrant software package into aiding their preferred style of analysis. Naturally, the less assistance the ethnographer requires from the computer, the less intrusive the grounded-theory perspective is likely to be. The computer also makes demands on the form of ethnographic data collected. At present, the computer still favors word-processed text over other forms of data such as sketches, maps, photographs, video images, or recorded sound. But as computers increase in power, analysts can look forward to gaining greater digital control over non-text data. The experience of flipping through pages of fieldnotes—sketches, diagrams and coffee stains—will never be replicated on the computer monitor. But if knotty problems such as protecting the identity of research subjects can be overcome, computers may soon provide a compelling auditory and visual alternative to this tactile experience.

CAQDA SOFTWARE

Computers can be programmed to accomplish four different kinds of analysis: numerical/arithmetic analysis, writing and document processing, data organization, and symbolic manipulation (Fielding & Lee 1991:2–3). Ethnographers use computers for all these kinds of analysis. Our overview of contemporary CAQDA software is organized around major distinctions in how data are organized and how symbols are manipulated by different packages. This overview is not meant as a thorough guide for the prospective purchaser of CAQDA software. That reader should read reviews of programs (Prein et al 1995; Tesch 1990; Tesch 1991a, especially volume 2; Weitzman & Miles 1995), consult published discussions of researchers' experiences with CAQDA software (cited passim below), and try out different software with his or her own data. In preparing this overview, we have drawn especially on *Computer Programs for Qualitative Data Analysis* (Weitzman & Miles 1995), which contained the most thorough and up-to-date reviews available at press time.

Document Processing: Searching and Retrieving

Word processing is the bread and butter of computer assistance for the ethnographer. The only computer assistance many ethnographers require is searching with a word processor. Basic searches retrieve a text string from a single computer file. More advanced searches count the occurrences of a string, and stand-alone search engines can search multiple files and produce extracts of search "hits" in context. The General Inquirer, the first CAQDA package, produced lists of word counts from a selected file as a preface to content analysis (Stone et al 1966). This ability is no longer considered the province of CAQDA packages, and for many ethnographers, text searching within a word-processing file is sufficient (Stanley & Temple 1995). Specialized programs developed for both CAQDA and commercial uses enhance the search and retrieval process. Many of these programs are designed for what Tesch called descriptive-interpretive work rather than theory building (Tesch 1990, 1991a). For searching and retrieving, packages including GOFER, Metamorph, Orbis, Sonar Professional, The Text Collector, WordCruncher, ZyIN-

DEX, and FYI3000PLUS expand on the capacities of word processors in several ways (for FYI3000PLUS, see Weaver & Atkinson 1994).

First, these packages create and manage the ethnographic database. Some of these packages manage files off-line (data remain in separate, unaltered text files); others manipulate the data directly. Usually, document processors work on documents that have already been produced in a word-processing package. Orbis manages files produced in XyWrite or NotaBene; MetaMorph and WordCruncher are particularly adept with WordPerfect documents. Others read files produced by a variety of word-processing, database, spreadsheet, and even drawing programs. Nearly all can manage plain text files, and some packages require files to be in this format before they can work with them.

The second value-added feature of document processors is their search features. As part of their management of the qualitative dataset, document processors allow the analyst to specify a variety of computer files in which to conduct a single search. ZyIndex, for example, searches documents that remain in their native format off-line, allows the analyst to keep track of changes to documents through several revisions, and indexes files so they can be readily included or excluded from particular searches. Document processors can mount complex searches: combinations or sequences of text strings; strings within specified proximity of each other; word synonyms, stems, and roots; and searches defined through Boolean, fuzzy, or set logic. Some display the results of searches interactively so that analysts can see how the addition or deletion of certain search terms in a complex search affects the number of hits produced.

Document processors are designed to make it easy for ethnographers to investigate data they have collected. Compared to word processors, document processors do a better job of placing the complete ethnographic dataset in the hands of the analyst. They allow the ethnographer to search more easily for desired pieces of text and to investigate how the text is arranged in the dataset. But document processors place some limitations on the format of data, especially on the use of non-text data such as drawings, figures, or other freehand notes. Although searching and retrieving text from an ethnographic database is a relatively non-invasive way of using CAQDA software, ethnographers must not be lulled into a false sense of security. CAQDA software betters the odds of finding significant material in the ethnographic database, but it does not assure it.

Data Organization

Searching and retrieving allows the analyst to inspect but not alter the ethnographic database. However, CAQDA packages such as askSam, Folio Views, MAX, Tabletop, HyperQual2, Kwalitan, Martin, QUALPRO, and The Ethnograph allow the analyst to alter the form of the ethnographic database by organizing its text.[4] Data organization is one of the dominant forms of contemporary CAQDA, and the packages listed here include some widely discussed in the literature (see Armstrong 1995; Mangabeira 1995; Smith & Hesse-Biber 1996; Sprokkereef et al 1995; Weaver & Atkinson 1994, 1995).

Organizers expand on document processors in two ways. First, organizers allow the ethnographer to attach a structure to the ethnographic database. Some document processors can retrieve text chunks in context. Organizers create context by giving analysts control over the structure of the ethnographic database, and this structure can be manipulated and analyzed by the researcher. Organizers can also structure the ethnographic database by adding database fields for factual information and for memos that are produced during analysis. The second addition of organizers is the ability to code ethnographic data according to a theoretical scheme developed by the analyst. Organizers are designed to tag chunks of text with analytical codes and to retrieve codes and tagged text. Retrieval of codes frequently includes the ability to search for multiple codes, to retrieve the text associated with codes, or to count codes.

ORGANIZING AND ANNOTATING Organizing and annotating are two basic tasks of qualitative data analysis. Some computer applications are designed to translate these activities with fidelity from hard copy to electronic form. For example, HyperQual2 and Martin use note cards as an organizing metaphor. Like their hard-copy counterpart, the note cards of these CAQDA packages each contain a single chunk of text. Electronic cards can be replicated and sorted into stacks, and these stacks then provide the raw materials to write up memos, annotations, and the ethnographic report. Another way to organize a hard-copy database is to use database-like fields. Fields can contain a variety of information including factual information that situates the ethnographic text to which it is attached (data collector, date of interview or observation, information about the subject of the note) or analytical information about the text itself. CAQDA software such as askSam facilitates the creation, insertion, and organization of these fields. Once organized, these CAQDA programs can quickly search and retrieve information from database fields and quickly count and tabulate the results of these searches.

Note cards, memos, and database fields are easily grasped metaphors for organizing data; they have been used by generations of ethnographers. Other CAQDA software draws on metaphors without long pedigrees in the ethnographic community. Some of these packages, such as MAX and Tabletop, move the qualitative researcher closer to a quantitative research style. MAX

[4]Most CAQDA packages have capabilities that defy easy categorization according to the kind of analysis they perform. Among document processors, Sonar Professional, ZyINDEX, GOFER, and FYI3000PLUS also include significant data-organizing features. Similarly, askSam, Folio Views, MAX, and Kwalitan are able to search for and retrieve text from the ethnographic database.

allows ethnographers who have also collected quantitative data to integrate both text and numbers into a single analytical space. Tabletop displays relationships between previously identified features of the ethnographic database in graphs such as Venn diagrams and scatter plots. Finally, packages such as Folio Views provide a menu of organizational tools that includes outline levels, database fields, and "pop-up" notes. It is up to the analyst to determine which tools facilitate appropriate organization of the ethnographic database and how they should be applied.

CAQDA packages that accommodate organizing and annotating the ethnographic database are useful in a variety of situations, but they are particularly useful in research projects as they expand in size and scope. Multisite or multiyear ethnographic projects generate a plethora of notes that beg for efficient organization. Flexible annotations are particularly valuable in multiresearcher projects in that each researcher provides her or his own analysis and commentary.

CODING, RETRIEVING, AND COUNTING Coding and retrieving is one of the central tasks of CAQDA software packages. Many of the software packages discussed above can code textual data, retrieve text based on applied codes, and tabulate which codes have been applied to which text. Most packages discussed in this section and below use coding and retrieving as their primary method of analysis or as a preface to other kinds of analysis. There are many ways to apply codes to text. Software such as Kwalitan, QUALPRO, or The Ethnograph number each line in the ethnographic database and apply codes to specific lines. Some packages encourage coding on the computer screen, whereas others encourage the analyst to code a numbered print-out of the text for later entry. Multiple codes can be applied to one line or chunk of text, but some packages place limits on the number of codes that can be applied (Coffey & Atkinson 1996). No CAQDA package eases the intellectual labor involved in coding, but code-and-retrieve software eases the administrative labor of applying and altering a coding scheme. This is especially so for software packages that take advantage of the graphical user interface of the Macintosh or Windows operating systems; in these, the analyst uses a mouse to highlight a text passage on the computer screen and then selects the code that applies to that section.

Once codes are applied to the ethnographic database, CAQDA software greatly accelerates analysis based on retrieving codes. Code-and-retrievers find codes using the same powerful features that document processors applied to the raw database. Multiple codes may be searched for at once. Hierarchies of codes can be established so that searches for higher-order terms also retrieve instances of lower-order terms. Complex searches can be formulated using Boolean, sequential, and proximity logic. Retrieval may yield a display of text associated with a code or a union of codes, or it may yield counts where those codes were applied. A number of CAQDA packages support cross-tabular displays of counts.

Organizing with CAQDA alters the ethnographic database in two ways. First, the database can be organized using database fields, hierarchical levels, or annotations so that the analyst has an easier time placing data in context and moving about in large ethnographic databases. Second, the database can be organized by applying codes to the text of the database so that the analyst can retrieve information from the database based on a theoretical mark-up of the text. CAQDA software facilitates the administration of both of these activities, but it does little to guide the intellectual work involved.

Symbolic Manipulation

A fine line separates CAQDA packages that organize data from those that manipulate symbols. Symbolic manipulation software helps the analyst develop or test theories about relationships in the ethnographic database. Like data organizers, symbol manipulators are a popular form of CAQDA, and software packages such as NUD.IST, AQUAD, ATLAS/ti, Inspiration, MECA, Meta-Design, SemNet, HyperRESEARCH, and QCA are widely discussed in published literature (Hesse-Biber et al 1991, Huber & García 1991, Muhr 1991, Ragin 1987, Richards 1995, Richards & Richards 1991b).

There are three kinds of CAQDA software for symbol manipulation. Some symbol manipulators begin where code-and-retrievers leave off. These packages focus analysts' attention on the coding process, encouraging them to create positive links between codes and to develop theory as they create a coding scheme. A second form of symbol manipulation is done by theory-building software. These packages take material that has been abstracted from the ethnographic database through coding or other means and analyze relationships between codes or concepts. The final kind of CAQDA software that facilitates symbolic manipulation is hypothesis testers. These packages facilitate the advancement and testing of causal statements about relationships between codes or concepts in multiple cases in the ethnographic database.

VALUE-ADDED CODERS The coding process already contains the seeds of symbol manipulation. Value-added coders add additional coding and analysis features to allow the analyst to move closer to the manipulation of concepts—usually by moving further from the ethnographic text. Software packages such as AQUAD allow the analyst to search purposefully through the ethnographic database for combinations of codes. The analyst can look for theoretically significant combinations of codes, tabulate the number of instances, and compare them to counts for combinations of codes that represent competing theories. Value-added coders consider the ethnographic database on a case-by-case basis so the counts and cross-tabulations they produce are a case-based numerical summary in contrast to the variable-based summaries provided by quantitative analysis.

A second way of transforming coding into symbol manipulation is to involve the computer in the construction of the coding scheme. NUD.IST and other packages force analysts to develop hierarchical relationships between codes as they apply them to the ethnographic database (Richards & Richards 1995). The construction of hierarchical categories theoretically concretizes the codes used and makes the logic of the coding scheme explicit as it is developed and applied. Hierarchical coding schemes are particularly useful for grounded-theory analysis, where new codes and elaboration of existing codes occur continuously as the analyst works with the ethnographic database.

Other value-added coders involve the computer in the coding process without imposing hierarchical constraints on the coding scheme. In ATLAS/ti, for example, the coding scheme is not constrained by the software but is retained to manipulate and analyze on its own. Text, codes, and memos can be linked in the program and these links later inspected and manipulated in conjunction with the original ethnographic text. Maps of relationships between elements in the database provide an analytical metaphor distinct from quantitative summary statistics or cross-tabulations.

THEORY BUILDERS Compared to value-added coders, theory-building CAQDA software moves the analyst a step further from the ethnographic text. Software packages such as ETHNO, Inspiration, MECA, and MetaDesign are designed to facilitate the conceptual manipulation of ethnographic data. Theory-building CAQDA software packages do not actually construct theory, of course. They construct a graphical map (node and links) of ethnographic data. Nodes represent data (fieldnotes, memos, codes, etc), and links represent relationships between data. Maps may help the analyst picture the project's theoretical shape, the concepts in use, the relationship between those concepts, and the ethnographic data that have been collected regarding each of those concepts and links. Theory-building software facilitates experiments with different concepts and links within the research project.

But theory-building CAQDA packages need not be reserved for the armchair ethnographer idly speculating on abstract relationships in field data. Theory builders can also incorporate links to the original ethnographic text that encourage grounding in the original data and checks on concept validity. In addition, theory builders need not be reserved for analyses of a nearly finished research project (nor need they be the exclusive province of the principal investigator). Theory builders can aid ethnographers who are mapping complex empirical concepts or events during the course of fieldwork.

HYPOTHESIS TESTING Some value-added coders such as HyperRESEARCH and AQUAD as well as stand-alone packages such as QCA use hypothesis testing, the third form of symbol manipulation. Hypothesis-testing software bridges the gap between qualitative and quantitative analysis by facilitating case-based analysis of qualitative data. These packages allow the analyst to specify hypotheses based on codes applied to text (in HyperRESEARCH and AQUAD) or based on a descriptive matrix of cases (in QCA). Hypothesis testers determine how causally antecedent features of cases are related to outcomes. Boolean algebra is used to define the antecedent conditions for each case in the database. CAQDA software reduces large numbers of cases into statements that identify under what conditions the outcome of interest prevails.

Qualitative hypothesis testing determines what qualities of cases are crucial for a specified outcome. In contrast, quantitative hypothesis testing focuses on the contribution of different variables to the outcome. Aside from this difference, CAQDA packages that include hypothesis-testing features are similar to statistics software that dominates computer-assisted analysis of quantitative data. Hypothesis testers encourage the analyst to develop ideas in the form of equations (Boolean rather than arithmetic) and to investigate how different terms (binary codes rather than multivalue variables) in the equation affect its ability to accurately explain outcomes.

Stand-alone hypothesis testers remove the analyst from the original ethnographic database. These software packages are useful in the analysis of data from a variety of sources and not only from ethnographic field studies. Hypothesis testers that include search-and-retrievers or data organizers may encourage the analyst to remain in contact with the ethnographic database even as analysis proceeds along more abstract and quasi-quantitative avenues. Ideally, hypothesis-testing software allows the analyst to ensure reliability through hypothesis checking and to maintain validity by returning frequently to re-examine the original ethnographic database and the codes, memos, and annotations that have accumulated over the course of the research project.

Symbol manipulation includes a variety of techniques for analyzing ethnographic data in ways that take advantage of microcomputers. Value-added coders encourage the analyst to develop explicit links between codes and data as the analysis proceeds. The software keeps track of the relationships between codes as they develop and then makes them available for later re-inspection and analysis. Theory builders facilitate exploration of concepts in ethnographic research projects through graphical displays and the ability to quickly move between different levels of detail. Finally, hypothesis testers move CAQDA closer to the practices of quantitative research by embracing the goals of reliability and explanation. Hypothesis-testing packages may even allow analysts to strive for reliability and causal explanation without losing the traditional advantages of qualitative data with respect to validity.

FUTURE DIRECTIONS AND RELEVANCE OF CAQDA

The current state of computer-assisted data analysis among qualitative researchers resembles the proverbial water glass that may be either half full or half empty. The large number of CAQDA software programs available suggests that we are in a preliminary stage of computer entry into the qualitative field. With time, the computer will do for qualitative data analysis what it has done in the quantitative realm: reduce labor, regularize procedures for data gathering and analysis, and establish conventions for the reporting of results. Moreover, the diversity of program options will allow these advances to occur along parallel methodological lines so that regularizing data-handling procedures will not require homogeneous epistemological stances. On the other hand, the still infrequent mention of CAQDA in ethnographic writing means that the expansion of software choices has not yet influenced the course of ethnographic research. CAQDA may be a significant advance for positivist ethnographers, but its potential for regularizing analysis in the qualitative field has not been reached. Of course, inertia among researchers and peer reviewers may account for some of the gap between expanding software choices and the dearth of CAQDA mention in published research (Lee & Fielding 1991:9). But there are fundamental issues about qualitative data analysis that inform the half-full and half-empty perspectives on CAQDA.

Lack of the "Killer App"

CAQDA software has proliferated in the last decade and a half, but no "killer app" has emerged from among the ranks of CAQDA software (Blank 1991). A killer app is a computer application that makes the use of the computer irresistibly compelling by doing tasks unmanageable without computer assistance, in the fashion that spreadsheet programs VisiCalc and Lotus 1-2-3 motivated United States businesses to place personal computers on employees' desks. Most CAQDA software diminishes the amount of labor needed to organize and code ethnographic data but does not fundamentally change the process of ethnographic analysis. In fact, ethnographers considering computer use must scale several learning curves (which programs are available, what are the basics of seemingly appropriate ones, what is the actual operation of the selected one) and then shape their data and analysis to the requirements of the chosen software package. Lacking an irresistibly compelling reason to adopt CAQDA, ethnographers may forgo computer assistance simply because the costs outweigh the benefits.

The computer offers three ways of facilitating qualitative analysis that may lead to, but are no guarantee of, the enthronement of a CAQDA killer app. First, CAQDA packages reduce the administrative burdens of ethnographic analysis. Administrative assistance is a strong reason to climb learning curves in some research projects, such as those that use grounded-theory methods or those large projects that involve multiple sites or multiple researchers. But given the diversity of techniques for ethnographic analysis, administrative reduction is compellingly attractive to only a fraction of qualitative researchers. Second, many CAQDA programs allow the user to analyze ethnographic materials that are difficult to access without the computer. These packages integrate text, graphics, sound, and video; they encourage analysis based on the creation of links between distinct pieces of the ethnographic database; and they open up new possibilities for the presentation of ethnographic research. However, not only do many ethnographers work exclusively with text, but also text and graphics are the dominant form of the ethnographic report. Multimedia capability alone does not create a killer app. Third, some of the features of symbol-manipulation software are not easily replicated without a computer. Potentially, these packages contain the seeds of a killer app.

Any CAQDA software that aspires to the title of killer app must accomplish two tasks. Like symbol-manipulation software, it must offer analysts the ability to perform analyses that are unmanageable without a computer. To be compelling, the CAQDA software package will have to constitute its own best marketing device. In addition, the methodological and epistemological diversity of ethnographic data analysis means that CAQDA software will have to offer different analytical facilities to different analysts. The challenge of the CAQDA killer app is to facilitate the analytical strategies of positivists and non-positivists with diverse analytical goals without disproportionately imposing barriers to entry on any one group. At present, popular software packages meet the challenges of one group or another, but no killer app appears to be on the horizon.

The Crisis of Representation and CAQDA

Part of the reason that no CAQDA package is poised to become a killer app is that contemporary methodological discussions in ethnography are not related to the integration of computers into qualitative data analysis—a fact our survey of recently published ethnographic work makes clear (see footnote 1). References, implicit and explicit, to the double crisis of representation and legitimation, what Denzin & Lincoln have termed the fifth "moment" of qualitative research, appear frequently in published ethnographies, and the crisis is of great concern to methodologists (Denzin & Lincoln 1994b, 1995; Snow & Morrill 1995a, but see also Snow & Morrill 1995b).[5]

In this climate of ferment, the rules for analysis are open to question, and one of the CAQDA paradigms may emerge to organize future qualitative work. Users and developers of hypertext software are particularly excited and

[5]We hope not to open the Pandora's box of ethnography's decades-long crisis of representation. Consult Denzin & Lincoln 1994a for a variety of perspectives on this question.

optimistic about this prospect. Hypertext not only makes the case for CAQDA as a killer app but also addresses the limitations of previous conceptions of computer use. Hypertext analysis is less rigid, more susceptible to interpretation, and most importantly, not lineally descended from the numerical processing paradigm used by quantitative researchers.

But the crisis in legitimation is a particularly hostile atmosphere for computer-assisted methods that are often associated with a positivistic approach to data analysis. Qualitative researchers have already expressed concerns about the use of CAQDA in practice. One fear is that the computer will "take over" qualitative data analysis—turning against the ethnographer like Frankenstein's monster. Theoretically, this fear is calmed by the reminder that the real work of qualitative data analysis lies not in the mechanics of searching for text, applying codes to data, or testing hypotheses using those codes. Rather, the work lies in the annotation and rewriting of notes, in the conceptualization and development of a coding scheme, and in the art of proposing reasonable hypotheses (Hesse-Biber 1995). Practically, researchers report that the use of CAQDA software encourages the exact opposite of the Frankenstein scenario. Outside the computer—in piles and files of note cards, transcripts, and memos or in boxes of audiotape—the data overwhelm the ethnographer. The computer allows the ethnographer to manage the overwhelming amount of data. This encourages the ethnographer to approach the data and become comfortable "playing" with it and learning it (Smith & Hesse-Biber 1996). In short, rather than distancing the ethnographer from the data, the use of the computer reduces the distance between analyst and data by making the latter less overwhelming and more approachable. The computer can facilitate the analyst's movement away from the data, but it does not cause this movement.

There remains, of course, the issue of what the ethnographic enterprise is. When it is based solely on "understanding," as it is for the traditions of ethnomethodology and symbolic interaction, computer assistance cannot make up for the shortcomings in the researcher's basic talent to interpret. However, for ethnomethodologists interested in analyzing indexical language patterns, for example, CAQDA software has the potential to be quite helpful (see, for instance, Schegloff 1996). In the case of anthropology, there remains the question of whether it is necessary for the ethnographer to penetrate the psychological world of the native or simply to interpret it through what Geertz identifies as a series of symbolic forms—words, images, institutions, and behaviors (Geertz 1983: 58). CAQDA can help the researcher identify social patterns, but it cannot substitute for the insight of the researcher. For example, Geertz found in his study of Moroccan society that the linguistic concept of "nisba" was important in separating people from each other and determining what it meant to be a person. Using suffixes, the people he studied were able to identify who belonged to what tribe, city, family, etc. Although Geertz found this pattern without the use of CAQDA, computer assistance would have increased the probability that a less insightful analyst would have seen this concept recur in a variety of contexts and grasped its significance. CAQDA can compensate for the limitations of the fieldworker by highlighting significant patterns recorded in the notes, even if the researcher did not recognize the pattern at the time the notes were recorded.

Systemization of Ethnographic Methods

For ethnographers not torn by the twin crises of representation and legitimation, the advent of CAQDA opens a couple of possibilities. First, the use of CAQDA software makes explicit the methods of analysis used in converting ethnographic data into ethnographic reports. The explicit discussion of methods of analysis in the grounded-theory school midwifed the development of much CAQDA software. Computer-assisted analysis goes beyond discussion, however, by allowing ethnographers to share details of their analysis process. Even when ethical concerns prevent the sharing of raw data, the use of CAQDA may increase reliability by making explicit the concrete steps taken in moving from data to conclusion.

Second, the use of computers fosters increased reliability and generalizability by expanding the amount of data that can be managed and exhaustively analyzed within a single ethnographic project. Data expand rapidly in ethnographies involving multiple sites or multiple researchers. In large-scale sociological and anthropological studies, the senior researcher becomes the analytical specialist (examples undertaken without CAQDA include Lewis 1963, Moore & Garcia 1978, Rainwater 1970, Sullivan 1989, Warner 1963). All members of the research team funnel data to the leader, who guides the analysis and writes research reports. Computer assistance makes it possible for researchers to collaborate more easily as data management devolves to the database system.

Combined, explicit systems of analysis and increased ability to generalize reliably suggest the development of a new way of organizing data, asking research questions, and systematically developing answers in ethnographic research. CAQDA software may allow ethnographers to access large ethnographic databases directly—without the theoretical intermediary of a single intellectual vision or research goal. The computer can accommodate data collected by multiple fieldworkers and facilitate coding, re-coding, linking, and re-linking by multiple investigators. Within this analytical space, differing understandings of the same database can be produced and compared, and analysts can examine the procedures undertaken to produce each account.

CONCLUSION

To date, all that many ethnographers have had to rely on was their memory of the data they collected and the meaning of those data in the context of their study. However, the workings of memory create two potential problems for researchers analyzing ethnographic field data. First, researchers may use those data that were most dramatic in the fieldwork and erroneously present them as being the most significant; second, they may use more data from the later stages of fieldwork and less of what happened in the middle or beginning because the later data are fresher and clearer in their minds. CAQDA can help the careful analyst avoid both of these problems, but it is no panacea. Researchers who use CAQDA still face issues related to representation. Data quality is directly tied to the ability of the researcher to observe significant phenomena in the course of fieldwork and to recognize what he or she has seen. While CAQDA can compensate for small failures of detailed observation or sharp insight, it is no substitute for either.

The use of CAQDA could stimulate team approaches in ethnographic research that would generate a wealth of data and make important analytic contributions (see the examples cited above), but CAQDA does not eliminate the validity problems inherent to team ethnography. Because data in ethnographic teams are gathered by a number of researchers who in many cases have different degrees of training (as well as different degrees of insight), there is no way to assure consistency in what each researcher thinks it important to record. Thus, there are validity problems for which CAQDA cannot compensate. Ethnographers spend much of their time engaged in filework rather than fieldwork (Plath 1990), but quality analysis that has a high degree of validity and reliability remains dependent on the competence and consistency of fieldworkers.

Literature Cited

Agar M. 1991. The right brain strikes again. See Fielding & Lee 1991, pp. 181–94

Armstrong D. 1995. Finding a “role” for The ETHNOGRAPH in the analysis of qualitative data. See Burgess 1995, pp. 63–79

Berg BL. 1995. *Qualitative Research Methods for the Social Sciences.* Boston: Allyn & Bacon

Blank G. 1991. Why sociological computing gets no respect. *Soc. Sci. Comput. Rev.* 9:593–611

Blumer H. 1969. *Symbolic Interactionism: Perspective and Method.* Berkeley: Univ. Calif. Press

Burawoy M. 1998. The extended case method. *Soc. Theory* 16:63–92

Burawoy M, Burton A, Ferguson AA, Fox KJ, Gamson J, et al. 1991. *Ethnography Unbound: Power and Resistance in the Modern Metropolis.* Berkeley: Univ. Calif. Press

Burgess RG, ed. 1995. *Studies in Qualitative Methodology,* Vol. 5. Greenwich, CT: JAI

Carsaro WA, Heise DR. 1990. Event structure models from ethnographic data. *Sociol. Methodol.* 20:1–58

Charmaz K, Olesen V. 1997. Ethnographic research in medical sociology: its foci and distinctive contributions. *Sociol. Methods Res.* 25:452–94

Coffey A, Atkinson P. 1996. *Making Sense of Qualitative Data.* Thousand Oaks, CA: Sage

Denzin NK, Lincoln YS, eds. 1994a. *Hand-*

book of Qualitative Research. Thousand Oaks, CA: Sage

Denzin NK, Lincoln YS. 1994b. Introduction: entering the field of qualitative research. See Denzin & Lincoln 1994a, pp. 1–19

Denzin NK, Lincoln YS. 1995. Transforming qualitative research methods. *J. Contemp. Ethnogr.* 24:349–58

Fielding NG, Lee RM, eds. 1991. *Using Computers in Qualitative Research.* Newbury Park, CA: Sage

Fischer MD. 1994. *Applications in Computing for Social Anthropologists.* London: Routledge

Garfinkel H. 1967. *Studies in Ethnomethodology.* Englewood Cliffs, NJ: Prentice Hall

Geertz C. 1983. *Local Knowledge: Further Essays in Interpretative Anthropology.* New York: Basic Books

Glaser BG, Strauss AL. 1967. *The Discovery of Grounded Theory: Strategies for Qualitative Research.* New York: Aldine

Hesse-Biber S. 1995. Unleashing Frankenstein's monster? The use of computers in qualitative research. See Burgess 1995a, pp. 25–41

Hesse-Biber S, Dupuis P, Kinder TS. 1991. HyperRESEARCH: a computer program for the analysis of qualitative data with an emphasis on hypothesis testing and multimedia analysis. *Qual. Sociol.* 14:289–306

Horowitz R. 1997. Barriers and bridges to class mobility and formation: ethnographies of stratification. *Sociol. Methods Res.* 25:495–538

Huber GL, García CM. 1991. Computer assistance for testing hypotheses about qualitative data: the software package AQUAD 3.0. *Qual. Sociol.* 14:342–48

Huberman AM, Miles MB. 1994. Data management and analysis methods. See Denzin & Lincoln 1994a, pp. 428–44

Kelle U, ed. 1995. *Computer-Aided Qualitative Data Analysis.* Thousand Oaks, CA: Sage

Kirk RC. 1981. Microcomputers in anthropological research. *Sociol. Methods Res.* 9: 461–72

Lee RM, Fielding NG. 1991. Computing for qualitative research: options, problems and potential. See Fielding & Lee 1991, pp. 16–37

Lewis O. 1963. *Life in a Mexican Village: Tepoztlan Restudied.* Urbana: Univ. Ill. Press

Lonkila M. 1995. Grounded theory as an emerging paradigm for computer-assisted qualitative data analysis. See Kelle 1995, pp. 41–51

Mangabeira W. 1995. Qualitative analysis and microcomputer software: some reflections on a new trend in sociological research. See Burgess 1995, pp. 43–62

Moore JW, Garcia R. 1978. *Homeboys: Gangs, Drugs, and Prison in the Barrios of Los Angeles.* Philadelphia, PA: Temple Univ. Press

Morrill C, Fine GA. 1997. Ethnographic contributions to organizational sociology. *Sociol. Methods Res.* 25:424–51

Muhr T. 1991. ATLAS/ti—a prototype for the support of text interpretation. *Qual. Sociol.* 14:349–72

Pfaffenberger B. 1988. *Microcomputer Applications in Qualitative Research.* Newbury Park, CA: Sage

Plath DW. 1990. Fieldnotes, filed notes, and the conferring of note. In *Fieldnotes: The Making of Anthropology,* ed. R Sanjek, pp. 371–84. Ithaca, NY: Cornell Univ. Press

Prein G, Kelle U, Bird K. 1995. An overview of software. See Kelle 1995, pp. 190–210

Ragin CC. 1987. *The Comparative Method: Moving Beyond Qualitative and Quantitative Strategies.* Berkeley: Univ. Calif. Press

Rainwater L. 1970. *Behind Ghetto Walls: Black Families in a Federal Slum.* Chicago: Aldine

Richards L. 1995. Transition work! Reflections on a three-year NUD.IST project. See Burgess 1995, pp. 105–40

Richards L, Richards T. 1991a. The transformation of qualitative method: computational paradigms and research processes. See Fielding & Lee 1991, pp. 38–53

Richards T, Richards L. 1991b. The NUDIST qualitative data analysis system. *Qual. Sociol.* 14:307–24

Richards T, Richards L. 1995. Using hierarchical categories in qualitative data analysis. See Kelle 1995, pp. 80–95

Richards TJ, Richards L. 1994. Using computers in qualitative research. See Denzin & Lincoln 1994a, pp. 445–62

Schegloff EA. 1996. Confirming allusions: toward an empirical account of action. *Am. J. Sociol.* 102:161–216

Smith BA, Hesse-Biber S. 1996. Users' experiences with qualitative data analysis software: neither Frankenstein's monster nor muse. *Soc. Sci. Comput. Rev.* 14:423–32

Snow DA, Morrill C. 1995a. Ironies, puzzles, and contradictions in Denzin and Lincoln's vision for qualitative research. *J. Contemp. Ethnogr.* 24:358–62

Snow DA, Morrill C. 1995b. A revolutionary handbook or a handbook for revolution? *J. Contemp. Ethnogr.* 24:341–49

Sprokkereef A, Lakin E, Pole CJ, Burgess RG. 1995. The data, the team, and The ETHNOGRAPH. See Burgess 1995, pp. 81–105

Stanley L, Temple B. 1995. Doing the business? Evaluating software packages to aid the analysis of qualitative data sets. See Burgess, pp. 169–93

Strauss AL. 1987. *Qualitative Analysis for Social Scientists.* New York: Cambridge Univ. Press

Sullivan M. 1989. *Getting Paid: Youth Crime and Work in the Inner City.* Ithaca, NY: Cornell Univ. Press

Tesch R. 1990. *Qualitative Research: Analysis Types and Software Tools.* New York: Falmer

Tesch R. 1991a. Introduction: computers and qualitative data II. *Qual. Sociol.* 14: 225–44

Tesch R. 1991b. Software for qualitative research: analysis needs and program capabilities. See Fielding & Lee 1991, pp. 16–37

Warner WL. 1963. *Yankee City.* New Haven, CT: Yale Univ. Press

Weaver A, Atkinson P. 1994. *Microcomputing and Qualitative Data Analysis.* Aldershot, UK: Avebury

Weaver A, Atkinson P. 1995. From coding to hypertext: strategies for microcomputing and qualitative data analysis. See Burgess 1995, pp. 141–68

Weitzman EA, Miles MB. 1995. *Computer Programs for Qualitative Data Analysis: A Software Sourcebook.* Thousand Oaks, CA: Sage

Werner O, Schoepfle GM. 1987. *Systematic Fieldwork,* Vol. 2: *Ethnographic Analysis and Data Management.* Newbury Park, CA: Sage

Winer LR, Carrière M. 1991. A qualitative information system for data management. *Qual. Sociol.* 14:245–62

Annu. Rev. Sociol. 1998. 24:499–516

SOCIOLOGICAL WORK IN JAPAN

Keiko Nakao

Department of Sociology, Tokyo Metropolitan University, 1-1 Minamiosawa, Hachioji-shi, Tokyo 192-0397, Japan; e-mail: nakao@bcomp.metro-u.ac.jp; and Department of Sociology, University of New Mexico, Albuquerque, New Mexico 87131

KEY WORDS: Japanese sociology, content analysis, theoretical trends, methodological trends

ABSTRACT

The aim of this paper is to provide an overview of contemporary sociology in Japan. The sociological discipline in Japan has made remarkable progress since World War II. The rapid economic growth during the 1960s, which was prompted by Western influence, had an effect on the direction of the discipline's development. After providing a brief overview of historical events, I consider scholarly publications during the last 30 years to illuminate substantive trends in sociological research. As might be predicted, the changing substantive interests of Japanese sociologists have been in many ways a response to societal changes and needs. I also examine the trends in theory, methods, and empirical research. A content analysis of articles published in the major Japanese sociological journals shows the growing emphasis on theoretical scholarship and the decreasing emphasis on empirical research in recent years. The conclusion presents some considerations concerning the future direction of Japanese sociology.

INTRODUCTION

The aim of this paper is to provide an overview of contemporary sociology in Japan. The development of sociology in any country is closely tied to its historical events and other circumstances in the society because the objects of sociological observation are society, social phenomena, and individuals in the society. Japanese sociology is no exception. The sociological discipline in Japan has made remarkable progress since World War II. The rapid economic

0360-0572/98/0815-0499$08.00

growth during the 1960s, which was motivated by Western influence, had an effect on the direction of the discipline's development. I first provide a brief overview of the historical events that helped shape the development of Japanese sociology. I then consider scholarly publications during the last 30 years to illuminate substantive trends in sociological research and the general state of the discipline. In this way, I show that the changing substantive interests of Japanese sociologists have been in many ways a response to societal changes and needs. I also examine the trends in theory, methods, and empirical research. A content analysis of articles published in the major Japanese sociological journals is provided to show the growing emphasis on theoretical scholarship and the decreasing emphasis on empirical research in recent years. My discussion concludes with some considerations concerning the future direction of Japanese sociology.

HISTORICAL BACKGROUND

The end of World War II marks the beginning of contemporary Japanese history. After the surrender in 1945, the country was economically devastated and its people demoralized. During the subsequent six years of American occupation, democratic systems, values, and ideologies were infused into Japanese politics, economics, education, and other social institutions. A new constitution was implemented in 1947 that guaranteed freedom of speech, religion, and assembly, and provided various civil liberties including the right to vote for both men and women. Reforms undertaken during the American occupation included the dissolution of the large family-based corporations called *Zaibatsu*, the authorization of workers to organize unions, and the implementation of agricultural reforms such as land redistribution.

The first decade after the war's end was a period of reconstruction and recovery from the damage resulting from the war. Following that, into the 1960s, Japan made a remarkable economic recovery as its GNP surged to become the second highest in the world. With the growing emphasis on industrialization as a means to economic growth, urban infrastructural investment and rapid rural-to-urban migration changed the nature of many Japanese cities.

By the mid-1960s, Japan had completed its economic rehabilitation; however, it also began to face new types of social problems such as environmental pollution, the undesired byproduct of rapid industrialization. Once basic economic needs were satisfied, the Japanese began to pay more attention to social issues, including the environment, social inequality, and civil rights. The movements by students and other civil groups in the late 1960s were partially responsible for the government's growing attention to social concerns.

The public's social awareness continued to grow throughout the 1970s despite the slowdown and stabilization of economic growth. The 1970s marked

Japan's emergence as a major contender in the world economy. With its inclusion in the economic summit in 1975 and the opening of its domestic market to foreign trade, Japan reversed its previous course of economic protectionism. Its increased immersion in the global economy stimulated steady economic growth that peaked in the late 1980s. Having become a key player in the world economy, Japan in the 1990s faces the crucial task of defining its international role within the global community.

Traditional Japanese Sociology

Prior to World War II, Japanese sociology closely reflected its origins in ethnological research, from which the substantive areas were beginning to emerge. Reflecting the influence of ethnology, two major areas of interest—rural sociology and family sociology—dominated the discipline. Most sociologists in the pre–World War II epoch were trained in these two areas, which focused on rural community and area studies and also on traditional Japanese family systems. The traditional Japanese family system, called *Ie*, not only was a family, as defined in Western society, but also functioned as an economic unit based on extended kin relations. The internal hierarchical structure of *Ie*, the acceptance of an authority structure, the pattern of relationships between *Ie* and the community, and the norms developed within the *Ie* system were all thought to be the basis for understanding the social structure and social organizations in Japan.

As sociologists expanded their substantive interests beyond the domain of the family, they continued to apply this concept to explain other aspects of social life (Kiyomi Morioka, personal communication). For example, internal structures of various social groups such as business and religious organizations, and the pattern of relationships—including labor relations—were related to the traditional *Ie* concept. While they had undergone some changes, family sociology and rural sociology remained dominant in sociological research after World War II.[1]

JAPANESE SOCIOLOGY IN A HISTORICAL CONTEXT: ANALYSIS OF SUBSTANTIVE AREAS

In this section, I depict the development of sociological research in Japan in a historical context. To capture the substantive trends in the discipline, I exam-

[1]Family sociology is currently considered to have two subfields: traditional and contemporary (Morioka et al 1993, Mitsuyoshi et al 1986, Mochizuki et al 1987). Traditional family sociology emphasizes a traditional family system typically seen in rural areas, while contemporary family sociology, which was developed after World War II, focuses on issues relating to families in more urbanized areas.

ine the data on publications, which is perhaps the best descriptor of sociologists' work.[2]

Every year, the Japan Sociological Society (JSS) publishes a list of books and articles, including reports and working papers, with sociological content. The list is compiled by soliciting information from over 2500 association members and by library search. Because of the difficulty of obtaining such information, these lists are by no means exhaustive; however, they are conceivably the best source of data currently available for my purpose.

Based on the primary substantive emphasis, each article is categorized into one of the substantive areas recognized and defined by the association. Table 1 displays the number (and the percentage in parenthesis) of publications in five-year periods for each substantive area. The area categories are arranged in decreasing order based on the number of publications during the most recent five-year period, 1990–1994.

The total number of articles in books, journals, and other outlets has increased over time, from 3297 in the early 1970s to 7882 in the early 1990s. The rate of increase was slightly higher in the 1970s through early 1980s than thereafter, indicating the discipline's growth in the 1970s.[3]

As the number of publications increased, so did their diversity. New categories were created to classify those articles as their numbers reached a critical mass. In the early 1970s, four categories were added (planning, sociology of law, social history, and leisure/sports). Economic sociology established its own category in the mid-1970s. The categories of discrimination, gender/generation, knowledge/science, and lifestyle/life structure were added in the early 1980s, while environmental sociology, the newest category, was established in 1993. Tracing the changes in the categories themselves is an indication of how the discipline has evolved to encompass a stronger emphasis on social issues in an industrialized society. The following section reveals that the changing rate of publications in the various substantive areas corresponds to the transformations in Japanese society since 1965.

[2]Other informative data about the growth in sociologists' activities over time is academic institutional data such as the number of departments, faculty, and degrees granted. Currently 122 Japanese university departments offer undergraduate curricula in sociology. Seventy-six universities provide graduate training, of which 47 offer Ph.D. programs (Asahi Shimbun 1996). However, accurate information on the number of sociology faculty and students is difficult to obtain. This is because sociology departments in Japanese universities are normally included under larger institutional units such as humanities, social sciences, and behavioral sciences, and data on faculty and students is publicly reported only for those larger units, not at departmental levels.

[3]It can be speculated that the increase in the total number of publications may be partly the result of improved data collection implemented over time, such as the electronic library search. Close examination of the data, however, found no single year that showed a dramatic increase that would clearly indicate such a possible artifact.

Japan's Post–World War II Industrialization and Sociology

Japanese sociology entered a new phase after World War II. Sociologists' interests reflected the nationwide commitment to industrialization and economic rehabilitation during the first two decades after the war. Thus, publications in industrial sociology, management, and labor relations proliferated during the late 1960s, becoming the third most popular substantive focus during that period. The declining popularity of this research focus during the subsequent decades (by the early 1990s, industrial and labor relations publications ranked behind eight other substantive foci) suggests that the flurry of interest in the 1960s reflected and perhaps stimulated the intense pursuit of industrialization in the immediate postwar period.

One of the most striking observations found in Table 1 is the changing proportions of publications in rural sociology and urban sociology over 30 years. Rural/community sociology ranked first (9.2%) in 1965–1969 but eighth (5.2%) in 1990–1994, while urban sociology increased its relative ranking from tenth (4.8%) in 1965–1969 to second (7.1%) in 1990–1994. The traditional dominance of rural sociology eroded as sociologists directed more attention to urban areas and the problems associated with urban life. Urban sociology established its dominance, at least in the number of publications, by the late 1980s. Indeed the preeminence of urban sociology since the 1980s is reflected in the emergence of one of its offshoots, lifestyle/life structure, as a distinctive substantive focus. This is an interdisciplinary substantive field dealing primarily with urban lifestyles and the structures around people in cities, including social networks. It is an area unique to Japanese sociology because of its focus on the traditional Japanese family system and community structure as they relate to contemporary social phenomena dealing with personal and family networks and community activities.

Social Awareness

The late 1960s and early 1970s was an era in which Japanese society began paying attention to the social costs of economic growth. Sociologists began focusing on various social problems, including environmental pollution. The number of articles in social problems/deviance soared from 60 (1965–1969) to 199 (1970–1974), and then to 284 (1975–1979). Concomitant with the students' movement of the late 1960s, the number of publications on social movements/collective behavior increased in the 1970s relative to the previous five-year period. Because environmental sociology was not recognized as a separate subfield until 1993, previously published articles dealing with environmental issues were categorized under either social problems or medical sociology, depending on their emphasis.

Table 1 Number and percentage (in parentheses) of sociological publications 1965–1994

Articles and working papers	1965–1969	1970–1974	1975–1979	1980–1984	1985–1989	1990–1994	TOTAL
Social thought/philosophy/ history of sociology	137 (7.2)	343 (10.4)	470 (9.6)	499 (7.7)	526 (7.0)	720 (9.1)	2695 (8.4)
Urban/life structure	91 (4.8)	206 (6.2)	314 (6.4)	398 (6.2)	567 (7.6)	562 (7.1)	2138 (6.7)
Theory	85 (4.5)	141 (4.3)	293 (6.0)	466 (7.2)	491 (6.6)	558 (7.1)	2034 (6.4)
Education	91 (4.8)	243 (7.4)	410 (8.4)	488 (7.6)	489 (6.5)	550 (7.0)	2271 (7.1)
Family	158 (8.4)	323 (9.8)	345 (7.1)	532 (8.2)	596 (8.0)	504 (6.4)	2458 (7.7)
Culture/religion/ethics	99 (5.2)	131 (4.0)	229 (4.7)	319 (4.9)	350 (4.7)	475 (6.0)	1603 (5.0)
Communication/infor-mation/symbols	90 (4.8)	173 (5.2)	156 (3.2)	245 (3.8)	330 (4.4)	426 (5.4)	1420 (4.4)
Rural/community	174 (9.2)	338 (10.3)	384 (7.9)	531 (8.2)	406 (5.4)	412 (5.2)	2245 (7.0)
Management/industrial/labor	142 (7.5)	210 (6.4)	302 (6.2)	343 (5.3)	410 (5.5)	397 (5.0)	1804 (5.7)
Social welfare/medical	99 (5.2)	130 (3.9)	370 (7.6)	411 (6.4)	382 (5.1)	393 (5.0)	1785 (5.6)
Comparative/area studies	80 (4.2)	94 (2.9)	89 (1.8)	143 (2.2)	238 (3.2)	296 (3.8)	940 (2.9)
Gender/generation				40 (0.6)	188 (2.5)	233 (3.0)	461 (1.4)
Deviance/social problems	60 (3.2)	199 (6.0)	284 (5.8)	278 (4.3)	347 (4.6)	205 (2.6)	1373 (4.3)
Social psychology/social perceptions	138 (7.3)	137 (4.2)	246 (5.0)	230 (3.6)	334 (4.5)	201 (2.6)	1286 (4.0)
Political/international relations	44 (2.3)	134 (4.1)	182 (3.7)	204 (3.2)	184 (2.5)	183 (2.3)	931 (2.9)
Social history		8 (0.2)	27 (0.6)	58 (0.9)	179 (2.4)	174 (2.2)	446 (1.4)
Groups/organizations	116 (6.1)	129 (3.9)	151 (3.1)	176 (2.7)	154 (2.1)	157 (2.0)	883 (2.8)
Social class/stratification/social mobility	46 (2.4)	91 (2.8)	125 (2.6)	153 (2.4)	195 (2.6)	153 (1.9)	763 (2.4)
Ethnicity/nationalism			43 (0.9)	87 (1.3)	66 (0.9)	149 (1.9)	345 (1.1)
Methods	26 (1.4)	29 (0.9)	66 (1.4)	86 (1.3)	136 (1.8)	143 (1.8)	486 (1.5)

(Continued)

	1965–1969	1970–1974	1975–1979	1980–1984	1985–1989	1990–1994	TOTAL
Demography	32 (1.7)	42 (1.3)	47 (1.0)	109 (1.7)	113 (1.5)	126 (1.6)	469 (1.5)
Social movements/collective behavior	22 (1.2)	55 (1.7)	64 (1.3)	66 (1.0)	127 (1.7)	125 (1.6)	459 (1.4)
Knowledge/science				24 (0.4)	66 (0.9)	119 (1.5)	209 (0.7)
Social change	47 (2.5)	40 (1.2)	60 (1.2)	79 (1.2)	87 (1.2)	101 (1.3)	414 (1.3)
Discrimination				105 (1.6)	103 (1.4)	101 (1.3)	309 (1.0)
Leisure/sports		12 (0.4)	54 (1.1)	63 (1.0)	69 (0.9)	78 (1.0)	276 (0.9)
Law		11 (0.3)	27 (0.6)	54 (0.8)	83 (1.1)	77 (1.0)	252 (0.8)
Environmental						73 (0.9)	73 (0.2)
Planning		46 (1.4)	61 (1.2)	83 (1.3)	128 (1.7)	71 (0.9)	389 (1.2)
Economic			29 (0.6)	49 (0.8)	68 (0.9)	48 (0.6)	194 (0.6)
Other	113 (6.0)	32 (1.0)	57 (1.2)	144 (2.2)	82 (1.1)	72 (0.9)	500 (1.6)
Total	1890 (100.0)	3297 (100.0)	4885 (100.0)	6463 (100.0)	7494 (100.0)	7882 (100.0)	31911 (100.0)
Books and monographs							
Books/edited books	426 (77.0)	523 (72.8)	655 (74.4)	902 (73.2)	946 (71.1)	1060 (77.5)	4512 (74.2)
Translated books of foreign sociologists	127 (23.0)	195 (27.2)	225 (25.6)	331 (26.8)	384 (28.9)	307 (22.5)	1569 (25.8)
Total	553 (100.0)	718 (100.0)	880 (100.0)	1233 (100.0)	1330 (100.0)	1367 (100.0)	6081 (100.0)

Data Source: *Shakaigaku Hyouron*, 1965–1994

Gender study is an area that has received great influence from American sociology. The women's movement of the 1960s in America captured Japanese public attention a decade later. A certain irony surrounded the fact that the country that had introduced Japan to the ideals of democracy, egalitarianism, and universal civil rights was now encountering political upheaval owing to a legacy of gender discrimination (Ishida 1996). Gender studies caught the attention of Japanese sociologists, who sought to alleviate similar contradictions in their own society. In the late 1970s several societies for women's studies were established and gender was recognized as a substantive area separated from social problems. Gender has yet to be formulated as a distinctive substantive category; it is currently combined with generation, which includes gerontology and issues surrounding generational differences. Nevertheless, the number of publications on gender issues has grown rapidly within the last ten years (40 in 1980–1984 to 233 in 1990–1994), and it has become one of the major fields in today's Japanese sociology.

International Relations

Although Japan's economic development was motivated by Western influence, it was not until the late 1960s that Japan began considering issues surrounding its relationships with the developed countries of the West. As Japan's economy caught up with Western standards and its products gained a growing share of global markets, Japanese sociologists focused more attention on international relations. Politicians, economists, and social scientists began their efforts to understand other countries and Japan's role in international relations. The surge of political/international relations publications in the 1970s reflects Japanese sociology's growing interest in global affairs.

Even though Japan assumed an increasingly central role in the global economy during the 1980s and 1990s, there was no proportionate increase in international relations publications in the sociological literature. It is possible that some internationally focused sociologists may have turned from international relations to area studies as an avenue for their global concerns. Compared to the 1970s, the number of articles in comparative/area studies increased in the late 1980s and early 1990s (from 1.8% in 1975–1979 to 3.8% in 1990–1994). Prior to the late 1980s, most area studies focused on the Western, developed countries that provided economic models for Japan's development. Since then, area studies reflect the growing interest of Japanese sociologists in the developing countries of East Asia with which the country has established increasing economic ties. Thus the shift in area studies reflects the changing political and economic alliances between Japan and other nations.

Another recent social issue relating to East Asian countries concerns the rising number of East Asian immigrants to Japan. Their growing presence is forcing the country, which has long been highly racially and ethnically homogeneous, to confront issues of ethnic discrimination, changing labor relations, and other effects of immigration. These demographic changes have stimulated a surge in sociological scholarship examining ethnicity, ethnic discrimination, and ethnic-based social movements.

Information and Technology

Consistent with its growing importance in other postindustrial societies, information became a valuable commodity as technological development accelerated in the 1980s in Japan. Mass media have begun to play an important role in the society. No longer merely a medium for communicating social events to the public, mass media have begun to shape peoples' perceptions of social reality. The sociological publication trend during the 1990s seems to reflect some of the characteristics common to information-based societies. Articles within the areas of culture/religion/ethics and communications/information/symbols have become more frequent, ranking sixth and seventh respectively in 1990 and 1994. The modest but steady increases in knowledge/science and leisure/sports also exemplify this trend.

Concluding Comments

As the quantity of publications within various substantive fields indicates, trends in sociological literature have been shaped by changes in the larger society. Clearly, publication rates alone are insufficient to fully capture the diverse changes occurring within a discipline and its subfields. Yet they do provide a rough picture of the trends within the discipline and the larger society it represents. They also illuminate both changes and continuities within the discipline.

While various subfields have waxed or waned in popularity, at least one, the sociology of education, has continually yielded numerous publications over the years. Its consistent predominance likely reflects the salient role of education, both within the discipline and within society at large, which affects such diverse social phenomena as socialization, social stratification, status attainment, and deviance. Yet while the quantity of sociology of education scholarship has varied little over time, by no means has the subfield been immune to social changes during the period. Under the American occupation after World War II, the Japanese educational curriculum was modified to place an increasing emphasis on liberal, instead of imperialistic, principles. Higher educational institutions were transformed to co-ed, allowing more opportunities for women. As rapid economic growth, urbanization, and technological advancement within Japanese society reshaped core institutions, the educational system was required to provide curriculum and pedagogical methodologies to adequately prepare students for new institutional roles. These trends within the educational system and the larger society have given rise to new social problems, such as the pressure on children to excel on examinations to compete for a limited number of university slots (see Takeuchi 1981), or the bullying of some students by their peers (see Morita & Shimizu 1986). Such changes have offered fertile avenues for research, stimulating Japanese educational sociologists to explore the implications of such trends for both the educational system and Japanese society as a whole.

In sum, while the evolution of the subfields to a large extent reflects social trends within relevant institutions, the development of each subfield has also depended on other factors, both systemic and accidental. My broad-based account of substantive trends is intended to provide an overview of the discipline rather than a detailed analysis of each subfield and its formative dynamics. Their analysis would provide fertile ground for future research in Japanese sociology.

For further information about the development of specific substantive areas, refer to e.g. Mitsuyoshi et al 1986, for traditional family sociology; Mochizuki et al 1987, for contemporary family sociology; Miura et al 1986, for lifestyle/life structure; Nakata et al 1986, for rural sociology; Suzuki et al 1985, for urban sociology; Naoi et al 1986, for social stratification and social mobility; Inagami et al 1987, for industrial sociology; Nitagai et al 1986, for social movements; Mitani et al 1988, for social problems; Mita et al 1989, for culture and social perception; Hougetsu et al 1986, for deviance and criminology; Akimoto et al 1985, for political sociology; Shibano et al 1986, for sociology of education; Shouji et al 1988, for social systems and social change; Miyake et al 1986, for religion; and Takeuchi et al 1987, for mass communications.

THEORY AND METHODS IN JAPANESE SOCIOLOGY: WESTERN INFLUENCE

Theoretical Paradigms

One striking observation suggested by Table 1 is the dominance of a substantive area called social thought/social philosophy/history of sociology. A prominent disciplinary subfield since the 1960s, it comprised over 9% of all sociological publications in 1990–1994. Most of the articles included in this category are writings about theories or philosophies of foreign social thinkers. Their primary purpose has been to introduce influential works of classical theorists such as Marx, Weber, Durkheim, and Simmel, and of contemporary theorists such as Parsons, Habermas, Foucault, Luhmann, and Giddens, to Japanese sociologists in light of each author's own commentary, insights, and elaborations. A separate category called general theory includes articles on and about theories that are more relevant to explaining the social phenomena in contemporary Japanese society. Many of these articles depart from the contemporary theories developed in foreign countries. Also evident are the numerous translated books written by foreign sociologists; as Table 1 indicates, approximately 25% of sociological books over 30 years are direct translations of foreign works. This demonstrates a clear tendency for Japanese sociology to incorporate theories formulated in Western societies.

Marxism, which was politically suppressed during World War II, quickly became a major theoretical interest among Japanese sociologists after the war ended. As theoretical sociologists strove to understand Marxism, they focused on the concepts most relevant to sociology. As Japan's industrialization peaked in the mid-1960s, sociologists began to embrace Parsonian theory. Following the trend in American sociology, Parsonian theory attracted the attention of a new generation of Japanese social theorists seeking to understand their industrialized society and the various social problems that accompanied it. This structural functional approach was applied and extended to various areas such as social change and modernization (e.g. Tominaga 1965), social psychology (e.g. Sakuta 1972), small groups (e.g. Aoi 1980), and social systems (e.g. Yoshida 1974) (see Shiobara et al 1997). Structural functionalism continued to be the main sociological paradigm until the late 1970s. At the same time, however, it was not immune to criticisms by Marxists, Weberians, and phenomenologists, as it was also in American sociology, which contributed to its declining dominance in the 1980s.

As Japan shifted from an industrialized society to an informational society in the 1980s, so did sociologists' interests. As information, rather than manufactured items, became the country's most valuable commodity, sociologists turned their theoretical interests to culture, mass communications, and the media. Accordingly, postmodernism rose to ascendance as the primary theoretical paradigm. Foucault, Habermas, and Luhmann are examples of foreign theorists whom Japanese theorists emulated (e.g. Hashizume, Uchida, Imada). Even today, no other theory has achieved preeminence over postmodernism (Koutou 1997), which continues to be the dominant theoretical paradigm in Japanese sociology.

The influential nature of Western theories has challenged Japanese theorists to apply them, with the necessary modifications, to Japanese society. Yet whether Western theories can explain Japanese social phenomena, and whether, in general, theories developed in one country are automatically applicable to a different social context, are questions deserving consideration. Japanese sociologists generally see the benefit of applying theoretical approaches formulated in foreign countries to their own society. Moreover, since Japan is currently one of the most economically developed countries in the world, theories meant to be generalizable to industrialized capitalist nations are in principle applicable to contemporary Japan. Yet every society contains a unique component resulting from a long series of historical events and coincidental circumstances. For example, according to many sociologists, many aspects of contemporary Japanese society, from family to corporate and political organizations, have been shaped by its traditional system rooted in feudalistic principles. The values formed within such traditional social structures, many scholars maintain, continue to govern the Japanese people's perception and behaviors. In a rapidly changing society, where traditional systems, structures, and values are quickly disappearing, Japanese social theorists are faced with the challenging task of constructing new theories that incorporate both the social conditions unique to Japan and those common to other developed countries.

Methodology and Empirical Research

During the 1960s the American sociological emphasis on empirical research took root in Japan, as Japanese sociologists increasingly came to recognize the advantages of applying a scientific approach to their scholarship. Applying quantitative techniques and other empirical methodologies learned from American researchers, Japanese sociologists enriched their discipline by using the new methodological approaches to probe important research questions. Their efforts spawned a proliferation of empirical research papers, which became the most common types of publications in the early 1970s. A content analysis of the articles appearing in the primary Japanese sociology journal *Shakaigaku Hyouron* illustrates the trends in empirical research. While no single journal can adequately characterize an entire discipline, *Shakaigaku Hyouron* is considered particularly appropriate because it is the official journal of the Japan Sociological Society and is targeted toward a general sociological audience.[4]

Table 2 categorizes the articles appearing in this journal between 1970 and 1994 according to their content type: empirical, purely theoretical, methodological, or review. We observe that 41.9% of the articles published in the early 1970s were based on empirical research, while only 31.4% were theoretical works. This pattern changed toward the end of the decade, however, in that theoretical papers outnumbered empirically based ones in the 1980s. The early 1990s showed a continuation of that trend, with only 20.8% of published articles representing empirical research and 63.5% reflecting purely theoretical scholarship.

[4]The anonymous referee system was implemented in 1979 for *Shakaigaku Hyouron*. As with any other professional journal, the selection of articles would be expected to reflect a certain degree of editorial judgement. To minimize such possible biases, articles that appeared in special issues were excluded from the present content analysis.

Table 2 Number and percentage (in parentheses) of articles in *Shakaigaku Hyouron*

	1970–1974	1975–1979	1980–1984	1985–1989	1990–1994	Total
Theory	27 (31.4)	26 (29.2)	33 (38.8)	38 (38.8)	61 (63.5)	185 (40.7)
Methods	0 (0.0)	3 (3.4)	3 (3.5)	4 (4.1)	6 (6.3)	16 (3.5)
Empirical	36 (41.9)	28 (31.5)	21 (24.7)	34 (34.7)	20 (20.8)	139 (30.6)
Review	23 (26.7)	32 (36.0)	28 (32.9)	22 (22.4)	9 (9.4)	114 (25.1)
Total	86 (100.0)	89 (100.0)	85 (100.0)	98 (100.0)	96 (100.0)	454 (100.0)

Data Source: *Shakaigaku Hyouron*, 1970–1994

Methodology is an area in which Japanese sociology has yet to achieve much strength, especially compared to American sociology. Quantitative methodological papers began to appear in *Shakaigaku Hyouron* in the late 1970s (see Table 2), but from this point until the early 1990s they accounted for a mere 3.5%, on average, of all published articles. Furthermore, the application of advanced methodological techniques has not yet become a common practice. Thus, among the empirical papers published in *Shakaigaku Hyouron* between 1970 and 1994, the content analysis presented in Table 3 reveals that only 17.9% employed multivariate statistical techniques to analyze data.

These trends do not imply that Japanese sociologists have been uninterested in empirical studies or methodological issues. A group of mathematical sociologists (e.g. Yasuda) founded its own subdiscipline and established a journal called *Riron-to-Houhou* (*Theory and Methods*) in 1985. Despite its recent beginnings, this journal has quickly become a prestigious outlet for empirical, methodological, and mathematical modeling papers.

In contrast to increased theoretical emphasis in recent years, the data indicates a decline in the proportion of papers devoted to quantitative methodological concerns. Even in a methodologically oriented journal such as *Riron-to-Houhou*, the proportion of quantitative methodological papers decreased from 60.6% in 1985–1989 to 39.3% in 1990–1994 (see Table 4). While the actual number has increased slightly (from 20 to 24), and still represents the most frequent type of article seen in this journal, a greater increase in the number of papers of the quantitative-methods type would have been expected from the increase in the total number of articles published.

In *Shakaigaku Hyouron*, the professional journal of the Japanese Sociological Society, empirically based papers not only constituted a diminishing proportion of publications, but they were less often based on quantitative data. In the early 1970s, 94.4% of empirical works were based on quantitative data; by

Table 3 Number and percentage (in parentheses) of empirical articles in *Shakaigaku Hyouron*

	1970–1974	1975–1979	1980–1984	1985–1989	1990–1994	Total
Analytical method						
Multivariate	2 (5.7)	6 (24.0)	3 (14.3)	9 (27.3)	4 (20.0)	24 (17.9)
Nonmulti-variate	33 (94.3)	19 (76.0)	18 (85.7)	24 (72.7)	16 (80.0)	110 (82.1)
Total (5 missing cases)	35 (100.0)	25 (100.0)	21 (100.0)	33 (100.0)	20 (100.0)	134 (100.0)
Data						
Survey	7 (19.4)	7 (25.0)	5 (23.8)	9 (26.5)	4 (20.0)	32 (23.0)
Secondary data	27 (75.0)	17 (60.7)	14 (66.7)	15 (44.1)	10 (50.0)	83 (59.7)
Intensive interview	2 (5.6)	4 (14.3)	2 (9.5)	10 (29.4)	6 (30.0)	24 (17.3)
Total	36 (100.0)	28 (100.0)	21 (100.0)	34 (100.0)	20 (100.0)	139 (100.0)

Data Source: *Shakaigaku Hyouron*, 1970–1994

the early 1990s, the proportion of quantitatively oriented empirical papers declined to 70.0% (see bottom half of Table 3). During this period, empirical publications based on secondary data showed a dramatic decrease over time, dropping from 75% in 1970–1974 to 50.0% in 1990–1994, while those using intensive interviews became more common during this period, rising from 5.6% to 30.0% in 20 years.

This decreasing interest in the quantitative approach may reflect the change in the discipline's dominant theoretical paradigm. The shift from structural functionalism to postmodernism likely stimulated a parallel movement away from quantitative analysis. Instead, qualitative methods and ethnomethodology are showing a gradual gain in popularity.

In short, these trends suggest that Japanese sociology has become more theoretically oriented in recent years, yet at the same time less inclined to verify theoretical propositions through empirical evidence. Because the link between theory and method is made through empirical research, the decline in empirically oriented works may contribute to the disarticulation between theoretical and applied scholarship as well as the stagnation of social methodology.

Although the overall number of empirical publications has decreased in recent years, there are particular substantive areas in which empirical research has been consistently strong over the years. These include family, rural, urban, and social stratification and social mobility. Family and rural sociologists have traditionally been trained to use empirical research. Having their roots in eth-

Table 4 Number and percentage (in parentheses) of articles in *Riron-to-Houhou*

	1985–1989	1990–1994	Total
Theory	6 (18.2)	17 (27.9)	23 (24.5)
Methods - quantitative	20 (60.6)	24 (39.3)	44 (46.8)
Methods - qualitative	1 (3.0)	1 (1.6)	2 (2.1)
Empirical	4 (12.1)	10 (16.4)	14 (14.9)
Review	2 (6.1)	9 (14.8)	11 (11.7)
Total	33 (100)	61 (100)	94 (100)

nology, they have relied on field work, intensive interviews, and historical documents for their empirical observations. With the introduction of scientific methods, they began using surveys as data-collection tools. As the discipline's focus shifted from rural to urban studies, surveys have become a dominant methodology applied among urban sociologists. Currently, many large-scale surveys are being funded within family and urban sociology.

Social stratification/mobility researchers have played an important role in the field of quantitative methods and empirical research. The most prominent survey in Japanese sociology is the SSM (Social Stratification and Social Mobility) survey, which has been carried out every ten years since 1955. It is based on a national sample of over 5000 individuals selected through a multistage stratified sampling method. These surveys contain interviews whose items are targeted primarily toward stratification research, including measures of family background, occupation, education, and social status (see Tominaga 1979 for details). Each wave of the survey also includes various questions reflecting the interests of researchers involved in the survey and the broader sociological community. The results from each wave of the survey have been published as monographs (e.g. Tominaga 1979, Naoi & Seiyama 1990, Hara 1990, Kikuchi 1990, Okamoto & Naoi 1990), which are regarded as the frontline of Japanese empirical research.

DISCUSSION

To summarize the development of an entire discipline is an ambitious task. Instead of introducing and critiquing major theories and research in selected areas, this paper focused on describing the overall substantive emphases within the discipline over time. The analyses in this paper are based on the available data on sociological publications, which proved to be useful in examining the dynamics of Japanese sociologists' interests and productivity.

The theoretical and methodological trends seen in Japanese sociology in the last 25 years raise a few issues for consideration. Ideally, theoretical direction and methodological focus should be related to each other, for the choice of methodology depends on the theoretical questions being explored. Yet the quantities of methodological and theoretical works should vary independently; an increased emphasis on one should not imply a decreased emphasis on the other. Moreover, if theory and methods were closely linked, the introduction of new theories would likely expand the quantity of empirical research. In the case of Japanese sociology, however, the observations of the above content analysis do not illustrate such linkages. The data shows an inverse pattern between the number of theoretical and empirical papers. It would appear that the emerging theories are not yet being substantiated sufficiently by empirical data. Japanese sociology would benefit from a closer consolidation between theory and research, both by formulating theories into verifiable propositions and by using theory to inform empirical research designs.

At the same time, more extensive methodological training is called for in Japanese universities. The lack of emphasis on methodological training is partly an unfortunate consequence of the structure of Japanese academic institutions. Consistent with the vertical structure in traditional Japanese organizations, mentorship is emphasized in graduate training. This results in a deficiency in structured curriculum covering a wide variety of core sociological courses at the graduate level. This type of training tends to produce highly qualified specialists in narrow fields.

The Japan Sociological Society has recently launched its effort to establish a system through which survey data is made available to researchers other than those who actually conducted the survey. An increase in empirical research might be stimulated by such a mechanism. In addition to the SSM survey, numerous large-scale surveys are funded and conducted each year. If shared and used appropriately, these results could provide a basis for empirical research that would otherwise require extensive data-collection efforts.

However, Japanese sociologists' efforts to stimulate empirical research may be tied to a more fundamental issue concerning the most effective way to position themselves and their discipline within the global sociological community. Their successful efforts to assimilate the sociological achievements of the United States and Europe have enriched their knowledge of theories and methods developed in foreign countries. Yet they have had less success in making their work visible to the international community of sociologists. The sociological discipline has reached a stage at which most practitioners appreciate the benefits of a global perspective. A more concerted interchange between Japanese sociologists and others in the discipline might be achieved through an emphasis on comparative research that illuminates both the uniqueness and universality of Japanese society. Such an exchange would not only benefit Japanese scholars but would be highly advantageous to the entire discipline.

ACKNOWLEDGMENTS

I wish to thank Professor Kiyomi Morioka for providing invaluable information about the history of Japanese sociological discipline. Comments and insights from Professors Kiyoshi Morioka and Keiko Yasukouchi were very much appreciated. I would like to express my gratitude to Drs. Susan Tiano, Robert Fiala, and Rogers Saxon for useful comments on the earlier draft of the manuscript. Special thanks go to Takuya Hayashi and Atsushi Hoshi for help in conducting content analyses.

Literature Cited

Akimoto R, Aiba J. 1985. *Seiji (Political Sociology)*. Readings Nihon no Shakaigaku Ser., Vol. 14. Tokyo: Tokyo Univ. Press

Aoi K. 1980. *Shoushuudan no Shakaigaku (Sociology of Small Groups)*. Tokyo: Tokyo Univ. Press

Asahi Shimbun. 1996. *Shakaigaku ga Wakaru (Understanding Sociology)*. AERA Mook Vol. 12. Tokyo: Asahi Newspaper Pub.

Hara J. 1990. *Gendai Nihon no Kaisou Kouzou: Kaisou Ishiki no Doutai (Social Stratification Structure in Contemporary Sociology: Trends of Perception About Class and Stratification)*. Tokyo: Tokyo Univ. Press

Hougetsu M, Ohmura E, Hoshino K. 1986. *Shakai Byouri (Deviance)*. Readings Nihon no Shakaigaku Ser., Vol. 13. Tokyo: Tokyo Univ. Press

Inagami T, Kawakita T. 1987. *Sangyou/Roudou (Industry and Labor)*. Readings Nihon no Shakaigaku Ser., Vol. 9. Tokyo: Tokyo Univ. Press

Ishida T. 1996. *Shakaikagaku Saikou (Rethinking Social Sciences)*. Tokyo: Tokyo Univ. Press

Kikuchi J. 1990. *Gendai Nihon no Kaisou Kouzou: Kyouiku to Shakai Idou (Social Stratification Structure in Contemporary Japan: Education and Social Mobility)*. Tokyo: Tokyo Univ. Press

Koutou Y. 1997. Nihon no shakaigaku: shakaigaku riron (Japanese sociology: sociological theory) In *Shakaigaku Riron (Sociological Theory)*, ed. T Shiobara, et al. Readings Nihon no Shakaigaku Ser., Vol. 1:3–11. Tokyo: Tokyo Univ. Press

Mita M, Yamamoto Y, Satou K. 1989. *Bunka to Shakai Ishiki (Culture and Social Perception)*. Readings Nihon no Shakaigaku Ser., Vol. 12. Tokyo: Tokyo Univ. Press

Mitani T, Ohyama N, Nakagawa K. 1988. *Shakai Mondai (Social Problems)*. Readings Nihon no Shakaigaku Ser., Vol. 11. Tokyo: Tokyo Univ. Press

Mitsuyoshi T, Matsumoto M, Masaoka H. 1986. *Dentou Kazoku (Traditional Family)*. Readings Nihon no Shakaigaku Ser., Vol. 3. Tokyo: Tokyo Univ. Press

Miura N, Morioka K, Sasaki M. 1986. *Seikatsu Kouzou (Life Structure)*. Readings Nihon no Shakaigaku Ser., Vol. 5. Tokyo: Tokyo Univ. Press

Miyake H, Koumoto M, Nishiyama S. 1986. *Shuukyou (Religion)*. Readings Nihon no Shakaigaku Ser., Vol. 19. Tokyo: Tokyo Univ. Press

Mochizuki T, Meguro Y, Ishihara K. 1987. *Gendai Kazoku (Contemporary Family)*. Readings Nihon no Shakaigaku Ser., Vol. 4. Tokyo: Tokyo Univ. Press

Morioka K. 1993. *Kazoku Shakaigaku no Tenkai (Developments in Family Sociology)*. Tokyo: Baifuukan

Morita Y, Shimizu K. 1986. *Ijime—Kyoushitsu no Yamai* (*Bullying—Problems in Classrooms*). Tokyo: Kaneko Shobou

Nakata M, Takahashi A, Sakai T, Iwasaki N. 1986. *Nouson* (*Rural Sociology*). Readings Nihon no Shakaigaku Ser., Vol. 6. Tokyo: Tokyo Univ. Press

Naoi A, Hara J, Kobayashi H. 1986. *Shakai Kaisou/Shakai Idou* (*Social Stratification and Social Mobility*). Readings Nihon no Shakaigaku Ser., Vol. 8. Tokyo: Tokyo Univ. Press

Naoi A, Seiyama K. 1990. *Gendai Nihon no Kaisou Kouzou: Shakai Kaisou no Kouzou to Katei* (*Social Stratification Structure in Contemporary Japan: Structure and Process of Social Stratification*). Tokyo: Tokyo Univ. Press

Nitagai K, Kajima T, Fukuoka Y. 1986. *Shakai Undou* (*Social Movements*). Readings Nihon no Shakaigaku Ser., Vol. 10. Tokyo: Tokyo Univ. Press

Okamoto H, Naoi M. 1990. *Gendai Nihon no Kaisou Kouzou: Josei to Shakai Kaisou* (*Social Stratification Structure in Contemporary Japan: Women and Social Stratification*). Tokyo: Tokyo Univ. Press

Sakuta K. 1972. *Kachi no Shakaigaku* (*Sociology of Values*). Tokyo: Iwanami Shoten

Shibano M, Asou M, Ikeda H. 1986. *Kyouiku* (*Education*). Readings Nihon no Shakaigaku Ser., Vol. 16. Tokyo: Tokyo Univ. Press

Shiobara T, Inoue S, Koutou Y. 1997. *Shakaigaku Riron* (*Sociological Theory*). Readings Nihon no Shakaigaku Ser., Vol. 1. Tokyo: Tokyo Univ. Press

Shouji K, Yazawa S, Takekawa S. 1988. *Taisei to Idou* (*Social System and Social Change*). Readings Nihon no Shakaigaku Ser., Vol. 17. Tokyo: Tokyo Univ. Press

Suzuki H, Takahashi Y, Shinohara T. 1985. *Toshi* (*Urban Sociology*). Readings Nihon no Shakaigaku Ser., Vol. 7. Tokyo: Tokyo Univ. Press

Takeuchi I, Okada N, Kojima K. 1987. *Mass Communication* (in Japanese). Readings Nihon no Shakaigaku Ser., Vol. 20. Tokyo: Tokyo Univ. Press

Takeuchi Y. 1981. *Kyousou no Shakaigaku—Gakureki to Shoushin* (*Sociology of Competition—Educational Attainment and Promotion*). Tokyo: Sekaishiousha

Tominaga K. 1965. *Shakai Hendou no Riron* (*Theory of Social Change*). Tokyo: Iwanami Shoten

Tominaga K. 1979. *Nihon no Kaisou Kouzou* (*Social Stratification Structure in Japan*). Tokyo: Tokyo Univ. Press

Yoshida T. 1974. *Shakai Sisutemuron ni okeru Jouhoushigenshori Paradaimu no Kousou* (*Information Management Paradigm in the Theory of Social Systems*). Gendai Shakaigaku, Koudansha, 1:7–27

Annu. Rev. Sociol. 1998. 24:517–54

NARRATIVE ANALYSIS—OR WHY (AND HOW) SOCIOLOGISTS SHOULD BE INTERESTED IN NARRATIVE

Roberto Franzosi

Trinity College, University of Oxford, Oxford OX1 3BH, United Kingdom; e-mail: roberto.franzosi@trinity.ox.ac.uk

KEY WORDS: narrative analysis, discourse analysis, content analysis, language and class and gender, science rhetoric, role of reader

ABSTRACT

In this paper I explore the questions of why and how sociologists should be interested in narrative. The answer to the first question is straightforward: Narrative texts are packed with sociological information, and a great deal of our empirical evidence is in narrative form. In an attempt to answer the second question, I look at definitions of narrative, distinguishing narrative from non-narrative texts. I highlight the linguistic properties of narrative and illustrate modes of analysis, paying close attention to both the structural properties of the text and its subtle linguistic nuances. I guide the reader through a detailed analysis of a short narrative text. I show how linguistics and sociology interplay at the level of a text.

> Narrative is present in myth, legend, fable, tale, novella, epic, history, tragedy, drama, comedy, mime, painting (think of Carpaccio's *Saint Ursula*), stained glass windows, cinema, comics, news items, conversations. Moreover, under this almost infinite diversity of forms, narrative is present in every age, in every place, in every society; it begins with the very history of mankind and there nowhere is nor has been a people without narrative. All classes, all human groups, have their narratives . . . narrative is international, transhistorical, transcultural: It is simply there, like life itself...
>
> Barthes 1977:79

0360-0572/98/0815-0517$08.00

NARRATIVE: WHAT'S IN IT FOR US?

Given a set of numbers—236, 435, 218, 767, 456, 367—most sociologists certainly would recognize the numbers as data. Most would also know what to do with them. They could plot those data, tabulate them, estimate statistical models. Some would easily deal with the problems of first-order correlation of the residuals that those data and those models may produce; they would try to overcome problems of heteroschedasticity, non-normality, influence, and all the other little and big problems that plague our statistical work. But take the following text.

> As soon as the water went down, I began to work digging the bodies out of the debris. I worked for eight days after the flood looking for bodies, and I recovered twenty-two of them. The last one I found was a little five-year-old boy. It reminded me so much of my own little boy that I could not take any more. That is when I went to pieces... (Erikson 1976:165)

As sociologists, what should we get out of this passage? Does the passage contain data (data?) of any interest to us? What are we to make of it? How are we to analyze it, to test hypotheses, to draw inferences? Paradoxically, we are more at ease in the artificial and (wo)man-made world of statistics than in the more natural world of language and words. After all, a course in statistics is part and parcel of any sociology graduate training. A course in the analysis of text certainly is not, and even courses in qualitative research methods pay little attention to texts and narratives as such. And, perhaps, before we even ask questions of method and analysis, there is a more fundamental question that begs an answer: Why should sociologists be interested in narrative?

In this article, I take up these questions. Do not expect a comprehensive or summary review of the literature on narrative—of necessity, I will be rather selective.[1] My goal is to introduce sociologists to the basic concepts, particularly as elaborated by linguists, and to show how linguistics and sociology interplay at the level of a text. I provide definitions of narrative, distinguishing narrative from non-narrative texts. I highlight the linguistic properties of narrative and illustrate modes of analysis. As a way to review the issues involved I guide the reader through a detailed analysis of a short narrative text. In this analysis, I pay close attention to both the structural properties of the text and its subtle lin-

[1] I found Chatman (1978), Genette (1980), Rimmon-Kenan (1983), Cohan & Shires (1988), and Toolan (1988) to be the best introductions to the issues. Ricoeur's (1984, 1985, 1988) three-volume work on time and narrative is not for the faint of heart. It provides a comprehensive review of the views on time and narrative of linguists, philosophers, historians, and sociologists. It may be hard for the novice to follow the intricacy of Ricoeur's account of the various authors' positions, despite Ricoeur's lucid and clear language. I would recommend reading it last.

guistic nuances.[2] After all, as Chatman (1978:94) writes, "For many narratives what is crucial is the tenuous complexity of actual analysis rather than the powerful simplicity of reduction."

The narrative analysis of the text helps to bring out not only the properly linguistic characteristics of the story—a task perhaps better left in the hands of those who know how to do this best: linguists—but also a great deal of sociology hidden behind a handful of lines. It is precisely because (*a*) narrative texts are packed with sociological information and (*b*) much of our empirical evidence is in narrative form that sociologists should be concerned with narrative. [Just think: Even the quantitative sociological method par excellence, the sample survey, often hides powerful narratives behind its numbers (Mishler 1986:72).]

NARRATIVE AND NARRATIVE ANALYSIS

Labov defined narrative as "one method of recapitulating past experience by matching a verbal sequence of clauses to the sequence of events which (it is inferred) actually occurred" [Labov (1972:359–60); see also Labov & Waletzky (1967:20)]. That definition has survived, more or less intact, through the years and through a number of hands that have pulled and pushed it from different angles. We find it in Rimmon-Kenan: "... narrative fiction ... [is] a succession of events" [Rimmon-Kenan (1983:2–3)]; in Cohan & Shires: "The distinguishing feature of narrative is its linear organization of events" [Cohan & Shires (1988:52–53)]; and in Toolan: "A minimalist definition of narrative might be: 'a perceived sequence of nonrandomly connected events'" [Toolan (1988:7)].

It is not surprising that all these definitions are in basic agreement. After all, they have common roots in the work of the Russian formalists of the beginning of the twentieth century, Propp (1968) and Tomashevski (1965) in particular. It is the Russian formalists who introduced the distinction between story vs plot in narrative (*fabula* vs *sjuñet*). Building upon Aristotle's idea of plot-structure or *mythos*—in the master's own words, "By this term 'plot-structure' I mean the organisation of the events" (Halliwell 1987:Ch. 6, p. 37)—Tomashevski (1965:67) wrote, "Plot is distinct from story. Both include the same events, but in the plot the events *are arranged* and connected according to the orderly sequence in which they were presented in the work." He continues in a note, "In brief, the story is 'the action itself, ... [the plot is] how the reader learns of the action.'" Basically, a *story* refers to a skeletal description of the fundamental events in their natural logical and chronological order (perhaps

[2]The latter type of analysis has fallen under the domain of discourse analysis [e.g. the four volumes edited by van Dijk (van Dijk 1985) or the easier treatment by Fairclough (Fairclough 1995)].

with an equally skeletal listing of the roles of the characters in the story) (Bal 1977:4; Toolan 1988:9).

The French structuralists adopted the basic distinction *fabula* vs *sjuñet*, coined their own terms for the dichotomy *histoire* vs *discours* [see Benveniste (1971:206–8); Barthes (1977); Chatman (1978:19); Toolan (1988:11–12)], story vs discourse, and further subdivided the plot/discourse level into text (or, more generally, discourse) and narrating or narration, i.e. "the act of narrating taken in itself" (see Genette 1980:27, Toolan 1988:10–11).

Bal also speaks of a "three-level hierarchy, *histoire, récit, narration*" (Bal 1977:5–6) and of the "three aspects of narrative," story, text, and narration (Genette 1980:25–26; see also Rimmon-Kenan 1983:3–4, Cohan & Shires 1988:53). As usual, the trouble is that subtle differences exist among authors not only in the narrative levels and labels, but also in their definitions that make ploughing through the literature an unnecessarily difficult task [see Toolan (1988:9–11) on this point]. Nonetheless, we could summarize the distinctions that linguists have introduced in the study of narrative in the following way:

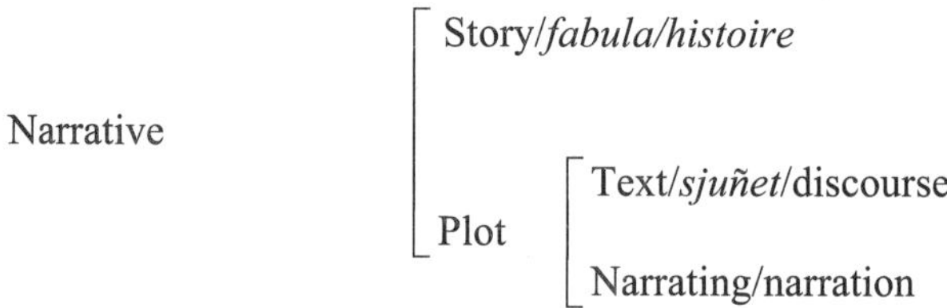

It is the story—the chrono-logical succession of events—that provides the basic building blocks of narrative. Without story there is no narrative. "The presence or absence of a story is what distinguishes narrative from non-narrative texts" (Rimmon-Kenan 1983:15). "A story may be thought of as a journey from one situation to another," wrote Tomashevski (Tomashevski 1965:70). A story, in other words, implies a change in situations as expressed by the unfolding of a specific sequence of events. The chronological sequence is a crucial ingredient of any definition of story. Tomashevski, Labov, Prince, Bal, Todorov, Rimmon-Kenan, and Cohan & Shires all drum away at that same point [Tomashevski (1965:70); Labov (1972); Prince (1973:23); Bal (1977:7); Todorov (1977:111); Rimmon-Kenan (1983:19); Cohan & Shires (1988:53–54)].

Not every sequence of any two temporally ordered events can constitute a story (Rimmon-Kenan 1983:19). Two sentences such as "Joan took her plane at 5 pm" and "Peter drove to the airport at 8 pm" would constitute a story only if later sentences established a logical connection between those two sentences, such as "They had both been looking forward to spending the weekend together." The temporal ordering of events in a story is a necessary but not sufficient condition for the emergence of a story. The events in the sequence must be bound together by some principles of logical coherence.[3] At the level of plot the events of a story can form complex sequences by combining events in a variety of ways through enchainment, embedding, and joining [Bremond (1966); Todorov (1981:52–53); Rimmon-Kenan (1983:23)]. Finally, the events in the story must disrupt an initial state of equilibrium that sets in motion an inversion of situation, a change of fortunes—from good to bad, from bad to good, or no such reversal of polarity, just an 'after' different from the 'before,' but neither necessarily better nor worse.

"The inversion of an event is one of the essential features of a story," sums up Prince (1973:28)—the other essential feature being the temporal ordering of events in a story.[4] In classical Aristotelian poetics, the turn of fortunes—a *reversal*—is the key characteristic of comedy and tragedy. "Reversal," wrote Aristotle, "is a complete swing in the direction of the action" (Halliwell 1987:Ch. 11, p. 42). While comedy marks an improvement of a situation, tragedy marks a worsening, the "transformation to prosperity or affliction" [Halliwell (1987:Ch. 18, p. 51); on Aristotelian reversals, see Chatman (1978:85) and Ricoeur (1984:43–44)]. Reversals can occur repeatedly in a story along the sequence: initial state → disruption → new state → disruption → new state → ... → final state (equilibrium). Each new state is both a point of arrival and a point of departure, sort of a temporary equilibrium between the "before and after," the past and the future. In Todorov's words, "The elements [of a story] are related [not] only by *succession*; ... they are also related by *transformation*. Here finally we have the two principles of narratives" [Todorov (1990:30)].

In a sequence, not all events are equally consequential for change of a situation. For Tomashevski, "Motifs [basically, actions and events] which change the situation are dynamic motifs; those which do not are static" (Tomashevski 1965:70). This distinction—between those actions and events that fundamentally alter a narrative situation and the ones that do not—recurs often in the field. Barthes, for instance, distinguishes between cardinal functions (or nuclei) and catalyzers (Barthes 1977:93–94). Catalyzers "merely fill in the narrative space," while cardinal functions alter current states of affairs, either by bringing them to a new equilibrium or by disrupting an existing equilibrium. "Catalyzers are only consecutive [i.e. chronologically ordered] units, cardinal functions are both consecutive and consequential" (Barthes 1977:94). Chat-

[3]However, as Chatman argues, readers will typically even attempt to make a story out of temporally sequenced but logically unrelated clauses by implicitly supplying logical connectives [Chatman (1978:47, 49)].

[4]See also Prince (1973:23). On the reversal of situation, see Tomashevski (1925:70–71); Todorov (1977:111–12, 1981:51); see also Aristotle, who first introduced the concept of reversal in his *Poetics* (Halliwell 1987:Ch. 11, p. 42). Bremond (1966) also believed that all sequences are either sequences of improvement or deterioration (see the discussion by Rimmon-Kenan 1983:27).

man (1978:32, 53–56) adopted Barthes' basic distinction with different labels: kernel and satellite events (labels also adopted by Rimmon-Kenan 1983:16). Again, although intuitively and in principle the separation of the clauses of a text into different functions should be straightforward, in practice, in the analysis of any specific text, what is kernel to one author may be satellite to another, and vice versa. Deletion of kernels would fundamentally destroy the narrative logic (Chatman 1978:53). Kernels open up narrative choices.

Dynamic motifs, cardinal functions, or kernel events have corresponding linguistic markers. For Labov (1972:360–61) "a minimal narrative ... [is] a sequence of two clauses which are temporally ordered. ... The skeleton of a narrative ... consists of a series of temporally ordered clauses" (called narrative clauses). And yet, while there may be no narrative without narrative clauses, not all clauses found in narrative are narrative clauses. [Danto (1985:143–81) similarly talks about "narrative sentences."]

Consider Labov's example:

(*a*) I know a boy named Harry.
(*b*) Another boy threw a bottle at him right in the head
(*c*) and he got seven stitches.

In this narrative passage, only clauses *b* and *c* are narrative clauses. Clause *a* is not. It is a "free clause," in Labov's terminology; a clause that, having no temporal component, can be moved freely up and down in the text without altering its meaning. Not so with narrative clauses.[5] A rearrangement of narrative clauses typically results in a change in meaning ("I punched this boy/and he punched me" vs "This boy punched me/and I punched him") (Labov 1972:360).

Labov not only draws a distinction between narrative and non-narrative clauses, he also posits the presence of six distinct functional parts in a fully formed narrative: (*a*) abstract; (*b*) orientation; (*c*) complicating action; (*d*) evaluation; (*e*) result or resolution; (*f*) coda. Of these six functional parts, "only ... the complicating action is essential if we are to recognize a narrative" (Labov 1972:370).[6] The complicating action constitutes "the main body of narra-

[5]In 1925, Tomashevski had already introduced the distinction between bound motifs and free motifs, where a motif is basically a unit of narrative. Free motifs are those that may be safely omitted from a story "without destroying the coherence of the narrative"; bound motifs are those whose deletion would disturb "the whole causal-chronological course of events" (Tomashevski 1965:68). As Todorov notes, "optional ('free') propositions ... are such only from the point of view of sequential construction; they are often what is most necessary in the text as a whole" (Todorov 1981:52–53). Indeed, it is likely that it is at the level of free motifs that the telling of the story (the plot) would differ (Tomashevski 1965:68). See also Barthes' distinction between cardinal functions (or nuclei) and catalyzers (Barthes 1977:93–94).

[6]Labov did not test his structural model of narrative. Peterson & McCabe (1983), however, did analyze a set of children's narratives using Labov's scheme. van Dijk also adopted a Labovian scheme in his analysis of narratives of ethnic prejudice (van Dijk 1984). For a more complete list, see Toolan 1988:176.

tive clauses," and that body of clauses "usually comprises a series of events" (Labov & Waletzky 1967:32). Implicitly,

> Labov works on the broad assumption that what is said ... will not be the core of a story; that, rather, what is done ... will be. The "what is done" then becomes (or may become) the core narrative text of clauses—actions—while the "what is said" becomes evaluative commentary on those actions... (Toolan 1988:157)

But the "doing vs saying" distinction implicitly or explicitly is at the core of linguistic theories of narrative structures. In Ricoeur's words, "there is no structural analysis of narrative that does not borrow from an explicit or implicit phenomenology of 'doing something'"(Ricoeur 1984:56). Bal similarly points out that "in general, narrative theorists rather tend to analyse the course of action to which they limit their story" (Bal 1977:89). Genette (1980:164, 169) distinguishes between narrative of events and narrative of words.

It is this emphasis on action (on "doing something") that has led to the privileged position of actions/events over actors in poetics. We first find this subordination of character to action in Aristotle, who wrote in his *Poetics*: "Tragedy is a representation not of people as such but of action and of life, and both happiness and unhappiness rest on action. ... and while men do have certain qualities by virtue of their character, it is in their actions that they achieve, or fail to achieve, happiness. ... without action you would not have a tragedy, but one without character would be feasible" [Halliwell (1987:Ch. 11, pp. 37–38); see also Ricoeur (1984:37); Barthes (1977:104); Rimmon-Kenan (1983:34)].

We find it also in Propp, the Russian formalist of the beginning of this century who left a seminal work on the structural analysis of narrative. In his study of Russian folk tales, Propp identified 31 basic functions (namely, spheres of action) that are invariant across different tales (Propp 1968). After spending the better part of a book discussing these functions and their roles in narrative sequences, Propp dedicated only a handful of pages to a quick discussion of characters (1968:79–91). All story characters can be reduced to a simple typology of seven "character roles" based on the unity of actions assigned to them by the narrative: the villain, the donor, the helper, the sought-for-person and her father, the dispatcher, the hero, the false hero.

We still find this emphasis in Greimas, who proposed to describe and classify narrative characters according to what they do (hence the name actants)—once more reproducing the subordination of character to action despite Greimas' focus on actants (Greimas 1966). According to Greimas, six basic actants can be found in all narratives, working in sets of three interrelated pairs (Greimas 1966: 172–91), sender/receiver, helper/opponent, subject/object, typically represented in the following way:

Sender → object → receiver

Helper → subject → opponent

In Greimas' model, (*a*) the sender initiates or enables the event; (*b*) the receiver benefits or registers the effects of the event; (*c*) the opponent retards or impedes the event by opposing the subject or by competing with the subject for the object; (*d*) the helper advances the event by supporting or assisting the subject [see also Toolan (1988:93); Barthes (1977:106–7); Rimmon-Kenan (1983:34–35)].

In general, a narrative text will comprise a mixture of both narrative and non-narrative clauses. In particular, descriptive and expository propositions typically enter into a minimal narrative (Tomashevski 1965:66; Bal 1977:13; Rimmon-Kenan 1983:14–15). "Description alone is not enough to constitute a narrative; narrative for its part does not exclude description" (Todorov 1990: 28). Narrative texts are those where the distinctive characteristics of the narrative genre are prevalent (Bal 1977:13).

Bal correctly points out that a theory of narrative presupposes a theory of text genres; she proposes three types of texts, lyrical, dramatic, and narrative (Bal 1977:12–13). The narrative text basically tells a story (just like drama, but unlike lyrical texts) in a complex way (contrary to the other two types of texts) wherein the ratio of narrator's discourse to actor's discourse is maximized (contrary to both lyrical and dramatic texts). "In modern theories of literature," states Bal, "description occupies a marginal role. The structural analysis of narrative relegates it to a secondary function: It is subordinate to the narration of action. It can occupy the catalyser function, but never that of nucleus" (Bal 1977:89). Description is a luxury, a narrative ornament (Bal 1977:89–90).

FURTHER FORAYS INTO A STRUCTURAL ANALYSIS OF NARRATIVE

"A narrative ... shares with other narratives a common structure which is open to analysis, no matter how much patience its formulation requires" [Barthes 1977:80 (1966)]. We have seen the results of that collective exercise in patience in search of "the invariant structural units which are represented by a variety of superficial forms" (Labov & Waletzky 1967:12); of the recurrent characteristics and the "distinguishable regularities" behind narrative (Greimas 1971:794); behind the "millions of narratives" [Barthes 1977:81 (1966)] to be more precise.

Propp took the first bold step toward a structural analysis of narrative when he identified an invariant pattern of 31 functions behind the large variety of Russian folktales. Regardless of the particular content of a folktale, regardless of how the story is told, all Russian folktales, according to Propp, will exhibit (at least some of) those 31 basic functions. Furthermore, the sequence in which those functions appear is fixed.[7] Greimas further aggregated Propp's 31 functions into a basic set of six functions (Greimas 1966). Labov found a six-part macrostructure in vernacular narratives of New York Harlem African-Americans: abstract, orientation, complicating action, evaluation, result or resolution, and coda (Labov 1972:362–70; see also Labov & Waletzky 1967).[8] More generally, van Dijk has argued that all texts are characterized by macrostructures ("schemata") that provide the "global schematic form" of a discourse—different discourse genres being characterized by different schemata (van Dijk 1983:24). Thus, the schema of a newspaper article comprises both a summary and a story; the story further comprises a situation and comments; the situation comprises episode and background; the episode includes main events and consequences; while background includes context (circumstances and previous events) and history (van Dijk 1988:51–59).

Of particular interest is the relationship between these deep, macrolevel structures and surface, microlevel structures. For Labov (1972:375), narrative, macrolevel structures can be mapped into surface structures through adverbial elements (for time and space), a subject-noun phrase, and a verb phrase. Other linguists, as well, have argued that narrative stories are characterized by a simple surface representation patterned after the canonical form of the language (subject/action/object) with some modifiers (Todorov 1969:27–41; 1977: 218–33; 1981:48–51; Halliday 1970; Chatman 1978:91; Prince 1973:32). Cognitive psychologists and computer scientists involved in artificial intelligence projects of computer understanding of natural languages have similarly represented stories in terms of a "story grammar" (e.g. Rumelhart 1975; Mandler 1978).

Over the last decade, sociologists have proposed various methods of analysis of narrative texts that are fundamentally based on these and other structural linguistic characteristics of narrative. Abell (1987), for instance, has proposed a methodology that he terms "comparative narratives" based on a formal representation of narrative structures in terms of actors and actions. In my own work, I have developed a story grammar (or semantic grammar) to structure the narrative information provided by newspaper articles on protest events (Franzosi 1989). A semantic grammar offers several advantages over more traditional content analysis schemes for the collection of text data (Franzosi 1989; 1990a,b). In particular, the re-expression of the grammar in set theoretical terms allows researchers to go "from words to numbers," i.e. to analyze

[7]For a critique of this aspect of Propp's morphology of stories, see Bremond (1964). Bremond argues that stories are not all characterized by a single, invariant macrostructural sequence. Rather, invariant sequences are characteristic of microstructures (i.e. parts of stories) and those sequentially invariant microstructures combine in a multiplicity of forever varying ways to form complex narrative macrostructures.

[8]For a comparison of Greimas' and Labov & Waletzky's schema, see van Dijk (1972:293).

narrative information statistically (Franzosi 1994). Furthermore, within a set theoretical notation, the basic structure of a semantic grammar translates easily into the mathematical structure underlying network models (Franzosi 1998). Intuitively, a semantic grammar structures narrative information within the basic template SAO, or subject, action, object, where both subjects and objects are typically social actors (e.g. "police charge demonstrators"). In other words, the basic structure of a semantic grammar links social actors around specific spheres of action. Network models can be used to analyze text data organized not only in SAO structures, but also in sets of relational concepts. Concepts, rather than social actors, represent the nodes of these networks (for this approach, see Carley 1993).

Other approaches proposed by sociologists similarly take off in fundamental ways from structural characteristics of narrative. Abbott (1995), for instance, investigates the sequential organization of narrative structures in search of patterns of recurrent sequences. "The sequence of events has its own laws," wrote Propp long ago. "Theft cannot take place before the door is forced. Insofar as the tale is concerned it has its own entirely particular and specific laws. The sequence of elements ... is strictly *uniform* [emphasis in original]. Freedom within this sequence is restricted by very narrow limits which can be exactly formulated" (Propp 1968:22). Abbott & Hrycak's method of analysis allows investigators to bring out those uniform sequences (and not just in narrative) (Abbott & Hrycak 1990).

Even more closely related to the structural characteristics of narrative is a method of analysis of text data proposed by Heise (Heise 1989; Corsaro & Heise 1990). Following the long philosophical and linguistic tradition of the difference in meaning between "things [that] happen because of one another, or only after one another," of dynamic and static motifs, of cardinal functions (or nuclei) and catalyzers, of kernel and satellite events, Heise developed a computer program, ETHNO, that forces investigators to make explicit the implicit assumptions built into causal arguments, as these arguments are reflected into the chronological sequence of skeleton narrative sentences. Griffin's analysis of the narrative of a lynching event that took place in Missisipi in 1930 (Griffin 1993) shows that Heise's approach does help to tease out the implicit and explicit causal patterns of a narrative. Furthermore, the approach helps to bring out research questions and broad patterns of social relations by focusing on a single narrative.

What is characteristic about these new techniques is that their real contribution does not seem to lie so much in the methodological but in the epistemological realm. As Abbott argues with reference to sequence analysis, sequence analysis is not just "a particular technique [of data analysis, but] ... rather a body of questions about social processes" (Abbott 1995:93). No doubt, a view of social reality fundamentally based on narrative data shifts sociologists' concerns away from variables to actors, away from regression-based statistical models to networks, and away from a variable-based conception of causality to narrative sequences. That view promises to bring sociology closer to history and to sociology's own original concerns with issues of human agency. It also blurs the line between quality and quantity, transcending the terms of a debate that has uselessly involved social scientists over the last 50 years (see Abell 1987:3–12). But whether a technique is worth its salt (particularly when it claims to rise above the methodological realm and into the epistemological one) fundamentally depends upon the substantive products it delivers. And as of yet, the researchers involved in peddling these wares have delivered substantive products of limited import (for some examples, see Abbott & Barman 1997; Franzosi 1997a,b; Griffin 1993). More to the point, these researchers have been less than forthcoming in spelling out the methodological and epistemological limitations of their techniques (see Franzosi 1999). Semantic grammars, they tend to mix syntactical and semantic categories (e.g. subject and object are syntactical categories—actor would be a better semantic alternative—but action is a semantic category; verb would be the syntactical equivalent). Furthermore, the processes that actors perform are broader than those implied by the term action. The high costs involved in the collection of event data may lead researchers to focus on particuarly transformative events (e.g. "the red years" and "black years" of 1919–1922 of my work, or Tarrow's focus on the cycle of protest around the Italian "hot autumn" of 1969; see Franzosi 1997b, Tarrow 1989). The event is back, from the ashes of Braudel's attack and that of his colleagues in the *Annales* school. Finally, the very richness of the event data that computerized semantic grammars deliver may lead researchers to adopt descriptive modes of explanation, the narrative of the evidence imposing its form on the mode of explanation. In going "from words to numbers" we may have inadvertently gone from "thin explanations" (based on variables and regression models) to "thick descriptions." The application of network models to narrative data may not necessarily improve things on this score. Laumann wrote that "the hallmark of network analysis ... is to explain, at least in part, the behavior of network elements (i.e. the nodes) and of the system as a whole by appeal to specific features of the interconnections among the elements" (Laumann 1979:394). Such emphasis on explanation (rather than description) is certainly part and parcel of our disciplinary mottos and of the legacy bequeathed to us by our "founding fathers." But a focus on the system of interconnections alone is unlikely to lead us beyond the descriptive.

With respect to Heise and Griffin's approach, their method leaves unresolved the issue of how investigators reach fundamental decisions about what is sequential and what is consequential. For all the logical questions that ETHNO asks, for all its probing, the decision-making process itself remains a "black box" hidden in the recesses of the human psyche. That being the case, and given that ETHNO has been applied to understand short narrative passages, why would a good linguist or a good historian not reach those same conclusions without ETHNO? (For a critique of one of Abbott & Bauman's contributions, see Franzosi 1997c.)

AN EXAMPLE

Consider the following text.

> Neville: After my wife kicked me out I spent several weeks living in my car. Being homeless she wouldn't let me see my son ... I really missed Ricky. A friend suggested I go to see Shelter. I was a little apprehensive ... frightened to go in, but they were brilliant. It's a bit like a hotel, it's very clean and the staff are great. Best of all my wife came round to check the place out and now lets my son visit me, it's let me rebuild me family life... (*Oxford Independent*, 1997)

It is not hard to recognize this text as narrative. The text deals with "the temporal character of human experience" (Ricoeur 1984:52), with a change in situation from bad (homelessness and breakdown of family life) to good (a place to live and the rebuilding of family life), and contains both narrative and non-narrative (mostly descriptive) clauses arranged in chronological order (see Table 1).

Many temporal references in Neville's story highlight the role of narrative as "recapitulation of past experience" (Labov 1972:359). But time in narrative has a dual function: It "is constitutive both of the means of representation (language) and of the object represented (the incidents of the story). Time in narrative fiction can be defined as the relations of chronology between story and text" (Rimmon-Kenan 1983:44). In Neville's story, the sequence of clauses coincides with the sequence of the narrated events (the sequences of both clauses and events are the same; see columns 1 and 2 in Table 1). Story and plot coincide, with minimum plot development. That is rather typical of simple stories. The plot is the realm where the narrative abilities of different authors can make something out of the basic raw material of a story (a sequence of events). Narrative theorists have highlighted three different aspects of narrative time—order, duration, and frequency—each dealing with three different sets of questions: When? For how long? And how often?[9]

Neville's story does not provide enough clues for a clear answer to the first question: When? Although extranarrative information tells us that the story

[9]The most comprehensive account of narrative time is Genette's treatment (Genette 1980). Ricoeur's three-volume treatment is more ambitious (Ricoeur 1984, 1985, 1988), but not as crisp as Genette's. Ricoeur's book deals with linguists', philosophers', and historians' views of time. It provides a comprehensive review of each author's position in lucid, clear language. For brief introductions to the issues, see Rimmon-Kenan (1983:43–58), Cohan & Shires (1988:84–89); Toolan (1988:48–61).

Table 1 Narrative and non-narrative clauses in Neville's story*

Clause sequence	Event sequence	Narrative clauses	Descriptive clauses
(01)	T_1	After my wife kicked me out	
(02)	T_2	I spent several weeks living in my car	
(03)			Being homeless
(04)		she wouldn't let me see my son	
(05)		I really missed Ricky	
(06)	T_3	A friend suggested	
(07)	T_4	I go to see Shelter	
(08)			I was a little apprehensive...
(09)			frightened to go in
(10)			but they were brilliant
(11)			It's a bit like a hotel
(12)			it's very clean
(13)			and the staff are great
(14)	T^5	Best of all my wife came round	
(15)		to check the place out	
(16)	T_6	and now lets my son visit me	
(17)		it's let me rebuild me family life	

*The distinction between "narrative" and "descriptive" units in Table 1 is based on the linguistic properties of the verb. Typically, the narrative characteristics of a story are linguistically marked by the use of (*a*) finite (rather than non-finite) verbs (e.g. walks or walked, rather than to walk) and (*b*) dynamic verbs that depict events and active processes, rather than stative verbs that describe states of affairs or descriptions (Prince 1973:29, Chatman 1978:31–2, Toolan 1988:34–5, 266). "Process statements are in the mode of DO or HAPPEN.... Stasis statements are in the mode of IS" (Chatman 1978:32). Yet, some static verbs in the mode IS hide process statements in the mode of DO. A good example is clause 10, "they were brilliant," which implies that the Shelter staff DID something to make Neville feel welcome, or comfortable and at home.

Also, strictly speaking, the numbered text units are not clauses (e.g. clause 4), although most of them are. The discourse analysts' terminology of "discourse units" may be more appropriate. I have kept the term "clause" to emphasize Labov's separation of narrative and descriptive, or "free," clauses (Labov 1973).

was published in January 1997, it does not tell us when exactly the narrated events took place. The deictic element "now" temporally anchors the story to the moment of narration—rather than to a moment prior to that of narration—but that narration could have occurred at any time in the past prior to publication. The temporal shift from the past tense of most clauses in the story ("kicked out," "spent," "missed," "suggested") to the present tense of clauses 11–13 is in line with the descriptive character of those clauses and with the static nature of those verbs. As for duration, we know that Neville spent several weeks living in his car, but we do not know how long he has been living in Shelter or how long his son's visits are. Finally, we do not know, for instance, how often Ricky visits his father Neville at Shelter. In clause 4, the aspect of the verb "wouldn't let me" indicates a repetition of the action (habitual action), a denial protracted in time.

The narrativists' duration and frequency do not just refer to the duration and frequency of the narrated (real-life) events. More generally, duration and frequency refer to the relationship between narrative clauses and narrated events. [On these points, see Genette (1983:33–160); Rimmon-Kenan (1983:43–58); Cohan & Shires (1988:84–89); Toolan (1988:48–62).] A narrator can sum up in one sentence events that took place over a long period ("After the fall of the Roman empire..."), or dwell for many pages on fleeting events lasting a few minutes [Geertz's thick description (1973:3–30)]. Neville dedicates the same textual duration (one clause) to events of unequal temporal duration ("I spent several weeks living in my car" and "my wife came round"). Similarly, a narrator can recount the same event several times (frequency). In the film *Groundhog Day* the events occurring in one day in the life of a TV news reporter are told several times as that day is relived over and over by the protagonist.

The narrative "game with time" (Genette 1980:155) is by no means confined to purely fictional narrative. Claude Lévi-Strauss has argued that chronology is the distinctive characteristic of history: Without chronology ("dates"), there is no history [Lévi-Strauss (1972:258–60); see also Barthes (1970); White (1987:1–25)]. But different periods of history are characterized by different densities of dates. There are "hot" chronologies such as World War II, where the historian closely follows the events day by day, hour by hour, and chronologies where the historian quickly jumps over long spans of thousands of years. This selection of dates and events (the "facts" of the historian), these narrative strategies are not "innocent." They reflect the (conscious and unconscious) intentions of the historian; they serve a fundamental ideological function (Barthes 1970; White 1987:35). That is true for even the simplest of historical work—the chronicle. Medieval chroniclers listed events sequentially, year after year, one event per year, one year per line, a blank entry for many years. Furthermore, events varied in duration from "Pippin, mayor of the palace, died" (714 AD) to "Theudo drove the Saracens out of Acquitaine" (721 AD) (White 1987:6–9). Yet, even this seemingly random and bizarre selection of facts—"712 flood everywhere; ... 722 Great crops; ... 725 Saracens came for the first time" (White 1987:7)— makes sense in light of the authors' fundamentally religious *weltanschauung* where only the "other world" counts and God's intentions for this world are inscrutable.

The choice of "facts" in Neville's narrative and the lack of correspondence between narrative duration and the duration of narrated events perhaps points to an ideological bias in Neville's narrative. Take Neville's dramatic entry into his story in the first clause: "After my wife kicked me out...." The clause does not have independent status. It is "backgrounded" with respect to the "foregrounded" main clause of the sentence, "I spent several weeks living in my car." (See Hopper 1979 on backgrounding and foregrounding.) As such, it downplays the event of being kicked out of the house, and up-plays the state of homelessness. Yet the clause is highly marked. It is the very first clause of the story. Neither in the first sentence nor in subsequent sentences does Neville tell the reader why his wife kicked him out. His narrative does not focus on the reason and causes of an action that has tragic consequences for his life. Rather, it focuses on those tragic consequences. Through careful backgrounding and foregrounding, through silence on causes and emphasis on consequences, Neville draws the reader's attention to Neville's point of view, rather than the wife's (indeed, we read "me," "me," "me," "my," "my," "my" throughout the story). It provides a male's, rather than a female's reading of the events.

The second sentence in the text is similarly introduced by a clause with no independent status: "being homeless." The participial form syntactically introduces a causal argument, without, however, explicitly stating causation ("because I was homeless"). As a result, subsequent actions are less clearly consequential. The aspect ("wouldn't") of the verb "let" indicates not only a habitual response (i.e. throughout this period of Neville living in his car), but also a volitional response (she did not want Neville to see his son—his son!). Backgrounding and foregrounding of clauses in the second sentence make the actions of Neville's wife appear unmotivated and mean-spirited.

Using similar rhetorical devices of silence and emphasis, of backgrounding and foregrounding, the media provide ideologically biased readings of social relations (Eco 1971). In one of the few systematic analyses involving English mainstream and radical papers, Hartmann (1975/1976) shows that the *Morning Star*, the daily newspaper of the British Communist Party, pays much more attention to the causes of industrial action than its consequences on the economy or on the public. According to Downing, the "refusal to explain the roots of any strike, ... [and the focus] on its disruptive effects, ... [makes] the strikers' decision all the more inexplicable and unforgivable" (Downing 1980:47).

The research of the Glasgow University Media Group on British television coverage of strikes highlighted similar patterns. The TV news reporting of the 1975 Glasgow garbage collectors' strike focused on the health hazard posed by the strike (the "effect" of the strike) with minimal attention paid to the reasons for the strike (Glasgow University Media Group 1976:244, 249, 253). Murdock's analysis of media coverage of radical groups shows that those same mechanisms of systematic bias operate in the media against other groups (Murdock 1973). Murdock writes, "Attention is (then) directed away from the underlying issues and the definitions of the situation proposed by radical groups, and fixes instead on the forms which this action takes. The 'issue' therefore becomes one of the forms rather than causes" (Murdock 1973:157). His case study of a mass demonstration against the Vietnam War held in London on 27 October 1968 shows how media emphasize form over content, how "the underlying causes of why there was a march to begin with" are neglected (Murdock 1973:160). Van Dijk's work on the role of the Dutch media in the reproduction of racism basically tells the same story with regard to ethnic minorities (van Dijk 1987:210, 218). "Topics are dealt with in terms of 'problems' and from the point of view of the authorities" (van Dijk 1987:210). "The causes or context of such problems are seldom analyzed in the press, and hardly ever explained in terms of White racism" (van Dijk 1987:218).

Careful backgrounding and foregrounding of information can certainly go a long way in ideologically coloring a text. But that ideological color can also be made quite explicit. According to Labov, the sequence of purely narrative clauses performs the referential function of narrative. Basically, that function deals with the question: What is the story? But narratives are also characterized by a second function—the evaluative function—which deals with the question: Why is the story told? (What is the story's point? See e.g. Toolan 1988:147.) A typical story will contain explicit evaluative statements that reveal the teller's attitudes to the events recounted. Many of the narratives collected by Erikson, after the Buffalo Creek flood that wiped out an entire mining community, express sentiments of anger towards the Pittston Mining Company:

> "We have bitterness toward the coal company."
> "They washed us out, killed all those people."
> "I don't think they thought of us as human beings."
> "All I can call the disaster is murder."
> "The coal company knew the dam was bad, but they did not tell the people."
> "All they wanted was to make money."
> "They did not care about the good people that lived up Buffalo Creek..." (Erikson 1976:183)

Indeed, the sense of moral outrage toward corporations and the profit motive may well be the point of the stories of at least some of the survivors. But stories do not necessarily have only one point. The Buffalo Creek survivors, while blaming the company for such devastating tragedy, may also want to convey to city people who have flocked to Buffalo Creek after the disaster what it means to have lost not just someone close to kin, but a community:

> "If you had problems, you wouldn't even have to mention it."
> "People would just know what to do. They'd just pitch in and help."
> "Everyone was concerned about everyone else."
> "Well, I have lost all my friends. The people I was raised up and lived with, they're scattered. I don't know where they are at. I've got to make new friends, and that's a hard thing to do..." (Erikson 1976:190–91)

The more complex the story, the more likely that it will explicitly satisfy the evaluative function with one or multiple story points. Children's ability to tell stories increases with age—simple chronological stories being characteristic of children less than four years of age. [For a brief review of children's narrative development, see Toolan (1988:193–202).] Between the ages of four and nine, children steadily improve their narrative competence: (*a*) The weight of the evaluative function increases at the expense of the purely narrative function—that function being marked by specific evaluative clauses; (*b*) stories become longer and plots more elaborate (older children present the events in the plot in a different sequential order than in the story); (*c*) direct speech or free indirect speech, completely absent in younger children, becomes more common with age; (*d*) main characters become "rounder," to use Greimas' expression; (*e*) stories become more coherent and causal arguments more explicit.

Neville's story presents none of the characteristics associated with high narrative competence. His story does not contain explicit evaluative clauses. That does not mean, of course, that there is no evaluation in Neville's account of a particular moment of his life. As Skinner has argued, the process of production of text is always inextricably linked to the production of ideology.[10] Even the referential function of narrative—the chronological sequence of narrative clauses—is not devoid of evaluation. Purely narrative sequences are never innocent. Narrative sequences imply causal sequences. As Aristotle wrote in the *Poetics,* "It makes a great difference whether things happen because of one another, or only *after* one another" (emphasis in the original) (Halliwell 1987:42). Todorov made that point explicit: "Most works of fiction of the past are organized according to an order that we may qualify as both temporal and logical; let us add at once that the logical relation we habitually think of is implication, or as we ordinarily say, causality" (Todorov (1981:41).[11] Certainly, Neville's story suggests (or is at least compatible with) the following causal proposition: Because a wife kicks out a husband, the husband ends up homeless. There is some truth to that. In a survey of three different populations of single homeless people conducted in England in 1991, the breakdown of a relationship is the main reason for homeless persons leaving their last home (Anderson et al 1993:70–73).[12] But that, of course, is dodging the question: Why did Neville's wife kick him out in the first place? After all, the in-depth study of 30 newly separated mothers in the Nottingham and Derby

[10]See the essays collected in Tully (1988).

[11]On the relationship between causality as chronologically ordered sets of propositions, see also Rimmon-Kenan (1983:17–19); Cohan & Shires (1988:17, 58).

[12]This does not in itself explain why people who have left their homes become homeless. In Britain this is primarily due to a shortage of affordable housing, so that people in low-paid jobs, the unemployed, and those with mental health, alcohol or drug abuse problems are at risk of homelessness if they lose their accommodation following the breakdown of a relationship.

areas shows that the most frequently reported reason for the breakdown of a relationship is the man's violence and adultery (Leeming et al 1994:19). Again, silence on causes and emphasis on consequences shifts the blame away from Neville and towards his wife.[13]

The implicit causal reading of Neville's narrative does give us some clues on how to interpret his story and his intentions—the story point. Perhaps Neville is suggesting that women are to be blamed for men's misfortune. The text, then, is a political manifesto against women. Both the causal arguments implicitly built in Neville's narrative and the subtle backgrounding and foregrounding of information point to that reading of the story point. Further evidence for that interpretation of the text comes from character traiting—the positive or negative portrayal of actors—and the attribution of actions to actors. There is minimum characterization of dramatis personae in Neville's story.[14] With the exception of Shelter, all actors—Neville himself, the wife, his son Ricky (indeed, always referred to as "my" son), the friend, Shelter staff—are human. Interestingly enough, and perhaps no differently from fairytales where the giver/sender in Greimas' model is often nonhuman and endowed with magical powers, the giver/sender is not a human being but an organization (Shelter). It is adjectives that provide basic information on character traiting (Todorov 1969:31).

For Chatman, "A trait may be said to be a narrative adjective ... labeling a personal quality of a character" (Chatman 1978:125). In qualifying the word "adjective" with the word "narrative," Chatman is stressing the fact that character traiting (or the adjectival function of narrative) does not necessarily fall on adjectives exclusively. Again, there is minimum use of adjectives in Neville's narrative for the purpose of character traiting. Of the five adjectives found in the text (apprehensive, frightened, brilliant, clean, great), however, two (apprehensive and frightened) are used by Neville to portray himself and the other three (brilliant, clean, and great) are lavished upon Shelter. While the first two adjectives describe negative psychological and emotional states, the other three are either hyperbolic (brilliant, great) or, when they are simply positive (clean), they are strengthened by a quantifier (very). Again, Shelter emerges as the real deus ex machina in Neville's narrative. In fact, setting him-

[13]The issue of narrative truth is not a linguistic problem. It becomes a problem when narrative is used to index social reality. It is a problem for historians. For Ranke, one of the "founding fathers" of the historical profession, history must relate things the way they actually happened (*wie es eigentlich gewesen*)—the historians' "noble dream" of objectivity (Novick 1988). It is a problem for ethnographers who draw broader inferences from informants' narratives—narratives always subject to selection, distortion, interpretation, evaluation (for a brief introduction to the issue of narrative truth, see Kohler Riessman 1993:21–23).

[14]We owe to Greimas the distinction between flat and round characters, characters with minimum characterization and characters presented with a relative degree of complexity and depth (Rimmon-Kenan 1983:40; Bal 1977:31).

self up as a "little guy" (frightened and apprehensive) helps Neville build up Shelter, by contrast.

In the absence of explicit character traiting, we can also infer character from action (Rimmon-Kenan 1983:60–61; Toolan 1988:102). Thus, the dramatic opening of Neville's story "After my wife kicked me out" implicitly points an accusatory finger towards the wife. After all, as far as we know, Neville did nothing to deserve this. In his narrative, Neville does not volunteer any information on the reasons why he was kicked out of the house. We are left to imagine: Because he abused his wife, because he refused to carry any responsibility around the house, because he had affairs, because he was a drunk or a drug addict.... In fact, the violence perpetrated against Neville in the opening clause—violence all the more senseless and gratuitous because it has no (narrative) explanation—helps to bring Neville into focus as a victim rather than a villain. We feel sorry and we sympathize for victims, while we are repulsed by villains. Further clues help to conjure up positive images about the moral fiber of Neville—after all, a man who ("really") misses his son, who has strong aspirations to family life, who appreciates cleanness, and who has friends.[15] Rather than a brazen and insolent villain, this narrative presents before us a man deserving of our pity—homeless, harmless, and deeply hurt in his paternal feelings (if not in his masculinity altogether). And so it is. We do extend him our pity. At which point, with the reader on his side, Neville, in the closing lines of his narrative, can even afford a more sympathetic portrayal of his wife. Again, characterization is not direct; we have to infer character from action. But the actions of Neville's wife in the last clause point to a caring mother, who, having the well-being of her son at heart, comes around to check Shelter, and then lets Ricky visit his father.

Whatever Neville's intentions, no doubt, the wife's actions associate her to a strong character: She kicks out, she would not let (combining volition and permission), she comes around, she checks, she lets. Indeed, these are actions of authority and power. By contrast, both directly and indirectly, Neville comes across as a weak character. Directly, Neville describes himself as apprehensive and frightened. Indirectly, we can infer who Neville is not only from what he did, but from what he could have done and did not do. Neville appears to passively accept his wife's authority and power. His story offers no signs of protest on his part to his wife's most damaging decisions: of kicking him out of the house and of not allowing him to see his son. He could have kicked the wife out. He could have argued and screamed, perhaps even resorted to physical violence. He could have run away with his son. He could have engaged a legal battle with his wife.

[15]Rossi's data on Chicago homeless show that homelessness does not necessarily imply complete loss of friendship (or family) ties (Rossi 1989:173–7).

He could have, but he did not. Why not? "The human capacity to withstand suffering and abuse is impressive," writes Barrington Moore (1978:13) in his *Injustice: The Social Bases of Obedience and Revolt*. It certainly helps if the sufferers believe in the fundamental justice of their suffering. [See Barrington Moore's discussion on responses of moral outrage or moral submission to injustice (Moore 1978:49–80).] Does Neville believe that he deserves having been kicked out of the house? And does he hold that belief because his wife's action was prompted by something he did and that he himself perceives as morally wrong—a breach of the social contract—or because he "take[s] pride and pleasure in ... [his] pain" (Moore 1978:50) and suffering, like religious ascetics or Indian Untouchables?

We do not know the answer to those questions. But the text does present an interesting reversal of stereotypical gender roles of male aggressiveness and female passivity. That is particularly true if we make the reasonable assumption that Neville is a member of the lower classes. As Bourdieu shows, a conception of masculinity in terms of toughness, virility, physical strength (with "enormous, imperative, brutal needs") is much more likely among working-class men (Bourdieu 1984:192; also 190, 382). There is nothing in Neville's traiting of his wife's decisiveness. Being apprehensive, frightened, and generally hesitant (as underscored by the choppy character of the narrative at this point—see the dots which imply a temporal pause in Neville's talk in clause 8) is not a traditional masculine trait. When considering that in Neville's story the wife is the prime mover, the initiator of a temporal sequence of clauses that, in the end, sees Neville in a homeless state, perhaps Neville is telling his fellow readers that his wife has emasculated him, broken him down as a man. That is something, of course, that no patriarchal society can accept. Peasant communities across Europe for centuries collectively "took care" of offenders of traditional community norms through public rituals known as "rough music" or *charivari* (Thompson 1993:467–538). Women who broke patriarchal values—the scold, the husband-beater, the shrew—were a prominent target in these rituals (Thompson 1993:476, 493). In an 1838 description:

> When any woman, a wife more particularly, has been scolding, beating or otherwise abusing the other sex, and is publicly known, she is made to ride stang. A crowd of people assemble towards evening after work hours, with an old, shabby, broken down horse. They hunt out the delinquent ... and mount her on their Rozinante ...astride with her face to the tail. So they parade her through the nearest village or town; drowning her scolding and clamour with the noise of frying pans &c.... (Thompson 1993:499)

Whether Neville believes his wife's actions to be just or unjust, the lack of resources would certainly put a limit to the available courses of action. If Neville were poor he could hardly engage his wife in a protracted legal battle over their son. Gamson et al (1982:60–64) argue that the range of possible responses to unjust authority vary from compliance to evasion, rim talk, resistance, direct action, and preparation for future action. But whether social actors chose one form of reaction or another in their encounters with unjust authority ultimately depends upon the availability of resources. Scott's (1985) study of Malaysian peasants makes that point quite clear: The relative lack of resources does not allow the peasants to take overt reactions. "Most forms of this struggle stop well short of outright collective defiance. Here I have in mind the ordinary weapons of relatively powerless groups: foot dragging, dissimulation, desertion, false compliance, pilfering, feigned ignorance, slander, arson, sabotage and so on" (Scott 1985:xvi). Newby, in his study of East Anglian peasants, similarly noted: "The agricultural worker has acknowledged his powerlessness and decided to make the best of his inferior situation, contriving to take it somewhat for granted while not necessarily endorsing it in terms of social justice" (Newby 1979:414).

We do not know Neville's thoughts on the justice/injustice of his wife's actions. But we can at least ask the question: What resources does Neville command? More generally, what do we know about Neville? Who is Neville? In one of Grimm's classical fairy tales, "Roland and Maybird," the parents of the two children abandon them in the thick of the woods. Cleverly, Roland leaves behind a trail of white pebbles that will help him find the way out. Neville has also left behind a trail of clues that help us understand who he is. We know that Neville is likely to be a young man. After all, Ricky, his son, is still a little boy in need of his mother's permission to see his father. Perhaps, he is also white. The majority of homeless people surveyed by Anderson et al in England were white, male and in the age group 25–44 (Anderson et al 1993:7–9).

We also know that Neville is likely to be poor. If he were not, he could have moved into a hotel or into a place of his own after being "kicked out." There is no mention of any financial transactions between Neville and his wife. Is Neville contributing child support? Unlikely, in his current situation; in fact, unlikely in any situation from what we know of divorced men's contributions to child support. Most ex-partners provide no child support to newly separated mothers (Leeming et al 1994:55).

We do not know whether Neville is also unemployed, although he is quite likely to be. In the 1991 English survey of homeless by Anderson et al, fewer than 10% of the homeless people surveyed were employed (Anderson et al (1993:15–16; see Rossi 1989:135 for similar data on Chicago homeless). But if he is gainfully employed it is likely to be in a low-pay, low-status occupation. How could he hold onto a more demanding job while living for weeks in a car? Rossi's data on Chicago homeless make it clear how difficult it must be to keep up appearances while living in the streets: Only 27.5% of the respondents living in the streets appear "neat and clean" to the interviewer vs 70.5% of those living in shelters (Rossi 1989:93). In England, according to the survey conducted by Drake et al, 65% of the currently unemployed homeless were semiskilled or unskilled in their last job (Drake et al 1982:26, 29). As for their current job, when the homeless do work, they do so prevalently in low-pay, low-status, casual jobs (Anderson et al 1993:15–16).[16]

Not only the facts of Neville's story tell us something about his social background. Purely linguistic markers also help to identify Neville as a member of speech communities more typically found among the lower ranks of British society. There is some evidence of a "women's language" (Lakoff 1975) or, more generally, a "powerless language" (O'Barr & Atkins 1980). [However, see the strong critique by Coates (1993:132–35).] That language is characterized by: (*a*) hypercorrect grammar; (*b*) higher frequency of accompanying gestures, hedges ("well," "I guess"), and intensifiers (e.g. "so," "very"); (*c*) "empty" adjectives ("divine," "cute," "charming," "ghastly"); (*d*) polite forms ("would you please ...?"); (*e*) rising (question-type) intonation in declarative sentences; (*f*) greater pitch range and more rapid pitch changes; (*g*) tag questions ("isn't it?") (Lakoff 1975:53–57; O'Barr & Atkins 1980; Toolan 1988:250; Coates 1993: 132–33). Linguistic research on courtroom transcripts has shown that defendants and witnesses with professional qualifications or positions of authority tend to use a language of power (see Toolan 1988:249–55 for a review). Furthermore, those defendants and witnesses who use a language of power tend to be perceived by judges, juries, and lawyers as more knowledgeable, more credible, and more trustworthy than those who use a powerless language.

In Neville's language we find many of these markers of powerless language. We find hedges (the dots in clause 8 are a marker of hesitation and uncertainty, further underscored by the adjectives "apprehensive," "frightened"), empty adjectives ("brilliant," "great"), and intensifiers ("really missed Ricky" in clause 5; "very clean" in clause 12). What Neville finds attractive about Shelter ("clean" and "like a hotel") is also more typical of working-class individuals. In his study of taste, Bourdieu provides quantitative evidence on the relationship between socioeconomic background and images of an "ideal home" (Bourdieu 1984:247–48). "The proportion of choices emphasizing overtly aesthetic properties (studied, imaginative, harmonious) grows as one moves up the social hierarchy, whereas the proportion of 'functionalist' choices (clean, practical, easy to maintain) declines" (Bourdieu 1984:247).

The text does not provide any information on posture, gestures, gaze, or voice pitch. That is unfortunate, because conversation analysts and ethnometh-

[16]The most common form of income for homeless people was Income Support or other state benefits with an average total income of £38 per week (Anderson et al 1993:15–16). On the income of homeless people in the US, see also Rossi's data on the Chicago homeless (1989:136).

odologists have shown how telling those extralinguistic characteristics can be (Maynard 1992; see also Coates 1993:188, 197–98; Kohler Riessman 1993:40).[17] Silences may speak even louder than words, as shown by the work by West & Zimmerman (West & Zimmerman 1980, 1983; see also Coates 1993:107–14) on gender differences in patterns of silences and interruptions in everyday conversations. In a careful analysis of interactions between doctors, patients, and family in the delivery of bad news, Maynard writes: "We must pay attention to the full sociolinguistic environment surrounding the bearing of bad news" (Maynard 1992:118). The evidence from Neville's text on hypercorrect grammar is mixed. If anything, the text contains several vernacular forms. "Me family life" in clause 17 should be "my family life." In "Being homeless, she wouldn't let me" (clauses 3 and 4), the semantically implied subject of the first clause is "I" but syntactically it is "she." Coates argues that hypercorrect language is more characteristic of women than men (Coates 1993:66–86); if anything, working-class men have a linguistic preference for nonstandard, vernacular language. That being the case, Neville's use of vernacular language is quite characteristic of both his gender and class. Not so characteristic, however, is Neville's use of formal adjectives (e.g. apprehensive) and of complex syntactical constructs (e.g. clauses 1 and 3 and the adverbial clause 14). Neville's text seems to contain a peculiar mix of lowbrow and highbrow linguistic codes.

Notwithstanding some contradictions in Neville's language, facts and language by and large go hand-in-hand in Neville's story, to project an image of Neville as a powerless character. Interestingly enough, for all the strength of Neville's wife as a character, for all the power she wields (by contrast), ultimately it is not up to her to reverse Neville's fortune. It is Shelter! Although Neville's wife is the grammatical subject (and the agent) in clauses 14, 15, and 16, the subject of the very last clause in that sentence (clause 17) is "it" (presumably Shelter, the only "it," i.e. the only non-human and inanimate character in the story with agentative characteristics). It is it—Shelter—that "lets" Neville rebuild his family life. In fact, in the very last clause of Neville's narrative, Shelter has replaced the wife as the agent we had come to expect as being associated with the verb "let."

It is that sudden and awkward transition in grammatical subjects in the conjoined clauses of the last clause that may leave the reader wondering whether, when Neville says "it's let me rebuild me family life," he does not mean, in fact, that he has moved back into the house. Neville does not tell us that. But

[17]Written text, of course, does not provide any information on accent and pronounciation. Sociolinguists have shown that, perhaps even more than any other linguistic markers, pronounciation can offer invaluable clues about the social background of individuals (Coates 1993:61–86; Romaine 1994:69–75).

neither did he tell us that he went to see Shelter. All he told us in clauses 6 and 7 was "A friend suggested I go to see Shelter." From there, Neville jumped directly to Shelter. There is a "gap" in the text that the reader fills ("I went to see Shelter").[18] Is Neville introducing another similar gap at the very end of his narrative? Only the deictic element "now" in clause 16 excludes the possibility that Neville has moved back with his wife. "Now" anchors the text to a concrete spatial and temporal situation (now = Neville at Shelter = rebuilding family life inside Shelter), which may shed some new light on the story point. Could Neville's narrative be just an advertisement for Shelter? The adjectival traiting of Shelter, the role of Shelter as deus ex machina of the narrative, and the ambiguity of the last clause certainly point in that direction. In that sense, a more explicit reference to Neville's return home in the last clause would have taken the referential focus away from Shelter, something no advertisement can afford.

To bring Neville's story into sharper focus as, perhaps, an advertising text, consider the following narrative: "You were leading a miserable life, without any friends and anyone to go out with, all because you had dandruff. But now, thanks to Best Shampoo, dandruff is gone and you have plenty of friends and dates." Best Shampoo (or Shelter) offers the magical solution to one's problems. When viewed that way, Neville's reversal of fortunes from bad to good brought about by the intervention of Shelter conforms quite closely to Greimas' basic narrative model: A subject (typically the hero) strives to win over an object (a beautiful princess) against the opposition of a villain but with the help of a friend or relative (helper) and the magic intervention of a sender [a sort of superhelper in Toolan's words (Toolan 1988:93)]. In Neville's story, Neville is acting as the subject missing his son Ricky (object) whom he cannot see because of his wife's interdiction (villain); with the help of a friend (helper) Neville gets in touch with Shelter (sender), which will allow Neville to attain his goal. Vestergaard & Schroder (1985:27–32, 94) showed that such a model is indeed one of the typical models of advertising narratives, where the advertised products take on Greimas' actant role of giver/superhelper. "Advertising ... does not try to tell us that we need its products as such, but rather that the products can help us obtain something else which we do feel that we need"—health, success, friends, and the like (Vestergaard & Schroder 1985:29).

In many advertisements, the power of the magic superhelper to bring about change in one's life is dramatized via the use of colors: The before is typically in black and white, the after in color—the temporal framework of the technical

[18]Gaps can be introduced to speed up the reading process—as in this case—or to arouse the reader's curiosity. On the linguistic concept of "gap" see Rimmon-Kenan (1983:127–29) and Perry (1979).

development of photography providing the simple temporal reading of the advertising narrative. Thus, in the advertisements for Virginia Slims cigarettes, the picture typically contrasts a black-and-white, small frame of a woman's life in the old days—a life of drudgery and hard work, particularly when compared to a man's life—to a larger and colorful frame of a woman's life now, a life of success and independence, as underscored by the fact that she can freely smoke (!).

There are no explicit references to colors in Neville's narrative. Yet, consider the role of the adjective "brilliant" in clause 10. Coming after the images of gloom and doom conjured up in the reader's mind by Neville's description of his homelessness, the adjective "brilliant," although used in reference to Shelter staff, floods the narrative space with bright light, ultimately opening a glimmer of new hope in Neville's life. The before (gloom and doom) and after ("brilliant") are starkly separated by the use of that adjective of light. The before and after are further underscored by the sudden shift in the use of verb tenses from the past tense to the present tense of clauses 11 through 13 (it's ... a hotel; it's ... clean; ... are great).

If Neville's story is nothing but an advertisement for Shelter, then perhaps Neville is a fictional character. He is not the author of his story. There is a real author behind the story. Chatman introduced different levels of narrators and narratees [Chatman (1978:151); see also Rimmon-Kenan (1983:86–89); Cohan & Shires (1988:89–94); Toolan (1988:76–80)]:

real author → implied author → (narrator) → (narratee) → implied reader → real reader

But that real author has hidden behind Neville, leaving no explicit markers of his/her role—after all, what Shelter can do for the homeless is all the more credible if it comes from a real character. (On verisimilitude, see Chatman 1978:48–53.)

And that quest for realism leads to a muffled authorial voice. A muffled authorial voice is a purely rhetorical device. It is the same device that authors normally use in scientific writing. To achieve objectivity, authors silence their authorial voice. Objectivity is "absence of clues to the narrator ... [a] referential illusion" (Barthes 1970:149) achieved by suppressing the emotive and conative functions of language and emphasizing the referential function (Jakobson 1960:357). In scientific writing, the authors' direct intervention is minimal if not nonexistent. Historians have worked hard at denying themselves a voice. Their narrative mode of writing puts them dangerously close to narrative fictional writers—dangerously close, that is, for anyone expected to tell a real rather than fictional story and, thus, to be more than a mere storyteller. "A narrator is no longer present [in historical writing]. ... The events appear to narrate themselves" (Benveniste 1971:206–8; see also Cohan & Shires 1988:93). Historical discourse is "a discourse without 'Thou'.... In historical discourse destination-signs are normally absent" (Barthes 1970:148).

Yet, the author of Neville's text has only partially succeeded in this. Just like Neville himself, the "real" author has left behind clues of his/her presence. The many gaps in the narrative suggest that, perhaps, the author was trying to compress the text, to summarize it. The beginning of Neville's story is strongly marked (i.e. unusual). We do not typically start a narrative in the form: "After my wife kicked me out." Rather, we might say: "This and that happened, then my wife kicked me out." "A friend suggested I go to see Shelter" would be followed by "so I went." Truly direct speech (by Neville) would also contain many utterances of the type "ehm," "well," "you know," "so ... then" commonly found in colloquial discourse.[19]

The real author has also introduced linguistic expressions that are atypical of colloquial direct speech, particularly for low-status individuals. The complex, syntactically subordinate clauses 1 and 3 and the adverbial clause 14 seem out of character. The adjective "scared" would have sounded more realistic in Neville's mouth than the formal synonym "apprehensive." "I lived in my car for several weeks" would have been more likely than "I spent several weeks living in my car." "Because I was homeless," or "I did not have a home ... so ... my wife wouldn't let me see my son" would have replaced the hypotactic "Being homeless." Perhaps Neville's text is the result of an educated writer trying hard to be Neville-like, to imitate the speech of a homeless person by putting words into the mouth of an imaginary Neville, or the result of that same type of writer tampering with the narrative (e.g. an interview) of a real Neville. The apparent contradictions noted above in Neville's mixture of both powerful and powerless language find a plausible explanation when we take into consideration issues of authorship.

Both a structural analysis of Neville's story and one that pays close attention to the linguistic nuances of the text have helped us shed light on the story point. The story may simply be an advertisement for Shelter rather than a male manifesto against women (or both). Indeed, the double reversal of a situation in Neville's narrative seems to support both story points. Neville's being kicked out of the house by his wife marks the first reversal, the first disruption of an equilibrium, the worsening of a situation characterized by homelessness and loss of family life, in a word, the beginning of tragedy. Neville's moving into Shelter marks the second reversal, the improvement of the situation that ultimately leaves the reader on a happy-ending note. Neville's wife plays a crucial role in this first reversal of fortunes, good→bad, which may lead to a

[19]That could be the result of poor transcribing, however, wherein an inexperienced interviewer has cut out many of the speaker's colloquial utterances; for a basic introduction to the problems of transcribing ethnographic text, see Kohler Riessman (1993:56–60).

reading of the story as a male manifesto. Shelter, the organization for the homeless, plays a pivotal role in the second reversal, bad→good, which may lead to a reading of the story as an advertising text. But in this double reversal, the first reversal is backgrounded and the second foregrounded. By parallelism, Neville's story foregrounds its advertising role and backgrounds its role as a male manifesto.

Perhaps if we had more information on the context of Neville's narrative we might be able to draw firmer inferences on the story point. Under what conditions was the text produced? All we know, besides Neville's story itself, is that the story comes from *The Oxford Independent*. That information excludes a range of options as a source of the excerpt. For sure, the narrative does not come from a social science investigation of the type that Elliott Liebow (*Tell Them Who I Am*) (Liebow 1993) and Peter Rossi (*Down and Out in America*) (Rossi 1989) have masterfully put together on the subject of homelessness. Particularly in Liebow we find many excerpts of Neville's kind: "One day I was a productive and respected citizen, the next day I was dirt," says Shirley to Liebow (Liebow 1993:217). Too close for comfort? Sandford, the author of *Down and Out in Britain*, put it pungently:

> I descended into the bilges of society. Wearing boots that gaped at the seams and an ancient great-coat, I allowed my beard to grow and my hair to become matted with dirt. I wanted to meet and talk with down and outs.... And I sensed a feeling of deep insecurity, the deep fear that I too might all too soon end up, derelict, on Britain's skid-row.... (Sandford 1971:9)

Not surprisingly, sociologists (and social scientists in general) have tried hard to put some distance between themselves and the people they study, both in their methods (e.g. surveys on the basis of questionnaires not directly administered by the "scientist") and in their language (e.g. talking about respondents as the "object" of study). (For a feminist critique of this last point, see Graham 1984.) What is of interest here is how science underscores objectivity at the level of language through the systematic elimination of any signs (*a*) of the subjectivity of authorship and of a direct relationship between author and reader (Barthes & Jakobson's "referential illusion"), and (*b*) of any relationship between the real authors (the "scientists") and their subjects (turned into objects) of inquiry (the double illusion of science). The development of a specialized jargon to express common concepts is another effective distance device (Lakoff 1975:53–57).

The name *The Oxford Independent* seems to suggest that the source of the excerpt is a newspaper. After all, *The Independent* is one of England's quality papers. *The Oxford Independent* could just be a local paper based in Oxford. If so, what kind of newspaper is *The Oxford Independent*? A daily, weekly, monthly? The fact that the issue is numbered (Number 12) and the fact that reference is made to a month (January), rather than a specific day (e.g. 1/3/1996) seems to point to a monthly publication. Perhaps even more telling is the year of publication of the article (1997). Together with the place of publication (Oxford, England), this information helps to contextualize Neville's misfortune. As it turns out, Neville was far from being alone in his homeless status in those years. Although it is no simple matter to get reliable estimates of the number of homeless people, it is widely acknowledged that (*a*) the number increased significantly throughout the 1980s and early 1990s in England, and that (*b*) homelessness became more visible, with makeshift beds in subways, shop doorways, and parks.[20]

Between 1975 and 1985, and then again in the early 1990s, the rate of unemployment soared despite changes in definitions (Gallie & Marsh 1994:3). On that score, England followed a path similar to that of other industrialized nations. What was more peculiar to England was that the policies of the Thatcher governments were systematically dismantling the welfare state, with devastating consequences for those living on the edge of poverty. As the poor were getting poorer, the richer were getting richer. Income inequality sharply rose in the United Kingdom from the late 1970s onward, reaching levels second only to those of the United States in the industrialized world (Johnson & Webb 1993; Atkinson 1997).

Why was *The Oxford Independent* running Neville's story? Could the excerpt be part of a larger reportage on homelessness? After all, one of the most compelling accounts of homelessness came from the English journalist and writer Jeremy Sandford in his book *Down and Out in Britain*, which inspired Rossi's own title. Alternatively, was the story part of a single article on homelessness? Since human-side stories are typically run around Christmas time, the date of the story (January) seems to confirm that assumption.

THE ROLE OF THE READER

On that scene of last-minute Christian pity, let us take leave from Neville and his world—the microcosm of his personal life and the macrocosm of British society at the turn of the second millennium. I could have said more, no doubt,

[20]It is difficult to quantify precisely the extent of or increase in homelessness. The 1991 Census provided the first official record with 2,827 homeless people and 19,417 hostel dwellers (Office of Population Censuses and Surveys 1993). Occasional surveys suggest higher figures of 5,000–6,000 homeless (Shelter 1991) and 50,000 hostel dwellers (Connelly & Crown 1994:15). Other official statistics exclude "single" homeless people, because single homeless do not qualify for housing under the terms of the 1977 Housing and Homeless Persons Act, the 1985 Housing Act Part III, and the 1996 Housing Act. Indirect measures also provide an indicator of the increase in homelessness. For instance, between 1971 and 1986 there was a seven-fold increase in housing applications from homeless people according to official statistics (Shanks & Smith 1992:35). The number of households statutorily accepted as homeless has also increased, from 63,013 (1978) to 111,757 (1985) to 169,966 (1992).

but my page limit is up. But within those limits, I hope to have given the reader enough token evidence on why (and how) sociologists should be interested in narrative. The analysis of Neville's story has brought out a wealth of both linguistic and sociological information.

"The analysis of Neville's story," but, really, come now! The analysis has brought out nothing; Roberto Franzosi has, in reading Neville's narrative—one time, two times, many times, "with steadily greater selectivity and attention ... [and forming] tentative hypotheses about the nature and intention of whatever was noted" (De Beaugrande 1985:55). I have brought out that wealth of both linguistic and sociological information.[21] And you—the reader—will have surely done the same, refracting Neville's story onto my story and ultimately building your own story.

Whatever else the analysis of Neville's story may have shown, one thing it has clearly shown: Our ability to understand and fully grasp the meaning of even such simple text as Neville's story is inextricably linked to a wealth of background knowledge that readers consciously or unconsciously bring to the text in the construction of meaning. "No knowledge without foreknowledge," the hermeneutics scholars maintain (Diesing 1991:108). Our ability to read Neville's story as an advertising text fundamentally depends upon our "foreknowledge" of advertising codes.[22] Our ability to pick up the deeply ingrained male viewpoint in Neville's story depends upon our linguistic competence in teasing out meaning embedded in language nuances. Finally, our ability to go beyond Neville's microcosm depends upon our knowledge of the social relations of his macrocosm (the interplay between text and *con*text).

Perhaps, when reading Neville's story, the average reader will not think of Culler, Liebow, Rossi—the linguistic and sociological paraphernalia of my own text. Eco distinguishes on this point between a "naive" and a "critical" reading of a text, "the latter being the interpretation of the former" (Eco 1979:205). There is never a single message uniquely encoded in a text; there are several messages ("a network of different messages") as decoded by different readers endowed with different "intertextual frames" and "intertextual encyclopedias," and different reading codes (Eco 1979:5).

[21]Indeed, according to hermeneutics scholars, text comprehension is an iterative process (the "hermeneutic circle"): A reader will (*a*) approach a text with some hypotheses in mind about the text; (*b*) search for evidence on those hypotheses in a reading of the text; (*c*) set up new hypotheses about meaning; (*d*) restart the reading process (Diesing 1991:109, 121). On the text and its reading, see also Rimmon-Kenan 1983:117–29, in particular 119–22, and Cohan & Shires 1988:114–33; on the dynamic of text reading as a system of hypotheses, see Perry 1979:43 and Culler 1975.

[22]"Code" is the concept used by Barthes in his *S/Z* (Barthes 1990). Eco talks about "intertextual frames" and Perry of "frames" (Eco 1979; Perry 1979:36). This process of assimilating the meaning of a text through the familiar is called "naturalization" by Culler (1975:138).

The role of the reader is far from passive. Narrators and authors, of course, may try to build a "preferred" reading of their texts. Neville's story is undoubtedly told from his point of view. For one thing, Neville is the narrator of the story. More to the point, Neville tells the story from his perspective. We know how Neville feels and what he has had to go through. But we do not know how his wife feels, the difficulties she had to face as a single parent. Had the wife told the story, she probably would not have chosen to begin it the same way as Neville, leaving out the reason for kicking him out. Perhaps the story is told from the point of view of a homeless organization in search of publicity.

Whatever the author's "preferred" reading, readers bring in their own preferences, their own points of view. Texts are hardly ever so "closed" as to allow only one type of reading to the exclusion of all others. (On the concept of "open" and "closed" texts, see Eco 1979:8–11.) Even when they try to be, the outcome of their reading by a different "model reader" is unpredictable. "Nobody can say what happens when the actual reader is different from the 'average' one" (Eco 1979:8). Contrary to the structuralist view of a text as a process closed by the author in production, Culler, Eco, and others see the text as something actually produced in the reading process. "The reader as an active principle of interpretation is a part of the picture of the generative process of the text" (Eco 1979:4).[23]

To Neville's text we bring our attitudes toward homelessness and gender. According to Millar (1982), in the 1970s the English public perceived homeless people as drunks, but by the 1980s they viewed them as "wandering mad people" and they blamed their presence on the streets on the closure of mental hospitals and the failure of community care. The result of an unplanned experiment has similarly revealed the role of our gender attitudes on the interpretation of texts. In discussing Neville's text in a graduate class, the women in the class were much less likely than the men to automatically grant Neville their pity, to unconditionally take his side regardless of what he had done to deserve his present condition. They were much more likely to view the woman in the story not as a ruthless wife but as a responsible mother. Neville must have done something heinous to drive such a woman to kick him out—a wimpy character who, while looking for our sympathy, does not even have the courage to tell us what he did. It is clear from the unfolding of the story that the wife's actions are motivated not by anger or revenge toward her husband, but only by her son's well-being. She is certainly not using Ricky as a weapon against Neville. No, Neville's story is just another story told by a man, in men's image, and for men's consumption.

[23]Significantly, the first section of the "Introduction" to Eco's collection of essays in *The Role of the Reader* bears the title "How to produce texts by reading them" (Eco 1979:3).

The point is: Understanding of even the simplest text requires a great deal of background knowledge, an "intertextual encyclopedia" in Eco's words (Eco 1979:7, 208). In fact, some would argue that our very ability to understand, to *really* understand Neville's story depends upon an empathetic understanding of the "other," upon having shared the same experiences as the "other"—a distinct kind of knowledge sociologists and philosophers of knowledge have referred to as *verstehen*.

CONCLUSIONS

Historian Carlo Ginzburg closes with the following lines from a wonderful little book on the trial by the Inquisition of a poor sixteenth-century miller called Menocchio: "About Menocchio we know many things. About this Marcato, or Marco—and so many others like him who lived and died without leaving a trace—we know nothing" (Ginzburg 1982: 128). Perhaps I can close similarly: About Neville we know very little. All we know is what he has left behind in a short narrative of a moment of his life. In fact, we cannot even be sure that Neville is a real or fictitious character. We do not know what the purpose of the story is.

Yet, the linguistic analysis of Neville's narrative has allowed us to shed light on many real lives like his. Narrative analysis has not only revealed the close relationship between the words in a text and between a text and other texts (e.g. stories and advertisements). Narrative analysis has brought out relationships between people—texts do not just index a relation between words and between texts, but between text and social reality. Sociology has crept in behind linguistics. Neville's simple (and perhaps, fictitious) narrative has sparked our sociological imagination; it has allowed us to get a glimpse of the broad social relations (especially of gender and class) of British society at the turn of the second millennium.

That, of course, may be too brazen a claim in the eyes of the sociological "scientist." Ginzburg and his fellow historians may deal with the life of Menocchio. Linguists may spend pages and whole tomes arguing over the structure and meaning of a four-line text. Other members of the academic community may make their living on the basis of a single story. But sociology is about discovering general laws. Sociology is a science. It is not interested in the particular; its objective is the universal.[24] We can hardly find any interest in this man's life, a man we do not even know is real. Much of the sociological debate between qualitative and quantitative approaches has centered on the issue of

[24]On these issues, see Windelband's 1894 inaugural lecture (Windelband 1980) and Rickert—Windelband's teacher (Rickert 1962:55–56).

sample size, of the small "N" of ethnographic approaches. The analysis of Neville's story may just be an extreme example of the study of the particular.[25]

That view of the sociological enterprise has led sociologists to their own way of approaching narrative texts: content analysis (for all, see Kúppendorf 1980). Notwithstanding the ethnomethodological approach to text, sociologists have typically not been interested in (nor do they have the theoretical and methodological tools for) analyzing the linguistic nuances of a text—what can one text tell them about broader social relations anyway? Nor have they been interested in the invariant, structural patterns of narrative—yes, it is patterns that sociologists are after, but not patterns of texts (that's linguists' business), rather patterns of social relations. (On this point, see also Todorov 1981:5–6). And in their search for patterns of social relations, they tease out of a text the common threads ("themes")—common to the texts, but as they apply to real human beings—and then they count and tabulate those themes (how many of these, how many of those). Alternatively, they provide snippets of those common themes (think, indeed, of such beautiful accounts as Erikson's and Liebow's). In analyzing "respondents' stories," sociologists cut up individual stories and recompose the pieces into new stories, with the coherence and context of each original narrative lost and forgotten. Upon the new stories, sociologists then impose the coherence of the "scientific" ethnographic text in the context of sociological "literature."[26]

Yet, "precisely because they are essential meaning-making structures, narratives must be preserved, not fractured, by investigators, who must respect respondents' ways of constructing meaning and analyze how it is accomplished" (Kohler Riessman 1993:4). That, of course, is easier said than done. Such close analysis of a handful of short texts is possible. But where does that leave researchers confronted with large bodies of narrative data (e.g. ethnographic material or unstructured interviews)? At the current state of linguistic formalization and computer-software development, there may be no escape from one form or another of the kind of thematic analysis proposed by content analysis [even when these themes or "concepts" are represented in terms of network relations (see Carley 1993)].

Ultimately, each technique has its advantages and limitations. Researchers should be aware of what is gained and lost with the use of each technique. To the extent possible, researchers approaching the study of textual material (in

[25] I should point out, however, that linguists have been no less interested than sociologists in building general theories and that they have been very successful in building such theories on the basis of case studies. The real issue, in fact, is not the number of cases scientists take into account in building their models, but, whether individual cases fit into a general model.

[26] For a brief sociological introduction to narrative, see Kohler Riessman (1993) and the literature cited there; for a more ethnographic view, see Van Maanen (1988); for an epistemological feminist manifesto on narratives, see Graham (1984).

fact, not just those) should use a variety of methods. Even simple frequency-counts of words have their value when properly used and backed up by other forms of evidence and analysis. As usual, what really counts is not the methods used but the questions asked.

Given the enormous difficulties and ambiguities that we have encountered in understanding and extracting meaning from even such a simple text as Neville's story, some of the key words that appear in most definitions of content analysis—"objective," "systematic," "scientific," "quantitative," "replicable and valid inference," "explicitly formulated rules"—will strike any reasonable reader as overly optimistic if not altogether misguided (see Shapiro & Markoff 1997 for a quick summary of definitions). In light of Eco's "network of different messages," "intertextual frames," and "intertextual encyclopedias" that go into the reading process (Eco 1979:5), how could we ever hope to squeeze it all in a handbook of coding rules that did not itself look like an encyclopedia? The emphasis on "objective," "systematic," or "scientific" in the process of going from text to coding may succeed in drawing attention away from the murky waters of text understanding, but ... it does not get us any closer to finding real solutions to the problem. The scientific claims of content analysis must not refer to this central aspect of the technique but, perhaps, to other, more peripheral aspects. That is indeed the case. Lasswell, one of the "founding fathers" of content analysis, concentrated his "scientific" efforts on such issues as statistical sampling of texts, design of coding categories, validity and reliability, unit of analysis, and methods of data analysis, but did not tackle the fundamental issue of meaning [see the many chapters in *Language of Politics* dedicated to methodological issues (Lasswell et al 1968)]. Taking the part for the whole—a rhetorical device or "figure of speech" technically known as synechdoche, one of the four "master tropes" with metaphor, metonymy, and irony—scientists effectively generalize their scientific claims.

The debate on the sex of the angels occupied some of the most brilliant minds of the Middle Ages. Within the Christian culture of medieval European societies, that issue addressed central concerns of dominant cultural frameworks. Has the current culture of scientific or pseudoscientific discourse blinded us to the point that we actually believe some of things we are writing? (As an exercise in the rhetoric of science, count the number of times such key words as "rigor," "power," "precision," and the like appear in my published work on semantic grammars). Perhaps, in light of the themes discussed in this chapter, what we need is more "open texts," scientific texts that are open to the conditions of their own production. Hopefully, in this process of self-reflectivity, we will not have fallen prey to postmodernist gibberish, nor will we have given up an honest search for rigor in the social sciences.

The narrative analysis of Neville's story also points to a different way of looking at the relationship between the micro and the macro, the particular and the universal. The process of contextualizing a text for narrative understanding—the foreknowledge of knowledge—quickly leads us away from Neville's microcosm to the macrocosm of British society. That same process quickly leads us away from narrow linguistic concerns. I have provided a handful of examples on how to link a linguistic analysis to a sociological analysis, how to go from text to context, from Neville's particular to the universal.

For sure I have picked and chosen here and there to shed light on context, selectively drawing from the "intertextual encyclopedia" of knowledge. The linkages I have explored between text and context, micro and macro, are more tentative and informative than definitive. Readers who approach narrative texts with more strongly substantive-driven problems will no doubt pursue those linkages more systematically. My goal was modest: Show the reader how to raise sociologically informed research questions and how to pursue them, rather than answer them, starting from a narrative text. Following that goal, I hope to have also shown that narrative analysis (broadly conceived here as the analysis of both linguistic and extralinguistic characteristics of speech acts) yields an understanding of social relations as embedded in linguistic practices. Many of the studies reviewed here have shed light on how specific linguistic mechanisms underline social relations of gender or class. Unlocking those mechanisms in one particular social setting may ultimately provide greater knowledge than that based on tenuous statistical relations between poorly measured and even more poorly understood concepts in the context of poorly estimated models, even if the rules on how to go from the particular to the universal are scientifically embedded in the procedures we use. (Think, for instance, of sampling statistics.) In that sense, narrative analysis may have also shown how social scientific practices involve specific language games in relation to the people we draw information from (our subjects/objects of study) and pass information to (our readers).

To the novice, all of this will surely sound like a daunting task (perhaps it is easier to let the computer run regressions). The understanding of the text has required us to zoom down on linguistic problems. The understanding of the context has required us to open up to neighboring and distant disciplines, to harness knowledge that comes from far afield. Don't despair! The good news is that literary competence is not intuitive but learned (Culler 1975:113–30; Toolan 1988:29; Cohan & Shires 1988:22; see also Bourdieu 1984:399). And so is the "competence" of linking a narrative analysis to a sociological analysis. Just start from Statistics 101 ... sorry ... *Narrative* 101.

ACKNOWLEDGMENTS

The writing has benefited from grants from the National Science Foundation (SBR-9411739) and the University of Oxford. I would like to thank Richard Lim and Sandra Whitlock for their help with some of the research. I am indebted to my linguist colleagues Diana Lewis and Martin Maiden for their close reading of an earlier draft. Only their many suggestions have rescued me from committing, I am afraid, the grossest of errors.

Literature Cited

Abbott A. 1995. Sequence analysis: new methods for old ideas. *Annu. Rev. Sociol.* 21:93–113

Abbott A, Barman E. 1997. Sequence comparison via alignment and Gibbs sampling: a formal analysis of the emergence of the modern sociological article. *Sociol. Methodol.* 27:47–87

Abbott A, Hrycak A. 1990. Measuring resemblance in sequence data. *Am. J. Sociol.* 96:144–85

Abell P. 1987. The syntax of social life. In *The Theory and Method of Comparative Narratives*. Oxford: Clarendon

Anderson I, Kemp P, Quilgars D. 1993. *Single Homeless People*. London: HMSO

Atkinson AB. 1997. Bringing income distribution in from the cold. *Econ. J.* 107: 297–321

Bal M. 1977. *Narratologie. Essais sur la Signification Narrative dans Quatre Romans Modernes*. Paris: Editions Klincksieck

Barthes R. 1970. [1967.] Historical discourse. In *Structuralism: A Reader*, ed. M Lane, pp. 145–55 London: Cape

Barthes R. 1977. [1966.] Introduction to the structural analysis of narratives. In *Image Music Text. Essays Selected and Translated by Stephen Heath*, pp. 79–124. London: Fontana

Barthes R. 1990. [1970.] *S/Z*. Oxford: Blackwell

Benveniste E. 1971. [1966.] *Problems in General Linguistics*. Coral Gables, FL: Univ. Miami Press

Bourdieu P. 1984. *Distinction: A Social Critique of the Judgement of Taste*. Cambridge, MA: Harvard Univ. Press

Bremond C. 1966. La logique des possibles narratifs. *Communications* 8:60–76

Carley K. 1993. Coding choices for textual analysis: a comparison of content analysis and map analysis. *Sociol. Methodol.* 23: 75–126

Chatman S. 1978. *Story and Discourse: Narrative Structure in Fiction and Film*. Ithaca, NY: Cornell Univ. Press

Coates J. 1993. [1983]. *Women, Men and Language*. London: Longman. 2nd ed.

Cohan S, Shires LM. 1988. *Telling Stories: A Theoretical Analysis of Narrative Fiction*. New York: Routledge

Connelly J, Crown J. 1994. *Homelessness and Ill Health: Report of a Working Party of the Royal College of Physicians*. London: Royal Coll. Physicians

Corsaro W, Heise D. 1990. Event structure models from ethnographic data. *Sociol. Methodol.* 20:1–57

Culler J. 1975. *Structural Poetics. Structuralism, Linguistics and the Study of Literature*. London: Routledge & Kegan Paul

Danto AC. 1985. *Narration and Knowledge*. New York: Columbia Univ. Press

De Beaugrande R. 1985. Text linguistics in discourse studies. In *Handbook of Discourse Analysis*. Vol. 1. *Disciplines of Discourse*, ed. T van Dijk. London: Academic

Diesing P. 1991. *How Does Science Work? Reflections on Process*. Pittsburgh, PA: Univ. Pittsburgh Press

Downing J. 1980. *The Media Machine*. London: Pluto

Drake M, O'Brien M, Biebuyck T. 1982. *Single and Homeless*. London: HMSO

Eco U. 1971. Guida all'interpretazione del linguaggio giornalistico. In *La Stampa Quotidiana Italiana*, ed. V Capecchi, M Livolsi. Milan: Bompiani

Eco U. 1979. *The Role of the Reader: Explorations in the Semiotics of Texts*. Bloomington, IN: Indiana Univ. Press

Fairclough N. 1995. *Critical Discourse Analysis: The Critical Study of Language*. London: Longman

Franzosi R. 1989. From words to numbers: a generalized and linguistics-based coding procedure for collecting event-data from newspapers. *Sociol. Methodol.* 19: 263–98

Franzosi R. 1990a. Strategies for the prevention, detection and correction of measurement error in data collected from textual sources. *Sociol. Methods Res.* 18:442–72

Franzosi R. 1990b. Computer-assisted coding of textual data using semantic text grammars. *Sociol. Methods Res.* 19:225–57

Franzosi R. 1994. From words to numbers: a set theory framework for the collection, organization, and analysis of narrative data. *Sociol. Methodol.* 24:105–36

Franzosi R. 1997a. Labor unrest in the Italian service sector: an application of semantic grammars. In *Text Analysis for the Social Sciences: Methods for Drawing Statistical Inferences from Texts and Transcripts*, ed. CW Roberts, pp. 131–45. Hillsdale, NJ: Erlbaum

Franzosi R. 1997b. Mobilization and countermobilization processes: from the "red years" (1919–20) to the "black years" (1921–22) in Italy. A new methodological approach to the study of narrative data. In *Theory and Society*,Vol. 26 (2–3), ed. R Franzosi, J Mohr, pp. 275–304

Franzosi R. 1997c. On ambiguity and rhetoric in (social) science. *Sociol. Methodol.* 27: 135–44

Franzosi, R. 1998. Narrative as data. linguistic and statistical tools for the quantitative study of historical events." *Int. Rev. Soc. Hist.*, spec. issue. In press

Franzosi R. 1999. *From Words to Numbers: Narrative as Data.* Cambridge, UK: Cambridge Univ. Press. In press

Gallie D, Marsh C. 1994. The experience of unemployment. In *Social Change and the Experience of Unemployment*, ed. D Gallie, C Marsh, C Vogler, pp. 1–30. Oxford: Oxford Univ. Press

Gamson WA, Fireman B, Rytina S. 1982. *Encounters with Unjust Authority.* Homewood, UK: Dorsey

Geertz C. 1973. *The Interpretation of Cultures: Selected Essays.* New York: Basic Books

Genette G. 1980. [1972.] *Narrative Discourse: an Essay in Method.* Ithaca, NY: Cornell Univ. Press

Ginzburg C. 1982. *The Cheese and the Worms. The Cosmos of a Sixteenth-Century Miller.* Harmondsworth, UK: Penguin Books

Glasgow University Media Group. 1976. *Bad News.* London: Routledge & Kegan Paul

Graham H. 1984. Surveying through stories. In *Social Researching: Politics, Problems, Practice*, ed. C Bell, H Roberts. London: Routledge & Kegan Paul

Greimas AJ. 1966. *Sémantique structurale.* Paris: Larousse

Griffin L. 1993. Narrative, event-structure analysis, and causal interpretation in historical sociology. *Am. J. Sociol.* 98: 1094–1133

Halliday MAK. 1970. Language structure and language function. In *New Horizons in Linguistics*, ed. J Lyons, pp. 140–65. Harmondsworth, UK: Penguin Books

Halliwell S. 1987. *The Poetics of Aristotle: Translation and Commentary.* London: Duckworth

Hartmann P. 1975/1976. Industrial relations in the news media. *Ind. Relat. J.* 6:4–18

Heise D. 1989. Modeling event structures. *J. Math. Sociol.* 14:139–69

Hopper PJ. 1979. Aspect and foregrounding in discourse. In *Syntax and Semantics. Vol. 12: Discourse and Syntax*, ed. T Givon, pp. 213–41. New York: Academic

Jakobson R. 1960. Closing statement: linguistics and poetics. In *Style in Language*, ed. TA Sebeok, pp. 350–77. Cambridge, MA: MIT Press

Johnson P, Webb S. 1993. Explaining the growth in UK income inequality—1979–1988. *Econ. J.* 103:429–35

Kohler Riessman C. 1993. *Narrative Analysis.* Newbury Park, CA: Sage

Krippendorf K. 1980. *Content Analysis. An Introduction to Its Methodology.* Beverly Hills, CA: Sage

Labov W. 1972. *Language in the Inner City.* Philadelphia: Univ. Pa. Press

Labov W, Waletzky J. 1967. Narrative analysis. In *Essays on the Verbal and Visual Arts*, ed. J Helm, pp. 12–44. Seattle: Univ. Wash. Press

Lakoff R. 1975. *Language and Women's Place.* New York: Harper Torch Books

Lasswell H, Leites N, et al. 1968. [1949.] *Language of Politics: Studies in Quantitative Semantics.* Cambridge, MA: MIT Press. 2nd ed.

Laumann E. 1979. Network analysis in large social systems: some theoretical and methodological problems. In *Perspectives on Social Network Research*, ed. PW Holland, S Lenhardt, pp. 379–402. New York: Academic

Leeming A, Unell J, Walker R. 1994. *Lone Mothers: Coping with the Consequences of Separation.* London: HMSO

Lévi-Strauss C. 1972. [1962.] *The Savage Mind.* London: Weidenfeld & Nicolson

Liebow E. 1993. *Tell Them Who I Am: The Lives of Homeless Women.* New York: Free Press

Mandler J. 1978. A code in the node: the use of

story schema in retrieval. *Discourse Process.* 1:14–35

Maynard D. 1992. On method: conversation analysis and the study of diagnostic news deliveries. *Adv. Group Process.* 9:113–29

Millar RJ. 1982. *The Demolition of Skid Row.* Lexington, MA: Heath

Moore B Jr. 1978. *Injustice. The Social Bases of Obedience and Revolt.* White Plains, NY: Sharpe

Murdock G. 1973. Political deviance: the press presentation of a militant mass demonstration. In *The Manufacture of News: Social Problems, Deviance, and the Mass Media*, ed. S Cohen, J Young, pp. 156–75. London: Constable

Newby H. 1979. *The Deferential Worker: A Study of Farm Workers in East Anglia.* Madison, WI: Univ. Wisc. Press

Novick P. 1988. *That Noble Dream: The 'Objectivity Question' and the American Historical Profession.* Cambridge: Cambridge Univ. Press

O'Barr W, Atkins BK. 1980. 'Women's language' or 'powerless language?' In *Women and Language in Literature and Society*, ed. S McConnell-Ginet, et al, pp. 93–110. New York: Praeger

Office of Population Censuses and Surveys. 1993. *Census 1991: Communal Establishments.* London: HMSO

Oxford Independent. 1997. Jan. No. 12, p. 1

Perry M. 1979. Literary dynamics: how the order of a text creates its meanings. *Poetics Today.* 1:35–64

Peterson C, McCabe A. 1983. *Developmental Psycholinguistics: Three Ways of Looking at a Child's Narrative.* New York: Plenum

Prince G. 1973. *A Grammar of Stories: An Introduction. De proprietatibus litterarum.* Ser. Minor, Vol. 13. Paris: Mouton

Propp V. 1968. [1928.] *Morphology of the Folktale.* Austin, TX: Univ. Texas Press

Rickert H. 1962. [1902.] *Science and History: A Critique of Positivistic Epistemology*, ed. A Goddard. Princeton, NJ: Van Nostrand

Ricoeur P. 1984, 1985, 1988. *Time and Narrative.* Vols. 1, 2, 3. Transl. K McLaughlin, D Pellauer. Chicago: Univ. Chicago Press

Rimmon-Kenan S. 1983. *Narrative Fiction: Contemporary Poetics.* London: Methuen

Romaine S. 1994. *Language in Society: An Introduction to Sociolinguistics.* Oxford: Oxford Univ. Press

Rossi P. 1989. *Down and Out in America: The Origins of Homelessness.* Chicago: Univ. Chicago Press

Rumelhart D. 1975. Notes on a schema for stories. In *Representation and Understanding*, ed. D Bobrow, A Collins, pp. 211–36. New York: Academic

Sandford J. 1972. *Down and Out in Britain.* London: New English

Scott J. 1985. *Weapons of the Weak: Everyday Forms of Peasant Resistance.* New Haven, CT: Yale Univ. Press

Shanks N, Smith SJ. 1992. British public policy and the health of homeless people. *Policy Polit.* 20:35–46

Shapiro G, Markoff J. 1997. A matter of definition. In *Text Analysis for the Social Sciences: Methods for Drawing Statistical Inferences from Texts and Transcripts*, ed. CW Roberts, pp. 9–31. Hillsdale, NJ: Erlbaum

Shelter. 1991. *Twenty-Fifth Anniversary Report: Building for the Future.* London: Shelter

Tarrow S. 1989. *Democracy and Disorder: Protest and Politics in Italy, 1965–1975.* Oxford: Clarendon

Thompson EP. 1993. *Customs in Common.* New York: New Press

Todorov T. 1969. *Grammaire du Décaméron.* Paris: Mouton

Todorov T. 1977. [1971]. *The Poetics of Prose.* Oxford: Blackwell

Todorov T. 1981 [1968]. *Introduction to Poetics.* Sussex: Harvester

Todorov T. 1990 [1978.] *Genres in Discourse.* Cambridge: Cambridge Univ. Press

Tomashevski B. 1965 [1925]. Thematics. In *Russian Formalist Criticism: Four Essays*, ed. L Lemon, M Reis, pp. 61–95. Lincoln: Univ. Nebraska Press

Toolan M. 1988. *Narrative: A Critical Linguistic Introduction.* London: Routledge

Tully J, ed. 1988. *Meaning and Context: Quentin Skinner and His Critics.* Princeton, NJ: Princeton Univ. Press

van Dijk T. 1972. *Some Aspects of Text Grammars.* Paris: Mouton

van Dijk T. 1983. Discourse analysis: its development and application to the structure of news. *J. Commun.* 33(2):20–43

van Dijk T. 1984. *Prejudice in Discourse: An Analysis of Ethnic Prejudice in Cognition.* Amsterdam: Benjamins

van Dijk T, ed. 1985. *Handbook of Discourse Analysis.* London: Academic

van Dijk T. 1987. Mediating racism: the role of the media in the reproduction of racism. In *Language, Power and Ideology: Studies in Political Discourse*, ed. R Wodak, pp. 199–222. Amsterdam: Benjamins

van Dijk T. 1988. *News as Discourse.* Hillsdale, NJ: Erlbaum

Van Maanen J. 1988. *Tales of the Field.* Chicago: Univ. Chicago Press

Vestergaard T, Schrøder K. 1985. *The Language of Advertising*. Oxford: Blackwell

West C, Zimmerman DH, eds. 1980. Language and social interaction. *Sociol. Inq.* 50: Special issue

West C, Zimmerman DH. 1983. Small insults: a study of interruptions in cross-sex conversations between unacquainted persons. In *Language, Gender and Society*, ed. B Thorne, C Kramarae, N Henley, pp. 102–17. Rowley, MA: Newbury

White H. 1987. *The Content of the Form: Narrative Discourse and Historical Representation*. Baltimore, MD: Johns Hopkins Univ. Press

Windelband W. 1980 [1894]. History and natural science. *Hist. Theory*. 19:165–85

SUBJECT INDEX

A

Abbott, A, 150, 154, 360–61, 526
Abell, P, 525
Abortion
attitudes towards, 29, 42, 219, 335
Abrahamson, E, 278–79
Abuse
See Spousal abuse; Violence
Acceptance, 383
Accountability
and audience effects, 249–50
Accounting, 322, 338–39
Accumulation, periods of, 175
Actions
actors and, 348–50
facilitating, 4
in networks, 59
and objects of, 348–50
Actors, 6, 348–50
collective, 286
in networks, 64
Adolescents
Black, 13
crime rates among, 224
Mexican-origin, 13, 17
violence among, 300
Advertising, 303, 540, 545
Africa
history making in, 125
moratorium on aid to, 170
See also South Africa
Agar, M, 484
Age and collective action, 225
Aggregations, eclectic, 179
Aggression
alibis for, 232–33
defined, 231–32
feedback model of, 97
and intoxication, 293, 299–300
AIDS epidemic
memories of, 124
modeling, 268
Alamo historical site, 128
Alaniz, ML, 302–3
Alcohol
consequences of availability, 302–4
and violence, 291–307
Alexander, JC, 458
Alfano, G, 200
Algorithmic control, 153
Alienating workers, 148
Alliances, 59–60, 63
Allport, GW, 97
Alonso, AM, 126
Altruism, 193
Amenta, E, 382
American Jewish Committee, 40
American National Election Studies, 35
American Sociological Association, 9
Ammerman, NT, 31–32
Amphetamines, 295–96
Analytical Marxism, 460
Analyzing
coded data with CAQDA, 482–83
links with CAQDA, 484
networks, 358–59
See also individual analytic methods
Anderson, B, 116–17
Anderson, E, 332
Anderson, RM, 29
Anheier, HK, 11, 363
Annotating data with CAQDA, 487–88
Anomie
antidote to, 2
Anonymity in solutions, 199
Anthropology
cognitive, 346
Anti-apartheid protests, 219
Anti-Communism, 171
Anti-discrimination remediation, 90–91
Antiepistemology, postmodern, 120
Anti-immigrant violence
increasing, 96–97
Anti-immigration parties, 91–95
Austria, 91–92
Belgium, 92
France, 92–93
Germany, 93
Great Britain, 93–94
The Netherlands, 94
southern Europe, 95
Switzerland, 94–95
Anti-positivism, 458
Anti-Semitism
legislating, 90
literature on, 429
Anything goes environments, 303
AQUAD software, 489–91
Aretxaga, B, 444
Argentina
overthrow of Frondizi, 171
Arguments
presenting, 246, 251
Aristotle, 190, 319, 519–23, 533
Arms-length transactions, 72, 74
Arnold, B, 131
Arrests
studying, 218
Arrighi, G, 174
Artists and intellectuals
social ties among German, 11
Asahi Shimbun, 502
Asian-American CPs, 27
Asian-American women
marrying more whites than Asian-American men, 412–13
Asian immigrants
companies, capitalization of, 12
mothers, 10
askSam software, 479, 486–87
Assmann, J, 113
Associative involvement, 18
Assortive mating
See Marriage
Assurance Game, 185–88
Asylum seekers, 81
violence against in Germany, 96
ATLAS/ti software, 489–90
Atran, S, 442
AT\& T, 148, 153
Attractiveness, 398, 416–17
Attribute similarity, 354
Audience effects
and accountability, 249–50
Aussiedler return, 80, 90

Australia
  anti-immigration sentiments in, 96
Austria
  anti-immigration parties in, 91–92
Authoritarian regimes
  making transition to democracy, 160
  traditional, 151
Autobiographical memory, 111
Automaticity, 256–57
Automatic knowledge activation
  unconscious influence of, 257
Autonomy
  personal, 16, 66
  for workers, 148
Axelrod, R, 195–99

B

Backgrounding information, 532
Baimbridge, M, 91
Baker, WE, 6, 67
Banking
  interfaces with markets, 67
Bankruptcy law, 355
Barley, SR, 278
Barthes, R, 517, 521–24, 541–42
Bartkowski, J, 35
Bartlett, FC, 106
Baudrillard, J, 467
Baum, JAC, 64–65
Bayesian probability theory, 258
Beck, U, 466
Becker, PE, 275
Beethoven, L, 130–31
Belgium
  anti-immigration parties in, 92
Beliefs of conservative Protestants, 35–36
Bellah, RN, 122
Belonging
  sense of, 81–82
Benchmarks in colleges, 328
Benefits to others, 200
Benjamin, W, 118
Berelson, B, 346
Berger, PL, 329
Bet-hedging, 334
Biases, 254
Biblical literalists, 26, 35–36
Bifurcation in the workplace, 142
Bigots, 85
Biological connotations of nationality, 82
Biotechnology industry, 67, 70
Black colleges, 404
Black men
  marrying more whites than black women, 412
Blacks
  adolescent, 13
  CPs, 26–27
  intermarriage among, 406
  oppression of, 33
  workers' connection to labor market, 4
  See also Conservative Protestantism (CP)
Blalock, HM Jr, 441
Blatant prejudice, 83–85
Blau, PM, 403
Blauner, R, 147
Bless, H, 246
Blockmodeling, 11
Blood bank
  donating to, 205
Blossfeld, 414
Blumer, H, 215
Bollen, KA, 36
Boolean analysis, 360, 482–83, 488, 491
Borges, J, 118
Born-again, 36
  See also Conservative Protestantism (CP)
Bornstein, G, 201
Boston Consulting Group, 71
Boundaries in solutions, 202–4
Bounded solidarity, 7
Bourdieu, P, 2–6, 11, 362, 427, 456–57, 536
Bourgois, P, 17
Bowen, JR, 428
B-phase models, 175–79
Bradach, JL, 59
Brass, PR, 428
Braverman, H, 146–47, 154
Brazil
  and core nations, 177–78
  youth movements in, 362
Breakdown theories of collective action, 215–36
  clash of civilizations and, 234–35
  recent advances in, 225–28
  routine-disorder and, 234
  social capital and, 233
Breines, W, 336
Brent Spar oil rig case, 373, 389
Brownstein, HH, 306
Brubaker, R, 426, 443
Buchanan, JM, 188
Buffalo Creek Flood, 532
Bundesverfassungsgericht (German Federal Constitutional Court), 90
Burke, P, 112
Burris, BH, 143–45, 151–54
Burstein, P., 380
Burt, RS, 6, 11
Burton, M, 357
Business scan, 273
Busing
  attitudes towards, 219
Button, 378
Byproduct hypothesis
  in marriage patterns, 415–16
Byrne, D, 399

C

Calhoun, CJ, 456, 463–64, 469
California
  See Los Angeles
Capitalism
  endorsements of, 91
  social relations within, 146
  undermining nondemocratic regimes, 169
Capitalist labor process
  See Labor, process tradition in
CAQDA software
  See Computer-Assisted Qualitative Data Analysis
Cardoso, FH, 177–78
Carley, KM, 358–59
Carter, GL, 236
Carter, J, 32, 44, 171
Castells, M, 169
Castles, S, 78, 81, 88–89
Catalyzers, 521
Catholic colleges, 404
Catholic-Protestant intermarriage, 410
Catholics, 30, 35
CATI skip patterns, 35
Causal effects
  dynamics of, 267
  shifts in during diffusion, 282
Celebratory tone, in concepts, 2
Censorship
  See Libraries; Textbooks
Census procedures, 338
Centrum Party (The Netherlands), 94

Cerulo, K, 351–52
Chafetz, JS, 455–56
Chaiken, S, 248
Chance
  in marriage patterns, 402
Change
  brought by opposition to Communists, 373
  cycles within, 279–80
  instrumentalist vs inertial accounts of, 129–30
  policy, 378
  in western Europe, 82–83
Character roles
  basic, 523–24
Charismatic renewal, 29–30
Charity
  private, 6
Chatman, S, 519–22, 534, 541
Chicago Board of Trade, 329–30
Chicken Game, 185–88
Children
  benefitting, 10
  testing, 333
  value of, 327–28
China
  peasant rebellions in, 274
Chinatown
  New York City, 12
Chirac, J, 97
Chirot, D, 163
Chitwood, DD, 297
Choice of partners solutions, 197–98
Christian Coalition, 37, 47, 337
Christianization of memory, 114
Christian pity, 544
Christian Social Union party (Germany), 93
Citizenship
  for new European minorities, 81–82
City-level data
  about urban riots of the 1960s, 222–23
Civic engagement, 233, 435
Civic virtue, 19–20
Civilizations, clash of
  and breakdown theories, 234–35
Civil Rights movement, 230, 380
  in Japan, 500
Civil service
  reforms in, 279
Clark, HH, 252
Classification models
  See Modeling
Clerical work
  upgrading, 148
Climate favorable to democratization, 164
Closure, 5
Clotfelter, CT, 229
Clustering
  multidimensional, 356–58
Coates, J, 539
Cocaine, 296–97, 305
  dealers in the Bronx, 17
Coding data, 428
  with CAQDA, 482, 488–89
  See also Value-added coders
Coffey, A, 483, 488
Cognition
  and communication, 252–56
  implicit, 256–57
  socially situated, 247–56
  warm vs cold, 240
Cognitive anthropology, 346
Cognitive social psychology
  recent developments in, 239–59
Cohabitation, rise of, 397
Cohen, WM, 69
Cohesion through strong ties, 273
Cold War era, 424–25
Cole, RE, 281
Coleman, JS, 4–7, 9–10, 12, 283
Collective action, 183–210
  and age, 225
  breakdown theories of, 215–36
  and crime, 223–24
  in European setting, 217–18
  future directions in, 233–35
  and moral sentiments, 230–33
  nonroutine, 233–35
  secondary groups in, 218–20
  social movements in, 218–20
Collective memory, 105–34
Collective violence, 215–36
Collectivities, 8–9
Colleges, 279
  administrative assistance in, 492–93
  Black, 404
  Catholic, 404
  grading in, 329
  implementing benchmarks, 328
  ranking, 313, 329
  teaching methodology, 514
  violence against minorities at, 98
Collier, D, 282
Collins, JJ, Jr, 293
Collins, PH, 464
Collins, R, 458, 465
Commemoration, 112–15, 118–19
Commensuration, 313–39
  in action, 334–39
  critics of, 330
  defined, 315–18
  degree institutionalized, 329–30
  discontent over, 332–34
  feminist, 334–36
  historical legacies of, 318–23
  importance of, 323–26
  incommensurables, 326–28, 332
  refracting power relations, 330–32
  strategic, 331
  studying, 328–34
Commentary
  a form of reading, 113
Commission for Racial Equality (Britain), 91, 94
Commodification, 313–39
Commons dilemmas, 185, 190–92
Communal contenders, 430
Communal groups, 396
Communication
  and cognition, 252–56
  society based on, 459
  solutions based on, 194
Communicative memory, 111
Communists
  attitudes towards, 41
  change brought by opposition to, 373
Communities
  constituted by their history, 122
  different, same practice, 280–81
  fashion-setting, 278–79
  identifying with, 7
  same, different practices, 281–82
  social capital of, 16–20
  See also Social ties
Compaq Corp., 68
Comparisons
  small-n, 435
Competition
  intergroup, 194–95
  marketplace, 58

and structural equivalence, 274–75
Computer-Assisted Qualitative Data Analysis (CAQDA)
analyzing coded data with, 482–83
analyzing links with, 484
coding data with, 482
crisis of representation and, 493–95
document processing with, 485–86
entering data with, 481
future directions in, 491–96
history of, 479–85
killer app lacking in, 492–93
linking data with, 483–84
manipulating symbols with, 489–91
organizing data with, 481–82, 486–89
relevance of, 492–95
retrieving with, 485–86
searching with, 485–86
software for, 485–91
Computerized numerical control (CNC), 144
Computers
for analyzing ethnographic field data, 477–96
getting texts into, 366
simulations by, 197
in the workplace, 141–55
See also Computer-Assisted Qualitative Data Analysis (CAQDA); individual software packages
Comte, A, 215
Conceptual innovation, 458–59
Conflict, 425
framing as ethnic, 443–44
group, 77
See also Violence
Confrontations, 431
mutual, 458
Connections
global, 163–79
Conscription, military, 203
Consequences
of social movements, 371–89
Conservative party (Britain), 94
Conservative Protestantism (CP), 25–50
beliefs of, 35–36
culture wars of, 42–44
defining, 25–27
denominational affiliation, 34–35
family issues and, 39–40
gender and, 38–39
growth of, 48–50
monographs defining, 28
movement identification, 36–37
religiosity of, 38
Southern, 30–33
tolerance among, 40–42
Constitutional Convention of 1787, 317
Constitutive incommensurables, 327
Contagion, 265–86
Contemporary social conditions
diagnosing, 465–66
Content
arbitrary nature of, 351
See also Narrative analysis
Contention
repertoires of, 270
Contestation
concept of, 126–28
Context-dependent methods of analysis, 480
Contracts
short-term, 59
Convergence
See Global convergence models
Conversational relevance
of irrelevant information, 252–56
and response effects, 254–55
Conversion theory, 250
Cooley, CH, 106
Cooperation
provided by network forms of organization, 66
in social dilemmas, 183–210
Cooptation
of organizations, 66
Cornes, R, 189
Corporal punishment, 39–40
Corporations
family-based, in Japan, 500
Correspondence analysis, 361–62
Counter-memory, 126
Counting with CAQDA, 488–89
CPs
See Conservative Protestantism (CP)
Crack
See Cocaine
Crane, D, 468–69
Credentials conferred, 3
Crenshaw, EM, 165
Cressy, D, 116
Crime and collective action, 81, 223–24
Criminal Victimization Survey, 307
Crisis of representation and CAQDA, 493–95
Critical mass
reaching, 202
Cronon, W, 329–30
Crossing effects
in marriage patterns, 416
CSC Index, 280
Csikszentmihalyi, M, 354
Cultural expectancies for alcohol use, 303–4
Cultural impacts of movements, 386
Culturalist approaches to ethnic violence, 441–46
Cultural memory, 112
Cultural negotiation, 126
Cultural resources in marriage patterns, 400, 409
Cultural status of the diffusion practice, 279–80
Cultural taste
education as proxy for, 412
Culture
bases of diffusion, 276–82
categories, 276
construction of fear by, 441–43
and marriage patterns, 399–400
See also Subcultural identity theory
Culture wars of conservative Protestants, 42–44
Cumulative adoption patterns, 283
Cycles
world-system, 175–79

D

Damanpour, F, 270
Dams
planning, 314, 317, 327
Dance traditions
study of, 361
D'Andrade, RG, 346, 357–58
Data
defining, 518
organizing with CAQDA, 486–89
See also Ethnographic field data; Large data sets

Data analysis
See Computer-Assisted Qualitative Data Analysis (CAQDA)
Davis, GF, 269, 280, 285
Davis, K, 399, 402–3
Davis, NZ, 445
Davis-Merton hypothesis, 416
Dawes, R, 191–92, 201, 204
de Boeck, P, 363
DEC Corp, 68
Decentralization
functional, 145
patterns of, 144–46
Decision-making, 527
Deconstructing identitarian mythology, 134
Deep structures of narrative, 525
Defection
diffusing the harm of, 191–92
mutual, 196
in social dilemmas, 185–86
Democratization
global, 159–80
Denominational affiliation
of conservative Protestants, 34–35
specifying, 34
Denzin, NK, 364, 493
Deprofessionalization, 149–50
Desacralization of tradition, 108
de Saussure, F, 351
Design
sociotechnical, 147–49
Deskilling of workers, 147–48
Determinism vs indeterminism, 153
Deus ex machina, 534
Developments
See Future directions
Diagnosing contemporary social conditions, 465–66
Dialogue among multiple theoretical approaches, 461
Diamandouros, PN, 164
Diani, M, 384
Dictators
US support of, 171
Diesing, 545
Different practices
same community, 281–82
Diffusion, 265–86
cultural bases of, 276–82
cultural status of, 279–80
definitions of, 266–69
formal models of, 283–85
future directions in, 285–86
initial elements of argument, 269–70
mediated by interpretive work, 277–78
notions underlying, 267–69
shifts in causal effects during, 282
Dilemmas
See Social dilemmas
DiMaggio, PJ, 42, 271, 349–50, 417
Direct discrimination, 87–90
Disaggregation, plea for, 446–47
Discourse, 265–86
Discourse analysis
See Narrative analysis
Discrimination, 87–91
remediating, 90–91
Disease categories
study of, 358
Disinhibition
selective, 300–2
Dismantling totalitarian regimes, 159
Disorganization, 215–17
Dispensationalism, 29
Disruption
effectiveness in protests, 376–79
of quotidian, 227–28
Dissociative anaesthetics, 297
Distortions, 249–50
Divorce
increase in, 397
Dobbin, F, 272
Doctrine
vs experience, 29
Document processing with CAQDA, 485–86
Domesticity
valuing, 334–36, 398–99
Dore, R, 60, 68
Dotson, JW, 297
Downmarrying, 413
Downward leveling, 17
Doz, YL, 72
Dramatic tragedy
defining, 184
Dresher, M, 185
Drug Related Involvement in Violent Episodes (DRIVE), 305
Drug Relationships in Murder Project (DREIM), 305
Drugs
and violence, 291–307
See also individual drugs
Dual-process models, 242
Durkheim, E, 2, 7, 107, 109, 215, 325, 508
Dworkin, R, 230
Dyadic social dilemmas, 185–88
Dynamic processes of social memory, 122

E

Eastern Europe
revolutionary tendencies in, 172
transition to democracy, 160, 172, 389
East Germany, 372–73
deprivations endured in, 9
Eccles, RG, 60, 323
Eclectic aggregations, 179
Eco, U, 546–47, 549
Economic benefits
provided by network forms of organization, 65–66
Economic compulsive
behavior, 306
violence, 304
Economic sociology, 502
Education
acquiring credentials, 4
effect in marriage patterns, 411, 413
in later life, 193–94
as proxy for cultural taste, 412
sociology of, 507
Effects
of social capital, 8–14
See also Causal effects
Efficiency
and Total Quality Management (TQM), 282
Elections, 159, 434
Electronic communications
impact of, 114
Elias, N, 464
Elks Club, 18
Ellinwood, EH, Jr, 295
Ellison, CG, 39–42
Embedded transactions, 72
Empirical research
constructing tools for, 455–57
in Japanese sociology, 511–13
Endogamy, 400–1
describing degrees of, 418
England, P, 329
Entering data with CAQDA, 481

Environment
  influence on individual behavior, 239
  protecting, 503
Equalitarians, 85
Equal Rights Amendment (ERA), 335
Equilibria
  disrupting, 521
  optimal vs deficient, 185–86, 206
Equivalence
  See Structural equivalence
Erikson, E, 122, 226, 518
Espeland, WN, 314, 327
Ethical concerns, 318–21
Ethnic cleansing, 226
Ethnicity
  in marriage patterns, 406–7
  and violence, 425–27
Ethnic memory, 114
Ethnic niches, 12
Ethnic violence, 423–35
  case studies of, 436–37
  culturalist approaches to, 441–46
  game theoretic approaches to, 438–40
  inductive approaches to, 430–37
  international relations approaches to, 437–38
  rational action approaches to, 437–41
  spiraling, 225–27
Ethnoclasses, 430
Ethnographic field data
  analyzing using computers, 477–96
  notebooks, 494–95
Ethnograph software, 486, 488
Ethnography
  systematizing, 495
  team, 496
Ethnomethodology, 480
Ethnonationalists, 430
ETHNO software, 361, 526–28
Eurobarometer Survey 30, 83–87
Europe
  collective action in, 217–18
  fundamental changes in, 371–89
  See also Eastern Europe; Southern Europe; Western Europe
European Green parties, 93
European Union (EU), 80
Evangelicals, 25–50
  history of, 27–29
Evans, P, 233
Events
  narratives of, 523
Event Structure Analysis (ESA), 361
Exchange hypotheses
  in marriage patterns, 416–17
Ex-colonial immigrants, 80, 82
Exogamy
  preventing, 400
Expectation of reciprocity, 208
Experience
  versus doctrine, 29
Experts, 272
Extended-case method of analysis, 480
Eye-witness testimony
  reliability of, 254

F

Factionalism, 375
Fagan, J, 299–300
Failed social movements, 382–87
Falwell, J, 29, 32, 45–47
Family support, 10–11
  compensating for inadequate, 13–14
  and conservative Protestantism (CP), 39–40
  in marriage patterns, 398
  traditional Japanese system, 501
Farm workers
  success of, 381
Fashion-setting communities, 278–79
Favoritism, creating ingroup, 198
Fear
  of being a sucker, 189
  cultural construction of, 441–43
Fearon, JD, 424, 438–39
Feedback model of aggression, 97
Feelings
  as information, 244–45
  interplay with thinking, 242–47
Feldman, A, 445
Female Drug Related Involvement in Violent Episodes (FEMDRIVE), 305
Feminist perspectives
  on commensuration, 334–36
  on recovering lost voices, 126–27
  on sociology, 463, 467
  on surrogate motherhood, 332–33
  See also Gender; Women; Women's Movement
Fernandez-Kelly, MP, 13
Fiat Inc, 147
Fiction, 519
Fictitious narratives, 541
  opinions about, 254–55
Field data
  See Ethnographic field data
Fielding, NG, 485
Finke, R, 49
Fischer, MD, 481
Fiske, ST, 242, 249, 258
Flood, M, 185
Flood
  poem about, 532
Florida
  See Miami
Folio Views software, 479, 486–88
Folktales
  telling, 524–25
Foregrounding information, 532
Foreign capital investment, 174–75, 177
Foreign intervention, 170–72
Forgas, JP, 245
Formal analysis
  advantages and disadvantages of, 364–65
  See also individual analytic methods
Formalizing of the professions, 150
Foucault, M, 331, 338, 508
Fragmentation of multiple theoretical approaches, 457–59
Framing conflict as ethnic, 443–44
France
  anti-immigration parties in, 92–93
  articles published in, fate of, 3
  desecration of Jewish graves in, 96
  Republican period in, 116
  revolutionary period in, 127
  rural Portuguese in, 80
  strikes in, 216–17, 375
Franchises, 59
Franco, F, 166–67

Franzosi, R, 355, 526, 545
Freedom
desiring, 179
Freedom Party (Austria), 91–92
Free-riding, 194
opportunities for, 15–16
preventing, 200
Free trade vs free enterprise, 174
Freidson, E, 149–50
Friedkin, NE, 273–74
Friedland, R, 332–33
Friedlander, S, 119
Friendship
value of, 327–28, 332
Front National party (France), 92–93
Fuegian language, 188
Fukuyama, F, 163, 226, 233
Functionality of violence
aggression, intoxication and, 299–300
Fundamentalism, 25–50
history of, 27–29
Fund raising strategies, 201
Future directions
in collective action, 233–35
in Computer-Assisted Qualitative Data Analysis (CAQDA), 491–96
in diffusion, 285–86
in intermarriage and homogamy, 409–12
in social dilemmas, 208–10
for sociological study, 467–70
FYI3000PLUS software, 486–87

G

Gaborieau, M, 445
Gagnon, VP, 433–34
Game theoretic approaches
to ethnic violence, 438–40
to social dilemmas, 190
Gamson, WA, 375–76, 380, 537
Gamson typology, 383–84
Gastarbeiter system, 79–80, 89–90
Gay, DA, 38–40, 42
Gedi, N, 112
Geertz, C, 15, 494–95
Gender
and conservative Protestantism (CP), 38–39
equal employment and, 144
and ethnic violence, 444
expectations in Maasai culture, 357
in Japanese sociology, 506
General Foods, 147
General Inquirer software, 485
Generalized memory trace, 129
General Social Survey (GSS)
coding, 34–36, 41–42
Genette, G, 528
Genocides
literature on, 429
Geographical grouping
in marriage patterns, 402–3
Germany, 79–80
anti-immigration parties in, 93
direct discrimination in, 88
management trends in, 281
myth of writer as loner in, 359
Russian Jews in Berlin, 78
social ties among artists and intellectuals, 11
violence against asylum seekers in, 96
See also East Germany; West Germany
Giannini, AJ, 296
Giddens, A, 454, 458, 465, 508
Ginzburg, C, 547
Giugni, MG, 384
Glaser, BG, 479
Glasgow University Media Group, 531
Glenn ND, 408
Global convergence models, 164–65, 170, 176–77
Global hegemon
shifting, 172–75
Global industrialization, 164–69
Globalization, 163–79
defining, 465–66
and democracy, 159–80
shocks to, 169–70
Global linkages
new, 176
GOFER software, 485, 487
Gold, SJ, 11
Golden parachutes, 276, 280, 285
Goldstein, PJ, 304–5
Goldstone, J, 380
Goodwill, 60
Gorbachev, M, 174, 372
Gore, A, 32
Gorsuch, RC, 38
Go together
things that, 354
Governance
forms of, 59, 73–74
Governments
attention paid to public opinion, 379
repression by, 228–30
Grading in school, 329
Graduated system of sanctions, 206
Graham, B, 32
Granovetter, MS, 11–15, 58–60, 63, 73, 273–74, 284
Grazing land disputes, 191
Great Britain
anti-immigration parties in, 93–94
direct discrimination in, 87–88
dramatizing history of, 125–26
parliamentarization of politics, 348–49
Somalis in London, 78
Green, DP, 98
Green, JC, 33, 38, 45, 48
Greenberg, SW, 293
Greenpeace activists, 372–73
Greenwald, AG, 256–57
Greimas, AJ, 523–25, 540
Greve, HR, 275
Griffin, L, 527
Grim triggers solutions, 198
Griswold, W, 347–48
Grounded-theory method of analysis, 479–80
Group closure, 396
Group identification, 3
in marriage patterns, 400–401
in solutions, 194–95
Group reciprocity solutions, 198–99
Groups
competition among, 194–95
conflict among, growing, 77
love for, 227
size in solutions, 201–2
Group sanctions
concerning loan repayment, 8
concerning marriage patterns, 401–2
Guest workers, 79–80, 82, 89–90
Guigni, MG, 373
Guillen, MF, 281
Gulati, R, 69–70, 73
Gurr, TR, 384, 426, 430–31
Guth, JL, 45–48

H

Habermas, J, 330, 462–65, 508
Habitus
 concept of, 456
Hacking, I, 324
Hagan, J, 9–10
Hage, P, 364
Hagerstrand, T, 284
Haider, J, 91–92
Halbwachs, M, 106–11, 129
Hamel, G, 62, 69
Hammond, NDC, 359
Handgun purchases, 229–31
Hannan, MT, 68
Hansen, TB, 444
Hao, L, 10
Hardin, G, 190, 202–4
Hartmann, P, 531
Hate crimes, 98
Healing, divine, 29
Health maintenance organizations (HMOs), 272
Hechter, M, 204–5, 440–41
Heckathorn, DD, 190
Hegemonic shifts, 172–75
Heimer, CA, 328, 332
Heise, D, 527
Heisler, M, 431
Hemingway, E, 363
Hendricks, J, 411
Herbst, S, 336
Hernes-type models, 283
Heroes
 corporate, 271
 in engineering, 265
 role of, 124
Heroin, 295, 298, 305
Hesse-Biber, S, 494
Heuristic power of concepts, 2
HICLAS software, 363
Hierarchical classification models, 299, 363–64
Hierarchical division of labor
 breaking down, 143–44
Hierarchies
 of codes, 488
 as form of organization, 58–59
 rationale behind, 66–70
Higgins, ET, 241
Hijacking attempts
 warding off, 269
Hill, SS, Jr, 31
Himmelfarb, G, 325
Himmelstein, JL, 337
Hiroshima
 bombing of, 127
Hirsch, EL, 219
Hirsch, PM, 277–78
Hirschhorn, L, 147
Hispanic category, 325, 331
Historical consciousness
 changing forms of, 125
Historical legacies
 of commensuration, 318–23
 of contemporary sociological projects, 469–70
Historical memory, 110–11
Historical sociology, 105–34
Historical writing
 narrator in, 541
History of memory, 112–22
HIV/AIDS spread
 See AIDS epidemic
Hobsbawm, E, 117, 122
Hochschild, A, 334–35
Hole, J, 335
Holiness denominations, 26
Holland
 See The Netherlands
Holocaust, 133
 as turning point, 119
Holocaust Memorial Center, 125
Holy Spirit
 gifts of the, 29
Home-based work, 145–46
Homelessness, 537–38, 543–46
Home schoolers, 333
Homicide
 and alcohol use, 301–2
 female offenders, 306
Homogamy
 and education, 404
 and intermarriage, 395–419
 preferences and, 400
Homosexuality
 attitudes towards, 41
 perspectives on sociology involving, 464, 467
Hopper, PJ, 531
Horizontal organizations, 216
Horowitz, DL, 431–34, 442, 444
Household possessions
 classifying, 354–55
Housework
 valuing, 334–36
Hubbuck, J, 88
Huberman, AM, 480
Human capital
 acquiring, 5
Human judgment
 faulty, 241
Human psyche
 probing, 527
Human relations movement, 278
Hungary
 development of organizations in postsocialist, 64–65
Hunter, JD, 42
Huntington, S, 160, 166–67, 169
Huntington, SP, 234
Hutton, P, 108–9
Huyssen, A, 120
Hypercentralization, 152
HyperQual2 software, 486–87
HyperRESEARCH software, 483, 489–91
Hypertext connections, 481, 483–84, 494
Hypothesis testing
 with CAQDA software, 490–91
 using Boolean analysis, 360

I

IBM Corp, 68
Identifiability in solutions, 199
Identitarian mythology
 deconstructing, 134
Identity
 concept of, 122–26
 See also Group identification
Immigration
 attitudes towards, 85–87, 506–7
 illegal, 81
 in western Europe, 79–80
Implicit cognition, 256–57
Impression formation, 246
Incommensurables, 326–28, 337
 claims made about, 332–34
Indexing system
 devising, 482
India
 riots in, 225–26, 232, 424, 435, 442–43
Indian States (US), 413
Indigenous peoples, 327, 430
Indirect discrimination, 87–90
Individual
 actively interprets environment, 239–40
Individualism, 193
Individual-level data, 293–98
 about drugs, alcohol and violence, 293–98
 about urban riots of the 1960s, 220–22

Inductive approaches to ethnic violence, 430–37
Industrial conflict, 376–77
Industrialization
  global, 164–69
  and post-war Japanese sociology, 503
Industrial revolution, 142
Information
  backgrounding and foregrounding, 532
  feelings as, 244–45
  and Japanese sociology, 507
Information society, 509
Ingroup favoritism, creating, 198
Inherited poverty, 4
Innovation
  conceptual, 458–59
  and diffusion studies, 270
Inside-the-head phenomena, 240, 247
Inspiration software, 489–90
Institutional sociology, 338–39
Institutions
  borders of, 332
  meanings of, 365
  record-keeping by, 130
  reification of, 330
  relationships with, 3
Insurance, 323–24
  actuary work, 318
Intelligibility of social world, 466
Intepersonal relations
  effect of drug use on, 293
Interactionism
  symbolic, 460–61
Interdependence
  and power, 248–49
Intergenerational mobility, 4
Intergroup competition, 194–95
Intermarriage, 78
  among different racial groups, 407, 410
  and homogamy, 395–419
Intermarriage index Z, 405
Internal Revenue Service (IRS)
  administering negative sanctions, 205
  changing regulations of, 272
  investigations by, 45
International climate favorable to democratization, 164
International Labor Organization (ILO), 276
International Monetary Fund (IMF), 169
International relations
  approaches to ethnic violence, 437–38
  and Japanese sociology, 506–7
Internet
  texts available on, 366
Interorganizational networks, 64
Interorganizational relations, 265–86
Interpretation
  constructing frameworks for, 456
  of history, 110–11
  of mediating diffusion, 277–78
  structural approach to, 351–53
Intertextual encyclopedias, 545, 549
  of knowledge, 550
Intertextual frames, 545, 549
Intervention
  foreign, 170–72
Intoxication, aggression and the functionality of violence, 299–300
Ireland
  See Northern Ireland
Irrational elements
  helping maintain social order, 117–18
Irrelevant information
  conversational relevance of, 252–56
Isen, AM, 243
Ishida, T, 506
Israel
  collective identity in, 125
  immigrant families in US, 11
  support for, 40
Italy
  anti-immigration parties in, 95
  community organizations in, 19
  contentious gatherings in, 355–56
  protest cycle in, 386
  Senegalese street vendors in, 78, 96
  tax laws in, 68
Iteration in solutions, 199–200

J

Jackson, RH, 424
Jacobs, JJ, 413
Jacoby, R, 116
James, W, 241
Japanese-Americans
  internment of, 127
Japanese corporations
  family-based, 500
  ties among, 69
Japanese sociology, 499–515
  after World War II, 503
  empirical research in, 511–13
  historical background, 500–8
  and information and technology, 507
  and international relations, 506–7
  methodology in, 510–11
  publications, 504–5
  theoretical paradigms, 508–10
  traditional, 501
Japan Sociological Society (JSS), 502, 510–14
Jervis, R, 437
Jesus
  representations of, 131
Jewish-Gentile intermarriage, 410
Jewish graves
  desecration of in France, 96
Jewish memory, 110, 113–14
Jews, 43
  coding of, 35
  as diamond merchants, 5, 15
  genocide of, 133
  living arrangements of, 403
  Russian, in Berlin, 78
  See also Holocaust
Jim Crow laws, 402
Joas, H, 462
Jobs
  complaints about, 91
  searches for, 63
Johnson, P, 544
Joint marriages, 399
Joint ventures, 59
Judgment
  faulty, 241, 252
  and memory, 243–45
Judiciary
  professionalism in, 150

K

Kahneman, D, 253
Kakar, S, 225–26, 232
Kalmijn, R, 398–400, 406–10, 413–53

Kapferer, B, 436
Kaplan, J, 295
Karp, D, 198–99
Katz, J, 427
Kelley, D, 48–49
Kelley, HH, 193
Kellstedt, LA, 26, 35–36, 42–43
Kernel events, 521
Kerr, N, 201
Ketamine, 297–98
Key-word computer searches, 236
Killer app
  lacking in CAQDA, 492–93
Kin support, 10, 16
Kirk, RC, 479
Kitschelt, H, 91, 384
Kneecapping, 433
Knowledge
  sociology of, 105, 130–33
  See also Automatic knowledge activation
Kohl, H, 95, 97
Kollock, P, 192, 195
Koopmans, R, 97–98
Korean businesspeople, 12, 15
Koutou, Y, 509
Krauss, RM, 252
Kriesi, HP, 269, 384
Kuhn, TS, 132
Ku Klux Klan, 96
Kula, W, 331
Kunda, G, 265–66
Kuran, T, 440
Kwalitan software, 486–88

L

Labor
  breaking down division of, 143–44
  commensuration and, 320–21
  internal markets for, 144
  process tradition in, 146–47
  See also Housework; Trade unionism
Labov, W, 519, 522–25, 528
LaFree, G, 224
Laitin, DD, 433–35, 438–40
Lakoff, G, 34
Landes, R, 78
Lang, GE, 130–31
Large data sets
  working with, 430–31
Large-n studies, 207, 436
  using the Internet for, 209
Larson, MS, 149
Lasswell, H, 549
Last-in, first-out, 89
Latency periods, 279
Latino-American CPs, 27
Lattice analysis, 362–63
Laumann, EO, 59
Law, 272
  professionalism in, 150
Layton-Henry, Z, 90
Lazerwitz, 410
League of Women Voters, 18
Learning
  about methodology, 514
  in network forms of organization, 62–64
  state-dependent, 243
Learning curves
  climbing, 492–93
LeBon, G, 215
Ledyard, JO, 189
Lee, BA, 406–7
Lee, R, 131
Lega Lombarda party (Italy), 95
Legitimacy
  provided by network forms of organization, 64–65
Le Goff, J, 114–15
Leigh, BC, 300
Lemann, N, 19
Lemarchand, R, 443
Lemert, CC, 466–67
Le Pen, J, 92–93
Leveling downward, 17
Leviathan solution, 202
Levine, DN, 461
Lévi-Strauss, C, 351–53, 530
Leydesdorff, S, 127
Libraries
  regulating, 41
  See also Textbooks
Lieberson, M, 403–4, 418
Liebow, E, 543
Liebrand, WBG, 193
Life-cycle effects, 224–25
Light, I, 12
Lin, N, 12
Lincoln, JR, 69
Linguistic analysis, 518–19, 547
Linking data with CAQDA, 483–84
Linz, JJ, 163
Literary study, 347–48, 358, 363, 524
Liturgical memory, 115
Local marriage markets, 403–4
Los Angeles
  Koreatown, 12
  riots in, 232
Loury, G, 4, 6
Lover, value of, 319
Lowenthal, D, 125
Lucas, HC, 326
Luhmann, N, 459, 508

M

MacEwen, M, 91
Machiavelli, N, 20
Macro diffusion research, 268–69
Macrolevel structures of narrative, 525
Macy, MW, 198
Mafia
  studies of, 208
Magic superhelper, 540
Major, J, 95
Majority
  influence over minority, 250–51
  prejudice of, 83–85
Malleability of memory, 128–30
Management
  control vs worker autonomy, 151–53
  fashions in, 278
  feeling threatened, 151
  in Germany, 281
Mannheim, K, 123
Manza, J, 42–44, 47
Mapping
  in meaning measurement, 358–59, 367
Maravall, JM, 166–67
March, JG, 317
Marcus, HR, 240
Mare, RD, 411, 413
Marijuana, 305
Market exchanges, 3
Marketing software, 493
Markets
  form of organization, 58–59
  interfaces with in banking, 67
  rationale behind, 66–70
Markoff, J, 165
Marriage
  commitment to, 40
  joint, 399
  patterns in, 395–419
  preferences of candidates, 398–400
  See also Spousal abuse
Marriage markets, 402–4
  local, 397, 403–4, 414
Marsden, GM, 27–28, 36

Martiniello, M, 80
Martins, L, 169
Martin software, 486–87
Marwell, G, 202
Marx, K, 2, 7, 107, 168, 319–21, 330, 508–9
Marxism
analytical, 460
Mass media
See Media
Material memory, 111
Mate selection
See Marriage
Matute-Bianchi, ME, 17
MAX software, 486–87
Mayan architecture
connectivity studies of, 359
Mayhew, LH, 91
Maynard, D, 539
McAdam, D, 272, 276
McCarthy, JD, 219
McClintock, CG, 193
McDonald, J, 134
McDowall, D, 229
McLanahan, S, 10
McLuhan, M, 114
Mead, GH, 106
Meaning structures
in human drives, 50
measuring, 345–67
Measurement
of conservative Protestant membership, 33–38
of the duality of social and cultural structures, 361–64
of intermarriage and homogamy, 404–6
of meaning structures, 345–67
of relations, 353–56
See also Commensuration
MECA software, 489–90
Media, 271
controllers of, 47
Mediational analysis, 240
Medicine, 274, 318
professionalism in, 150
special cases in, 328
Melich, A, 86
Melting pot concept, 81
Memory
augmenting, 495–96
Christianization of, 114
contemporary crisis of, 120
contestation, 126–28
history of, 112–22
and judgment, 243–45
malleability of, 128–30
mood-congruent, 243–44
neglect of, 107
persistence of, 128–30
popular, 127
triggering, 442
Memory-nation, 121
Memory studies, 105–34
lineages of, 106–8
Memory trace
generalized, 129
Memory training, 113
Mental control, 257
Merton, RK, 364, 416, 461
Message elaboration, 247
Messick, DM, 203, 207
MetaDesign software, 489–90
Metalanguage
codifying, 457
Metamorph software, 485
Metaphors of social dilemmas, 185
Methadone, 305
Methodology
in Japanese sociology, 510–11
Metropolitan Statistical Areas (MSAs), 414
Mexican-origin adolescents, 13, 17
Mexican-origin students, 13
Mexico
debt crisis in, 169–70
Meyer, JW, 339
Miami
Little Havana, 12
riots in, 232
Microdynamics of the workplace, 142
Microlevel structures of narrative, 525
Micro-linguistic analysis, 457
Microprocesses of diffusion, 270
Miczek, KA, 296
Migration
massive, 77
Miles, R, 80–81
Militant sects, 430
Military conscription, 203
Miller, AH, 221
Miller, NS, 296
Mimetic memory, 111
Minorities
citizenship and, 81–82
and majority influence, 250–51
See also New minorities
Mishler, EG, 519
Mnemonic consensus, 127
Mnemonic practices, 105–34
Mobilization spiral, 438
Modeling
aggression, 97
diffusion, 283–85
hierarchical classification, 363–64
HIV/AIDS spread, 268
intermarriage and homogamy, 406
social dilemmas, 184–92
See also individual models
Moderation/disruption axis, 373–74
Modernity
defining, 465–66
Mohr, JW, 349–50, 359, 362–63
Moluccans in The Netherlands, 79
Money, 322
See also Commensuration
Monitoring workers, 152
Mood-congruent memory, 243–45
Moods
effect on processing strategies, 245–47
exploring, 241
Moore, B, Jr, 536
Moral Majority, 45
Moral relativism, 41
Moral rot, 163
Moral sentiments
in collective action, 230–33
Morioka, K, 501
Morita, Y, 508
Morphology of stories, 525
Morris, A, 272
Moscovici, S, 251
Mosse, GL, 118
Motherhood, 546
out-of-wedlock, 10
surrogate, 332–33
See also Parental support
Mothers Against Drunk Driving (MADD), 219
Motivated Tactician
limits on, 256–58
in social situations, 242, 248–51, 258
Motivation
for commensuration, 316
exploring, 241
in solutions to social dilemmas, 192–95
Motorola Corp, 280
Movement gurus, 272
Movement identification of conservative Protestants, 36–37
Movements
cultural impacts of, 386
See also Social movements
Movimento Sociale Italiano, 95

Mowery, DC, 69
Multidimensional scaling (MDS) analysis, 356–58, 361–64
Multiple-person social dilemmas, 185, 188–92
Multiplexity, 16
Multiyear or multisite projects, 488
Murdock, G, 531–32
Museum
  concept of, 119, 124
Music
  meaning of, 351–52
Muslims
  fundamentalists, 27, 37
  immigrants to Europe, 78
Muus, P, 81–82
Myth of writer as loner, 359

N

Narcotic and Drug Research, Inc, 304–5
Narrative analysis, 517–51
  defined, 519–24
  golden age of, 366
  reconstruction in, 113
  role of reader in, 253, 544–47
  of sample text, 528–50
  and social processes, 134
  structural, 524–28
  See also Historical legacies; Literary study; Storytelling; Texts
Narratives
  of events and of words, 523
Narrator
  in historical writing, 541
Nash equilibria, 186
National Action Against the Swamping of the People and Homeland (Switzerland), 94
National Advisory Commission on Civil Disorders (NACCD), 220–24
National anthems
  meaning of, 352
National Cooperative Research Act, 58
National Criminal Victimization Survey, 294
National Endowment for Democracy, 171
National Front party (Great Britain), 94
National Institute of Justice, 294
Nationalist violence, 423–35
Nationality, 123
  biological connotations of, 82
  social capital of, 17–20
National Manufacturing Sector Congress, 178
National Music Week, study of, 349
National Research Council, 145, 291–92
National treasures
  valuing, 328
Native American concerns, 327, 430
Naturalization of immigrants, 82
Nazi ideology
  legislating against, 90, 119
  literature on, 429
Necklacing, 433
Negative attitudes towards foreigners
  rising, 86–87
Negative sanctions
  administering, 205
Negative social capital, 14–17
Negotiation
  cultural, 126
Neo-evangelical CPs, 28
Neoinstitutionalists, 339
Neo-Taylorists, 142, 152
Nested contexts models, 299
The Netherlands
  anti-immigration parties in, 94
  religious endogamy in, 411
  South Moluccans in, 79
Network analysis, 265–86, 358–59
Network forms of organization, 57–74
  defined, 59–62
  functions in, 62–66
  markets and hierarchies and, 66–70
  success rate of, 70–74
Networks
  among German artists and intellectuals, 11
  dense, 6
  dysfunctionalities within, 71
  interorganizational, 64
  small firm, 61
  social, 3
  wife accessing for husband, 399
Neuropsychological perspectives
  on memory, 109
New Era
  dawn of, 132
Newer institutionalism, 348–51
New Left activists, 336
New minorities, 77–99
  defined, 78–83
  discrimination against, 87–90
New Orleans
  Vietnamese community in, 9
News
  delivering bad, 539
  through weak ties, 273–74
New York City
  Chinatown, 12
  intermarriage patterns in, 410
  Jewish diamond merchants in, 5, 15
  Puerto Rican crack dealers in the Bronx, 17
  social welfare agencies in, 349–50
Nichiro Shoshu/Sakagakkai (NSS), 277
Nietzsche, FW, 118
Nixon, R, 32, 96, 131
Non-governmental organizations (NGOs)
  representation by, 446
Nonstate communal groups, 430
Nora, P, 120–22
Norms
  conversational, 253
  observance of, 5
  proscriptive, 300–1
  violations of, 241
Northern Ireland, 96, 435, 444
North Sea, 372–73
Nostalgia
  commercialization of, 125
Notebooks of ethnographic field data, 494–95
N-person social dilemmas, 185–88, 188–92, 198–204
Nuclear power
  crisis at Three-Mile Island, 227
  discussion of, 279
NUD.IST software, 489–90
Nuer people
  study of, 106
Nussbaum, MC, 318–19

O

Oberschall, A, 216, 225–26, 372

Objects of actions
  and actions, 348–50
Observation
  of diffusion, 269–70
Occupation
  See Professional work; Work; Workplace
Office of Technology Assessment, 143, 145
Oil prices
  rise in, 80, 169
Olick, JK, 130
Oligopolistic industries, 66
Olivetti Inc, 147
Olson, M, 189, 205
Olzak, S, 431
Opinions on fictitious issues, 254–55
Opportunity
  See Political opportunity
Oppression
  shaping beliefs, 33
Oral history, 126–27
Orbell, J, 194, 196, 207
Orbis software, 485
Ordaining women, 38–39, 276
Organization/disorder axis, 374
Organizations
  diffusion in, 265–86
  horizontal, 216
  impact of, 374–76
  networks within, 57–74
  restructuring, 142–46
Organizing data with CAQDA, 481–82, 486–89
Osgood, CE, 346
Ostracism, 207
  threat of, 5
Ostrom, E, 198, 204–8
Outcomes of social movements, 371–89
Outgroup members, 396
Out-of-wedlock motherhood, 10
Outsourcing agreements, 59
Oversampling, 30

P

Paleoanthropological perspectives
  on memory, 110
Panopticon
  advanced version of, 152
Paranoia
  feelings of, 296
Parastatals, 168
Parcel, TL, 10
Parental support, 10
  of intermarriage, 401
  See also Corporal punishment
Parent Teacher Association (PTA), 18
Paris Club, 170
Paris Commune, 274
Park, R, 215
Parker, RN, 300–3
Parkhe, A, 72
Parliamentarization of politics in Britain, 348–49
Parsonian action theory, 458
Parsons, T, 215, 458, 508–9
Participatory involvement, 18
Partito Repubblicano Italiano, 95
Pasteur, L, 130
Patriarchal perspectives, 39, 536
  See also Gender
Pattern-picking, 352
Patterns
  case-based, finding, 431–35
  of centralization and decentralization, 144–46
  of intermarriage and homogamy, 406–9
Payoff structure in solutions, 200
Pearsonian correlation, 405
Pentecostal denominations, 26
  history of, 29–30
Peoplehood
  sense of, 400
Perez, L, 12
Perrow, C, 61, 66
Persistence of memory, 128–30
Personal autonomy, 16
Persuasion, 246–47
Peters, T, 280
Petro dollars, 169
Pettigrew, TF, 83–88, 98
Pfeffer, J, 66
Phencyclidine (PCP), 297–98
Phenomenological sociology, 329
Plato, 319
Plot, 519
Podolny, JM, 64, 69
Poem about Buffalo Creek Flood, 532
Pogroms
  literature on, 429
Point-to-point processes, 283–84
Poison pills, 269, 273, 280, 285
Poland
  Solidarity movement in, 165
Polarization
  in the professions, 150–51
  in the workplace, 142
Police action
  See Repression
Policy change, 378
Political culture profiles, 111
Political opportunity, 381
Political power
  and opportunity structures, 380–82
  of the religious right, 44–48
  and social movements, 336–38
Political-process model, 381
Political refugees, 81
Political sociology, 346–47
Political violence, 427
Politics in Britain
  parliamentarization of, 348–49
Pollitt, K, 19
Popular memory, 127
Porter, TM, 317–18
Portes, A, 12, 70
Portugal, 172–75
Posen, BR, 437
Possessions
  classifying, 354–55
Postmodern antiepistemology, 120
Postmodern gibberish, 549
Postmodernity, defining, 134
Poulantzas, N, 173–75
Poverty
  inherited, 4
  measuring, 362–63
Powell, E, 94
Powell, WW, 58–63, 67, 70–73, 268
Power
  and interdependence, 248–49
  refracted by commensuration, 330–32
  See also Political power
Power elite, 47
Powerholders, 378
Prayer in public schools, 31
Prechel, H, 152–53
Preferences of marriage candidates, 398–400
Prejudice, 83–85
Prestige, 275
Prince, G, 521
Prisoner's Dilemma, 185–88
Private property rights, 204
Probability theory
  Bayesian, 258

Process data
obtaining relevant, 240
Processes
point-to-point, 283–84
of social memory, 122
threshold, 284–85
Processing strategies
effect of moods on, 245–47
Professional work, 149–51, 318
measuring reputations in, 324
Profitability, 338
Progressive Era, 278, 337, 349, 358
Proletarization of the professions, 149
Property rights, 204
Prophecy, 29–30
Propp, V, 523–26
Protest, 265–86, 375
cycles of, 386
violent and disruptive, 376–79
See also Riots
Protestant-Catholic intermarriage, 410
Protestantism, conservative
See Conservative Protestantism
Proust, M, 114
Provocation
rituals of, 445
Proximity logic, 488
See also Spatial proximity
Prunier, G, 436
Przeworski, A, 161, 178
Psychopharmacological violence, 291–307
Psychosis
toxic, 295
Publications in sociology, 502–5
Public Goods dilemmas, 185, 188–90
Public welfare
See Social welfare
Puerto Rican crack dealers in the Bronx, 17
Puritan entrepreneurial success, 15
Putnam, R, 18

Q

QCA software, 489–91
Qualitative data analysis (QDA), 547
See also Computer-Assisted Qualitative Data Analysis (CAQDA)
Qualitative hypothesis testing, 491
Quality circles, 277
QUALPRO software, 486, 488
Quantification
by commensuration, 313–39
debate over, 547
Questionnaires, 255
Quillian, L, 83
Quotidian
disruption of, 227–28

R

Race
equal employment and, 144
income inequality and, 4
in marriage patterns, 401–2, 406–7
perspectives on sociology involving, 463–64, 467
See also Slavery
Race Relations Act (Britain), 94
Radical Right
literature on, 429
Radin, MJ, 333
Radio station management, 275
Ragin, C, 360
RAND Corp, 185
Range land disputes, 191, 208
Rapoport, A, 188
RATE software, 283
Rational action approaches to ethnic violence, 437–41
Rational-choice theory, 460
Raz, J, 326–27
Reader
role in narrative analysis, 544–47
Reading
commentary, a form of, 113
Reagan, R, 131, 171
Real estate prices, 326
Rebellions
See Breakdown theories of collective action
Reciprocity
expectations, 3, 208
solutions, 195–97
Reconstruction
of current theoretical approaches, 462–64
Recontracting, 61–62
Red Cross, 18
Redemocratization, 161
Reed, R, Jr, 37, 46, 337
Refugee seekers, 81
Regional differences
in marriage patterns, 413–15
Regression models
spatial, 284
Reif, K, 83
Reification
institutionalization as, 330
Relational similarity, 354–55
Relational sociology, 457
Relations
episodic, in markets, 59
interorganizational, 265–86
measuring, 353–56
Relativity
of values, 324
Relevance
of CAQDA, 492–95
See also Conversational relevance
Reliability
of eye-witness testimony, 254
Religion
in marriage patterns, 407–8, 410–11
switching for marriage partner, 404
Religiosity of conservative Protestants, 38, 41
Religious Identity and Influence Survey, 37
Religious Right, 44–48, 336–37
See also Conservative Protestantism
Renewal movement
charismatic
See Charismatic renewal
Rent strikes, 374
Representation, crisis of, and CAQDA, 493–95
Repression
governmental, 228–30
Reputation studies, 130–33
in professional work, 324
Research programs
protecting identity of subjects, 485
refinement of theoretical, 459–61
Resource mobilization (RM) theory, 217–25
Response effects
conversational relevance and, 254–55
Restructuring
the organization, 142–46
the workplace, 141

Retrieving data with CAQDA, 485–86, 488–89
Revisionist studies
of urban riots of the 1960s, 220–23
Revolt, 535–36
Rich, PB, 79
Ricoeur, P, 518, 523, 528
Riessman, K, 542
Right, religious
See Conservative Protestantism
Right brain analysis, 484
Riots
ghetto, 377
of the 1960s, 220–24
Risk society, 466
Rituals, 536
classification of, 349
commemorative, 112
and ethnic violence, 444–45
of provocation, 445
Ritzer, G, 454, 457, 459
Robertson, P, 30, 37, 45–47
Robinson, WI, 178
Robots
mapping meaning of, 359
Rogers, EM, 268, 280
Role of reader
in narrative analysis, 544–47
Roof, WC, 34
Rorschach test analogy, 367
Rosenberg, S, 363–64
Ross, L, 251
Rossi, P, 537–38
Rotating credit associations (RCAs), 12
Rothchild, D, 439
Rough music, 536
Rouquie, A, 171
Routine-disorder
and breakdown theories, 234
Rowan, B, 281
Rueschemeyer, D, 166, 170
Rule, JB, 456
Rumbaut, RG, 16
Rwanda
killing in, 424

S

Safe country of origin principle, 81
Salience of technical expertise
increased, 151
Salzman, H, 142–43, 146
Same practice, different communities, 280–81
Sanctioning intermarriages, 401
Sanctions
administering negative, 205, 536
graduated system of, 206
in solutions, 204–6
See also Group sanctions
SAO structures, 526
SAS software, 283, 478
Savings, 328
Scaling
multidimensional, 356–58
Scapegoating, 83, 95
Scatter plots, 488
Schiff, M, 6
Schoen, R, 405, 412
Schoenhuber, F, 93
Schools
busing, attitudes towards, 219
as local marriage markets, 414–15
Schudson, M, 128
Schumm, WR, 36
Schwartz, B, 108, 111, 124, 128–31
Schwartz, N, 244–45, 248, 252–55
Schweizer, T, 354, 363
Science-fiction novels
mapping meaning in, 358–59
Science rhetoric, 517–51
Scopes Trial, 28
Scott, J, 537
Scripts
reliance on, 246
Searching, 236
with CAQDA, 485–86
Secondary groups in collective action, 218–20
Securities and Exchange Commission
investigation by, 45
Seidman, G, 167–68
Seidman, S, 467
Selective disinhibition, 300–2
Self-defeating behaviors, 196
Self-employed professionals, 149
Self-vindicating numbers, 331
Selznick, P, 66
Semantic grammars, 527
Semiperiphery nations, 167, 176
SemNet software, 489
Sequential analysis, 360–61, 488, 520–21
Settlement houses, 350
Sexuality
of angels, 549
perspectives on sociology involving, 464, 467
role attitudes about, 419
selling, 328
and teen drinking, 300
Shakespeare, W, 363
Shallow structures of narrative, 525
Shapeability of social world, 466
Shell Oil Co, 372–73
Shibley, MA, 32
Shils, E, 107
Shocks
global, 169–70
Shorter, E, 374, 376–77
Shweder, RA, 354
Signaling, 209
Silicon Graphics Corp, 68
Similarities, 353–56
in marriage patterns, 399
Simmel, G, 16, 322, 433, 508
Simulations
computer, 197, 283–84
Skills
changes in worker, 146–51
portfolios of, 62
Skocpol, T, 19, 359
Skogan, WG, 234
Slavery, 317, 402
Small firm networks, 61
Small-n studies, 435–36, 548
Smelser, N, 215
Smidt, C, 35, 41
Smith, A, 15
Smith, BA, 494
Smith, T, 46–47
Snider, JG, 346
Snow, DA, 227–28, 277
Sociability, 14
negative side to, 16–17
Social awareness
in Japanese sociology, 503, 506
Social capital, 1–21
and breakdown theories of collective action, 233
of communities and nations, 17–20
defined, 2–6
effects of, 8–14
negative, 14–17
resources obtained through, 5
sources of, 6–8
Social change agents, 272
Social cognition, 247–56

Social conditions
  diagnosing contemporary, 465–66
Social contingency model, 249
Social control, 1–21
Social dilemmas, 183–210
  futures directions in, 208–10
  metaphors of, 185
  modeling, 184–92
  multiple-person, 188–90
  n-person, 198–204
  solving, 192–206
  studying, 207–8
  two-person, 185–88
Socialism
  attempts to salvage, 177
Socialization, 418
Social judgment, 243–45
Social learning solutions, 198
Socially situated cognition, 247–56
Social memory, 105–34
  delimiting the field of, 109–12
  processes of, 122
Social movements
  in collective action, 218–20
  diffusion in, 265–86
  outcomes and consequences, 371–89
  and politics, 336–38
  problems remaining in, 385, 388–89
Social networks
  See Networks
Social psychology, 109
  See also Cognitive social psychology
Social theory
  CAQDA software for building, 490
  dialogue among multiple approaches, 461
  engagement with, 464–65
  enlargement of, 462–64
  in Japanese sociology, 508–10
  reconstruction of, 462–64
  refinement of research programs, 459–61
  synthesis of multiple approaches, 457–59
  taking stock of itself, 453–54
Social ties among German artists and intellectuals, 11
Social traps, 188
Social value orientations solutions, 192–94
Social welfare
  agencies in New York City, 349–50
  dependency on, 13, 30
  provided by network forms of organization, 66
Socioeconomic resources
  in marriage patterns, 398–99, 408–9, 411–12
Sociological publications
  in Japan, 502–5
Sociological theory
  fragmentation and division within, 459
  See also Social theory
Sociology
  contemporary theoretical developments in, 453–70
  dissolution of theories of, 466–67
  economic, 502
  of education, 507
  historical, 105–34
  institutional, 338–39
  in Japan, 499–515
  of knowledge, 105, 130–33
  phenomenological, 329
  political, 346–47
  publications in, 502–5
  relational, 457
  of science, 453–70
  value of narrative to, 517–51
  of work, 154
Sociotechnical design perspectives, 147–49
Software
  marketing, 493
  See also Computer-Assisted Qualitative Data Analysis (CAQDA); individual packages
Solidarity, 216
Solitary lifestyle, 295
Solving social dilemmas, 192–206
  motivational solutions to, 192–95
  strategic solutions to, 192, 195–99
  structural solutions to, 192, 199–206
Sonar Professional software, 485, 487
Sorenson, O, 66
Sorrentino, RM, 241
Soule, SA, 276
Sources and structural mechanisms, 270–76
  external, 271–72
  internal influences, 272–76
South Africa, 219–20, 277
Southern conservative Protestantism, 30–33
Southern Europe
  anti-immigration parties in, 95
South Moluccans in The Netherlands, 79
Spain
  breakdown of Franco regime, 166–67
  Peruvian servants in Barcelona, 78
Spar case
  See Brent Spar oil rig case
Spatial proximity, 275–76
  and violence, 302–4
Spatial regression models, 284
Speech
  analyzing, 542
Spilerman, S, 222–23
Spousal abuse, 39, 306
Spread
  See Diffusion
Spunt, B, 305
SSM survey, 514
SSPS software, 478
Stagnation, periods of
  See B-phase models
Stand-alone hypothesis testing, 491
Standardized performance measures, 333
Standard Metropolitan Statistical Areas (SMSAs), 414
Stanley, L, 485
Stanton-Salazar, RD, 13
Stark, D, 64
Stasiulis, DK, 82
State-dependent learning, 243
Static processes of social memory, 122
Statistical analysis, 430–31
Statist ideologies, 117
Status
  among new minorities, 80–81
  of the diffusion practice, 279–80
  provided by network forms of organization, 64–65
  See also Socioeconomic resources
Status group closure, 396
Steinbrunner, JD, 323
Stepick, A, 17
Stereotyping, 246
  automatic, 257
Stevens, ML, 333
Stinchcombe, A, 68

Stone, C, 485
Stories, 519
  hiding behind, 548
  morphology of, 525
Story grammar, 525
Storytelling, 524–25
  conditions for, 118
Strang, D, 277, 279, 283
Strategic alliances, 59–60
Strategic commensuration, 331
Strategic solutions to social dilemmas, 192, 195–99
Stratification research, 396
Strauss, AL, 479
Strikes
  in France, 216–17, 375
  in Glasgow, 531
  rent, 374
Strong ties
  cohesion through, 273
Structural amnesia, 106
Structural analysis of narrative, 524–28
Structural approach to interpretation, 351–53
Structural equivalence
  and competition, 274–75
Structural function
  similarity of, 355–56
Structural holes, 6, 11
Structuralism, 351–53
Structural mechanisms, 270–76
Structural models, 364–65
Structural solutions
  to social dilemmas, 192, 199–206
Structuration theory, 459, 465
Structure
  finding, 356–61
Stuart, TE, 63–64
Suarez-Orozco, MM, 17
Subcultural identity theory, 49–50
Subjectivity similarity, 353–54
Subjects
  protecting identity of, 485
Subtle prejudice, 83–85
Success in social movements, 382–87
  differential evaluation of, 387
Sucker
  fear of being, 189
Sudman, S, 346
Sullivan, M, 13, 41
Sun Computers Corp, 68
Sung, BL, 412
Superhelper
  magic, 540
Supply side theory, 49
Survey measurement, 33–38
  using multiple measures, 38
Switzerland
  anti-immigration parties in, 94–95
Symbolic interactionism, 460–61, 480
Symbolism
  commemorative, 112
  and ethnic violence, 444–46
  manipulating with CAQDA, 489–91
Syndicates, 60
Synechdoche, 549
Synthesizers of theoretical approaches, 457–59, 468
Systematizing ethnographic methods, 495
Systemic violence, 304

T

Tabletop software, 486–87
Tactics
  See Motivated Tactician
Takeovers, 274
  hostile, 277–78
  warding off, 269
Takeuchi, Y, 508
Tambiah, SJ, 432, 446
Tamil separatists, 433
Tarde, G, 215
Tarrow, S, 377, 383, 386, 431
Taste
  See Cultural taste
Taxes
  collecting, 203
  See also Internal Revenue Service (IRS)
Taylor, FW, 146, 152–53, 325
Taylor, SE, 240, 242
Taylor, SP, 293
Taylorism, 281
  See also Neo-Taylorists
Team ethnography, 496
Technical expertise
  increased salience of, 151
Technobureaucratic professionalism, 149
Technocratic ideology, 153
Technology
  accommodating vs assimilating, 146
  and Japanese sociology, 507
  See also Computers
Telecommuting, 145–46
Temporality, reifying, 134
Tesch, R, 480–82, 485
Testing hypotheses
  CAQDA software for, 490–91
Tetlock, PE, 249–50, 259
Textbooks
  influencing, 48
Text Collector software, 485
Texts
  examining in meaning measurement, 366
  narrative vs non-narrative, 520, 529
  preferred form of ethnographic data, 484
  size of chunks analyzed, 481
Thatcher, M, 94–95, 97, 544
Theory
  See Social theory
Theory-building software, 490
Thinking and feeling
  interplay of, 242–47
Third parties in marriage patterns, 400–2
Third wave literature, 160
Third wave of democratization, 175
Third World
  development in, 20
  revolutionary tendencies in, 172
Thomas, DL, 38
Thomas, RJ, 153
Thraenhardt, D, 81–82, 95–96
Thraenhardt thesis, 95–96
Threat
  felt by housewives, 336
  felt by managers, 151
Three-Mile Island nuclear crisis, 227
Threshold
  models, 284
  points, 189, 200
  processes, 284–85
Thymos quotient, 163
Ties
  relative absence of, 6
Tilly, C, 216–18, 228, 231, 348–50, 355, 377, 385–89, 426–27
Time
  anomalies in, 530
  violence across, 302–4
  See also Temporality
Tit-For-Tat strategy, 196–97, 208, 336

Todorov, T, 521, 533–34
Tolbert, PS, 282
Tomashevski, B, 519–22
Tominaga, K, 513
Tongues
  speaking in, 29–30
Toolan, M, 533
Tool builders among sociologists, 468
Tools
  constructing sociological, 455–57
Totalitarian regimes
  dismantling, 159
Total Quality Management (TQM), 280, 282
Touraine, A, 466
Toxic psychosis, 295
Trade
  See Free trade vs free enterprise
Trade-offs, 315–17, 326
Trade unionism, 168, 275–76, 278
Tradition
  desacralization of, 108
  neglect of, 107
Traditional authority, 151
Traditional Japanese family system, 501, 510
Tragedy
  of the commons, 185, 190–92
  defining, 184
Transaction cost perspective, 65
Transactions
  embedded vs arms-length, 72, 74
Transnational perspectives
  See Globalization
Trends
  See Future directions
Tripartite framework, 302–4
Triple melting pot, 415
Trist, E, 147
Trust, 60–62, 72–73, 187, 208–9, 220
Tucker, A, 185
Turner, BS, 454, 459, 462
Turner, JH, 454
Two-person social dilemmas, 185–88
Two-tier occupational structures, 142

U

Unconscious influences
  by automatic knowledge activation, 257
Unemployment, 13
Uniform Commercial Code (UCC), 355
Unions
  See Trade unionism
United Nations
  defining political refugees, 81
Upskilling, 147–49
Urban riots of the 1960s, 220–23
US Bureau of Alcohol, Tobacco and Firearms (BATF), 236
US Bureau of Justice Statistics, 294
US Bureau of the Census, 406
US Commission on Civil Rights, 98
Use, finding
  in meaning measurement, 366–67
Uunk, 411, 414–15
Uzzi, B, 61, 72

V

Valenzuela, A, 13
Value-added coders, 489–90
van de Kragt, A, 200
van Dijk, T, 532
van Lange, PAM, 192
Veenman, J, 89
Venn diagrams, 488
Ventresca, M, 338
Verdery, K, 177
Vertical integration, 68
Vietnamese community in New Orleans, 9
Vietnam War
  memorial, 127
  memories of, 124
Violence
  and aggression, 299–300
  among adolescents, 300
  collective, 215–36
  defining, 427–30
  and drugs and alcohol, 291–307
  economic compulsive, 304
  effectiveness in protests, 376–79
  political, 427
  systemic, 304
  See also Ethnic violence; Spousal abuse
Vlaams Blok party (Belgium), 92
Volksunie party (Belgium), 92
Volunteering, 225
von Hofmannsthal, H, 106

W

Wacquant, LJD, 13
Waldinger, R, 15
Waldmann, P, 435
Waldrauch, H, 82
Wallace, RA, 454
Wallace, WL, 457
Wallerstein, I, 160, 172, 176
Warburg, A, 106
Warner, RS, 49
Watergate affair, 128
Weak ties
  news through, 273–74
  strength of, 11
Weather
  effect on mood, 244
Weaver, A, 483, 486
Weber, M, 15, 321–22, 396, 424, 442, 508
Weed, FJ, 219
Wegner, DM, 256–57
Weingast, B, 439
Weitzman, EA, 481, 485
Welfare
  See Social welfare
Weller, SC, 361
Wellman, B, 145, 152
Werner, O, 482
Western Europe
  change in, 82–83
  new minorities in, 77–99
West Germany
  economic miracle in, 79
Westphal, JD, 282
Whig history, 118
White, H, 530
White, RW, 435
White CPs
  See Conservative Protestantism (CP)
Whitehead, L, 171
White House Office of National Drug Control Policy, 298
Williamson, O, 58, 62, 65
Wilpert, C, 89–90
Wilson, JQ, 232, 234
Winer, LR, 482
Wish, ED, 297
Wittgenstein, L, 455
Wolfe, T, 363–64
Women
  as homicide offenders, 306
  ordaining, 38–39, 276
  role in society, 398
  shrewish, 536
  See also Motherhood

Women's Movement, 380
Women's Studies
  See Feminist perspectives; Gender
Woodberry, RD, 30
Woodward, SL, 436
Woolcock, M, 20
WordCruncher software, 485
Words
  narratives of, 523
Work
  designing, 147
  socioeconomic homogamy in, 409
  sociology of, 154
  See also Housework; Labor; Professional work; Strikes; Unemployment
Worker participation
  experiments in, 151–52
Workers
  See also Farm workers
  alienating, 148
  autonomy vs managerial control, 151–54
  changes in skill levels, 146–51
  self-employed professionals, 149
Workplace
  computerization of, 141–55
  restructuring, 141
  switching for marriage partner, 404
World Council of Churches, 87
World fairs
  concept of, 124
World polity, 425
World-system cycles, 175–79
Writer as loner, myth of, 359
Wrong, D, 7

Y

Yamagishi, T, 190, 193, 197–98, 206–9
Yamaguchi, K, 283
Yates, FA, 113, 122
Yavapai tribe, 327
Yerushalmi, YH, 110–11, 116
Youth
  See Adolescents
Yugoslavia
  dissolution of, 423, 425, 431, 436

Z

Zaibatsu, 500
Zeal, 7
Zelizer, B, 122
Zelizer, V, 327–28
Zero-sum game metaphor, 197
Zerubavel, E, 123
Zhou, M, 9, 12
Z-scores, 236
Zuboff, S, 148, 151–52
ZyINDEX software, 485–87

CUMULATIVE INDEXES

CONTRIBUTING AUTHORS, VOLUMES 1–24

A

Abbott A, 19:187–209; 21:93–113
Adams J, 13:237–57
Adler PA, 13:217–35
Agger B, 17:105–31
Alderson AS, 19:321–51
Aldous J, 3:105–35
Aldrete-Haas JA, 7:157–75
Aldrich HE, 2:79–105; 16:111–35
Alexander JA, 19:89–112
Alexander KL, 19:401–23
Alford RR, 1:429–79
Allan E, 22:459–87
Allardt E, 15:31–45
Allen WR, 12:277–306
Althauser RP, 15:143–61
Amenta E, 12:131–57
Andorka R, 13:149–64
Aneshensel CS, 18:15–38
Anheier HK, 16:137–59
Anthony D, 5:75–89
Aponte R, 11:231–58
Archer M, 19:17–41
Arditi J, 20:305–29
Astone NM, 12:109–30
Atchley RC, 8:263–87
Atkinson P, 14:441–65
Auerhahn K, 24:291–311

B

Bahr HM, 9:243–64
Bainbridge WS, 20:407–36
Baldassare M, 4:29–56; 18:475–94
Barchas PR, 2:299–333
Barker E, 12:329–46
Barkey K, 17:523–49
Barnett WP, 21:217–36
Baron JN, 10:37–69
Bechhofer F, 11:181–207
Ben-David J, 1:203–22
Ben-Yehuda N, 20:149–71
Berezin M, 23:361–83
Berg I, 4:115–43
Berger J, 6:479–508
Berk RA, 9:375–95
Berk SF, 9:375–95
Bertaux D, 10:215–37
Biddle BJ, 12:67–92
Bielby DD, 18:281–302
Bielby WT, 3:137–61
Billings DB, 20:173–202
Billy JOG, 11:305–28
Birkbeck C, 19:113–37
Blalock HM, 10:353–72
Blau JR, 14:269–92; 19:17–41
Blau PM, 21:1–19
Block F, 7:1–27
Blumstein P, 14:467–90
Boli-Bennett J, 1:223–46
Bollen KA, 19:321–51
Bonacich P, 4:145–70
Boocock SS, 4:1–28
Boorman SA, 6:213–34
Boruch RF, 4:511–32
Bottomore T, 1:191–202
Bourque LB, 21:447–77
Bradach JL, 15:97–118
Braithwaite J, 11:1–25
Branch K, 10:141–66
Braungart MM, 12:205–32
Braungart RG, 12:205–32
Breiger RL, 21:115–36
Brenner J, 15:381–404
Brent EE, 20:407–36
Brinkerhoff D, 7:321–49
Brint S, 11:389–414
Brooks C, 21:137–62
Brubaker R, 24:423–52
Bucholz KK, 15:163–86
Burris BH, 24:141–57
Burstein P, 7:291–319; 17:327–50
Burt RS, 6:79–141
Buttel FH, 13:465–88

C

Calavita K, 23:19–38
Calhoun C, 19:211–39
Camic C, 24:453–76
Campbell JL, 19:163–85
Canak W, 7:225–48
Caplow T, 9:243–64
Carley KM, 20:407–36
Carroll GR, 10:71–93; 21:217–36
Catton WR Jr, 5:243–73
Centeno MA, 20:125–47
Cerulo KA, 23:385–409
Chadwick BA, 9:243–64
Chafetz JS, 23:97–120
Charng H-W, 16:27–65
Chase ID, 17:133–54
Chase-Dunn C, 1:223–46; 21:387–417
Cheng L, 9:471–98
Cherlin AJ, 9:51–66; 20:359–81
Chirot D, 8:81–106
Choldin HM, 4:91–113
Cicourel AV, 7:87–106
Clark TN, 1:271–95; 11:437–55
Clarke L, 19:375–99
Clayman SE, 17:385–418
Cohen E, 10:373–92
Cohen EG, 8:209–35
Collins C, 21:349–86
Collins HM, 9:265–85
Conrad P, 18:209–32
Cook KS, 9:217–41; 18:109–27
Corcoran M, 21:237–67
Cornfield DB, 17:27–49
Corsaro WA, 16:197–220
Coser LA, 2:145–60; 19:1–15
Crenshaw EM, 17:467–501
Crittenden KS, 9:425–46
Croteau D, 18:373–93
Cunnigen D, 7:177–98

D

Dauber K, 15:73–96
Davis DE, 18:395–417
DeLamater J, 7:263–90
Demerath NJ III, 2:19–33

Demo DH, 18:303–26
DeVault ML, 22:29–50
Dillman DA, 17:225–49
DiMaggio P, 23:263–87
DiMaggio PJ, 16:137–59
Dimitrova D, 22:213–38
DiPrete TA, 20:331–57
DiRenzo GJ, 3:261–95
Dobratz BA, 8:289–317
Dobson RB, 3:297–329
Dohan D, 24:477–98
Dornbusch SM, 15:233–59
Duncan CM, 16:67–86
Duncan GJ, 15:261–89
Dunlap RE, 5:243–73
Dunn D, 14:227–48
Dynes RR, 3:23–49

E

Eccles RG, 15:97–118
Eckberg DL, 6:1–20
Edelman LB, 23:479–515
Eder D, 16:197–220
Eitzen DS, 17:503–522
Elder GH Jr, 1:165–90
Elder JW, 2:209–30
Elliott B, 11:181–207
Emerson RM, 2:335–62; 7:351–78
England P, 14:227–48
Entwisle B, 19:321–51
Entwisle DR, 19:401–23
Erickson ML, 1:21–42
Eschbach K, 21:419–46
Espeland WN, 24:313–43
Espenshade TJ, 21:195–216
Esping-Andersen G, 18:187–208
Estes SB, 23:289–313
Evans PB, 7:199–223

F

Fantasia R, 21:269–87
Farley R, 12:277–306
Feagin JR, 6:1–20
Featherman DL, 4:373–420
Felson RB, 22:103–28
Fennell ML, 12:255–75; 19:89–112; 23:215–31
Fine GA, 10:239–62; 19:61–87
Fischer CS, 1:67–89
Fisher GA, 11:129–49
Fishman JA, 11:113–27
Flache A, 21:73–91
Flacks R, 4:193–238
Fligstein N, 15:73–96; 21:21–43
Foley DL, 6:457–78
Fonda S, 18:419–48
Foner A, 5:219–42
Fontana A, 13:217–35
Form W, 5:1–25; 13:29–47
Forristal JD, 20:331–57
Fox MF, 21:45–71
Fox RC, 2:231–68
Frank AW III, 5:167–91
Franzosi R, 24:517–54
Freeland R, 21:21–43
Freese L, 6:187–212
Freidson E, 10:1–20
Freudenburg WR, 12:451–78
Frey JH, 17:503–22
Friedland R, 1:429–79; 10:393–416
Friedman LM, 15:17–29
Frisbie WP, 3:79–104
Fuguitt GV, 11:259–80
Furstenberg FF Jr, 16:379–403; 20:359–81

G

Gagliani G, 13:313–34
Galaskiewicz J, 4:455–84; 11:281–304
Galtz N, 22:437–58
Gamson WA, 18:373–93
Ganzeboom HBG, 17:277–302
Garrison HH, 8:237–62
Garton L, 22:213–38
Gartrell CD, 13:49–66
Gecas V, 8:1–33; 15:291–316
Gelles RJ, 11:347–67
George LK, 19:353–73
Gereffi G, 18:419–48
Gerstein D, 11:369–87
Ghazalla I, 12:373–99
Gibbs JP, 1:21–42
Giele JZ, 5:275–302
Giugni MG, 24:371–93
Glasberg DS, 9:311–32
Glass JL, 23:289–313
Glenn ND, 3:79–104
Goldstein MS, 5:381–409
Goldstone JA, 8:187–207
Goode E, 20:149–71
Gordon C, 2:405–33
Gordon G, 1:339–61
Gortmaker SL, 23:147–70
Gottfredson MR, 7:107–28
Gray LN, 16:405–33
Greeley AM, 5:91–111
Greenfeld L, 14:99–123
Grimes P, 21:387–417
Griswold W, 19:455–67
Grob DB, 22:377–99
Gross N, 24:453–76
Groves RM, 16:221–40
Guillemard A-M, 19:469–503
Gulia M, 22:213–38
Gusfield JR, 10:417–35

H

Hagan J, 12:431–49
Haggerty T, 17:205–24
Hall JR, 16:329–51
Hall TD, 8:81–106
Hallinan MT, 14:249–68
Hannan MT, 5:303–28
Hare AP, 5:329–50
Hareven TK, 20:437–61
Harris AR, 8:161–86
Hasenfeld Y, 13:387–415
Haug MR, 3:51–77
Hauser RM, 3:137–61
Hawley AH, 18:1–14
Haythornthwaite C, 22:213–38
Hechter M, 23:191–214
Heer DM, 11:27–47
Hegtvedt KA, 9:217–41
Heilman SC, 8:135–60
Heimer CA, 14:491–519
Hein J, 19:43–59
Heise DR, 20:407–36
Henshel RL, 8:57–79
Hermassi E, 4:239–57
Hernandez DJ, 12:159–80
Hickson DJ, 13:165–92
Hill GD, 8:161–86
Hindelang MJ, 7:107–28
Hirschman C, 9:397–423; 20:203–33
Hogan DP, 12:109–30
Holden KC, 17:51–78
Hollander P, 8:319–51
Holz JR, 5:193–217
Homans GC, 12:xiii–xxx
Horwitz AV, 10:95–119
House JS, 14:293–318
Hout M, 21:137–62
Hoynes W, 18:373–93

I

Ihinger-Tallman M, 14:25–48

J

Jacobs JA, 22:153–85

Janson C-G, 6:433–56
Jaret C, 9:499–525
Jenkins JC, 9:527–53; 18:161–85
John D, 22:299–322
Johnson MP, 2:161–207
Jones RA, 9:447–69
Juster SM, 13:193–216

K

Kalleberg AL, 5:351–79; 14:203–25
Kalmijn M, 24:395–421
Kalton G, 12:401–29
Kanazawa S, 23:191–214
Kandel DB, 6:235–85
Kanter RM, 2:269–98; 7:321–49
Kariya T, 16:263–99
Kasarda JD, 11:305–28; 17:467–501
Katz AH, 7:129–55
Keating KM, 14:149–72
Kennedy MD, 22:437–58
Kerckhoff AC, 21:323–47
Kertzer DI, 9:125–49; 17:155–79
Kiecolt KJ, 14:381–403
Kimeldorf H, 18:495–517
Kluegel JR, 7:29–56
Knoke D, 12:1–21
Kohli M, 10:215–37
Kollock P, 14:467–90; 24:183–214
Kolosi T, 14:405–19
Komarovsky M, 17:1–25
Kourvetaris GA, 8:289–317
Kozloff MA, 4:317–43
Krecker ML, 16:241–62
Kreps GA, 10:309–30
Kuklick H, 9:287–310
Kurz K, 13:417–42

L

Lachmann R, 15:47–72
LaFree G, 19:113–37
Laitin DD, 24:423–52
Lammers CJ, 4:485–510
Land KC, 9:1–26
Landis KR, 14:293–318
Laslett B, 15:381–404
Laub JH, 18:63–84
Laumann EO, 4:455–84
Lehrer E, 12:181–204
Leicht KT, 23:215–31
Leifer EM, 12:233–53
Lenski G, 20:1–24
Lever H, 7:249–62
Levine S, 4:317–43
Levitt B, 14:319–40
Levitt PR, 6:213–34
Lewis GF, 2:35–53
Lichter DT, 23:121–45
Lie J, 23:341–60
Light J, 4:145–70
Lincoln JR, 13:289–312
Lipman-Blumen J, 1:297–337
Lipset SM, 22:1–27
Liska AE, 13:67–88; 23:39–61
Lo CYH, 8:107–34
Long JS, 21:45–71
Longshore D, 11:75–91
Lubeck PM, 18:519–40
Lumsden CJ, 16:161–95
Luschen G, 6:315–47
Lye DN, 22:79–102

M

Machalek R, 10:167–90
Machlis GE, 14:149–72
Macke AS, 4:57–90
Macy MW, 20:407–36; 21:73–91
Maddox GL, 5:113–35
Maier T, 16:263–99
Maines DR, 3:235–59
Manza J, 21:137–62
March JG, 14:319–40
Mare RD, 18:327–50
Marini MM, 15:343–80
Markovsky B, 20:407–36
Marks C, 17:445–66
Marsden PV, 4:455–84; 16:435–63
Martindale D, 2:121–43
Marx GT, 1:363–428
Massey DS, 7:57–85
Matras J, 6:401–31
Matthews R, 22:401–35
Mauss AL, 10:437–60
Mayer KU, 15:187–209; 23:233–61
Maynard DW, 17:385–418
McBride K, 13:289–312
McCall GJ, 10:263–82
McEwen CA, 6:143–85
McFalls JA Jr, 16:491–519
McLanahan S, 13:237–57
McMahon AM, 10:121–40
McNicoll G, 18:85–108
McPhail C, 9:579–600
McQuail D, 11:93–111
Mechanic D, 1:43–65; 16:301–27; 22:239–70
Meier RF, 8:35–55
Menaghan EG, 17:419–44
Merton RK, 13:1–28
Meyer JW, 1:223–46; 6:369–99; 10:461–82
Michalowicz J, 10:417–35
Miller J, 8:237–62
Mirowsky J, 12:23–45
Mizruchi MS, 22:271–98
Model S, 14:363–80
Modell J, 17:205–224
Moen P, 18:233–51
Mohr JW, 24:345–70
Morgan DL, 22:129–52
Morgan SP, 22:351–75
Morse EV, 1:339–61
Mortimer JT, 4:421–54
Moseley KP, 4:259–90
Moskos CC Jr, 2:55–77
Mukerji C, 12:47–66
Muller W, 13:417–42
Munger F, 22:187–212
Myles J, 20:103–24

N

Nakao K, 24:499–516
Nathanson CA, 10:191–213
Nee V, 22:401–36
Nerlove M, 12:181–204
Nettler G, 5:27–52
Newby H, 9:67–81
Nielsen F, 20:267–303
Niemi RG, 3:209–33

O

Oberschall A, 4:291–315; 12:233–53
Olick JK, 24:105–40
Oliver PE, 19:271–300
Olzak S, 9:355–74; 15:119–41
Oppenheimer VK, 23:431–53
O'Rand AM, 16:241–62
Orbuch TL, 23:455–78
Orloff A, 22:51–78
Ouchi WG, 11:457–83

P

Page KL, 24:57–76
Palloni A, 12:431–49
Palmer D, 10:393–416
Pampel FC, 21:163–94

Parikh S, 17:523–49
Parish WL Jr, 3:179–207
Parker RN, 24:291–311
Patterson O, 3:407–49
Peattie L, 7:157–75
Pedraza S, 17:303–25
Pepinsky HE, 12:93–108
Peters ME, 21:163–94
Petersen T, 19:425–54
Petersen W, 4:533–75
Peterson RA, 5:137–66
Pettigrew TF, 11:329–46; 24:77–103
Pfeffer J, 2:79–105
Pichardo NA, 23:411–30
Piliavin JA, 16:27–65
Podolny J, 24:57–76
Pontell HN, 23:19–38
Porter JR, 5:53–74; 19:139–61
Portes A, 7:225–48; 13:359–85; 24:1–24
Prager J, 11:75–91
Preston SH, 3:163–78

Q

Quadagno J, 13:109–28
Quarantelli EL, 3:23–49

R

Rabow J, 9:555–78
Rafferty JA, 13:387–415
Ramirez FO, 6:369–99
Rein M, 19:469–503
Reskin B, 19:241–70
Riecken HW, 4:511–32
Riesman D, 14:1–24
Riley JW Jr, 9:191–216
Riley MW, 16:1–25
Risman B, 14:125–47
Ritchey PN, 2:363–404
Robbins J, 24:105–40
Robbins T, 5:75–89
Roberts BR, 16:353–77
Robins LN, 15:163–86
Rochefort DA, 16:301–27; 22:239–70
Romanelli E, 17:79–103
Roof WC, 2:19–33
Rosa EA, 14:149–72
Rosenbaum JE, 16:263–99
Rosenfeld RA, 18:39–61
Rosenholtz SJ, 6:479–508
Ross CE, 12:23–45
Ross HL, 10:21–35
Rossi PH, 10:331–52; 18:129–60
Rothschild J, 12:307–28
Roy WG, 10:483–506
Rumbaut RG, 17:351–83
Russell R, 12:307–28

S

Sabagh G, 12:373–99
Salaff J, 22:213–38
Sampson RJ, 18:63–84
Sánchez-Jankowski M, 24:477–98
Sanders IT, 2:35–53
Sassen S, 16:465–90
Sasson T, 18:373–93
Savage M, 5:329–50
Scheff TJ, 9:333–54
Scheppele KL, 20:383–406
Schneider JW, 11:209–29
Schock K, 18:161–85
Schoen R, 14:341–61
Schoenberg R, 15:425–40
Schoepflin U, 15:187–209
Schooler C, 22:323–49
Schudson M, 12:47–66
Schuessler KF, 11:129–49
Schuman H, 2:161–207
Schwartz M, 9:311–32
Schwartz P, 14:125–47
Schwartz RD, 4:577–601
Schwartzman KC, 24:159–81
Schwarz N, 24:239–64
Schwirian KP, 9:83–102
Sciulli D, 11:369–87
Scott J, 17:181–203
Scott SL, 20:173–202
Scott WR, 1:1–20
Seeman M, 1:91–123
Segal DR, 9:151–70
Segal MW, 9:151–70
Seltzer J, 20:235–66
Seron C, 22:187–212
Settersten R, 16:263–99
Settersten RA, 23:233–61
Sewell WH, 15:1–16
Shalin DN, 4:171–91
Shapin S, 21:289–321
Shelton BA, 22:299–322
Shepard JM, 3:1–21
Shlay AB, 18:129–60
Short JF, 19:375–99
Simmons RG, 4:421–54
Simpson M, 6:287–313
Simpson RL, 11:415–36
Singer JD, 6:349–67
Singh JV, 16:161–95
Skocpol T, 12:131–57
Skvoretz J, 20:407–36
Sloane D, 22:351–75
Smith CS, 24:25–56
Smith DH, 1:247–70
Smith ER, 7:29–56
Smith KR, 15:261–89
Smith V, 23:315–39
Smock PJ, 17:51–78
Sniderman PM, 22:377–99
Snipp CM, 18:351–71
Snow DA, 10:167–90
So A, 9:471–98
Sobieszek BI, 3:209–33
Sorensen A, 20:27–47
Sorensen AB, 4:345–71; 5:351–79
Soule SA, 24:265–89
Spates JL, 9:27–49
Spenner KI, 4:373–420; 14:69–97
Spitzer S, 9:103–24
Steffensmeier D, 22:459–87
Stepan-Norris J, 18:495–517
Stevens ML, 24:313–43
Stewman S, 14:173–202
Stinchcombe AL, 23:1–18
Strang D, 24:265–89
Stryker S, 4:57–90
Suchman MC, 23:479–515
Sudman S, 2:107–20; 12:401–29
Sullivan TA, 1:203–22
Summers GF, 10:141–66; 12:347–71
Suttles GD, 2:1–18
Swedberg R, 17:251–76
Sweet JA, 3:363–405
Swidler A, 20:305–29

T

Tallman I, 16:405–33
Tarrow S, 14:421–40
Thoits PA, 15:317–42
Thomas GM, 10:461–82
Tickamyer AR, 1:297–337; 16:67–86
Tillman R, 23:19–38
Treas J, 13:259–88
Treiman DJ, 17:277–302
Truelove C, 13:359–85
Tuma NB, 5:303–28
Turegun A, 20:103–24
Turkel G, 4:193–238
Turner RH, 16:87–110
Tyler WB, 11:49–73

U

Uhlenberg P, 18:449–74
Ultee WC, 17:277–302

Umberson D, 14:293–318
Useem B, 24:215–38
Useem M, 6:41–78

V

van Kersbergen K, 18:187–208
Vega WA, 17:351–83
Vinovskis MA, 4:603–27; 13:193–216
Vogel EF, 3:179–207

W

Walaszek Z, 3:331–62
Walder AG, 15:405–24
Waldinger R, 15:211–32; 16:111–35
Walker HA, 12:255–75
Wallerstein I, 4:259–90
Walton J, 13:89–108; 19:301–20
Washington RE, 5:53–74; 19:138–61
Waters MC, 21:419–46
Wegener B, 18:253–80
Wellman B, 22:213–38
Wethington E, 18:233–51
Whetten DA, 13:335–58
White L, 20:81–102
Whitmeyer JM, 18:109–27
Whyte MK, 3:179–207
Wilkins AL, 11:457–83
Williams DR, 21:349–86
Williams RM Jr, 1:125–64; 20:49–79
Willie CV, 7:177–98
Wilson FD, 10:283–307
Wilson J, 6:21–40
Wilson WJ, 11:231–58
Winship C, 18:327–50
Wise PH, 23:147–70
Witten M, 14:49–67
Wohlstein RT, 9:579–600
Wood JL, 1:363–428
Woodberry RD, 24:25–56
Wright CR, 5:193–217
Wright JD, 10:331–52
Wuthnow R, 14:49–67

Y

Yago G, 9:171–90
Yinger JM, 11:151–80

Z

Zablocki BD, 2:269–98
Zald MN, 4:115–43; 13:387–415
Zelditch M Jr, 6:479–508
Zhou M, 23:63–95
Zucker LG, 13:443–64
Zukin S, 13:129–47
Zussman R, 23:171–89

CHAPTER TITLES, VOLUMES 1–24

PREFATORY CHAPTERS

Title	Author(s)	Volume:Pages
Fifty Years of Sociology	GC Homans	12:xiii–xxx
Three Fragments from a Sociologist's Notebooks: Establishing the Phenomenon, Specified Ignorance, and Strategic Research Materials	RK Merton	13:1–28
On Discovering and Teaching Sociology: A Memoir	D Riesman	14:1–24
Some Reflections on the Golden Age of Interdisciplinary Social Psychology	WH Sewell	15:1–16
The Influence of Sociological Lives: Personal Reflections	MW Riley	16:1–25
Some Reflections on the Feminist Scholarship in Sociology	M Komarovsky	17:1–25
The Logic of Macrosociology	AH Hawley	18:1–14
A Sociologist's Atypical Life	LA Coser	19:1–15
Societal Taxonomies: Mapping the Social Universe	G Lenski	20:1–26
A Circuitous Path to Macrostructural Theory	PM Blau	21:1–19
A Biographical Essay on Judith Blake's Professional Career and Scholarship	LB Bourque	21:447–77
Steady Work: An Academic Memoir	SM Lipset	22:1–27
On the Virtues of the Old Institutionalism	AL Stinchcombe	23:1–18
Social Capital: Its Origins and Applications in Modern Sociology	A Portes	24:1–24

THEORY AND METHODS

Title	Author(s)	Volume:Pages
Competing Paradigms in Macrosociology	T Bottomore	1:191–202
Sample Surveys	S Sudman	2:107–20
Attitudes and Behavior	H Schuman, MP Johnson	2:161–207
Comparative Cross-National Methodology	JW Elder	2:209–30
Measurement in Social Stratification	MR Haug	3:51–77
Trend Studies with Survey Sample and Census Data	ND Glenn, WP Frisbie	3:79–104
Structural Equation Models	WT Bielby, RM Hauser	3:137–61
Laboratory Experimentation in Sociology	P Bonacich, J Light	4:145–70
Radical Sociology: The Emergence of Neo-Marxian Perspectives in US Sociology	R Flacks, G Turkel	4:193–238
Mathematical Models in Sociology	AB Sorensen	4:345–71
Environmental Sociology	RE Dunlap, WR Catton Jr.	5:243–73
Methods for Temporal Analysis	MT Hannan, NB Tuma	5:303–28
Models of Network Structure	RS Burt	6:79–141
Formal Theorizing	L Freese	6:187–212
The Comparative Evolutionary Biology of Social Behavior	SA Boorman, PR Levitt	} :213–34
Observational Field Work	RM Emerson	7:351–78

World-System Theory	D Chirot, TD Hall	8:81–106
Social Indicators	KC Land	9:1–26
Marxist Perspectives in the Sociology of Law	S Spitzer	9:103–24
Middletown, Ill: Problems of Replication, Longitudinal Measurement, and Triangulation	HM Bahr, T Caplow, BA Chadwick	9:243–64
The Sociology of Knowledge: Retrospect and Prospect	H Kuklick	9:287–310
The Two Social Psychologies: Postcrises Directions	AM McMahon	10:121–40
The Life Story Approach: A Continental View	D Bertaux, M Kohli	10:215–37
Systematic Field Observation	GJ McCall	10:263–82
Evaluation Research: An Assessment	PH Rossi, JD Wright	10:331–52
Contextual-Effects Models: Theoretical and Methodological Issues	HM Blalock	10:353–72
Social Problems Theory: The Constructionist View	JW Schneider	11:209–29
Social Theory and Talcott Parsons in the 1980s	D Sciulli, D Gerstein	11:369–87
Efficiency and Social Institutions: Uses and Misuses of Economic Reasoning in Sociology	A Oberschall, EM Leifer	12:233–53
New Developments in the Sampling of Special Populations	S Sudman, G Kalton	12:401–29
Time Budgets and Their Uses	R Andorka	13:149–64
New Directions in Environmental Sociology	FH Buttel	13:465–88
Practical Uses of Multistate Population Models	R Schoen	14:341–61
Ethnomethodology: A Criticial Review	P Atkinson	14:441–65
Covariance Structure Models	R Schoenberg	15:425–40
Theories and Methods of Telephone Surveys	RM Groves	16:221–40
Concepts of the Life Cycle: Their History, Meanings, and Uses in the Social Sciences	AM O'Rand, ML Krecker	16:241–62
Epistemology and Sociohistorical Inquiry	JR Hall	16:329–51
Network Data and Measurement	PV Marsden	16:435–63
Critical Theory, Poststructuralism, Postmodernism: Their Sociological Relevance	B Agger	17:105–31
Vacancy Chains	ID Chase	17:133–54
The Design and Administration of Mail Surveys	DA Dillman	17:225–49
The Diversity of Ethnomethodology	DW Maynard, SE Clayman	17:385–418
Two Approaches to Social Structure: Exchange Theory and Network Analysis	KS Cook, JM Whitmeyer	18:109–27
Models for Sample Selection Bias	C Winship, RD Mare	18:327–50
The Sad Demise, Mysterious Disappearance, and Glorious Triumph of Symbolic Interactionism	GA Fine	19:61–87
Macrocomparative Research Methods	KA Bollen, B Entwisle, AS Alderson	19:321–51
Recent Advances in Longitudinal Methodology	T Petersen	19:425–54
Sociobiology and Sociology	F Nielsen	20:267–303
The New Sociology of Knowledge	A Swidler, J Arditi	20:305–29
Multilevel Models: Methods and Substance	TA DiPrete, JD Forristal	20:331–57
Legal Theory and Social Theory	KL Scheppele	20:383–406
Artificial Social Intelligence	WS Bainbridge, EE Brent, KM Carley, DR Heise, MW Macy, B Markovsky, J Skvoretz	20:407–36

Beyond Rationality in Models of Choice	MW Macy, A Flache	21:73–91
Sequence Analysis: New Methods for Old Ideas	A Abbott	21:93–113
Talking Back to Sociology: Distinctive Contributions of Feminist Methodology	ML DeVault	22:29–50
Focus Groups	DL Morgan	22:129–52
An Introduction to Categorical Data Analysis	D Sloane, SP Morgan	22:351–75
Innovations in Experimental Design in Attitude Surveys	PM Sniderman, DB Grob	22:377–99
Feminist Theory and Sociology: Underutilized Contributions for Mainstream Theory	JS Chafetz	23:97–120
Sociological Rational Choice Theory	M Hechter, S Kanazawa	23:191–214
People's Accounts Count: The Sociology of Accounts	TL Orbuch	23:455–78
Diffusion in Organizations and Social Movements: From Hybrid Corn to Poison Pills	D Strang, SA Soule	24:265–89
Commensuration as a Social Process	WN Espeland, ML Stevens	24:313–43
Measuring Meaning Structures	JW Mohr	24:345–70
Contemporary Developments in Sociological Theory: Current Projects and Conditions of Possibility	C Camic, N Gross	24:453–76
Using Computers To Analyze Ethnographic Field Data: Theoretical and Practical Considerations	D Dohan, M Sánchez-Jankowski	24:477–98
Narrative Analysis–or Why (and How) Sociologists Should be Interested in Narrative	R Franzosi	24:517–54

SOCIAL PROCESSES

Convergence and Divergence in Development	JW Meyer, J Boli-Bennett, C Chase-Dunn	1:223–46
Voluntary Action and Voluntary Groups	DH Smith	1:247–70
Strands of Theory and Research in Collective Behavior	GT Marx, JL Wood	1:363–428
Social Exchange Theory	RM Emerson	2:335–62
Response to Social Crisis and Disaster	EL Quarantelli, RR Dynes	3:23–49
Social Organization and Social Structure in Symbolic Interactionist Thought	DR Maines	3:235–59
Theories of Social Conflict	A Oberschall	4:291–315
Sociology of Contemporary Religious Movements	T Robbins, D Anthony	5:75–89
Sociology of Mass Communications	JR Holz, CR Wright	5:193–217
Status Organizing Processes	J Berger, SJ Rosenholtz, M Zelditch Jr.	6:479–508
The Role of Cognitive-Linguistic Concepts in Understanding Everyday Social Interactions	AV Cicourel	7:87–106
Sociological Aspects of Criminal Victimization	MR Gottfredson, MJ Hindelang	7:107–28
Self-Help and Mutual Aid: An Emerging Social Movement?	AH Katz	7:129–55
Countermovements and Conservative Movements in the Contemporary U.S.	CYH Lo	8:107–34
Expectation States and Interracial Interaction in School Settings	EG Cohen	8:209–35

Distributive Justice, Equity, and Equality	KS Cook, KA Hegtvedt	9:217–41
Contemporary Ethnic Mobilization	S Olzak	9:355–74
Resource Mobilization Theory and the Study of Social Movements	JC Jenkins	9:527–53
Individual and Collective Behaviors within Gatherings, Demonstrations, and Riots	C McPhail, RT Wohlstein	9:579–600
Sociological Inquiry and Disaster Research	GA Kreps	10:309–30
Class Conflict and Social Change in Historical Perspective	WG Roy	10:483–506
Sociology of Mass Communication	D McQuail	11:93–111
Associations and Interest Groups	D Knoke	12:1–21
Efficiency and Social Institutions: Uses and Misuses of Economic Reasoning in Sociology	A Oberschall, EM Leifer	12:233–53
Religious Movements: Cult and Anticult Since Jonestown	E Barker	12:329–46
Theory and Research on Industrialization	J Walton	13:89–108
Analysis of Events in the Study of Collective Action	S Olzak	15:119–41
The State and the Life Course	KU Mayer, U Schoepflin	15:187–209
Role Change	RH Turner	16:87–110
Deinstitutionalization: An Appraisal of Reform	D Mechanic, DA Rochefort	16:301–27
Choices, Decisions, and Problem-Solving	I Tallman, LN Gray	16:405–33
The Economic Costs of Marital Dissolution: Why Do Women Bear a Disproportionate Cost?	KC Holden, PJ Smock	17:51–78
Medicalization and Social Control	P Conrad	18:209–32
The Concept of Family Adaptive Strategies	P Moen, E Wethington	18:233–51
Commitment To Work and Family	DD Bielby	18:281–302
Formal Models of Collective Action	PE Oliver	19:271–300
Sociological Perspectives on Life Transitions	LK George	19:353–73
Entry into School: The Beginning School Transition and Educational Stratification in the United States	DR Entwisle, KL Alexander	19:401–23
Comparative Patterns of Retirement: Recent Trends in Developed Societies	A-M Guillemard, M Rein	19:469–503
The Sociology of Ethnic Conflicts: Comparative International Perspectives	RM Williams Jr.	20:49–79
Coresidence and Leaving Home: Young Adults and Their Parents	L White	20:81–102
Moral Panics: Culture, Politics, and Social Construction	E Goode, N Ben-Yehuda	20:149–71
Why Fertility Changes	C Hirschman	20:203–33
The Division of Household Labor	BA Shelton, D John	22:299–322
Modeling the Relationships Between Macro Forms of Social Control	AE Liska	23:39–61
New Forms of Work Organization	V Smith	23:315–39
New Social Movements: A Critical Review	NA Pichardo	23:411–30
Breakdown Theories of Collective Action	B Useem	24:215–38
Warmer and More Social: Recent Developments in Cognitive Social Psychology	N Schwarz	24:239–64
Was It Worth the Effort? The Outcomes and Consequences of Social Movements	MG Giugni	24:371–93

INSTITUTIONS AND CULTURE

The Comparative Study of Health Care Delivery Systems	D Mechanic	1:43–65
Sociology of Science	J Ben-David, TA Sullivan	1:203–22
Religion–Recent Strands in Research	NJ Demerath III, WC Roof	2:19–33
The Military	CC Moskos Jr.	2:55–77
Advanced Medical Technology–Social and Ethical Implications	RC Fox	2:231–68
Family Interaction Patterns	J Aldous	3:105–35
Slavery	O Patterson	3:407–49
The Social Organization of the Classroom	SS Boocock	4:1–28
Status Inconsistency and Role Conflict	S Stryker, AS Macke	4:57–90
Moral Order and Sociology of Law: Trends, Problems, and Prospects	RD Schwartz	4:577–601
Criminal Justice	G Nettler	5:27–52
Sociology of American Catholics	AM Greeley	5:91–111
Revitalizing the Culture Concept	RA Peterson	5:137–66
The Sociology of Mental Health and Illness	MS Goldstein	5:381–409
Sociology of Leisure	J Wilson	6:21–40
Sociology of Sport: Development, Present State, and Prospects	G Luschen	6:315–47
Comparative Education: The Social Construction of the Modern World System	FO Ramirez, JW Meyer	6:369–99
Black Students in Higher Education: A Review of Studies, 1965–1980	CV Willie, D Cunnigen	7:177–98
Retirement as a Social Institution	RC Atchley	8:263–87
The Sociology of Values	JL Spates	9:27–49
Changing Family and Household: Contemporary Lessons from Historical Research	A Cherlin	9:51–66
Change in Military Organization	DR Segal, MW Segal	9:151–70
Supply-Side Sociology of the Family: The Challenge of the New Home Economics	RA Berk, SF Berk	9:375–95
The Changing Nature of Professional Control	E Freidson	10:1–20
Social Control Through Deterrence: Drinking-and-Driving Laws	HL Ross	10:21–35
The Sociology of Tourism: Approaches, Issues, and Findings	E Cohen	10:373–92
Secular Symbolism: Studies of Ritual, Ceremony, and the Symbolic Order in Modern Life	JR Gusfield, J Michalowicz	10:417–35
Sociological Perspectives on the Mormon Subculture	AL Mauss	10:437–60
The Impact of School Desegregation: A Situational Analysis	D Longshore, J Prager	11:75–91
Macrosociolinguistics and the Sociology of Language in the Early Eighties	JA Fishman	11:113–27
Popular Culture	C Mukerji, M Schudson	12:47–66
A Sociology of Justice	HE Pepinsky	12:93–108
Toward a Structural Criminology: Method and Theory in Criminological Research	J Hagan, A Palloni	12:431–49
Network Approaches to Social Evaluation	CD Gartrell	13:49–66
Research on Stepfamilies	M Ihinger-Tallman	14:25–48

New Directions in the Study of Culture	R Wuthnow, M Witten	14:49–67
Study of the Arts: A Reappraisal	JR Blau	14:269–92
Litigation and Society	LM Friedman	15:17–29
Children's Peer Cultures	WA Corsaro, D Eder	16:197–220
Divorce and the American Family	FF Furstenberg Jr.	16:379–403
The Social Impact of War	J Modell, T Haggerty	17:205–24
Ethnic Minorities and Mental Health	WA Vega, RG Rumbaut	17:351–83
Sport and Society	JH Frey, DS Eitzen	17:503–22
Social Organization and Risk: Some Current Controversies	L Clarke, JF Short Jr.	19:375–99
Recent Moves in the Sociology of Literature	W Griswold	19:455–67
Here and Everywhere: Sociology of Scientific Knowledge	S Shapin	21:289–321
Comparative Medical Systems	D Mechanic, DA Rochefort	22:239–70
Cultural and Social-Structural Explanations of Cross-National Psychological Differences	C Schooler	22:323–49
Culture and Cognition	P DiMaggio	23:263–87
The Family Responsive Workplace	JL Glass, SB Estes	23:289–313
Fundamentalism Et Al: Conservative Protestants in America	RD Woodberry, CS Smith	24:25–56

FORMAL ORGANIZATIONS

Organizational Structure	WR Scott	1:1–20
Environments of Organizations	HE Aldrich, J Pfeffer	2:79–105
Technology, Alienation, and Job Satisfaction	JM Shepard	3:1–21
The Comparative Sociology of Organizations	CJ Lammers	4:485–510
Corporations and the Corporate Elite	M Useem	6:41–77
Continuities in the Study of Total and Nontotal Institutions	CA McEwen	6:143–85
Recent Research on Multinational Corporations	PB Evans	7:199–223
Organizational Performance: Recent Developments in Measurement	RM Kanter, D Brinkerhoff	7:321–49
Ownership and Control of Corporations	DS Glasberg, M Schwartz	9:311–32
Organizational Perspectives on Stratification	JN Baron	10:37–69
Organizational Ecology	GR Carroll	10:71–93
Negotiated Orders and Organizational Cultures	GA Fine	10:239–62
White Collar Crime	J Braithwaite	11:1–25
The Organizational Structure of the School	WB Tyler	11:49–73
Interorganizational Relations	J Galaskiewicz	11:281–304
Organizational Culture	WG Ouchi, AL Wilkins	11:457–83
Associations and Interest Groups	D Knoke	12:1–21
Gender Differences in Role Differentiation and Organizational Task Performance	HA Walker, ML Fennell	12:255–75
Alternatives to Bureaucracy: Democratic Participation in the Economy	J Rothschild, R Russell	12:307–28
Decision-Making at the Top of Organizations	DJ Hickson	13:165–92
Japanese Industrial Organization in Comparative Perspective	JR Lincoln, K McBride	13:289–312
Organizational Growth and Decline Processes	DA Whetten	13:335–58
Institutional Theories of Organization	LG Zucker	13:443–64
Organizational Demography	S Stewman	14:173–202
Organizational Learning	B Levitt, JG March	14:319–40

Structural Change in Corporate Organization	N Fligstein, K Dauber	15:73–96
Price, Authority, and Trust: From Ideal Types to Plural Forms	JL Bradach, RG Eccles	15:97–118
Internal Labor Markets	RP Althauser	15:143–61
The Sociology of Nonprofit Organizations and Sectors	PJ DiMaggio, HK Anheier	16:137–59
Theory and Research in Organizational Ecology	JV Singh, CJ Lumsden	16:161–95
The Evolution of New Organizational Forms	E Romanelli	17:79–103
Networks of Corporate Power: A Comparative Assessment	J Scott	17:181–203
Sociological Perspectives on American Indians	CM Snipp	18:351–71
Media Images and the Social Construction of Reality	WA Gamson, D Croteau, W Hoynes, T Sasson	18:373–93
Perspectives on Organizational Change in the US Medical Care Sector	ML Fennell, JA Alexander	19:89–112
Theoretical and Comparative Perspectives on Corporate Organization	N Fligstein, R Freeland	21:21–43
Modeling Internal Organizational Change	WP Barnett, GR Carroll	21:217–36
Computer Networks as Social Networks: Collaborative Work, Telework, and Virtual Community	B Wellman, J Salaff, D Dimitrova, L Garton, M Gulia, C Haythornthwaite	22:213–38
What Do Interlocks Do? An Analysis, Critique, and Assessment of Research on Interlocking Directorates	MS Mizruchi	22:271–98
The Changing Organizational Context of Professional Work	KT Leicht, ML Fennell	23:215–31
Sociology of Markets	J Lie	23:341–60
The Legal Environments of Organizations	LB Edelman, MC Suchman	23:479–515
Network Forms of Organizations	J Podolny, KL Page	24:57–76
POLITICAL AND ECONOMIC SOCIOLOGY		
Community Power	TN Clark	1:271–95
Political Participation and Public Policy	RR Alford, R Friedland	1:429–79
Political Socialization	RG Niemi, BI Sobieszek	3:209–33
Business and Society	I Berg, MN Zald	4:115–43
Comparative Industrial Sociology and the Convergence Hypothesis	W Form	5:1–25
Sociology of Labor Markets	AL Kalleberg, AB Sorensen	5:351–79
Corporations and the Corporate Elite	M Useem	6:41–77
Accounting for International War: The State of the Discipline	JD Singer	6:349–67
The Fiscal Crisis of the Capitalist State	F Block	7:1–27
Recent Research on Multinational Corporations	PB Evans	7:199–223
The Sociology of Democratic Politics and Government	P Burstein	7:291–319
Political Power and Conventional Political Participation	GA Kourvetaris, BA Dobratz	8:289–317

Title	Authors	Volume:Pages
Contemporary Ethnic Mobilization	S Olzak	9:355–74
Resource Mobilization Theory and the Study of Social Movements	JC Jenkins	9:527–53
The Economy and Social Pathology	AV Horwitz	10:95–119
Economic Development and Community Social Change	GF Summers, K Branch	10:141–66
Park Place and Main Street: Business and the Urban Power Structure	R Friedland, D Palmer	10:393–416
The Expansion of the State	GM Thomas, JW Meyer	10:461–82
The Petite Bourgeoisie in Late Capitalism	F Bechhofer, B Elliott	11:181–207
The Political Attitudes of Professionals	S Brint	11:389–414
Social Control of Occupations and Work	RL Simpson	11:415–36
Life-Course and Generational Politics	RG Braungart, MM Braungart	12:205–31
Efficiency and Social Institutions: Uses and Misuses of Economic Reasoning in Sociology	A Oberschall, EM Leifer	12:233–53
Theories of the Welfare State	J Quadagno	13:109–28
Income Inequality and Economic Development	G Gagliani	13:313–34
The Welfare State, Citizenship, and Bureaucratic Encounters	Y Hasenfeld, JA Rafferty, MN Zald	13:387–415
Evaluating Work and Comparable Worth	P England, D Dunn	14:227–48
National Politics and Collective Action: Recent Theory and Research in Western Europe and the United States	S Tarrow	14:421–40
Origins of Capitalism in Western Europe: Economic and Political Aspects	R Lachmann	15:47–72
Price, Authority, and Trust:From Ideal Types to Plural Forms	JL Bradach, RG Eccles	15:97–118
Ethnicity and Entrepreneurship	HE Aldrich, R Waldinger	16:111–35
The Sociology of Nonprofit Organizations and Sectors	PJ DiMaggio, HK Anheier	16:137–59
Peasants and Proletarians	BR Roberts	16:353–77
The US Labor Movement: Its Development and Impact on Social Inequality and Politics	DB Cornfield	17:27–49
Major Traditions of Economic Sociology	R Swedberg	17:251–76
Comparative Perspectives on the State	K Barkey, S Parikh	17:523–49
Global Structures and Political Processes in the Study of Domestic Political Conflict	JC Jenkins, K Schock	18:161–85
Contemporary Research on Social Democracy	G Esping-Andersen, K van Kersbergen	18:187–208
Regional Paths of Development	G Gereffi, S Fonda	18:419–48
Refugees, Immigrants, and the State	J Hein	19:43–59
The State and Fiscal Sociology	JL Campbell	19:163–85
Between Rocky Democracies and Hard Markets: Dilemmas of the Double Transition	MA Centeno	20:125–47
Religion and Political Legitimation	DB Billings, SL Scott	20:173–202
Social Structure and the Phenomenology of Attainment	RL Breiger	21:115–36
Gender in the Welfare State	A Orloff	22:51–78
Market Transition and Societal Transformation in Reforming State Socialism	V Nee, R Matthews	22:401–35
From Marxism to Postcommunism: Socialist Desires and East European Rejections	MD Kennedy, N Galtz	22:437–58

Politics and Culture: A Less Fissured Terrain	M Berezin	23:361–83
Computerization of the Workplace	BH Burris	24:141–57
Globalization and Democracy	KC Schwartzman	24:159–81

DIFFERENTIATION AND STRATIFICATION

Race and Ethnic Relations	RM Williams Jr.	1:125–64
Age Differentiation and the Life Course	GH Elder Jr.	1:165–90
Sex Roles in Transition: A Ten-Year Perspective	J Lipman-Blumen, AR Tickamyer	1:297–337
The Differentiation of Life-Styles	BD Zablocki, RM Kanter	2:269–98
Measurement in Social Stratification	MR Haug	3:51–77
Mobility and Stratification in the Soviet Union	RB Dobson	3:297–329
Achievement Ambitions	KI Spenner, DL Featherman	4:373–420
Black Identity and Self-Esteem: A Review of Studies of Black Self-Concept, 1968–1978	JR Porter, RE Washington	5:53–74
Ascribed and Achieved Bases of Stratification	A Foner	5:219–42
Discrimination: Motivation, Action, Effects, and Context	JR Feagin, DL Eckberg	6:1–20
Comparative Social Mobility	J Matras	6:401–31
Status Organizing Processes	J Berger, SJ Rosenholtz, M Zelditch Jr.	6:479–508
Beliefs About Stratification	JR Kluegel, ER Smith	7:29–56
Black Students in Higher Education: A Review of Studies, 1965–1980	CV Willie, D Cunnigen	7:177–98
The Sociology of American Jewry: The Last Ten Years	SC Heilman	8:135–60
Expectation States and Interracial Interaction in School Settings	EG Cohen	8:209–35
Sex Roles: The Division of Labor at Home and in the Workplace	J Miller, HH Garrison	8:237–62
Generation as a Sociological Problem	DI Kertzer	9:125–49
America's Melting Pot Reconsidered	C Hirschman	9:397–423
Organizational Perspectives on Stratification	JN Baron	10:37–69
Ethnicity	JM Yinger	11:151–80
The Petite Bourgeoisie in Late Capitalism	F Bechhofer, B Elliott	11:181–207
Urban Poverty	WJ Wilson, R Aponte	11:231–58
New Black-White Patterns: How Best To Conceptualize Them?	TF Pettigrew	11:329–46
Social Control of Occupations and Work	RL Simpson	11:415–36
The Shifting Social and Economic Tides of Black America, 1950-1980	WR Allen, R Farley	12:277–306
On the Degradation of Skills	W Form	13:29–47
The Effect of Women's Labor Force Participation on the Distribution of Income in the United States	J Treas	13:259–88
Making Sense of Diversity: Recent Research on Hispanic Minorities in the United States	A Portes, C Truelove	13:359–85
Class Mobility in the Industrial World	K Kurz, W Muller	13:417–42
Social Stratification, Work, and Personality	KI Spenner	14:69–97
Comparative Perspectives on Work Structures and Inequality	AL Kalleberg	14:203–25
Equality of Educational Opportunity	MT Hallinan	14:249–68

Stratification and Social Structure in Hungary	T Kolosi	14:405–19
The Rising Affluence of the Elderly: How Far, How Fair, and How Frail?	GJ Duncan, KR Smith	15:261–89
Sex Differences in Earnings in the United States	MM Marini	15:343–80
Poverty and Opportunity Structure in Rural America	AR Tickamyer, CM Duncan	16:67–86
Market and Network Theories of the Transition from High School to Work: Their Application to Industrialized Societies	JE Rosenbaum, T Kariya, R Settersten, T Maier	16:263–99
Peasants and Proletarians	BR Roberts	16:353–77
Household History and Sociological Theory	DI Kertzer	17:155–79
Comparative Intergenerational Stratification Research: Three Generations and Beyond	HBG Ganzeboom, DJ Treiman, WC Ultee	17:277–302
Job Mobility and Career Processes	RA Rosenfeld	18:39–61
Concepts and Measurement of Prestige	B Wegener	18:253–80
The Sociology of Work and Occupations	A Abbott	19:187–209
Sex Segregation in the Workplace	B Reskin	19:241–70
Women, Family, and Class	A Sorensen	20:27–47
Comparative Studies in Class Structure	J Myles, A Turegun	20:103–24
Scientific Careers: Universalism and Particularism	JS Long, MF Fox	21:45–71
Class Voting in Capitalist Democracies Since World War II: Dealignment, Realignment, or Trendless Fluctuation?	J Manza, M Hout, C Brooks	21:137–62
Rags to Rags: Poverty and Mobility in the United States	M Corcoran	21:237–67
From Class Consciousness to Culture, Action, and Social Organization	R Fantasia	21:269–87
Institutional Arrangements and Stratification Processes in Industrial Societies	AC Kerckhoff	21:323–47
US Socioeconomic and Racial Differences in Health: Patterns and Explanations	DR Williams, C Collins	21:349–86
Gender Inequality and Higher Education	JA Jacobs	22:153–85
Law and Inequality: Race, Gender... and, of Course, Class	C Seron, F Munger	22:187–212
Intermarriage and Homogamy: Causes, Patterns, and Trends	M Kalmijn	24:395–421

INDIVIDUAL AND SOCIETY

Major Developments in the Sociological Study of Deviance	JP Gibbs, ML Erickson	1:21–42
The Study of Urban Community and Personality	CS Fischer	1:67–89
Alienation Studies	M Seeman	1:91–123
Attitudes and Behavior	H Schuman, MP Johnson	2:161–207
Physiological Sociology: Interface of Sociological and Biological Processes	PR Barchas	2:299–333
Development of Evaluated Role Identities	C Gordon	2:405–33
Family Interaction Patterns	J Aldous	3:105–35
Political Socialization	RG Niemi, BI Sobieszek	3:209–33
Socialization, Personality, and Social Systems	GJ DiRenzo	3:261–95
Human Spatial Behavior	M Baldassare	4:29–56

Status Inconsistency and Role Conflict	S Stryker, AS Macke	4:57–90
The Sick Role: Assessment and Overview	S Levine, MA Kozloff	4:317–43
Adult Socialization	JT Mortimer, RG Simmons	4:421–54
Black Identity and Self-Esteem: A Review of Studies of Black Self-Concept, 1968–1978	JR Porter, RE Washington	5:53–74
Sociology of Later Life	GL Maddox	5:113–35
Reality Construction in Interaction	AW Frank III	5:167–91
The Sociology of Mental Health and Illness	MS Goldstein	5:381–409
Drug and Drinking Behavior Among Youth	DB Kandel	6:235–85
The Sociology of Cognitive Development	M Simpson	6:287–313
Sociological Aspects of Criminal Victimization	MR Gottfredson, MJ Hindelang	7:107–28
The Social Control of Sexuality	J DeLamater	7:263–90
The Self-Concept	V Gecas	8:1–33
Perspectives on the Concept of Social Control	RF Meier	8:35–55
The Social Psychology of Deviance: Toward a Reconciliation with Social Structure	AR Harris, GD Hill	8:161–86
Dying and the Meanings of Death: Sociological Inquiries	JW Riley Jr.	9:191–216
Toward Integration in the Social Psychology of Emotions	TJ Scheff	9:333–54
Sociological Aspects of Attribution	KS Crittenden	9:425–46
Psychoanalysis and Sociology	J Rabow	9:555–78
The Economy and Social Pathology	AV Horwitz	10:95–119
The Sociology of Conversion	DA Snow, R Machalek	10:167–90
White Collar Crime	J Braithwaite	11:1–25
Effects of Sibling Number on Child Outcome	DM Heer	11:27–47
Quality of Life Research and Sociology	KF Schuessler, GA Fisher	11:129–49
Family Violence	RJ Gelles	11:347–67
Social Patterns of Distress	J Mirowsky, CE Ross	12:23–45
Recent Developments in Role Theory	BJ Biddle	12:67–92
The Transition to Adulthood	DP Hogan, NM Astone	12:109–30
Childhood in Sociodemographic Perspective	DJ Hernandez	12:159–80
Everyday Life Sociology	PA Adler, P Adler, A Fontana	13:217–35
Parenthood and Psychological Well-Being	S McLanahan, J Adams	13:237–57
Sociological Research on Male and Female Homosexuality	B Risman, P Schwartz	14:125–47
Structures and Processes of Social Support	JS House, D Umberson, KR Landis	14:293–318
Recent Developments in Attitudes and Social Structure	KJ Kiecolt	14:381–403
Personal Relationships	P Blumstein, P Kollock	14:467–90
Social Structure, Psychology, and the Estimation of Risk	CA Heimer	14:491–519
The Sociology of Adolescence	SM Dornbusch	15:233–59
The Social Psychology of Self-Efficacy	V Gecas	15:291–316
The Sociology of Emotions	PA Thoits	15:317–42
Altruism: A Review of Recent Theory and Research	JA Piliavin, H-W Charng	16:27–65
Role Change	RH Turner	16:87–110
Concepts of the Life Cycle: Their History, Meanings, and Uses in the Social Sciences	AM O'Rand, ML Krecker	16:241–62

Title	Authors	Volume:Pages
Work Experiences and Family Interaction Processes: The Long Reach of the Job	EG Menaghan	17:419–44
Social Stress: Theory and Research	CS Aneshensel	18:15–38
Crime and Deviance in the Life Course	RJ Sampson, JH Laub	18:63–84
Social Science Research and Contemporary Studies of Homelessness	AB Shlay, PH Rossi	18:129–60
The Self-Concept Over Time: Research Issues and Directions	DH Demo	18:303–26
The Situational Analysis of Crime and Deviance	C Birkbeck, G LaFree	19:113–37
Minority Identity and Self-Esteem	JR Porter, RE Washington	19:139–61
Nationalism and Ethnicity	C Calhoun	19:211–39
Consequences of Marital Dissolution for Children	JA Seltzer	20:235–66
Stepfamilies in the United States: A Reconsideration	AJ Cherlin, FF Furstenberg Jr.	20:359–81
Immigration and Ethnic and Racial Inequality in the United States	MC Waters, K Eschbach	21:419–46
Adult Child-Parent Relationships	DN Lye	22:79–102
Mass Media Effects on Violent Behavior	RB Felson	22:103–28
The Measurement of Age, Age Structuring, and the Life Course	RA Settersten Jr, KU Mayer	23:233–61
Identity Construction: New Issues, New Directions	KA Cerulo	23:385–409
Reactions Toward the New Minorities of Western Europe	TF Pettigrew	24:77–103
Social Memory Studies: From "Collective Memory" to the Historical Sociology of Mnemonic Practices	JK Olick, J Robbins	24:105–40
Social Dilemmas: The Anatomy of Cooperation	P Kollock	24:183–214
Alcohol, Drugs, and Violence	RN Parker, K Auerhahn	24:291–311
Ethnic and Nationalist Violence	R Brubaker, DD Laitin	24:423–52

DEMOGRAPHY

Title	Authors	Volume:Pages
Explanations of Migration	PN Ritchey	2:363–404
Mortality Trends	SH Preston	3:163–78
Demography and the Family	JA Sweet	3:363–405
International Migration	W Petersen	4:533–75
Recent Trends in American Historical Demography: Some Methodological and Conceptual Considerations	MA Vinovskis	4:603–27
Dimensions of the New Immigration to the United States and the Prospects for Assimilation	DS Massey	7:57–85
Sex Differences in Mortality	CA Nathanson	10:191–213
The Nonmetropolitan Population Turnaround	GV Fuguitt	11:259–80
Social Mobility and Fertility	JD Kasarda, JOG Billy	11:305–28
Female Labor Force Behavior and Fertility in the United States	E Lehrer, M Nerlove	12:181–204
The Effect of Women's Labor Force Participation on the Distribution of Income in the United States	J Treas	13:259–88
Immigration and Urban Change	R Waldinger	15:211–32

Title	Author(s)	Volume:Pages
The Risks of Reproductive Impairment in the Later Years of Childbearing	JA McFalls Jr.	16:491–519
Women and Migration: The Social Consequences of Gender	S Pedraza	17:303–25
Third World Urbanization: Dimensions, Theories, and Determinants	JD Kasarda, EM Crenshaw	17:467–501
Changing Fertility Patterns and Policies in the Third World	G McNicoll	18:85–108
The Easterlin Effect	FC Pampel, HE Peters	21:163–94
Unauthorized Immigration to the United States	TJ Espenshade	21:195–216
Gender and Crime: Toward a Gendered Theory of Female Offending	D Steffensmeier, E Allan	22:459–87
The First Injustice: Socioeconomic Disparities, Health Services Technology, and Infant Mortality	SL Gortmaker, PH Wise	23:147–70
Women's Employment and the Gain to Marriage: The Specialization and Trading Model	VK Oppenheimer	23:431–53

URBAN AND RURAL COMMUNITY SOCIOLOGY

Title	Author(s)	Volume:Pages
The Study of Urban Community and Personality	CS Fischer	1:67–89
Urban Ethnography: Situational and Normative Accounts	GD Suttles	2:1–18
Rural Community Studies in the United States: A Decade in Review	IT Sanders, GF Lewis	2:35–53
Urban Density and Pathology	HM Choldin	4:91–113
Community Structure as Interorganizational Linkages	EO Laumann, J Galaskiewicz, PV Marsden	4:455–84
Factorial Social Ecology: An Attempt at Summary and Evaluation	C-G Janson	6:433–56
The Sociology of Agriculture: Toward a New Rural Sociology	H Newby	9:67–81
Models of Neighborhood Change	KP Schwirian	9:83–102
The Sociology of Transportation	G Yago	9:171–90
Recent Neo-Marxist Urban Analysis	C Jaret	9:499–525
Economic Development and Community Social Change	GF Summers, K Branch	10:141–66
Urban Ecology: Urbanization and Systems of Cities	FD Wilson	10:283–307
Park Place and Main Street: Business and the Urban Power Structure	R Friedland, D Palmer	10:393–416
Urban Poverty	WJ Wilson, R Aponte	11:231–58
The Nonmetropolitan Population Turnaround	GV Fuguitt	11:259–80
Rural Community Development	GF Summers	12:347–71
Gentrification: Culture and Capital in the Urban Core	S Zukin	13:129–47
Immigration and Urban Change	R Waldinger	15:211–32
Poverty and Opportunity Structure in Rural America	AR Tickamyer, CM Duncan	16:67–86
Economic Restructuring and the American City	S Sassen	16:465–90
The Urban Underclass	C Marks	17:445–66

Suburban Communities	M Baldassare	18:475–94
Urban Sociology: The Contribution and Limits of Political Economy	J Walton	19:301–20
Growing Up American: The Challenge Confronting Immigrant Children and Children of Immigrants	M Zhou	23:63–95

POLICY

Evaluation Research	G Gordon, EV Morse	1:339–61
Political Participation and Public Policy	RR Alford, R Friedland	1:429–79
Advanced Medical Technology–Social and Ethical Implications	RC Fox	2:231–68
Social Experiments	HW Riecken, RF Boruch	4:511–32
Social Policy and the Family	JZ Giele	5:275–302
The Sociology of Housing	DL Foley	6:457–78
Sociology and Social Forecasting	RL Henshel	8:57–79
Social Control Through Deterrence: Drinking-and-Driving Laws	HL Ross	10:21–35
Evaluation Research: An Assessment	PH Rossi, JD Wright	10:331–52
Urban Policy Analysis	TN Clark	11:437–55
States and Social Policies	T Skocpol, E Amenta	12:131–57
Social Impact Assessment	WR Freudenburg	12:451–78
A Critical Examination of Macro Perspectives on Crime Control	AE Liska	13:67–88
Energy and Society	EA Rosa, GE Machlis, KM Keating	14:149–72
Sociological Research on Alcohol Use, Problems, and Policy	KK Bucholz, LN Robins	15:163–86
Deinstitutionalization: An Appraisal of Reform	D Mechanic, DA Rochefort	16:301–27
Policy Domains: Organization, Culture, and Policy Outcomes	P Burstein	17:327–50
Population Aging and Social Policy	P Uhlenberg	18:449–74
The Savings and Loan Debacle, Financial Crime, and the State	K Calavita, R Tillman, HN Pontell	23:19–38
Poverty and Inequality Among Children	DT Lichter	23:121–45
Sociological Perspectives on Medical Ethics and Decision-Making	R Zussman	23:171–89

HISTORICAL SOCIOLOGY

American Sociology Before World War II	D Martindale	2:121–43
Sociological Theory From the Chicago Dominance to 1965	LA Coser	2:145–60
Precapitalist Social Structures	KP Moseley, I Wallerstein	4:259–90
Recent Trends in American Historical Demography: Some Methodological and Conceptual Considerations	MA Vinovskis	4:603–27
Accounting for International War: The State of the Discipline	JD Singer	6:349–67
The Comparative and Historical Study of Revolutions	JA Goldstone	8:187–207
Changing Family and Household: Contemporary Lessons from Historical Research	A Cherlin	9:51–66

The New History of Sociology	RA Jones	9:447–69
The Expansion of the State	GM Thomas, JW Meyer	10:461–82
Class Conflict and Social Change in Historical Perspective	WG Roy	10:483–506
Changing Perspectives on the American Family in the Past	SM Juster, MA Vinovskis	13:193–216
The Economic Progress of European and East Asian Americans	S Model	14:363–80
Gender and Social Reproduction: Historical Perspectives	B Laslett, J Brenner	15:381–404
Historical Studies of Labor Movements in the United States	H Kimeldorf, J Stepan-Norris	18:495–517
Class Formation in Nineteenth-Century America: The Case of the Middle Class	M Archer, JR Blau	19:17–41
Aging and Generational Relations: A Historical and Life Course Perspective	TK Hareven	20:437–61
SOCIOLOGY OF WORLD REGIONS		
Convergence and Divergence in Development	JW Meyer, J Boli-Bennett, C Chase-Dunn	1:223–46
Social Structure of World Regions: Mainland China	MK Whyte, EF Vogel, WL Parish Jr.	3:179–207
Mobility and Stratification in the Soviet Union	RB Dobson	3:297–329
Recent Developments in Polish Sociology	Z Walaszek	3:331–62
The Development of Soviet Sociology, 1956–1976	DN Shalin	4:171–91
Changing Patterns in Research on the Third World	E Hermassi	4:239–57
Sociology of South Africa	AP Hare, M Savage	5:329–50
"Marginal" Settlements in Developing Countries: Research, Advocacy of Policy, and Evolution of Programs	L Peattie, JA Aldrete-Haas	7:157–75
Latin America: Social Structures and Sociology	A Portes, W Canak	7:225–48
Sociology of South Africa: Supplementary Comments	H Lever	7:249–62
World-System Theory	D Chirot, TD Hall	8:81–106
Research on Marxist Societies: The Relationship Between Theory and Practice	P Hollander	8:319–51
The Reestablishment of Sociology in the PRC: Toward the Sinification of Marxian Sociology	L Cheng, A So	9:471–98
Gender Differences in Role Differentiation and Organizational Task Performance	HA Walker, ML Fennell	12:255–75
Arab Sociology Today: A View From Within	G Sabagh, I Ghazalla	12:373–99
Soviet Sociology and Sociology in the Soviet Union	L Greenfeld	14:99–123
Recent Developments in Scandanavian Sociology	E Allardt	15:31–45
Social Change in Post-Revolution China	AG Walder	15:405–24
The Sociology of Mexico: Stalking the Path Not Taken	DE Davis	18:395–417
The Crisis of African Development: Conflicting Interpretations and Resolutions	PM Lubeck	18:519–40
World-Systems Analysis	C Chase-Dunn, P Grimes	21:387–417

Sociological Work in Japan K Nakao 24:499–516

BICENTENNIAL ARTICLES

American Sociology Before World War II D Martindale 2:121–43
Sociological Theory From the Chicago Dominance to 1965 LA Coser 2:145–60

Annual Reviews

A nonprofit scientific publisher
4139 El Camino Way • P.O. Box 10139
Palo Alto, CA 94303-0139 USA

BB98

STEP 1: ENTER YOUR NAME & ADDRESS

NAME

ADDRESS

CITY STATE/PROVINCE COUNTRY POSTAL CODE

TODAY'S DATE DAYTIME PHONE

E-MAIL ADDRESS FAX NUMBER

Phone Orders **800-523-8635** (U.S. or Canada)
650-493-4400 ext. 1 (worldwide)
8 a.m. to 4 p.m. Pacific Time, Monday-Friday

FAX Orders **650-424-0910**
24 hours a day

Mention priority code **BB98** when placing phone orders

STEP 4: CHOOSE YOUR PAYMENT METHOD

❑ **Check or Money Order Enclosed** (US funds, made payable to "Annual Reviews")

❑ **Bill Credit Card** ❑ AmEx ❑ MasterCard ❑ VISA

Account No. ____

Signature ____

Exp. Date MO/YR Name ____
(print name exactly as it appears on credit card)

STEP 2: ENTER YOUR ORDER

QTY	ANNUAL REVIEW OF:	VOL.	Place on Standing Order? SAVE 10% NOW WITH PAYMENT	PRICE	TOTAL
		#	❑ Yes, save 10% ❑ No	$	$
		#	❑ Yes, save 10% ❑ No	$	$
		#	❑ Yes, save 10% ❑ No	$	$
		#	❑ Yes, save 10% ❑ No	$	$
		#	❑ Yes, save 10% ❑ No	$	$

30% STUDENT/RECENT GRADUATE DISCOUNT (past 3 years) Not for standing orders. Include proof of status. $

CALIFORNIA CUSTOMERS: Add applicable California sales tax for your location. $

CANADIAN CUSTOMERS: Add 7% GST (Registration # 121449029 RT). $

STEP 3: CALCULATE YOUR SHIPPING & HANDLING

HANDLING CHARGE (Add $3 per volume, up to $9 max. per location). **Applies to all orders.** $

SHIPPING OPTIONS: (No UPS to P.O. boxes)
U.S. Mail 4th Class Book Rate (surface). Standard option. FREE. $ **N/C**
UPS Ground Service ($3/ volume. 48 contiguous U.S. states.) $

Please note expedited shipping preference: ❑ UPS Next Day Air ❑ UPS Second Day Air ❑ US Airmail ❑ UPS Worldwide Express ❑ UPS Worldwide Expedited

Note option at left. We will calculate amount and add to your total

Abstracts and content lists available on the World Wide Web at www.AnnualReviews.org. E-mail orders: service@annurev.org

TOTAL $

Orders may also be placed through booksellers or subscription agents or through our **Authorized Stockists.**
From Europe, the UK, the Middle East and Africa, contact: **Gazelle Book Service Ltd., Fax** (0) 1524-63232.
From India, Pakistan, Bangladesh or Sri Lanka, contact: **SARAS Books, Fax 91-11-941111.**